# ADOBE® INDESIGN™ 1.5

## *Introduction to Electronic Mechanicals*

AGAINST THE CLOCK
PERFORMANCE SUPPORT & TRAINING SYSTEMS

**PRENTICE HALL**
Upper Saddle River, NJ 07458

**Executive Editor:** Elizabeth Sugg
**Developmental Editor:** Judy Casillo
**Supervising Manager:** Mary Carnis
**Production Editor:** Denise Brown
**Director of Manufacturing and Production:** Bruce Johnson
**Manufacturing Buyer:** Ed O'Dougherty
**Editorial Assistant:** Lara Dugan
**Formatting/Page Make-up:** Against the Clock, Inc.
**Prepress:** Photoengraving, Inc.
**Printer/Binder:** Press of Ohio
**Cover Design:** Joe Sengotta
**Icon Design:** James Braun
**Creative Director:** Marianne Frasco

Prentice Hall International (UK) Limited, London
Prentice Hall of Australia Pty. Limited, Sydney
Prentice Hall Canada Inc., Toronto
Prentice Hall Hispanoamericana, S.A., Mexico
Prentice Hall of India Private Limited, New Delhi
Prentice Hall of Japan, Inc., Tokyo
Pearson Education Asia Pte. Ltd., Singapore
Editora Prentice Hall do Brasil, Ltda., Rio de Janeiro

10 9 8 7 6 5 4 3 2 1

ISBN 0-13-090449-X

# CONTENTS

## PURPOSE

The Against The Clock series has been developed specifically for those involved in the field of graphic arts.

Welcome to the world of electronic design and prepress. Many of our readers are already involved in the industry — in advertising and design companies, in prepress and imaging firms, and in the world of commercial printing and reproduction. Others are just now preparing themselves for a career somewhere in the profession.

This series of courses will provide you with the skills necessary to work in this fast-paced, exciting, and rapidly expanding business. Many people feel that they can simply purchase a computer, the appropriate software, a laser printer, and a ream of paper, and begin designing and producing high-quality printed materials. While this might suffice for a barbecue announcement or a flyer for a yard sale, the real world of four-color printing and professional communications requires a far more serious commitment.

## THE SERIES

The applications presented in the Against The Clock series stand out as the programs of choice in professional graphic arts environments.

We've used a modular design for the Against The Clock series, allowing you to mix and match the drawing, imaging, and page-layout applications that exactly suit your specific needs.

Titles available in the Against The Clock series include:

*Macintosh: Basic Operations*
*Windows: Basic Operations*
*Adobe Illustrator: Introduction and Advanced Digital Illustration*
*Macromedia FreeHand: Introduction and Advanced Digital Illustration*
***Adobe InDesign: Introduction and Advanced Electronic Mechanicals***
*Adobe PageMaker: Introduction and Advanced Electronic Mechanicals*
*QuarkXPress: Introduction and Advanced Electronic Mechanicals*
*Microsoft Publisher: Creating Electronic Mechanicals*
*Microsoft PowerPoint: Presentation Graphics with Impact*
*Microsoft FrontPage: Designing for the Web*
*MetaCreations Painter: A Digital Approach to Natural Art Media*
*Adobe Photoshop: Introduction and Advanced Digital Images*
*Adobe Premiere: Digital Video Editing*
*Macromedia Director: Creating Powerful Multimedia*
*File Preparation: The Responsible Electronic Page*
*Preflight: An Introduction to File Analysis and Repair*
*TrapWise and PressWise: Digital Trapping and Imposition*

**Pencil** icon indicates a comment from an experienced operator. Whenever you see the pencil icon, you'll find corresponding sidebar text that augments or builds upon the subject being discussed at the time.

**Bomb** icon indicates a potential problem or difficulty. For instance, a certain technique might lead to pages that prove difficult to output. In other cases, there might be something that a program cannot easily accomplish, so we might present a workaround.

**Pointing Finger** icon indicates a hands-on activity — whether a short exercise or a complete project. Note that sometimes this icon will direct you to the back of the book to complete a project.

**Key** icon is used to point out that there is a keyboard equivalent to a menu or dialog-box option. Key commands are often faster than using the mouse to select a menu option. Experienced operators often mix the use of keyboard equivalents and menu/dialog box selections to arrive at their optimum speed.

If you are a Windows user, be sure to refer to the corresponding text or images whenever you see this **Windows** icon. Although there isn't a great deal of difference between using these applications on a Macintosh and using them on a Windows-based workstation, there are certain instances where there's enough of a difference for us to comment.

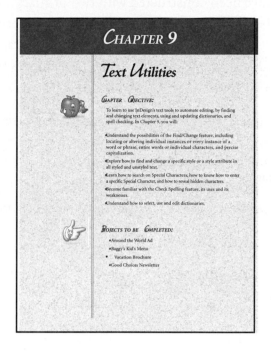

**Chapter Openers** *provide the reader with specific objectives.*

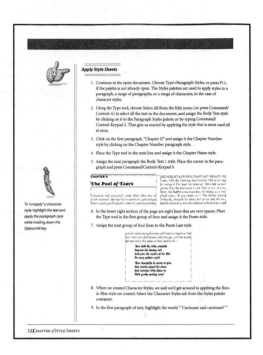

**Sidebars and Hands-on Activities** *supplement concepts presented in the material.*

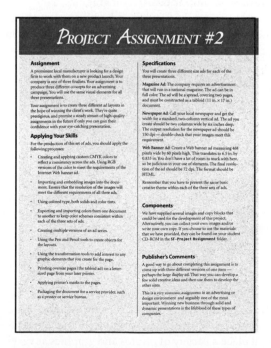

**Project assignments** *allow you to use your imagination and your new skills to satisfy a client's publications needs.*

**Step-by-step projects** *result in finished artwork — with an emphasis on proper file construction methods.*

Against The Clock course materials have been constructed with two primary building blocks: exercises and projects. Projects always result in a finished piece of work — digital imagery typically built from the ground up, utilizing photographic-quality images, vector artwork from illustration programs, and type elements from the library supplied on your student CD-ROM.

This course, *Adobe InDesign 1.5: Introduction to Electronic Mechanicals,* uses several step-by-step projects that you will work on during your learning sessions. (There are also open-ended project assignments following the two reviews.) You will find images of the step-by-step projects that you will complete by the end of the course displayed on the inside front cover of the book. Here's a brief overview of each:

## PROJECT A: AROUND THE WORLD AD

This project helps you apply the skills you have learned in the first four chapters — an overview of design, efficient use of the many palettes, and varied ways of working with text. Beginning with a shell, you will create text frames, type and tweak a headline, insert and format text, and import and format a block of body text, managing its flow across multiple columns. This project will give you the feel for combining text and graphics for a clean, striking design.

## PROJECT B: BAGGY'S KID'S MENU

Once you have learned to work with graphics, we turn you loose on a menu just for kids. This document you create from scratch. You'll manufacture a happy background using InDesign's Polygon tool, and spice up the menu with a number of imported cartoon graphics. You'll work with paragraph styles to simplify and speed your progress, and you'll embed images in the text flow to ensure that they're properly spaced in relation to their surrounding text. Finally, you'll add some finishing touches using the versatile Bézier tool. When you've finished with this menu project, you'll have the knack for placing images and type, effectively and efficiently.

## PROJECT C: VACATION BROCHURE

By the time you've progressed this far, you'll want to sink your teeth into a more complex project. You'll set up a six-panel brochure, complete with folds. Establishing your color scheme will take some work, as will the demanding job of creating style sheets. Each element requires exacting placement in this project, and you'll be dropping your pictures in "by the numbers," to ensure that they interact well with the surrounding text. This project reinforces the skills you've learned in rotating text and images, bleeding elements off the page, and ensuring that your type and background interact effectively with one another.

## PROJECT D: GOOD CHOICES NEWSLETTER

So, how involved can a two-page newsletter be? You'll find out when you create this "final exam" project. We help you stretch your skills, from establishing preferences to utilizing special dictionaries, as you begin to set up this document. You'll use the powerful step-and-repeat feature as you prepare the master pages, and you'll place a variety of photos and graphics at varying percentages to create a newsletter that grabs the reader's eye. You'll also insert and format text using style sheets, and utilize InDesign's powerful text-management tools to ensure that the document not only looks good, but also employs accurate spelling and hyphenation. Finally, you'll prepare this document for printing, so the whole world (or at least the organization's mailing list) can enjoy it.

## FOR THE STUDENT

On the CD-ROM you will find a complete set of Against The Clock (ATC) fonts, as well as a collection of data files used to construct the various exercises and projects.

The ATC fonts are solely for use while you are working with the Against The Clock materials. These fonts will be used throughout both the exercises and projects.

A variety of student files have been included. These files are necessary to complete both the exercises and projects.

## FOR THE INSTRUCTOR

The Instructor Kit consists of an Instructor's Manual and an Instructor's CD-ROM. It includes various testing and presentation materials in addition to the files that come standard with the student books.

- **Overhead Presentation Materials** are provided and follow along with the course. These presentations are prepared using Microsoft PowerPoint and are provided in both "native" PowerPoint format as well as Acrobat Portable Document Format (PDF).

- **Extra Projects** are provided along with the data files required for completion. These projects may be used to extend the course, or may be used to test the student.

- **Finished artwork (in PDF format)** for all projects that the students complete is supplied on the CD-ROM.

- **Test Questions and Answers** are included on the instructor CD-ROM. These questions may be modified, reorganized, and administered throughout the delivery of the course.

- Halfway through the course is a **Review** of material covered to that point, with a **Final Review** at the end.

I would like to give special thanks the writers, illustrators, editors, and others who have worked long and hard to complete the Against The Clock series. Foremost among them are Robin McAllister, Dean Bagley, and Lisa Bochatey, whom I thank for their long nights, early mornings, and their seemingly endless patience.

Thanks to the dedicated teaching professionals whose comments and expertise contributed to the success of these products, including Doris Anton of the Wichita Area Technical College, Bonnie George of Pittsburg State University, Carin Murphy of the Des Moines Area Community College, and Dee Colvin of the University of North Florida.

And a big thanks to Terry Sisk Graybill, copy editor and final link in the chain of pro–duction, for her tremendous help in making sure we all said what we meant to say.

A big thanks to Judy Casillo, developmental editor, and Denise Brown, production editor, for their guidance, patience, and attention to detail.

A special thanks to my husband, Gary Poyssick, for his unswerving support and for living in a publishing studio.


Ellenn Behoriam, June, 2000

## OUR HISTORY

Against The Clock (ATC) was founded in 1990 as a part of Lanman Systems Group, one of the nation's leading systems integration and training firms. The company specialized in developing custom training materials for such clients as *L.L. Bean, The New England Journal of Medicine, Smithsonian,* the *National Education Association, Air & Space Magazine, Publishers Clearing House,* The *National Wildlife Society, Home Shopping Network,* and many others. The integration firm was among the most highly respected in the graphic arts industry.

To a great degree, the success of Systems Group can be attributed to the thousands of pages of course materials developed at the company's demanding client sites. Throughout the rapid growth of Systems Group, Founder and General Manager Ellenn Behoriam developed the expertise necessary to manage technical experts, content providers, writers, editors, illustrators, designers, layout artists, proofreaders, and the rest of the chain of professionals required to develop structured and highly effective training materials.

Following the sale of the Lanman Companies to World Color, one of the nation's largest commercial printers, Ellenn embarked on a project to develop a library of training materials engineered specifically for the professional graphic artist. A large part of this effort is finding and working with talented professional artists, writers, and educators from around the country.

The result is the ATC training library.

## ROBIN MCALLISTER

**Robin McAllister** has been speaking and writing about creating effective pages since before desktop publishing was invented. In the process of teaching others, he has written various "how to" guides and training manuals. Rob serves as a contributing editor for numerous publications and publishers, and has authored a variety of desktop publishing and prepress titles.

In addition to other activities, Rob is the team leader for America Online's Applied Computing Community. Rob is a technical editor for *Electronic Publishing* and contributing editor for *Printing News* in addition to project manager for Against The Clock.

## DEAN BAGLEY

**Dean Bagley** is an experienced marketing and advertising expert. One of Dean's most effective skills is the development of hands-on activities, which, as you'll see is the foundation of the ATC series.

Dean is a professional cartoonist, well-known for his imaginative and entertaining "Baggy Gator" series of characters. Dean has been working with the Against The Clock series for more than six years.

## LISA BOCHATEY

**Lisa Bochatey** has been involved with graphics and computers for more than 20 years. She spends her time training and consulting for newspapers, publishers, designers, and general business clients in the Midwest. Lisa has Masters degrees in both Print Technology and Management, as well as in Instructional Design from Rochester Institute of Technology.

# GETTING STARTED

## Platform

The Against The Clock series is designed to apply to both Macintosh and Windows systems. InDesign runs under Macintosh, Windows 98, and Windows NT. There are separate student files for Macintosh and Windows students.

## Naming Conventions

In the old days of MS-DOS systems, file names on the PC were limited to something referred to as "8.3," which meant that you were limited in the number of characters you could use to an eight-character name (the "8") and a three-character suffix (the "3"). Text files, for example, might be called *myfile.txt*, while a document file from a word processor might be called *myfile.doc* (for document). On today's Windows systems, these limitations have been, for the most part, overcome. Although you can use longer file names, suffixes still exist. The Macintosh does not rely on the file extension at all. You see the characters as part of the file name. The suffixes for InDesign documents and templates have four characters, INDD and INDT, respectively. Whether you see them or not is another story.

When your Windows system is first configured, the Views are normally set to a default that hides these extensions. This means that you might have a dozen different files named *myfile*, all of which may have been generated by different applications and consist of completely different types of files.

You can change this view by double-clicking on *My Computer* (the icon on your desktop). This will open the file. Select View>Folder Options. From Folder Options, select the View tab. Within the Files and Folders folder is a checkbox: Hide File Extensions for Known File Types. When this is unchecked, you can see the file extensions. It's easier to know what you're looking at if they're visible. While this is a personal choice, we strongly recommend viewing the file extensions. All the files used in this course have been named using the three- or four-character suffix.

## Key Commands

There are two keys generally used as *modifier* keys — they do nothing when pressed, unless they are pressed in conjunction with another key. Their purpose is to alter the normal functions of the other key with which they are pressed.

The Command (Macintosh) or Control (Windows) key is generally used when taking control of the computer. When combined with the "S" key, it functions to save your work. When combined with "O," it opens a file; with a "P," it prints the file. In addition to these functions, which work with most Macintosh and Windows programs, the Control key may be combined with other keys to take control of specific functions in InDesign.

Another special function key is the Option (Macintosh) and Alt (for alternate) (Windows) key. It, too, is a modifier key, and you must hold it down along with whatever other key (or keys) is required for a specific function. The Option and Alt keys are often used in conjunction with other keys to access typographic characters having an ASCII number higher than 128. Under Windows, they are used in conjunction with the numeric keypad. For example, Alt-0149 will produce a bullet character. Alt-F4 will close the program. The Option key is combined with alphanumeric keys, instead of the numeric keypad. Option-8, for example, will produce a bullet.

The keys on the top row of the keypad, F1–F12, also accomplish specific tasks in conjunction with the computer. F1 will bring up the Help menu. F6 and Shift-F6 will move elements to the front or the back of a "stack" of text and graphic objects.

The Macintosh and Windows access context-sensitive menus in similar but different ways. On the Macintosh, holding down the Control (not the Command) key while clicking the mouse button will bring up context-sensitive menus. Under Windows, this is accomplished by clicking the right mouse button (right-clicking). We generically call accessing the context menu "context-clicking."

## The CD-ROM and Initial Setup Considerations

Before you begin using your Against The Clock course book, you must set up your system to have access to the various files and tools to complete your lessons.

### Student Files

This course comes complete with a collection of student files. These files are an integral part of the learning experience — they're used throughout the course to help you construct increasingly complex elements. Having these building blocks available to you for practice and study sessions will ensure that you will be able to experience the exercises and complete the project assignments smoothly, spending a minimum of time looking for the various required components.

In the Student Files folders, we've created sets of data. Locate the **SF-Intro InDesign** folder and drag the icon onto your hard disk drive. If you have limited disk space, you may want to copy only the files for one or two lessons at a time.

We strongly recommend that you work from your hard disk. However, in some cases you might not have enough room on your system for all the files we've supplied. If this is the case, you can work directly from the CD-ROM.

### Creating a Project Folder

Throughout the exercises and projects you'll be required to save your work. Since the CD-ROM is "read-only," you cannot write information to it. Create a "work in progress" folder on your hard disk and use it to store your work. Create it by context-clicking, while at your desktop, then selecting New Folder (Macintosh) or New> Folder (Windows). This will create the folder at the highest level of your system, where it will always be easy to find. Name this folder "Work in Progress".

## Fonts

You must install the ATC font library to ensure that your lessons and exercises will work as described in the course book. These fonts are provided on the student CD-ROM.

Instructions for installing fonts are provided in the documentation that came with your computer. In general, drag them into your System>Fonts folder on the Macintosh, or, under Windows, from your Start>Settings>Control Panel>Fonts, select File>Install New Font. Navigate to the Fonts folder on the CD, select the fonts, and click OK.

## System Requirements

On the Macintosh, you will need a Power PC 604 processor or above, running OS 8.5 or later; 48 MB of RAM using virtual memory, or 96 MB with virtual memory off; a monitor with a resolution of at least 832×624 pixels; Adobe PostScript Level 2 or higher printer; and a CD-ROM drive. You will need 120 MB of free hard drive space for installation.

On a Windows operating system, you'll need a Pentium II or faster processor; Windows 98/NT 4.0 or higher; 48 MB RAM; a monitor with a resolution of at least 800×600 pixels; Adobe PostScript Level 2 or higher printer; and a CD-ROM drive. You will need 75 MB of free hard drive space for installation.

## Prerequisites

This book assumes that you have a basic understanding of how to use your system.

You should know how to use your mouse to point and click, and how to drag items around the screen. You should know how to resize a window, and how to arrange windows on your desktop to maximize your available space. You should know how to access pull-down menus, and how checkboxes and radio buttons work. Lastly, you should know how to create, open, and save files.

If you're familiar with these fundamental skills, then you know all that's necessary to utilize the Against The Clock courseware library.

**Notes:**

# *I*NTRODUCTION

Adobe InDesign is a powerful, design-oriented publishing tool. It is designed to integrate text and graphics — prepared in the program itself or imported from other sources — and to produce a file that may be printed to a local or networked printer, taken to a commercial printing service (called a GASP, or Graphic Arts Service Provider), or published to the World Wide Web.

It has been our goal, in creating exercises and projects, first to help you see that you can create "cool stuff" quickly and easily, in InDesign. Then we have built on those principles, to show you that going beyond the basics enables you to work even more quickly, and with far less repetitive action than using only basic skills. One example of this is using the power of InDesign's style sheets. While becoming expert is hard work, it should also be fun and fulfilling.

As you progress through this course, we encourage you to pay attention not only to the details — how to do the tasks associated with the exercises and projects — but also to the principles behind them. While there are some projects and exercises that demand absolute attention to each detail, many give you more latitude. We encourage you to experiment, rather than limit yourself solely to ideas that the authors find interesting, and so expand your creative vision.

Additionally, we encourage you to look at the big picture — what you're actually creating — and make decisions based on that reality, rather than establishing a blanket rule for production.

The goals of this course are to:

- Build on your existing knowledge.

- Expand your vision of creative and production techniques.

- Temper creative technique with production reality.

- Explore expanded uses of Adobe InDesign.

This course is targeted toward design and print production techniques and functions. We also recognize the limitations of InDesign, and you'll note a number of cautions in the form of our "Bomb" icon. You'll also find interesting tidbits, coupled with solid information, in our "Teacher" (pencil icon) sidebars.

InDesign is an evolving program. We believe you will enjoy working and playing with it as you take advantage of its tools for graphic design and production.

# CHAPTER 1

## Creating the Electronic Mechanical

### CHAPTER OBJECTIVE:

To become familiar with the origins and growth of publishing, from prehistory through today's computer age. To become acquainted with industry terms and concepts used referring to typefaces and parts of documents. To learn the basic process of publishing from initial concept to delivered file, whether a mechanical for print use or components for Web application. In Chapter 1, you will:

- Explore the major steps in the history and maturation of publishing, including key inventions, improvements on systems and media, and some of today's possibilities through computers and software.

- Meet the members of the team who produce and publish documents, and understand the roles they serve.

- Review the creative and production stages needed to produce a document, from initial thumbnail sketches and comps to the delivered electronic mechanical.

- Learn the impact purposing and repurposing documents has on the final product.

- Explore the development of type design, and some of the notable features and advantages of specific categories of type.

- Learn to distinguish the design elements of the letterform and elements of typographic usage, including spacing around words and paragraphs.

- Review publishing industry terminology and customs.

- Begin to learn about types of images and preparation for effective use.

# Creating the Electronic Mechanical

The "electronic mechanical" is a result of the evolution of the process of publishing. That process has created rules, protocols, and a language unique to the printing and publishing industry. Publishing has expanded to include electronic publications in addition to printed documents, presenting us with a variety of methods of communication.

This chapter will acquaint you with a history of publishing, and with the basics of creating documents for publication. Its purpose is to get you off to a good start, so that the terms we use will make sense, rather than simply being new words you must memorize.

## A History of Publishing

Humans have a history of "publishing" from earliest times, even in primitive cultures. Their communications with their gods or fellow men appear on cave walls, preserving for posterity the story of the artists and the culture of their day.

Over the centuries, the human race developed many formalized systems of writing. Egyptian hieroglyphs were not only pictorial representations of ideas but phonetic symbols. Cuneiform, the writing of Sumerians and others in ancient Mesopotamia, used wedge-shaped characters to represent both ideas and syllabic sounds. Writing systems developed by one people were often used and adapted by others. Eventually alphabets were developed, using symbols representing consonants and later vowels to correspond to the sound of the language, rather than to ideas. In the East, the Chinese written language evolved quite differently as a logographic system. In this system, a word is represented by two graphs: one represents the meaning and the other indicates pronunciation. Since Chinese has so many words that sound the same, an alphabet sound-based system would not be as efficient as it is for Western languages. Each system works well for the languages and dialects it represents.

The media evolved too — from earliest rock carvings and paintings to writing on animal skins, clay tablets, vellum, fine papyrus, and eventually the high-quality papers (and low-quality newsprint) we have today. Media have been created to fulfill specific needs, including coated papers which give superior presentation of photographs and textured papers (often used by commercial and fine artists to create a specific effect) as they interact with the medium being applied (charcoal, watercolor, and ink, for example). Other media include plasticized substrates that are suitable for outdoor advertising, papers that will survive for decades to preserve an image, even T-shirts are a medium for graphic designs and communicated messages.

Documents also developed greater portability and ease-of-use. The scroll was portable, but required great skill to turn to the exact spot to resume reading. Leaved publications, forerunners of today's books, made such reading and the production of documents much easier.

Written language was often limited to the priests, bureaucrats and scribes — the first publishing professionals — who became the writers and readers of the written word. In those days, the rules for writing were relatively simple — the words had to be captured, and captured accurately. (In time, these "keepers of the written word" would embellish their work with art in the form of the beautiful illuminations we find in documents such as the *Book of Kells*.)

*Even with our modern technology, we still call each sheet of paper that goes through a printing press an* **impression***.*

*Moveable type, reusable elements employed to compose and print text, was developed in China in the 11th century. The Chinese ideographic language was so complex, however, that this printing innovation did not develop further.*

*Many typographic and other terms are defined in this chapter in the section "Typographic Terms and Customs."*

While we applaud their skills, we also note that, in some cultures, these people had great power as the writers and sole readers of the recorded word. They often acted as spokespeople and interpreters for the gods of that society, thereby controlling the people. Limited literacy and access to written material throughout the centuries also often restricted the spread of ideas to only the privileged and wealthy.

For thousands of years, documents were painstakingly written and copied by hand, character-by-character, making them extremely valuable. A revolution occurred in the mid-1400s that would finally make "publishing" a reality. The documents would become "public," in the sense that they could be produced in sufficient quantity to be distributed to larger groups of people, and could be afforded by other than the very wealthy.

## Automating the Publishing Process

In 1450, Johannes Gutenberg invented a printing press that used movable type, changing forever the way people communicate. Because of his invention, multiple copies of documents could be made with relative ease. The process involved coating metal castings of type with ink by hand, and then pressing those plates against the paper with a lever or screw, causing an imprint of the plate to be made on the paper. Printing was born.

Over the next five centuries, the basic concept of printing did not change. Ink was applied to a raised surface, then literally *pressed* onto the paper. There were, however, a number of improvements to that original approach.

One such improvement had to do with the letterform. Since words had been written in typefaces we recognize today as Blackletter or Uncial, Gutenberg fashioned his original type to emulate that lettering style. If you've ever tried to read a long document prepared in Olde English, American Uncial, or Goudy Text, you know how difficult this style is to read. However, it continued for about 50 years, until Nicholas Jensen designed the first Roman typeface. The following year, Aldus Manutius designed the first Italic face. The results of those changes are reflected in all our type libraries — there are literally thousands of faces to choose from today.

More than just the look of type changed over the years. In a variety of ways, the process of printing became automated. As a result of the industrial revolution, presses were driven by steam and by electricity, making them faster and capable of printing larger sheets of paper, and publications became less expensive to produce.

One of the most extraordinary changes came about in 1890. For over 400 years, type was handpicked and literally set in place (hence, "typesetting") one piece at a time. In that year, Ottmar Merganthaler developed a machine that would set an entire line of type at one time. He called it, appropriately, the "Linotype."

The Linotype, and other typesetting machines of this era (often called "linecasters"), set their lines of type by placing brass matrices (called "slugs") on a line, which was then clamped into a typesetting form called a "chase." A mold was made of the brass slugs, and a lead plate (sometimes coated with nickel) was produced from the mold. The slugs were returned to the linecaster to be reused. Because the lead was heated prior to being poured into the molds, the process of typesetting of this era is sometimes referred to as "hot metal."

At approximately the same time, the modern typewriter emerged (the Underwood, 1897), which used the infamous "QWERTY" keyboard developed by Remington in 1873. Interestingly, Merganthaler did not use a keyboard even remotely similar to the QWERTY, and subsequent developers of typesetting machines created their own keyboard layouts.

*The "QWERTY" keyboard, so called from the first six letters in the top letter row of the typewriter (and now the computer), was used in the early prototypes for a commercial typewriter. It was thought to be more efficient than an alphabetic arrangement. Keys were placed in combinations less likely to hit each other and stick during rapid typing.*

*The Photon was a **phototypesetter** — a machine that printed directly to photosensitive paper. Phototypesetters are often referred to as "second-generation typesetters" to distinguish them from earlier machines that made impressions with lead type.*

Gradual changes brought typesetting and typing increasingly closer. In 1928, the TTS (punched tape) system was introduced, using a standard typewriter keyboard. Using this system, three linecasters operated by tape could produce the same volume as seven linecasters employing manual typographic input. In time, the first commercially viable typesetting machine resembling a typewriter emerged (the Photon, 1953).

## A Merger of Two Cultures

In the early 1950s, Varityper and Compugraphic corporations each introduced a stand-alone photocomposition system reasonably priced compared to the price of other systems of that time. In these photocomposition systems, the keyboard and monitor were directly wired to the imaging devices, including a turret of lenses or a zoom lens, which would project light through a filmstrip or disk onto photosensitive media. On those early terminals, you could see only two lines of type: the one you were working on and the one that you had just finished typing. These machines evolved into powerful, text-based, dedicated machines that were, until recently, the standard of the publishing industry.

A true merger of the print and office environment occurred after word processing began with the introduction of the IBM MT/ST (Magnetic Tape Selectric Typewriter) in Germany in 1964. After that, it wasn't until 1972 that a functional word processing system with video display terminal was available.

With word processing came the opportunity to use lesser-skilled typists to input large amounts of text. Now typists with limited training were able to capture a majority of the keystrokes needed to convert word-processed files to typesetting. This was still a far cry from what we know as desktop publishing (DTP) today, but it was a vast improvement over machines that required that all text be composed on the keyboard attached to them, and could not accept text from an outside source.

In the late 1970s, two system standards were emerging: Apple-DOS and CP/M. IBM had yet to get involved with personal computers. August 1981 brought the IBM PC and MS-DOS into the market. Hewlett-Packard introduced the LaserJet, bringing about a new quality level for printing, and some interesting possibilities for both office and printing environments. In 1984, Apple introduced the Macintosh.

At about the same time, Adobe introduced the PostScript page description language, Aldus released PageMaker, and Apple released the LaserWriter printer. Of course, PageMaker was not the first desktop publishing program. There were many that predated it on the PC (before Windows), on the Apple IIe, and on the Macintosh.

## Merged Text and Graphics

Until approximately this time, merging text and graphics into a document was a manual, time-consuming process. If you examine early newspapers, you'll note that they are almost entirely devoid of graphics of any kind, and photographs were all but unheard of.

The reason for this is that every element in a publication, other than type, had to be manually inserted. In the days of hot metal, this meant literally engraving the lead with a stylus to produce such simple elements as rules. More complex graphics were etched in metal, included with the type, and plated.

When lithography became the technology of choice, art elements were inserted photographically, or were combined with the type on a stiff board, called a *mechanical*, then the entire page was photographed. It was still a laborious process.

With the introduction of desktop publishing programs came the ability to combine text and graphics quickly and easily — provided they were both in electronic form. Drawing programs, such as Adobe Illustrator, Macromedia FreeHand, and CorelDRAW!, could now create vector-based illustrations. Painting programs, such as MetaCreations Painter, Canvas, and Adobe Photoshop, could create raster-based images. Desktop scanners could import picture data into the computer so it could be manipulated and used in documents.

## The Design/Content/Production Team

As publishing migrated to the computer, the need for individual skills increased. Designers today also handle page-layout responsibilities, although they'd often rather leave the mundane operations to technicians. As documents produced on the desktop have become more complicated, users often make more and more serious and expensive mistakes. The sought-after benefits of greater control of documents and lower prices are realized only by those who prepare documents that they can control and who keep up with technology. Somewhere in this process we realize that we have strengths to exploit and weaknesses to consider.

Publishing has always been a team effort. We may wish that we could do it all, but there are very few 20th-Century Renaissance people out there. In addition, as we've mentioned earlier, those who are very good at one thing usually prefer to do what they're good at and have been trained to do. Of course, there's often some overlap, particularly with today's publishing technology. Let's look at the "team" in its purest sense, and each distinct job.

*Designers* determine the overall look of a document, including the selection of fonts and decisions regarding art and color. They are usually responsible for bringing the document through the comprehensive sketch phase and often work with illustrators and photographers to ensure that their ideas are implemented. They generally approve the final product before it is sent to the client.

*Content providers* include writers, editors, illustrators, photographers, and others who provide the information contained in a document. As an example, text creators provide the words and the hierarchy of elements (such as Headline 1, Headline 2, and so forth). The designer determines the appearance of those words and headlines. The photographer provides an image, but the designer decides how the photo is to be cropped, or whether it will have a background.

*Production team members* combine material from all the content providers according to the instructions from the designer. This specialty requires technical knowledge of a number of programs and of either the printing process or the intricacies of the Web. There must be a close interaction between those assembling pages and the service provider to ensure that the document can be reproduced efficiently, so that the client is happy with the result.

*The word **mechanical** derives from the assembly process. Those who assembled the artboards were skilled craftspeople, "mechanics," so their work was termed **mechanical**.*

*Throughout this course, we will refer to the **GASP** — Graphic Arts Service Providers. They are technical professionals who have high-end imaging devices and who may also have printing presses. No job should be undertaken without first consulting with the GASP who will eventually image or print it.*

## Assembling Documents

When a document is ready to be assembled, all the parts are ready to go. The last thing page layout specialists want to see is "Pix #14 TK," (*TK* is the standard abbreviation for "to come.") A size difference of just a fraction of an inch can throw an entire page off.

Page layout specialists quickly assemble the pages, using the comp (comprehensive sketch) as a guide. They create Masters so elements that will appear on every page do not have to be recreated each time. Style sheets are prepared, to make consistent application of character and paragraph features quick and easy. They flow text onto the pages, position artwork, and fine-tune the details. When the page layout specialists are finished, there should be no more changes to the document; such changes are very expensive to make after the document passes through this stage, because even a minor change can affect the flow of text throughout the entire document. Additionally, changes made at this point may require that other elements be changed. It is not difficult to double the cost of a project by making a change at this stage.

As the process of document production has evolved, a division of powers has developed. Content providers produce text, illustrations, and photographs. Production artists combine these elements in electronic documents. Prepress technicians color-correct scans and otherwise prepare the electronic document for printing. At the printing house, press, bindery and other specialists complete the process.

Today, many of us fulfill multiple functions. Many times, an artist will produce illustrations, perform production art roles, and even color-correct photos. However, the process and the specific skills needed are unchanged.

## From Concept to Mechanical: The Design Process

Design is creating the look of a document. Technically speaking, it has little or nothing to do with the content, and everything to do with the way that content speaks to its audience. It includes managing the geometry of pages: their size, orientation (portrait/vertical or landscape/horizontal), and the grid that will be followed to lead the viewer's eyes through the document. Design includes making decisions about the type of pictures that will illustrate the text, and determining every aspect of the typographic elements.

### Sketches from Thumbnail to Comp

Designing a document requires creativity and imagination, in addition to understanding the advantages and limitations of the media used. We recommend that initial sketches (called *thumbnails*) be created with paper and pencil, not on the computer. This is the way designers have traditionally created their designs, and it's still the best way. Many designs still originate on cocktail napkins or restaurant placemats.

Once the thumbnail sketch has been made, it can be refined quickly and easily on the computer. The computer is a wonderful production tool, but it is not particularly efficient as a design tool. You can take a pencil and paper anywhere and allow inspiration to strike. You probably won't lug your computer around everywhere you go.

*In the real world, the cost of producing a document is extremely important.* **Authors' Alterations (AAs)** *are defined as any change made to the original specifications. Excessive AAs late in the process add substantially to the cost of the job. Avoid them whenever possible by planning carefully and proofing thoroughly before going to press.*

*Although this thumbnail doesn't look like much, award-winning campaigns have been created on the backs of cocktail napkins.*

*Thumbnail sketch showing section chapter opener and standard page.*

After the basic idea has been sketched, your design will probably progress to the stage known as the *comprehensive sketch* or *comp*. This stage refines the thumbnail by providing graphic answers to the following questions:

- Trim size of the finished piece? Bleeds? Folds?
- Number of pages?
- Balance of pages? Margin size? Number of columns?
- Picture placement and cropping?
- Type specifications?
- Colors to be used?

An object that prints to the edge of the page is said to "bleed," because when it is created, it actually goes beyond (bleeds off) the edge of the page. Notice how these images do this.

III

Lorem ipsum dolor sit amet consectetuer adipiscing elit, sed diam nonummy nibh euismod tincidunt ut laoreet dolore magna aliquam erat volutpat. Ut wisi enim ad minim veniam, quis nostrud exerci tation ullamcorper suscipit lobortis nisl ut aliquip ex ea commoda consequat. Duis autem vel eum

III

Boats of all sizes and types arrive at Coco Head for the annual CocoLoco clambake and beach party. The event has been held every year since its founding in the mid-'60s, when The Beachboys and other rock 'n' roll entertainers were in their heyday. 400 people turned out for the event in 1998.

*Comp and finished Section Page, following the thumbnail shown earlier.*

Notice the refinements introduced in the final versions.

**Chapter 2**

L orem ipsum dolor sit amet consectetuer adipiscing elit, sed diam nonummy nibh euismod tincidunt ut laoreet dolore magna aliquam erat volutpat. Ut wisi enim ad minim veniam, quis nostrud exerci tation ullamcorper suscipit lobortis nisl ut aliquip ex ea commodo consequat. Duis autem vel eum iriure dolor in hendrerit in vulputate velit esse molestie consequat, vel illum dolore eu feugiat nulla facilisis at vero eros et accumsan et iusto odio dignissim

**Seashells by the Seashore 2**

L istening to the "sea" by holding a shell up to the ear was one of life's grand experiences when we were young. Discovering sea shells is still a delight. Every morning, when on vacation on Florida's Gulf Coast, you can see adults discovering again the almost-fogotten pleasures of child-hood as they strain through piles of shells deposited by the most recent high tide. Their oohs and aahs and squeals of delight when they find a treasure can't help but bring a smile.

---

Body Text 1-No Indent. consectetuer adipiscing elit, sed diam nonummy nibh euismod tincidunt ut laoreet dolore magna aliquam erat volutpat.
Body Text. Ut wisi enim ad minim veniam, quis nostrud exerci tation ullamcorper suscipit lobortis nisl ut aliquip ex ea commodo consequat. Duis autem vel eum iriure dolor in hendrerit in vulputate velit esse molestie consequat, vel illum

- Bulleted List 1-Space Above. Adolore eu feugiat nulla facilisis at vero eros
- Bulleted List. Luptatum zzril delenit augue duis dolore te feugait nulla facilisi
- Bulleted List 2-Space Below. Tincidunt ut laoreet dolore magna aliquam erat volutp

1. Table   Table   Table
2. Table   Table   Table

**Headline 1**

Lorem ipsum dolor sit amet consectetuer adipiscing elit, sed diam nonummy nibh euismod tincidunt ut laoreet dolore magna aliquam erat volutpat. Ut wisi enim ad minim veniam, quis nostrud exerci tation ullamcor

**Headline 2**

Per suscipit lobortis nisl ut aliquip ex ea commodo consequat. Duis autem vel eum iriure dolor in hendrerit in vel illum dolore eu feugiat nulla facilisis at vero eros et accumsan et iusto odio

*Caption Text*

**Headline 3**

Lorem ipsum dolor sit amet consectetuer adipiscing elit, sed diam nonummy nibh euismod tincidunt ut laoreet dolore magna aliquam erat volutpat. Ut wisi enim ad minim veniam, quis nostrud exerci tation ullamcorper suscipit lobortis nisl ut aliquip ex ea commodo consequat. Duis autem vel eum iriure dolor in hendrerit in vulputate velit esse molestie consequat, vel illum dolore eu feugiat nulla facilisis at vero eros et accumsan et iusto odio dignissim qui blandit praesent luptatum zzril delenit augue duis dolore te feugait nulla facilisi.

---

Often we forget the all-important fact that shells are not simply deposits of calcium — they're the "home" and protective coating of some sea critter. Occasionally, one animal grabs the shell for its home after the original occupant has died.
It's a little bit disconcerting, when you pick up a shell on the beach, to have a crab crawl out and nip your finger. Yet, that's exactly what can happen! To say that it's a "rude awakening" is quite an understatement.
Because shells may be the exoskeleton of a living animal, it is important to teach children that shells deserve the respect of other living creatures. When a live one is found, the appropriate response is to return it to its habitat.

*Typical shell by the sea*

**More About Shells**

It's no wonder we are intrigued by the variety of shells we discover. at,variety of shells we discover. They have been admired universally by civilizations from the earliest times of recorded history.
Ancient Phoenicians used the shells they harvested both as money and as jewelry. (It's always been common practice to make jewelry from one's valuables.) In the "New World," the natives who greeted Columbus and those who later met Miles Standish's party used shells in the same manner.
Of course, it's hard to even think about shells without considering the Polynesians. With them, shells, and the creatures who originally filled them, were a part of their daily life.

*The King of Shells*

It's no wonder the conch shell is held in such high regard. To begin with, it's a wonderful source of food. The conch is large, and its flesh is delectable. Although it's most often served in a chowder (with lots of pepper) or in a highly-spiced conch fritter, this sea creature can be prepared in a variety of ways. It's delicious and nutritious, as well.
In addition to being part of the food supply, these large shells were used for communication by a number of cultures. The Maya of Mexico's Yucatan peninsula removed the broad end of the shell, exposing the beginning of a spiral. This was smoothed and altered to individual taste, so the shell would produce a mellow, horn-like sound. The "voice" of the conch shell can be heard for miles — especially when played in either open mountain areas or across open water. It is this latter use that made it so valuable to the Polynesian sailors.

---

*Comps (left) and finished pages (right) for chapter openers and inside text pages. Note that the comp for the text page shows a variety of features (levels of headlines, body text, bulleted text, and caption formats), but does not attempt to show a full page layout.*

In the past, the comp was often prepared with colored markers and rubdown letters. Today, it is more often prepared on the computer, sometimes using nonsense type, called "greeking," at the appropriate size and line spacing. Pictures may be low-resolution versions of the actual images, or, more often, are images from stock libraries that give the look and feel of the image to be used.

The comp is often the first proof that a client approves. For documents that have a number of types of pages, or a number of styles, the comp includes samples of each. For example, a document might have a special look for section starts, one for chapters, and a still different look for pages of running text. Each type of page would be shown, but it wouldn't be necessary to show all 5 sections and all 30 chapters. There may also be specific styles for tables, sidebars, footnotes, and each level of headline.

Each of these would be included in the comp, allowing the client to approve or alter them at this preliminary stage, rather than when the document is completed.

When the comp is approved, the job moves into production. A close interaction among creatives, prepress production, and print professionals is vital in order to avoid costly mistakes, which can easily hide in a digital mechanical. The advantage of the digital mechanical is that changes can be made in text, images can be replaced, and colors can be changed, up to the very last minute — when the file is sent off to the service provider.

## Prepurposing and Repurposing Documents

*Although many programs supposedly can repurpose a document designed for print to the Web, the results are seldom acceptable unless the document has been prepurposed for multiple uses.*

Today's documents often do double- or even triple-duty. A magazine ad may be featured on the company's Web page; it may be included with sales kits. For that matter, it may even be screen printed on T-shirts or enlarged to wall size for use at trade shows. Because of this, it is important to know how each graphic element in the document is to be used, and to determine in advance how it should be produced for maximum flexibility.

### Understanding the Medium

When a document is designed — and this is a factor that even experienced designers often forget — the first consideration should be the medium or media in which it will be reproduced. Are you designing a newspaper ad? Will the ad appear in a magazine on glossy paper? Will it be photocopied and stuck under windshield wipers? Will it be displayed on a Web page?

In every case it is necessary to determine the resolution, and sometimes the structure, of the graphics, including their file type. Font decisions must be made, as must decisions affecting the number of colors to use and the color mode in which they will be presented on your page.

Nor should we think that we are limited to the choices we've just considered. It is also possible that a design will be screen printed, so six discrete colors may be desirable, rather than the standard four process colors. And if the design is to be screen printed, perhaps on T-shirts, it becomes important to consider the porosity of the medium, to avoid creating either clunky type and graphics, or elements that will disappear or break up because they are too delicate.

*The standard four process colors are Cyan, Magenta, Yellow, and Black, commonly referred to as "CMYK."*

Sometimes a document will be used in multiple media. When this is the case, even more planning must go into the document — and it will often need to be manufactured in different formats. One size does not fit all.

## Components of an Electronic Mechanical

Electronic mechanicals, like their physical predecessors, are comprised of text and images. Even though we have become a more picture-oriented society, text still comprises the majority of information in documents. And, believe it or not, text is much more difficult to manage than graphic elements.

### Type and Typography

Even in this age of multitudes of pictures, the fact remains that about 70%–80% of printed matter is text. While pictures help us demonstrate our point, text is an extension of speech. Since this is the case, we have a responsibility to present text in our documents in a highly readable form, taking advantage of technology, but more importantly, understanding how we can make the text in our documents best perform its task of communication.

### The Evolution of Type

As we explored a brief history of publishing, a part of that necessarily included references to the evolution of type. Type has evolved along two axes. The first is the design axis. This is the area that often interests people in type — the nuances and variety of design. The second axis is the mechanical and technological one — the area people begin to appreciate after they have used type for some time, or when they decide that they, too, would like to design a typeface.

### From Chancery to Garage

Although man has been recording his exploits from antediluvian times, we can reasonably assert that the first typographers were the scribes and other professionals charged with creating official records. The early letterforms — even as they were copied for use with early printing presses — were flowing, often ornate, and not nearly as readable as our modern type faces.

*Poetica Chancery*

**Goudy Text**

**Engravers Olde English**

**Fette Fraktur**

**american uncial**

*These examples of Blackletter type include chanceries, the German Fractura style, uncials, and others based on manuscript writing styles that predate the invention of moveable type.*

From these beginnings, type designers decided that changes were in order. Nicholas Jenson designed the first *Roman* font about 1470, followed by Aldus Manutius, who designed the first *Italic* a year later. Garamond and Caslon were also noted designers of this period. This style of type (*Oldstyle*) is characterized by letters that have some (but not great) contrast between their thick and thin strokes. The stress on curved strokes is inclined to the left. Early expressions of the style have a diagonal stroke on the lowercase "e" and the ascenders are approximately the same height as the capital letters. Later expressions make the stroke on the "e" more horizontal, and ascenders became taller.

ITC Berkeley Oldstyle *& Berkeley Oldstyle*
Adobe Caslon *& Adobe Caslon*
Stemple Garamond *& Stemple Garamond*
Goudy Oldstyle *& Goudy Oldstyle*
Minion *& Minion*
Poliphilus Roman *& Blado Italic*

*Oldstyle is one of the early styles of lettering designed for printing. Note the variation in the "e" and in the height of ascenders in comparison with uppercase letters. Notice also the evolution of the ampersand (&) as it progresses from the Latin "et" to the stylized figure we use today.*

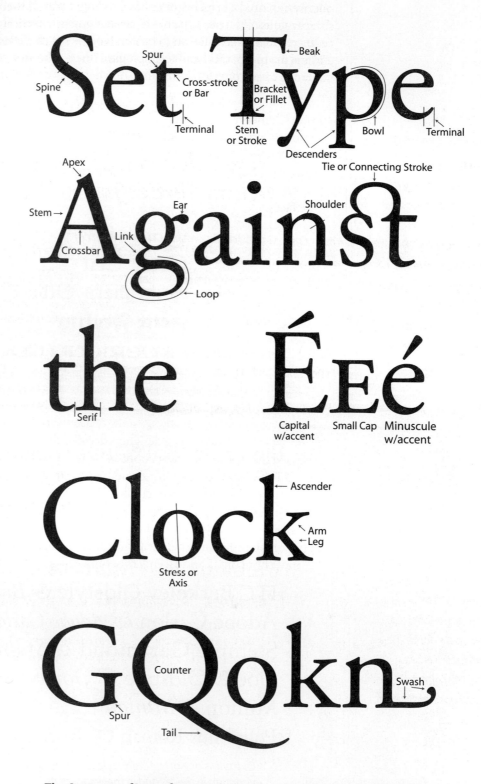

**The Anatomy of Letterform.** *Each part of a character has a specific name. Sometimes we confuse ourselves by using different terminology. Here are named parts of different letterforms.*

As you have noted, the development of lettering styles has undergone transition throughout history. As time passed, type was developed that showed greater stroke contrast with sharper serifs. The stress on curved strokes is nearly vertical. Near the end of the 17th century, this new style began to evolve. Notables such as Baskerville designed type in this era, and a typeface was developed for the *Times of London* that, with few changes, we know today as Times Roman.

ITC New Baskerville *& New Baskerville*
Bulmer *& Bulmer*
New Caledonia *& New Caledonia*
Janson Text *& Janson Text*
Life *& Life*
ITC Stone Serif *& Stone Serif*
Times New Roman *& Times New Roman*

*Transitional type styles show sharp serifs, a more vertical structure of the typeface itself, and a greater contrast between thick and thin strokes.*

As the *Transitional* style was developing, another style, known as *Modern* was building upon its structure, and creating a look and feel all its own. Designers Bodoni, Didot, and Walbaum contributed to the modern look, which is characterized by extreme contrast between thick and thin strokes. The serifs are usually very thin, and almost flat, displaying little of the bracketing of the Roman faces. Stress on the rounded letters is vertical.

Bauer Bodoni *& Bauer Bodoni*
Linotype Centennial *& Centennial*
ITC Fenice *& Fenice Oblique*
Melior *& Melior*
Walbaum *& Walbaum*
**Poster Bodoni & *Poster Bodoni***

*The Modern family of typefaces displays very strong changes between its thick and thin strokes, carried almost to caricature in the case of Poster Bodoni. Interestingly, ITC Fenice's "italic" is actually an oblique — the letter shape does not change.*

**Roman** *typefaces are so-named because they are based on serif variations developed by ancient Romans, and later by Italian humanistic lettering. A Roman typeface is neither italic nor bold, and is generally the primary typeface of its family.*

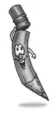

*Many of the examples of typefaces on these pages will show a prefix or foundry name (such as ITC or Linotype) prior to the Roman face; it is often missing from the italic due to space considerations.*

It would seem a logical extension of the Modern serif design to introduce a heavier *Slab Serif* to typefaces. However, these faces, first appearing in the early 19th century, differed radically from their historical predecessor because, instead of having a radical difference between thick and thin strokes, the strokes are almost invariably uniform. Stress on the rounded letters is almost vertical.

Candida & *Candida*
ITC Cheltenham & *Cheltenham*
**Berthold City** & *Berthold City*
**Clarendon**
ITC Lubalin Graph & *Lubalin Graph*
ITC Officina Serif & *Officina Serif*
Serifa & *Serifa*

*Slab Serif letterforms, from the very round letters of Lubalin Graph to the very narrow Officina and City typefaces, are unique in that the color is almost completely monotone. Some typefaces in this group have been adopted for use with the typewriter. Others, such as City, Lubalin, and Serifa, use an oblique rather than a true italic.*

*San Serif* means "without serif" even though some typefaces of this category have a flair in areas where serifs normally occur. Sans serif faces are also called *Grotesques* or *Gothics*. Primary subgroupings of this category include *Geometric* sans serifs, such as Futura and Kabel; *Neo-Grotesques*, such as Helvetica and Univers; and *Humanist* faces, such as Gill Sans and Optima.

Akzidenz Grotesk
Futura & *Futura*
Gill Sans & *Gill Sans*
**Neue Helvetica** & *Neue Helvetica*
ITC Kabel
Optima & *Optima*
Univers & *Univers*

*Sans Serif typefaces have a relatively consistent line weight. While some have a true italic, others simply oblique the letterform. A number of sans serifs have no italic at all.*

Beyond the typefaces used for creating books, brochures, and other text-heavy publications, are those used for invitations, announcements, certificates, and so forth. Often these are produced using typefaces we know as *Scripts*. They first appeared as distinct typefaces in the mid-16th century. We generally include in this group any typeface that looks as though it

*The "color" of type is its optical appearance, based on the typeface itself and the density of type on the page. Slab Serif typefaces have a consistent density.*

*Many families of type do not contain an italic.*

has been written with a pen or brush. (We've made the exception of uncials, which, in our estimation, belong with the earlier letterforms.) Scripts may be formal or informal.

| | |
|---|---|
| *Belleview* | *Isadora* |
| *Brush Script* | *Linoscript* |
| *Caflisch* | *Mistral* |
| **Cascade** | *Palace* |
| *Cataneo* | *Pepita* |
| *Coronet* | *Reporter 2* |
| **Dom Casual** | *Snell Roundhand* |

*Script faces are unique. Believe it or not, each of these scripts is the same size, 21 pt. The substantial variety available within this family of type makes for interesting applications within documents not requiring a great deal of text.*

All the typeface categories we've discussed are usable as text. There are some faces, though, that are designed specifically for use as headlines, or for fanciful applications. While the first use of a *Decorative* face was likely in 1690 (the typeface was Union Pearl), they came into extensive use in the 19th century in response to the need for advertising typography. Today there are some type foundries that create almost nothing but display or decorative type.

| | |
|---|---|
| **Aachen Bold** | IRONWOOD |
| ITC ANNA | JUNIPER |
| Arnold Boecklin | Latino Elongated |
| **Blackoak** | PONDEROSA |
| BROADWAY | ITC MACHINE |
| CASTELLAR | Revue |
| CHARLEMAGNE | ROSEWOOD |
| Giddyup | STOP |
| Hobo | UMBRA |

*Decorative typefaces are designed, generally speaking, for use in headlines. Notice the variety with these fonts. While they are clearly unsuited for mainstream text use, they still follow the rules for readability and form. Even Ponderosa, which is very scrunched at 21 pt., is a usable face in much larger sizes. Decorative type should not be used in small sizes.*

While the Modern class of typefaces was regarded as somewhat outrageous in the early days of its development, it had nothing on today's typefaces, called, alternately *Grunge*, *Garage* (because many of the developers work out of their homes or garages), and *Garbage* (for obvious reasons). They are wild, whimsical, and follow few rules but their own. However, they are usable (in moderation) to make a strong statement.

Chilada UNO          Chilada Dos
Chilada Tres         Chilada Cuatro
Sand  Screwed  Up  Typewriter
Weimar               Zeitgeist MT Craz Paving

*Grunge, Garage, or Garbage fonts can really affect your vision if you look at them for too long. Even their baselines are not apparently regular. Many fonts such as these are available from online services as shareware.*

There is one last category of typeface we should consider — *Pi*, *Symbol*, *Logo* and *Ornamental* type. Typefaces in this category are not alphabetical, but play an important role in communication. We'll take a look at representative typefaces from this category. Think of ways you might be able to use symbol type for your applications.

Caslon Ornaments

Carta

Monotype Directions

MiniPics-Lil Dinos

Monotype Signs

Stone Phonetics IPA

ɑßçðɛɸɢʜɪɟɨʟɯɲɔʼɹʀʃθʊʊʋʘʎχʏʒˇ..‗

Universal Greek with Math Pi

αβψδεφγηιξκλμνοπ + − × ÷ ∓° √

*As you see, even though these typefaces are not comprised of letters, they can still communicate effectively. When doing special kinds of work, such as math, engineering, or map creation, such fonts are all but indispensable.*

## Type Mechanics

Now that we've explored the varieties of type, we want to know how it functions, and how we can work with it within InDesign. To understand type, we need to understand its various parts.

To begin with, type is different from graphics because there is literally more to it than meets the eye. The characters of a typeface are designed to interact with one another. Some typefaces have hundreds or even thousands of sub-commands, known as "kerning pairs," that allow the individual letters to interact with no operator intervention. Other typefaces have few, if any, kerning pairs. You often find the latter situation when you purchase shareware fonts, or low-priced CDs with thousands of fonts on them. Generally speaking, if the designer has taken the time to create a large number of kerning pairs, you have a good font. If the kerning pairs are absent, the font may be well drawn, but you'll have to work harder to get it to look good on the page in paragraphs of text.

## *Dissect the Letterform*

1.  On a sheet of paper, neatly print your first and last name.

2.  Without referring to the illustration on page 18, identify the primary parts of the letters in your name.

3.  With the page still in front of you, flip back to the illustration and note how many additional elements you can find.

4.  Paying attention to the stress of the letters and the relationship between x-height, ascenders and cap height, what family of typefaces does your style most nearly represent?

## Measuring Type

To talk intelligently about type, we should recognize the design elements that comprise the letterform. Both horizontal and vertical measure are important as we work with type in our documents.

The *baseline* is the imaginary line upon which each standard character rests. (There are a few figures that do not rest on the baseline.) Even with Grunge fonts, this line exists in the design process.

The height of the lowercase letter is defined by the *x-height*, which is the measured height of the lowercase letter "x," from the baseline to the flat top of the letter. You'll note, in the following example, that some rounded letters, such as the "p," push above the x-height. This is the letter's *shoulder height*, and is generally not measured.

Stems of lowercase letters that project above the x-height, such as the "b," "d," "f," "h," "k," and "l," are called "ascenders." Portions that project below the baseline are called "descenders" ("g," "j," "p," "q," and "y"). In many alphabets, the ascender is actually taller than the height of the capital letter, called the "cap height."

Most typefaces have a built-in space above the ascender, and extending to the height of the nominal size of the letter. This is called the "body clearance line," and is designed into the typeface so that ascenders from one line and descenders from another will not collide.

*Over the next week, collect as many examples of different typefaces as possible. Classify them according to their main categories.*

*The **nominal** size of a letter is the size that we call it, or name it. While a 72-point letter does not measure 72 points, there are 72 points from its descender to the top of the body clearance line.*

Few typefaces from different families are the same height. Matching a type size requires knowledge of the typefaces involved. Perseverance, and a little luck doesn't hurt.

Clearance
Ascender
Cap Height
Small Cap
X-Height

Baseline

Descender

72 Points

This example has been constructed of Adobe Minion, in uppercase, lowercase, and small capital letters. The type size is 72 pts. (measured from the descender to the body clearance line).

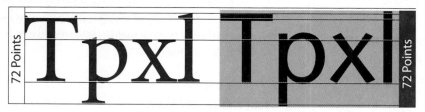

72 Points

72 Points

In this example, we have compared Adobe Minion with Stone Sans. Notice how much deeper the descender drops, and how much taller the ascender rises. Minion is approximately 68 pts. from descender to ascender, while Stone Sans is nearly 71 pts. If we measured these typefaces with a ruler, we would not be able to tell their exact point size. Stone Sans' cap height alone is 3 pts. taller.

Type has dimension — we must deal with its width as well as its height. Just as each character has space built-in above it to allow for fit, it also has a space allocation to allow it to fit with the next letter in a line of type. The entire character width includes a *left sidebearing* and a *next-character origin point*. Between them is the space actually taken up by the character, called the "bounding box." The bounding box is measured from the character's leftmost point to its rightmost point. The three widths together make up the *character width*.

That all seems pretty basic. The problem arises when we try to align type that is radically different in size. Because the left sidebearing and next-character origin point are empty space around a character, and are defined as a percentage of the overall width, the space varies with the point size, so type may not align properly on the right and left margins. Let's see how this looks.

The ***bounding box*** of a single typographic character, also called a "glyph," is similar to the bounding box of a graphic. It includes every element within its assigned area, creating the boundary of that character.

# Headline

Because the left sidebearing is based upon the point size, it is proportionately larger in headlines than it is in body text, giving the impression that there is an error in the alignment of the headline,

To overcome the problem, it is necessary to determine (by experimentation) the value of the left sidebearing for larger point sizes, relative to body text, and adjust the indents appropriately.

*When large headlines are set, especially with fussy ad copy, the inset caused by the left sidebearing can create problems.*

When characters are kerned or tracked, this affects the character origin points, resulting in more tightly or more loosely structured type, as shown here.

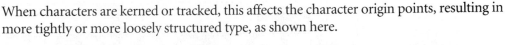

# Type Type Type
# TYPE TYPE TYPE

*In the example above, the word is shown with tight kerning and tracking, built-in kerning, and loose kerning and tracking. Notice that the words typed in all capital letters are more readable with looser kerning and that caps and minuscules look better set tighter.*

### Type Technology

Over the years, type has evolved from wood blocks and metal castings, from which the document was printed directly; to brass matrices, from which type was cast into lead molds (which, for lengthy press runs were coated with nickel to make them last longer); to negative images on a glass or plastic matrix, to be imaged to photographic paper or film; to the digital images we use today. In the past, font technology was proprietary, and generally worked with only one typesetting system. Linotype type would work with Linotype typesetters, Monotype with Monotype, AlphaType with AlphaType, and so on. There were many manufacturers of typesetting systems — both hardware and software — and to change systems meant purchasing another entire type library.

Today, there are two dominant type standards: PostScript, developed by Adobe Systems, and TrueType, developed by Apple Computer and later codeveloped by Microsoft Corporation. TrueType is integrated into both the Windows and Macintosh operating systems, and PostScript type works well when Adobe Type Manager is also in use. PostScript type is a subset of the PostScript page description language used in professional publishing.

Regardless of whether they are TrueType or PostScript, fonts are constructed from outlines, and are entirely editable — in fact, they may be converted into graphics by illustration programs, so that they may be altered into logotypes, or simply saved in a graphics format, reducing the opportunity for errors to be introduced into documents. The letters are designed for either system on a one-em square grid.

*Although there were conflicts between PostScript and TrueType fonts when TrueType was in earlier stages of development, those problems are not relevant today. You should note, however, that PostScript fonts and TrueType fonts may contain different metrics, so they are not interchangeable. If you create a document using the PostScript version of a font, you should print it using a PostScript, not a TrueType, font.*

*If you learn the typographic terms and customs, you will be able to discuss the typographic aspects of your job intelligently with others. If you don't learn them, you'll likely have problems communicating your needs and desires to other industry professionals.*

*Type is constructed using outlines. It may be reproduced at virtually any size at the highest resolution of the imaging device (monitor or printer) without any deterioration in quality.*

## Typographic Terms and Customs

Many of the terms we use to describe page elements, spacing, measurement, and other features when working with documents can well be described as *typographic terms.* In addition, many customs have evolved over the years. Some of these are noted here for your reference:

### Letterform & Character Construction

**Ascender.** The part of a lowercase letter, such as a "d" or a "b," that extends above the body of the letter or the x-height of the typeface.

**Baseline.** The imaginary line on which the "base" of type sits. In most typeface designs, rounded and pointed letters dip below the baseline.

**Bounding Box.** Space taken up by the width and height of the character itself, with no allowance for spacing.

**Cap Height.** The height of a capital letter, measured from the baseline to the top of the capital letter.

**Character Set.** The entire group of characters that make up a typeface, including alphanumeric and nonalphanumeric symbols. The set can be specific to the typeface or to the computing platform on which it is used.

**Character Space.** The space between two bounding boxes, including the left sidebearing and the space between the bounding box and the next character point.

**Font.** A typeface. Traditionally, one size of a typeface, such as 10-pt. Minion. PostScript and TrueType fonts contain all sizes of the typeface.

*Many italic letters actually change shape. Note the differences here between the Roman and italic letterforms:*

a    *a*

e    *e*

f    *f*

w    *w*

&    *&*

**Italic.** One of the primary styling options for type. Usually, but not always, related to a Roman font. Italic fonts slant to the right at approximately 12°. Often, italic letters in a type family change form from the Roman letter.

**Letterspace.** Space designed between letters; alternately, the alteration of that space which may be inserted using kerning, tracking, and H&J routines.

**Ligature.** A combination of two letters, which functions as a single letter. Common ligatures are ff, fi, fl, ffi, and ffl. They are available in the Expert series of some fonts.

**Lowercase.** The 26 letters of the alphabet. Minuscules. In the days of metal type, capital letters were stored in the top (upper) case, minuscules were stored in the lower case.

**Minuscule.** The 26 letters of the alphabet when not capitalized.

**Oblique.** A mechanical slanting of Roman letters to achieve the effect of italics. Unlike true italics, the letterform does not change shape.

**Pi.** Type that is not part of the character set of the font and is generally a symbol character.

**Roman.** One of the primary styling options for type. It is generally the base, or primary font in a family, such as Times Roman.

**Sans Serif.** Typeface in which the strokes simply end. There is no finishing stroke at an angle to the stroke which comprises the primary letterform. This is Myriad, a sans serif typeface.

**Script.** A decorative typeface that resembles handwriting.

**Sentence Case.** A headline style wherein only the first word and any proper nouns are capitalized.

**Serif.** Typeface with a finishing stroke at the end of most primary strokes which comprise the primary letterform. This is Minion, a serif typeface.

**Shoulder.** The height to the curve of rounded lowercase letters, such as "n."

**Size.** The height of the letters of a typeface, measured in points from the descender to the body clearance line. We call this the "nominal point size" because, while it is not measurable (the height of the body clearance area is variable), it is the "named" size of the type, such as 12 point.

**Small Caps.** Capital letters which are approximately the same height as lowercase letters. They are often used when acronyms, such as CD-ROM are included in lines of text, or for common abbreviations, such as AM or PM. Although small caps can be "faked" using the publishing program, it is better to use a font designed with small caps, such as the Expert series available with some fonts.

**Title Case.** A headline style wherein all words, except articles and prepositions, are capitalized.

**Type.** Any characters which comprise a font. The term originally referred to the raised character that would be inked and then struck against paper. The word originated from the Greek *typos*, meaning "a blow" or "the mark of a blow."

**Typographic Characters.** Characters which differentiate typography from word processing or typewriter-generated text. These include quotation marks, en and em dashes, and spaces, among many others.

**Uppercase.** The 26 letters of the alphabet. Capitals. In the days of metal type, capital letters were stored in the top (upper) case, minuscules were stored in the lower case.

**Word Space.** Space between words as defined by the designer of the typeface.

**X-Height.** The height of a lowercase "x" measured from the baseline.

### Horizontal and Vertical Measurement

**Pica.** Unit of measure. Twelve points. In modern usage, a pica is 1/6 inch.

**Point.** Unit of measure. In modern usage, 1/72 inch.

**Vertical Spacing.** The space between lines of type. In addition to the spacing between lines in a single paragraph, additional vertical spacing between paragraphs may be achieved using "Before Paragraph" and "After Paragraph" spacing.

### Letter Space and Line Space

**Em Space.** A space equal in width to the nominal point size. In 10-pt. type, an em space is 10 pts. wide.

**En Space.** A space equal to half the width of an em space.

**Figure Space.** A space equal to the width of a single number

**French Spacing.** Double spaces after a period or colon.

**Kerning.** Adjusting two consecutive letters so that the space between them is pleasing to the eye.

**Kerning Pair.** Any two letters which have been kerned. Well-designed fonts have many kerning pairs prebuilt into them.

**Leading.** The space between lines of type, measured from baseline to baseline. It may be defined in relative or absolute terms. Hence, 10-pt. type set with 12-pts. baseline to baseline may be defined as 10/12 or 10+2. However, "plus" spacing is usually reserved for interparagraph space, so we could see a specification of 10/12+3 meaning that the paragraph would be set with 12 pts. between lines, with an additional 3 pts. between paragraphs. The term originates from the compositor's practice of placing thin strips of lead between lines of type to space them further apart.

**Line Length.** The overall space allocation of any line, measured from the left-hand margin to the right-hand margin.

**Paragraph Indent.** A space before the first word which identifies a new paragraph.

**Thin Space.** A fixed (non-justifying) space one-fourth the width of an em space.

**Tracking.** The spacing of a group of letters. To maintain the overall effect of uniformity, entire paragraphs, not short phrases or lines within the paragraph, should be assigned the same tracking value.

*The definition of **widows** and **orphans** is sometimes flip-flopped, depending upon the manufacturer of the software program. That's why we usually refer to them collectively as "widows and orphans." Remember that you don't want them in your documents.*

### Hyphenation and Justification

**H & J.** Hyphenation and Justification. The process by which a page layout program applies the rules and parameters specified for hyphenating text and allowing proper spacing.

**Hyphenation.** Separating or joining words using the hyphen character. Hyphenation follows language-specific rules for separating words.

**Justification.** Alignment of text, specifying which margin(s) will align. Normally, *justified* means both margins align; *flush left* or *flush right* indicates which margin is aligned (they may also be expressed as *ragged right* or *ragged left*); *centered* indicates that the text is centered horizontally within the text area of the page, with neither margin aligning.

**Orphan.** A single line of a paragraph that falls at the bottom of a column or page.

**Ragged Text.** Text set with one or both margins variable.

**Widow.** A condition where the last line of a paragraph falls at the top of a column. Also, when the last line of a paragraph consists of only one word or is very short with relationship to the line length.

### Typographic Characters

**Accents.** When typesetting foreign words that originate in non-English languages, it is important to insert the proper accent. Examples: resumé, entrée, pâté, jäger, mañana.

**Ellipses.** Also dots of ellipsis or ellipsis points. Three spaced periods (…) indicating the omission of words from a quotation.

**Em Dash.** ( — ) A long dash, used to indicate a change of thought in a sentence.

**En Dash.** ( – ) A dash approximately half the width of an em dash. It replaces the words "to" or "through," and is used as a minus sign for mathematical purposes.

**Feet/Inches.** These marks ( ′ ″ ) must often come from the Symbol font or another font. They are different from the primes ( ' " ).

**Mult.** The multiplication symbol ( × ). It is not an "x."

**Quotation Marks.** These marks may be single ( ' ' ) or double ( " " ). Often the program will allow them to be automatically substituted for single and double primes ( ' " ).

### Typographic Terms

**Bulleted List.** A series of entries in a document, each entry of which begins with a nonalphanumeric character, such as a traditional bullet ( • ) or another character, such as this one ✔.

**Folio.** Page number.

**Grid.** A system of dividing a page into sections to ensure readability and continuity of design.

**Guides.** Nonprinting elements of a page, designed to assist the page layout specialist in placement of text and graphics.

**Gutters.** Vertical space between adjacent columns within a page or table, between the inside margin and binding, or between the three trim margins and the image area. Internal gutters are sometimes called "alleys." Outside gutters are also called "margins."

**Headers, Footers.** Text that prints in the top or bottom margin of each page of a document. They usually include information such as page number, title, date, and so forth.

**Margin.** The space between the edge of the page and the beginning of the standard grid of text and graphics to allow for visual space, trimming, and binding.

**Numbered List.** A series of entries in a document, each entry of which begins with a number. Typically, the decimal points align.

**Paragraph Rules.** Lines above or below a paragraph.

**Pull Quote, Callout.** Text "pulled" or "called" out from the body of text and used as a graphic element.

**Reverse Type.** Type that is white on a colored or black background. It is the nonprinting, rather than the printing area.

**River.** Wide areas of white running through a column of type, caused by poor H&J routines in justified type.

**Spellcheck.** A tool available to check the spelling of words against a dictionary, rules, and algorithms. It is not a substitute for a proofreader.

**Style Sheet.** A group of character attributes and paragraph formats that can be applied in one step to a paragraph or to a range of characters. Collectively, all the styles in a document, and their interactivity with one another.

**Typography, Typographic.** The arrangement, style, and general appearance of matter printed from type. Typography takes into consideration elements such as line spacing, word and character spacing, and the shape of individual letters. The application of art to the science of type.

**Typographic Customs**
**Line Spacing.** Never press the Return key twice. Allow InDesign to set up space before and space after paragraphs instead.

**Paragraph Indents.** InDesign will insert paragraph indents automatically, so inserting a tab is unnecessary. Inserting spaces using the Spacebar is unacceptable; in justified paragraphs, spaces are of variable width, which would result in indents of variable width.

**Sentence Spacing.** When typing documents, put only one space after sentences. In the "old days" when each character had the same width space, two spaces were necessary to make reading easier. Today, one space does the job, and if the line of text is justified, two spaces following a period will create a huge hole.

**Tabs.** Insert only one tab if you are entering your text in a word-processing document. InDesign may be set up to properly align tabs.

## Images

As you are aware, there's more to creating attractive publications than using text. InDesign's images can come from a variety of sources. Some will be computer-generated from programs such as CorelDRAW!, Adobe Illustrator, or Macromedia FreeHand. Others will be scanned from photographs, traditionally produced sketches, line art, or illustrations. Still others may be created within InDesign.

*Raster images used in print publishing generally have a resolution of 266–300 dots per inch — that's a total of 5,660,480–7,200,000 spots in an 8×10 photo.*

*Conversely, images published to the Web have a resolution of 72 dots per inch — a total of only 414,720 spots in an 8×10 photo.*

Inserting graphics is straightforward. However, unlike text, it is critical to understand the benefits and limitations of different types of graphic files. Ultimately, what is important is whether the picture will print to the desired medium.

Graphics fall into two categories: vector and raster. *Vector* graphics are described as being object-oriented, resolution-independent, or "draw" type graphics. *Raster* graphics are described as bitmap, resolution-dependent, or "paint" type graphics.

Vector objects are mathematically defined as a series of straight lines, arcs, circles, and squares. They are sets of mathematical instructions that can be scaled in any direction with no loss in resolution. When they are printed to a high-resolution printer or imagesetter, they will print with no "jaggies."

Raster images are defined by individual pixels (picture elements). The number of pixels making up the raster image is fixed, and will remain the same no matter how much you magnify the graphic. As magnification increases, pixels get larger and are visible to the naked eye, rather than leaving smooth curves or subtle gradations.

*Cattleya orchid (see below) at high magnification, low-resolution.*

Commonly used raster images include BMP and TIFF files for print, and JPEG and GIF files for the Web. Raster graphics are created in programs such as MetaCreations Painter and Adobe Photoshop, and include scanned images.

*Pixels are picture elements, a measure of monitor resolution. Dots refer to the screening of a halftone. Spots refers to the printer's resolution.*

*Vector lily in EPS format (left) and Cattleya orchid in TIFF format (right).*

High-end painting, photo-retouching programs, and scanners can all create TIFF images. These images can be bitmapped (black and white), grayscale (up to 256 levels of gray), or color. The resolution of a TIFF image is directly related to the resolution at which it was created. If you enlarge a TIFF image too much, it will deteriorate when printed.

For printing, you'll ideally want to use EPS (if you are printing to a PostScript printer) and TIFF images, and for the Web, JPEG and GIF. These files are all compatible with the environments in which they will be used.

## Publishing for Print and Electronic Distribution

We mentioned earlier that creating documents for Web publication is different than creating them for print. The differences are made clear when we examine the following table.

| Element | Print | Web |
|---|---|---|
| **Format** | Usually vertical. 8.5″× 11″ is standard | Usually horizontal (to fit monitor). 640 × 480 pixels (approximately 9″× 6.7″) |
| **Type** | Fixed. What you produce is what is seen | Variable. Often depends on what the reader has in the computer |
| **Graphics** | High-Resolution CMYK or spot color TIFF or EPS format | Low-Resolution RGB JPEG or GIF format |
| **Color Display** | Fixed. What you produce is what is seen | Variable. Depends on the color depth of the viewer's computer, and on how color is calibrated on that system |
| **Interaction** | May be read | May be read, may link to other documents, may be used for commerce |
| **Modification** | Once a document is printed, it cannot be modified, except at substantial expense | May be modified at will, even automatically updating itself from a database |

While the difficulties presented in designing for both print and Web media are not insurmountable, they are a design issue that must be addressed when the project is being defined. All too often, a document will be prepared for print, then the decision will be made to adapt the print document for the Web. This not only is impractical, but also results in documents that do not work well and get poor results.

When designing for both media, the document will be produced in two distinct formats, usually using different fonts. There will also be a separate set of graphics files. While color is critical for print documents, it is far less so on the Web, since color is dependent on the monitor of the viewer rather than on an element that the creator can control. One of the greatest benefits of Web documents is that there can be extensive interaction with the viewer, as opposed to a static print page.

### Documents Purposed for Print Publishing

Programs designed to help you produce documents for print publishing in quantity are somewhat more complicated than word processing programs. This is because they need to be more flexible in determining page structure and in assigning printing parameters.

### Structuring the Published Document

Documents designed for print publishing, whether they are highly structured books or freewheeling, design-heavy advertisements, are generally going to be much more involved than office documents.

Because of the intricacies of its design, a book may have dozens, or even hundreds, of styles. Five levels of headlines are not unusual, nor are nine different styles for bullets. For documents such as these, the powerful style-sheet feature of InDesign comes into play.

Although ads have much less structure than do books and annual reports, they have a variety of type styles and sizes much of the time. When ads are done as a series, the style-sheet feature is again valuable to ensure consistency from document to document. In addition, it is important to be able to adjust the fit of letters with one another to make them visually pleasing. This is called "kerning," "tracking," or "mortising."

Finally, a smooth interaction with text and graphics must be achieved. It isn't enough to be able to place a picture on the page. The type must be able to flow around the graphic, and the graphic element should be able to flow with the text.

## Printing the Document

While an office document will usually have just a few copies printed, a published document can reasonably be expected to print hundreds, thousands, or even more, depending upon the nature of the publication. Alternately, one each of thousands may be indicated, as in the case of massive mail merges and customized documents.

Sometimes a black-and-white version of a color presentation is needed, so instead of printing to a color printer, the document is printed to black and white as a *composite*. This preserves the tonality of the colors by printing colors as shades of gray. Documents printed on a color laser printer are also composites.

Black-and-white documents are the mainstay of much of the printing done in the business community today. Often these are printed to very fast, high-resolution laser printers, to be assembled into books "on the fly."

Although these are usually printed over a network, there is not a lot of difficulty associated with this type of printing. Often, the file is simply sent to the server for an in-plant printer, or it is delivered to an outside service provider for imaging.

On the other hand, documents that will be printed on a printing press must have their colors *separated*; each color must appear on a separate printing plate. There are two kinds of color-separated documents.

*Spot Color* is a second color that is made up of one ink, such as Pantone 186 (PMS 186) which is bright red. If a document is black and PMS 186, each color will print on its own printing plate.

*Process Color* is color comprised of the process inks — cyan, magenta, yellow, and black — known in the industry as "CMYK." If you mix the equivalent of PMS 186 from process inks, you will have percentages of magenta, yellow, and black, each on their own printing plate. (There is no cyan in this ink equivalent.)

Colors defined as RGB will not always separate correctly for the lithographic printing process, although they work well for other processes, such as printing to color copiers, large-format inkjet printers, and other RGB-savvy devices.

### Documents Purposed for the World Wide Web

Documents that will end up on the Web must meet different standards than documents to be printed. In our nice, neat world of print publishing, the person who assembles the page defines exactly how it will appear when it is printed. On the Web, the standards are different.

Although fonts can be made a part of a graphic, it is more difficult to define specific fonts to display as editable fonts. For the most part, it is necessary to define your page to the lowest common denominator, so virtually every computer will have the proper fonts.

It is also important that pages load quickly. If graphics are poorly created (they take too long to load), a person accessing a Web site will simply "turn the page" and move to another one, possibly another Web site.

Additionally, while it is important to use CMYK for graphics to be printed, it is equally important to use RGB for Web-based color. And don't expect that everyone will see the same colors that you see. Monitors have different fluorescents, different color palettes, and different color depths — while you're looking at millions of colors, someone else may only be able to see 256.

## Summary

You've become acquainted with the historical origins and the progress of publishing, from its ancient beginnings through the Renaissance and into the computer age. In addition, you've become familiar with a number of terms used when referring to elements of documents.

We've considered the process of publishing, from thumbnail sketch to digital mechanical. We've compared files designed for print with files designed for use on the Web, and have noted some different parameters for each.

As you continue with this course, you'll discover more facets of publishing and will learn to create documents for print, for the Web, or for multiple applications.

# CHAPTER 2

# Getting Acquainted with InDesign

## CHAPTER OBJECTIVE:

To become familiar with the basic tools, windows, menus and palettes of InDesign. To learn to navigate within a document, managing the many palettes and maximizing screen space. In Chapter 2, you will:

- Learn to move comfortably from page to page, and from one size view of the page to another.

- Explore the Toolbox and the functions of each tool.

- Practice grouping and arranging palettes as well as minimizing and maximizing palette size, to work most efficiently.

- Review menu basics and learn to use the Properties menus.

# Getting Acquainted with InDesign

InDesign, like many other page layout applications, offers a variety of ways to perform tasks. For now, we'll break them into three categories — tools, menus, and palettes. Don't try to memorize the information that follows; we just want you to be aware of some of your available options.

In this chapter we will present various tools and features available in InDesign. Learning which tool to access for a particular task is key to increased productivity. Time is money, and your ability to streamline the production cycle of any project will bring you one step closer to meeting your deadlines.

## The Document Window

A new or existing InDesign document is restricted visually by the available screen space. The Toolbox, palettes, and document page quickly fill the document with task-specific items.

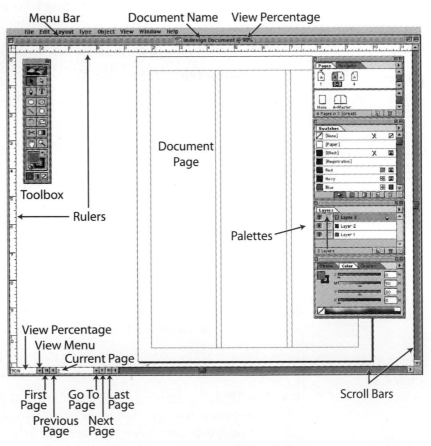

*Macintosh Document Window. The Windows version is very similar.*

**View Percentage.** This box shows the current level of magnification your document displays. Highlight this box at the bottom left of the screen and type in your desired percentage of magnification. Apply this with Return or Enter to change the view.

**View.** Next to the View Percentage box, is a pop-up menu selection of set percentages from which to choose.

**First Page.** This button takes you to the initial page of the document.

**Previous Page.** The Previous Page button moves you back one page.

**Current Page.** This box shows the current page number. You can go to another page by highlighting this box and typing in the desired page number. Press Return/Enter to apply.

**Go To Page.** Next to the Current Page box is a pop-up menu allowing you to go to any page in the document.

**Next Page.** This button moves you from the current page to the following page.

**Last Page.** The Last Page button moves you to the final page of the document.

## The Toolbox

The Toolbox contains tools that serve a particular function, with no other menu or palette able to create the same effect in the same manner. The other tools are used for selecting, creating transformations, modifying paths, painting, and moving the page.

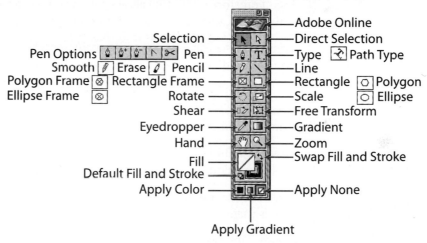

**Adobe Online.** This tool allows you to receive the most up-to-date technical and creative information about Adobe Corporation. You must have Internet access, be online, and have a Web browser to use this feature.

**Selection.** This tool selects an entire object or group of objects by clicking on them or dragging a selection marquee around the target objects.

**Direct Selection.** This tool directly isolates and selects specific parts of an object or path. It can also be used to select groups of objects and nested groups of objects.

**Pen.** The Pen tool is the primary drawing tool, creating straight or curved vector paths. The fly-out menu of the Pen tool offers three optional tools: Add Anchor Point, Delete Anchor Point, and Convert Anchor Point. The Scissors tool (see below) is included with the Pen tools.

**Type.** This is the only tool that allows you to directly type text into the document. The Selection tool adjusts the handles of text frames. The fly-out menu accesses the Path Type tool, used to set type on a Bézier path.

**Rectangle Frame.** This tool is used to create frames into which type is flowed or graphics are placed. The Ellipse Frame and Polygon Frame tools are also accessed from this button, by holding down the mouse button until they appear in the fly-out menu.

*Shortcuts for accessing the Toolbox tools:*

*Except with the Type tool selected, hold down the Shift Key to cycle through tools that are layered.*

*Selection tool – V*

*Direct Selection tool – A*

*Pen tool – P*
  *(also Scissors)*

*Type tool – T*

*Pencil tool – N*
  *(also Smooth & Erase)*

*Line tool – \*

*Frame tools – F*

*Rectangle tool – M*
  *(also Ellipse & Polygon)*

*Rotate tool – R*

*Scale tool – S*

*Shear tool – O*

*Free Transform tool – E*

*Eyedropper tool – I*

*Gradient tool – G*

*Hand tool – H*

*Zoom tool – Z*

*Fill/Stoke – X (this toggles)*

*Swap Fill/ Stroke – Shift-X*

*Default Fill /Stroke – D*

*Apply Color – <*

*Apply Gradient – >*

*Apply None – /*

*Double-clicking on the Line tool icon brings up the Stroke palette.*

*Double-clicking on the Polygon tool icon brings up the Polygon Settings dialog box, which can then be used to modify the Polygon.*

*Create a circle or a square by holding the Shift key while dragging the Ellipse or Rectangle tool.*

*To activate the Hand tool with any other tool selected, press the Spacebar.*

**Rectangle.** This tool is used to draw rectangles, which may be constrained to squares by holding down the Shift key when dragging. The Ellipse and Polygon tools are also accessed from this button, by holding down the mouse button until they appear in the fly-out menu.

**Line.** Dragging the Line tool, then releasing it creates a single, straight line with no internal Bézier points. Lines may be constrained to 45° angle increments by holding down the Shift key as the Line tool is dragged.

**Rotate.** The Rotate tool is a transformation tool that spins a selected object (or objects) around a set Origin Point.

**Scale.** This tool enlarges or reduces an object around a set Origin Point. To constrain the object's proportions, hold down Command/Control-Shift when dragging the Scale tool on the object.

**Shear.** Shearing an object skews (slants) an object along a horizontal axis or rotates the object along horizontal and vertical axes.

**Free Transform.** This tool allows you to perform a variety of transformations — move, scale, reflect, rotate, and shear — upon an object without changing tools.

**Scissors.** When clicked on a vector path, the Scissors tool will split the path at the selected point, providing separate anchor points that can be moved or deleted. It is located under the Pen tool.

**Eyedropper.** This tool copies and applies type, fill, and stroke attributes as well as color from the element it samples.

**Gradient.** The Gradient tool works in conjunction with the Gradient palette to change the angle, direction, and type of gradient that fills the selected object.

**Hand.** The Hand tool moves the document around within the enclosing window screen. This is useful for better viewing of a page or specific items.

**Zoom.** This tool enlarges or reduces a document's view to preset percentages. Clicking without holding a complementing key enlarges the view. Holding the Option/Alt key while clicking reduces the view. When the tool is dragged around an object, "marqueeing" it, the selected area fills the center of the screen.

**Fill box.** The Fill box applies a chosen color, gradient, or pattern to the interior of an object. It works with the Apply Color palette, which has a Fill box as well.

**Swap Fill and Stroke.** This tool reverses the two, allowing the Fill to acquire the Stroke color, and the Stroke to acquire the Fill color.

**Default Fill and Stroke.** With just one mouse click, this tool will return the Fill and Stroke tools to their defaults of a Fill of None, and a Black Stroke.

**Stroke.** The stroke box is the defining outline of a vector path. The Stroke tool in the Toolbox applies color to the stroke of a selected object. Attributes of the stroke are defined in the Stroke palette.

**Apply Color.** Clicking with this tool applies its set color to either the Fill or Stroke of a selected object, determined by whichever tool (Fill or Stroke) is active. The Color palette appears if this tool is double-clicked.

*A **palette** is a collection of related commands or operations used to help monitor and modify your work. By default some palettes are grouped together.*

**Apply Gradient.** Clicking this tool applies its set gradient to the Fill or Stroke of a selected object. Double-clicking on this icon activates the Gradient palette.

**Apply None.** Do not be misled by seeing white within an object. Since the page is white, looks can be deceiving. None is the same as transparent. An object Filled or Stroked with None has no color applied to it.

## Palettes and Screen Space

No matter how large your monitor is, it will soon be cluttered by palettes, and your artwork will be obscured. The fastest way to get rid of all palettes is by pressing the Tab key. You can use the Tab key to toggle back and forth between hiding or showing the palettes. To toggle all the palettes except for the main Toolbox, hold the Shift key while pressing Tab. Open only the palettes you need.

Some palettes, however, are needed, and sending them away, then bringing them back again can become tedious. Palettes can be manipulated to fill less screen space, and yet still be available for instant access. The two functions for controlling the palettes are Grouping and Minimize/Maximize.

### Grouping

You have seen palettes that contain multiple name tabs. These name tabs are the means for relocating individual palettes. By clicking and dragging on these name tabs, palettes can be moved to another destination. *Grouping* is defined as dragging a palette's name tab to a different palette and combining them. Many individual palettes can be grouped together, or one can be dragged from a group to become a stand-alone, individual palette.

One example of this is the default grouping of the Paragraph Styles and Character Styles palettes, which are grouped with the Swatches palette. They are all three visible, accessible with a single click, and yet out of the way. To accomplish this, the name tabs of the component palettes were dragged to the name tab area of the Swatches palette.

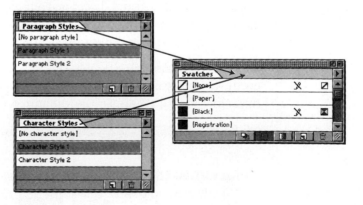

*To group palettes, drag and drop a palette's name tab to the palette in which you wish it to reside.*

*Default palette groupings are:*

*Paragraph Styles, Character Styles, and Swatches*

*Transform, Character, and Paragraph*

*Pages, Layers, and Navigator*

*Stroke, Color, Gradient, and Attributes*

*The Minimize/Maximize button toggles back and forth between palette sizes. If the palette is in its truncated state, the Minimize/Maximize button will toggle between truncated and minimized sizes, ignoring the full size.*

## Minimize/Maximize

This economical use of screen space with palettes can go further by using the Minimize/Maximize button on the right of the title bar. When this button is pressed, everything except the title bar of the palette folds up like a window shade, leaving only the title bar and the name tabs visible.

Minimize/Maximize button

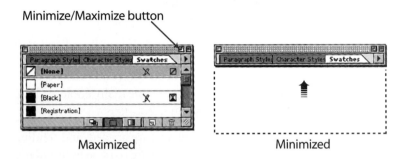

Maximized          Minimized

## Options

The arrow at the upper right of the palette reveals the options available. These include the ability to create a new element, duplicate, edit, and delete an element, plus other, palette-specific options.

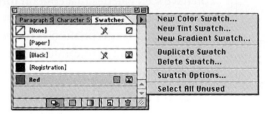

## Double-clicking Name Tabs

Double-clicking a palette's name tab changes the palette into one of three sizes. When a palette is first accessed and shown on your monitor, it is at its full size. The amount of the palette that is visible, though, depends on whether Show Options is selected from the Palette menu located in the top-right corner of the palette.

If the palette's name tab is double-clicked a second time, the palette truncates (is shortened), displaying only a limited number of its items. If the name tab is double-clicked a third time, the palette displays its Minimized state.

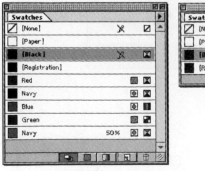

Minimized

Truncated

Full Size

## Menus

The menus in the Menu Bar are critical for accessing certain features not found in either the Toolbox or palettes. As the features of InDesign are showcased, the menu options will be illustrated. Some menus have nested, fly-out menus that offer additional choices. These are marked by the triangle symbol, which will show other options when you rest the mouse button on the triangle.

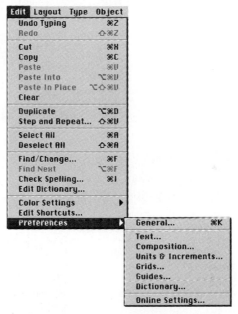

*Macintosh Menus*

*Windows Menus*

## Properties Menus

Properties of objects may be viewed by Control-clicking (Macintosh) or right-clicking (Windows) the mouse button to display a mini-menu that flies out from the cursor, wherever it is located. This menu varies, depending on what type of object is selected, or if no object is selected.

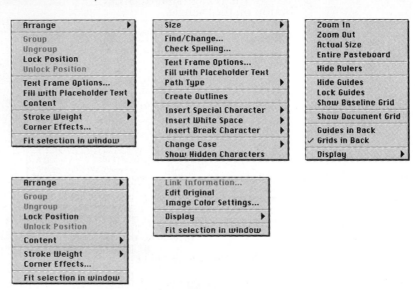

*The Properties menus change content based on what they are referencing. Top row: Text Frame, Text, Nothing selected. Bottom row: Picture Frame, Picture.*

**Text Frame selected.** With a text frame selected, you may access the Text Frame options — fill the frame with placeholder text, change the content of the frame, or affect the frames properties, such as Stroke Weight, Corner Effects, arrangement, and position.

**Text selected.** This menu becomes available when the text cursor is active within a text frame. It provides options for Text Size, Find/Change, Check Spelling, Text Frame Options, inserting special characters and white space, changing text to outlines, filling the text frame with placeholder text, defining a path (if the text is bound to a path), inserting a break character, changing case, or showing hidden characters.

**Object selected.** Refers to objects such as placed graphics. Link Information, Edit Original, Image Color Settings, Display and Fit Selection in Window become available.

**Object Frame selected.** Refers to objects such as placed graphics, frames, paths drawn with the Pen tool, or graphic objects drawn with the Ellipse, Rectangle, Polygon or Line tools. The fly-out menu gives the ability to Arrange Front/Back, Group or Lock objects, apply the Content of the frame, or set Stroke Weight and Corner Effects to graphics drawn with the InDesign tools.

## Explore the InDesign Tools

1. From the File menu, use New to create a new document. At the Document Setup window, set the number of pages to 8. Set the Margins to 3p0, leaving all other settings at default. Click OK.

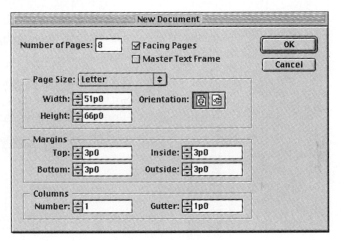

2. The document will open to page 1.

3. Hold the Shift key while pressing the Tab key to put away all palettes (except the Toolbox), which are on the screen. If they don't disappear when these keys are pressed, the toggle may be set to On. Press Tab again to toggle them to Off.

4. In the View menu, select Zoom Out for a better view of the page. Look at the View Percentage box to see the percentage of the page view. It will be set at 75% or 50%, depending upon the size at which you started.

5. In the Toolbox, select the Hand tool and click-drag on the document page. Notice how you can change the location of the view for more precise work.

6. In the View menu, select Fit Page in Window. The page reverts to its original size.

7. If the rulers are not visible, press Command/Control-R to show the page Rulers in the document.

8. Click on the Rectangle tool in the Toolbox. Click-hold the mouse button and drag the tool cursor diagonally on the page, drawing a rectangle approximately 18 picas wide, referring to the rulers as you drag.

9. Click on the Default Fill and Stroke icon in the Toolbox. This will give the rectangle a black outline.

10. Now click on the Selection tool in the Toolbox. Click the pointer arrow cursor on the outline of the rectangle. You will notice the Selection tool cursor turns into a single arrowhead. This indicates that the object is selected and ready to be moved. With the mouse button depressed, drag the rectangle to the center of the page.

11. Click on the Zoom tool in the Toolbox. Drag a marquee around the rectangle. The area you marquee will fill the document view.

12. Leave the document open for the next exercise.

## Navigate the Document

1. In the View Percentage box at the lower left of the document window, highlight the number and type "90". Press the Enter/Return key to view the document at 90%. Press the Delete key to remove the rectangle

2. To the right of the View Percentage box is the Current Page box showing the number of the page you are working on. Highlight the number 1 and type "6". Press Return/Enter to go to this page.

3. You will be on page 6, but page 7 adjoins it. The two pages together are called a "spread." We want to see both of these pages centered in the screen. From the View menu, select Fit Spread in Window. Both pages will move to the center of the screen.

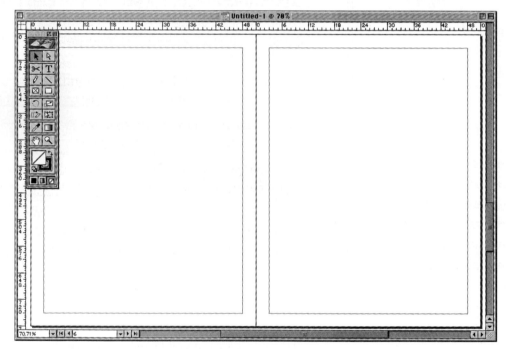

*The **Pasteboard** is an area the width of a page, to the left and right of a spread when Facing Pages are selected, and to the left and right of a single page when a single page layout is selected.*

4. Look at the Current Page box. Notice that it now says "6," (Macintosh) or "7," (Windows) although both pages are visible.

5. Press the Next Page button, which is to the right of the Current Page box. Notice how the Current Page changes to the next page number, and that page is centered in the window.

6. Press the Previous Page button. The previous page centers in the window. Press the Previous page button again and you will be on page 5 (Macintosh) or 6 (Windows).

7. Go to page 4 by selecting it from the Go To Page pop-up menu on the right side of the Current Page box. Page 4 is centered in the view. Press Next Page to center page 5 in the view.

8. Select View>Entire Pasteboard. The document changes to show smaller pages in its window, so the entire pasteboard is visible.

*Drag the window of the Pages palette so you can see all the pages*

9. Press the Last Page button to the right of the Next Page button. The document view moves up to show the last page — page 8.

10. Press the First Page button, to the left of the Previous Page button. The screen jumps back to this page in the document.

11. Press Command/Control-0 (zero) to Fit Page in Window. Page 1 will now fill the document screen.

12. Leave the document open for the next exercise.

## Work with the Palettes

1. Select Window>Pages. This will display the Pages palette, which also contains the Navigator and Layers palettes. Return to the Window menu and select Transform, which will show the Transform palette grouped with the Paragraph and Character palettes.

2. Click-hold on the Navigator name tab and drag it away from the Pages palette. Release the mouse button. You now have separated the two palettes.

3. Click on the Paragraph name tab in the Transform palette and drag it out to separate it. Do the same with the Character palette.

4. You now have four single palettes and one double palette on your screen. Drag the Layers palette from its grouping. Drag the Character and Paragraph palettes back into the grouping with the Transform palette.

5. Click on the title bar (the strip across the top of the palette) of the Navigator palette. Drag it under the Pages palette. The two palettes snap together when they come close to each other.

*Your Pages palette may be set at a vertical default as you see below. In addition, the Masters may be on top. This is defined using the Pages palette Options fly-out menu.*

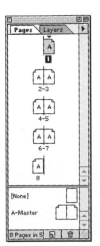

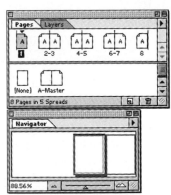

6. Move the other three palettes under the Navigator palette, so that all the palettes are lined up in one column.

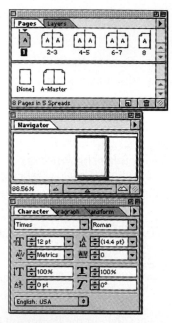

7. In each palette, click the Minimize button so that the palette disappears, leaving only the title bar.

8. Click and drag on the title bars of each palette and move them so that they are all stacked against each other. This made it easier to view more of the document screen.

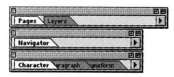

9. Click on the Minimize button of the Pages palette. This will toggle the palette to Maximize. You will now see the entire Pages palette.

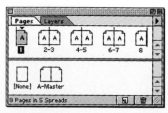

10. Double-click on the Pages name tab. Observe how this also makes the palette smaller. Double-click again to minimize it.

11. Drag the Navigator name tab into the Pages palette, next to the Pages name tab. You have now grouped the Pages and Navigator palettes back together.

*The palettes take on a stacking order, with the first one dragged into position being on the bottom and the last on top. Your Pages palette may be on the bottom of the stack. If so, drag it out of the stack and then drop it in again.*

12. Now move the Transform palette up under the Pages palette, so that they snap together. This snapping only occurs when the left sides of the palettes are flush.

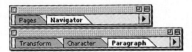

13. You have experienced many facets of the InDesign environment, using features such as page navigation, view adjustment, and palette manipulation. Close the document without saving.

## Summary

In this chapter, you have become acquainted with the Toolbox, windows, menus, and palettes of InDesign. You have learned to manage a number of palettes to maximize your available screen space, and to navigate within an InDesign document. You are now ready to begin working with InDesign.

**Notes:**

# CHAPTER 3

# Working with Files

## CHAPTER OBJECTIVE:

To learn the settings to build and control documents and the basic anatomy of a document page. To learn how to create new, and open, close, and save existing documents. To become familiar with options for working with multiple page documents. In Chapter 3, you will:

- Explore InDesign's many preferences and defaults for setting up an individual document or for working on many documents.

- Review the basics of opening, closing, and saving documents.

- Become familiar with the structural elements of a page, including live areas, gutters, and margins.

- Learn how to create new documents and work with InDesign's initial settings.

- Explore working with multi-page documents, basing the document on single or multiple Masters.

- Learn the functions of the Grabber Hand and the Navigator palette for moving easily around a document page.

# Working with Files

The key to creating effective pages with a minimum of effort is understanding how InDesign manages the document file and its many parts. This section will help you understand preferences and default settings, and will guide you through the basics of document structure and management.

## Working with Preferences and Defaults

Many elements can be set to function as a program default, or as a document default or preference. As a general rule, setting a preference with no document open will establish it as a program default, affecting all documents created subsequently. Most preferences, when set with a document open, will affect that document only. Preferences are found within the Edit menu.

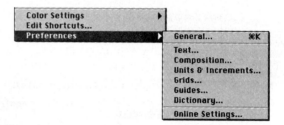

### General Preferences

General preferences affect the display of elements in the document.

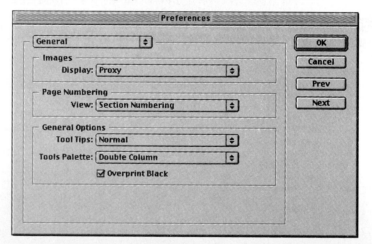

Images may display as Full Resolution, Optimized Resolution, Proxy, or Gray Out images. Full Resolution images take a long time to draw, so it is generally best to use the Proxy images setting. Optimized Resolution downsamples images to a resolution appropriate to display with high quality. Vector graphics are displayed at full resolution. The resolution for Proxy Images is specified in dots per inch when each image is imported. You may find it desirable to Gray Out images when working with a computer that has inadequate RAM, or when tweaking text, and when you do not need to view the pictures. Proxy Images is the default.

Page numbering is viewed by section or by absolute numbers. Section Numbering shows actual page numbers; if the document contains front matter that is numbered with Roman numerals, it will display that section labeled with those numbers. Similarly, if a chapter begins on page 61, it will number the chapter with the actual numbering of its pages. Absolute Numbering displays the pages in a document as 1–x, regardless of the actual numbering of pages. Section Numbering is the default.

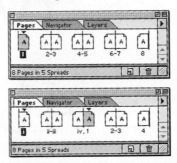

*Layouts showing Absolute Numbering (above) and Section Numbering (below).*

General Options are Show Tool Tips, Tools Palette, and Overprint Black. Tool tips display the name of the tool selected when the cursor is placed over the tool. The Tools palette (also referred to as the Toolbox) may be displayed as a double column, single column, or single row. Overprint Black, which causes black ink to print on top of all colors, should almost always be used. By default, these options are selected.

### Text Preferences

You will find that setting text preferences requires serious thought and attention to detail. As we discussed in Chapter 1, typefaces are unique, so setting text defaults is not a one-size-fits-all solution, and should be performed on a document-by-document basis.

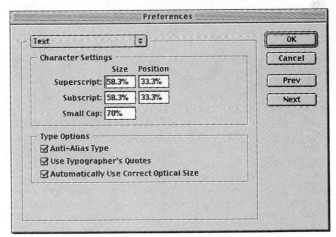

The size and position of Superscript and Subscript characters is defined based on the size of the standard letter and a percentage of the set size of the letter above and below the baseline. (A superscript, 36-pt. letter with a size of 50% and a position of 33.3% will be the size of an 18-pt. letter and will have its baseline 12 pts. above the baseline.)

Ideally, the top of a capital superscript letter will align with the top of a capital base letter. Sometimes you need to play with the adjustment to achieve this. Subscripts are not as precise. In many cases it is necessary to determine what size and position the author wants the character to occupy. When setting mathematical type, superscript and subscript numbers must work together.

$$40^{\text{TH}} \qquad X^y_k$$

$$40^{\text{TH}} \qquad X^y_k$$

*This illustration clearly shows that care must be taken when determining the size and offset of super- and subscript numbers. An offset of 33% is too great for the raised TH, which should be at the same position as the cap height. However, it is needed when super- and subscript letters are used together in equations.*

Small Cap size is defined as a percentage of the size of the capital letter. Whenever possible, if you are using small caps, select a font designed with actual small-cap characters. When you create small caps by reducing the point size, the vertical strokes become narrower than those of the typeface, and the characters look "not quite right." If you have such a font loaded on your computer, InDesign will automatically swap out the small cap in place of the "defined" small cap. The percentage size you specify will be automatically overridden and true small caps will be used instead.

# Capsp Capsp

*Times Roman (left) when converted to small caps, has a very visible reduction in size of its vertical stroke (compare the lowercase "p"). Minion was swapped out to its true small cap, which is much better looking.*

Superscript, Subscript, and Small Caps definitions are retroactive. If the definition is changed partway through the document, the definition of these characters will be affected document-wide.

The Type Options may be a little confusing. Check Anti-Alias Type to make type appear sharper on the monitor. It does not affect the quality of the letters when the document is printed.

The Use Typographer's Quotes option will automatically substitute typographer's quotes (sometimes called "curly quotes") when the prime or double prime key is pressed. This usually speeds production.

The final option, Automatically Use Correct Optical Size, is for use with Multiple Master fonts. It will use a font mastered for a smaller text size for small type, and type mastered for a larger text size for display type, achieving a cleaner letterform.

*To interactively toggle typographer's quotes with the prime or double prime, press Command-Option-Shift-" (Macintosh) or Control-Alt-Shift-" (Windows).*

*Preferences shown in the screen shots reflect the preferences to which we will set InDesign, not the default settings.*

## Composition Preferences

This section, more than any other, affects the productivity of your typographic page. It employs features that formerly were available only on high-end composition terminals.

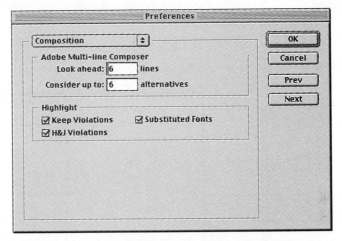

Adobe Multi-line Composer, when used in conjunction with the Paragraph palette menu, will determine line breaks and hyphenation based on what is happening a given number of lines ahead in the document. It makes these determinations in conjunction with hyphenation and justification rules that you have set for the document. Typically, DTP programs have based line-breaking decisions only on what has occurred in the current line. The downside of using the Multi-line Composer is that the more decisions it must consider, the slower composition of your document will be. It also takes control away from the user. Some documents may be more easily managed using Adobe Single-line Composer.

In addition, Composition Preferences can highlight instances that InDesign is unable to resolve automatically. These include Keep Violations, H&J Violations, and Substituted Fonts. Keep Violations are instances when the Keep with Next rules are not enforceable. When hyphenation and justification rules can't be followed, an H&J Violation occurs. If a font is missing, InDesign will substitute a font and flag the substitution.

## Units and Increments Preferences

This section determines your units of measurement. Ruler units may be defined in a variety of ways. Keyboard increments define how much movement or change occurs with the keyboard shortcut for increase and decrease of an element.

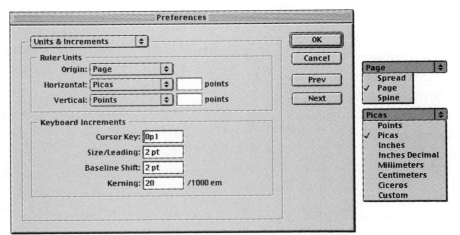

*If the ruler origin is set for the spread's binding spine, the origin point is locked. The ruler may not be repositioned.*

*There are traditionally 72.27 points in an inch and 12 points to a pica.*

*When a group of characters is selected, holding down the Option/Alt and → or ← keys will increase or decrease the tracking by the preset amount. When the cursor is placed between two characters, the same command will increase or decrease the kerning between those letters. Adding the Command/Control key increases or decreases the kerning or tracking by five times the amount.*

The origin of the ruler unit may be defined as Spread, Page, or Spine. When defined as Spread, the width of the entire spread is used contiguously. When defined by Page, each page begins at zero, with the zero point beginning at the upper-left corner. When defined as Spine, the measurement begins in the upper-left corner, but if there are multiple pages that originate from the binding spine, such as might be the case in a fold-out, the measurement continues the width of the pages on that side of the binding spine.

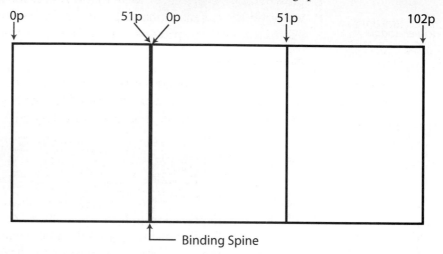

*When Spine is selected, the horizontal units are cumulative across the spread.*

Although the standard unit of measure in the United States is inches, and metric measure is used elsewhere, we will generally use picas for our unit of horizontal measure and points for the vertical unit. This is standard within the graphic arts industry, and ensures greater consistency. There are 72 PostScript points per inch, with 12 points to a pica. PostScript points are the current industry standard. The following chart shows a conversion of inches to inches decimal, picas and points, and points using this standard:

| Inches | Decimal | Picas | Points |
|--------|---------|-------|--------|
| 1/16 | 0.0625 | 0p4.5 | 4.5 |
| 1/8 | 0.125 | 0p9 | 9 |
| 3/16 | 0.1875 | 1p1.5 | 13.5 |
| 1/4 | 0.25 | 1p6 | 18 |
| 5/16 | 0.3125 | 1p10.5 | 22.5 |
| 3/8 | 0.375 | 2p3 | 27 |
| 7/16 | 0.4375 | 2p7.5 | 31.5 |
| 1/5 | 0.5 | 3p | 36 |
| 9/16 | 0.5625 | 3p4.5 | 40.5 |
| 5/8 | 0.625 | 3p9 | 45 |
| 11/16 | 0.6875 | 4p1.5 | 49.5 |
| 3/4 | 0.75 | 4p6 | 54 |
| 13/16 | 0.8125 | 4p10.5 | 58.5 |
| 7/8 | 0.875 | 5p3 | 63 |
| 15/16 | 0.9375 | 5p7.5 | 67.5 |
| 1 | 1 | 6p | 72 |

*Command/Control-Shift>*
*increases the point size of*
*selected characters and*
*Command/Control-Shift-<*
*decreases their point size by*
*the Size/Leading increment.*
*Adding the Option/Alt key*
*increases or decreases the*
*point size by five times the*
*amount.*

*Option/Alt- [Up Arrow key]*
*increases the leading and*
*Option/Alt- [Down Arrow*
*key] decreases the leading*
*by the Size/Leading*
*increment of a paragraph.*
*Adding the Command/*
*Control key increases or*
*decreases the leading by*
*five times the amount.*

*Option/Alt-Shift-↑ shifts the*
*baseline up and Option/Alt-*
*Shift-↓ shifts the baseline*
*down by the Baseline Shift*
*increment. Adding the*
*Command/Control key*
*increases or decreases the*
*baseline shift by five times*
*the amount.*

The Keyboard Increments section of this menu determines how much an element will move when an action is performed. The units of measurement menus will auto-convert to the units set in Preferences. For example, if your Units Preferences are set to picas, a 0.5 in entry will convert to 3p0.

The Cursor Key increment determines how far a selected object will be moved when you press the Up, Down, Left, or Right Arrow keys. If you hold down the Shift key, the object will move 10 times that distance. Size/Leading, Baseline Shift, and Kerning affect highlighted text when you press the appropriate key combination.

## Grids Preferences

There are two different grids used in documents. The Baseline Grid is used to align columns of text. The Document Grid is used to align objects. These grids cannot be assigned to an individual Master Page or to individual layers.

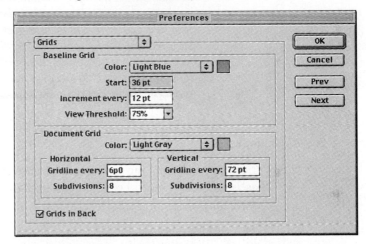

The Baseline Grid looks like lined paper, and interacts with each paragraph's Indents and Spacing command. Paragraphs that align to the Baseline Grid will always jump to the next grid line, regardless of how the spacing is defined. In other words, if the grid is 12 pts., and the paragraph is designed to have a leading of 12 pts. with 6 pts. above, it will advance an additional 6 pts., to the next available grid line.

| Alice was beginning to get very tired of sitting by her sister on the bank, and of having nothing to do: once or twice she had peeped into the book her sister was reading, but it had no pictures or conversations in it, 'and what is the use of a book,' thought Alice 'without pictures or conversation?'  So she was considering in her own mind (as well as she could, for the hot day made her feel very sleepy and stupid), whether the pleasure of making a daisy-chain would be worth the trouble of getting up and picking the daisies, when suddenly a White Rabbit with pink eyes ran close by her.  There was nothing so very remarkable in that; nor did Alice think it so very much out of the way to hear the Rabbit say to itself, 'Oh dear! | Alice was beginning to get very tired of sitting by her sister on the bank, and of having nothing to do: once or twice she had peeped into the book her sister was reading, but it had no pictures or conversations in it, 'and what is the use of a book,' thought Alice 'without pictures or conversation?'  So she was considering in her own mind (as well as she could, for the hot day made her feel very sleepy and stupid), whether the pleasure of making a daisy-chain would be worth the trouble of getting up and picking the daisies, when suddenly a White Rabbit with pink eyes ran close by her.  There was nothing so very remarkable in that; nor did Alice think it so very much out of the |
|---|---|

*This example shows how text is affected by the baseline grid so care must be exercised in its use. The text block on the left is specified identically to the one on the right in every typographical respect with 12-pt. leading and 6 pt. additional space between paragraphs. The only difference is the paragraphs in the right text block have Align to Baseline Grid turned on. This grid feature overrides interparagraph spacing that does not exactly equal the space between grids, resulting in a different look than is specified.*

The color of a grid may be any color you choose. When setting up grids, pick a color that is not used in the document if you choose to turn on the Baseline Grid.

The Start position of the grid should be one grid increment above the position of the first baseline of text. The grid will always start at the upper-left corner of the page, regardless of where the zero point is set. The grid increment should equal your line spacing (leading).

The View Threshold is the page magnification at or below which the grid will not show, even if it is turned on in the view menu.

The Document Grid, on the other hand, resembles graph paper. Like the Baseline Grid, it aligns itself to the upper-left corner of the page, and may be colored however you wish. The default grid structure is to put a main grid line every 6 picas (1 inch), and to divide that into 8 subdivisions. When working with picas, you may want to change the Subdivisions to 6 or 12 — or turn the grid off completely. Horizontal and vertical grids may be defined individually.

### Guides Preferences

Guides are designed to provide placement for columns and other page-related elements. The colors may be adjusted to your taste, and should be selected so as to minimize confusion between them and printing elements on the page. Unlike grids, guides may be assigned to layers and master pages.

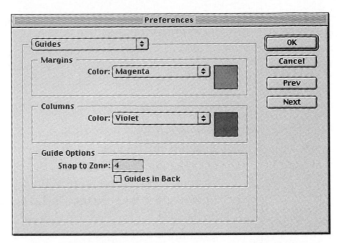

The Snap to Zone is defined in pixels. A Macintosh monitor usually has 72 pixels per inch; a Windows monitor usually has 96 pixels per inch.

Guides, by default, are placed in front of all objects on the page. Some people think this gets in the way, and would rather be able to use the snap-to effect of guides but not have them clutter up their view. To send the guides to the back, click the Guides in Back box.

## Dictionary Preferences

InDesign provides dictionaries for spelling and hyphenation in a number of languages. A default dictionary is selected for the document, but individual paragraphs, or even individual words, may be assigned a different dictionary. For example, you may have a manual in English, Spanish, French, and German. Each language is supported by its own dictionary.

Hyphenation Exceptions allow composition employing a user-defined dictionary, changes made in the document only, or both. The User Dictionary may be merged into the document, so the exceptions will not alert another user's spell check. When a change is made to the user dictionary, all stories may be recomposed using the new dictionary exceptions.

*All the dictionaries do not load when the program is installed using the normal defaults. A custom install will make all the dictionaries available.*

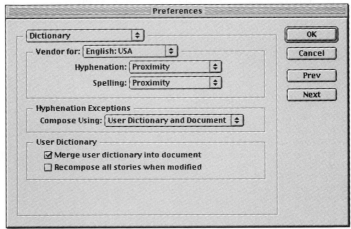

Applications Color Settings and Document Color Settings are used in conjunction with color management software. They should be used only when a workstation and its components have been properly calibrated. These settings are located at Edit>Color Settings, not under the Preferences menu.

## Set the Preferences

Close any documents that are open. We are going to set InDesign's default preferences, so it will appear this way every time you open the program.

1.  Select Edit>Preferences>General. Click on Images Display. Display choices are Full Resolution, Optimized Resolution, Proxy, or Gray Out. Leave the default of Proxy images. Click on Page Numbering View. The choices are Absolute Numbering or Section Numbering. Leave the default of Section Numbering. Click on Tool Tips. The options are for Normal, None, or Fast. Leave them at the default of Normal. These options affect the speed at which Tool Tips display. Click on Tools Palette. The options are Single Column, Double Column, and Single Row. Accept the default of Double Column.

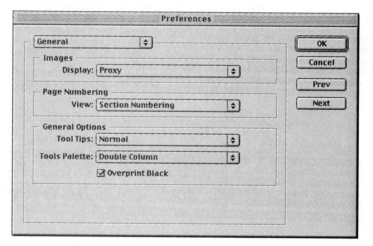

2.  From the drop-down menu at the top of the form (which currently reads "General"), select Text. Leave the default preferences.

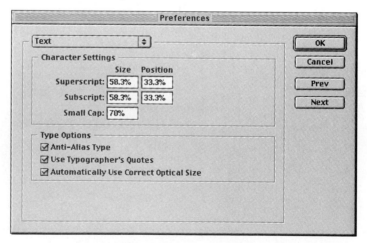

3. From the drop-down menu at the top of the form, select Composition. In the Highlight section, check Substituted Fonts.

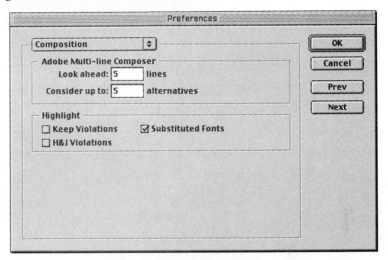

4. From the drop-down menu, select Units & Increments. Set the Ruler Units to Origin: Page, Horizontal: Picas and Vertical: Points. Leave the Keyboard Increments at their defaults.

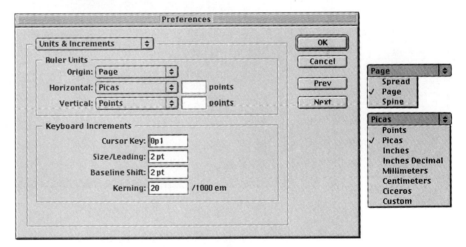

5. Select Grids. Review the options available and leave the preferences at their default.

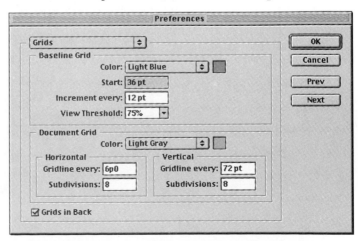

6. Select Guides. Review the options available and leave the preferences at their default.

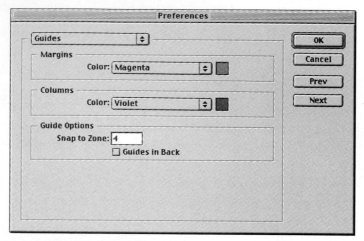

7. Select Dictionary. Click on the Vendor For (Language) drop-down menu to view the variety of languages supported. Leave the preferences at their default.

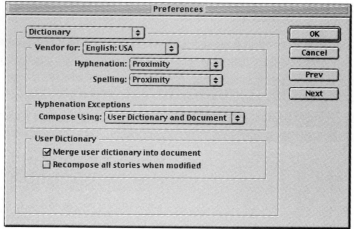

8. Click OK.

9. We're going to set one more preference — one that is not included in the Preferences menu. If the Pages palette is not already open, select Window>Pages.

10. Click on the arrow on the top right of the palette and select Palette Options.

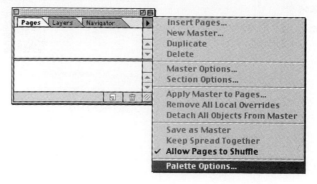

11. From the Pages Palette Options, select
    Pages Icon Size: Medium
    Masters Icon Size: Small
    Palette Layout: Pages on Top with Resize: Masters Fixed

    Be sure that Show Vertically is unchecked.

*Command/Control-O will bring up the Open menu*

*Command/Control-W will close the document.*

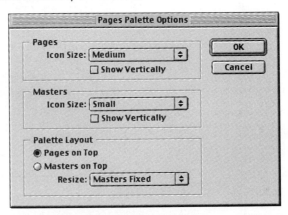

12. Click OK.

Now that you have set your preferences with no document open, these preferences will be observed each time you open InDesign, unless you override them.

## Opening, Closing, and Saving Documents

For the most part, these actions become automatic — and you may have performed these functions many times with other programs. They are all performed from the File menu.

*An alternate method for opening a file is to double-click on the file's icon.*

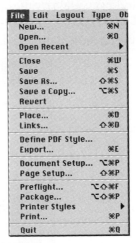

*Command/Control-S
executes a simple Save.
Command/Control-Shift-S
executes Save As. Com-
mand/Control-Option/Alt-S
executes Save a Copy.*

To Open a document, you simply select File>Open. You are presented with a number of options and icons.

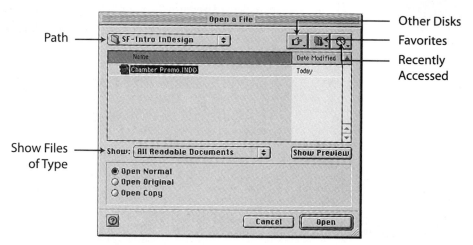

*Macintosh Open menu*

At the top of the menu are navigation features. The bar at the left provides the familiar path navigation. On the Macintosh, the pointer icon allows direct access to other disks on the network. The next icon is used to save a file as a Favorite, immediately accessible from the Favorites menu. The clock icon is a connector to recently accessed files (which may not be InDesign documents).

The main menu reveals documents in the current folder, with the date modified. Below it is the opportunity to show All Readable Documents or All Documents (Macintosh). Windows users have the options of Files of type: InDesign, PageMaker 6.5, QuarkXPress 3.3–4.04, or All Formats. If the document has been saved with a preview, the first page of the document may be displayed by clicking the Show Preview button (Macintosh only).

*It's a good idea to Save As
when you have finished
work on a document. This
cleans out extraneous data
that a simple Save leaves,
reducing the file size.*

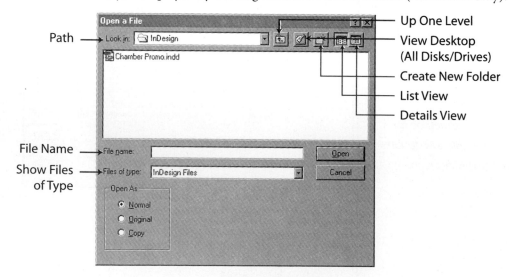

*Windows Open menu*

Under Windows, the Up One Level icon allows you to access a parent folder. View Desktop provides a view of all disks and drives. Create New Folder allows you to create a new folder on the fly. List and Detail View convert to these Windows views.

Your choices are to Open Normal, Open Original, or Open Copy. You will almost always want to Open Normal.

To Close a document, select File>Close. If no changes have been made, the file will close immediately. If you have made any changes to the document, you will be presented with the following menu.

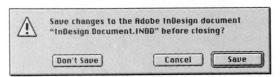

When you see this menu, don't automatically press the Return/Enter key. That will save the document with any changes you have made. Take a second to think about whether you made changes consciously, and if you want to save them. If so, press Return/Enter to Save. If not, click Don't Save to close the document without saving changes, or click Cancel to leave the document open.

There are three options for saving a document. The Save command is most frequently used. It saves the document, plus any changes you have made, to the same folder on your computer. Save As, which we'll use often in this course, allows you to rename the file or to save the current version of the file to a different folder; the renamed file is left open. The Save a Copy command is similar to Save As, except the original file is left open; as a default, the file name is preserved, and the word "copy" appended prior to the file extension.

## Page Anatomy

A typical page is made up of a number of standard elements. Good designers employ these to enhance the readability of the document and to guide readers from one element to another. We are discussing elements of the page itself, not graphic or typographic devices.

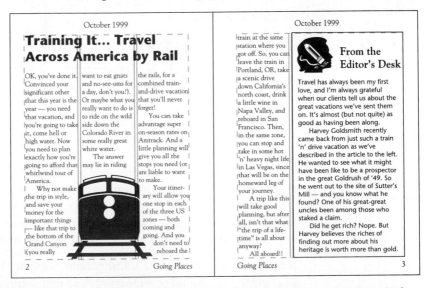

A "page" as we know it, is technically larger than the finished page size. A typical 8.5″ × 11″ page will have at least an extra 1/8″ all around to allow for "bleed." *Bleed* occurs when an image or other graphic element (such as a line) prints to the edge of the page. To allow for slight inconsistencies in the printing process, the element must actually extend beyond the page boundaries.

*Even though a "page" includes space around it to allow for bleed, we still select the finished (trimmed) size of the document we're producing. Bleed area extends onto the pasteboard.*

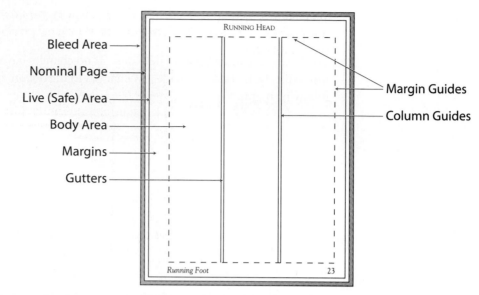

The area that is to contain non-bleeding elements is called the "live area." It may also be called the "safe area." This area is generally at least 1/8″ inside the actual page boundary.

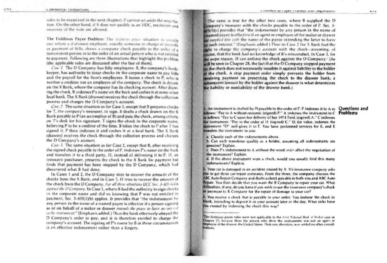

*Documents such as this 1197-page book need larger inside margins to compensate for the curl that develops due to the bulk of the book.*

*When designing pages, be sure to take into account the physical characteristics of the document, including its thickness and how it will be bound.*

The majority of text and graphics are placed within the body of the page. Surrounding this area are *margins*. Margins may all be the same size, or they may vary, depending upon the document's structure and what is to be placed in them. For example, a document with facing pages may require a larger inside margin than an ad. Books may have elements such as running heads and running feet in the top and bottom margins.

If a page has more than one column, there is a space between each column, often referred to as a "gutter." It should be wide enough so that columns of type do not appear to run into one another. To ensure this, one device that is often used is to place a vertical rule in the gutter to act as a "stopper" for the eye.

The *Zero Point* is an element that is used to establish relative page positions. By default, it is positioned in the upper-left corner of the first page of a spread. However, it can be moved, when it is appropriate to do so. To move it, you click on the Zero Point then drag it to its new position. To return the Zero Point to its original position, you just double-click the Zero Point icon.

Zero Point ———

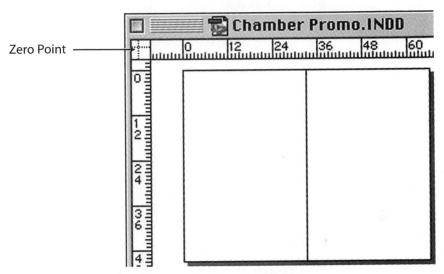

*The Zero Point is at the top left of the screen, where the two rulers meet.*

### Explore a Document

*InDesign remembers exact pathnames when identifying linked files. Throughout this course, when opening documents containing linked files, you will usually encounter the Fix Links warning box. When this occurs, simply click Fix Links. Unless the links have been moved to a folder other than that which contains the InDesign document, they will be updated automatically.*

1. From File>Open, navigate to your **SF-Intro InDesign** folder, and double-click on **Chamber Promo.INDD** to open it. It will open to the spread of pages 2–3.

2. If it is not already visible, open the Pages palette from Window>Pages.

3. Note in the Pages palette that there are three sections (the pages beginning each section have an arrow above them). The two sections for the covers of the booklet (using the C-Master) are numbered 1, 2, 3, and 4. The pages that will hold booklet content (using the A-Master) are numbered 1–8.

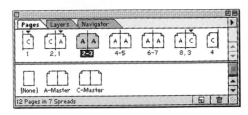

4. In the View menu, be certain Show Frame Edges is checked. Viewing the frames will help you identify the page geometry.

5. Identify the following on pages 2–3:

   Bleed Area
   Live Area
   Body Area
   Margins
   Columns
   Gutters
   Running Feet (Footers)

6. Select File>Save As. Navigate to your **Work In Progress** folder, and click Save to save the document, leaving the name the same.

7. Close the document.

Now that you've looked at some real document pages, it's time to create your own document. It's really easier than you might imagine. We'll start with the basics, and by the time you're done with this chapter, you'll be able to effectively structure the underlying document.

## Creating New Documents

New documents are created using the File>New command. When the New Document window appears, you are presented with a number of options.

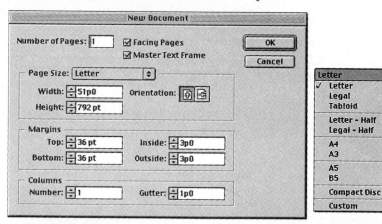

*For documents with pages requiring a number of text frames, or frames of different lengths, do not select Master Text Frame.*

The Number of Pages may be simply a starting number, or it may be the actual number of pages the document will contain. Most people leave the default at one and simply add pages as needed. Checkboxes offer options to create a Facing Pages view, where the page margins are mirrored, or to select single pages. When the Master Text Frame box is checked, a single text frame is created for each page. You may type text into this frame by pressing Command/Control-Shift and clicking on the frame.

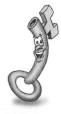

*You may activate the Pages palette by pressing F12.*

The page may be a standard size, such as Letter, Legal, Tabloid, Letter-Half, or Legal-Half, for those who use US specifications, or A4, A3, A5, or B5 for European paper specifiers. A Compact Disk size is also available. In addition, you may type in a specific Width and Height, creating a Custom page. (You don't have to select Custom before typing into these dialog boxes.) You have the option of selecting a Portrait (vertical) or Landscape (horizontal) orientation for your page. If you type the page dimensions width first, then height, the orientation will be determined automatically.

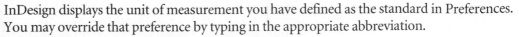

InDesign displays the unit of measurement you have defined as the standard in Preferences. You may override that preference by typing in the appropriate abbreviation.

| System | Type As | Comment |
| --- | --- | --- |
| Picas | #p# | Where the first # is the number of picas and the second is the number of points (up to 11) |
| Points | #pt | |
| Inches | #in | |
| Millimeters | #mm | |
| Centimeters | #cm | |
| Ciceros | #c# | Where the first # is the number of ciceros and the second is the number of Cicero points (up to 11) |

*To advance from section to section in the Pages palette, use the Tab key.*

If your Preferences are set to display in picas, and you wish to set up an 8.5 × 11-in. page, simply type "8.5 in" and "11 in" for the Width and Height dimensions.

The Margin amount is applied or selected in the next section. Alternately, you may use the up and down arrows. When Facing Pages are specified, the dimension of Left and Right Margins changes to Inside and Outside, because the pages are horizontally mirrored.

Finally, the number of columns and the gutter width is specified. All this information is displayed on the underlying Master.

## Pages and Spreads

Earlier, we discussed the makeup of individual pages. However, when we design a multi-page publication, we realize that a single page is only half the view. The entire spread must be appealing to the eye. After all, when we view a publication other than a comic book or a magazine we're reading on the subway, we usually view the facing pages simultaneously. The two pages should work together as a unit. The arrangement of columns should complement one another. In addition, the placement of elements on the spread should be pleasing, so as not to present a lopsided appearance.

### *Set Up the Newsletter*

1.  From File>New, create a new document with facing pages. Be sure the Master Text Frame is unchecked.

2.  Make the Page Size Letter with a Portrait orientation.

3.  The margins should be as follows:

    Top:     36 pt     Inside:   3p6
    Bottom:  48 pt     Outside:  3p0

4.  Set the Column Number to 3, with a Gutter of 1p3.

5.  Click OK or press the Return/Enter key.

6.  From File>Save, save the document to your **Work in Progress** folder. Name the file "Newsletter Master.INDD", and click Save.

7.  Leave the document open for the next exercise.

## Masters

Masters are the underpinnings of your InDesign documents. If you ignore the opportunity to tailor them to the document, you simply make your work that much harder.

Every element that you want to repeat on document pages can be included in a Master Page. Elements you want to repeat on spreads in your document may be included in the Master Spread (both facing pages together). These elements may include guides, running heads and feet, automatic page numbering, and even graphic elements.

Since you can have several different Masters per document, long documents can be created by applying different Masters to specific types of document pages. For example, you may have a section title, a chapter opener, and a text page, all with different parameters. Applying them is as easy as clicking a mouse button.

### Set the Underpinning of the Document

1. Continue in the document you just created.

2. Be sure the Pages (F12) and Transform palettes (F9) are visible.

3. You should see two sections in the Pages palette. The upper section is for document pages, and the lower section holds the Master Pages.

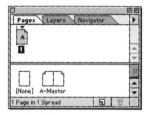

4. Double-click on the left page of the Master Page spread labeled "A-Master" to select it. The left Master Page should display in your window.

5. Click on the Type tool icon in the Tools palette.

6. Below the three-column box in the left Master Page, click and drag to create a text frame. A blue box will appear.

7. Click on the Selection tool.

8. If it is not highlighted, click on the Transform tab, then click on the upper-left proxy handle. (It will turn black).

*Command/Option-N (Macintosh) or Control-Alt-N (Windows) will insert the automatic page number.*

*The page proxy allows you to reference the object's axis from nine distinct points.*

9. Type the following dimensions into the Transform palette:

X: 3p0      W: 44p6
Y: 756 pt    H: 18 pt

Press Return/Enter to apply these settings and exit the menu.

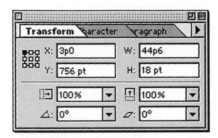

10. Double-click the right Master Page icon and create another text frame. Choose the Selection tool, and using the Transform palette, make the frame the following dimensions:

X: 3p6      W: 44p6
Y: 756 pt    H: 18 pt

Press Return/Enter to apply these settings and exit the menu.

11. Select the Type tool, and click in the frame you created first on the left Master page.

12. Type the word "Page" and press the Spacebar.

13. Select Layout>Insert Page Number. An "A" will appear in the text frame. This is the placeholder for InDesign's automatic page number.

14. Click on the Paragraph palette to select it. Click on the Align Center icon to center the page number in the text box.

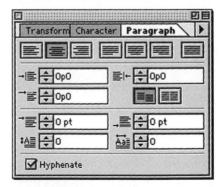

15. Position the Type tool in the text frame you created in the right Master Page.

16. Type the word "Page" and press the Spacebar.

17. Select Layout>Insert Page Number to place the automatic page number placeholder in this text frame.

18. Using the Paragraph palette, click Align Center to center this text.

19. Double-click on page 1 in the Pages palette. You'll notice that the items placed on A-Master appear on page 1. The "Page A" that resulted from inserting the automatic page number is now "Page 1."

20. Save the document (Command/Control-S), and leave it open for the next exercise.

We commented that a document can have multiple Masters. Each Master may be created from scratch, or it may be built from information contained on another Master. We're going to base the next two Masters on the one we've already created.

### Add Multiple Masters

1. Continue in the open document. Be sure the Pages (F12) and Transform palettes (F9) are visible.

2. From the Pages palette, click the arrow on the palette Options menu, and select New Master.

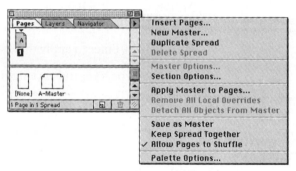

3. Name the new Master "Nameplate", based on A-Master. Leave the number of pages at 2 and click OK. The newsletter is opened to the new Master. InDesign will automatically assign the new Master the Prefix of "B." This is going to be the Master for page 1 of the newsletter. We're going to remove the page number and add the nameplate.

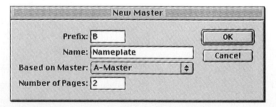

4. Choose the Selection tool. On the right-hand Nameplate Master Page, Command/Control-Shift-click on the text frame containing the page number placeholder. (Simply clicking will not unlock the frame for editing.)

5. Choose Edit>Cut to remove it.

6. From File>Place, choose the file **ST Nameplate.EPS** from your **SF-Intro InDesign** folder. Uncheck the Show Import options box. Click Choose/Open or double-click the file icon.

7. When the paintbrush icon appears, click in the upper-left corner of the live area (inside the margin guide) of the right Master Page.

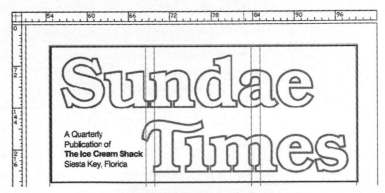

8. Check the Transform palette and make any necessary changes. The upper-left corner of the image you just placed should be at X: 3p6, Y: 36 pt.

9. We have one more Master to create. This one is for page 2 of the newsletter, which will carry the masthead. From the Pages palette, use the Options fly-out menu to select New Master.

10. Name this page "Masthead", and base it on A-Master. Leave the number of pages at 2. (To see this Master in the Pages palette, you may need to increase the size of the palette window or scroll down.)

11. From File>Place, choose the file **ST Masthead.EPS** from your **SF-Intro InDesign** folder. Click Choose or double-click the file name.

12. When the paintbrush icon appears, click it in the lower part of the third column on the left page.

13. Using the Transform palette, adjust the position of the upper-left corner of the image to X: 33p6, Y: 555 pt.

14. Save the document and leave it open for the next exercise.

## Document Pages

Once the Masters are constructed, the document can take shape. Longer documents are usually based on Masters, while shorter documents are frequently built interactively, using page-based frames for text and graphics. This allows for a smooth workflow from design through the finished document stage.

### Basing Document Pages on Masters

New pages are added to the document either by clicking on the page icon at the bottom of the Pages palette, by selecting Insert Pages from the palette Options menu, or by dragging a Master into the Document Pages section. When a page is added by clicking on the page icon, it will have the same Master as the page immediately previous to it. When you use the drop-down menu, you can specify the number of pages to be added, the Master to be used, and the position of the page(s) in the document.

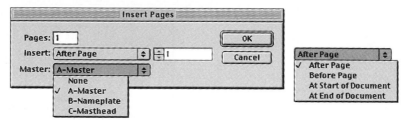

To apply a Master to a document page, simply click on the Master, drag it on top of the document page (which will have a heavy border around it), and release the mouse button. To apply a Master to a single spread, click the name of the Master and drag it to the spread and release the mouse button. (The spread will have a heavy border around it.) Alternately, you can select Apply Master to Pages from the Options drop-down menu. You may specify a single page, a spread, or a larger range of pages. To apply a Master to noncontiguous pages, separate the pages with a comma.

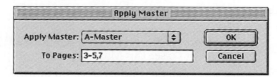

*In this example, A-Master is to be applied to pages 3-5 and page 7.*

While Master elements appear on all pages to which the specific Master is applied, these Master elements may be altered or overridden, as appropriate. To do so, Command/Control-Shift-click on the element. It then becomes a "live" object and may be altered.

If you discover that you have accidentally overridden a master element and wish to undo your override, select the overridden element, and select Remove Selected Local Overrides from the Pages palette Options menu. To remove overrides from all Master elements, Select Remove All Local Overrides from the Pages palette Options menu with no Master elements selected.

*Allow Pages to Shuffle is on (checked) by default. This allows pages to be added as spreads. If it is unchecked, single pages will be added.*

If a Master is modified, those modifications affect all pages to which the Master has been applied, except in instances where master elements have been altered on the document page.

It may be desirable to create a series of frames on the Master Page, either frames that will contain graphics or text frames linked to other text frames, to create a specific text flow. We'll explore the many text flow options available in the next chapter.

### Apply Masters to Your Document

1. Continue in the open document. Double-check that the Pages and Transform palettes are visible.

2. Click on the Pages palette Options menu and select Insert Pages.

3. Insert seven pages after page 1, based on the A-Master. Click OK.

Let's apply information from the Masters.

4. In the Pages palette, click on the B-Nameplate Master icon and drag it on top of page 1. Release the mouse button.

5. Click on the C-Masthead Master icon and drag it on top of page 2 . Be certain only page 2 is highlighted. Your Pages palette should look like this.

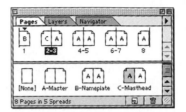

Now let's see what making a modification to a Master will do.

6. In the Pages palette, double-click on the left-hand C-Masthead Master icon.

7. Select the Rectangle Frame tool and draw a frame with the following definition:

X: 3p0        W: 29p3
Y: 36 pt      H: 708 pt

8. From the Object menu, select Content>Text.

9. Select View>Hide Guides. Double-click on the icon for document page 2 to view the change.

*While you can reapply a Master , this simply places the master elements below other elements on the page. It will not undo changes you have made to the document page. If you have removed master elements, it will reestablish them.*

*To protect a Master object on a document page from updating when a Master is altered, select the object and choose Detach Selection from Master from the Pages palette Options menu. To detach all objects on a spread from the Master, the objects must be released (Command/Control-Shift-click), then Detach All Objects From Master may be selected.*

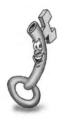

*To activate the Zoom tool, press the letter "Z". To temporarily switch to the Zoom In tool when using another tool, press and hold Command/Control-Spacebar. To temporarily switch to the Zoom Out tool, press and hold Command-Option-Spacebar (Macintosh) or Control-Alt-Spacebar (Windows).*

10. Let's alter the frame on page 2. Using the Selection tool, Command/Control-Shift-click on the new frame. Shorten its height to 500 pt.

11. Click on the C-Masthead icon in the Pages palette and drag it over the document page-2 icon. Note that the Master Page frame has been applied below the frame you altered.

12. The frame you altered should still be selected. If it is not, click on it with the Selection tool.

13. Access the Pages palette Options. Note that Remove All Local Overrides is grayed out and unavailable. Because the Master was reapplied, the altered frame is no longer regarded as a Master element. Press Command/Control-X to delete it.

14. Command/Control-Shift-click on the frame with the reapplied Master and shorten its height to 600 pt.

15. Activate the Pages palette Options menu and click on Remove Selected Local Overrides to return the Master elements to their original specifications.

16. Save the document. From the File menu, select Close.

### Basing Document Pages on Frames

Text and graphics are placed in frames in InDesign. It is not necessary to predraw the frame, as is the case with some other programs, but it is often useful to do so. When you place a graphic, or enter or flow text, the graphic or text automatically creates its own frame, which can be edited through the Options menu. Alternately, you can create frames using the Ellipse, Rectangle, Polygon, Frames, Pen, or Pencil tool.

As we noted earlier, frames smooth the workflow, from design through production, because they provide continuity. As with frames on Masters, text frames on document pages can be linked to create a specific text flow. For example, text may be linked from a frame on page 3 to a frame on page 6.

We will discuss frames in the context of text and graphics in upcoming chapters.

## Viewing and Controlling the Page

It is often necessary or advisable to change the page view. InDesign provides a number of ways to do so.

The first is the Zoom tool. It will zoom in 25% increments from 25% to 100% and will double (or halve) the zoom percentage each time it is clicked from 100% to 4000%. With the tool selected, click to enlarge. Hold down Option/Alt to reduce. Pressing Command/Control - "=" (equal) and Command/Control - "-" (hyphen) accomplishes the same function.

To go directly to a specific predefined view, access the View Percent box in the lower left of the window. Select the desired view from the pop-up menu. Alternately, you may type the view percentage you wish in the window.

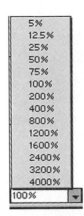

To toggle between the last two views, press Command-Option-2 (Macintosh) or Control-Alt-2 (Windows). You must use the "2" key on the first row of the standard keyboard, not the numeric keypad.

Other features that will help you maneuver the page effectively are the Hand tool, the Navigation palette, and the ability to have multiple views of the document open simultaneously.

The Hand tool allows you to "grab" the page and move it so you can better see what you are working on. Simply select the Hand tool icon from the Toolbox, click the mouse button on the page, and drag. To temporarily switch to the Hand tool as you are working, press the Spacebar, then drag the page with your mouse.

When you are working on a small area of a page, it's helpful to get a picture of the entire page structure. For that, use the Navigator palette. To use it, position the red box in the palette's proxy image over the portion of the page you wish to view, and enlarge as needed. You will still have a feel for how the overall page looks, even when you are zoomed into a very small area.

*Command/Control-W will close the document.*

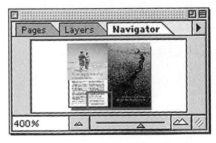

A total of 28 (Macintosh) or 60 (Windows) windows may be open at one time. You can, for example, open additional windows to see how Master changes affect different pages of the document, compare different spreads, or work on details. You can observe how the changes you make affect the entire layout, which may be displayed at a smaller percentage of view.

## Summary

In this chapter, you have learned the basic structure of electronic mechanicals, and have explored the settings you will use to control your documents. You learned how to open, close, and save documents, and how to build on the document's structure. You also learned how to maneuver around the page quickly and easily.

## Notes:

# CHAPTER 4

# Working with Text

## CHAPTER OBJECTIVE:

To learn the basic properties of and how to work with text frames. To understand formatting of text characters and entire paragraphs. In Chapter 4, you will:

- Learn to create text frames, then enter and work with text within the frames.
- Understand how to navigate through and edit text, and work with text overflow.
- Learn to format text (such as setting the font, font size, leading, tracking, and more) using the Character palette.
- Explore Special Characters and some keyboard shortcuts.
- Learn to format paragraphs (including alignment, indents, hyphenation, and spacing between paragraphs) using the Paragraph palette.
- Become familiar with the use of tabs and tabular columns.
- Understand importing and exporting text files, including the formats of word processing that InDesign supports.
- Learn how to place and thread text between multiple frames.

## PROJECTS TO BE COMPLETED:

- **Around the World Ad (A)**
- Baggy's Kid's Menu (B)
- Vacation Brochure (C)
- Good Choices Newsletter (D)

# Working with Text

In Chapter 1, we learned about the evolution of type and typography. We also discussed a number of text terms that we will use throughout the rest of the course. Text makes up approximately 70%–80% of printed matter, so it is important to learn to handle it well. This course will help you learn ways to handle text most efficiently.

Text is always created in frames, which you might think of as containers for text. You may create a text frame, or you may allow InDesign to create the frame for you when you type or place text into your document. A text frame is identified by the ports on the upper left (in) and lower right (out) of the frame. The ports indicate whether or not text in the frame is part of a stream coming from and going to other frames in the document. The Type tool is used to insert text into the frame or to edit it. To position and size the text frame, you use the Selection tool or Transform palette. To alter the shape of the frame, you use the Direct Selection tool, sometimes in conjunction with elements of the Pen tool.

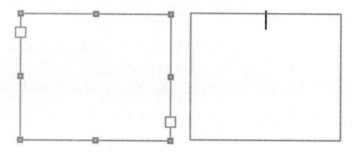

*The frame on the left shows the "in" and "out" ports of the text frame. The frame on the right shows the text insertion point for centered text.*

## Setting Text Frame Properties

When a text frame is created, the document default is one column containing no text. Columns and frames can, however, be modified. Text Frame Options are accessed from Object>Text Frame Options, from Control-click>Text Frame Options (Macintosh), right-click>Text Frame Options (Windows), or by pressing Command/Control-B.

*Command/Control-B will access the Text Frame Options menu.*

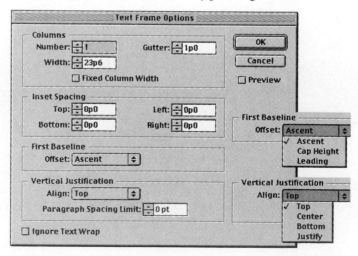

*The New Document dialog box also has a Columns Number option that can set the number of columns the new document will have.*

When the number of columns is changed, or if the gutter width is changed, the column width changes as well. If the Fixed Column Width box is checked, the overall width of the text frame will change if the number of columns is changed.

Text may be inset from the edges of the frame independently. If the frame is not rectangular, only one inset value may be entered. The baseline position of the first line of text in a frame is set through First Baseline Offset. It may be set to Ascent (the height of the ascenders of the typeface), to Cap Height (the height of the capital letters of the typeface), or to Leading (the leading value of the paragraph, exclusive of any Space Before values). If Cap Height or Ascent are chosen and a capital letter is accented, the accent mark will print above the text frame.

Vertical Justification Alignment options are Top, Center, Bottom, and Justify. The Top, Center, and Bottom options will position the text in the assigned position in the frame, allowing empty space to occupy the balance of the frame. The Justify option will add space between lines to completely fill the frame with text. The Paragraph Spacing Limit defines how much extra space is allowed between paragraphs, in addition to any space already assigned. InDesign first tries to fill the frame using inter-paragraph space, up to the maximum you have allowed. After the limit has been reached, it will add space between lines to fill the frame.

If the Ignore Text Wrap box is chosen, text wrap values of an image placed in the paragraph will be ignored, and the text will overprint the graphic.

## Editing Text

Almost as important as getting text into a frame is modifying it once it's there. You can cut, paste, move, or simply modify the properties of its text.

### Viewing Hidden Characters

*You may access the Properties menu for a frame by Control-clicking (Macintosh) or right-clicking (Windows).*

A number of characters commonly inserted in text are *hidden*, that is, they are not seen when the document is printed. Often, however, it is useful to view these characters when editing text, particularly if you are working with text someone else has entered. To view them, with the Type tool active, you select Type>Show Hidden Characters, or you select Show Hidden Characters from the Properties menu. The unseen characters will appear in the same color as the guides and text frame (the default is light blue).

### Selecting Text

InDesign offers several methods for selecting text. You can double-click the mouse button to select the word on which the Type tool rests and the space band following. A triple-click will select the entire paragraph.

Another text selection method is to click at a location within the paragraph, then, holding down the Shift key, click on another location. All text between the two clicks is selected.

If you use the keyboard to select text, you position the Type tool in front of the text to be selected, then with the Shift key depressed, use the keyboard arrow keys to select the text. If the Command/Control-Shift is depressed, and the Up and Down Arrow keys pressed, the entire paragraph before or after the insertion point is selected. Each time the arrow key is depressed, another paragraph is selected.

To select all the text in a text stream or story, make certain the Type tool is selected and that there is an insertion point in the text block. Choose Edit>Select All or press Command/Control-A.

### Using Cut, Copy, Delete, and Paste Text

To move text, select it and press Command/Control-X. The selected text is cut from the text frame and placed onto the Clipboard. Place the Type tool at the new insertion point, where the type is to be relocated, and press Command/Control-V to paste.

To duplicate text, you select it and press Command/Control-C. The selected text is copied into the Clipboard, the original remaining in the text frame. You can then position the insertion point at a new location, and press Command/Control-V to paste the text.

To delete text, select it and press either the Delete or Backspace key.

## Navigating Through Text Blocks

An InDesign paragraph could be defined as "any information that is followed by pressing the Return/Enter key (¶)." Whether it is a word or several lines of text, if it is followed by a ¶, it's a paragraph. Headings, bulleted items, and captions are examples of paragraphs. Each time you press the Return/Enter key, you have created a paragraph.

As you've learned, you can navigate through blocks of text using the arrow keys or the mouse. The commands below will help you edit text more efficiently:

- Command/Control-Left/Right Arrow will move the insertion point one word in the direction of the arrow.

- Command/Control-Up/Down Arrow will move the insertion point to the beginning of the paragraph preceding or following the insertion point.

- Command/Control-Home will move the insertion point to the beginning of a story.

- Command/Control-End will move the insertion point to the end of a story.

These commands may be used with the Shift key to select text. For example, if you use the Command (Macintosh) or Control (Windows) key with Home, all text from the insertion point to the beginning of the story will be selected.

Whenever text is selected, if you begin typing, the selected text is deleted and replaced with the text you are typing.

## Text Overflow

When there is too much text to fit the frame, an overflow icon will alert you to the problem. If this happens, the out port of the text frame will turn red and a small, red plus sign ( + ) will appear. (If the text were flowing into another frame, the plus sign would turn to a blue arrow.)

*You don't want to see an overflow icon in a text frame. Even though it won't print, it is a warning. You should do something about text that's not in view. Make the frame larger, make the type smaller, delete the text, or link the text to another frame. A simple paragraph return can create an overflow state.*

think it so very much out of the way to hear the Rabbit say to itself, `Oh dear! Oh dear! I shall be late!' (when she thought it over afterwards, it occurred to her that she ought to have wondered at this, but at the time it all seemed quite natural); but when the Rabbit actually took a watch out of its waistcoat-pocket, and looked at it, and then

*The text frame above shows the "in" and "out" ports. If this frame is linked to another frame, the "+" on the "out" port will be a blue ▶. If it is not linked, the + sign will turn red to indicate that there is still more text to be placed.*

## Formatting Text

Elements that affect the appearance of the individual characters, rather than of the paragraph as a whole, are entered and modified using the Character palette.

### The Character Palette

The Character palette is divided into four main sections. The first identifies the Font and Style. The second describes Font Size, Leading, Kerning, and Tracking — all pertaining to the spacing of letters and lines of type. The third section modifies the type's physical attributes with Vertical/Horizontal Scale, Baseline Shift, and Skew. The fourth defines which dictionary language will be used for spelling and hyphenation. All items have a drop-down menu from which to select. Values may be selected from the menu, or the values you desire may be typed into the appropriate fields. The Return or Enter key must be pressed to apply the values you have entered.

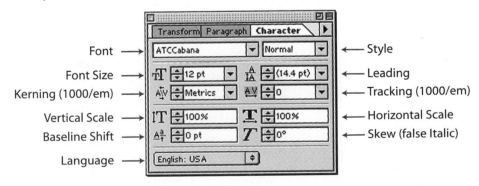

The Font is the name of the family of type selected from the drop-down menu or typed into the dialog box. Fonts must be installed in the computer in order to be accessible. Within font families you will find various weights, such as Regular, Semibold, Bold, and Ultra, and varieties, such as Italic, Oldstyle, and Roman. These are called "styles." Only styles available to the computer are displayed in the Style portion of the Character menu.

Minion Regular                **Minion Bold**
*Minion Regular Italic*          ***Minion Bold Italic***
Minion Semibold              **Minion Black**
*Minion Semibold Italic*        Minion Regular Small Caps & Oldstyle Figures

*In this example, the varieties of Minion are styles. Although Minion Regular Small Caps & Oldstyle Figures is listed as a style, it is technically an extension of the Minion Regular character set.*

For example, if you were to make a headline ATC Daquiri, then use the keyboard shortcut Command/Control-Shift-B to make it bold, the style would appear in brackets [Bold] in the menu and the headline would be highlighted with a pink background, indicating that the font is not present. You would not be able to apply a bold style to the type, because it does not exist.

The *Font Size* is the height of a typeface, measured in points. This is not just the visible size of a character, but includes the distance from the descender to the clearance allowance above the ascender.

This 72-pt. example in Minion Regular shows the breakdown of the vertical spacing of type, including the clearance allowance above the ascender. (Notice that the cap height is different from the ascender height.)

*Leading* is the space between lines of type, measured in points. If Auto leading is selected, the value of the leading (by default 120% of the point size) will appear in parentheses. Be careful that the leading values you choose ensure good readability of the text.

10 pt Minion Regular with 10 pt leading is what many people call "tight" line spacing. Too little linespacing creates dark, uninviting "color" that causes the eye to take in other lines.

10 pt Minion Regular with 12 pt leading is what many people call "normal" line spacing. A proper amount of linespacing allows the eye to travel easily from one line to the next.

10 pt Minion Regular with 15 pt leading is what many people call "open" line spacing. Too much linespacing creates disruptive jumps from line to line.

*The function of the printed piece dictates the proper line spacing or leading. Text for prolonged reading, novels, for example, should be more openly spaced than directories, catalogs, reference works, or ads.*

*ATC typefaces are created with no built-in kerning pairs. To view how InDesign uses robust kerning pairs, change the typeface to Arial, Helvetica, or Times New Roman, type the word "Wordy." and place the cursor between the "Wo" pair and the "y." pairs of letters. The kerning values will display in the palette.*

*Many commercial fonts have a large number of built-in kerning pairs, so you don't have nearly as much hands-on intervention in the kerning. This is called "Robust Kerning," and is one reason these fonts are more expensive than shareware.*

The spacing between two letters is called a *kerning pair*. Kerning is defined in thousandths of an em. Metrics, Optical, or Manual kerning options are available. In body text, it is usually best to use Metrics kerning if you are working with a typeface with robust kerning pairs.

# WATCH YOUR WHITESPACE
# WATCH YOUR WHITESPACE
# WATCH YOUR WHITESPACE

*The first line above has had all kerning stripped out, so one letter begins at the end of the preceding letter's allotted space. The second line uses only the built-in font metrics. The third line is kerned more heavily, to match the white space throughout the entire line. When kerning headlines, pay attention to the white space. It should be relatively even throughout.*

*Tracking* is the spacing between ranges of letters and is defined in thousandths of an em. Kerning and tracking are cumulative in InDesign, so a word might be tracked −10 and a character pair could have an additional −35/1000s of kerning.

When tracking lines of text is it best to track the entire paragraph, rather than a single line. Tracking just one line, either to make it tighter, or to make it looser, simply calls attention to the line. At any rate, tracking, like kerning, should be exercised with discretion.

Proper letterspacing depends on many factors, such as the typeface, the amount of copy, line spacing, size, and weight of the type, as well as individual taste.

When letterspacing is set at its optimum, text has enhanced readability. The tighter the letterspacing, the darker the lines of type become; the looser, the grayer they are.

When letterspacing is set at its optimum, text has enhanced readability. The tighter the letterspacing, the darker the lines of type become; the looser, the grayer they are.

*In the example above, the third line in the first paragraph was tracked to force the word "just" up. Notice how tracking the single line makes it stand out. Lower left is tracked normally, upper right is tracked to -35, lower right is tracked to +35.*

Generally speaking, you should not make alterations to a font. The appearance of the typeface is usually destroyed, as you can see in the following image:

# EᴇEaɑɑ

*Here, respectively, are a Minion Regular "E" with no scaling applied, an "E" vertically scaled to 50%, and an "E" horizontally scaled to 50%. Notice how the thick and thin strokes are radically altered. To the right are a Minion Regular lowercase "a," true italic "a," and skewed italic "a." Many characters change their shapes when true italics are applied.*

*Underlined text is a holdover from typewriter days and should not be used. It is a poor replacement for italics.*

*An **em** is the width of the point size in actual points. An em in 10-point type is 10 points wide. In 24-point type it is 24 points wide.*

*Selecting **Metrics** as the kerning option causes InDesign to use the kerning built into the font, known as Font Metrics.*

*Keyboard shortcuts may be used instead of selecting from the Character palette or the Character palette Options menu. These commands toggle the style on and off.*

*Command/Control-Shift-B*
*Bold*
*Command/Control-Shift-I*
*Italic*
*Command/Control-Shift-Y*
*Normal*
*Command/Control-Shift-U*
*Underline*
*Command/Control-Shift-/*
*Strikethrough*
*Command/Control-Shift-K*
*Caps*
*Command/Control-Shift-H*
*Small Caps*
*Command/Control-Shift-+*
*Superscript*
*Command-Option-Shift-+*
*Subscript (Macintosh)*
*Control-Alt-Shift-+*
*Subscript (Windows)*

*Text may be assigned any color from the swatch libraries, or a special color may be mixed.*

The effect of vertically scaling type is to keep the vertical stroke width the same and to compress or expand the horizontal stroke. The effect of horizontally scaling type is to keep the horizontal stroke width the same and to compress or expand the vertical stroke.

Skewed type may be used for special effects, but should never be substituted for italics. It is simply a distortion of the letterform.

The imaginary line that letters sit on is called the "baseline." Moving the baseline of letters up or down is called "baseline shift." A baseline shift may be useful in a number of instances. For example, it may be used to create fractions, or to alter a character that should be superscripted (such as in a name like M$^c$Arthur). Baseline shifts are also used to "bounce" type in headlines, such as the one pictured below.

# F$^o$ll$_o$w the B$^o$uncing B$^a$ll.

The final section allows you to select a specific language for hyphenation and spelling when that feature is needed. This is particularly useful when more than one language is used within a publication.

The Character palette Option menu has four sections. The first deals with the display of the palette itself. The second deals with case and position of text. The third has to do with styling text, and the fourth allows the user to cause a word not to hyphenate.

| **Hide Options** | |
|---|---|
| **All Caps** | TEXT IS SET IN ALL CAPITAL LETTERS. |
| **Small Caps** | TEXT IS SET IN SMALL CAPITAL LETTERS. |
| **Superscript** | Text has $^{superscript}$ characters. |
| **Subscript** | Text has $_{subscript}$ characters. |
| **Underline** | Text characters are underlined. |
| **Strikethrough** | Text characters are ~~struck through~~. |
| **Ligatures** | Ligatures are used if available ff = ff, fl = fl, fi = fi |
| **Old Style** | OldStyle numbers are used if available 1976 = 1976 |
| **No Break** | Hyphenation is disallowed for the word selected. |

*Many of the elements found in the Character palette Options menu may be accessed from the keyboard.*

Hide/Show Options will hide or show the vertical and horizontal scale, baseline shift, skew, and language features. It shrinks the size of the palette to include only the most-used features.

When characters are highlighted, the All Caps, Small Caps, Superscript, and Subscript styles may be applied. The size (and position in the case of super- and subscript) is determined by the Character Settings, set at File>Preferences>Text. When the Small Caps option is selected, InDesign will access true small caps, if such a font is available.

The styling options — Underline, Strikethrough, Ligatures, and Old Style — are somewhat confusing. Underline and strikethrough characters are always available. Ligatures are available only if they are supported by the font. If the document will be used cross-platform, and you're working on a Macintosh, *do not* use this option. Ligatures are not usually included in alphabets on Windows machines. Even though your "fi" ligature is returned to "f" and "i" characters, the difference may be substantial enough to rewrap the text. Old Style characters are contained in Open Type fonts as extended glyphs. This option may be selected only when Open Type fonts are used.

When a word is highlighted and the No Break option is selected, that word will not hyphenate.

## Enter Text

1.  Select File>New. Create a letter-size document, using the default margins. Facing Pages and Master Text Frame should not be checked.

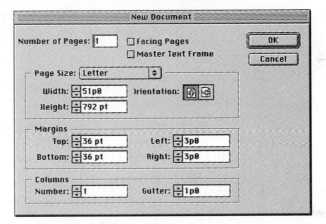

*To Show Hidden Character (think of them as invisible), press:*

*Command-Option-I (Macintosh)*

*Control-Alt-I (Windows)*

2.  From the Type menu, select Show Hidden Characters.

3.  The Transform palette should be open.

4.  Select the Type tool, click at the upper-left corner of the live area of the page, and drag diagonally until you have a frame with the following dimensions:

    X: 3p0      W:  22p0
    Y: 36 pt    H:  220 pt

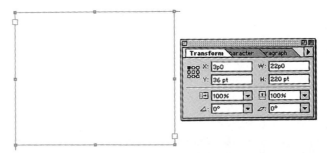

    The insertion point indicates where the text will be typed. As you fill the depth of the text frame, you can either stretch the frame to make it taller, or wider to fit the text, or you can link two text frames. Alternately, you can change the type size to fit it to the frame.

5.  Click on the Character tab to go to this section of the palette.

6. Type "Alice's Adventures in Wonderland" in the text frame. Observe the Font, Size, and other information in the Character palette.

7. Select the text and, in the Character palette, change the typeface to ATC Plantation Plain/Regular. Make the Size 36 pt.

8. Change to the Selection tool, and click on the text frame.

9. Resize the frame to a width of 17p6 by clicking and dragging on the right-hand adjustment handle or by typing the new width into the Transform palette. This allows "Adventures" to flow as we wish, but "Wonderland" is still hyphenating.

10. Switch back to the Type tool and, following the space band before the word "Wonderland," hold down the Shift key and press Return/Enter. This inserts a *soft return*, or forced line break, while not ending the paragraph.

11. "Wonderland" is still hyphenating, but now it's repairable with tracking. Select all the type.

12. In the Tracking dialog box, set the Tracking to –20. This fixes our problem, and the type looks better, as well.

13. Let's kern the "Wo" letter pair. Place the Type tool between the "W" and "o".

14. In the Kerning section of the Character palette, set the Kerning to –75. Press Return/Enter.

15. Kern any other letters that look particularly bad to you. (The "Ad" pair needs help.)

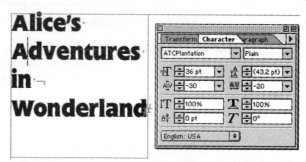

16. Change to the Selection tool, and move the text frame to the right side of the page.

17. Create a new text frame with a width of 12p and a height of 144 pt. below the text frame containing "Alice's Adventures in Wonderland".

18. With the Type tool selected, choose as the typeface ATC Cabana Normal, 12 pt.

19. Type the following:

"Alice was beginning to get very tired of sitting by her sister on the bank, and of having nothing to do; once or twice she had peeped into the book her sister was reading, but it had no pictures or conversations in it, and what is the use of a book, thought Alice, without pictures or conversation?"

20. Notice the Overflow icon in the lower right of the text frame. This icon indicates that the text frame is not large enough to display all the text in the story.

21. Hold down the Command/Control key to temporarily switch to the Selection tool. Resize the text frame so that all text typed in step 19 will fit.

22. Double-click on the word "bank" in the first sentence, and replace it with "fence". Notice how the selected word is replaced by the newly typed text.

23. Select the first word, "Alice". In the Character palette, click on the arrow in the upper right to reveal the palette Options menu. Select the Small Caps text style. Notice how the lower case letters became small capitals, but the capital letter was unaffected.

24. Save the document to your **Work in Progress** folder as "Working Text.INDD". Leave it open for the next exercise.

## Inserting Extended Characters

*Extended characters* are those which cannot be accessed directly from the keyboard, as shift or unshift characters can. They are, for the most part, characters with an ASCII value higher than 128. Windows users are accustomed to entering these characters by holding down the ALT key, then typing the ASCII value, 0### (a zero followed by three numbers) using the numeric keypad. Macintosh users access the characters by holding down the Option or Option-Shift keys in combination with another character. Some characters not typically available on both Macintosh and Windows are now cross-platform accessible. Access these characters through Type>Insert Character.

## Inserting Special Characters

Special Characters in InDesign include some extended characters, but also include "characters" which are not really characters at all, but are commands telling the printer how to treat specific types of spacing. The Special Characters menu is accessible through Control-click (Macintosh) or right-click (Windows). They are also available as keyboard shortcuts.

## List of Special Characters:

| Character/Result | Macintosh | Windows |
|---|---|---|
| Bullet • | Option-8 | Alt-8 |
| Copyright © | Option-G | Alt-G |
| Registered Trademark ® | Option-R | Alt-R |
| Degree º | Option-Shift-8 | Alt-Shift-8 |
| Ellipsis … | Option-; | Alt-; |
| Paragraph ¶ | Option 7 | Alt-7 |
| Quote, Single ' or ' | Option-] or Option-Shift-] | Alt-] or Alt- Shift-] |
| Quote, Double " or " | Option-[ or Option-Shift-[ | Alt-[ or Alt-Shift-[ |
| Trademark ™ | Option-2 | Alt-2 |
| Section symbol § | Option-6 | Alt-6 |

### Hyphens and Dashes

| | | |
|---|---|---|
| Discretionary Hyphen | Command-Shift- - (hyphen) | Control-Shift- - (hyphen) |
| Nonbreaking Hyphen | Command-Option- - (hyphen) | Control-Alt- - (hyphen) |
| Em Dash — | Option-Shift- - (hyphen) | Alt-Shift- - (hyphen) |
| En Dash – | Option- - (hyphen) | Alt- - (hyphen) |

### Spaces

| | | |
|---|---|---|
| Em Space/En Space | Command-Shift-M or -N | Control-Shift-M or -N |
| Thin Space (1/4 Em) | Command-Option-Shift-M | Control-Alt-Shift-M |
| Hair Space (1/24 Em) | Command-Option-Shift-I | Control-Alt-Shift-I |
| Figure Space | Command-Option-Shift-8 | Control-Alt-Shift-8 |

*(Width of a numeric character)*

| | | |
|---|---|---|
| Nonbreaking Space | Command-Option-X | Control-Alt-X |
| Flush Space | Command-Option-Shift-J | Control-Alt-Shift-J |

*(Will insert space, so that all text following is set flush with the right margin)*

| | | |
|---|---|---|
| Soft Return | Shift-Return | Shift-Enter |

Auto Page Numbering and Section Numbering are available from the Special Characters list, but not from a keyboard combination.

### Special Commands

| | | |
|---|---|---|
| Column Break | Enter | Enter |

*(Moves cursor to next column)* — enter on numeric keypad

| | | |
|---|---|---|
| Frame Break | Shift-Enter | Shift-Enter |

*(Moves cursor to next threaded frame)* — enter on numeric keypad

| | | |
|---|---|---|
| Page Break | Command-Shift-Enter | Control-Shift-Enter |

*(Moves cursor to next threaded page)* — enter on numeric keypad

| | | |
|---|---|---|
| Right Indent Tab | Shift-Tab | Shift-Tab |

*(Inserts right-aligned tab at right indent)*

| | | |
|---|---|---|
| Indent to Here | Command-\ | Control-\ |

*(Indents all subsequent text in the paragraph to that point)*

| | | |
|---|---|---|
| Continued From | Command-Option-Shift-[ | Control-Alt-Shift-[ |

*(Inserts page number where story is continued from)*

| | | |
|---|---|---|
| Continued To | Command-Option-Shift-] | Control-Alt-Shift-] |

*(Inserts page number where story is continued to)*

## Format Characters

1.  Open the document **Working Text.INDD** from your **Work in Progress** folder, if it is not already open.

2.  Following the word "Wonderland" in the headline, insert the text cursor and press Return/Enter to make a hard return.

*The manner in which text is aligned affects its readability.*

*This paragraph is set **Align Left**. The left margin is in a constant position. Its value lies in the fact that there are consistent spaces between words and a consistent spot to which the eye returns.*

*This paragraph is set **Justified**. Left and right margins are even, but spaces between words are uneven. This style gives documents a formal, finished look.*

*This paragraph is set **Align Right** which should be used sparingly, perhaps as picture captions. They are difficult to read because there is no consistent spot for the eye to return to.*

*            **Align Center***
*is generally used for invitations, captions, and headlines. It is pretty, but hard to read.*

3. Change the font to ATC Mai Tai Normal, 12 pt. Set the tracking to 0.

4. Type the following on two lines, separated by a soft return:

   "—by Lewis Carroll <hold Shift key to make a soft return>
   © [Public Domain]"

   You may use either the keyboard shortcuts from the chart above or the Insert Special Characters menu to find these characters.

5. Save the file to your **Work in Progress** folder and close it.

## Formatting Paragraphs

The appearance or type style of text influences the character of a page. The formatting of paragraphs also affects how your page looks and reads.

Paragraph formatting issues you should consider include:

- Alignment of text (left, right, centered, both margins justified)
- Indents (left, right, and first line)
- Spacing above and below paragraphs
- Drop caps, if any
- Hyphenation and justification
- Widow and orphan control
- Paragraph rules

To apply paragraph formatting, simply place the Type tool anywhere in a paragraph. Since paragraph formatting affects the entire paragraph, all the text does not have to be manually selected. The Paragraph palette is found in the same container as the Transform and Character palettes, or it may be activated through Type>Paragraph (Command/Control-M).

### Paragraph Palette

The Paragraph palette is divided into four primary sections. The first manages the overall justification of the paragraph. The second section controls indents and determines whether or not the paragraph will align with the underlying baseline grid. The third controls space before and after the paragraph, and drop cap specifics. The fourth section determines whether or not the paragraph will be hyphenated.

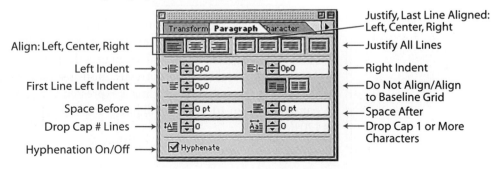

The first section, justification options, is grouped into three subsections. The first is for *unjustified text* — text which is aligned to the left or right margins, or is centered on the page. The second section determines how the last line of paragraphs of justified text will be addressed — right, left, or centered. The third forces all lines of text in the paragraph to justify to both margins.

The top two boxes in the next section are for setting a left or right indent for the entire paragraph.

The first line indent adds its indent to any existing paragraph indent. So, if a paragraph is indented one pica from the left margin, with a first line indent of one pica, the first line will be indented two picas from the margin. Additionally, the first line may be given a negative indent or *outdent* by typing a hyphen (minus) in front of the indent amount; this is also called a "hanging indent."

The Do Not Align to Baseline Grid/Align to Baseline Grid boxes determine, on a paragraph-by-paragraph basis, whether or not the underlying grid for the document will affect the linefall of the paragraph. In most cases, aligning to the baseline grid is not a good idea.

Space Before and Space After dialog boxes allow the placement of a specific amount of space before or after a paragraph. They are usually used between elements in a bulleted list, between headlines and text, and between paragraphs that do not have first line indents.

Drop Cap Number of Lines and Drop Cap One or More Characters are reasonably self-explanatory. When paragraphs have a drop cap, these dialog boxes control the number of lines a paragraph will drop and the number of characters to include in the drop. (If a quotation opens a section, it is appropriate to include both the quotation mark and the first character of the quote as a two-character drop cap.)

The Hyphenate check box turns hyphenation on or off for that paragraph. Generally speaking, callouts, headlines, and captions will have their hyphenation turned off.

Behind the triangle at the top right of the Paragraph palette is the "behind the scenes" power of paragraph controls. Most of these are advanced features and will be considered in the *InDesign: Advanced Electronic Mechanicals* course. We'll give a brief overview here.

| Hide Options | |
| --- | --- |
| **Justification...** | Justification standards |
| **Keep Options...** | Defines which lines are kept together |
| **Hyphenation...** | Hyphenation standards |
| **Paragraph Rules...** | Rules (Lines) Above and Below |
| **Adobe Single-line Composer** | Hyphenation based on either a |
| ✓ **Adobe Multi-line Composer** | single line or a number of lines |

Justification rules take effect primarily when the text alignment is justified to both margins. They control Word Spacing, Letter Spacing, and Glyph (character) Scaling that will be used to force a paragraph to justify. InDesign uses the parameters, in the order that they appear, to cause a paragraph to justify correctly. Non-justified text uses the Desired column to determine its spacing. Auto Leading is expressed as a percentage based on the point size. A paragraph set in 10-pt. type will have a leading value of 12 pts. if the Auto Leading value is 120%.

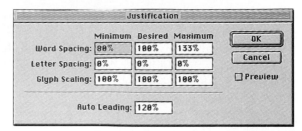

Keep Options is very useful in production situations. Keep with Next forces a paragraph (such as a headline) to stay with the number of lines stipulated. It can save you from some very unattractive (and embarrassing) composition errors. Keep Lines Together refers to a single paragraph. It protects against a single line of the paragraph falling at the bottom of a page or column, or a single line being forced to the next paragraph or column. Paragraphs may start anywhere, or they may be forced to the next column or the next threaded frame. They may also be forced to the next page, the next odd page, or the next even page.

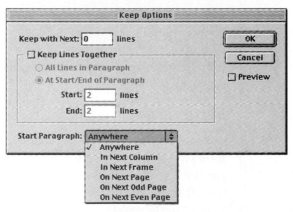

*The **Hyphenation Zone** is the distance from the end of the line in which a hyphenable point must fall in order for the word to be hyphenated.*

Automatic hyphenation is controlled on a paragraph-by-paragraph basis, through the Hyphenation options. Of course, operators may manually override any automatic hyphenation decisions. The minimum length of words that will hyphenate is controlled here, as is the number of hyphens allowed in successive lines. The zone in which hyphenation will occur is also determined. In addition, this menu gives a control for automatic hyphenation of capitalized words. (Capitalized words are not usually hyphenated because they are often proper nouns.)

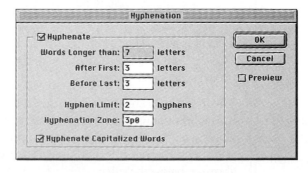

*Press Command/Control-Shift-T to access the Tabs palette.*

*Tabs may be used for positioning text in a paragraph, but their primary function is to provide columnar alignment for rows of text.*

*If text is highlighted in pink, it was originally set with a font you do not have.*

*Typographers specify the size of the type with the leading by separating them with a slash. If the type is to be set in 10-pt. size with 12-pt. Leading, they would write "10/12." This is referred to as "10 over 12."*

Instead of drawing lines under or over paragraphs with the Line tool, we make them a part of the paragraph using InDesign's Paragraph Rules options. Stipulate the rule's weight, and whether the stroke will overprint colors below, the color, and tint. Define whether the rule is to be the width of the column or of the text, its position relative to the baseline, and its indents (or outdents).

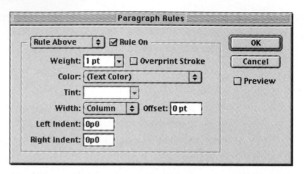

Adobe Single-line Composer and Adobe Multi-line Composer are linked to InDesign's Composition Preferences which control advanced features of the program. Essentially, the Composer takes into account all the paragraph rules you have invoked and makes composition decisions based on them, spreading the decision out over several lines or over only a single line.

## Setting Tabs

Tabs are another type element often used. The Tabs palette is accessed at Type>Tabs. The most effective way to access this palette is to create your text frame, then select the Tabs palette. It will be placed in the ideal position above your text frame. The palette may be moved above the text frame you're working on by clicking the magnet-shaped icon on the right of the tab palette.

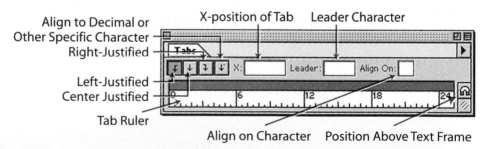

Tabs may align left, center, right, or to a character (the decimal, or period, is the default). The tab leader may be blank or a combination of multiple characters, including spaces. (Fixed spaces will not work.)

The first step in creating tab settings is to determine the number of tabular columns that the table contains. Once you've determined the number of columns, then decide on their alignment. To create a tab, click the appropriate location on the Tab ruler. To move a tab, select it on the Tab ruler and drag it to a new location. To delete a tab, select it and drag it above or below the ruler.

Precise tab settings aren't necessary when you first begin typing information — just set them at approximate positions. When the Tab key is pressed, the selected text moves to the positions defined in the Tab menu. After the text is typed, if tab settings are not positioned where you wish, select the entire table and reposition the tabs. InDesign interactively applies your tab settings, so you immediately see the effects of your changes.

We're going to put what you've just learned to work as we format an invoice from the Mad Hatter.

### Format the Invoice Header

1. Open the document **Hattery.INDD** from your **SF-Intro InDesign** folder.

2. Select Type>Show Hidden Characters, or press Command-Option-I (Macintosh) or Control-Alt-I (Windows). Take a moment to see how the document is put together. The Character and Paragraph palettes should be available.

3. Select all the text in the first line and style it ATC Holiday, 30 pt.

4. Switch to the Paragraph palette and change the Alignment to Center.

5. Add 9 pt. Space After.

6. Return to the Character palette, highlight the next three lines of text and style them ATC Mai Tai Normal, 12 pt., with 15-pt. Leading. (We will normally write this "ATC Mai Tai Normal 12/15".)

7. Switch to the Paragraph palette and center the text, or simply type Command/Control-Shift-C.

*Use these shortcuts to format paragraph alignment:*
*Command/Control-Shift-L*
*Align Left*
*Command/Control-Shift-R*
*Align Right*
*Command/Control-Shift-C*
*Align Center*

*Command/Control-Shift-F*
*Justify (except last line)*
*Command/Control-Shift-J*
*Justify all lines*

---

## The Mad Hattery

1227 Offkilter Road
Carrolland, NH 03308
(603) 894-1784

---

8. In the Character palette, select the word "Invoice" and style it ATC Holiday 24/27.

9. Leave the file open for the next exercise.

### Create a Reversed Heading

1. In the Paragraph palette, align the text Centered, add 6 pts. Space Before and 6 pts. Space After.

2. Select the invoice number and, from the appropriate palettes, style it ATC Mai Tai Bold 12/15, aligned right.

3. Triple-click to highlight the next paragraph.

4. Style it ATC Mai Tai Normal, 8.5/10, with 6 pts. Space Before and After, Justified with last line aligned left.

5. Select the header line for the invoice and style it ATC Mai Tai Bold 10/12, with left and right indents of 0p9, and 6 pts. Space After.

*Toggle quickly between*
*Character & Paragraph*
*palettes*
*Command/Control-T*
*Character palette*
*Command/Control-M*
*Paragraph palette*

6.  Select the next four lines and style them ATC Mai Tai Normal 10/18, with left and right indents of 0p9.

7.  Select the final line and style it ATC Mai Tai Bold 10/18, with left and right indents of 0p9.

8   Place the cursor in the paragraph with the centered word "Invoice." Select the Paragraph palette, and click on the Options arrow. Select Paragraph Rules.

9.  With Rule Above selected, click the Rule On button. Make the Weight 18 pt. and the Color Black.

10. Choose Rule Below, and click the Rule On button. Make the Weight 6 pt. and the Color Black. Click OK.

11. Double-click on the word Invoice to highlight it.

12. Select Window>Color. Double-click on the Color tab to expand the palette, if necessary.

13. Be certain the Fill, not the Stroke, icon is selected. Type "0" (zero) in the box next to the color slider and press Return/Enter, or slide the small triangle all the way to the left. (If you use the slide, do not press Return/Enter.)

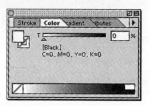

14. Leave the file open for the next exercise.

## Apply Tabs

1.  Place the cursor in the line that begins with "Item #".

2.  Activate the Tab palette from Type>Tabs or by pressing Command/Control-Shift-T.

3.  Set a left-aligned tab at 5p6, a center-aligned tab at 15p0, a center-aligned tab at 20p0, and a center-aligned tab at 25p0.

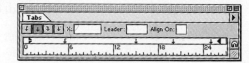

4.  Highlight the next four lines and set tabs as follows: left-aligned at 5p6, decimal-aligned at 15p3, center-aligned at 20p0, decimal-aligned at 24p10.

5.  Place the cursor in the last line (Total Due…). Set a decimal-aligned tab at 24p10. We're getting there, but there's still some work to do. The dollar signs need help. We want to align them. We'll use the figure space.

*Activate the Paragraph Rules palette by pressing Command-Option-J (Macintosh) or Control-Alt-J (Windows)*

*You may directly access the Figure Space by pressing Command-Option-Shift-8 (Macintosh) or Control-Alt-Shift-8 (Windows)*

6. Place the cursor between the dollar sign ($) and the "8" in the second line item. Control-click/right-click to activate the context-sensitive menu. Select Insert White Space>Figure Space. The dollar sign will align with the dollar sign above it.

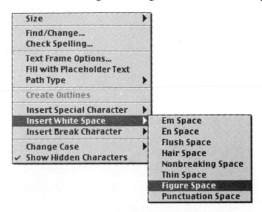

*When coloring type, make sure the Fill icon, not the Stroke, is active.*

7. Do the same thing for the other items in this column and in the "Ext." column. Use two figure spaces when necessary.

8. Let's make a couple of adjustments to the tabbed header for our invoice (the one that begins with "Item #"). Place the cursor in the line. From the Paragraph palette, set the Space Before at 6 pt. and the Space After at 9 pt.

9. Click on the Paragraph palette, and select Paragraph Rules from the Option's fly-out menu.

10. Turn the Rule Above on by clicking in the box. Make its Weight 3 pt., the Width Column, and the Offset 10 pt.

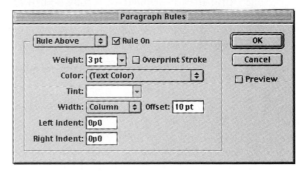

11. Select Rule Below and turn it on. Make its Weight 1 pt, the Width Column, and the Offset 4 pt. Click OK.

12. Go to the "Total Due" line. Make the Space Before 12 pt.

13. Click on the Options triangle and select Paragraph Rules.

14. Select Rule Above and turn the rule on.

15. Make its Weight 2 pt., the Width Column, and the Offset 12 pt. Click OK.

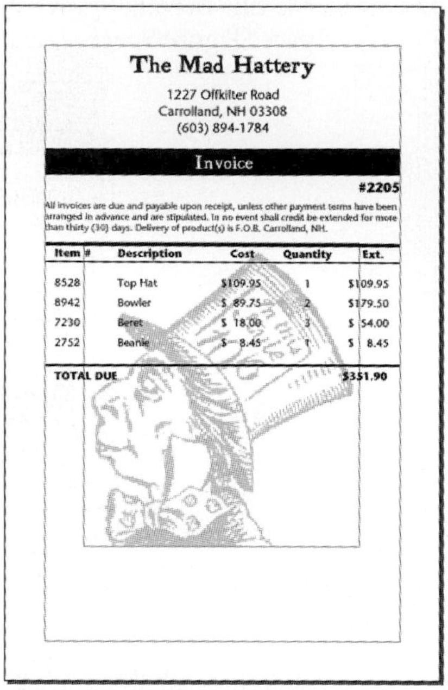

16. Save the document to your **Work in Progress** folder. Close the document.

## Importing and Exporting Text Files

Often you will not be typing the bulk of your text into InDesign. Instead, you will import it from a word processing program. The text may be either *tagged text*, i.e. text with formatting already applied, or it may be *raw text*. It may also be a hybrid (what you'll get most often) — raw text with boldface and italic noted.

InDesign supports a variety of word processing formats:

- Microsoft Word 97/98 and later

- Microsoft Word 6.0 – 7.0

- Microsoft Word 4.0 – 5.0

- WordPerfect 6.1 – 8.0

- Excel 97/98

- RTF (Rich Text Format)

- Tagged Text

- Text

When a file is imported, the Import Options may be set. Options will vary, depending upon which word processing program was used to produce the text file. In general, these are the steps to follow when importing a file:

With a document open, you would choose File>Place (Command/Control-D). A menu similar to this would appear:

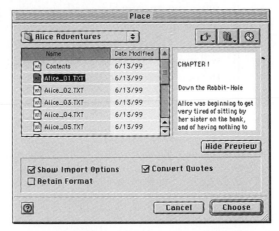

With the Show Import Options selected, you would double-click the file you wish to import. Alternately, you could hold down the Shift key and double-click the file you wish to import.

You would then set the desired options and click OK. The cursor will change to a loaded text icon.

If the text icon is clicked anywhere on the page, the text will flow the width of the live area (from left to right margin) from the vertical position at which the icon is clicked to the bottom of the page.

If there is an active frame on the page, the text will flow into the frame. A frame may be created by clicking the icon, then dragging to a point on the page.

InDesign will notify you if the document you are importing requires unavailable fonts.

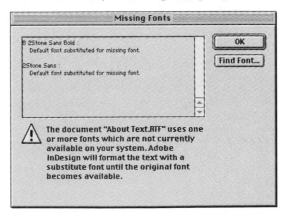

If you get this dialog box, you may click the Find Font button. You will then be presented with a palette showing all the fonts in the document, and you will have the option of replacing missing fonts with fonts that are in the system. Click the More Info button to obtain more information about the missing font. When you have finished making the necessary font substitutions, click Done. Alternately, you can simply click OK, and the file will import with missing fonts. If you're going to apply different font styles anyway, this is the best approach to take.

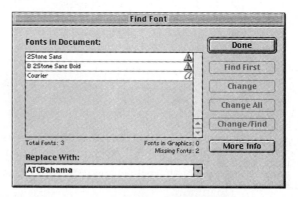

Text may also be exported in a number of formats. To do so, you should be certain the Type tool is active, and select File>Export (Command/Control-E). You would then select the file option in which you wish to export the text. The options are:

- Adobe InDesign Tagged Text

- Adobe PDF

- EPS

- HTML

- Prepress File

- Rich Text Format

- Text-only

*You may receive the message that there is a modified link. If so, click Update in the Links menu. (It is automatically opened when such an event occurs).*

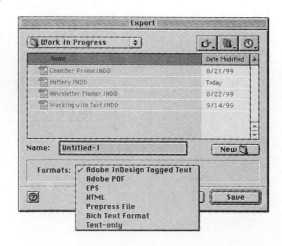

## Linked Text Files

Text placed into an InDesign document contains a link to the original file. The link is not automatically updated when the original file is altered, but it may be manually updated through the Links Manager. This can be especially useful when importing files containing dynamic data, such as price lists. However, if body text is altered, the document may reflow, causing a real mess. Update text links with caution. It is usually better to embed the text files through File>Links, then selecting Embed in the Links options.

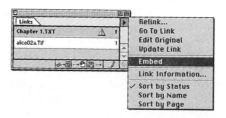

## Threaded Text

As you noted earlier, sometimes text will not fit in the frame. Much of the time, you will not be able to simply resize the frame or the type, as we did earlier. When that is the case, the text must be linked to another frame. This is accomplished by clicking on the out port (the red "+" sign at the lower right) with the Selection tool. The cursor will change to a loaded text icon. Simply drag the icon to form another text frame, while holding down the mouse button. Release the button and the text will fill the new frame.

'Well!' thought Alice to herself, 'after such a fall as this, I shall think nothing of tumbling down stairs! How brave they'll all think me at home! Why, I wouldn't say anything about it, even if I fell off the top of the house!' (Which was very likely true.) Down, down, down. Would

the fall never come to an end! 'I wonder how many miles I've fallen by this time?' she said aloud. 'I must be getting somewhere near the centre of the earth. Let me see: that would be four thousand miles down, I think—' (for, you see, Alice had learnt several things of this sort in

her lessons in the school-room, and though this was not a very good opportunity for showing off her knowledge, as there was no one to listen to her, still it was good practice to say it over) '—yes, that's about the right distance—but then I wonder what Latitude or Longitude

*Text that is threaded flows from frame to frame.*
*You can see this when you access View>Show Text Threads.*

### Place and Thread Text

1. Open the file **Alice_01.INDD** from your **SF-Intro InDesign** folder.

2. Select the Type tool, hold down the mouse button, and drag a text frame to the following dimensions:

   |         |          |
   |---------|----------|
   | X: 3p0  | W: 45p0  |
   | Y: 36 pt | H: 216 pt |

*Press F9 to activate the Transform palette.*

(Switch to the Selection tool, click on the frame, and adjust the dimensions in the Transform palette.)

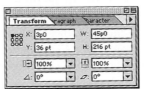

3.  From File>Place, choose **Chapter 1.TXT** from your **SF-Intro InDesign** folder. Show Import Options, Retain Format, and Convert Quotes should be checked. (If you elect to Show Preview (Macintosh only), you'll notice that the "text" contains a lot of code. This is because the file we're placing is an InDesign Tagged Text file.) Click Choose.

*Because of the slight differences between the metrics of Macintosh and Windows fonts, the line breaks may be a little different than shown here.*

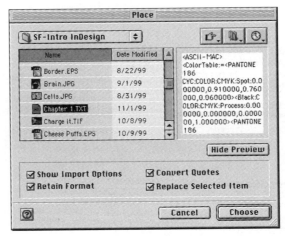

4.  The InDesign Tags Import Options box appears. Select Tagged File Definition and ensure that the Show List of Problem Tags before Place box is checked. This is useful if any tags have been improperly entered. Click OK.

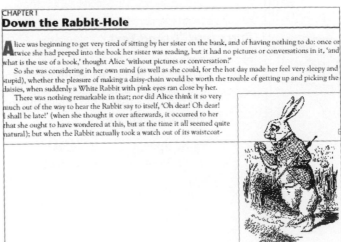

5. Notice that the exit port displays a red "+". This tells us there is more text to flow. With the Selection tool, click on the port. The cursor changes to a loaded text icon.

6. Drag a text frame as follows:

   X: 3p0          W: 20p0
   Y: 264 pt       H: 492 pt

   When you release the mouse button, the text will fill the frame, and you will see there is still more text to place. (Adjust the size of the frame using the Transform palette, if necessary.)

7. Click on the exit port and drag another text frame as follows:

   X: 24p0         W: 24p0
   Y: 264 pt       H: 492 pt

   Release the button to fill the frame with text. Adjust the size of the frame in the Transform palette, if necessary. There may be more text to place.

   We're going to handle this a little differently, since there are some paragraphs that have word widows (one word on a line).

8. Select the Type tool and place the cursor in the third paragraph (which begins with "There was nothing so very remarkable…"); triple-click the mouse button to select the entire paragraph.

9. If your text is overset (the red + appears in the exit port), make the tracking amount −5 in the Character palette. The balance of text flows into the frame and the red "+" disappears.

   If you did not have overset text, make the tracking amount +5 to force more words into the line to get rid of the widow.

10. Save the document to your **Work in Progress** folder and close the document.

## Summary

You have learned the properties of text frames, including columns, insets, and first baselines. You have learned to format text characters and to format paragraphs. You can also manage text in frames by enlarging the frame, linking frames, and by working with the text itself to achieve a better fit. Now you're ready to go on to some more advanced text features that will make working with text even easier.

*Complete Project A: Around the World Ad*

**Notes:**

# CHAPTER 5

# Style Sheets

## CHAPTER OBJECTIVE:

To learn to create, apply, and edit styles, and to base a new style upon another. To learn how styles interact with each other and with other elements in InDesign. In Chapter 5, you will:

- Understand what style sheets are and how they can make production work extremely efficient.

- Learn how to style selected text efficiently with attributes such as Font, Font Size, Leading, Kerning, Color, and more, by applying Character Styles.

- Learn how to apply and change attributes such as Indents and Spacing, Drop Caps, Justification, Tabs, Hyphenation, Rules, Keep Options, and more to paragraphs throughout an entire document with Paragraph Styles.

- Understand when to create a new style, when to base one style on another, and how to edit an existing style.

## PROJECTS TO BE COMPLETED:

- Around the World Ad (A)
- Baggy's Kid's Menu (B)
- Vacation Brochure (C)
- Good Choices Newsletter (D)

# Style Sheets

Whenever you're building a document with more than a few paragraphs of copy, you will find yourself spending a great deal of time formatting the text. Style sheets allow you to format both characters and entire paragraphs with a single click or keystroke, eliminating the need to apply each attribute individually.

Character and paragraph styles can be created by formatting a paragraph or text selection, then using that formatted text to create a named style in the Character Styles or Paragraph Styles palette. Later, the named styles can be applied to paragraphs or text elements from the appropriate palette or by using keyboard shortcuts.

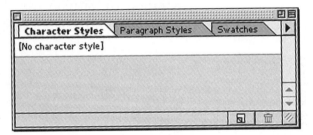

*Character Styles and Paragraph Styles palettes are included in the same palette container as the Swatches palette.*

Style sheets can contain predefined settings for almost any available attribute. Character styles may include Font, Size, Color, and other character attributes. Paragraph styles may include character attributes plus any information available from the Paragraph Options palette: Formats, Tabs, and Rules. Character styles may be based on other character styles. Paragraph styles may be based on other paragraph styles; their character attributes are defined directly by the paragraph style.

Styles are used to greatest advantage when working with long, text-intensive documents that have recurring editorial elements, such as headlines, subheads, captions, sidebars, and so forth. They are useful for documents on which several people work concurrently, such as a book, where chapters may be composed by different individuals. They are also useful in documents with specific stylistic requirements, such as catalogs. In cases such as these, style sheets ensure consistency in text and paragraph formatting throughout a publication. This course book — with its variety of headers, body copy, and sidebars — is an example of a document that benefits from the use of styles. Styles ensure that similar editorial elements are treated with design consistency throughout the document.

Another major advantage of using style sheets is the ease with which changes can be made to all text defined as a particular style. For example, a 24-pt. headline style can be modified to increase the font size to 28 pts.; a run-in head that appears a hundred or more times in a book can change its color from red to green, by simply changing that element in the character style. All text defined will be changed instantly.

*Press F11 to bring the Paragraph Styles palette to the front of the styles palette container and press Shift-F11 to bring the Character Styles palette to the front of the container.*

## Character Styles

We could view a character style as the primary building block of all elements in our document. Let's take a look at how a character style is constructed. In the Character Styles palette, there are a series of options available through the drag-down menu below the style name: General, Basic Color Formats, Advanced Color Formats, and Character Color.

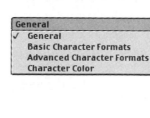
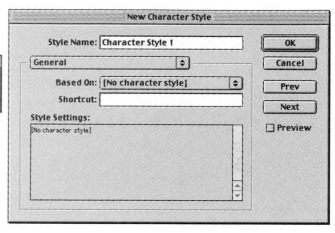

*When you change your selection in the drag-down menu under the style name, notice that the attributes available in the dialog box change.*

The name assigned to the character style should be a descriptive one, related to paragraph-style names, that will reveal the qualities of the character style without having to constantly refer back to them. If, for example, the character style is identical to the body-text style with the exception of its color, and body text is called "BT," then the character style could be called "BT_Blue." We can also assign a keyboard Shortcut with General selected in the menu under the style name. In this case we assigned Command-1 (Macintosh) or Control-1 (Windows). To access the shortcut, we would press Command/Control and "1" on the numeric keypad.

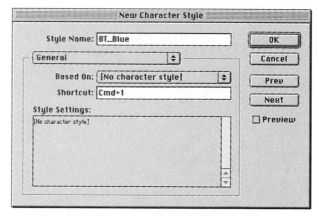

With Basic Character Formats selected in the menu under the style name, you can assign the primary character attributes of Font, Style, Size, Leading, Kerning, Tracking, Case and Position. You may also assign Underline, Strikethrough, Ligature, Old Style characters, and non-breaking options.

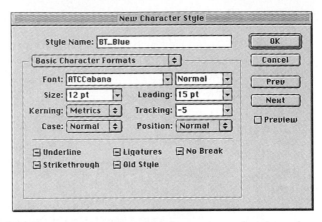

With Advanced Character Formats selected in the menu under the style name, you can scale the character horizontally or vertically, apply a Baseline Shift, or Skew the character (apply false italic). You may also select any of the active languages for spelling and hyphenation.

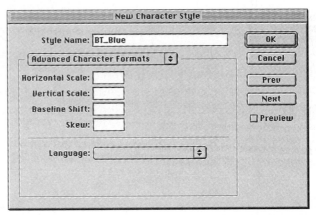

With the final option — Character Color — selected in the menu under the style name, you are able to assign a color from the Swatches palette to the characters selected. In addition to assigning an overall color to the text, a stroke may be assigned as well. Stroke and fill may be forced to overprint.

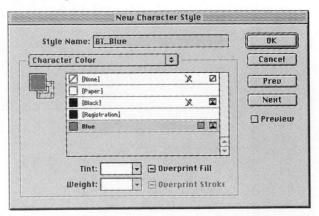

*In the illustration above, the Fill has been set to Blue and the Stroke has been left with no color applied.*

— *A "–" symbol (Macintosh) indicates that the character will pick up attributes from the underlying paragraph.*

*A gray checkmark (Windows) indicates that the character will pick up attributes from the underlying paragraph.*

*A checkmark indicates that the attribute will be added.*

*A blank box indicates that the attribute will not be applied.*

If an element is left blank, it will pick up that characteristic from the overall style of the paragraph. Where there are buttons, a hyphen "–" symbol (Macintosh) indicates that the character style will pick up the attribute from the underlying paragraph. This is comparable to a gray checkmark under Windows. A checkmark ( ✓ ) indicates that the attribute will be added, and a blank box indicates that the attribute will not be applied.

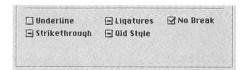

*In this example, the underline style will not be applied, even if text in the paragraph is underlined. The words selected will not be allowed to hyphenate. (No Break has been selected.) All remaining attributes will be picked up from the underlying paragraph.*

**A bold, run-in headline in color** differentiates the character style in this paragraph from the rest of the paragraph. It is handled through the Character Styles palette and can be applied with a keystroke, such as Command/Control-keypad-1 (assigned by the user). This character style's name, BT_Blue, suggests that it is the same as body text, but has the added characteristics of being a different color.

If you were to apply these style options individually, you would find the process very time-consuming, particularly if you had a number of paragraphs with run-in headlines.

When you create your own style sheets, you begin to see the real power in publishing. There are two ways to create styles from scratch. The method we call "the designer method" is to apply formatting to the text until it looks good to the eye, then click in the paragraph with the Type tool, and create a new style (Character or Paragraph). All of the attributes thus defined will be applied to the new style automatically. The *compositor method* is to create the styles using the Character Styles and Paragraph Styles palettes. This is the preferred method when you are given style specifications. We will use the compositor method in constructing our styles.

*Note the last item in the Character Styles and Paragraph Styles Options palettes. Small Palette Rows is useful when you have many styles in the palette. The disadvantage to the small rows, however, is that it's easier to accidentally click on the wrong style.*

### Build Character Styles

1. From the **SF-Intro InDesign** folder, open the document **Working with Style.INDD**. If the document does not open to the first page (the first line is "CHAPTER II"), double-click on the page-1 icon in the Pages palette to go there.

2. If it is not already open, open the Character Styles palettes by selecting it from Type>Character Styles or by pressing Shift-F11.

3. Select New Style from the Character Styles fly-out menu.

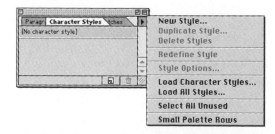

4. Make the Style Name "Run-in Blue". Place the cursor in the Shortcut dialog box and press Command/Control-keypad-1 to assign the shortcut. Click on the Next button to advance to the next option — Basic Character Formats.

5. With Basic Character Formats selected in the menu under the style name, define the style as ATC Mai Tai Bold, 12 pt. We'll pick up the leading from the paragraph style.

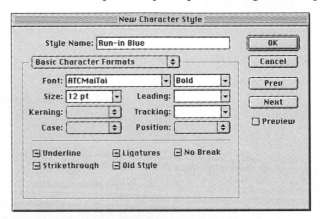

6. Click Next to advance to the next option in the menu under the style name — Advanced Character Formats. We're not going to use any of these attributes, but this gives you an opportunity to see what they look like.

7. Click Next to advance to Character Color in the menu under the style name. With the Fill icon active, click on Pantone 286 CVC to assign it the color. Click Next again to return to the General menu. Note that the Style Setting box displays all the options you selected for this character style. Click OK to add the style to the Character Styles palette.

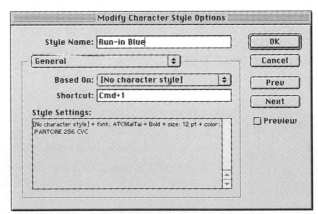

8. We'll apply this style later in the chapter.

9. Save the document to your **Work in Progress** folder.

*This textbook is an example of a document built with styles. All the headers, body text, and hands-on exercises are formatted using styles. This helps make the document consistent. There are many books in the series, and each uses the same fonts, paragraph formats, indents, tabs, and character styles.*

## Paragraph Styles

All the elements that may be applied to a paragraph may be stored in a paragraph style. They may be entered directly or referenced from another paragraph style. We discussed the basics of paragraph formatting earlier in this course, but it is with paragraph styles that we harness the power of the paragraph features.

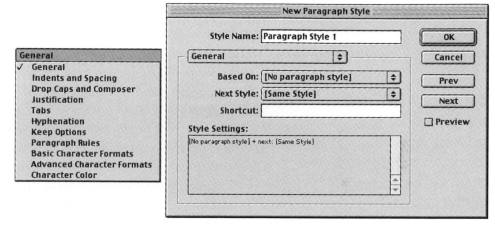

### General

With General selected in the menu under the style name in the New Paragraph Style dialog box, each paragraph can have its own distinctive name. A paragraph style may have the same name as a character style, and this is often desirable for easy cross-reference. Like character styles, paragraph styles may be assigned keyboard equivalents. They may also be based on another paragraph style having similar character style, leading, or indents for convenience — or to maintain a relationship between styles.

*As wonderful as the "Next Style" feature is when typing text directly into InDesign, it is of no value when you import text from a word processor. If you are working with imported text, don't waste your time trying to work with the Next Style feature. Instead, use a similar feature in the word processing software (if it has that capability).*

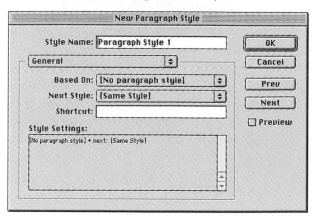

A powerful feature of paragraph styles, if text is being entered directly into InDesign, is the Next Style menu. For example, an H2 style (level-two headline), may be followed by a BT1 (similar to a BT but with no paragraph indent), followed by a BT. If the Next Style box is checked, the operator would simply select H2, type the headline, press Return/Enter to change to BT1, type the text, press Return/Enter and type in the BT style. The text might look something like this:

**H2**   **I. Down The Rabbit-hole**

**BT1**   ALICE was beginning to get very tired of sitting by her sister on the bank, and of having nothing to do: once or twice she had peeped into the book her sister was reading, but it had no pictures or conversations in it, "and what is the use of a book," thought Alice, "without pictures or conversation?" So she was considering in her own mind (as well as she could, for the hot day made her feel very sleepy and stupid) whether the pleasure of making a daisy-chain would be worth the trouble of getting up and picking the daisies, when suddenly a White Rabbit with pink eyes ran close by her.

**BT**   There was nothing so very remarkable in that; nor did Alice think it so very much out of the way to hear the Rabbit say to itself, "Oh dear! Oh dear! I shall be too late!" (When she thought it over afterwards, it occurred to her that she ought to have wondered at this, but at the time it all seemed quite natural); but when the Rabbit actually took a watch out of its waistcoat pocket, and looked at it, and then hurried on, Alice started to her feet, for it flashed across her mind that she had never before seen a rabbit with either a waistcoat pocket or a watch to take out of it, and burning with curiosity, she ran across the field after it, and fortunately was just in time to see it pop down a large rabbit-hole under the hedge.

When defining attributes, the attribute may be specific to the paragraph style, or it may be based on another paragraph style. A number of paragraph features, such as leading and alignment, can be based on another paragraph style. It would be better to base the new paragraph style on an existing one to take advantage of the similar features of the sample style.

For example, Body Text, Body Text-First Paragraph, Bulleted Lists, and Numbered Lists may retain the same font and size, but may have different indents, tabs, and space above and below.

## Indents and Spacing

Alignment, indents and spacing are included in this option in the menu under the style name. Many of the elements available here should be familiar already. Alignment may be Left, Center, Right, Justified with the last line being flushed left, right, or centered, or Full Justified, forcing the last line of the paragraph to both right and left margins. Left and Right indents affect the left and right margins of the paragraph in reference to the text frame in which it resides. First Line Indent places the left margin of the first line of the paragraph with relation to the paragraph indents. Space Before and Space After indicate space in addition to the leading between paragraphs. Here you may also elect to align a paragraph to the Baseline Grid.

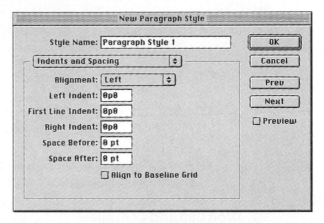

This is the default Baseline Grid setting — found at File>Preferences — and most people leave it set this way.

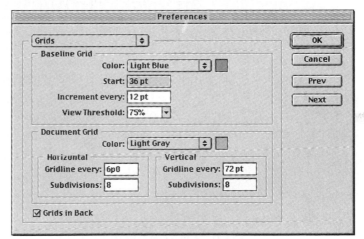

Notice how it affects the placement of text on the page.

*The block of text on the left is set with the grid off, the block at the right with the grid on. With these settings, the grid interferes with the design specifications.*

*For a review of the features of Multi-line Composer, refer to Chapter 3.*

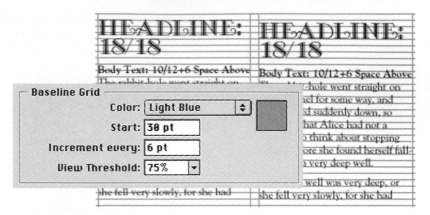

*In this example, with the same two text blocks, the grid has been reset to a 6-pt. increment to better work with the document's parameters.*

### Drop Cap and Composer

This option in the menu under the style name allows automatic application of drop caps to a paragraph. The number of Lines for the Drop Cap and the number of Characters that will be affected may be specified. This is particularly useful when used in conjunction with character styles. In addition, multi-line or single-line composition routines may be selected here.

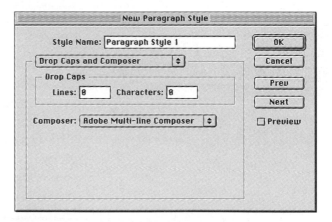

### Justification

The Justification option in the menu under the style name controls InDesign's automatic features for making lines fit in order to avoid excessive hyphenation. These features are Word Spacing, Letter Spacing, and Glyph Scaling. The percentage for Auto Leading is also included here. Auto Leading is set by default to 120% of the nominal type size. Generally speaking, Auto Leading should not be used, because it will adjust line spacing if a character from another font or a graphic is inserted in the line, making line spacing uneven.

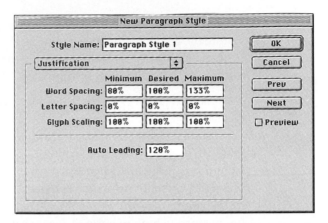

*Although character spacing can be managed using tracking, this should be approached with caution. Tracking in InDesign compresses word space in addition to compressing letterspace; this is usually undesirable.*

To properly justify a line or a paragraph of type, the interplay between the words and their space and the individual characters and their space must be taken into consideration. The default word space allows InDesign to crunch word space to 80% of what the designer intended, and to stretch it to 133% when copy is justified. Glyph Scaling allows InDesign to compress or expand the actual letterform. If this feature is used at all, the scaling percentages should be minimal.

The three choices for spacing are Minimum, Desired, and Maximum. InDesign will always try to give the desired spacing. It will then apply the parameters defined in H&Js to make each line fit, looking ahead several lines, if Multi-line Composer is used. Word space percentages are expressed as a percentage of the word space designed into the font. Character space percentages are a percentage of the space between characters, as designed into the font.

## Tabs

Tab settings may also be included in a paragraph style. This is particularly useful when tabular data follows a consistent format, as in menus, tables of contents, and some financial tables. The tab location (horizontal position on the line), Leader characters, and alignment within the tab area may be set here.

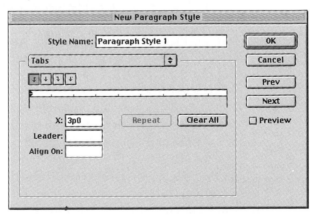

## Hyphenation

Automatic Hyphenation may be checked on or off, the length of the shortest word to be hyphenated may be controlled, and the smallest word you will allow to be hyphenated, in number of characters, may be stipulated.

Too many hyphens in a row creates an appearance called "ladders"— similar to the rungs of a ladder at the end of lines — and is very distracting. Many publishing standards set this number at two or three. Advertising standards usually allow no more than one, and that with caution. The Hyphenation Zone determines how close to the end of a line the text must come before a hyphen is inserted. Hyphenation will be inserted only if the previous word ends before the Hyphenation Zone begins and there is an acceptable hyphenation point within the word. The Hyphenation Zone only applies to text that is not justified to both margins. A Hyphenation Zone value of 0 means there is no zone, and InDesign will hyphenate according to all other hyphenation criteria, or will wrap the entire word to the next line. The Hyphenation Zone should be considered carefully, taking into consideration the overall line length and type size. A zone of 3 picas (the default) may be appropriate for 12-point type on a 22-pica line, but entirely inappropriate for 9-point type on a 10-pica line.

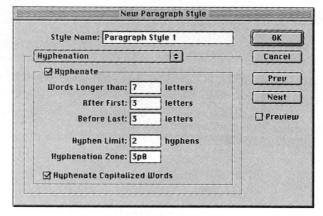

Generally speaking, it is not proper to hyphenate capitalized words. However, if the documents being worked on have very short lines, and there are a number of long proper nouns, allowing them to break is often a good idea (the page looks a lot better). The Hyphenate Capitalized Words checkbox is at the bottom of the page.

## Keep Options

The Keep Options are sometimes thought of as widow and orphan control. At least two lines of a paragraph should remain together in running text. However, there are some types of text, such as headlines, and bulleted and numbered lists, that should keep all lines in the paragraph together. In addition, some paragraphs, such as headlines, should be kept with the next paragraph. To enable that function, enter the number of lines in the following paragraph that should be kept with the headline in the Keep with Next:___ Lines area. Paragraphs may start anywhere, or they may be forced to the next column or the next threaded frame. They may also be forced to the next page, the next odd page, or the next even page.

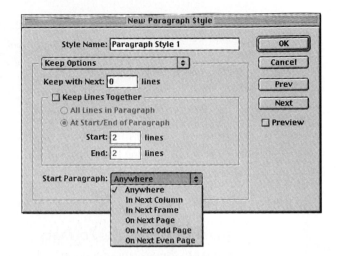

## Paragraph Rules

Many times, rules interact with tabs to create effective tables. At other times they can be used to create more effective headlines, by creating a reversed headline that will flow with text, in concert with financial elements, or to set off such items as callouts, or pull quotes. Being able to access them quickly, easily, and repeatedly is a function of including them in style sheets.

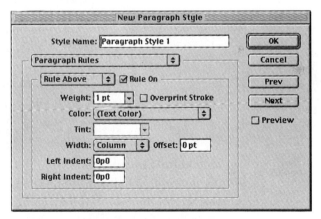

## Basic Character Formats

Much like Character Styles, the Basic Character Format sets the character style for the entire paragraph. The Font, Style, Size, Leading, Kerning, Tracking, Case, and Position are all assigned using this option in the menu under the style name. In addition, options for Underline, Strikethrough, Ligatures, Old Style characters, and No Break are accessed here. No Break means that the entire paragraph will be forced to fit on one line. You will rarely want to use this feature.

*The character Skew function is a distortion of letterform and should not be used in place of italics.*

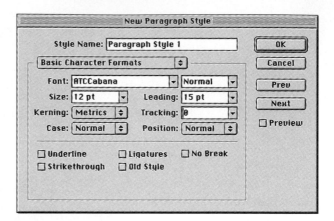

### Advanced Character Formats

Similar to the Advanced Character Formats in the Character Styles palette, this option in the menu under the style name allows you to specify Horizontal Scale, Vertical Scale, Baseline Shift, Skew (false italics), and Language for the entire paragraph.

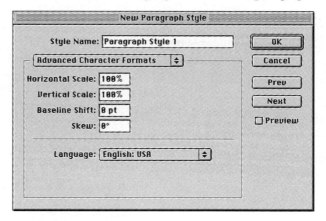

### Character Color

The final option in the menu under the style name in the New Paragraph Style dialog box, Character Color, allows you to set the color of the type in the paragraph, and to assign a stroke to it, if appropriate.

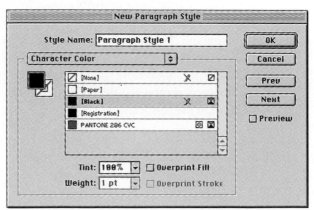

### Create the Body Text Paragraph Style

1. If it is not already open, open **Working with Style.INDD** from your **SF-Intro InDesign** folder. Nothing should be selected in the document.

2. Click on the Paragraph Styles tab in the styles palettes container.

3. Select New Style from the Options menu. The General option in the menu under the style name in the New Paragraph Style dialog box appears.

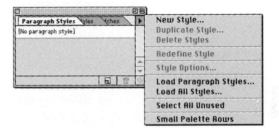

4. In the Style Name field, type "Body Text". Press Command/Control-keypad-2 to assign it as the shortcut. Notice in the Style Settings box that the last style information that was entered has been picked up automatically. Click Next to advance to the next option.

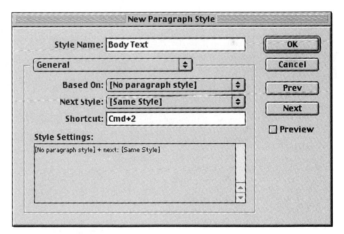

5. In the Indents and Spacing option in the menu under the style name, set Alignment to Left Justify and the First Line Indent to 1p6. Leave everything else at zero (0). Leave Align to Baseline Grid unchecked. Click Next.

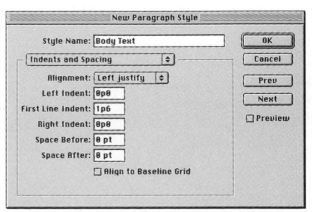

6. We will not assign Drop Caps. Ensure that the Composer is set to Adobe Multi-line Composer. Click Next.

7. Click Next to exit the Justification option in the menu under the style name. Make no changes.

8. We will not set any tabs for this style. Click Next.

9. In the Hyphenation option in the menu under the style name, uncheck Hyphenate Capitalized Words. Click Next.

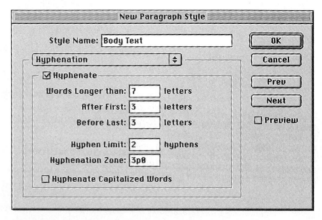

10. In the Keep Options selection in the menu under the style name, check the Keep Lines Together box, and enter "2" for both Start and End Lines. Click Next.

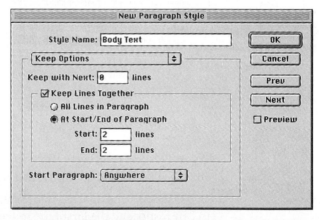

11. We will not set any rules above or below this paragraph. Click Next.

12. In the Basic Character Formats option in the menu under the style name, select ATC Cabana Normal, 12 pt., with a Leading of 15 pt. (12/15). Click Next.

*In the previous chapter, you learned that in typographer's shorthand, 12/15 means 12-pt. type with 15 pts. of leading.*

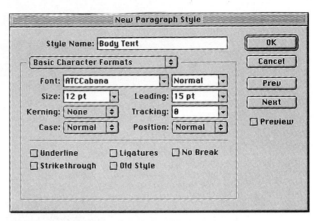

13. We will not apply any Advanced Character Formats. Click Next.

14. Make the Character Color Black. Click Next.

15. Back at the General menu, note the Style Settings. Click OK.

16. Leave the document open for the next exercise.

## Create the Headline Paragraph Style

1. Select New Style from the Paragraph Styles palette Options menu. Be certain that you are using [No Paragraph Style] as the basis for your new style.

2. Name the style "Chapter Number". Do not assign it a shortcut.

3. Select Indents and Spacing in the menu under the style name.

*Unless you are basing one paragraph style on another to duplicate style elements, it is always best to click on [No Paragraph Style] before you begin to create the new style. Otherwise, you may include unwanted elements in your style.*

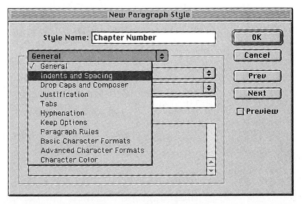

4. Set the Alignment to Left (the default). All Indents and Space Before and After should be set to zero.

5. Select Hyphenation from the menu under the style name and uncheck Hyphenate.

6. Navigate to Keep Options, and select Start Paragraph: On Next Odd Page.

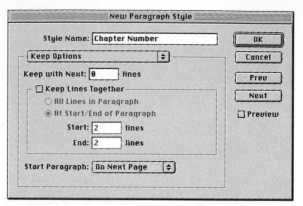

7. Navigate to Paragraph Rules. Turn Rule Above on. Assign it a weight of 2 pt., a color of Pantone 286 CVC, and an offset of 12 pt.

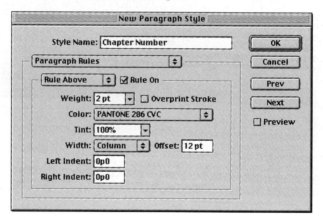

8. Navigate to Basic Character Formats and assign ATC Mai Tai Bold, 12 pt. as the font.

9. From Character Color, assign Black. Click OK.

10. Leave this file open for the next exercise.

## Create the Chapter Name Style

1. Create another new paragraph style. Name this style "Chapter Name".

2. From the Indents and Spacing option in the menu under the style name, set Alignment to Left and Space After to 30 pt. Indents and Space Before should be set to zero.

3. From the Hyphenation option in the same menu, be certain that the Hyphenate box is unchecked.

4. From the Keep Options selection in the menu under the style name, keep all lines in the paragraph together. The paragraph may start Anywhere.

5. From the Paragraph Rules menu, be certain Rule Above is unchecked. Turn the Rule Below on. Assign it a Weight of 2 pt., a color of Pantone 286, and an offset of 6 pt.

6. From the Basic Character Formats option in the menu under the style name, assign ATC Cabana Heavy Italic, 18/30.

7. Assign Black as the Character Color. Click OK

8. Save the document and leave the document open for the next exercise.

## Create Styles Based on One Another

1. Continue in the open document. Click on the Body Text style to highlight it, and create a new paragraph style. Name it "Body Text 1". Note that the style is automatically based on Body Text. Set the Next Style to Body Text, and the Shortcut to Command/Control-keypad-0 (zero).

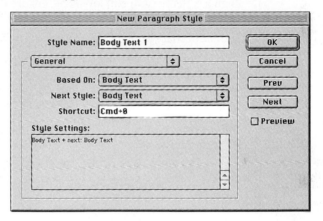

2. Click on the drop-down menu under the style name, and select Indents and Spacing.

3. Set the First Line Indent to 0p0. Click OK.

   That's all it takes to set up a new style based on another. Let's set up another style, based on Body Text 1.

4. Click on Body Text 1 and select New Style.

5. Name the style "Poem".

6. From the same drop-down menu, select Indents and Spacing.

7. Set the Alignment to Left, Left Indent to 3p0, and Space Before to 6 pt.

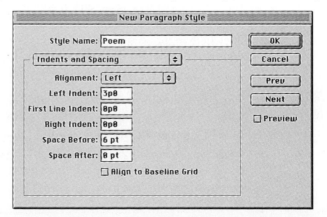

8. Navigate to Keep Options.

9. Click the All Lines in Paragraph button. Click OK.

10. Click on the Poem style, and create a new style named "Poem Last".

11. Navigate to Indents and Spacing and add Space After of 6 pt. to the current definition. Click OK.

12. Save the document and leave it open for the next exercise.

### Editing Existing Styles

You may discover that you made a mistake when you created a style, or (more likely) someone else may change the design parameters. Editing an existing style is easy — but you must be aware of the structure of the document's style sheet before making wholesale changes. Before you edit anything, ensure that the style you're going to change doesn't have other styles dependent on it, unless they are going to be similarly altered. After you're confident that you won't hopelessly ruin the document, select the style to be altered from the list of styles in the styles palettes (double-click on it) and make the necessary changes. Click Save to store the changes you have made to the document.

### *Edit styles*

1. Click on the Poem style and select Style Options (or simply double-click on the style name) to open it.

2. Navigate to Basic Character Formats. Change the font to ATC Coral Reef Plain (Macintosh) or ATC Coral Reef Regular (Windows). Click OK.

3. Open the Poem Last style and navigate to Basic Character Formats. You'll notice that it has already been changed to ATC Coral Reef Plain (Macintosh) or ATC Coral Reef Regular (Windows). This is because we based this style on the Poem style. Click OK to close the style.

4. Save the document and leave it open for the next exercise.

## Using the Styles Palettes to Apply Styles

There is a difference between the ways in which character styles and paragraph styles are applied. To apply the character style, all the characters to which the style is to be applied must be selected (highlighted). If you miss a letter, the style will not be applied to it. After selecting the text, select the style to be applied. To apply a paragraph style, simply click anywhere in the paragraph and select the style. You may apply the style to multiple consecutive paragraphs. It doesn't matter whether character styles or paragraph styles are first applied. Character styles override paragraph styles.

The fastest way to apply a style is to use the keyboard equivalent that you previously assigned while creating your styles. For example, if you define the paragraph style Body Text to use Command/Control-2, simply click the type tool anywhere in a paragraph, type Command/Control-2 (on the keypad), and the paragraph will automatically be assigned the Body Text style. To apply a character style, follow the same procedure, except you must first highlight the text to which the style is to be applied.

*To "unapply" a character style, highlight the text and apply the paragraph style while holding down the Option/Alt key.*

You may also apply styles from the styles palettes (Type>Character Styles or Shift-F11, or Type>Paragraph Styles or F11). Most people work with the styles palettes open.

### Apply Styles

1. Continue in the open document. Choose Type>Paragraph Styles, or press F11, if the palette is not already open. The styles palettes are used to apply styles to a paragraph, a range of paragraphs, or a range of characters, in the case of character styles.

2. Click the Type tool in the frame and choose Select All from the Edit menu (or press Command/Control-A) to select all the text in the document, and assign the Body Text style by clicking on it in the Paragraph Styles palette or by typing Command/Control-keypad-2. That gets us started by applying the style that is most used all at once.

3. Click on the first paragraph, "Chapter II" and assign it the Chapter Number style by clicking on the Chapter Number paragraph style.

4. Place the Type tool in the next line and assign it the Chapter Name style.

5. Assign the next paragraph the Body Text 1 style. Place the cursor in the paragraph and press Command/Control-keypad-0.

| **CHAPTER II** | ting along in a great hurry, muttering to himself as he came, `Oh! the Duchess, the Duchess! Oh! won't she |
| **_The Pool of Tears_** | be savage if I've kept her waiting!' Alice felt so desperate that she was ready to ask help of any one; so, when the Rabbit came near her, she began, in a low, |
| `Curiouser and curiouser!' cried Alice (she was so much surprised, that for the moment she quite forgot how to speak good English); `now I'm opening out like | timid voice, `If you please, sir--' The Rabbit started violently, dropped the white kid gloves and the fan, and skurried away into the darkness as hard as he could |

6. In the lower-right section of the page are eight lines that are very spacey. Place the Type tool in the first group of four and assign it the Poem style.

7. Assign the next group of four lines to the Poem Last style.

as if she were saying lessons, and began to repeat it, but her voice sounded hoarse and strange, and the words did not come the same as they used to do:--

`How doth the little crocodile
Improve his shining tail,
And pour the waters of the Nile
On every golden scale!

`How cheerfully he seems to grin,
How neatly spread his claws,
And welcome little fishes in
With gently smiling jaws!'

8. When we created character styles, we said we'd get around to applying the Run-in Blue style we created. Select the Character Styles tab from the styles palette container.

9. In the first paragraph of text, highlight the words " `Curiouser and curiouser!' "

10. Press Command/Control-keypad-1. Click anywhere in the document to view your work.

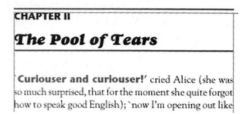

You probably noticed that the rule above "Chapter II" is above the text frame.

11. Click on the left text frame with the Selection tool.

12. From Object>Text Frame Options (Command/Control-B), set the top Inset Spacing to 0p3 to bring the rule inside the text frame, and click OK.

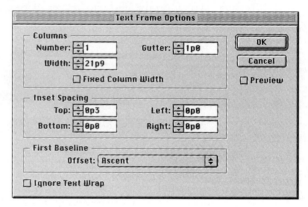

13. The page now looks much better.

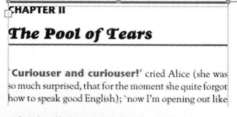

14. That's all there is to it. Save the document to your **Work in Progress** folder.

## Summary

In this chapter you have learned how to create and apply character styles and paragraph styles, how to edit styles, and how to base one style on another. You have learned how styles can interact with one another, and with other elements of InDesign, such as the underlying Baseline Grid and the Text Frame Options.

# Working with Graphic Elements

## CHAPTER OBJECTIVE:

To learn to use the graphic frame tools and graphic creation tools to draw Bézier curves and create basic objects. To learn to manage those objects and rearrange them, as needed. In Chapter 6, you will:

- Explore the uses of the Pen, Line, Ellipse, Rectangle, and Polygon tools in creating lines, paths, and basic shapes.

- Learn what Bézier curves are, and practice drawing them.

- Learn how to draw and constrain lines, and to create drawn frames.

- Learn to use the Stroke palette to determine the thickness of line, type of join, characteristics of dashed lines, and more.

- Become familiar with the painting tools, and learn how to apply color and gradients.

- Learn the anatomy of frames, how to manipulate objects within frames, and how to alter the size of the frame and its content, independent of each other.

- Become familiar with the power of the Arrange menu for moving objects in front of and behind each other.

- Explore methods of rotating, scaling, and shearing objects directly and using the Transform palette.

## PROJECTS TO BE COMPLETED:

- Around the World Ad (A)
- Baggy's Kid's Menu (B)
- Vacation Brochure (C)
- Good Choices Newsletter (D)

# Working with Graphic Elements

If you look at the pages of any magazine, or at Web pages on the Internet, when you take away the glitz, pages are composed of only two elements: text and graphics. The text is typed and edited; the graphics are drawings, scans, photos, or animations. You have already experienced how to create and format type in earlier chapters. There are two categories of graphics: (1) objects drawn within InDesign and (2) graphic objects that are imported from an outside source. In this chapter, we are going to examine the objects that can be drawn with InDesign's tools.

## Object Drawing Tools

There are six tools for drawing lines and objects: the Pen, Pencil, Ellipse, Rectangle, Line, and Polygon tools.

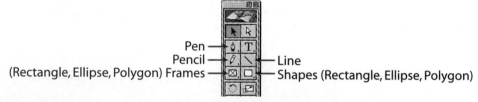

**Pen.** The Pen tool is InDesign's most versatile drawing tool, providing you with the ability to draw both straight and curved lines with a great deal of control. The curved lines are Bézier curves, and can be modified with the Direct Selection tool. If the Pen tool icon is selected and held, a fly-out menu appears showing further options: the Add Anchor Point, Delete Anchor Point, Convert Direction Point, and Scissors tools.

*Shift-P toggles through the various Pen tools.*

**Pencil.** The Pencil tool is used to draw freehand lines as well as both open and closed paths. Its lines and paths become Bézier curves and may be edited with the Direct Selection tool. If the Pencil icon is selected and held, a fly-out menu reveals the Smooth tool and Erase tool. The Smooth tool is used to remove unwanted bumps from an existing path while retaining, as much as possible, the existing shape. The Erase tool is used to remove portions of a path.

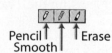

**Rectangle, Ellipse, and Polygon.** These tools are used to draw rectangles, ellipses, and polygons (3–100 sides). Horizontal and vertical dimensions are constrained by pressing the Shift key when dragging the mouse. When the Option/Alt key is held down, the object is drawn from the center.

**Line.** The Line tool is used to draw a line from the point where the mouse is initially clicked to the point where the mouse button is released. Holding the Shift key constrains the lines to 45° increments as it draws.

*Ellipse, Rectangle and Polygon tools automatically apply the stroke specified in the Stroke palette, in the active stroke color. The respective frame tools apply no stroke automatically.*

*Holding the Option/Alt key while using the Pen tool turns the tool into the Convert Direction tool.*

*The Ellipse, Rectangle and Polygon tools automatically create closed paths. The Line tool can only create open paths.*

*Holding the Shift key while clicking the Pen tool constrains it to a 45˚ increment.*

## The Bounding Box

Before we show you how to draw objects with the InDesign tools, we should show you what you will see when the drawn objects are selected with the Selection tool. While the objects are being drawn by the various tools, you will see only the object being created. However, even if the object is in the midst of being created, and the Selection tool is clicked on this object, a blue box with handles will appear around the selected artwork.

This blue box is known as the "bounding box." All objects, whether selected individually or as a group of objects, have an imaginary box that marks the extreme perimeter of the selected objects. The following example shows how objects and groups of various sizes and shapes have bounding boxes.

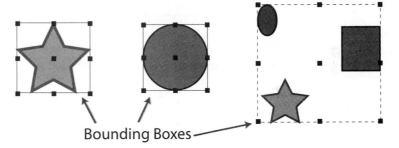

Bounding Boxes

## What Does This Box Do?

The bounding box not only shows the perimeter of the selected piece(s), but gives instant access to modify the object it contains. There are four corner handle, four side handles, and a center point. Dragging the corner handles will scale the object both horizontally and vertically. Holding the Shift key while dragging a corner handle will scale the object proportionally.

Drag the handles on the left and right sides to scale the object horizontally. Drag the top and bottom handles to enlarge or reduce the object vertically.

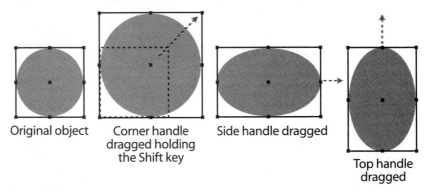

Original object     Corner handle dragged holding the Shift key     Side handle dragged     Top handle dragged

## Bézier Drawing Tools

The Pen and Pencil tools create paths comprised of Bézier curves. These are complex mathematical formulae that are entered by actually positioning the points with the Pen tool, or by drawing a freeform shape with the Pencil tool.

### Pen Tool

The Pen tool works by clicking its pen-tip cursor on the page. The object it creates as it is clicked is called a "path." As long as the tool is clicked and never deselected, you could theoretically draw an unending path. To deselect the path, choose the Selection tool, the

*The symbols on the right of the Pen tool give insight into the status of the drawing process.*

*The **X** means the tool is not in progress and free to either start a new path, or continue an existing one.*

*The **O** appears when the tool touches an open path endpoint signifying that it will close the path if clicked.*

*The **/** appears when the tool touches an open path endpoint, signifying that it will continue drawing the path when clicked on.*

*The ⌐ appears when the tool touches an endpoint of an open path that is active.*

*No symbol means that the Pen tool is active and ready to continue the path in progress.*

Direct Selection tool, the Type tool, or any other drawing tool, and click on an empty area of the page.

The anatomy of a path is simple. Each click of the Pen tool creates anchor points. Each anchor point is connected by a single segment. Paths are categorized as *open paths* or *closed paths*. Open paths are easily identified by their beginning and ending points, which are at either end of the path. Closed paths are continuous, having no apparent beginning or end to their form.

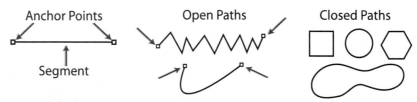

Curved lines are drawn with the Pen tool by click-dragging on an anchor point, which pulls out a direction line that can adjust the curve.

## Corner Point

The *Corner Point* is an anchor point at which a path abruptly changes direction. It may connect two straight segments, two curved segments, or a straight and a curved segment.

In this example, the Pen tool was clicked (A), and moved to point B with the Shift key held down to constrain the path to a straight line, then clicked again. The Pen tool was then clicked on this endpoint, and a direction line dragged out. The mouse button was released. The mouse was then moved to the right and clicked while holding the Shift key (C), giving the curved segment an anchor point to which to extend. The corner point or the curving segment can be clicked on by the Direct Selection tool to access the direction line to make adjustments. The corner point is the only anchor to have no visible direction line.

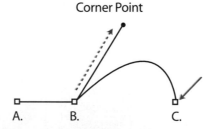

## Smooth Point

The Smooth Point gets its name from the type of curved segments it produces, which are smooth in their flow and continuity as they extend from the point. The clearest identifying aspect of the Smooth Point is that it has two direction lines that adjust both segments attached to the anchor point.

In the example that follows, the Pen tool was clicked on the page, the mouse button held down, and an initial curve direction line dragged from it (A). The Pen tool was moved to the right and again clicked and a direction line was dragged from this, the Smooth Point (B). The Pen tool was moved to the right and clicked, then a direction line was dragged from this point, ending the drawing process. The result is a path possessing a Smooth Point. When its direction lincs are moved, both the segments (prior and secondary) are moved with it (D). Either segment, however, may be adjusted independently by dragging on the appropriate direction line.

When using the Pen tool, be aware that there is an Automatic Add and Delete Points function that becomes active when touching an anchor point or segment of a selected path.

If the Pen tool touches the segment, the Pen takes on the Add Anchor point symbol (+) in its lower-right corner. This works on any segment of a selected path.

If the Pen tool touches an anchor point of a selected path, the symbol becomes the minus sign (-) for the Delete Anchor point tool.

For this to work on an anchor point, it must not be a beginning or endpoint of the path. It will only work on those anchor points that occur on the segment, between the beginning and endpoints.

Smooth Point

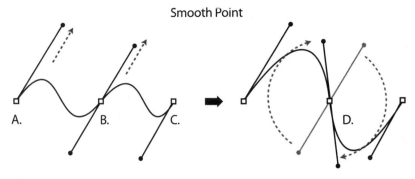

### Editing Paths

The fly-out tools for the Pen tool are used primarily for editing or modifying existing paths that need further enhancements. The Add Anchor Point tool must be clicked on a segment in order to add a point. The Delete Anchor Point tool must be clicked on an anchor point to delete it. The Convert Direction Point tool may be dragged on an anchor point, or single-clicked on the point, to change its point type. Dragging on a point converts it to a Smooth Point (A). Single-clicking on a Smooth Point removes the curves from the segments (B).

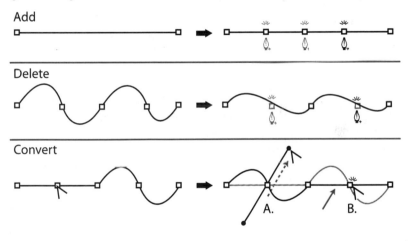

### *Draw with the Pen Tool*

1. Select File>New to create a new document with one page, one column, and margins of 3 picas.

2. In the Toolbox, click on the Default Fill and Stroke icon to set the Stroke to a black line.

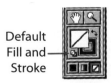

Default Fill and Stroke

*The Default Fill and Stroke icon in the Toolbox paints the selected object with a Fill of None and a Black Stroke.*

3. From the vertical ruler on the left of the screen, drag a guide out to about the 12-pica mark of the horizontal ruler at the top. Make certain that Snap to Guides is checked in the View menu. Click on the Pen tool icon in the Toolbox. Single-click the tool on the guide to create a beginning point. This acts as a guide for keeping the alignment straight when the final clicks are applied to create this object. Move the cursor over to the right about 24 picas, press the Shift key to constrain, and click on the page again. You will have created a single segment or line. Do not deselect.

4. Move the Pen tool about an inch (72 pt.) below this point, hold the Shift key, and click again to continue the path. Do not deselect.

5. Move the Pen tool to the left and hold the Shift key as you click on the guide again. The anchor point that you click will snap to the guide.

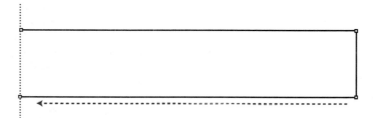

6. Holding the Shift key, move the Pen tool up to click on the beginning point. The result will be a rectangle drawn from scratch. Select this object with the Selection tool and delete it.

7. Select the Pen tool in the Toolbox. Click near the center of the page to create a beginning point. Move the tool up and to the right, then click again.

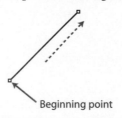

*The single click of the Pen tool creates an anchor point. If a single anchor is clicked, then the path is aborted and deselected, this initial point will remain invisible — a potential PostScript error waiting to happen! Clean up your work. When you are finished, switch to the Selection tool, Select All, then select stray anchor points and delete them.*

*When using the Pen tool, Option/Alt toggles to the Convert Direction Point tool.*

8. Move the Pen tool down and to the right, below the beginning point, and click again.

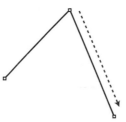

9. Move the tool lower and to the left, then click once more. Notice how the path is growing with each click of the Pen tool.

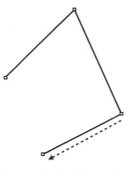

10. Move the Pen tool up to perform a final click on the beginning point, closing the path. You have created a freeform object, without the constraint of the Shift key.

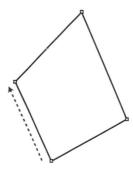

11. Click on the Selection tool in the Toolbox. This will automatically select the object you just drew. Notice the blue bounding box that surrounds it.

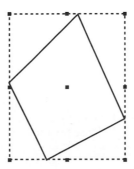

*The bounding box is also capable of reflecting the selected object. By dragging the selected handle toward and past the opposing handle, on the other side of the object, you will succeed in changing the horizontal or vertical appearance. This is also known as "mirroring" the object.*

12. Click on the right-middle handle, and drag to the right.

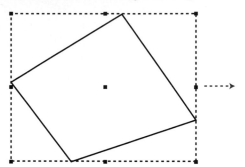

13. Click on the bottom handle and drag it upward. Notice that the bounding box has fast modifying features that eliminate the need to use the Scale tool (covered later in this chapter) for fine-tuning purposes.

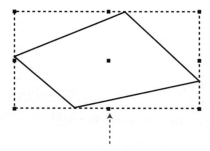

14. Click on the bottom-right corner handle and drag it down to the right, but do not hold the Shift key. Notice how the object transforms with a freeform effect.

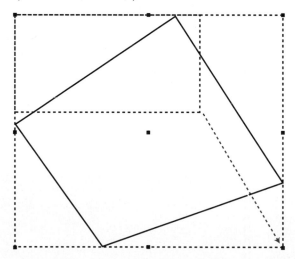

15. Release the mouse button and observe the object's alteration. Click-hold on this bottom-right corner handle and drag toward the upper-left corner of the bounding box. Hold the Shift key as you drag, and notice how the object retains its proportions. Release the mouse button.

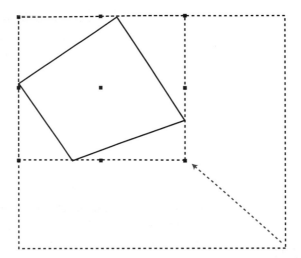

*Shaping the object with the corner handles of the bounding box is actually scaling the object, which we discuss in greater detail in the Transformations section of this chapter.*

16. You have now learned how to draw objects containing straight line segments with the Pen tool; you have used the Shift key to constrain the angles of the drawing process, and used the bounding box to modify the object. We will now create curves with the Pen tool. Select all objects in the document and delete them.

17. Keep the document open for the next exercise.

### Create Curved Segments

1. If the document from the previous exercise is not open, create a new document.

2. Select the Pen tool and click its cursor on the page. Move the cursor about 6 picas to the right. Holding the Shift key, click again to create a segment (A). Click the Pen tool on the endpoint and drag out a direction line for a curve. Release the mouse button. You have created a Corner Point (B).

A.                                    B.

3. Move the Pen tool 6 picas further to the right, hold the Shift key, then click-drag on the page, creating a Smooth Point with a double handle.

*When using the Pen tool to draw a path, it is best to set the Fill to None (which is the system default), so that the Fill does not confuse the eye while drawing.*

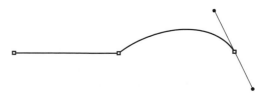

4. Move the Pen tool 6 picas further to the right while holding the Shift key. Single-click the Pen tool on the page to finalize the path.

5. With the Direct Selection tool, click on the second point. You will see the direction line of the curved segment following the corner point. Click on the tip of the direction line and drag it, changing the shape of the curve.

6. Now click on the third point made. You will see its two direction lines. Click on either tip of this handle and drag it, altering the curve. The curving segments on either side of the anchor point will change as you drag.

7. You have now used the Pen tool to draw the two types of curve points, and have adjusted them. Close the document without saving.

## Pencil Tool

Using the Pencil tool is much like freehand drawing with a mouse. Simply click a starting point and draw the shape. InDesign automatically creates appropriate Bézier points as you draw. Unlike the Pen tool, when the mouse button is released, the path is ended. Closed paths are created with the Pencil tool by pressing the Option/Alt key. If there is a gap between the beginning and ending points on the path, InDesign will fill that section with a line based on the attitude of the beginning and ending Bézier points.

### Smoothing Paths

Beneath the Pencil tool is the Smooth tool. This tool is used to retain the general shape of the drawing, while getting rid of unwanted raggedness. Drag the Smooth tool along (not across) the part of a path that you want to smooth.

### Erasing Sections of Paths

To erase portions of a path, use the Erase tool, also located beneath the Pencil tool. Drag it along (not across) the part of a path you wish to erase. The Erase tool removes only paths, not filled areas.

*The Stroke palette is quickly accessed by double-clicking on the Line tool in the Toolbox.*

## Create a Freehand Drawing

1. From your **SF-Intro InDesign** folder, open the document **Pencil Play.INDT**. We have created the template so you can practice using the Pencil and related tools. The owl is on a locked layer (you'll learn about layers in *InDesign: Advanced Electronic Mechanicals*) beneath the layer on which you'll be working.

2. Select Window>Stroke, or press F10 to activate the Stroke palette.

3. Set the Stroke weight at 2 pt.

*The keyboard shortcut to access the Ellipse, Rectangle, and Polygon tools is to press the "M" key.*

4. Double-click the Pencil tool to access its Tolerance settings. Set the Fidelity for 2 Pixels and the Smoothness at 0%. Click OK.

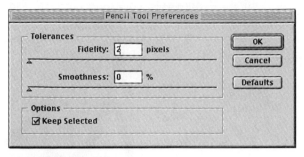

5. Select the Pencil tool and begin drawing the outline of the owl. Try to draw logical segments in one smooth stroke.

6. Before drawing the claws, double-click on the Pencil tool and set the Fidelity for 0.5 pixels.

7. For the line across the owl's forehead, and for the center line of the beak, switch to a 1-pt. stroke weight.

8. Before drawing the breast feathers, switch to a 4-pt. stroke weight and, in the Stroke palette, change to the Round endcap. The Fidelity should be 0.5.

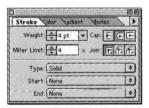

9. Before drawing the eyes, switch to a 0.5-pt. stroke weight. Set the Fidelity to 0.5.

10. When drawing the eyes, press the Option/Alt key when you complete the path. A circle will appear showing you the path will close. Release the mouse button to close the path.

11. With the path closed, select the Fill button and click Apply Color to fill the eye with black.

12. When the owl is drawn, use the Selection tool to select a line that is jaggy. Click on the Pencil tool and hold the mouse button down. Select the Smooth tool and go back over your work to smooth any jagginess. Drag the smooth tool the length of the line — do not rub across the line.

*When smoothing a line, drag the Smooth tool along the line's path, not across it.*

13. When you are happy with your work, choose Window>Layers to activate the Layers palette (or press F7). Click on the Template layer and, from the palette's Options menu, choose Delete Layer "Template".

14. Save your drawing to your **Work in Progress** folder and close.

## Primitive Tools

The four tools that are used for creating basic shapes, referred to as "primitive objects," are the Ellipse, Rectangle, Line, and Polygon tools. The nature of these tools is that they create objects merely by dragging the tool cursor on the page. Holding the Shift key while drawing a line constrains it to 45° increments when the cursor is dragged. Holding the Shift key also constrains the Ellipse tool to draw circles, the Rectangle tool to draw squares, and the Polygon tool to draw equilateral polygons.

*The Stroke palette is quickly accessed by double-clicking on the Line tool icon in the Toolbox.*

### The Line Tool

The Line tool draws a single line from the first click-drag of the cursor on the page until the mouse button is released, ending the line (A). If the Shift key is held while dragging, the line is constrained to 45° angles (B).

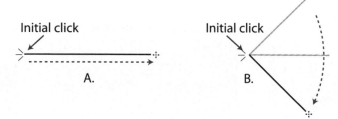

### The Ellipse Tool

The Ellipse tool creates ellipses. To use the Ellipse tool, select its icon from the Toolbox. Drag the cursor on the page to draw ellipses.

Hold down the Shift key to constrain the ellipses to circles.

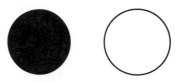

## The Rectangle Tool

The Rectangle tool creates rectangles. The Rectangle tool is dragged on the page to create rectangles of any size. Holding the Shift key while dragging the tool cursor constrains the drawn object to a square.

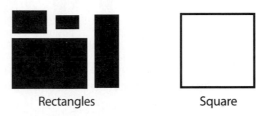

Rectangles    Square

## The Polygon Tool

The Polygon tool draws polygons and stars. The Polygon tool is dragged on the page to create objects of any size and shape. Holding the Shift key while dragging the tool cursor constrains the drawn object to an equilateral shape.

## Stroke Palette

The Fill of an object requires no decision beyond the color, tint, or gradient with which it is painted. The Stroke of an object, however, has many variables that determine its appearance. When the appearance of the stroke has been determined, press the Return/Enter key to apply it.

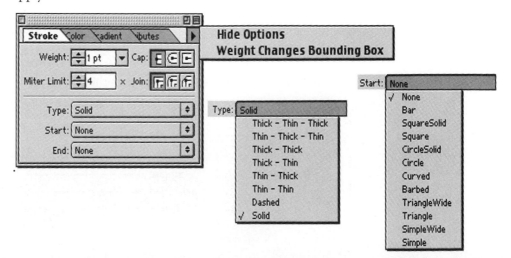

*The keyboard shortcut to access the Ellipse, Rectangle, and Polygon tools is to press the "M" key.*

*Double-click the Polygon icon in the Toolbox to access the Polygon palette to change the number of sides or to create a star effect.*

*Objects can have both Fill and Stroke attributes simultaneously. This rectangle was painted as: Fill of 30% Black, with a Stroke of Black, 8 pt. wide.*

**Stroke Weight.** This option sets the thickness of the stroke, measured in points.

**Miter Limit.** This option determines how rounded or angular the Joins of a path will be where the two segments meet.

**Cap and Join.** *Caps* are the ends of open paths. A *Join* is the corner where two segments meet at an anchor point.

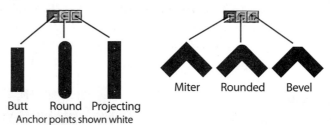

Butt  Round  Projecting
Anchor points shown white

Miter  Rounded  Bevel

**Stroke Type.** The default stroke attribute is a single solid line. If the stroke is to have dashed lines, this option must be selected from this part of the Stroke palette.

**Dash, Gap.** When the Dashed line option is chosen, the Dash/Gap section of the Stroke palette appears. The increments typed in these boxes (measured in points) determine the length of the dashes and space between them (the gap). If only the first two boxes (dash, gap) are used, the dashes and gaps will remain constant for the length of the stroke. By entering numbers in the other dash/gap boxes, the appearance of the dashed line can be made more creative, even alternating the size of the dashes and spaces. The Caps section also controls how the dash looks. If the Rounded Caps button is selected, the dashes will have rounded endcaps as well.

*The color attribute (Fill or Stroke) which is in front of or on top of the other box, is the **active** color attribute.*

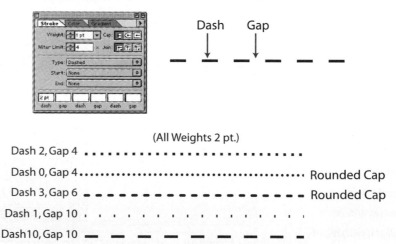

Dash  Gap

(All Weights 2 pt.)

Dash 2, Gap 4
Dash 0, Gap 4 ........................................ Rounded Cap
Dash 3, Gap 6 – – – – – – – – – – – – – Rounded Cap
Dash 1, Gap 10
Dash 10, Gap 10 — — — — — — — —

**Start/End.** The Start and End options in the Stroke palette determine what type of symbol appears at the two ends of a path. The beginning point of a path is the Start, and the finishing point is the End.

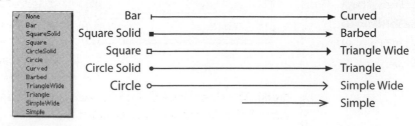

Bar
Square Solid
Square
Circle Solid
Circle

Curved
Barbed
Triangle Wide
Triangle
Simple Wide
Simple

## The Painting Tools

An attribute applied to a path's interior is known as a Fill, because it "fills" the object. The three attributes that can fill an object are a color, a gradient, and an imported graphic. One should be careful when filling an open path that has no stroke, since both open and closed paths can be filled. The fill will connect between the two anchor endpoints.

Let's review the two most important painting elements: Fill and Stroke. The correct attributes must be active (in front of the other icon) in order to paint the object's Fill or Stroke correctly. In this example, Fill is active; it is in front of the Stroke icon. Clicking the icon brings it forward and makes it active.

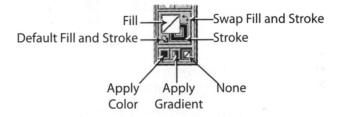

**Fill icon.** This icon, when active, fills the selected object with the applied color, gradient, or pattern.

**Stroke icon.** The Stroke icon, when active, applies selected colors to the stroke of a selected object. A gradient should rarely be applied to a stroke.

**Swap Fill and Stroke.** This icon will reverse whatever color attributes are assigned to Fill and Stroke. Fill will take on the Stroke color; Stroke will take on the Fill color.

**Default Fill and Stroke.** This icon is set for fill of None, and a stroke of Black. The Stroke will take on the weight set in the Stroke palette.

**Apply Color.** This box, when double-clicked with an object selected, displays the Color palette, where colors can be created or modified. The resulting color will be instantly applied to the object as the colors are adjusted.

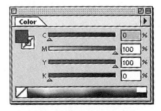

**Apply Gradient.** The Gradient palette appears when the Apply Gradient box is double-clicked. A selected object will receive a gradient fill if this button is clicked. (Creating custom gradients will be covered in Chapter 8.)

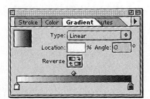

**None.** The None box will apply no color to either Fill or Stroke. When None is clicked, the active Fill or Stroke will have no color applied.

*If you have the Transform palette active on the screen, you will immediately be able to see the exact size and position of your circle as you draw and move it.*

## Painting Methods

There are several ways to apply colors to your objects. They fall into these categories:

- By clicking on the color swatch in the Swatches palette with the object selected.

- By clicking Apply Color, Apply Gradient, or the None box in the Toolbox with the object selected.

- By moving the color sliders in the Swatch Options dialog box (from the Swatches palette Options menu) and applying a Global change — all objects with that color are changed to the new color.

- By adjusting the color sliders in the Color palette with the object selected.

- By dragging and dropping a swatch of the color on the object to be colored.

- By using the eyedropper tool.

### Use the Line Tool

1. Select File>New to create a new document.

2. Click on the Default Fill and Stroke icon in the Toolbox, then select the Line tool.

3. Click and drag the Line tool on the page without holding down any additional keys. The tool creates a line to wherever you now move the cursor.

4. Continue dragging the Line tool around near the initial click while still holding down the mouse button. Add the Shift key as you move the Line tool. Observe how the dragging becomes jerky, snapping to 45° angles as you drag up and down.

5. Drag the Line tool 90° to the right, about 12 picas from the initial click, then release the mouse button. You will have created a single line. Leave the line selected.

6. Double-click on the Line tool icon in the Toolbox. This will bring up the Stroke palette on the screen. Use the palette Options menu to access Show Options, which will bring up the full-sized palette.

*Hold down the Command/ Control key to temporarily convert any tool to the Selection tool.*

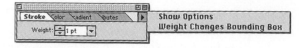

*The default colors appear within brackets. They are None, Paper, Black, and Registration.*

7. To the right of the Weight box is a drop-down menu of weights. Click on this menu and select 3 pt. Pull down the Type menu in the Stroke palette and select Dashed. The Dash/Gap section will appear. Type a "2" in the first Dash box, and a "5" in the next Gap box. The line will now be a 3-pt. dashed line, with 2-pt. segments and 5-pt. gaps.

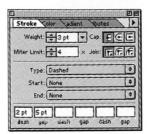

8. Click on the middle Caps option, which is Rounded Caps.

The line that you drew becomes 3 pt. in thickness with Rounded Caps.

● ● ● ● ● ● ● ● ● ● ● ● ● ● ● ● ● ● ● ● ● ● ●

9. Pull down the End menu in the Stroke palette, and select Triangle Wide.

*Pressing the "D" key invokes the Default Fill and Stroke paint attribute of a Fill of None, and a Black Stroke.*

The right side of the line will take on this arrowhead.

10. Delete the object and leave the file open for the next exercise.

### Draw and Paint Using Shapes

1. With the document from the previous exercise open, select the Ellipse tool from the Toolbox. Drag the tool cursor on the page and note how the object changes as the tool is moved. Hold the Shift key and notice how the shape is constrained to a circle. Draw a 6-pica circle on the page. With the Selection tool, move the circle to the upper-left corner of the page.

2. Click on the Rectangle tool in the Toolbox. Drag its tool cursor on the page and note how the rectangle can be made any size or shape. Hold the Shift key as you drag to constrain the rectangle to a square. Draw a 6-pica square and move it to the right of the circle. Deselect the square.

3. Double-click on the Polygon tool in the Toolbox. In the dialog box, set the Number of Sides to 8. Leave the Star Inset at 0%. Click OK.

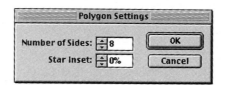

4. With the Polygon tool selected, drag the cursor on the page and note that the polygon grows disproportionately as you drag the cursor. Hold the Shift key and observe that the sides are constrained to the same size.

5. Draw a Polygon 6 picas wide and 72 points high, and move it up to the right of the square. You should have three objects lined up — the circle, square, and polygon.

6. We will now paint these objects using the methods we previously discussed. Select Window>Swatches to access the Swatches palette. The default colors appear. (Creating colors is covered in Chapter 8.) For this exercise, we will use the existing colors.

7. With the Fill active (on top), click on the circle with the Selection tool. In the Swatches palette, click on the yellow swatch (C=0, M=0, Y=100, K=0). The circle will be filled with yellow.

8. From the Window menu, select Stroke to display the Stroke palette. In the Weight pop-up menu, select 4 pt. to give apply a stroke of 4 pt. to the circle.

9. In the Toolbox, click on the Stroke icon to make it active. Now the Stroke will receive a color. Click on the green swatch in the Swatches palette (C=75, M=5, Y=100, K=0). The circle is now painted yellow with a green border.

10. Click on the square with the Selection tool. In the Toolbox, click Fill to make it active. In the Swatches palette, click the magenta swatch (C=0, M=100, Y=0, K=0). The square will fill with this color. The Apply Color box takes on this color as well.

11. In the Stroke palette, set the Weight to 3 pt. Set the Stroke Type to Dashed, giving the square a 2-pt. dash. Leave the gap box blank.

12. Make the Stroke box active in the Toolbox. Click on the blue color swatch in the Swatches palette (C=100, M=90, Y=10, K=0). The square will be painted with a blue dashed stroke.

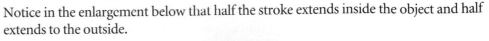

Notice in the enlargement below that half the stroke extends inside the object and half extends to the outside.

13. Click on the Fill icon to make it active.

14. Next, select the polygon you drew. This object currently has a Fill of None, but the Apply Color box is still holding the magenta color that was applied to the square. Click the Apply Color box. The polygon fills with this same color. This is a shortcut for applying the last-used color to objects filled with None, rather than having to scroll through a Swatches palette that may be full of colors.

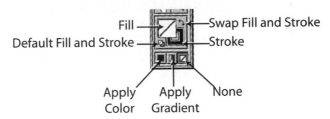

15. Click the Stroke icon in the Toolbox to make it active. In the Stroke palette, set the Weight to 8 pt. In the Swatches palette, click the red swatch (C=15, M=100, Y=100, K=0).

    The polygon will be filled with the magenta color, and will possess an 8-pt. red border.

16. We will perform one more color adjustment. Select all three objects, click the Fill box in the Toolbox, and click the red swatch in the Swatches palette to fill them all with red. Now deselect these objects.

17. Close the document without saving.

## Frames

Frames are like containers. They hold objects and assist in achieving the desired design elements with graphic objects and text. When the Type tool is dragged on the page, it instantly creates a text frame that has one purpose — to hold the text typed or imported into the text frame. Graphic frames are similar to text frames in the sense that they hold objects, but graphic frames are customized for artistic needs. The three standard graphic frames are found as the optional tools with the Ellipse, Rectangle, and Polygon tools. Click-hold on the tool icons found in the Toolbox to bring up a fly-out menu showing an optional tool image with an "X" inside. This icon is the frame tool for that shape.

*Options for the frame tool include Rectangle, Ellipse, and Polygon shapes.*

*The Preview option in the Swatch Options dialog box will show the selected objects changing as the color sliders of the box are moved.*

*The two ways to insert objects into frames are to use Edit>Paste Into, or File>Place to place an external image into the selected frame. (Placing images will be covered in Chapter 7.)*

If a frame tool is dragged on the page, it creates a box with an "X" inside. This is the visual way to distinguish a frame from another, similarly shaped object.

## Anatomy of Frames

When a frame is selected, a box with handles surrounding the frame appears. This is the frame's bounding box. It normally acts on the frame, not the image contained within the frame.

The frame of the Rectangle Frame tool is not easy to see because the shape of the frame closely adjoins the bounding box. However, when observing the Ellipse and Polygon frames, the bounding box is more apparent. Here are the three frame shapes, with the bounding box rendered as a dashed line. They are selected to show their bounding boxes and handles.

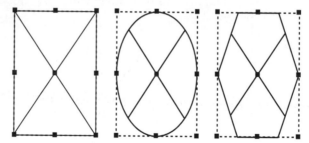

Moving the box handles resizes the frame accordingly. If the Shift key is held while moving the corner handles, the frame will enlarge or reduce proportionally on both the vertical and horizontal axis.

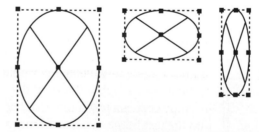

Frames are not just generic containers. Frames, like objects made with the drawing tools, can be filled or stroked.

No Fill or Stroke          Fill only          Fill and Stroke

*If you have two objects, for example a circle and a rectangle, and use Paste Into to paste one inside the other, the graphic that is Pasted Into becomes a graphic frame.*

*The Selection tool moves both the frame and its contents.*

*When handles are moved with the Selection tool, the frame sections are moved.*

*Command/Control and the Selection tool allows both the frame and its contents' handles to be moved.*

*The Direct Selection tool moves either the frame or the contents, independent of each other.*

*A frame can be pasted into another frame. This is called **nesting** frames.*

## Manipulating Objects and Frames

Once an object is placed inside a frame, the first consideration is how to move either the frame or the object around so that the object has a more practical location. There are four ways to organize the frame and object's position.

- By adjusting the frame's control handles

- By clicking on the object with the Direct Selection tool and repositioning it

- By clicking on the frame with the Direct Selection tool and repositioning it

- By using the Object>Fitting menu selections

Where, exactly, does an object position itself when placed inside a frame? If Paste Into is used, the object defaults to the upper-left corner of the frame's bounding box.

The following circle was drawn with the Ellipse tool. It was then selected and cut. The Polygon frame was drawn and selected. Edit>Paste Into was used to put the circle inside the frame. When the circle went into the frame, the circle went into the upper-left area of the polygon frame's bounding box.

We show this with dashed lines, though it actually looks like the circle is cut off at the frame's edges.

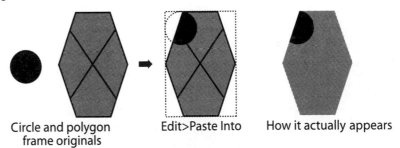

Circle and polygon frame originals          Edit>Paste Into          How it actually appears

### Adjusting the Frame Handles

To fine-tune the fit of a frame around an object, the frame's handles can be dragged to resize the frame. Here is a sample of how a frame is manipulated for correct object placement. This turtle artwork was pasted into a frame (A). The box handles of the frame were moved inward (B, C) to better fit the art.

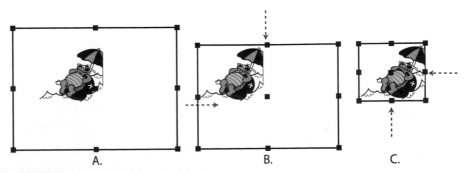

A.          B.          C.

### Using the Direct Selection Tool

The fastest way to move the frame or the object is to click on either the frame or the object with the Direct Selection tool and drag.

*Press the "A" key as a shortcut to select the Direct Selection tool.*

*Frames can only hold one object at a time. If a frame holds one object, and Paste Into is performed on the frame, the old object is replaced with the new object.*

*Frames automatically become the frame type of their content. If the Type tool is clicked in an empty graphic frame, the frame becomes a text frame.*

The turtle image was selected with the Direct Selection tool and dragged to the right (A). The other method used was to select the frame with the Direct Selection tool and drag it to the left (B). Remember, when moving objects, the Shift key constrains the movement to 45° angles.

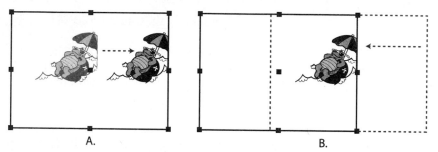

A.                    B.

### Fitting Objects by Menu

There are four options found in the Object>Fitting menu to automatically fit objects with their frames. These options are Fit Content to Frame, Fit Frame to Content, Center Content, and Fit Content Proportionally.

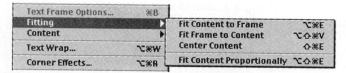

Fit Content to Frame scales the object as large as it will go, without fully exceeding the contours of the frame. The horizontal and vertical proportions may not be retained.

Fit Frame to Content collapses the frame to the contours of the object that it holds, as nearly as its frame structure will allow.

Center Content does not scale the object in the frame, but centers it within the frame.

Fit Content Proportionally enlarges or reduces the object to fit the frame, while maintaining the object's horizontal and vertical proportions.

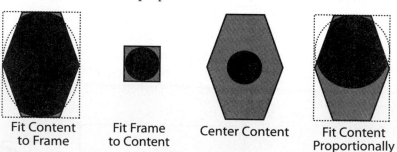

Fit Content to Frame    Fit Frame to Content    Center Content    Fit Content Proportionally

## Converting Paths and Frames

It is not always necessary to use one of the frame tools to create a frame. You are not restricted to only these three shapes (ellipse, rectangle, polygon). If you draw a path with the Pen tool, or alter an existing path, it can be converted to a frame by using the Content option of the Object menu.

There are three frame types: Graphic, Text, and Unassigned.

The Graphic option converts a path to a graphic frame. Empty text frames can be converted to a graphic frame, and vice versa. Both graphic and text frames can be converted to Unassigned, which is a generic path. Whatever the frame type, the name of its type will be gray in this menu. For example, if the frame selected is a graphic frame, the word "Graphic" in the menu becomes gray.

## Work with Frames

1.  Select File>New to create a new document.

2.  In the Toolbox, select the Ellipse tool and draw a 6-pica circle on the page. Paint the circle with a fill of red, and a yellow stroke.

3.  With the Rectangle tool, draw a rectangle, 12 picas × 72 points, painting it with a Fill of blue, and a Stroke of green.

**Important!**

*Frames that contain objects or text cannot be converted to other frame types.*

4.  With the Polygon tool, draw a 6-sided polygon, 72 pts. high, with its width constrained to height. (You'll note that even though the polygon is symmetrical, the width is actually greater than the height, according to the Transform palette.) Paint it with a Fill of yellow, and a Stroke of red.

    You will now have three objects to work with and place inside the upcoming frames. Select all three objects and use the Stroke palette to set their stroke weights to 2 pt.

5.  Click-hold the Frame tool icon to bring up its fly-out menu. Select the Ellipse Frame tool and drag its cursor on the page to draw an oval frame 12 picas × 288 points.

6.  Continue to select the Rectangle Frame and Polygon Frame tools, and draw a sample of their frames next to the ellipse frame. The frames should all be approximately the same size.

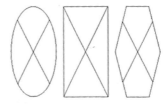

7.  Select the circle object created earlier and cut it. (Edit>Cut or Command/Control-X). Click on the oval frame and paste the circle inside the frame (Edit>Paste Into or Command-Option-V [Macintosh] or Control-Alt-V [Windows]).

8. Use the Direct Selection tool to click on the circle and move it around inside the oval. Move it so that part of the circle is outside of the oval boundary. The frame masks out part of the circle. Leave the circle where it is.

9. Select this frame with the Selection tool. Choose Object>Fitting>Center Content. The circle will move to the exact center of the frame.

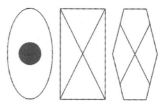

*A frame is literally a mask which holds an object and cuts off its image at the edge of the frame shape.*

10. Click on the control handles of the frame and reduce the size of the oval frame until it tightly surrounds the circle. In the Toolbox, click the Fill box to make it active. In the Swatches palette, click on the cyan swatch to color the oval frame. Notice that the color of the frame goes behind the circle.

11. Select the polygon object and use Edit>Cut to cut it. Select the rectangle frame and use Edit>Paste Into to place the object inside the frame. Click on the frame with the Direct Selection tool and move the frame to center the object.

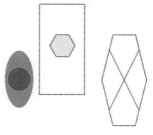

12. Select the rectangle frame with the Selection tool. In the Object menu, choose Fitting>Fit Frame to Content. The frame shrinks to conform to the edges of the polygon. Click on the control handles of the frame to drag them outward, enlarging the frame to see more of its interior.

13. The Fill box should still be selected, so click on the cyan swatch to paint the frame. Click the Stroke box in the Toolbox to make it active. Click on the green swatch. Access the Stroke palette from the Window menu and change its Weight to 4 pt.

14. Click on the polygon with the Direct Selection tool and move it around within the rectangle frame. Reselect the rectangular frame. From the Object menu, select Fitting>Fit Content Proportionally. The polygon enlarges to fill the frame's narrowest dimension, while retaining it proportions.

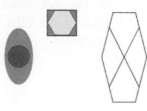

15. Select the rectangle object with the Selection tool and use Edit>Cut to cut it. Select the polygon frame and use Edit>Paste Into to paste the object inside the frame.

16. Press the "A" key to instantly switch to the Direct Selection tool.

17. Click on the border of the frame to move it around and better center inside it. (If you click inside the frame, you will move the rectangle instead.)

18. In the Object menu, use Fitting>Fit Content to Frame to enlarge the rectangle. Notice that the entire polygon is filled. The rectangle has not just filled the polygon shape — it has filled the entire bounding box area.

19. Paint the frame with a Fill of red, and a Stroke of yellow. Change the Weight to 3 pt. in the Stroke palette. You won't see the fill because the rectangle is covering it.

20. Click on the oval frame that you first created. Cut this frame with Edit>Cut, then, with the Direct Selection tool, click on the Rectangle within the polygon frame and use Edit>Paste Into. You have now "nested" one frame inside another.

21. Use the Direct Selection tool to click on any of the objects or frames and observe how the elements can be moved around individually.

22. You have seen how frames can be utilized as a grouping and masking design element to create artwork using objects drawn in InDesign. Close the document without saving.

## Manipulating Objects

When drawing multiple objects or frames, one object may obscure another by being in front of it. Layers allow the stacking of objects in front of or behind other objects. This subject will be explored in the *InDesign: Advanced Electronic Mechanicals* course. There is another way, however, to arrange objects and their relationship to each other.

The arrangement of objects from front to back is known as the "stacking order." This order has two basic rules:

- Newly created objects (graphics and text frames) are automatically placed in front of all other objects in the document.

- Any object that is pasted into the document goes in front of all other objects in the document.

*Use Command/Control-Option-V to Paste Into.*

In the following example, the circle was drawn first. The other objects were drawn in the order you see, left to right (A). The polygon was then selected, cut, and pasted. By being pasted, the polygon was placed in front of all other objects (B), because InDesign treats it as the most recently inserted item.

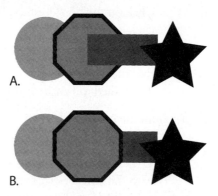

A.

B.

## The Arrange Menu Options

How does one move objects to a better Front/Back hierarchy? With the Arrange feature in the Object menu. This menu offers four basic options for stacking objects.

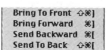

The keyboard shortcuts for the four Arrange options are:

**Bring To Front**
*Command/Control-Shift- ]*

**Bring Forward**
*Command/Control- ]*

**Send To Back**
*Command/Control-Shift- [*

**Send Backward**
*Command/Control- [*

- Bring To Front moves all selected objects to the immediate front of all other objects, while retaining their relative stacking order.

- Bring Forward moves the selected object up one level in the stacking order.

- Send Backward moves the selected object back one level in the stacking order.

- Send To Back moves all selected objects to the immediate back of all other objects, while retaining their relative stacking order.

  *In our example, the polygon was copied and pasted, which made it the front object.*

- Next, the rectangle was selected and Bring Forward was applied. This moved it in front of the star, but kept it in back of the polygon (A).

- The circle was then selected and Bring To Front applied to it. This made it the new first object, putting it in front of the polygon (B).

- The polygon was selected and Send To Back was chosen from the menu. This put it behind all other objects (C).

- The rectangle needed to be behind the star, but in front of the polygon. It was selected, then Send Backward was applied.

These four Arrange menu options save valuable time of in moving objects forward and backward, as desired.

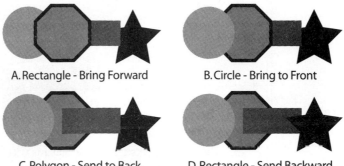

A. Rectangle - Bring Forward

B. Circle - Bring to Front

C. Polygon - Send to Back

D. Rectangle - Send Backward

## Arrange Objects

1. From the File menu, navigate to the **SF-InDesign Intro** folder and open the document **Timber's Used Cars.INDD**. You will find a piece of art that has objects obscured by other objects. This can all be fixed by using the Arrange options to get everything in order.

*Without the Object> Arrange options, taking 10 different objects and arranging them with only Bring To Front or Send To Back would be very time-consuming.*

2. The first thing that you'll notice is that the sign is in front of the two faces. With the Selection tool, click on the sign and use Object>Arrange>Send To Back to put it behind them.

3. Next, select Timber, the car salesman, and press Command/Control-Shift-] to Bring To Front this honest dog.

4. The lady dog is in front of the sign, but behind the ground object. Select the ground rectangle and use Object>Arrange>Send Backward.

5. Blackie, the washer/waxer, has his wash rag obscured by Timber's tail. Select Blackie and use Object>Arrange>Bring Forward to put him in front of Timber.

6. Blackie is still hiding his bucket, so click on the bucket and press Command-Shift-] (Macintosh) or Control-Shift-] (Windows) to see it better.

7. You have used Object>Arrange to straighten up this formerly messy artwork. Now Timber can sell the car and everyone will be happy.

8. Save the document to your **Work in Progress** folder and close the file.

## Transformation Basics

Objects can be transformed two ways:

**Transform Palette.** The Transform palette offers the ability to apply numeric transformations that are typed into its input fields. This is the method to use when numbers or angles must be exact, such as a 45° rotation.

**Manually.** In this process, the user accesses the tool and drags the selected object. This method relies on the way the selected object looks as it is being dragged. You can, however, observe the precise percentages and angles in the Transform palette as you manipulate the object.

## The Transform Palette

The palette you will use most often when making these transformations is the Transform palette. It has eight fields in which to type numbers to create these effects. Press the Return/Enter key to apply this information to the selected object.

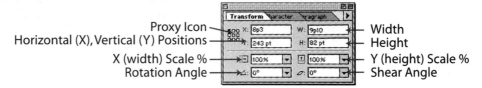

Proxy Icon — Horizontal (X), Vertical (Y) Positions — X (width) Scale % — Rotation Angle — Width — Height — Y (height) Scale % — Shear Angle

## The Proxy Icon

Starting at the left side of the Transform palette, we find a pattern of squares, with one square painted black when an object is selected. This black square is the Reference Point. All nine points, taken together, are a proxy of the bounding box of the object selected. This is the point, or axis, on which the transformation performs its operation. All objects default to the Standard mode, where all the points are perpendicular. If, however, an object is rotated 22.5° or more, the Proxy Icon symbol changes to represent a more angular appearance.

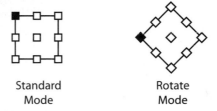

Standard Mode          Rotate Mode

To show how the Reference Point affects a transformation, we have used a square and indicated the original position by the dashed square. The angle of "45" was typed into the Rotate field of the Transform palette. The square was rotated using a different Reference Point each time. Example (A) uses the point at the upper-left corner of the object. When this was applied, the square rotated, pivoting on this axis.

For example (B), the Reference Point was set at the lower-right corner, which meant that the square would rotate, pivoting on this corner as an axis. With example (C), the Reference Point was set for its exact center. The square rotated around this point. The Reference Point is Standard here, showing the point prior to rotating.

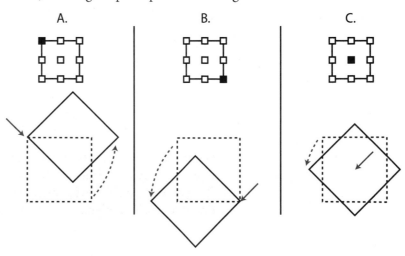

A.          B.          C.

## Direct Transformations

To transform a selected object manually, pull or move the object to change its appearance. This is done in sequence: the object is selected, the Transformation tool (Rotate, Scale, or Shear) clicked in the Toolbox, then the cursor dragged near the object, transforming its appearance. The cursor turns into an arrowhead ( ▶ ) shape when clicked on the object to transform it. When the object is selected for transformation, there will not yet be a crosshair symbol designating the Reference Point.

The crosshair becomes visible when a transformation tool is selected from the Toolbox. The Reference Point crosshair appears on the object, in the place designated in the Transform palette's proxy. The Reference Point may be changed by clicking on any of the other squares in the proxy.

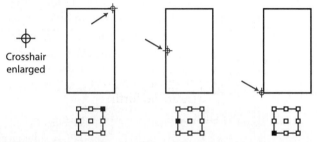

There is another way to set this Reference Point crosshair — by dragging it. For example, let's say that you want to rotate the object from a far off point. The Transform palette's Reference Point makes no provision for this. When the object is selected, and the Rotate tool clicked in the Toolbox, the crosshair will appear (A). To move the crosshair, simply click on it and drag to where you want it (B).

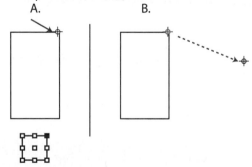

When the Reference Point is manually relocated, the transformed object uses the new location as its axis. The Reference Point for the rectangle above (B) was moved while the Rotate tool was clicked in the Toolbox. The rectangle was then dragged by the tool cursor, and revolved around the relocated Reference Point.

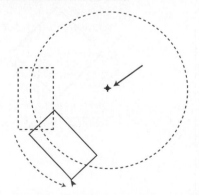

### Duplicating while Transforming

In some instances it becomes necessary to transform a duplicate of the selected object. It can be tedious to have to first duplicate the path, then select this copy to make transformations. What if the original object could be duplicated while making the transformation? This is possible by holding the Option/Alt key while clicking with the chosen transformation tool. The transform dialog box for that tool will appear.

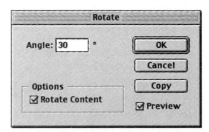

*Transform dialog box for the Rotate tool.*

In this example, the square was duplicated while being rotated (A), scaled (B), and sheared (C). There are no further repeats of this transformation/duplication. You get one duplicate per click.

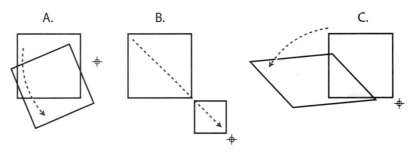

## The Transformation Tools

Drawing objects with the InDesign tools, as well as painting and arranging them, only begins to achieve the desired design. Most objects need further enhancements, such as altering their size to fit a layout, rotating them, or shearing them to give a simulated perspective view. All these modifications come under the heading of *transformations*. To transform an object implies that its original state is altered. The tools used for this purpose are:

> **Rotate.** The Rotate tool spins the selected object around an axis called the "Reference Point."

> **Scale.** The Scale tool reduces or enlarges an object, as either uniform (proportional) or nonuniform.

> **Shear.** The Shear tool skews a selected object to make it appear as if it were being viewed from an angle.

> **Free Transform.** The Free Transform tool allows you to move, rotate, scale, shear, and reflect objects without changing tools.

*Another way to apply numbers typed in a Transformation palette field to a selected object is to click the cursor into another field. If "45" were typed into the Rotate field, the mouse button could be clicked in any other field in the palette and the selected object would rotate 45 degrees.*

*Positive numbers, such as 45, rotate objects toward the left, or counterclockwise. To rotate an object clockwise, a minus sign must be placed in front of the number, such as –45.*

## Rotating Objects

The Rotate tool revolves the selected object around the set Reference Point, using the Transform palette, or by manually dragging the point to a new location. The rotation is performed either by typing the angle into the Rotate field of the Transform palette, or clicking the Rotate tool in the Toolbox and dragging the object. To use the Transform palette to rotate does not require clicking on the Rotate tool in the Toolbox. When rotating by manual dragging, keep the Transform palette on the screen, because as you drag, the angle of the rotation will appear as the object moves.

The Transform palette has a fly-out menu that offers three other rotating options: Rotate 180°, Rotate 90° CW (Clockwise), and Rotate 90° CCW (Counterclockwise).

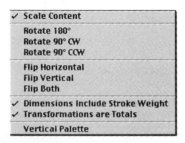

### Reflecting an Object

Objects often need to be reflected, mirrored, or flipped. There is no Reflect tool, so how can this done? By using the Transform palette menu to select Flip Horizontal, Flip Vertical, or Flip Both to meet the need.

## Scaling Objects

Scaling objects can be accomplished using the Transform palette or by manually dragging. The Transform palette can be set to maintain uniform (proportional) scaling. When scaling by dragging the object with the Scale tool, it is necessary to hold the Shift key to constrain the object to uniform proportions.

*The Reference Point in the Transform palette is the point that the object will use as the anchor for the transformation, even when dragged manually.*

### Scaling with the Transform Palette

When the Transform palette is used, a selected object is sized based on the units typed into the Scale fields: X Scale Percentage and Y Scale Percentage. The X Scale Percentage represents the width (horizontal) of the object. The Y Scale Percentage is the height (vertical).

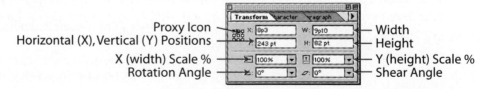

To keep the scaling proportional, the two percentage fields must be identical in number. 100% is the object's original size. Higher numbers increase the size; lower numbers reduce it. In this example, the star was scaled with both uniform and nonuniform units.

*The Reference Point will not be visible on the selected object until a transformation tool is clicked in the Toolbox.*

If the scaled object needs to be returned to its original size, the number 100 must be typed into both the Scale X Percentage and Scale Y Percentage fields.

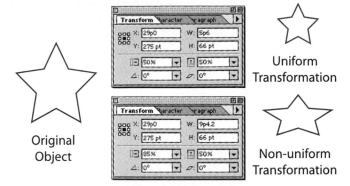

Original Object

Uniform Transformation

Non-uniform Transformation

If the Reference Point is set for the center of the object, the object will remain centered on its current position when it is scaled.

### Scaling with the Scale Dialog Box

You may prefer to use the Scale dialog box. To access it you would double-click on the Scale tool.

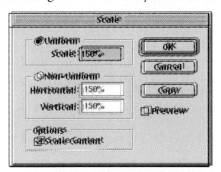

*If the Reference Point is relocated for a selected object, and then the object is deselected for other purposes, when selected again, the Reference Point will default to the Transform palette settings.*

With this dialog box, you may select Uniform Scale to scale both horizontal and vertical dimensions to the same percentage, or you may select Non-uniform to scale disproportionately. Content of the frame may be scaled or not, at the user's option.

### Direct Scaling

To directly scale an object, click on the Scale tool. The cursor appears as crosshairs, and will change to an arrowhead when the object is selected and the transformation begins. Dragging sizes the object, anchored to its Reference Point. The arrowhead cursor is used to drag the object. If the Shift key is held down while dragging, the object will scale uniformly, constrained horizontally and vertically.

In this example, the art object was selected, then the Scale tool was clicked. The Reference Point defaulted to the upper-left corner of the object (A). The cursor was then placed on the lower-right corner and dragged down, holding the Shift key to constrain. The image was enlarged uniformly (B).

Remember, keep the Transform palette on the screen as you make manual transformations. The proportions of the scaling will appear in the scale fields as you drag.

## The Shear Tool

The Shear tool distorts or skews objects. This might be used to create the impression that an object is being viewed from a different perspective. Another use of the Shear tool would be to transform a duplicate of an image to look like the object's cast shadow. Here are some samples of sheared objects.

Original

Sheared samples

### Direct Shearing

Shearing is best performed directly. The Transform palette can seem restrictive when used to shear an object because exact units must be typed into the Shear field. This can be tedious when you are experimenting with effects. By manually shearing an object, you see the effect as you drag the object.

The location of the Reference Point is important when shearing manually. The best choices for the Reference Point are the four corners outside of the object's bounding box. The worst location for the Reference Point is the center of the object. If this is the shearing axis, erratic skewing is almost impossible to control. Be certain to set the Reference Point in the Transform palette. Relocate it manually, according to the your shearing needs.

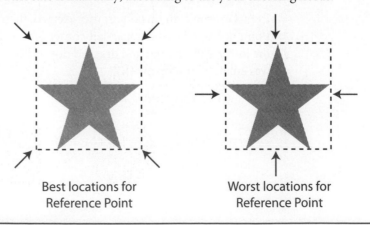

Best locations for
Reference Point

Worst locations for
Reference Point

The Reference Point's location is important, but even more important is where the Shear tool is clicked and dragged. Wherever the Reference Point is set, you should then drag the tool cursor from the diametrically opposite corner.

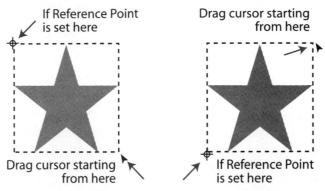

In the following example, first the star was selected, then the Shear tool was selected. The Reference Point was set for the upper-left corner, then the tool was placed on the lower-right corner, dragging upward. The star sheared as the tool was dragged.

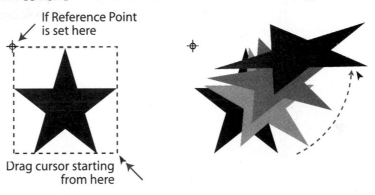

### *Transform Objects*

1. Create a new document from the File menu.

2. Use the Ellipse, Rectangle, and Polygon tools to draw three objects 6 picas wide by 72 points high: a circle, a square, and a 6-sided polygon.

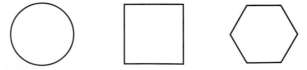

3. Fill the circle with red. Give it a 3-pt. stroke of yellow. Fill the rectangle with green, and apply a 2-pt. stroke of yellow. The polygon should be filled with cyan, and stroked with 1 pt. of blue.

4.  Click the square with the Selection tool. If the Transform palette is not on the screen, use the Window menu to access Transform. Make sure that the Reference Point is set for the middle point. In the Rotate field, type "45". Press Enter/Return to apply the rotation. The square will rotate 45°.

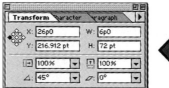

5.  With the polygon active, select the Transform palette and click the middle-right point to set the Reference Point. Click the Rotate tool in the Toolbox and drag it down on the left side of the polygon. The object rotates on the axis set by the Reference Point.

6.  Holding the Shift key, select all three objects. Click on the Rotate tool in the Toolbox to see the Reference Point crosshair. Drag it to the right, relocating the point for a manual rotation.

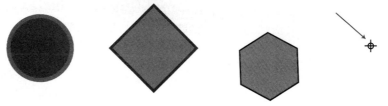

7.  Click the Rotate cursor on the left side of the circle and drag downward. All three selected objects rotate as you drag.

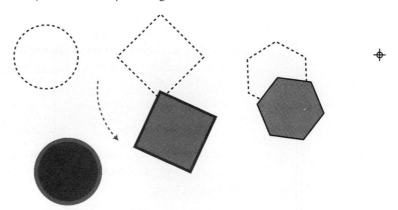

8. With the objects still selected, click on the Scale tool in the Toolbox. Drag the crosshair to the upper left of the area surrounding the three objects.

9. Drag the Scale cursor toward the crosshair, holding the Shift key to constrain the scaling to uniform proportions. Observe the Transform palette's scale fields as the numbers change while you drag. Stop at approximately 50%.

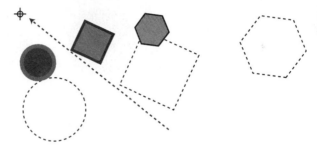

10. In the Transform palette, set the Reference Point for the center of the objects. In the scale fields, type "200" for both the X and Y percentages. Press the Enter/Return key to apply this. The objects will scale to approximately their original sizes.

11. Click on the Transform palette menu and select Flip Vertical. The three objects flip across a vertical axis in their combined center.

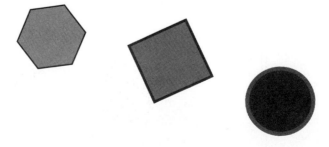

12. Click on the Palette menu again to select Flip Horizontal. The objects flip again, this time over a horizontal axis.

13. Click the Rotate tool in the Toolbox. The Reference Point is still set for the center of the objects. Drag the cursor on the circle and drag down to rotate them.

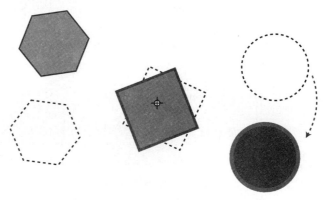

14. Select the Shear tool. Drag the Reference Point crosshair to the upper-left corner of the surrounding area near the polygon. Drag the Shear tool cursor from the bottom-right of the circle, dragging up and to the left, shearing all the objects.

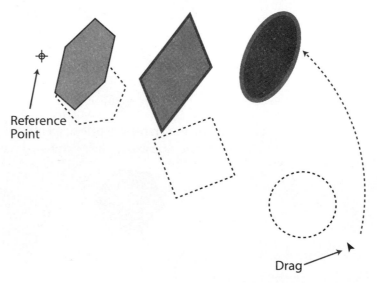

15. In the Transform palette, click the center Reference Point to set the point to the middle of the objects. Drag the cursor to the right of the circle, moving it up and to the left, shearing the objects even more.

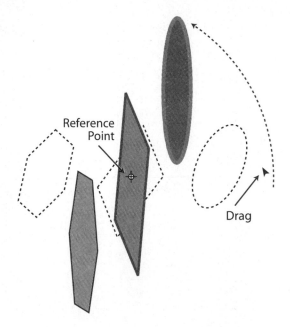

16. Click the Rotate tool in the Toolbox and relocate its Reference Point to the left center of the selected objects. Drag the cursor from the circle, pulling down. While you drag the objects, press Option/Alt to duplicate the rotated objects.

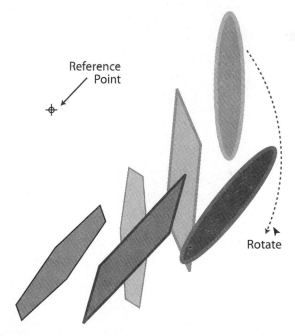

17. Close the document without saving.

## Summary

You have learned to use InDesign's graphic creation tools and its frame tools. You have learned to draw Bézier objects with the Pen tool and to create primitive shapes with the Rectangle, Ellipse, and Polygon tools. You have also learned how to manipulate those objects using the transformation tools and to change their stacking order.

**Notes:**

# PROJECT ASSIGNMENT #1

## Assignment

A client comes into your office seeking a new corporate identity. The company for which you are creating the logo and stationery package is a candy company.

Your assignment is to create a name and logo for this company, and generate a stationery and business card package, complete with a graphic that can be used on the envelopes and in other applications that the client might require in the future. Be imaginative — you can lay out the cards and stationery any way you want.

## Applying Your Skills

For the production of these identity publications, you should apply the following processes:

- Opening a new document with multiple pages to provide sufficient space for developing all of the objects you'll need to produce.

- Combining text elements, special characters, and spacing techniques to create a unique corporate identity package.

- Using multiple fonts in combination with each other. Employ italics or bold styles of fonts to add color and texture.

- Constructing frames to contain the objects when creating the business cards. This will allow you to "step and repeat" the frames in order to meet the eight-per-page requirement. Make up names and titles for the eight different cards.

- Creating objects with the painting tools.

- Aligning objects properly on the cards.

- Using Style Sheets to make it easy to try different fonts and sizes. Design and apply styles for the different elements such as titles, names, and addresses.

- Create and combine primitive objects to add graphic interest to the logo creation. Combine primitive elements with type objects. Use the Pen and Pencil tools, as well.

- Use transformations, such as mirroring, rotation, and scaling to modify elements.

## Specifications

| | |
|---|---|
| Business Card: | 3.5 in. × 2 in. |
| Stationery: | 8.5 in. × 11 in. |
| Envelope: | #10 envelope |

Construct eight aligned versions of the business cards, (two across by four high). Use the Line tool to create marks where they will be cut apart. Each card should be the same, so that you can simply change the names and print them eight sets at a time, as the client requires.

Create one document with three separate pages. Put the business cards on one page, the envelope graphic on another page, and the stationery layout on a third page.

## Publisher's Comments

Some of the most highly regarded work is done with simple tools. Combining type and primitive shapes has resulted in such recognizable brands as Niké, Volkswagen, Pepsi, and many other internationally recognized designs. Use your imagination, and don't be afraid to experiment.

Secondly, be sure that the finished results are sized correctly. Problems in sizing requirements lead to a majority of the problems encountered when attempting to reproduce your work at a commercial or digital printing company.

# REVIEW #1

## CHAPTERS 1 THROUGH 6:

In Chapters 1 through 6, you learned the basic operations necessary to set up InDesign documents and work with text. You learned the principal tools, menus, dialog boxes, and palettes, as well as how to navigate within documents. You practiced working with text in text frames, using Masters and styles, creating primitive objects, and working with images. After completing the discussions and exercises, you should:

- Understand the electronic mechanical and the stages that a publication goes through, from concept to delivery. You should be able to distinguish the design elements of the letterform and know the distinctions and advantages of specific type styles. You should be familiar with key industry terminology and publishing customs.

- Be familiar with InDesign's tools, windows, menus, and palettes. You should be comfortable grouping and arranging palettes to configure your workspace efficiently. You should be able to begin a new project and enter basic settings. You should be familiar with InDesign's preferences for individual or many documents.

- Be comfortable with the structural elements of a page, and working with multi-page documents and Masters. You should know the safe work areas, how to set margins and gutters, and how to handle bleeds.

- Know how to work with text frames. You should be able to create frames, import text, place and thread text between multiple frames, and work with the text within the frames. You should know how to navigate through and edit text. You should also know how to handle text overflow, tabular columns, special characters, and more.

- Understand the convenience and efficiency of using styles. You should be able to set and change character-style and paragraph-style attributes. You should know how to base one style on another and how to edit existing styles for rapid global changes within a document.

- Be familiar with the graphic creation tools and the use of graphic frames. You should be able to create Bézier curves on lines and paths, draw and constrain lines, and create dashed lines with different types of joins.

- Know how to create basic objects in InDesign. You should also know how to determine the thickness of lines, and apply color and gradients.

- Be comfortable manipulating objects and images within frames. Know how to use the Transform palette tools to rotate, scale, and shear objects, as well as how to do this manually.

# CHAPTER 7

# Working with Images

## CHAPTER OBJECTIVE:

To learn the types of images that can be imported into InDesign, and how to place and transform them. To distinguish vector from raster images, and use the Links palette to manage images. In Chapter 7, you will:

- Understand the types of images which InDesign can import, and their purposes and advantages.

- Learn to distinguish vector and raster images, considerations with scaling, and their typical applications.

- Explore issues with image resolution and how to determine the appropriate resolution for specific uses.

- Learn how to work with images in frames — placement, transformation, sizing, position within the frame, and borders.

- Understand how to work with linked images, including reestablishing broken links through the Links palette.

- Become familiar with a variety of methods for placing images.

- Learn techniques for scaling and cropping images.

## PROJECTS TO BE COMPLETED:

- Around the World Ad (A)
- Baggy's Kid's Menu (B)
- Vacation Brochure (C)
- Good Choices Newsletter (D)

# Working with Images

Documents are usually a combination of text and graphic images, which work together to achieve the document's purpose — to communicate. Although InDesign can create rules and irregular shapes, more complex line art and photographs should be generated in software designed for drawing and photo manipulation. Once complete, these images are imported into InDesign, positioned, cropped, scaled, and framed on the page alongside text and graphic elements constructed using InDesign.

A computer manipulates and records graphics using two different methods. The *raster* method records and manipulates pixels in the image. A *pixel* is a tiny square of color. Thousands of pixels next to each other in different colors and shades create the illusion of smooth shading, as in a photograph. Scanned images are raster images. Adobe Photoshop is a raster-based program. This type of program uses paintbrushes and pixel-based filters to adjust the image's color, sharpness, and composition.

The *vector* method records and manipulates paths and shapes that make up the image. Each line or shape is described mathematically, not pixel-by-pixel. It is assigned a color and layered over other shapes to form the graphic. Technical illustrations are an example of vector graphics. Adobe Illustrator and Macromedia FreeHand are vector-based programs. This type of program uses pen tools to create points defining the object's outline, much as the Pen tool works in InDesign. The object or points are selected to adjust the shape and assign attributes for each object.

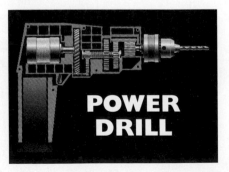

While sophisticated programs have blended the use of vector and raster technology, the distinctive look and editing methods for each type remain. Image file formats are also divided by these two categories. Each format has special characteristics and capabilities that make it suitable for specific uses and final output.

# Graphic File Formats Imported by InDesign

| | | Desktop Printer | Internet / Screen | Publication Print |
|---|---|:---:|:---:|:---:|
| **Illustrator (.ai)** | Native **Illustrator** 5.5–8.0 file format. Use Place for best results. Objects are editable but may be grouped. Text is not editable. Copy/Paste or drag & drop from Illustrator† but gradients aren't preserved and patterns become individual objects. | Vector | • | • | • |
| **BMP (.bmp)** | Standard Windows/DOS **bitmap** file format. Minimal color support. Not suitable for print or Web. | Raster | | | |
| **CT (.ct)** | **Scitex Continuous Tone** Used in high-end prepress workflow. | Raster | | | |
| **DCS (.dcs)** | **Desktop Color Separations** Type of EPS that supports grayscale, RGB, CMYK, spot color and alpha channels. Useful in specialized prepress workflow. Clipping paths supported. | Vector | | | • |
| **EPS (.eps)** | **Encapsulated PostScript** Standard cross-platform file format for prepress. May contain raster and vector images. Includes support for OPI image replacement workflow. Resolution-independent. Must print to PostScript printer. (Raster preview displayed in InDesign.) | Vector | • | * | • |
| **GIF (.gif)** | **Graphics Interchange Format** Supports only 256 (indexed) color. High compression suitable for solid-color illustrations and graphs displayed on the Web. | Raster | • | • | |
| **JPEG (.jpg)** | **Joint Photographic Experts Group** Standard cross-platform format for photographs. Includes compression that progressively degrades image quality but retains quality if high setting is used. Grayscale, RGB, and CMYK, as well as clipping paths from Photoshop are supported. | Raster | • | • | • |
| **PCX (.pcx)** | **Picture Exchange** Common image format for Windows applications. Limited color support and only RLE compression. | Raster | • | | |
| **PDF (.pdf)** | **Portable Document File format** Standard cross-platform format for fully designed pages, ads, and other documents that must retain graphic layout & formatting. | Vector | • | • | • |
| **PICT (.pct)** | Macintosh **Picture** Standard system clipboard format used by Macs and some clip art. May contain raster and vector information. InDesign imports PICTs on both platforms and supports RGB, CMYK and QuickTime images. | Raster | • | | |

\* Appropriate for online publishing if contained in a PDF file.
† Object Linking and Embedding and Publish & Subscribe are not supported by InDesign

*If the document is exported to HTML for the Web, InDesign converts all imported graphics to JPEG or GIF.*

## Graphic File Formats imported by InDesign

| | | | Desktop Printer | Internet/Screen | Publication Print |
|---|---|---|:---:|:---:|:---:|
| **Photoshop (.psd)** | Native **Photoshop 4–5** file format<br>While original isn't altered, in InDesign the file is flattened and alpha channels aren't recognized for transparency. | Raster | • |  | • |
| **PNG (.png)** | **Portable Network Graphics**<br>Designed with lossless compression to display 24-bit RGB photos and solid color illustrations or graphs online. Supports alpha channel or designated color transparency. | Raster |  | • |  |
| **TIFF (.tif)** | **Tagged Image File Format**<br>Standard cross-platform file format for photos and other raster art. Supports alpha channel and clipping path, but InDesign uses only the clipping path to create transparent background. Use grayscale, RGB, CMYK, Lab, indexed color, or bitmap. | Raster | • | * | • |
| **WMF (.wmf)** | Microsoft **Windows MetaFile**<br>Standard Windows system format. May contain raster and vector information, but InDesign only recognizes the vector data. 16-bit RGB only. | Vector | • |  |  |

\* Appropriate for online publishing if contained in a PDF file.

† Object Linking and Embedding and Publish & Subscribe are not supported by InDesign

## Resolution

Another difference between raster and vector images is how resolution affects them. Every physical device in digital graphics makes use of resolution, from digital cameras to digital copiers. They use a tiny grid of colored pixels or spots to capture and display images because they do not see shading and color as film does, in continuous tone. This grid of pixels is referred to as "resolution." Each type of device uses a different resolution, however, so it's important to understand when and how to apply resolution when preparing graphics for import into InDesign.

Raster graphics rely on a specified resolution in the graphic file to render properly on a device; they are *resolution-dependent*. Vector graphics do not rely on a specified resolution to be rendered properly; they are *resolution-independent*.

The difference between these two methods is one of timing. Resolution-dependent files are defined first by the resolution, then output. If the output device needs more pixels, it cannot generate new ones, it can only duplicate and stretch the existing ones, so it's important to create raster images using a resolution that's appropriate for the final output. Resolution-independent files are created and manipulated without a specified resolution because the file is defined by mathematical shapes not pixels. At the time of output, the shapes are drawn and filled by the number of pixels (or resolution) available to that output device. Resolution-independent, vector files are assigned a resolution at the end of the creation process.

*Output devices include your desktop printer (laser and non-laser), high-resolution printers, and your monitor for Internet and multimedia use.*

*Resampling an image involves changing its resolution in the native graphics program to accommodate the final output size or resolution. Images can be **down-sampled**, brought to a lower resolution, without loss of quality. **Upsampling** images beyond their original capacity forces the program to invent pixels and results in unacceptable reproduction quality.*

## Resolution-dependent Raster Files

Resolution-dependent files are assigned a resolution at the beginning of the creation process, then resampled, if necessary to satisfy the output. Preparing a raster graphic for import into InDesign requires assigning a resolution appropriate for the output.

Image resolution refers to how many pixels or dots per square inch (ppi for input devices or dpi for output devices) are contained in the raster graphic, a TIFF for example. Every pixel is one block of one color. When each block or pixel is very small, it blends with the pixels surrounding it to smoothly form the shapes in the picture, their coloring, and their shading.

Each graphic below is a tiny diamond shape filled with a gradient. The pixels have been outlined and enlarged to demonstrate the effect of resolution. The graphic on the left is a higher resolution, showing more tonal variations and a cleaner edge. The graphic on the right appears as large chunks and has a noticeable stair step edge. If the left graphic were enlarged, it would appear much like the right graphic, thus raster images are resolution-dependent. Their appearance depends on their resolution.

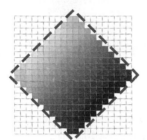 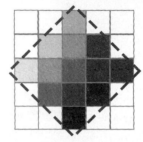

*The left image is higher resolution than the right image.*

The comparison implies that higher resolution is always better, but that is not necessarily the case. Since output devices use resolution to render type and graphics, the most important criteria is to match image resolution to the requirements of the output device. If the graphic will be output to the screen for a Web page, its resolution should be set to 72 ppi, an adequate match to the monitor's resolution. The graphic will contain one pixel for each pixel displayed on the monitor (1:1) at 100% size. The Macintosh's resolution is 72 ppi. Windows computers generally have a 96-ppi resolution, but 72 ppi is the standard for Internet display.

From this rule, we might assume that an image which will be output to a 600-dpi desktop printer should be scanned and saved at a resolution of 600 ppi. That assumption is also incorrect because printers and imagesetters don't print pixels — they print halftone dots made up of printer spots. These two other resolutions complicate the 1:1 rule slightly.

Printers and imagesetters use the image's resolution to create halftone dots, a resolution in lines per inch. Halftone dots are made up of printer spots, another resolution. If the image will be reduced or enlarged, additional calculation must be made when the image is created to maintain the picture's graphic integrity when it is rendered. The key is to reproduce a minimum of 256 levels of gray on the output device. The following two equations will provide the appropriate image resolution for any output device. Consult with your graphic arts service provider to ensure appropriate resolution for the processes involved.

Output resolution (dpi) / $\sqrt{256}$ = acceptable screen ruling (lpi) [ $\sqrt{256}$ =16 ]

Screen ruling (lpi) × 1.5 × reduction or enlargement % = Image resolution (ppi)

*Saving a raster graphic at the same resolution as the output device is necessary only for bitmaps, black and white (no gray) pixel images. Since bitmaps are not halftoned during output, they do not require the conversion discussed.*

If the imagesetter is set for 2400 dpi, the maximum acceptable screen ruling would be 150 lpi. Image resolution is calculated as follows:

| Actual size | 100% | $150 \text{ lpi} \times 1.5 \times 1.0$ | = | 225 ppi |
|---|---|---|---|---|
| Enlarge to | 200% | $150 \text{ lpi} \times 1.5 \times 2.0$ | = | 450 ppi |
| Reduce to | 50% | $150 \text{ lpi} \times 1.5 \times 0.5$ | = | 113 ppi |

An imagesetter running a resolution of 1200 dpi can accommodate a maximum line screen of 75 lpi. Running 3600 dpi, a resolution of 225 lpi may be achieved.

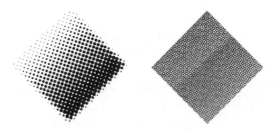

*Enlargement of halftone dots and the rosette halftone pattern of process color.*

These two gradient-filled diamonds display examples of printer and halftone resolution. The left diamond shows halftone dots for a single color, usually black. The right diamond shows the rosette pattern of halftone dots necessary for process color. These dots each consist of printer spots at 2540 dpi, a common resolution for high-quality imagesetters. The RIP calculated the size, or level of gray, for each printer halftone dot from the information contained in the image's pixels.

If resolution is grossly overestimated, the information will not help the printer render a better image. It will, however, consume file space and processing time. If the resolution is too low or the image is further enlarged in InDesign, the printed picture will be blurry and contain insufficient detail and color definition to accurately reproduce the image. This is the result of scaling a resolution-dependent graphic.

### Resolution-independent Vector Files

While TIFF and other raster file formats cannot be scaled successfully without resampling, vector file formats, such as an EPS, can be enlarged or reduced without affecting the clarity or color of the printed image. They are resolution-independent.

Vector files describe an image and its components mathematically. When the graphic is reduced or enlarged, that percentage is merely applied to the equations that represent the position, size, and shape of each path or object. After the computer has calculated how the image will look at the new size, it applies whatever resolution is used by the output device to render it. The graphic will render smooth output at any size. The EPS file, however, will look somewhat jaggy when placed in the document. This is because it will display a low-resolution screen image of the actual image as it will appear when printed to a PostScript output device. Although it looks jaggy on the screen, the image will be smooth when it prints to a PostScript printer.

*The factor 1.5 is a common average. If an image contains fine detail or delicate coloring, increase the factor to as much as 2. If special screening processes will be applied, an even higher factor is required.*

*The **RIP**, or Raster Image Processor, is software contained in the imagesetter or printer that calculates where and how the image is rendered on the page from your graphic files.*

*Vector EPS files are not resolution-dependent. However, raster files may be saved in EPS format, and are resolution-dependent.*

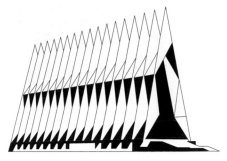

*The same EPS image imported to InDesign and scaled to 25% and 200%.*

*Command/Control-D is the keyboard shortcut for File>Place.*

## Place and Position Images

1.  Open a new document. Choose File>New. In the New Document dialog box, choose…
    **No. of pages:**  1
    **Facing Pages:**  Uncheck
    **Page Size:**  Letter
    **All margins:**  3p
    **Columns:**  1
    Click OK.

2.  With the Selection tool, choose File>Place. Navigate to the **SF-Intro InDesign** folder. Click the Show Preview button (Macintosh only) to view a thumbnail of each file. Select **Academy.EPS** and click the Choose/Open button.

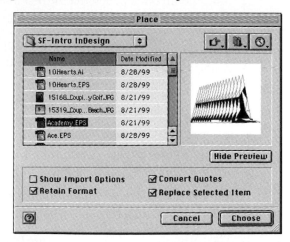

*Macintosh Place dialog Box*

3.  The cursor will transform into a loaded graphics icon, marking where the upper-left corner of the graphic will be placed. Click this icon near the top-left margin. A proxy image of the graphic will appear at 100%.

*Loaded graphics icon.*

4. With the Selection tool, click on the image and drag it to the upper-left corner of the page until the margin guides grab it. The Selection tool moves the bounding frame and the image it contains.

5. Select the Zoom tool and drag a marquee around the placed graphic to enlarge the view.

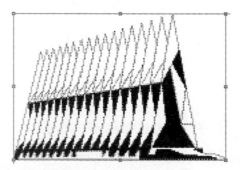

This is a vector graphic, but it appears jaggy on screen. Why? The graphic is vector, but the image seen on the screen/page is a low-resolution raster thumbnail. Using proxy images on the page for imported EPS files saves memory and allows faster screen draw while the page is being composed. The graphic can be sized, positioned, and cropped to suit the layout. When the page is printed, the image will look crisp because the actual vector graphic is sent to the printer with all the adjustments made to the proxy image in InDesign.

The resolution of the proxy or preview image can also be changed when the graphic is placed. The recommended resolution for proxy images is 72 dpi.

6. Zoom out and deselect the first image. Choose File>Place and choose the file named **BallRoll.EPS**. Click Choose/Open.

7. When the loaded graphics icon appears, click on the top margin at the center of the page and drag a frame across to the right margin and down to 216 pt. on the vertical ruler.

8. Save the document as "Picture Practice.INDD" in your **Work in Progress** folder and leave it open for the next exercise.

Placing an image, then creating its frame, is one technique of composition. Images can also be placed into specific frames built before the graphic is imported.

*Hold Shift to constrain the graphic frame to a square.*

*Import options provide several settings appropriate to each file format. Topics such as using clipping paths and color management are discussed in **InDesign: Advanced Electronic Mechanicals**.*

*If a placed image is not suitable, or you have accidentally placed the wrong image, use Command/Control-Z to Undo. Go back to File and Place the image again in a different manner.*

## Place Images Within Frames

1. Continue in the open document. First, Choose Window>Transform to bring up the Transform palette in order to view and enter information about elements being created.

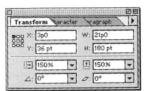

2. Select the Rectangle Frame tool (both tool and shape display an "X" inside the frame). Drag the tool to create a frame on the page under the Academy.EPS image. Fine-tune the Transform palette coordinates to:

   X: 3p0      W: 24p0
   Y: 216 pt   H: 198 pt

3. Now choose File>Place and select the file **Farmer.TIF** to import. In the Place dialog box, click Show Import Options. Choices in the Image Import Options dialog box vary depending on the file type selected. All images allow you to specify the resolution for their preview or proxy image. Enter "72" dpi, and click OK. The resolution you specify will be retained until you change it.

4. In the Image Import Options dialog box, click Choose/Open.

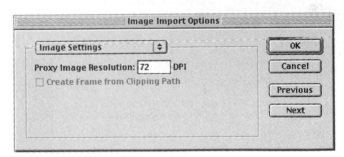

5. The image is obviously smaller than the frame, so we need to resize either the frame or the picture. Resize the frame this time. With the Selection tool, drag the bottom-right corner point up and left to the edge of the image, and deselect.

*Any closed path shape created in InDesign can be designated as a frame for containing imported images.*

*If the frame edges are no longer visible when the graphic is selected, choose View>Show Frame Edges.*

*To center a graphic in the frame, select the frame and image using the Selection tool. Then choose Object>Fitting>Center Content. Depending on the composition of the image, this may not yield the desired results. Still, this is one way to move the image into position for you to fine-tune afterwards.*

6. The frame tools, designated by the "X" in the shape, are designed to hold imported graphics. You can also use any of the regular shape tools and later convert the shapes drawn to either text or graphic frames. Select the Rectangle tool and drag to the right of the farmer to create a frame that is 9p0 wide by 234 pt. high.

7. At this point, the rectangle is a graphic element (the border will print), but may be used as a frame. To designate it as a frame, we will simply import a graphic into it. Choose File>Place and select **Flowers2.TIF** from the **SF-Intro InDesign** folder. Click Choose/Open.

8. The frame container is smaller than the imported graphic at 100%. To expand the frame, use the Selection tool to drag the bottom-left handle toward the middle of the page, until the frame is approximately 16p6 wide by 252 pt. tall. Click the handle, not inside the frame. If you click the pointer on the image, it will move the frame and image rather than resizing the frame.

9. To reposition the image inside the container, click on the Direct Selection tool. Click on the image itself and drag to the left until the outline of the placement box matches the outline of the frame container.

Notice how the different selection tools manipulate the imported graphic and its frame container. When you click on the image with the Selection tool, it moves the frame and graphic together on the page. If you click on the handle with the Selection tool, it resizes the frame. To move the image inside the container without moving the frame, use the Direct Selection tool instead of the Selection tool to click and drag on the image.

10. Save this file ton your **Work in Progress** folder. Leave it open for the next exercise.

## Linking vs. Embedding

It's important to understand how InDesign deals with placed image files because managing imported graphics ensures accurate output. Placing a graphic *imports* the image onto the InDesign page, but it does not necessarily copy the graphic into the InDesign file. If the graphic file is larger than 48k, InDesign utilizes a technique known as *linking* to store and display a preview of the image on the page and also store the location of the original graphic. Linking does not store a copy of the graphic file in the InDesign document file. When the file is printed, InDesign locates the graphic, applies position, cropping and scaling of the preview to the original graphic, and sends it to the output device in place of the preview.

Linking allows page designers to position, crop, and scale graphics alongside page elements, without significantly increasing the document's file size. Keeping the file size small helps minimize memory requirements and maintains efficient processing speeds while the document is being composed or printed. Linking also offers convenience when the original graphic needs to be modified. Once the changes have been saved to the graphic file, appearances of that graphic on the InDesign page can be updated without having to reimport every copy of the graphic in each document.

All this is accomplished because the path to the graphic file, when it was imported, is specified in the link. If the file has been moved, renamed, or deleted, when the document is reopened or printed, a message will appear saying that some graphics are missing. This also occurs when graphic files from a CD or network server are not available (removed from the drive or not connected) when the document needs them.

### *Manage and Update Image Links*

1. Continue in the open document. Choose File>Links to view the Links palette. The name of each graphic file is listed with the page number on which the graphic is placed at the right. If no symbol appears between the name and page number, the graphic is linked and ready for output.

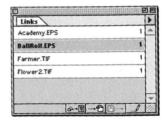

2. For the purpose of demonstration, we're going to break the links. Close the file.

3. Go to the desktop, locate the **SF-Intro InDesign** folder and move the following files (do not copy them) to the computer's hard drive: **Academy.EPS**, **BallRoll.EPS**, **Farmer.TIF**, and **Flowers2.TIF**.

4. Change the name of **Flowers2.TIF** to "Flowers2new.TIF".

5. If you have been working from the Student CD, eject it so the links will no longer be accessible.

6. Reopen the file.

You will receive the following warning:

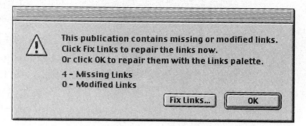

The Links palette should look like this...

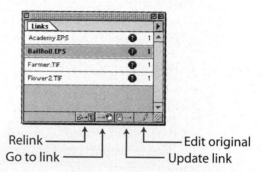

Relink ——
Go to link ——
—— Edit original
—— Update link

The question mark symbol indicates that these graphics are not located where they were when originally placed. They must be relinked.

7. Select Academy.EPS in the Links list and click the Relink button, furthest left at the bottom of the palette. When the Relink dialog box appears, click Browse and navigate to where the graphics were moved on your hard drive. Select the Academy.EPS file. Click Choose/OK.

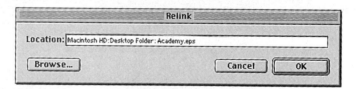

8. Select the next graphic in the list, BallRoll.EPS, and click the Relink button. It is relinked. Once a new location is designated, all other graphics that now reside in this location will be relinked without specifying the path. Select Farmer.TIF and click the Relink button for InDesign to reestablish the link.

9. Select Flowers2.TIF and click the Relink button. Click Browse. Go to the Desktop and select the file that was renamed Flowers2new.TIF. A dialog box will warn you, "The name specified is different … Link to this new name?" Click Yes. All of the broken links will be resolved.

10. To simulate updating modified graphics, move the files (except Flowers2new.TIF) back to the **SF-Intro InDesign** folder. Delete Flowers2new.TIF.

**Note:** if you are working from the Student CD, delete the files you moved, and reinsert the CD.

*Hold the Shift key while repositioning the graphic inside the frame with the Direct Selection tool to constrain its movement horizontally or vertically.*

*Another type of broken link occurs when the original graphic has been modified and resaved in the original program. In this case, the link must be updated to display and print the latest version of the graphic.*

*Relinking graphics can be time-consuming. Be careful not to rename or move graphics once they are linked. Do not delete the graphic files once they are imported! Remember to send copies of the graphic files with the document for output. If images are pulled from CDs or networked servers, make sure they are mounted or copy the image files to a folder that resides with the InDesign document.*

11. From the Links palette Options menu, choose Sort By Status. This will first list broken links and missing files, then graphic files that have been modified, and then the files with links that do not require attention. Select each file and click the Relink button to redirect InDesign to use the graphic files from the **SF-Intro InDesign** folder.

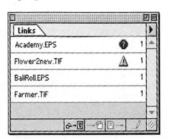

12. The Flowers2new.TIF file will display a different symbol indicating this graphic has been modified. Select Flowers2new.TIF, and, from the palette menu, choose Link Information. From this dialog box, you can discover pertinent information about the selected graphic file, including the file format, color space, color profile, file size, last modified date, and on which page it can be found in the document. If desired, the path name can be changed by typing in a new location. This dialog box indicates that the original file was in RGB Color Space and the Status indicates that the file has been modified. In our simulation, the Flowers2new.TIF file on the CD has been changed to grayscale and resampled to 30% of its original size. Click OK.

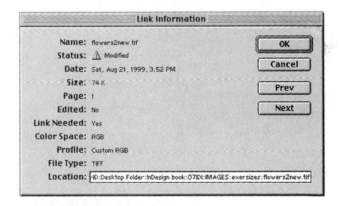

13. With Flowers2new.TIF selected, click the Go To Link button, second from the left at the bottom of the palette. The document window will shift the page view to display this graphic in the upper-left corner of the document window. This function helps you identify which graphic in the document the name refers to, and ensures that content is not accidently altered when links are updated.

14. With Flowers2new.TIF still selected, click the Update Link button, second from the right at the bottom of the palette. The image on screen should change to reflect that the linked file is now grayscale rather than the RGB and the file size will be quite a bit smaller than the original.

15. Save the document and keep it open for the next exercise.

### Embedded Graphics and File Size

A copy of the original placed image file can be embedded into an InDesign file. *Embedding* a graphic means a copy of the graphic file is resident in the document file, which makes the file larger. The advantage of embedding is that it makes the document completely self-sufficient, with no linking problems when it is output or transported to another computer system. Every embedded image is packaged inside the document. Graphics smaller than 48k are embedded into InDesign documents by default. Every time the graphic is copied in the document, the copy is stored in the file, adding to the file size. If necessary, larger graphics can be embedded into the InDesign document manually.

### *Embed Placed Graphics*

1. Continue in the open document. You will embed a graphic manually. Select Flowers2new.TIF in the Links palette. From the Links palette menu choose Embed. The following warning box will appear. Click Yes.

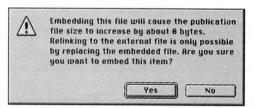

2. The graphic file is now copied into the InDesign document and its name is removed from the Links palette because it is no longer a linked file. If the original file is altered, the image in the document must either be deleted from the InDesign page and the altered image imported again, or the image in the document could be selected and Relink applied to the altered image.

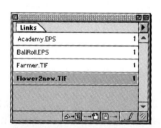

*If you have placed a file in a document, and you own the program that created it, select the file name in the Links palette and click Edit Original, the far-right button at the bottom, to edit the file in its original program.*

3. Save and close this file.

### Alternate Methods for Placing Graphics

Importing graphic files using the Place command offers the most control and highest quality for including images in an InDesign document, but there are additional methods that may be suitable in certain circumstances. While InDesign does not utilize Object Linking and Embedding (OLE), or Publish and Subscribe, it does permit graphics to be copied to the system clipboard and pasted into a document. It also supports drag-and-drop placement of graphic files from Adobe Illustrator documents or file windows on the desktop into the InDesign page.

*Using file formats such as WMF, PICT, and BMP may cause printing problems. As a rule of thumb, TIFF and EPS files are the standard formats to use when preparing files for print.*

### Copy & Paste Graphic

If the graphic is copied from one InDesign page to another, the graphic acts and prints the same as it would if you had placed it directly onto the page, including its linking information. Embedded graphics also transfer smoothly.

### Drag & Drop Graphic from Another InDesign Document

If two InDesign documents are open, a graphic image from one document can be dragged into the other document window.

### Drag & Drop Graphic from File Window or Illustrator

Files can also be dragged directly from an Adobe Illustrator document window or a file listing window on the desktop. Both methods, however, are limited because InDesign must use the system clipboard format to transfer the graphic: PICT format (Macintosh) and Metafiles (.WMF) for Windows-based systems. When dragging or copying Illustrator files, for example, gradient fills are not supported. The shapes that comprise pattern fills appear in InDesign as individual, grouped objects, not as pattern fill. This may cause printing and editing problems. Type contained in files copied from Illustrator must not be in editable text format, but should be converted to paths. All vector outlined path elements can be transformed and manipulated like an imported graphic. The shapes are usually grouped, which means the Direct Selection tool is needed to select and change each element.

### Importing other Adobe Native File Formats

Native Illustrator and Photoshop images can be placed onto the InDesign page without first saving them in a standard format such as an EPS or TIFF. To edit the graphic in its native program, select its name in the Links palette, and click the Edit Original button on the far right. The graphic will be opened in its originating program for alterations. When you return to the InDesign program, the graphic in InDesign will be updated automatically. Imported Photoshop graphics with layers are flattened for purposes of placement, and alpha channel transparency effects are not recognized, but the original files are untouched and fully editable.

## Scaling and Cropping Placed Graphics

Placed images are imported at 100% scale as they were created in their native application. During composition, however, that size may not fit the page layout. InDesign provides several ways to reduce or enlarge imported graphics to suit the needs of any design. Remember that vector graphics may be scaled to any percentage larger or smaller without concern for resolution and print quality, but resolution-dependent raster images must contain a sufficient number of pixels per inch to print at the resolution and scaling percentage chosen in the document. For each image, check the resolution against the scaling percentage assigned in InDesign to ensure it is still within acceptable parameters. If not, the raster image will need to be *resampled* (its resolution changed) or rescanned in the original application and updated in InDesign before the document is output.

Another way to control how placed images appear on the page is to crop them in InDesign. Image areas outside the frame are masked and will not display on the page or print; they are cropped. Cropping may involve importing the image into a small or irregularly shaped graphic container. Cropping is also done by making the frame smaller than the image after it is placed. A combination of scaling and cropping is used to format imported images and blend them with other InDesign elements.

### Create a Newspaper Ad

1. Start a new document. Choose File>New. In the New Document dialog box, make the following changes:

   **No. of pages:** 1
   **Facing Pages:** Uncheck
   **Page Size:** Custom
   **Width:** 25p
   **Height:** 360 pt
   **All margins:** 0p
   **Columns:** 1
   Click OK.

2. If the Transform palette is not already visible, choose Window>Transform.

3. With the Selection tool, choose File>Place. Be certain Show Import Options is not selected. Select **TravelLogo.EPS** from your **SF-Intro InDesign** folder. Click Choose/Open.

4. Position the loaded graphics icon in approximately the middle of the document and click (don't drag).

5. This file is an EPS graphic and scaling it a reasonable amount will not have an adverse affect on the output. With the image still selected, go to the Transform palette and enter 70% for both width and height scaling. Press Return/Enter.

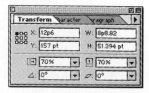

*Scaling, skewing and rotating graphic images is easy in InDesign, but not recommended in some cases. If imagesetter output is intended for the document, do not transform TIFF images. Limit transformation of EPS images to small percentages and amounts. Failure to heed this may cause the printing device to crash.*

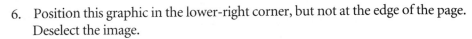

6.  Position this graphic in the lower-right corner, but not at the edge of the page. Deselect the image.

7.  Place the image named **Border.EPS** from your **SF-Intro InDesign** folder. Click the loaded graphics icon on the upper-left corner of the page.

*In the Transform palette, select an anchor point to scale from a specific position. Choose the center anchor point to scale the image or frame evenly on all sides from the center.*

8.  This, too, is a vector graphic. It will be scaled disproportionately to fill the ad area. With the Selection tool, while holding down the Command/Control key, click and drag the lower-right corner of the image frame to the right edge of the page, about 36 pts. below the bottom edge of the page.

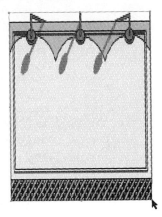

*Transforming placed images (especially rotating) may affect print quality and slow output to some imagesetters. Significant transformations should be completed in the original drawing program, before placing the image.*

Select the graphic with the Direct Selection tool and look at the Transform palette. It should indicate that the image was scaled approximately: Vertical 125% by Horizontal 276%. Deselect.

9. We would also like to crop the bottom of this image. With the Selection tool, click the bottom-center handle of the frame. Drag the frame edge up until the wood fencing portion of the image disappears. Leave the solid black line showing. Choose Object>Arrange>Send to Back. Deselect the image.

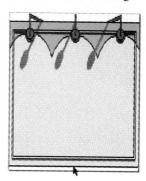

10. Save the document and leave it open for the next exercise.

## Add and Manipulate Images

1. Continue in the open document. Place the image named **Cruiseship.EPS** from your **SF-Intro InDesign** folder. Click the loaded graphics icon on the inside of the left border and under the shadow of the overhead lights.

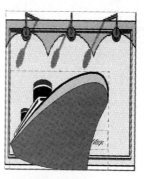

2. The ship needs to fit on the left side of the ad and nestle into the top of the border. We will shape the frame to the space and then fit the image. With the Selection tool, click on the right control handle of the frame and drag it left until the frame is about 10p6 wide (double-check using the Transform palette).

*When manually scaling an image in a frame, click-hold the Direct Selection tool on the frame handle and wait until the pointer changes to a two-headed arrow. You will then see the actual image transforming as you scale, instead of an empty frame.*

*Pressing the Command/ Control key while resizing with the Selection tool resizes both frame and contents simultaneously. If scaling uniformly, the Shift key should be added after the frame handle has been moved.*

*Hold Command/Control while dragging the control handle of a graphic frame to dynamically resize it. Hold Shift (after the move has begun) to constrain its proportions.*

*Click and hold the pointer a moment when using the Scale or Skew tool to view live preview results of the cursor motion.*

3. With the graphic still selected, choose Object>Fitting>Fit Content to Frame. It needs to be a little taller; while holding the Command/Control key, use the Selection tool to drag the frame's top-center control handle up to meet the points of the arches in the border. Deselect the frame.

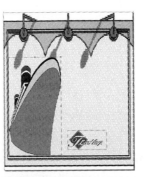

4. The casino ship needs a winning hand. Place the image named **Ace.EPS** from your **SF-Intro InDesign** folder. Click the loaded graphics icon at the bottom of the ship's hull. Leave the card image selected.

5. Select the Scale tool. With the Selection tool, click-hold on the lower-right control handle of the card image frame. Drag the handle up and to the left to make the image smaller. Add holding the Shift key to constrain proportions. Watch the Transform palette, and drag until the image is approximately 3-picas wide.

6. Select the Rotate tool. Click-hold the tool cursor outside the bottom-right corner, dragging counterclockwise until the Transform palette indicates approximately 20° rotation. Choose the Selection tool, reposition the card image if necessary, then deselect.

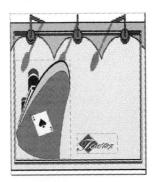

7. Place the image named **10Hearts.EPS** from your **SF-Intro InDesign** folder. Click the loaded graphics icon near the ace card.

8. Deselect the graphic and choose the Direct Selection tool. Click on the 10-of-Hearts image inside the frame. In the Transform palette, enter 50% in both Horizontal and Vertical Scale fields. Press Return/Enter.

9. With the Selection tool, select the image frame. Choose Object>Fitting>Fit Frame to Content. Position the card on top of the ace card, and deselect.

10. Place the image named **Ad Text.AI** from your **SF-Intro InDesign** folder. Click the loaded graphics icon at the bow tip of the ship. With the Selection tool drag the image into place as shown, so that the dollar sign is just touching the ship's bow. Deselect.

*If you have a copy of Adobe Illustrator, and lots of RAM, you may want to practice dragging and dropping files. Launch the program and open two files from the* **SF-Intro InDesign** *folder:* **Ad Text.AI** *and* **10Hearts.AI***.*

*Drag and drop, or copy and paste these files from their Illustrator document to this InDesign document, instead of placing the EPS file and creating the type.*

11. Place the image **Midnight.TIF** from your **SF-Intro InDesign** folder. Click the loaded graphics icon above the phone number and logo.

12. Adjust the frame on all sides to crop the image to show only the 12 in the image. Reposition to the lower-right corner of the ad, as shown.

13. Open the InDesign document **Picture Practice.INDD** from your **Work in Progress** folder. Select Window>Tile to see both document windows at the same time. In the Picture Practice.INDD document, locate and select the Flowers2new.TIF image. Click and drag this image to the ad file on which we have been working. Position it inside the double border in the lower-left corner. Deselect.

14. We are going to crop this graphic irregularly. Zoom into the area and select the Direct Selection tool. Click and drag the top-right corner point to the left about 1p6. Hold the Shift key to constrain movement. Click and drag the top-left corner point to the right about 1p6, holding Shift to constrain.

15. To the right of this image, create the following text styled as ATC Papaya, sized 22 pt., with 18-pt. leading, aligned left. Each word should be on a separate line.
"Ladies <return>
Night <return>
Tonight!"

16. Save this file as "Ad.INDD" in your **SF-Intro InDesign** folder, and close this document. Leave Picture Practice.INDD open for the next exercise.

## Adding Borders to Imported Images

Depending on the layout, some images will require a border. With InDesign, the frame container itself, or another frame behind the image, can provide the border. Borders may be added to rectangular, circular, or irregularly shaped graphic containers using the Stroke and Swatches palette.

### Create Borders for Imported Graphics

1. Continue in the open document.

2. Adjust the view to see the Academy.EPS image. Select the frame's handles with the Selection tool and resize it so that it is slightly larger than the image itself. Choose Object>Fitting>Center Content.

3. With the image frame still selected, click on the Stroke box in the Tools palette. Then click on the Default Fill and Stroke icon (small icon at the immediate left of the Stroke box) to assign a Black stroke to the frame border.

4. Choose Window>Stroke to display the Stroke palette. From the palette menu, choose Options to display the entire palette. Select 5 pt. weight from the drop-down menu. Choose Solid from the Type pop-up menu.

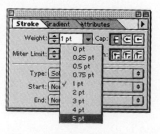

5. Select the BallRoll.EPS graphic with the Selection tool. Make certain Stroke is selected, then click on the Black swatch in the Swatches palette. In the Stroke palette, change the Weight of this frame to 2 pt.

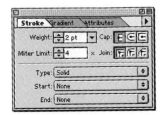

6. Choose Object>Corner Effects from the menu. First check Preview, then change the Effect to Fancy in the pop-up menu. The frame will not appear to change until the size is increased. Type "3p" into the Size field for this frame and click OK. Deselect the image.

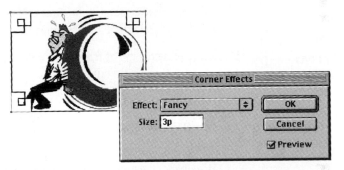

7. Select the Farmer.TIF image with the Selection tool. Choose Black for the Stroke color of this frame and assign it a 10-pt. weight in the Stroke palette. Choose Window>Color to open the Color palette and enter "50" in the percentage (%) field. Press Return/Enter to create a 50% Black tint border to this graphic.

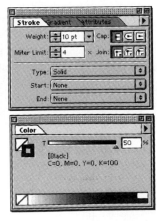

8.  Choose Object>Corner Effects and check its Preview option to view your selection. For the effect displayed, choose Rounded and enter 1p6 in the Size field. Click OK and deselect.

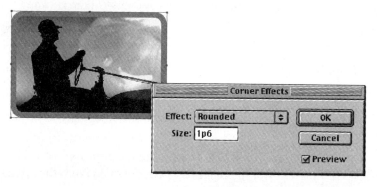

9.  Borders can also be made separately using an empty frame. To the right of the farmer image, create a rectangular frame 25p6 × 360 pt. in the empty space on this page. (Move or scale the Flowers2new.TIF image, if more room is required.)

10.  For the next type of frame, we will import the newspaper ad created in the last section. You could cut and paste or drag and drop the ad from the other file, but we have provided a completed ad in another file format that InDesign can both export and import. With the frame active, choose File>Place and select **Ad.PDF** from the **SF-Intro InDesign** folder. The ad will be placed in the frame just drawn.

11.  From the Transform palette Options menu, ensure that Dimensions Include Stroke Weight is checked. Open the Stroke palette menu and make certain that Weight Changes Bounding Box is not checked. These two options combined will ensure that the graphic and border will not grow beyond your dimension settings in the Transform palette. Adjust the scale of the image proportionally, and position the graphic in the ad to center in the empty frame that will become the ad border.

12.  Select the empty frame with the Selection tool. Check the Toolbox to ensure that its Fill is None, then change its Stroke to Black. Select 4 pt. Weight for this frame in the Stroke palette.

13.  Also in the Stroke palette, choose Dashed in the type pop-up menu, and enter the following values to define a special style of dashed border:
Dash: 10 pt.,  Gap: 3 pt.,  Dash: 6 pt.,  and Gap: 8 pt. Press Return/Enter.

*Dimensions Include Stroke Weight changes a setting in the Transform palette to display the item's dimensions around the outside of the graphic, including the border. When it is unselected, thick borders may add to the size of the image beyond your expectations.*

14. Toward the top of the stroke palette, click on the far-right icons for Cap and Join Style. These two are called Projecting Cap and Bevel Join, respectively, and will ensure that the border has clean-edged corners and a fuller appearance. Select combinations of the Cap and Join Style, then zoom in for a magnified view of their effect.

15. Save this file and close the window.

## Summary

In this chapter you have learned the types of images that can be imported into InDesign, the differences between vector and raster images, and how to determine the necessary resolution for resolution-dependent images. You have placed and transformed a variety of images, and you have learned how to manage images using the Links palette. You have learned how to effectively use the Selection and Direct Selection tools when working with graphics.

## Notes:

# CHAPTER 8

# Working with Color

## CHAPTER OBJECTIVE:

To learn the basics and uses of color, including RGB, CMYK, and spot color. To learn to create custom colors and gradients in both spot and process colors. To learn to import color and add it to bitmap and grayscale images, to fill and stroke, and to type. In Chapter 8, you will:

- Understand the different color models and how color behaves in different uses.

- Become familiar with standard terms for discussing color and its uses.

- Learn to use InDesign's Color Swatch palette to mix new CMYK and RGB colors, to adjust colors, and to store colors already created in this document or from other documents.

- Understand how to bring in spot colors from the variety of spot color libraries and how to make tints.

- Become familiar with gradients and how to create successful blends.

- Understand how to import color from other documents and from placed EPS files.

- Learn to apply color to created and imported elements such as InDesign objects, frames, images, and text.

## PROJECTS TO BE COMPLETED:

- Around the World Ad (A)
- **Baggy's Kid's Menu (B)**
- Vacation Brochure (C)
- Good Choices Newsletter (D)

# Working with Color

Although we can communicate perfectly well using black-and-white (or black-and-white with shades of gray), color gives pages pizazz, allows us to highlight elements, and lends variety to the document. However, not all color is created equal, and the colors we use must be created or specified with the end product in mind.

We must also concern ourselves with the interaction of colors: visually, in the manner in which they interact in each program we use, and how they work when the ink hits paper. Documents to be printed to an ink jet printer, to a printing press, or to be published to the Web all have different color criteria.

In order to deal effectively with color, we must become familiar with its components, so we can be understood when describing specific colorspace to colleagues and vendors. We also should understand why the same color image can look different from monitor to monitor, in various color proofs, and in the final printed piece.

## Understanding Color

In its purest form, color is light. So, while we may speak of the color of one's shirt being red, what we really mean is that red rays of light are reflected into our eyes. Because we see color as a result of reflection, objects that have smooth surfaces usually appear more brilliant than those with textured surfaces. When light strikes a surface, both the density of the surface and the pigments bend the light rays to allow us to see them as colors.

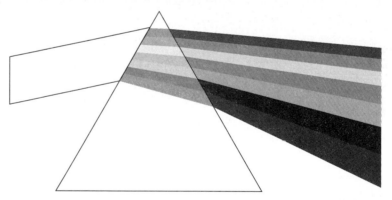

*When light passes through an object that is denser than air, it is bent or refracted. Since white light is comprised of a number of waves in varying lengths, each wave is refracted differently, giving us a spectrum, or rainbow. These colors progress from the shortest wave length, violet, to the longest one, red. The colors are violet, indigo, blue, green, yellow, orange, and red. Many of us learned them from longest to shortest, creating the memory hook "Roy G. Biv."*

We notice this phenomenon particularly with paper. Glossy paper, such as is used in leading magazines, is coated with clay and is *calendared* (shined up), and the ink remains on the surface. Other papers have a more porous coating and more of the ink is absorbed into the paper fibers (for example, the daily newspaper); the same color ink looks darker on uncoated papers than on coated papers. Of course, color looks brightest of all on our computer screens, because light is being transmitted, not reflected.

## The Interaction Between Color and Pigment

The "color" of an object is created by the reflection of light waves. When light strikes an object containing pigment, some of the light waves are absorbed and others are reflected. The examples below show how this occurs using several colors.

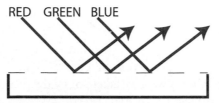

An object that reflects all light from an object appears white.

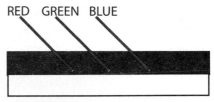

An object that reflects no light from an object appears black.

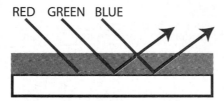

A cyan object reflects green and blue light and absorbs red.

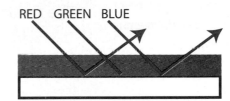

A magenta object reflects red and blue light and absorbs green.

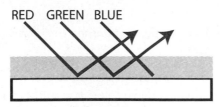

A yellow object reflects green and red light and absorbs blue.

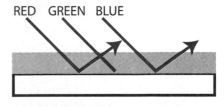

A violet object reflects some red and blue light, and absorbs green, plus some red and blue.

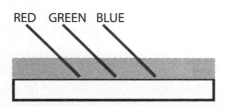

What does a green object do?

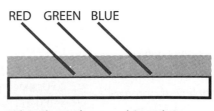

What does a brown object do?

*Can you figure out the bottom two interactions without turning the page upside down and reading the answers?*

*A green object reflects green light, absorbs red and blue.*

*A brown object absorbs some of all colors and reflects a portion of the red and green, and sometimes blue.*

When we attempt to reproduce a scene we've just enjoyed, we often are faced with disappointment. The reds may be a little orange, or the blues a trifle green on the prints or slides we receive from the color lab. Then we scan it on our desktop scanner, and it loses still more when we view it on the monitor. When the photo is included in a printed piece, all the luster may seem gone.

Each element along the way has affected the final product, from the introduction of color cast on the film to the ability of the color guns on the monitor to produce only 256 shades of each of the *primary colors* (red, green, and blue). The human eye can differentiate only 256 shades of any individual color — the magical 16.8 million colors computer monitors produce. However, we can perceive even more color, and that's why we're occasionally disappointed by the photos we have taken, or by the printed documents we produce.

To further complicate matters, color looks different when viewed in different lighting conditions. Incandescent lights create a yellowish hue, and fluorescent lighting often gives a bluish appearance. Add to that the fact that no two people see color exactly the same, and you are faced with difficulties in producing colors appealing to the eye.

## The Color Models

There are four color models that concern us. *L\*a\*b* defines color by its luminance, and chromatic components across two axes, the "a" axis ranges from green to magenta, and the "b" axis ranges from blue to yellow. *RGB*, also known as the *additive primaries*, combines the colors of light (all colors added together make white). *CMYK*, the *subtractive primaries* (*additive secondaries*), combines the pigments cyan, magenta, yellow, and black; when all pigments are removed, white results. *Spot color*, which includes the Pantone ink specification system, is used when exact color matches must be achieved, or when the budget allows for only up to three colors.

### L\*a\*b

CIE L\*a\*b was introduced by the *Commission Internationale de l'Eclairage*, an international standards-making body.

In the late 1920s, as color printing became more prevalent, it was seen that a standard for color description was needed. If two colors appear the same, they should be described in the same manner. For example, we might define "pure red" as R: 255, G: 0, B: 0 using RGB colorspace, or C: 0, M: 100, Y: 100, K: 0 using CMYK space. Of course, someone else might call it simply "bright red."

Because different programs and monitors describe color differently, and printing devices create it differently, there are widely divergent definitions for the same color. This is particularly true if we describe it in one space (RGB) and create it in another (CMYK).

In 1931, CIE developed the first widely used independent colorspace, known as CIE XYZ, named for the three axes used to describe the location of the colors. The values in this colorspace are derived from the relative amounts of RGB present in the color, and expressed as a percentage of luminance, together with 256 levels (ranging from −128 to +128) across two axes. In 1976, CIE XYZ was redefined and renamed CIE L\*a\*b. InDesign simplifies the spelling and calls the color model "LAB."

*To view colors in the best possible light, purchase fluorescent 5,000°K (Kelvin) lighting. This is the measurement of "daylight."*

*In school, many of us learned that the primary colors were red, yellow, and blue. What we were working with was paint, which although it is a pigment, does not have the properties of printing ink. The printing process uses the* **subtractive primaries**, *cyan, magenta, and yellow.*

*Hue* is the property we refer to when we call a color by its name: red, purple, or teal, for example. Hue changes as we travel in a circle around the axis of the color wheel. As you see, hue is defined as beginning from red (0°) and travelling counterclockwise around the wheel.

**Colorspace** *is the entire range of colors of any color model plotted within the three-dimensional CIE L\*a\*b\* coordinate system, which is a colorspace itself.*

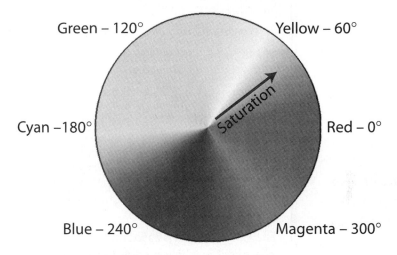

*A slice of CIE colorspace, with all hues represented.*

*Saturation*, also called "chroma" or "intensity," is the clarity of the color. Color is dulled by the introduction of elements of the color opposite it in the color wheel. When the center of the wheel is approached, the color becomes a neutral gray. Red is neutralized by the addition of cyan, or of blue and green.

*Luminance*, or *value*, is the amount of white or black added to the pure color. A luminance of 50 means there is no addition of white or black. Luminance of 100 is pure white, luminance of 0 is pure black.

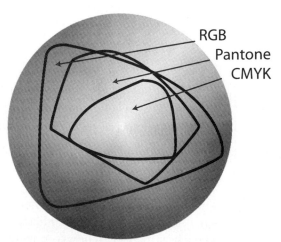

*The color gamuts we use take up only a portion of the visible spectrum. Above are the relative size and shapes of colors available in the RGB, Pantone (Spot), and CMYK color gamuts.*

## RGB

The *RGB* color model is capable of displaying the largest area of the color spectrum, with the exception of the entire LAB model. Red, Green, and Blue are known as the additive primary colors. When they are all added in equal quantity, the result is white. Where they overlap, they create a version of the additive secondary colors: cyan, magenta, and yellow. RGB colors are the colors of light, and are used by monitors and scanners.

The RGB color model may be used if documents are to be printed to RGB-savvy printers, such as inkjet and laser printers, or if they will be distributed electronically, and viewed on monitors, such as CD distribution, or publication on the Internet.

*Indexed color* is a subset of RGB, and is used to create GIF files. Indexed color is used in drawn images with areas of flat color, as opposed to photographs. The greatest number of colors that may be contained in an indexed-color image is 256. When creating indexed color images, you should always use the Web-safe palette, and should use as few colors as possible, so the image will paint up quickly.

## CMYK

The *CMYK* model is based on the absorption and reflection of light, as opposed to the transmission of light used by the RGB model. A portion of the color spectrum is absorbed when white light strikes ink-coated paper (or any pigment-coated material). The color that is not absorbed is reflected.

Theoretically, a mixture of equal parts of cyan, magenta, and yellow would produce black. Pigments, however, as opposed to light, are not pure, so the result of mixing these colors is a muddy brown. To obtain vibrant colors (and so that elements, such as type, can be printed cleanly), we add black to the palette. CMYK is also called "process color."

Process color is used to print documents that contain multiple distinct colors, or that contain color photos. A pattern of dots in varying sizes (called a "rosette") fools the eye into thinking that, although it is actually seeing cyan, yellow, magenta, and black dots, it is seeing distinct colors. The resolution of these dots, when used in the printing process, is described in lines per inch. If there are 150 lines per inch, there can be as many as 22,500 distinct spots in a one-inch square area. The resolution of the printer itself is usually about 2,400 spots per inch, giving it the capability to place 5,760,000 minuscule spots in that one-inch square.

## Spot

*Spot color* is used in two- and three-color documents, and is added to process color documents when a special color, such as a corporate color, must be achieved. It is also used as a stand-alone color, when black is not used. There are many specifications for spot color, but the most popular in the United States is the Pantone Matching System, also known as "PMS."

The PMS system defines most colors by number (although some colors are named). After you use it for a while, you'll be likely to start referring to colors using their PMS numbers. You'll hear many designers comments "Oh, that's about 327" instead of referring to the color as "teal." They are speaking of the Pantone 327 color.

InDesign supports Pantone color, and other spot and process color libraries, and allows you to define another color as "spot" if you choose to. Spot and process colors may be combined in the same document.

*The color **Paper** may be changed to give a better on-screen representation of a document that does not use white paper. Simply double-click on the swatch and change its color definition. Regardless of its on-screen appearance, this represents the nonprinting areas of the document. The color will not print.*

## InDesign's Color Swatch Palettes

The set of colors used in your InDesign document may be created and placed in the Swatches palette. Colors placed in the Swatches palette are called *Named* colors. Colors may also be mixed in one of the basic color modes (LAB, CMYK, or RGB) and applied directly to the object. Colors applied directly, without being placed in the Swatches palette, are called *Unnamed* colors. The advantage to placing mixed colors in the palette is that they are then reproducible elsewhere in the document, or may be imported into other documents. InDesign makes no provision for sampling a color to determine its makeup.

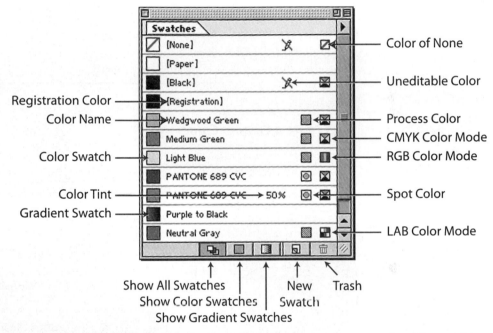

When a new document is created, the Swatches palette contains a swatch with no color, one named "Paper," which is the color of the background, Black, and a unique color called "Registration." None of these colors may be deleted. It also contains the primary colors for printing, Cyan, Magenta, and Yellow; and the primary colors for monitors, Red, Green, and Blue. These colors may be deleted.

*The color **Registration** is used to print printer's registration marks on the oversized printing sheet. Registration prints in every color the document uses.*

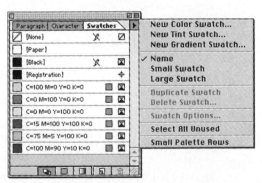

When a new color swatch is created, it may be a Color Type of either Process or Spot, and may be created in the LAB, CMYK, or RGB Color Mode.

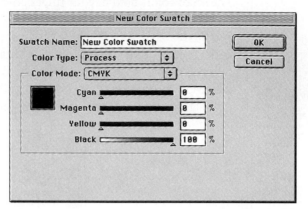

## *Create a Custom Color*

1. Create a new document.

2. Select Window>Swatches to display the Swatches palette.

3. From the fly-out menu, select New Color Swatch.

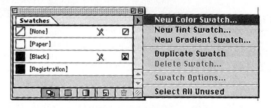

*To simplify the palette, we have removed the Cyan, Magenta, Yellow, Red, Green, and Blue swatches.*

4. We're going to create a soft blue, similar to that used for Wedgwood china. Uncheck the Name with Color Value box, and, In the Swatch Name box, type "Wedgwood Blue".

5. Leave the Color Type Process and the Color Mode CMYK.

6. Set the sliders, or type the numbers, as follows: C: 25, M: 10, Y: 0, K: 10. Click OK.

*When creating a new named color swatch, always create it in the mode in which the document will be published. If the document will be printed, use CMYK; if it is for electronic distribution, use RGB.*

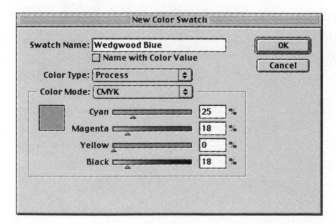

When colors are created in the CMYK color mode, we refer to them as C, M, Y, and K, instead of writing out the name. A formula comprised of 25% Cyan, 10% Magenta, 0% Yellow, and 10% Black is written C: 25, M: 0, Y: 0, K: 10.

Be careful when specifying Pantone colors. Pantone Coated colors have "CVC" endings to the color names; Pantone Uncoated colors end in "CVU". If the same color is specified in both Coated and Uncoated versions, two printing plates will be generated. We recommend using either one, but never both systems.

7. The color is added to the palette and becomes the active fill color.

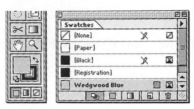

8. In the Swatches palette, double-click on the Wedgwood Blue swatch to bring up the Swatch Options menu.

9. In the Swatch Options menu, change the Color Type to Spot. Click OK.

10. Note that the Color Type icon changes to indicate that the color is spot, not process, and the CMYK icon indicates that it was created in CMYK mode.

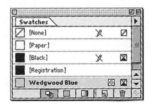

11. Let's create another color compatible with the color scheme. Select New Color Swatch.

12. Name this swatch "Medium Blue". The Color Type should be Process and the Color Mode CMYK.

13. Either use the sliders or type the following percentages into the dialog boxes: C: 50, M: 30, Y: 0, K: 20. Click OK.

14. Save the document to your **Work in Progress** folder as "Color Work.INDD". Leave the document open.

What we have just done is the best way to create a process color that is not part of an existing swatch library. Often, we will want to "steal" a color from an existing InDesign document to create consistency. To do this, we simply drag the color from the Swatches palette of the old document into the new document.

### Add Colors from Other Documents

1. With Color Work.INDD still open, open the document **Color Swiper.INDD** from your **SF-Intro InDesign** folder.

2. Use Window>Tile to reduce the window so you can see both documents.

3. Click on the color Wedgwood Green in the Swatches palette and drag it into the Color Work.INDD document. InDesign will automatically switch to the document into which you dragged the color.

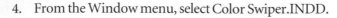

*Always check with your service provider before specifying an ink matching system. If you specify a Toyo ink and your vendor uses Pantone, you have a problem.*

4. From the Window menu, select Color Swiper.INDD.

5. Drag the Medium Green color into Color Work.INDD.

6. Save Color Work.INDD and leave it open. Close Color Swiper.INDD without saving.

RGB colors are created in the same way.

Much of the time, you will be working with spot colors, using the Pantone Matching System (PMS) or another color system. To access these you must use the appropriate swatch library. The swatch libraries are found under Window>Swatch Libraries.

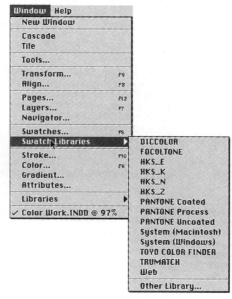

There are quite a few swatch libraries. They can be broken down into three types: spot, process, and RGB.

*When spot colors are converted to process, they do not convert cleanly. You will get unexpected results unless you rely on accurate conversion tables, such as Pantone's Process Color Simulator.*

Spot libraries include Pantone Coated, Pantone Uncoated, Toyo Color Finder, DICColor, and the four HKS libraries. Process libraries are Pantone Process, TruMatch, and Focoltone. RGB libraries are the Macintosh and Windows System colors, and the optimized Web palette.

Pantone is the most popular spot-color library in the United States. The Pantone Process library uses a different numbering system than the Coated and Uncoated libraries do. TruMatch and Focoltone are also used in the United States. HKS is a complex system used primarily in Germany. Toyo and DICColor (Dainippon Ink & Chemicals) are used primarily in Japan.

Throughout this course, when using a spot-color system, we will use Pantone Coated. We will usually mix process colors, or may convert them from Pantone Coated.

### Create Spot Colors

1. With the document Color Work.INDD still open, select Windows>Swatch Libraries>Pantone Coated. You may have a palette container with Pantone Coated, Uncoated, and Process libraries included. Make sure Pantone Coated is the topmost library.

2. Scroll down to Pantone 185 (from now on, we will refer to Pantone colors as PMS (Pantone Matching System), so this color would be called "PMS 185").

3. Double-click the color to add it to the Swatches palette.

4. Scroll down to PMS 286 and single-click it.

5. Hold down the Command/Control key, scroll to PMS 320, and click it. (Be sure to select 320, not 320 2X.)

6. From the fly-out Options menu, select Add to Swatches. Both swatches will be added to the Swatches palette.

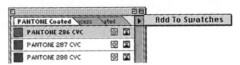

*Pantone colors, although they are spot, contain a built-in CMYK definition. Both spot and CMYK icons display with Pantone colors.*

7. Close the Swatch Library, save the document and leave it open.

## Tints of Colors

Often, you will want to use a lighter version of the same color. This is called a "tint." Tints are created using the Swatches palette. Although tints may be created from process colors, the results are somewhat unpredictable. You should create tints from spot colors only.

### Create a Tint

1. With the document Color Work.INDD open, select PMS 185 from the Swatches palette.

2. From the fly-out Options menu, select New Tint Swatch.

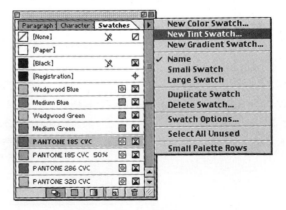

*Colors on the screen are different from colors on paper. Be sure to use a current swatch book so you are not disappointed with the color produced. When swatch books are exposed to light, the colors become faded or distorted, so you should replace them regularly to ensure a reliable reference.*

3.  Move the slider, so the Tint percent reads 50%, or type "50"% in the dialog box. Click OK.

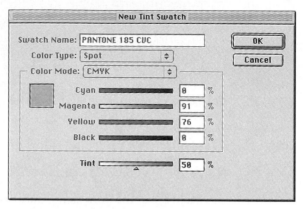

4.  The tint will now be added to your Swatches palette.

5.  Colors are added to the palette in the order they are created. For better palette organization, click on the tint with the Selection tool and drag it up so that it is placed just below the PMS 185 swatch. This has nothing to do with the way the computer handles the colors — it's simply easier to find things that are grouped in logical (in this case numeric) order.

Another way to accomplish the same thing is to manually adjust the color percentages.

6.  Double-click the Pantone 286 CVC swatch in the Swatches palette. The Swatch Options dialog box will appear. Although it is a spot color, we are given its CMYK equivalents.

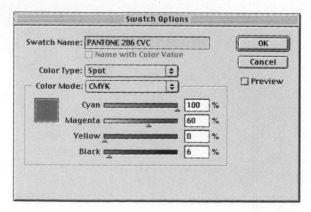

7. To ensure the color will be corrected uniformly, hold down the Shift key and click on the Magenta slider (this doesn't work with colors set to zero). Drag to the left to reduce the percentage to 40. Notice how the Magenta and Black percentages changed proportionately. Holding the Shift key makes all other sliders move as one.

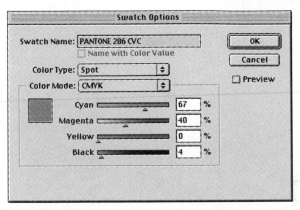

8. Click Cancel. We never want to adjust the representation of a Pantone ink when the document is being printed using spot color, because it will affect the screen representation and not the ink that is actually applied by the printing press.

9. Save the document and leave it open for the next exercise.

## Gradients

A *gradient* is a fill consisting of two or more colors or tints that blend into one another. A gradient can be linear or radial. Because a gradient creates a smooth blend of colors from one to the other, it employs the mathematics of PostScript in order to work. Perhaps you have seen gradients that have stairsteps between tones. This "stairstepping" is called "banding."

*InDesign works with all three levels of PostScript: Level 1, Level 2, and Level 3.*

*When there are too few steps for the length of the gradient at a specific resolution, the result is the banding effect you see here.*

There are 256 discrete steps in a gradient from 0% to 100%. If any step is greater than 2 points, it is visible to the eye. Therefore, if we have a gradient from black to white, it can be no longer than 512 points, or 7.1 inches. A gradient from 0% to 50% can be no longer than 256 points, or 3.5 inches.

You cannot, therefore, create a gradient that goes from the top of a letter-sized page to the bottom and have it look good, using versions of PostScript earlier than PostScript 3, which does away with the limitations we mentioned earlier.

### Create Gradients with Named Colors

1. With the document Color Work.INDD still open, place the cursor on the color Black, and select New Gradient Swatch from the Options fly-out menu.

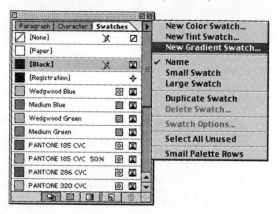

2. Name the swatch "Black to White".

3. Click on the leftmost Stop icon in the Gradient Ramp.

4. Leave the Type Linear and make the Stop Color Named Color.

5. Click Black as the named color.

6. Click on the rightmost Stop icon in the Gradient Ramp and click Paper.

7. Click on the diamond icon above the bar and move it to the left and right. Note how it affects gradient. When you are finished, reposition it at 50% and click OK.

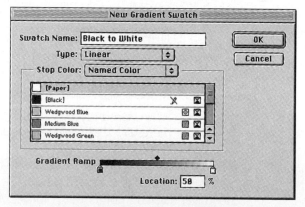

*If the diamond is moved to 70%, how does this affect the maximum length of the gradient? The 20% difference will make the maximum length of the gradient 40% shorter, because it increases the length of 50% of the black. It's easy to see why so many banding problems occur because of this.*

If the swatch does not appear, check Show All Swatches or Show Gradient Swatches in the Color palette.

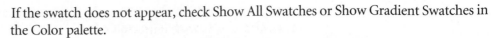

Show All Swatches
Show Color Swatches
Show Gradient Swatches
New Swatch
Delete Swatch

*Whenever a new stop is created, InDesign reverts to the CMYK color mode.*

8. Let's create another blend. This time, we'll blend using three colors.

9. Select New Gradient Swatch from the Swatches fly-out menu.

10. Now let's create a CMYK gradient. Select New Gradient Swatch from the Swatches Options fly-out menu.

11. Name it "Red, White & Blue."

12. Click on the left stop icon in the Gradient Ramp.

13. Leave the Type Linear and make the Stop Color Named Color.

14. Click PMS 185 as the named color.

15. Click on the right stop and apply PMS 286.

16. Click just below the Gradient Ramp bar, beneath the diamond at 50%. This inserts a new stop. Apply the color Paper to this stop. Click OK. Click any blank area within the Swatches palette to deselect the Red, White & Blue gradient.

17. Save the document and leave it open for the next exercise.

### Create CMYK Gradients

1. With the document still open, select New Gradient Swatch.

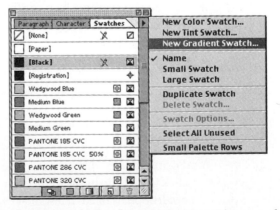

2. Name this gradient "Blue to Yellow". Leave its Type Linear and the Stop Color CMYK. Drag the middle stop down to remove it.

3. Click on the leftmost stop. The Stop Color will change to Named Color. Change it to CMYK. Assign the color as follows: C: 0, M: 20, Y: 100, K: 0.

4. Click on the rightmost stop. Change the Stop Color to CMYK. Assign the color as follows: C: 100, M: 80, Y: 0, K: 0. Click OK.

   Let's reverse this gradient.

5. With the Blue to Yellow gradient still selected, select Window>Gradient, then select Show Options from the palette's Options menu. The Gradient palette will appear.

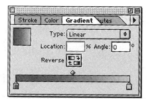

6. Click the Reverse button to cause the gradient to correctly reflect its name.

7. Save the file. Leave it open for the next exercise.

## Imported Color

There is still another way to add color to your palette. When you import an EPS graphic, any colors not already included in your palette will be added. If the graphic contains a color that is defined differently from a color already in the palette, you will be asked which color definition you wish to use.

### Import Color Files

1. With the document Color Work.INDD still open, place the graphic **Dragon.EPS** from your **SF-Intro InDesign** folder (File>Place).

2. Notice that five spot colors have been added to the palette. They may be changed from Spot to Process, but are otherwise not editable.

3. As you will learn in Chapter 10 (Printing & Packaging), these colors also may be converted to process when the file is imaged, so the graphic does not have to be reworked.

   Now we're going to use another method to create colors from an imported graphic.

4. Place the image **Your Vacation.TIF** from your **SF-Intro InDesign** folder.

5. Be sure the Fill icon is active (on top). Select the Eyedropper tool from the Tools palette.

6. Position the eyedropper over one of the hot-pink areas of the woman's blouse and click the mouse button. The icon will change from ✒ to ✎, indicating that the eyedropper is filled. It also makes the color you selected the active fill color

7. Drag the new color from the fill block in the Toolbox into the Swatches palette. Notice that it is named by its CMYK equivalents and that it is a CMYK color.

## Applying Color

Now you're ready to apply the colors in the document to a variety of created and imported elements. In the next exercise, we're going to apply color to an InDesign object, to a frame, to images, and to text. You'll see how applying color is straightforward and consistent across the variety of color applications.

### Use the Colors

1. With the document Color Work.INDD open, place the graphic **ATWU Logo.BMP** from your **SF-Intro InDesign** folder.

2. Be sure the Fill icon is in front in the Tool palette.

3. With the Direct Selection tool active, click on the logo (not the frame). You'll know if you selected the logo, because the fill color will turn black.

4. Click on PMS 320 to colorize this bitmap graphic.

5. Deselect by clicking anywhere on the page and switch to the Selection tool.

6. Enlarge the frame to a width of 12p and a height of 144 pt.

7. Select Object>Fitting>Center Content (Command/Control-Shift-O) to center the logo in the new frame.

8. With the Selection tool still active, choose PMS 286 to fill the frame with blue.

9. Press the "X" key to make the Stroke box active, and press F10 to activate the Stroke palette.

10. Assign the Stroke a weight of 4 pt.

11. Click on Gold (a color that was imported with the dragon art) to apply it to the stroke.

12. Click anywhere on the page to deselect this art.

13. Place the grayscale image **Charge It.TIF** from your **SF-Intro InDesign** folder.

14. Switch to the Direct Selection tool, click on the image, and return the fill icon to the top (press the "X" key).

15. Click on the color Medium Green to colorize the artwork. This looks a little washed out. Let's alter the color.

16. Double-click on the color Medium Green to bring up the Swatch Options dialog box.

17. Hold the Shift key and drag the Cyan slider to 70%, altering all colors.

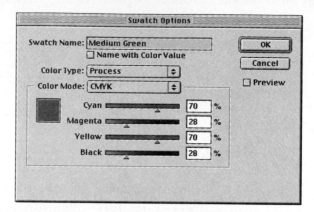

Unfortunately, if we had a number of other images using Medium Green in a document, they would also have been affected. Let's do this another way.

18. Press Command/Control-Z to undo the color change.

19. With Charge It.TIF selected, click on the color Medium Green, and select Duplicate Swatch from the fly-out menu.

20. Double-click on the color Medium Green copy and shift-drag the Cyan slider to 70%. Assign it a new name: Dark Green. Click OK.

21. Create a Text frame and type your name in 48 pt. ATC Cozumel. Press Return/Enter, and type "Gradient Type" on the next line.

22. Make sure the Fill icon is in front. Highlight your name, and select PMS 185 from the Swatches palette.

23. Bring the Stroke icon to the front and click on Chinese Red for the stroke color. (You can't just type an "X" to switch to the Stroke because you're using the Text tool.)

24. Highlight the Gradient Type line with the Text tool and assign a stroke of Black.

25. Switch to the Fill icon, and click on the Red, White and Blue gradient swatch.

26. Save and close the document.

## Summary

You've learned the basics of color, which types of documents require RGB color and which require CMYK, and when to use spot colors. In addition, you've learned to create custom colors and gradients in both spot and process color models, and have imported color from other InDesign documents and through EPS graphics. You have added color to bitmap and grayscale images, to the fill and stroke of frames, and to type.

***Complete Project B: Baggy's Kid's Menu***

# CHAPTER 9

# Text Utilities

## CHAPTER OBJECTIVE:

To learn to use InDesign's text tools to automate editing, by finding and changing text elements, using and updating dictionaries, and spell checking. In Chapter 9, you will:

- Learn to use the features of the Find/Change function, including locating or altering individual instances or every instance of a word or phrase, entire words or individual characters, and precise capitalization.

- Explore how to find and change a specific style or style attribute in all styled and unstyled text.

- Learn how to search on Special Characters, to know how to enter a specific Special Character, and to reveal hidden characters.

- Become familiar with the Check Spelling feature, its uses and its weaknesses.

- Understand how to select, use, and edit dictionaries.

## PROJECTS TO BE COMPLETED:

- Around the World Ad (A)
- Baggy's Kid's Menu (B)
- **Vacation Brochure (C)**
- Good Choices Newsletter (D)

# Text Utilities

Working with large amounts of text can be cumbersome when clients make changes, or when quickly typed text must be proofed for accurate spelling. To hunt for these changes by reading the text, word for word, takes considerable time. With deadlines looming, there usually is very little time for this degree of scrutiny.

InDesign has several text utilities to find and replace words or phrases, and to check spelling. Its dictionary can be edited to include words you use that are not found in most dictionaries, such as proper nouns. The text utility features are found at the bottom of the Edit menu:

- Find/Change

- Find Next

- Check Spelling

- Edit Dictionary

## Find/Change

The Find/Change feature enables one to search for specified text, and determine, in each case, whether or not to apply a change. The Find/Change dialog box offers several options for making text changes.

*If no text or text frames are selected, the Search menu of the Find/Change dialog box defaults to Document, which will search all the text frames in the document.*

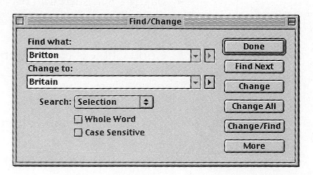

*The Find Next option in the Edit menu is not a separate function like Find/Change or Check Spelling. Instead, it is one of the Find/Change dialog box features. Find Next will locate a word or phrase that is still in the Find What input field. The Find/Change dialog box does not have to be open for this to work.*

**Find what.** This option can search for a single letter, word, or phrase. If the search is for a phrase, the entire phrase will be changed. Find/Change will not single out individual words from the phrase and change them elsewhere in the document.

**Change to.** This option can change the text to a single letter, word, or phrase.

**Find Next.** With this option, when the text is found, it can be replaced or ignored. Whether the text is changed or not, Find Next sends the searcher to the next text meeting the criteria.

**Change.** This option replaces the found text with the text typed into the Change To input field.

**Change All.** This feature goes through the selection, story, document, or all open InDesign documents, changing the text listed in the Find What field. This gives no option to pick and choose, so be careful that there are no words in a different context that will be affected.

**Change/Find.** When text is found, this option changes it, then proceeds to the next instance. It relieves the user of the necessity of having to constantly click the Find Next and Change buttons.

**More.** Additional search criteria becomes available by selecting this option. It enables searches for and changes to specified style settings.

**Search.** Often a document contains multiple text frames. This pop-up menu gives several options for determining where to search. The Document option searches all the text frames in the document. All Documents performs the search on every open InDesign document. Story searches starting from the cursor's present location to the end of the story, then returns to the beginning of the story and searches back to its starting point. To End of Story searches the text from where the cursor is located to the end of the story, then stops. Selection searches only the highlighted words.

*A continuous unit of text, whether it occupies one frame or multiple threaded frames, is considered one **story**.*

**Whole Word.** Sometimes words are sections of other larger words, such as "cat" and "catastrophe." If a search for the word "cat" is run, the word "catastrophe" will also be selected. To restrict the search to only the target word, click the Whole Word option. When this word appears within larger words, it will be ignored.

**Case Sensitive.** When the Case Sensitive option is clicked, the capitalization of the word must match exactly. The words "caterpillar," "Caterpillar," and "CATERPILLAR" would each require a separate Case Sensitive search.

### Find and Replace Text

1. Open the document **Cloud Factory.INDD** from the **SF-Intro InDesign** folder. This is a first draft of the story, and the author wants to make some changes. The Find/Change feature will be used to alter these words.

2. Select the Type tool and click in the text frame on page 1. In the Edit menu, choose the Find/Change feature. The dialog box appears.

*Some special characters have unique search codes. For a paragraph line break, type: "^p" (Shift-6, and p).*

*As long as the input fields of Change Format Settings are empty, no criteria are set to search on and replace to with new changes. The current settings of the text being searched remain the default settings of the styles.*

*If a found word is to be ignored, the Find Next button will move on to the next word that meets the search criteria.*

*Press Command/Control-F to access Find/Change from the keyboard.*

3. The author has decided to name the king Kumulo, rather than Kumulus. In the Find What field, type "Kumulus". In the Change To field, type "Kumulo". Select Story in the Search pop-up menu, if it is not already selected, to search this story only. Click the Find Next button.

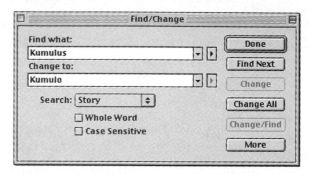

4. The first example of Kumulus is highlighted. Click the Change button. The word changes to Kumulo. Click Find Next again. The next example of Kumulus is highlighted.

5. To go faster, click Change/Find, which will change this word and move on immediately to the next example. You could continue clicking Change/Find, avoiding the Find Next and Change buttons, but you can cut your time down to a single click.

6. The author knows that only the name Kumulus needs to be changed, and there are no contextual variations in the name. In this case, by clicking the Change All button, all instances of Kumulus will change to Kumulo, avoiding the tedious task of clicking Find Next each time. Click Change All. When Find/Change is complete, InDesign will tell you how many changes were made. Click OK.

7. The next change is "chef" to "cook." This is not a simple task for Change All. There are other instances of "chef" with an initial letter, such as in "Head Chef." Only lower case instances of the word "chef" need changing.

8. With the Type tool in the text frame, return to the Find/Change dialog box. In the Find What field, type "chef". In the Change To field, type "cook". Click on the Case Sensitive box. Now the search is narrowed to only lower case "chef."

**Note:** The word "chefs" also appears in the story, but this is acceptable. Had we wanted "chefs" to remain untouched, we would click the Whole Word button, which would restrict the search for only the exact word "chef" and nothing else.

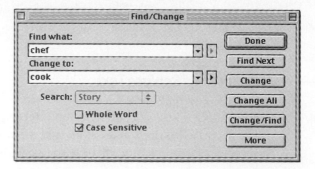

9. Click the Change All button to change every instance of the word "chef." When the dialog box informs you of how many changes are made, click OK.

10. The word "glutton" also appears in the story, and the author wants this changed to "gourmet." The problem is that Thermidor P. Guzzleglutton's name contains the word "glutton." Change All cannot be used here. It would take too many clicks of Find Next to locate the single word "glutton." This is where the Whole Word option is needed. It will look for the word exactly as typed in the Find What field. If any words contain "glutton" with other letters, they will be ignored.

Click the First Page button to jump to page 1, if necessary. Place the Type tool in the text frame and press Command/Control-F. In the Find What field, type "glutton". In the Change To field, type "gourmet". Click the Whole Word box to select it. Deselect the Case Sensitive box, if selected. Click the Find Next button. The document should jump to a section showing the word "glutton" highlighted. Click the Change button. The word will change to "gourmet."

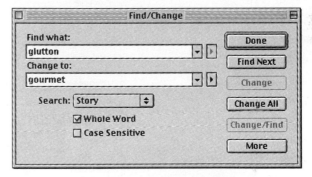

11. Click the text cursor after the word you just changed to "gourmet". In the Find What field, type "King". In the Change To field, type "king". This will give the searcher some criteria. Be sure to check Case Sensitive; if you don't, no changes will be made. Use the Search pop-up menu to select To End of Story. Click Find Next and continue to click this button, ignoring all found words, until you come to the end of the story text. When the end is reached, a warning that the Search is Complete appears. Click OK.

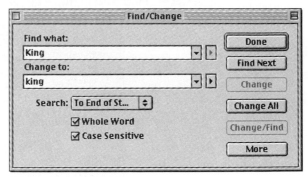

12. Click the First Page button to return to page 1. Use the text cursor to highlight only the text on this page. You can search on selected text. It is not mandatory to search an entire story. Change the scope of the search to Selection in Find/Change.

13. In the Find What field, type "King". In the Change To field, type "Emperor". Make certain Whole Word and Case Sensitive are not checked. Click Find Next. What happened? Notice that the "king" of the word "making" was highlighted. This is because without Whole Word or Case Sensitive checked, the searcher looks for anything containing the Find What words.

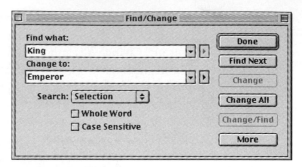

*If **Story** is searched, all linked text frames — even those that precede the present cursor position — will be checked. When **To End of Story** is searched, only text between the cursor position and the end of the story will be checked. This is a real time-saver when dealing with long stories (such as book chapters).*

14. Use the text tool to highlight this page of text. In the Find/Change box, select both the Whole Word and Case Sensitive options. Click Find Next. Now the first example of "King" is found. Click Change/Find to move to the next instance. Continue clicking Change/Find. When it reaches the last "King" in the selected text, the searcher gives notice that the Search is Completed. Click OK.

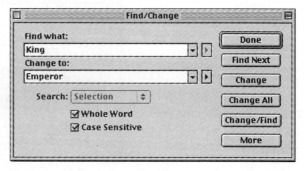

15. Find/Change does not require a complete word to be typed into the Find What or Change To fields. If part of a word is all that needs changing, this can be searched on as well. Place the Type tool at the beginning of the text on page 1. In the Find What field, type "easy". In the Change To field, type "eezy". We will change the names of the Junior Chefs from "Greasy" to "Greezy" just for fun. Keep in mind that "easy" is an actual word, so use the Find Next button with care to avoid changing other words accidentally .

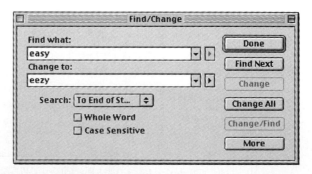

*The computer only knows what to look for by what you tell it. Always check whether or not the Whole Word or Case Sensitive boxes are selected appropriately.*

16. The Whole Word and Case Sensitive boxes should not be checked in order to be able to access the internal letters of the name "Greasy". Now click Find Next and the next word found will contain the word "easy". Ignore this by clicking Find Next again. The first "easy" in "Greasy" should be highlighted. Click change. Continue to Find Next and Change only the "easy" letters that are in the name "Greasy". When there are no more examples to find and change, notice that Search is Complete message will appear. Click Done.

17. Close the document without saving.

## More Options

In the Find/Change dialog box, there is a More button that will add two extra find options. The Less button hides these extra settings. These two options may be used to change overall style settings applied, or to limit a search to words in a particular typeface or that match a specific character or paragraph style: Format Settings, Find Style Settings, or Change Style Settings.

*Some writers have the old habit of typing two spaces after a period at the end of a sentence, which drives compositors crazy. Resolve this by doing a search on double spaces and replacing them with single spaces.*

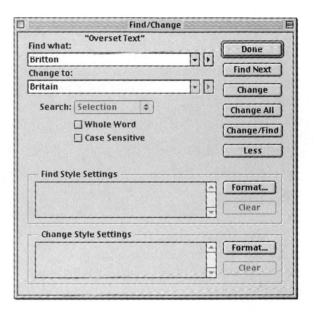

## Format Settings

These style search settings are made by clicking on the Format button of either the Find Style Settings or the Change Style Settings. Seven windows determine what text attributes are applied to the searched text. Alternately, text of a named character or paragraph style may be searched.

### Style Options

The Style Options drop-down menu is used to limit the text being searched to specific parameters, or to replace parameters. For example, if ATC Mai Tai 10 pt. is selected in the Style Options menu for Find Style Settings, the search engine will only look for words that meet those criteria. All other words in the story will be ignored. Similarly, text can be replaced by parameters entered in Style Options. To access Style Options formatting, push the Next button, or select the top, drop-down menu.

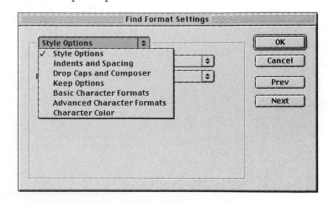

### Indents and Spacing

This setting allows a search based on paragraph attributes, including Alignment, Indents, and Space Before and After a Paragraph.

### Drop Caps and Composer

If the searched text contains Drop Caps, this dialog box provides fields for setting the number of lines and characters as criteria. The Adobe Multi-line or Single-line Composers may also be used as a search criterion.

*Settings in the Style Options windows do not search for actual styles as set by the Styles palette. They will look for any text that is styled with the criteria in these dialog boxes.*

*However, when styles are selected from the character styles or paragraph styles drop-down menus, only text having that character or paragraph style will be included in the search.*

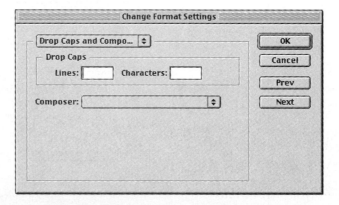

### Keep Options

Text may also be searched on the basis of its Keep Options. For example, a paragraph with Keep Attributes of All Lines in Paragraph could be searched to correct bad pagination.

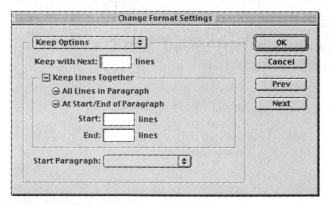

*The Format Settings windows can be accessed either through the top pop-up menu in the dialog box, or by clicking the Prev (Previous) or Next buttons.*

### Basic Character Format

With Basic Character Format, text can be searched by Font, Size, Leading, and other character attributes. For example, you might want to change all ATC Daquiri 14-pt. text to 12 pt.

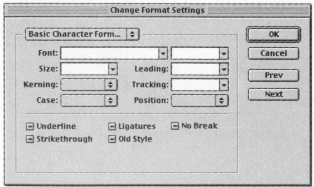

### Advanced Character Formats

If the text being searched has been modified with Scaling, Baseline Shift, Skewing, or Language, this too can be a criterion for either the search or change. For example, you might have a document that will be published in Canada and wish to change French to French: Canadian.

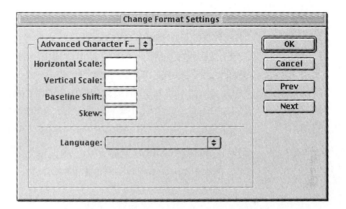

### Character Color

A character's Stroke or Fill can be a criterion for text to find or change.

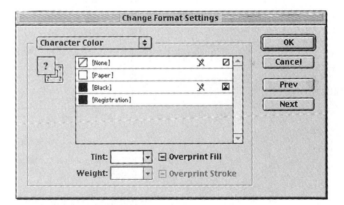

## Character Style and Paragraph Style

Searches may also be conducted based on character and paragraph styles. Choices for these searches are "Don't Care," "No Character [or Paragraph] Style," or any character style or paragraph style in the document.

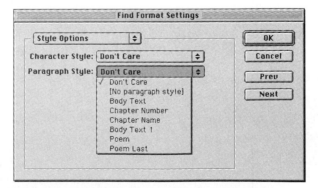

*These paragraph styles are from the Working with Styles.INDD document.*

Find/Change Format Settings defaults to character and paragraph styles of "Don't Care." When the default is accepted, the character or paragraph style will be ignored in the search. When the "No Character [or Paragraph] Style" option is chosen, only text that has no character or paragraph style applied will be included in the search. When any character or paragraph style is selected, only text of that style will be affected by the Find/Change function.

### Once Settings Are Made

After the settings are made in the Find Style Settings and Change Style Settings windows, the Find/Change dialog box will show these changes in the appropriate box. The Clear button will delete all the settings. If only the style settings and no particular word are to be changed, leave the Find What and Change To boxes empty. The search defaults to all words. Then click Find Next and make changes as usual.

The caution symbols above the Find What and Change to boxes alert you that a search will take place based solely or partially on style parameters.

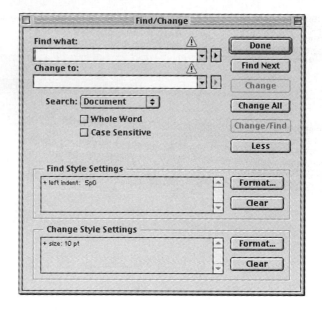

*Don't confuse the End of Paragraph marker (an invisible character accessed by typing "^p") with the visible Paragraph Symbol (¶, accessed by typing "^7").*

*Similarly, the Section marker (an invisible character defining an InDesign section, and accessed by typing "^x") should not be confused with the visible Section Symbol (§, accessed by typing "^6").*

## Special Characters

Not all searches must look for words. Other aspects of a block of text have definite attributes that can be looked for, such as the End of Paragraph marker, which is "^p". The Find What and Change To fly-out menu will place in the input fields the correct special characters for a variety of text characters and attributes.

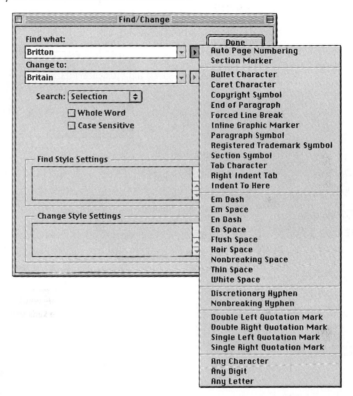

Be very careful when searching for the *wildcard characters* "Any Character," "Any Digit," and "Any Letter." They may be entered in the Find What dialog box, but are not available from the menu for the Change To dialog box. If you manually enter one of the search elements (^?, ^9, or ^$ respectively), InDesign will treat those symbols as text, and perform a literal replacement.

### Change Text Styles

1. Open the document **Formatted Text.INDD** in the **SF-Intro InDesign** folder. This document contains several recipes that must fit on a single page. The text was not formatted correctly, and global changes must be made to fit the text.

2. There are a number of extraneous empty paragraphs (two hard returns) entered to space out the document. We'll get rid of those first. Click the Type tool before the word "Recipes" so that it will be at the beginning of the story. From the Edit menu, select Find/Change. Remove the words remaining in the Find/Change dialog box from the last exercise. In the Find/Change dialog box, select End of Paragraph from the Find What fly-out menu to insert the "^p" special character into this field. Go back to the fly-out menu and select this option again to search for two end-of-paragraph markers (^p^p).

Click the cursor in the Change field to make its fly-out menu available. Select the End of Paragraph option only once in order to create a single end-of-paragraph marker. Make sure the Search option is set for Story. Click Change All. Click OK at the Search Is Completed notice.

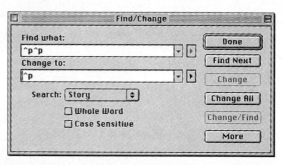

*When InDesign performs a Find/Change, it looks for the entire group as typed, then looks for the next match. So, when looking for ¶¶, there may be three paragraphs in a row. InDesign finds the pair of returns it is looking for…*

*¶*

*¶*

*¶*

*and deletes one.*

*¶*

*¶*

*It then looks for the next pair of returns.*

*When the Find/Change is executed again, it sees the two returns and again deletes one of them.*

3. Not all changes were made. To make sure that all returns are changed, press Command/Control-F to activate the Find/Change menu, and click Change All again. Click OK at the Search Is Completed notice. Check the document to be sure there are no extra spaces between lines.

4. From the Type menu, select Show Hidden Characters. You'll notice that even the listings of ingredients end with End of Paragraph markers (*hard returns*). We want to change these to *soft returns*, also known as "Forced Line Breaks."

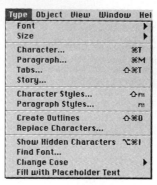

5. With the Type tool, select the first four lines of the ingredients for Orange-glazed Bananas Foster. Be sure your selection includes the ¶ markers.

6. In Find/Change, set Find What as "^p" and Change To as "^n" (the symbol for the Forced Line Break). Set the search for Selection. Click Change All. Click OK at the Search Is Completed notice.

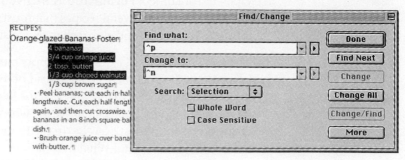

*Double-click any style to bring up the Style Options menu.*

7.  Repeat for the ingredients of Keylime Pie, Chocolate-Orange Pudding, Florida Orange Bread, and Orange Sunshine Cookies. Save to your **Work In Progress** folder.

    Now let's make some modifications to the text itself.

8.  The recipe titles are set in 14-pt. type, and they are the only elements using that type size. Select Edit>Find/Change and click on the More button.

9.  Delete the information in the Find What and Change To dialog boxes.

10. Click the Format button in the Find Style Settings section, and, in the Find Format Settings window, click the drop-down Style Options menu. Select Basic Character Formats. Set the Size at 14 pt. Click OK.

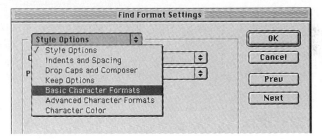

*What does the Check Spelling function look for? It looks for three things: words that do not match its dictionary, duplicate words together, and possible capitalization errors.*

11. Click the Format button of the Change Style Settings section, and, from the Paragraph Style drop-down menu, select Recipe Title. Click OK.

12. Position the Type tool at the beginning of the document and click Change All. Click OK at the Search is completed notice. Go to page 1 to see the changes.

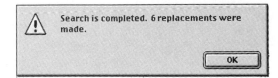

*Spell checkers, while useful, are not flawless and should not be relied upon absolutely.*

13. Next, we want to search the ingredients list. This was set with an indent of 5p0, a searchable parameter. In the Find/Change dialog box, click on the Clear buttons for both Find Style Settings and Change Style Settings to clean out the information you entered in your last search.

14. Again click the Format button in the Find Style Settings window, and, from the Style Options drop-down menu, select Indents and Spacing. Type "5p0" in the Left Indent field to search for text with that indent. Click OK.

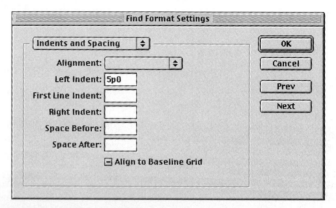

15. Click on the Format button for the Change Style Settings section. In the Change Format Settings window, select the style Ingredients from the Paragraph Style drop-down menu. Click OK.

16. In the Find/Change window click Change All. Click OK when informed that the search is complete.

17. The body text could be set to fill the margins. Access the Find/Change dialog box (Command/Control-F) and click the Clear buttons for both the Find and Change Style Settings sections.

18. Click on the Format button for Find Style Settings. Select Basic Character Formats from the drop-down menu. Since body text is the only text still set in 12 pt., this is a good search parameter. In the Size field, choose 12 pt. from the menu. Click OK.

19. Click on the Format button for Change Style Settings. From the Paragraph Style drop-down menu, select Body Text. Click OK.

20. Position the Type tool at the beginning of the document, and click Change All. Click OK when the search is completed. Save the file.

21. With the Type tool, highlight the word "Recipes" at the top of the page. Change the font to ATC Margarita Bold 24 pt. in the Character palette. In the Paragraph palette, make its alignment centered, with no Space Before and 16 pt. Space After.

22. Save the document to your **Work in Progress** folder and leave it open for the next exercise.

## Fine-tune the Document

1. Continue in the open document. The Chocolate-Orange Pudding recipe should remain together as a unit. Let's first modify the style sheets to make this happen automatically. Deselect by clicking outside the text frame.

2. Click the Ingredients paragraph style and select Style Options from the Options menu.

3. From the drop-down menu under the style name, select Keep Options. Keep all lines in the paragraph together. Click OK.

4. Now select the Recipe Title style>Style Options>Keep Options. Type "1" in the Keep with Next box. Click OK.

5. Now we have some space to fill in. With the Selection tool, click on the picture of a pie in the upper left of the pasteboard and cut it.

6. Click the Type tool at the end of the Keylime Pie heading. Press Return/Enter. In the Character menu, change the leading of the empty paragraph to 75 pt.

7. Paste the picture into the text frame. The text will flow to make room for the pie.

8. Turn off Show Hidden Characters in the Type menu. In the View menu, select Hide Guides and Hide Frame Edges. You will now see the page correctly formatted with the help of Find/Change's Style windows.

9. Save the document to your **Work in Progress** folder, and keep it open for the next exercise.

## Check Spelling

We all make mistakes, and giving text that is going to press a last-minute spell check can save a lot of embarrassment. The InDesign Check Spelling dialog box has features that can give you much control over finding and changing words, as well as the ability to add your own words to the dictionary.

**Not in Dictionary.** This field shows the word which the spell checker questions.

**Change To.** When a word is selected in the Suggested Corrections box, it appears as the preferred choice for replacing the highlighted word.

**Suggested Corrections.** These are words from the dictionary that the program suggests as possible replacements for the questioned word.

**Ignore.** When Ignore is clicked, the spell checker makes no change and moves on to select the next word it questions.

**Change.** When clicked, Change replaces the questionable word with the Change To word.

**Ignore All.** This button tells the spell checker to ignore all future instances of the high-lighted word.

**Change All.** This button changes all instances of the highlighted words to the replacement words in the Change To field.

**Search.** This pop-up menu allows you to choose the range of text to be spell checked.

## Edit Dictionary

Most dictionaries contain basic words in the chosen language. There are, however, many other words that are specific to a particular profession or discipline, even falling into the realm of slang or jargon. If the spell checker continuously finds words the writer uses frequently, it's best to add these words to the dictionary.

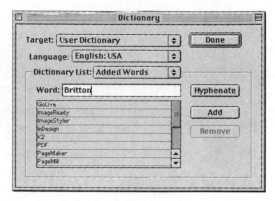

**Target Dictionary.** This menu allows you to place or remove the word from a specific dictionary.

**Language.** This menu provides an extensive list of language options for the dictionary. These options can be particularly helpful in matching the Check Spelling to the language of the text, or to handle selected foreign words incorporated into the text. Note that there are even options for some specialized professional fields — US Legal and US Medical.

**Dictionary List.** This menu allows you to view words that have been added or removed from the dictionary.

**Word.** The word that appears or is typed here will be added to the dictionary.

**Hyphenate.** When the Hyphenate option is clicked, the word in the Word field will be separated to show where hyphens will appear, should the word come at the end of word-wrapped text and require hyphenation.

**Add.** The word appearing in the Word field will be added to the dictionary.

**Remove.** Words clicked on in the dictionary list (below the Word field) will be deleted from the dictionary if Remove is then clicked.

### Check the Spelling

1. Continue in the open document. Deselect all text or text frames that may be selected. Go to Edit>Check Spelling.

2. Click the Start button to begin. If, by some chance, the button says Ignore, press it. Either button will start the Check Spelling search.

3. The first word to be questioned is "tbsp", the abbreviation for tablespoon. Recipes use this quite frequently, so there will probably be more in the document. Click Ignore All to keep the checker from questioning this again.

4. The next word questioned is "butter." The checker offers a capitalized replacement. Why? Because if you look at the top of the dialog box, you will see the words "Capitalization Error." It sees the abbreviated word prior to "butter" ends with a period. The checker thinks this is the end of a sentence, and that "butter" should start a new sentence with a capital letter. Press Ignore.

5. The next word is "choped." This is a misspelled word. The suggested replacement "chopped" appears in the dictionary list. Click on this word and press Change.

6. The checker moves on and finds "8-inch". Click Ignore.

7. "KEYLIME" is the next word to question. The replacement in the dictionary list breaks the two words up "KEY LIME." Select this and press Change. The lower case version of the same word will be questioned next. Replace with "key lime".

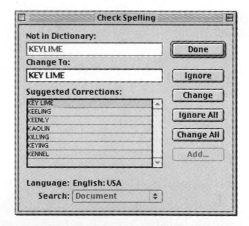

8. Next, the word "tsp" is questioned. This is the abbreviation for teaspoon and is used in recipes. Click Ignore All, in case there are further examples of this.

9. The next word to appear is "cream." The checker thinks this should be capitalized because it follows a period. It does not need a capital letter, so click Ignore. It also questions "9-inch." Ignore this as well.

10. Next up is the "9-in," which is almost correct. In the Change To input field, add "ch" to the word inch, then click Change. Even though this is correct, the checker still questions it as "9-inch." Click Ignore to move on.

11. The next word to appear is "orange." The checker thinks this should be capitalized because it follows a period. Click Ignore.

12. Now the checker has caught something you might have skimmed over were you proofing by sight. Have you ever noticed how similar a lower case letter "l" and the number "1" appear?

13. In the Change To input field, change the letter "l" to the number 1. Click Change.

14. The next words are questioned for Capitalization Error — baking, salt, cinnamon, and baking again. Press Ignore for these.

15. The next questioned word, "cinnaminn," is a misspelled word. There is a correct version in the dictionary list. Select "cinnamon" in this list and click Change.

16. The word "ungreased" is correct, even though the checker does not find it in its dictionary. If further recipes were to be spell checked, this would be a constant word that the checker would question. So, let's add it to the dictionary. Click Add in the dialog box. It will change to the Dictionary dialog box. Click Hyphenate in case the word needs to be hyphenated at any time. Click Add, then Done.

17. You will be back to the Check Spelling dialog box. Click Ignore to move on.

18. You will find yourself back at the beginning of the text. The Check Spelling session is finished. Click Done to close the dialog box.

19. Now, let's prove to ourselves that a proofreader is also required.

20. The third ingredient in the Key Lime Pie recipe is "1 /3" which has an extra space. It should be "1/3". Remove the extra space.

21. The second bulleted item of Key Lime Pie includes the word "tarter." While that is a word, we want to use "cream of tartar". Make this change to "tartar."

22. Florida Orange Bread's first item is listed as "smell oranges." We'd probably prefer to use "small oranges". Make this change also.

23. Save the changes and close the document.

## Summary

In this chapter you used InDesign's powerful text tools to automate the editing process. You learned to find and change text elements based on a variety of criteria. You became acquainted with the dictionaries and with the power of InDesign's spell checker. You also became aware of some of the deficiencies of spell checking programs in general.

*Complete Project C: Vacation Brochure*

**Notes:**

# Printing & Packaging

## CHAPTER OBJECTIVE:

To learn to prepare the document properly and collect all required elements before sending to the appropriate service provider. To learn to use and understand printer's marks, to set up and print a color document on a color or black and white desktop printer, and to manage printing oversized documents for proofing purposes. In Chapter 10, you will:

- Understand how to set up the proper driver and print settings for your printer.

- Learn how to proof a color document, whether printing on a color or black-and-white printer, and what type of printout to send to the service provider.

- Become familiar with how to work with oversized documents by tiling and scaling.

- Understand the purpose of different printer's marks and how to set them in InDesign.

- Explore the many options available through the Print dialog box, and how to set them appropriately for the document and use desired.

- Learn how to package documents for graphic arts service providers.

## PROJECTS TO BE COMPLETED:

- Around the World Ad (A)
- Baggy's Kid's Menu (B)
- Vacation Brochure (C)
- **Good Choices Newsletter (D)**

# Printing and Packaging

During composition and, of course, when the document is finished, it will need to be printed. Even pages designed for Web viewing are printed to desktop printers occasionally so that the data and images may be proofed, reviewed at a meeting, or referenced. InDesign utilizes several technologies and features which allow you to create just about any page design you can imagine. In the case of printing, some of those capabilities are handled by the operating system, and you'll need to install or enable them in order to print the document successfully. An InDesign document also uses graphic files, fonts, and page settings that must be checked before printing. If your document is larger than the paper size in your printer, or if you want to proof specifications for commercial printing such as bleed, trim, and color, some of those settings can be changed to get the output you need. Lastly, when you're ready to pass the file on to the Graphic Arts Service Provider, a special feature of InDesign, called "Package," can be employed to simplify the process and ensure the service provider gets all the necessary components to output your InDesign file successfully.

## Setting up to Print

When printing to a desktop printer that is connected to your computer, a few steps are required to prepare the document and the computer system. Because InDesign creates PostScript files, making the documents suitable for high-end commercial printing, you must have a PostScript printer driver installed on your computer. While older version drivers and non-PostScript drivers will output the page, some printing features and document elements, such as EPS files, will not work. In addition, the recommended PostScript drivers create a smaller, more efficient PostScript file, making the document faster to print and easier to transport.

The following drivers are recommended and included with the application. Follow the instructions they contain to install them, or check your system to ensure that these drivers are available and currently selected.

*Adobe PS 8.6 driver for Mac OS 8.5 or above*
*Adobe PS 4.3 driver for Windows 98 or above*
*Adobe PS 5.1 driver for Windows NT 4 or above*

Along with the PostScript printer driver, InDesign also requires that the appropriate PostScript printer description (PPD) file be chosen. The appropriate PPD file is the one that matches the printer you're going to use. Do this on Windows and Windows NT computers by adding a printer through the Printer Settings, or on a Macintosh computer through Printer Setup in the Chooser. Your printer should be selected as the default printer before trying to output a document from InDesign.

Once the PostScript driver and the PostScript Printer Description (PPD) are correctly selected, you're ready to prepare for the specific document.

## Macintosh Page Setup Preparations

1.  Open the document **Travel Brochure.INDD** from the **SF-Intro InDesign** folder. This is a process color brochure that will eventually be commercially printed, front and back, trimmed to 8.5-in. × 11-in., and folded into a three-panel brochure. You will first send a composite of this file to your desktop printer to proof copy, placement, and the general design of the piece.

2.  Choose File>Print.

3.  When you create a document in InDesign, you establish the page size and orientation of your document design. Page Setup allows you to position that page on the paper that comes out of your printer. From the Paper drop-down menu, choose US Letter. Click on the Landscape icon of the Orientation options. This depicts how the document will appear on that paper. The Scale should be 100%.

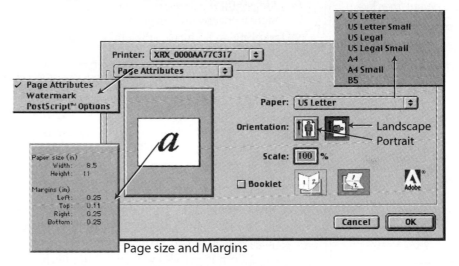

Page size and Margins

*You should ensure that graphic links are updated before selecting Print. Open the Links palette by selecting File>Links. Scroll through the palette. There should not be any symbols indicating broken or modified graphics.*

4.  The Page Attributes drop-down menu contains two other options: Watermark and PostScript Options. Select the Watermark option. The Watermarks option allows you to make universal notations, such as Confidential, Copy, and Draft on each page. You can create your own Watermarks, if you wish. None should be selected.

*Separations produce an individual page for each ink color, whether process or spot. Separations are discussed more in depth in our **InDesign: Advanced Electronic Mechanicals** course book.*

*If you are printing several copies of a multipage document, you might want to check Collate to have the printer output the pages in order, rather than five copies of page 1, then five copies of page 2, and so on. Be aware, though, that this method of printing is slower.*

*If you are printing a final copy of the document to special textured paper or cover stock, select Manual for the Paper Source and hand-feed the paper as your printer manual recommends.*

5. Go to the PostScript Options dialog box and be certain that nothing is selected. Click OK.

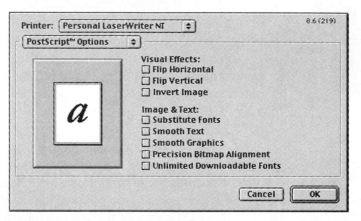

6. The computer is ready to print the document. Choose File>Print (Command-P). If there were any broken graphic links, this message would appear. You should cancel printing and return to the Links palette to update them.

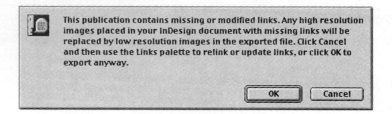

7. The Print dialog box has a drop-down menu under the Printer option. This menu offers a list of options, varying by which printer you have selected. Each option serves a specialized function. The first to appear is Advanced Page Control. The radio button beside All Pages should be selected. In the Options drop-down menu, select Both Pages. (View Section Numbering is irrelevant for this document. It is checked by default.)

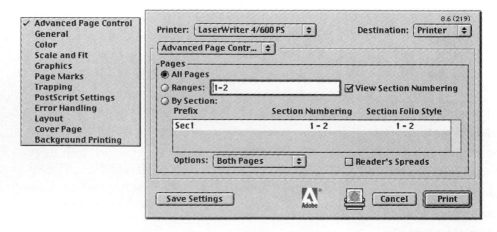

*Foreground printing is not often used unless there is a problem printing the document. The advantage of Foreground Printing is that you see messages describing what is being sent to the printer. Another advantage is that less free hard disk space is required.*

8. From the drop-down menu below the printer name, select General. The number of Copies should be set to "1". The Pages option should have All selected. For Paper Source, leave Cassette selected if you have 8.5-in. × 11-in. paper in the paper tray of your printer. Otherwise, select the appropriate Upper or Lower Cassette.

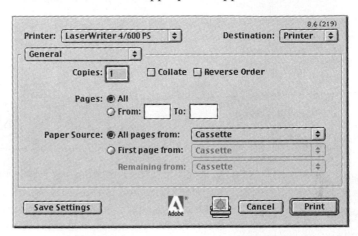

9. Select the Color option from the drop-down menu below the printer name. Select the Composite radio button. This will reproduce the color document in grayscale on a black-and-white printer. It should also be selected if printing to a color printer. The Screening drop-down menu should be set to Default. This enables the printer description file to dictate the optimum line screen value for the printer's resolution. Leave Frequency and Angle set with the numbers the Default option applied, based on the selected printer.

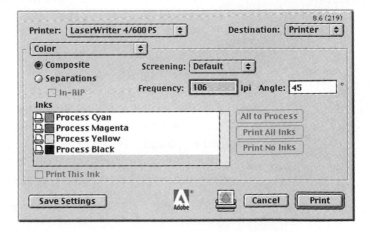

10. Select Background Printing from the drop-down menu below the printer name. Select the Foreground (No Spool File) radio button. This means that the information to print the file will be compiled and sent to the printer as a *foreground* function of the computer. You will not be able to continue working until the file is sent to the printer.

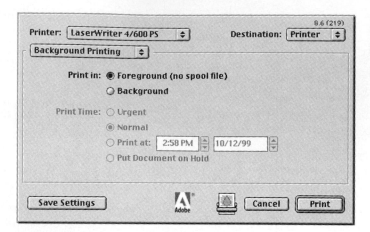

11. Click Print. Watch the message box as InDesign processes this file. It will display names of fonts and graphics files as they are being sent to the printer. These files are not included in the InDesign file and must be supplied by the computer. In a few minutes, you should see two printed pages coming out of your printer.

12. Proof the output. You will notice that the outside page of this brochure doesn't print the ink up to the edge of the paper as the file shows in the document. The ink stops printing about 1/4″ from the edge of the sheet. This is because laser and color printers cannot let the toner or ink print to the edge of the paper or it will inadvertently bleed onto the other side of the page and smear. The part that does print represents the imageable area of your printer.

13. Save the document to your **Work in Progress** folder. Leave it open for the next exercise.

## *Windows Page Setup Preparations*

1. Open the document **Travel Brochure.INDD** from the **SF-Intro InDesign** folder. This is a process color brochure that will eventually be commercially printed, front and back, trimmed to 8.5 in. × 11 in., and folded into a three-panel brochure. You will first send a composite of this file to your desktop printer to proof copy, placement, and the general design of the piece.

2. Choose File>Print (Control-P). If there were any broken graphic links, this message would appear. You should cancel printing and return to the Links palette to update them.

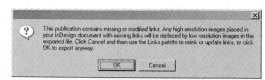

3. Click the Properties box. The Paper option is preselected.

*You should always be certain that graphic links are updated before selecting Print. Open the Links palette by selecting File>Links. Scroll through the palette. There should not be any symbols indicating broken or modified graphics.*

*If your default printer driver is not AdobePS 4.3 or later (which ships with InDesign), you will get the message: "Install and use AdobePS 4.3 or later PostScript driver for best results."*

*If you are printing several copies of a multipage document, you might want to check Collate to have the printer output the pages in order, rather than five copies of page 1, then five copies of page 2, and so on. Be aware, though, that this method of printing is slower.*

*If you are printing a final copy of the document to special textured paper or cover stock, select Manual for the Paper Source and hand-feed the paper as your printer manual recommends.*

4. When you create a document in InDesign, you establish the page size and orientation of your document design. Properties allows you to position that page on the paper that comes out of your printer. Choose the Paper size you'll be printing on, in this case US Letter. Click the page Orientation (Portrait or Landscape) — for this document, select Landscape.

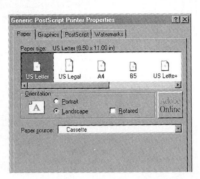

5. Select the Graphics option. Here you select the print properties for the document: Resolution, Negative, and Mirroring (used by service providers when creating film positives and negatives), Paper Handling, and Scaling. We're only interested in Scaling, which should be set to 100%. Make no other changes.

6. There are two other options: PostScript and Watermark. The PostScript Output Format menu allows the choice of PostScript (Optimize for Speed), which will most often be used when proofing. The other choices are PostScript (Optimize for Portability) ADSC, Encapsulated PostScript (EPS), and Archive format. Leave it set at default, PostScript (Optimize for Speed). The Watermarks option allows you to make universal notations, such as Confidential, Copy, and Draft on each page. You can create your own Watermarks, if you wish. None should be selected. Click OK. This returns you to the main Print menu. You are now ready to print the document.

7. Select the number of copies. Leave the number at the default of 1.

8. The balance of the Print dialog box consists of six options, each serving a specialized function. The first is Advanced Page Control. The radio button beside All Pages should be selected. In the Options drop-down menu, select Both Pages. (View Section Numbering is irrelevant to this document. It is checked by default.)

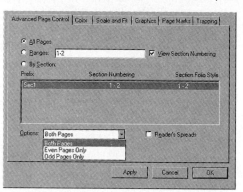

9. Select the Color option. Select the Composite radio button. This will reproduce the color document in grayscale on a black-and-white printer. It should also be selected if printing to a color printer. The Screening drop-down menu should be set to Default. This enables the printer description file to dictate the optimum line screen value for the printer's resolution. Leave Frequency and Angle set with the numbers the Default option applied, based on the selected printer.

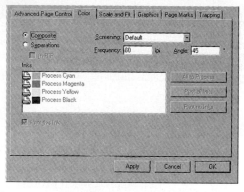

11. Click OK. Watch the message box as InDesign processes this file. It will display names of fonts and graphics files as they are being sent to the printer. These files are not included in the InDesign file and must be supplied by the computer. In a few minutes, you should see two pages emerging from your printer.

12. Proof the output. You will notice that the outside page of this brochure doesn't print the ink up to the edge of the paper as the file shows in the document. The ink stops printing about 1/4″ from the edge of the sheet. This is because laser and color printers cannot let the toner or ink print to the edge of the paper or it will inadvertently bleed onto the other side of the page and smear. The part that does print represents the imageable area of your printer.

13. Save the document to your **Work in Progress** folder and leave it open for the next exercise.

*Separations produce a page for each ink color, process or spot. Separations are discussed in our **InDesign: Advanced Electronic Mechanicals** course book.*

## Printing Oversized Documents

If you have a printer that prints 11 in. × 17 in. , you can print letter-size documents that have bleeds and trim them back to the edge of the 8.5 in. × 11 in. size, retaining the true bleed. At some point, however, you will need to print an oversized document to a printer that cannot handle this paper size. There are two options to help you, depending on what qualities you need to proof: tiling and scaling.

### Tiling

*Tiling* prints an oversized document by cropping blocks of the document page and printing the sections onto several sheets of paper. Once printed, you will have a full size-proof that can be cut out of the different sheets, assembled, and taped together.

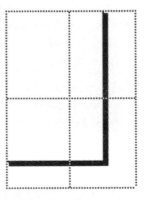

*Documents too large to fit on one page are tiled — split into overlapping sections — so they may be pieced together.*

### Scaling

Scaling offers a different approach, when proofing at exact size is not a critical factor. The Scaling option of the Print dialog box reduces the document, allowing more of the image to print on the sheet. Elements in the document are proportionally sized, but are not true to the finished size. For proofing purposes, this is sufficient.

## Printer's Marks

One of the key factors used in proofing is printer's marks, such as trim, bleed, and registration. Printer's marks can also include file and color information, which is printed outside the margin of the document to identify what was printed on the page and when. InDesign can automatically print five kinds of printer's marks to ensure that the commercial printer has the proper instructions to reproduce your document.

**Crop Marks.** These short lines outside the image area indicate where to trim or cut the sheet to its final size.

**Bleed Marks.** These short perpendicular lines indicate the edge of the image area including ink that prints beyond the final size trim or crop.

**Registration Marks.** These marks are small concentric circles intersected by a cross hair. These fine lines are used to align color separations precisely, ensuring that elements printed in different inks fit and appear as you designed them. These marks can also be used to overlay different versions on the same base design (e.g., different names printed in the exact same position alongside the art and address of a preprinted, generic business card).

## Apply the Final Touches

1. The last phase of this menu design is to add decorative graphic accents that give a special touch to the appearance of the page. These are wavy lines or squiggles that conform to the casual, childlike, scribbled design look.

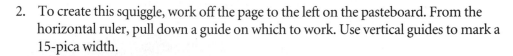

2. To create this squiggle, work off the page to the left on the pasteboard. From the horizontal ruler, pull down a guide on which to work. Use vertical guides to mark a 15-pica width.

3. Select the Pen tool and click the pen tip at the intersection of the horizontal and left vertical guide, and drag upward to start a Smooth Point. Release the mouse button. Move the Pen tool slightly to the right and click on the guide, dragging slightly upward again while holding the Shift key to constrain the angle to 45°. Release the mouse button. Continue this process of creating smooth points along the guide. The result will be a wavy line. Use the Direct Selection tool to fine-tune the curves so that they look almost uniform.

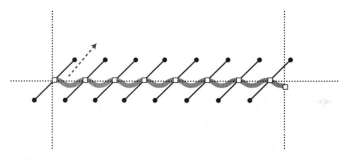

4. Choose Window>Stroke. Set a 2.5-pt. Weight to this squiggle line, adding Rounded Caps. Paint the Stroke with the Squiggle color you created, and a Fill of None.

5. Move the squiggle underneath the "Mom, I'm Not Very Hungry" headline. If necessary, manually resize the squiggle to fit between the headline and the "Little Nipper" food name.

6. Duplicate this squiggle and move the copy under the "Silly Side Orders" heading. All of the headings should have a squiggle to underline them, so copy and fit the squiggles now.

7. When the squiggles are all in place, Presto! the menu is complete and should look like this.

8. Save your changes and close the document.

# Project C: Vacation Brochure

A travel agency may feature many vacation packages, but more important than those packages is the necessity of convincing customers to use that agency rather than booking vacations for themselves. This brochure will require that you use most of the skills you have learned as you create the standard marketing piece, the six-panel brochure.

### *Set Up the Brochure Format*

1. Create a new document by selecting File>New. Set the Number of Pages to 2, and uncheck Facing Pages and Master Text Frame. Set the Page Size to Letter and the Orientation to Landscape. Set the Top and Bottom Margin to 18 pt., and the Left and Right margins to 1p6. Set the Columns to 1. Click OK.

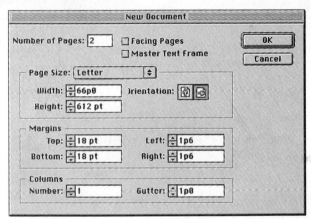

2. We're going to adjust the Guides for the fold marks. These can be tricky, and require exact specifications. Simply creating three columns would not work, because automatic folders require that the panel folding inward be shorter than the two outside panels.

3. From Edit>Preferences>Units and Increments, set the Horizontal Ruler Units to Picas, and the Vertical Ruler Units to Points, if you have not previously set these as your default.

4. Place two vertical guides on the first page, at 22p1 and 44p2. This will be the inside sheet. If necessary, adjust their position using the Transform palette.

5. Double-click on page 2 in the Pages palette. Place vertical guides at 21p9 and at 43p10. This will be the outside sheet, including the front and back cover.

6. From the left ruler, drag the guides for your live copy areas 1p6 to either side of the fold marks. They should be positioned as follows — page 1: 20p7, 23p7, 42p7, 45p7; page 2: 20p3, 23p3, 42p4, 45p4. This is most easily accomplished using the Transform palette.

7. Choose View>Lock Guides, so you won't accidentally move them.

8. Save your file as "ATWV_Brochure.INDD" in your **Work in Progress** folder.

*Items in dialog boxes which are not mentioned in the instructions should be left at the default settings.*

## Establish the Color Scheme

Our brochure will use process color. All colors we specify will have a Color Type of Process and a Color Mode of CMYK.

1. If you wish, select the six standard colors in the Swatches palette and delete them. This will result in a smaller palette. From the Swatches palette, select New Color Swatch.

2. Name the swatch "Dark Green". Set the specifications to C: 100, M: 0, Y: 75, K: 50.

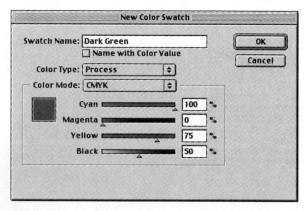

*It might seem easy to simply create three equal columns, but this doesn't work with the folding equipment used to mechanically fold brochures. The "tuck in" panel must be about 1/16" shorter than the other pages.*

3. Click OK to save this color.

    We will set up two additional colors, "Dark Blue," and "Light Blue".

4. Set up Dark Blue as C: 100, M: 75, Y: 0, K: 25.

5. Set up Light Blue as C: 85, M: 35, Y: 0, K: 0.

6. Save the document to preserve your changes.

## Set up the Text Styles

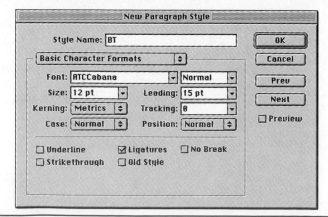

1. From the Paragraph Styles menu, select New Style.

2. The first style we're going to create is for body text. Name it "BT".

3. From the General drop-down menu, select the Basic Character Formats. Set the Font to ATC Cabana Normal, the Size to 12 pt., and the Leading to 15 pt.

4. Select Indents and Spacing from the drop-down menu under the style name, and make the Alignment Left and the First Line Indent 1p0.

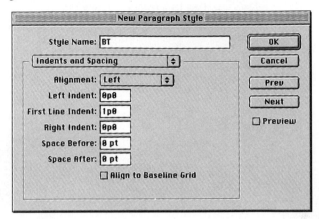

5. Click OK to save the style.

6. Create a new style. Name it "BT1". It will be the style for first paragraphs following heads and subheads. Base this style on BT.

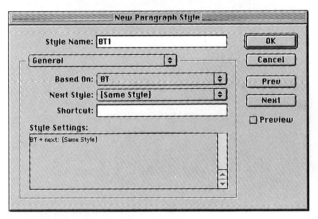

7. Choose Indents and Spacing in the top drop-down menu. Change the First Line Indent to 0p0.

8. Click OK to save the style.

9. The next style will be a subhead style, based on No Paragraph Style. Create a new style, and name it "SH". Set the Basic Character Formats as follows:

Font: ATC Mai Tai Bold
Size: 12 pt. on 15 pt. Leading
Alignment: Left, with all indents at zero
Space Before: 10 pt., and Space After: 5 pt.
Character Color: Fill of Dark Green, and a Stroke of None
Options: Keep with Next 1 Line, and Keep All Lines in Paragraph together

10. Click OK to save this style.

11. Create another new style. Name it "LB" and base it on the BT1 style. This is a bulleted list (List, Bulleted) style. In Indents and Spacing, set the Left Indent to 3p0 and the first line to –0p9. Click OK.

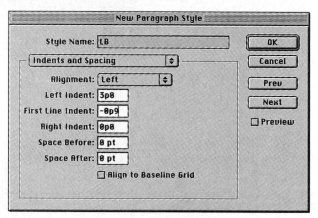

12. Select LB and create a new style based on it. Name this style "LB1", the first item of a bulleted list. In Indents and Spacing, specify 7.5 pt. Space Before the paragraphs. Click OK to save.

13. Create another style based on LB. Call this one "LB2". It will be for the last item of a bulleted list. Specify 7.5 pt. Space After the paragraphs. Save the style.

14. Create a new style based on BT1. Name it "Bio". In Indents and Spacing, specify 7.5 pts. after the paragraphs. Save this style.

15. Save the document.

### Apply Styles

1. Be sure you are on page 1. Create three rectangular text frames with the following specifications:

| X: | 1p6 | W: | 19p1 |
|----|-----|----|------|
| Y: | 18 pt | H: | 576 pt |

| X: | 23p7 | W: | 19p1 |
|----|------|----|------|
| Y: | 18 pt | H: | 576 pt |

| X: | 45p7 | W: | 18p11 |
|----|------|----|-------|
| Y: | 18 pt | H: | 576 pt |

2. Select View>Show Text Threads.

3. With the Selection Tool, click in the first frame to activate it, then click on the exit port at the lower right. Click in the middle frame to link the two.

4. Repeat, linking the middle frame with the right frame. Select View>Hide Text Threads to hide the visual threading.

5. Select File>Place (Command/Control-D) and place the file **ATWU_Brochure Text.RTF** from your **SF-Intro InDesign** folder.

*Text frames may be created by dragging the Type tool or by using the Rectangle Frame tool, then selecting Object>Content>Text.*

6.  With the Selection tool, click on the red overflow icon at the lower right of the text frame. The tool tip will turn into a loaded text icon.

7.  Place the Text tool in the first paragraph and select BT1 style from the Paragraph Styles palette.

8.  Select the second paragraph and define it as BT.

9.  Choose the third paragraph, "Meet Our Travel Specialists," and define it as SH.

10. Select the next paragraphs, down to the "How Can We Serve You?" subhead, and choose Bio as the style.

11. Choose the next paragraph, "How Can We Serve You?" and define the style as SH.

12. The next paragraph is BT1.

    Note that the text has automatically flowed into the third frame.

13. Bulleted List text begins with the next paragraph. Click at the beginning of the line containing the "Guided Tours" text and insert a bullet. Press Option/Alt-8.

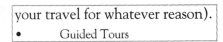

your travel for whatever reason).
•        Guided Tours

    Type a bullet in front of the remaining lines of bulleted text.

14. Place the cursor in the Guided Tours line. Define its style as LB1.

15. Select the text "The British Isles" through "Cruises" and define them as LB.

16. Select "Theatre and On the Town" and define it as LB2.

17. Select the last paragraph and define it a BT1.

18. Return to the first paragraph and select it. We're going to add a drop cap. From the Paragraph palette, assign the number of lines as 4 and the number of characters as 1.

19. Place the cursor between the "W" and the "h" of the first word, and force a line break (Shift-Return/Enter).

20. Highlight the "W" and define it as ATC Daquiri Plain (Macintosh) or ATC Daquiri Regular (Windows), with a color of Dark Blue.

> **W**hether your next vacation is designed to take you around the world in eighty days (more or less), or you're constrained to a long weekend closer to home, we're the people who can make your vacation fun, exciting, romantic, or relaxing

21. Highlight the entire paragraph (except the drop cap) and assign it a tracking value of "2", to remove the bad break in the last line.

22. Save the file and leave it open for the next exercise.

## Place the Images in Frames

1. Open the document **ATWV_Brochure.INDD** from your **Work in Progress** folder, if it is not already open.

   Under the subhead "Meet Our Travel Specialists" is a paragraph about each person. We're going to place the faces beside the names, so clients can identify with the people who are booking their travel arrangements.

2. Using the Rectangle Frame tool, create the first picture frame with the following specifications:

   | | | | |
   |---|---|---|---|
   | X: | 1p6 | W: | 6p0 |
   | Y: | 320 pt | H: | 102 pt |

3. Select Object>Text Wrap. Choose the second button, Wrap Around Bounding Box. Set the Bottom Offset to 9 pt. and the Right Offset to 0p9. You will use these margin settings for all the Bio pictures.

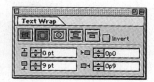

4. Select File>Place (Command/Control-D) to place the picture **Judy.TIF** from your **SF-Intro InDesign** folder.

5. Track the text of the paragraph next to Judy's picture at –2.

6. Set the picture frame for Max as follows:

   | | | | |
   |---|---|---|---|
   | X: | 1p6 | W: | 8p6 |
   | Y: | 480 pt | H: | 86 pt |

7. Set the Bottom and Right offsets for text wrap as before.

8. Place the picture **Max.TIF** from your **SF-Intro InDesign** folder.

9. Set Laurie's picture frame as follows:

   | | | | |
   |---|---|---|---|
   | X: | 23p7 | W: | 5p8 |
   | Y: | 148 pt | H: | 94 pt |

10. Place the picture **Laurie.TIF** from your **SF-Intro InDesign** folder. Set the offsets for the text wrap as before.

11. Track the text of the paragraph next to Laurie's picture at –3.

12. Set John's picture frame as follows:

    | | | | |
    |---|---|---|---|
    | X: | 23p7 | W: | 5p8 |
    | Y: | 351 pt | H: | 92 pt |

13. Place the picture **John.TIF** from your **SF-Intro InDesign** folder. Set the offsets for the text wrap as before.

14. Glen's picture obviously will not fit in the remaining space. Place the Type tool immediately before the paragraph and press Shift-Enter (on the numeric keypad) to move the blurb about Glen to the top of the next column.

15. Set Glen's picture frame as follows:

    X: 45p7      W:   4p9
    Y: 18 pt      H:   81 pt

16. Place the picture **Glen.TIF** from your **SF-Intro InDesign** folder. Set the offsets for the text wrap as before.

17. Draw another rectangular frame as follows:

    X: 45p7      W:   18p11
    Y: 378 pt    H:   180 pt

18. Place the picture **Your Vacation.TIF** from your **SF-Intro InDesign** folder. Apply text wrap with no offsets.

19. We're going to insert a mini-ad.

20. Create a text frame with the following specifications:

    X: 23p7      W:   19p1
    Y: 546 pt    H:   48 pt

21. Make the Fill color of the text box Dark Blue.

22. Type the following, line for line:

    "For your next vacation, call
    414/555-ATWV"

23. Set the first line of text to ATC Mai Tai Bold, 10/18, and the second line ATC Mai Tai Bold, 18/18. Color the text Light Blue.

24. Center the text horizontally.

25. From Text Frame Options, select Vertical Justification Align: Center.

*Press Command/Control-B to quickly access Text Frame Options.*

26. Congratulations! You're more than halfway done. One side of the brochure down, and one side to go. Save the file and leave it open to continue.

 hether your next vacation is designed to take you around the world in eighty days (more or less), or you're constrained to a long weekend closer to home, we're the people who can make your vacation fun, exciting, romantic, or relaxing — in other words, the kind of vacation you're looking to have. Located in "vacation central" — Florida's sunny Gulf coast, we're familiar with what people want from their vacations, and, with two decades behind us, we have the experience to help you maximize your vacation.

We'll work with your desires (and your budget) to help you get the most from a guided vacation, a cruise, an "on your own" experience, or a combination of any of these.

**Meet Our Travel Specialists**

Judy, believe it or not, is our resident ski bum. Last winter she was the guide for six (count 'em) trips to the American Rockies and Sierras. This summer where else would she be but taking ski tours "down under" to the Chilean Andes and to New Zealand. Seems like all she knows how to do is take fun to the max!

 And speaking of Max — she's a typical Floridian. Hates winter. (That's because she moved here from North Dakota about eight years ago.) Since she's been here she's been comfortable showing up at work in shorts and a polo shirt — except when she's having fun with our customers diving off the Keys, or sailing the Caribbean. Max is a registered dive instructor and holds her pilot's license for sailing craft. She also knows when the big fish are running for those of you who really enjoy big game fishing.

 What can we tell you about Laurie, except that she's a Celtophile. Her specialty is trips to Ireland, Scotland, England, Wales, Australia and New Zealand. Whether it's helping folks get the most from their trip to "the Homeland" or accompanying them on cycling and hiking trips through the beautiful mountains, trying to spy Nessie, exploring the towns, or watching the changing of the guard at Buckingham Palace, she's right at home in the British Isles and Down Under.

 John is our computer geek. He keeps track of all the best airfares and cruise line fares, so we can pass them along to you. Like everybody else, he has a "life." In addition to living online, he's our resident expert on Florida theme parks — and has extended that expertise to cover other parks, like Colonial Williamsburg. Since we're so close, he's been known to take a mid-week theme park break, just to see what's new and exciting that he can share with you.

For your next vacation, call
414/555-ATWV

 Glen is the person we all rely on to keep us together. He's the manager of the mailing list, keeper of the schedule — and all 'round expert on night life, concerts, and theatre. If you're planning an evening On the Town (New York, Chicago, San Francisco, Rome, or wherever) Glen will help you find the kind of fun you seek.

**How Can We Serve You?**

By now, you have a pretty good idea of what we can do for you. We specialize in vacation travel (but, of course, we'll be happy to book your travel for whatever reason).

- Guided Tours
- The British Isles
- Trips "Down Under"
- Dive Trips and Tours
- Sailing Trips
- Cruises
- Theatre and On the Town

Call us and see for yourself just how much fun you can have!

## The Special Offer Panel

We want to give our customers something special to look for over the next few months. This Special Events panel requires some new styles, and we'll make it stand out with color, as well.

1. With the publication ATW_Brochure.INDD open, go to page 2 by clicking on the page-2 icon.

2. We want this panel to stand out against the other panels in the document, so we're going to make it a shade of blue. Using the Rectangle tool, draw a rectangle with the following specifications:

X: –0p9      W:   22p6
Y: –9 pt     H:   630 pt

This extends the panel beyond the page parameters, bleeding the color off the page so we will have no problems with trim.

3. With the Fill icon active, click on the color Light Blue. From the Swatch menu, select New Tint Swatch. Set the Tint to 50% and click OK. You have now created a 50% tint of Light Blue and applied it to the rectangle.

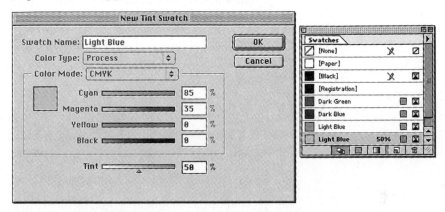

4. Assign a Stroke color of None.

5. Create a text frame with the following specifications:

   X: 1p6    W: 18p9
   Y: 18 pt   H: 576 pt

6. Control-click (Macintosh) or right-click (Windows) to access the Text Frame Options. Set the Inset Spacing to 0p6 for all sides.

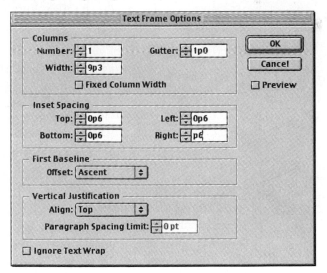

7. With the Selection tool active, set the Stroke to a Weight of 1 pt. Assign Black as the color.

8. Switch to the Text tool. From your **SF-Intro InDesign** folder, place **ATWU_Special Events.RTF**. Remove any extra spaces at the bottom of the text, to assure that you will not receive a "false" text overset warning.

   We're going to set up styles that are specific to this text.

9. Create a new paragraph style named "BTS" (Body Text Special). Set the Basic Character Format to ATC Mai Tai, Normal, 9/11 with 3 pt. Space After Paragraphs. Click OK to save the style.

10. Create a new style, based on BTS, named "BTS2". Set its specifications to ATC Mai Tai Italic, 8/9, with 5 pt. Space After.

11. Create a new style, based on BTS, name it "BTSH". Set its specifications as ATC Mai Tai Normal, 10/11, 5 pt. Space Before, and 5 pt. Space After. Set the Fill to Dark Blue.

12. Create a new style, based on SH, and name it "SH2". Set its specifications as ATC Mai Tai Bold, 14/14, All Caps, with 14 pt. Space After. Set the Alignment to Center and the Fill Color to Dark Green.

13. Select the first paragraph, "Special Events", and assign the SH2 style.

14. Select the second paragraph and assign the BTSH style. Highlight the words "Caribbean Sail and Dive" and change them from Normal to Bold.

15. Assign the BTS style to the next paragraph.

16. The following paragraph should be formatted with the BTS2 style.

17. Format the next two events the same way: the event name as the BTSH style, the description as the BTS style, and the prerequisite as the BTS2 style.

> **SPECIAL EVENTS**
> **AROUND THE WORLD**
>
> **Caribbean Sail and Dive.** April 23 – 29.
> ATW's Max Taylor leads you in this 7-day, 6-night sail and dive in the pristine waters of the West Indies. You'll sail the 51-foot sloop Ligatre, with a home port of Nassau, Bahamas. This combination sail and dive will provide a variety of experiences for all participants. We dive in the clear waters of the West Indies, and come face-to-face with a variety of flora and fauna. A Gala in Nassau ends your week of frolic on and in the water. This tour fills up fast!
> *Beginning and intermediate sailors. Dive certification requires. Call for rates and details.*

18. Deselect the frame. Save the document and leave it open for the next steps.

### Add the Mailing Panel

This brochure is designed to be a self-mailer. The back panel is designated as the mailing panel. It needs to include the return address and the First Class permit stamp.

1. Place the graphic **ATWU Logo_4C.EPS** from your **SF-Intro InDesign** folder. You may place it anywhere in the middle panel. We'll position it later.

2. Hold down Command-Option-Shift (Macintosh) or Control-Alt-Shift (Windows) and scale the graphic so the width is 9p0. The graphic will be scaled proportionally.

3. From the Transform palette, rotate the graphic 90°.

*A soft return is created by holding down the Shift key while pressing Return/Enter.*

4. With the upper-left Proxy Reference Point selected, position the logo at X: 23p6, Y: 480 pt.

5. Create a text box approximately 9p wide by 48 pt. in height. Type, line for line, with soft returns as line endings:

"Suite 100
Dockside Quay
Sarasota, FL 34231"

6. Make sure that no style was applied. Format the text as ATC Mai Tai Normal, 12/15. Set the Alignment to Center.

7. Change to the Selection tool, rotate the text frame 90°, and, with the upper-left Proxy Reference Point selected, position the frame at X: 32p9, Y: 480 pt.

8. Create another text frame 6p by 72 pt.

9. Type the following, line for line, with soft returns as line endings.

"Bulk Rate
U.S. Postage
PAID
Permit # 112
Sarasota, FL"

10. Format the text as ATC Mai Tai Normal, 10/12, with no additional Space Above or Below. Set the Alignment to Center.

11. Control-click (Macintosh) or right-click (Windows) and access the Text Frame Options. Set the Vertical Justification to Align Center. Click OK.

12. With the Selection tool active, set the Stroke to 1pt. and the color to Black.

13. Rotate the frame 90°.

14. With the upper-left Proxy Reference Point selected, position it at X: 23p3, Y: 18 pt.

15. Save your document. Just one panel to go — the easy one.

### Finish Up

1. Using the Rectangle Frame tool, create a picture frame with the following specifications:

X:  43p10    W:  22p10
Y:  −9 pt    H:  630 pt

2. Press Command/Control-D to place **ATWV_BroCover.TIF** from your **SF-Intro InDesign** folder.

   There are just a couple of things left to do. First, let's clean up the text.

3. Go back to page 1. You'll notice there is a red overset box at the lower right of the third panel. This could indicate that there's a problem. Remove the last paragraph return (after the exclamation point) and the box will vanish.

4. From Edit>Check Spelling, run a spell check on the entire story. You'll note that InDesign considers the drop cap "W" a single word, which then makes "hether" questionable. There are actually two spelling errors in the document.

5. Check your document over for bad hyphenation or for kerning in headlines that you think should be repaired.

6. Save the document to your **Work in Progress** folder. Close the document.

*Proper nouns and unique words such as "Celtophile" and "geek" do not appear in the standard dictionary.*

Creating a brochure is, as you see, demanding. However, when style sheets are used, the job is made much simpler. Using the techniques you have learned in the exercises and in this project will help you produce better-than-average publications.

# Project D: Good Choices Newsletter

Many organizations produce newsletters to keep members, clients, or employees abreast of happenings. Sometimes the newsletters are designed to serve a particular purpose, as is this one from a health care organization.

## Set Up the Document

1.  Start a new document with the following parameters:

    | | |
    |---|---|
    | No. of pages: | 2 |
    | Page Size: | Custom |
    | Facing Pages: | Uncheck |
    | Orientation: | Portrait |
    | Width: | 46p0 |
    | Height: | 54p0 |
    | Top margin: | 3p0 |
    | Left margin: | 10p0 |
    | Bottom margin: | 2p6 |
    | Right margin: | 3p0 |
    | Columns: | 4 |
    | Gutter: | 1p0 |

    Click OK.

2.  From Edit>Preferences, make the following settings:

    General Preferences palette: Leave defaults and check Overprint Black text.

    Text Preferences palette: Select Superscript Size 75% and Position 25%, Subscript Size 75% and Position 25%. Check Anti-Alias Type and Use Typographers Quotes.

    Composition Preferences palette: Accept the Multi-line Composer default of 5 lines and 5 alternatives. Select only Substituted Fonts for Highlight.

    Units and Increments: Ruler Units Origin: Page, Horizontal Picas, Vertical Inches. 1 pt. Size/Leading, and 1 pt. Baseline Shift.

    Dictionary: Choose English: USA Medical.

3.  Open these palettes —
    Tools, Swatches, Stroke, Navigator, Paragraph, Character, Color, Transform, Paragraph and Character Styles, and Pages. Your screen should look similar to the one on the next page.

*The Medical Dictionary will not be available unless it was included with a custom installation of InDesign.*

*Type any units of measure into one of the Transform palette coordinate fields to position objects or guides.*

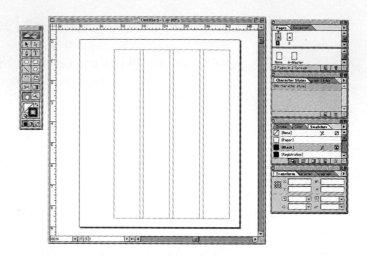

*While moving a guide, watch the Transform palette to view its position. To position the guide precisely, select the guide with the Selection tool (its color will darken) and type in the measurement.*

4. Double-click the ruler intersection to make certain that the zero point is at the upper-left corner. Double-click on the Master-Page icon in the Pages palette. Zoom into the upper-left corner of the page using the Zoom tool or Navigator palette.

5. Drag a horizontal guide from the ruler to Y: –0.125 in. Drag a vertical guide to X: – 0p9. Scroll down and drag another horizontal guide to Y: 9.125 in., (0.125 in. below the page border). These guides will edge the three-sided bleed.

6. Drag vertical guides to X: 4p6 and 9p. Release these guides outside the page border. Drag a horizontal guide to Y: 0.75 in. Drop this guide inside the page border, then select it with the Selection tool.

7. Choose Edit>Step and Repeat. Enter Repeat Count of 10, Horizontal Offset of 0p0, and Vertical Offset of 0.75 in. Click OK to complete the design grid.

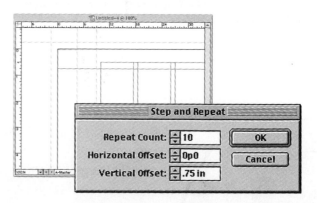

*To use the Zoom tool temporarily, hold the Command/Control key along with the Spacebar to zoom in.*
*Hold Command-Option/ Control-Alt along with the Spacebar to zoom out.*

8. Still on the Master page, select the Rectangle tool and create a box off the edge of the upper-left corner of the page. Click where the first guides intersect, then release at the next set of intersecting guides. Deselect the box.

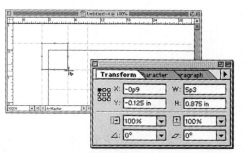

9. This will be a two-color newsletter, Black and PMS 547. To add this Pantone color to the Swatches palette, choose Window>Swatch Libraries>Pantone Uncoated. When the Pantone palette opens, scroll down about halfway to locate Pantone 547 CVU. Double-click on this swatch to add it to the palette, then close the Pantone palette. If you wish, remove the other colors from the palette.

10. We will also use a 10% tint of this color quite often. Be certain nothing in the document is selected. To add the tint swatch, select Pantone 547 in the Swatches palette. From the Swatches palette Options menu, choose New Tint Swatch. At the bottom of the New Tint Swatch dialog box is a slider to specify the tint value. Drag the slider or type into the field to establish a 10% tint of this color. Click OK.

11. With the Selection tool, select the box you created in step 8 by marqueeing the area. Make certain Fill is selected in the Toolbox, then click on the Pantone 547 10% tint swatch in the palette. Select Stroke in the Toolbox and click on the None swatch.

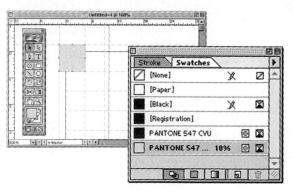

12. This box will form a tile pattern down the left side of the page, in two columns aligned with the guides. Select the box with the Selection tool and choose Edit>Copy. Deselect the box and choose Edit>Paste. Drag the box down past one space to the third space down. Resize the box to fit within the guides using the Selection tool.

13. Zoom out to see the entire page. Instead of copying the box again to make the pattern, select the resized box and choose Edit>Step and Repeat to duplicate four more boxes down the page. Horizontal offset should be set to 0p and Vertical offset should be set to 1.5 in., so that a space is skipped between each box.

*In all dialog boxes and palettes, the position of an object is moved using positive and negative numbers. Positive numbers move objects to the right and down. Negative numbers shift objects up and to the left of the original position.*

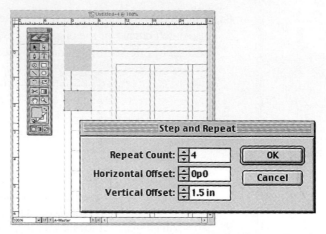

14. The second column of boxes is offset like a checkerboard. Start this section by selecting the last box at the bottom of page. Hold Option/Alt and drag a copy of this box one space to the right and one space down, to the very bottom of the page.

15. Drag the lower corner of the box to resize it to fit within the guides and off the bottom page edge to the bleed guide. Option/Alt drag this box two spaces directly up to start the checkerboard pattern.

16. Resize the box you just moved to fit within the guides, then duplicate it using Step and Repeat. This time the vertical offset should be -1.5 in. so that the four duplicate boxes appear above each other, rather than below as in step 13.

17. The Master Page of your newsletter is complete. Save this file as "Newsletter.INDD" in your **Work in Progress** folder.

*To ensure that the grayscale images trap (have no white space between) to the tinted color boxes, add a Stroke to the first image frame which will be duplicated. Before adding the Stroke, check Weight Changes Bounding Box in the Stroke palette menu. The Stroke should be 1 pt. and colored Pantone 547 10%. Open the Attributes palette and check Overprint Stroke.*

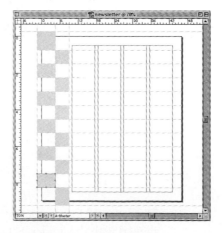

### Add Page Design Elements

1. Double-click on page 1 in the Pages palette. Page 1 looks very similar to the Master Page so far (except that the guides dragged outside the page area are missing). Four images will nestle into the checkerboard pattern on page 1 and four different images on page 2. Instead of sizing the image or cropping it to fit the space, we'll create a frame that fits within the guides first, then place the graphic into it, masking the edges to a perfect fit.

2. Zoom into the upper-left corner of page 1. With the Rectangle Frame tool, drag a frame that snaps to the guides in the first white space down in the first column. Both Stroke and Fill should be None. The Transform palette should read:

| | | | |
|---|---|---|---|
| X: | -0p9 | W: | 5p3 |
| Y: | 0.75 in | H: | 0.75 in |

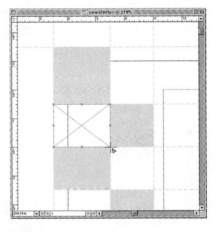

3. Choose File>Place. Select **Cells.JPG** from the **SF-Intro InDesign** folder and check Show Import Options. Click Open. In the Image Open/Import Options dialog box, make certain that the proxy image will be displayed at 72 dpi. Click OK.

4. Deselect the frame. Switch to the Direct Selection tool. Click on the image and position it inside the frame as shown.

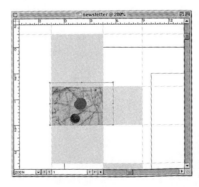

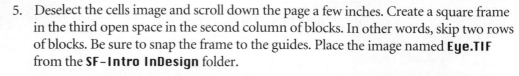

*Once you've checked that both image types (JPG and TIF) are being previewed at 72 dpi, uncheck Show Import Options.*

5. Deselect the cells image and scroll down the page a few inches. Create a square frame in the third open space in the second column of blocks. In other words, skip two rows of blocks. Be sure to snap the frame to the guides. Place the image named **Eye.TIF** from the **SF-Intro InDesign** folder.

6. Deselect the frame. With the Direct Selection tool, select the image. In the Transform palette, reduce this image to 90% horizontally and vertically. Reposition the image inside the frame, if necessary, to match this example.

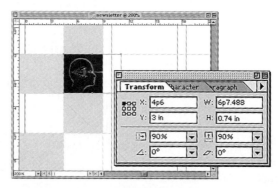

7. Deselect and switch back to the Selection tool. Select the Cells image (and frame) and Option/Alt copy it to the first column white space that is approximately 5.5 in. down the page. With the frame still selected, choose File>Place or type Command/Control-D to place another image. Choose **Veggies.JPG** in the **SF-Intro InDesign** folder. Be sure the Replace Selected Item box is checked. The Veggies image will replace the Cells image in this frame.

*Press Command / Control -; to show guides. Press Command/Control -H to show/hide frame outlines.*

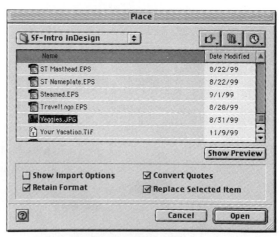

8. With the Direct Selection tool, scale this image to 110% proportionally and reposition it to match the example.

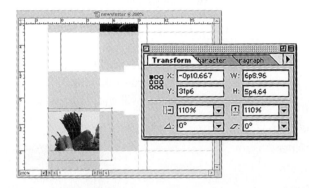

9. With the Selection tool, Option/Alt copy the Eye.TIF image to the last white space in the second column. Import here, in its place, the image named **Moonlitjog.TIF** from the **SF-Intro InDesign** folder. Do not scale this image, but move it straight up within the frame to show primarily the jogger and the sunrise.

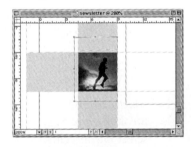

10. Complete the images on page 2 in the same manner and using the same pattern of white spaces. From top to bottom, the images to use from the **SF-Intro InDesign** folder are: **Salad.TIF** at 100%, **DNA.TIF** at 100%, **Salmon.JPG** at 100%, and **Brain.JPG** at 95% proportionally.

   Position the images to highlight each interesting, eye-catching section of the graphic. Page 2 and your links palette should appear as shown.

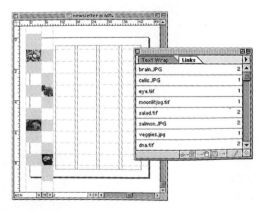

11. Save the file and continue.

12. Return to page 1. Zoom and position the page on your screen to view the top 3-4 inches of the page. You will now create the nameplate to the right of the checker-board pattern.

13. Select the Line tool. Using the third guide from the top of the page and the margin guides, draw a rule across all four columns. In the Transform palette, the Y coordinate should be 2.25 in. Draw another rule above it to span all four columns as well. Select the second rule and enter 11p6 in the Transform palette for its Y coordinate position. The palette will translate this to 1.9167 in.

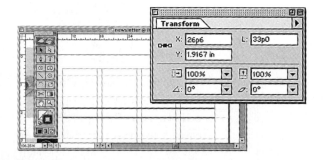

Select each of these rules in turn. In the Transform palette, click the left and right anchor point to check the X coordinate of their start and end points. Both rules should be the same — with left anchor selected, X: 10p0, and with the right anchor selected, X: 43p.

14. Marquee both rules with the Selection tool. Assign them a 1-pt. solid stroke in the Stroke palette by typing "1" in the dialog box and pressing Return. In the Toolbox, select Fill and click on the None swatch below it, then select Stroke, click on the black swatch and then deselect.

15. Select the Type tool and change the Fill to Pantone 547 (100%) and Stroke to None. Click and drag a text frame, filling the space between the rules starting near the left margin. In the Character palette, choose ATC Colada, 10 pt. In the Paragraph palette, choose the Centered icon. Type the following: "Published by the Center for Practical Research • St. Charles, Alabama".

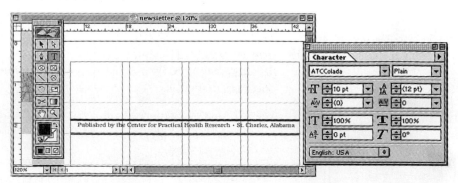

16. Adjust the text frame with the Selection tool so that it fits vertically around the type quite snugly. Choose Window>Align to open the Align palette. With the Selection tool, marquee both rules and the text frame. In the Align palette, first click the second icon in the top row to center-align the objects horizontally. Then click the second icon in the bottom row to distribute the center axis of the objects vertically. Close the Align palette and deselect.

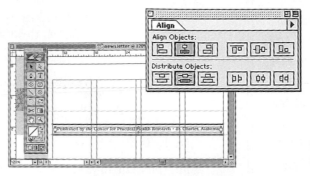

17. The next task is to create the title art. Choose File>Place and select **GDCHbglight.TIF** from the **SF-Intro InDesign** folder. Click to place the graphic inside the upper-left corner of the margin guides. Select the image with the Selection tool. Using the arrow keys, nudge the graphic to the right and up slightly so that it clears the rule below, then deselect it. This will act as a drop shadow for the solid type.

18. Switch to the Direct Selection tool and select the image. Click on Fill in the Toolbox. In the Swatches palette, select Pantone 547 to color this grayscale image, then deselect.

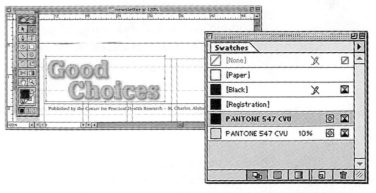

19. Now we are going to layer black type over the shadow graphic. Using the Type tool, click and drag a text frame over the graphic. In the Character palette, choose ATC Coconuts Extra Bold, 57 pt., with 48-pt. leading. Type "Good Choices" on two lines.

20. Move the text frame over the graphic shadow so that the first word lines up exactly, then nudge the box up and to the left approximately 2 pts. to position its offset from the shadow graphic.

21. To move "Choices" over, select the Type tool and place the cursor to the left of the "C". We'll add some special characters.

   • Control-click (Macintosh) or right-click (Windows) on the text. A properties menu appears. Choose Show Hidden Characters.

*Do not crop images that contain shadows and feathered edges. The proxy image will not allow you to judge successfully where the lightest part of the image fades out.*

*Press Command-Option-I (Macintosh) or Control-Alt-I (Windows) to Show or Hide Hidden Characters.*

• Control/right-click again, and choose Insert White Space>En space.

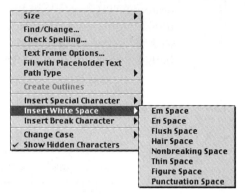

• Repeat this process to add two thin spaces and two hair spaces.

• Nudge the graphic again to reposition it as needed.

A little bit of highlight color should peek out from under and to the right of the characters. When you are done, turn off Show Hidden Characters.

22. Shift the view of your page to the upper-right corner. Here we'll combine InDesign and imported graphics. In the last column, create a rectangular frame that goes from the top margin almost down to the top rule. Its dimensions are 7p6 by 1.33 in. Click Fill in the Toolbox.

23. The Stroke and Fill of this frame will use a gradient. From the Swatches palette menu, choose New Gradient Swatch. Name this gradient "547 10-100/75". Choose Linear gradient and click on the left color stop. Choose Named Color from the Stop Color pop-up menu and select Pantone 547 10% from the list. For the right color stop, select Pantone 547 (100%). Drag the diamond to the right to 75% and click OK.

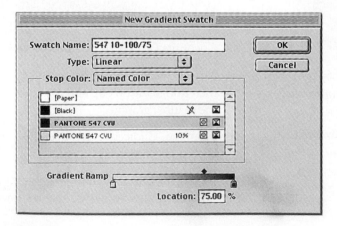

24. With the frame selected, the Fill tool should indicate that the gradient is chosen. Select the frame and click on the swatch, if it is not filled with the gradient. Then select the Gradient tool and drag from the top-right of the box to the lower-left to direct the fill. Do not start or release very far from the frame boundary, since that would extend the lightest and darkest colors outside the visible frame.

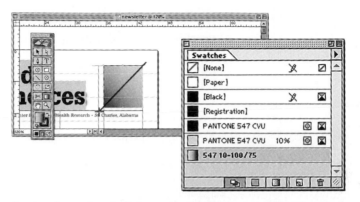

25. Switch to the Stroke tool and click on the gradient swatch. In the Stroke palette menu, make certain the Weight Changes Bounding Box is unchecked. Change the Stroke Weight to 4 pt. Select the Gradient tool and drag over the frame in the opposite direction, lower left to upper right.

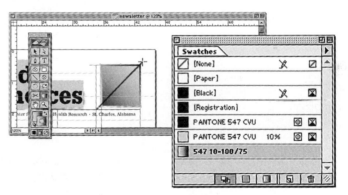

26. With the Selection tool, select the frame and place the image **YY.EPS** from your **SF-Intro InDesign** folder in the frame and then deselect. Change to the Direct Selection tool and select the placed graphic. Drag the lower-right corner of the graphic to the lower-right corner of the frame to scale it. Select the Rotate tool and move the anchor point to the center of the graphic. Rotate this image counterclockwise 45°.

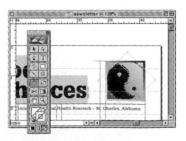

27. The nameplate is complete. Save the file and continue.

## Format the First Article

1. Shift your view of page 1 to see primarily the lower and right two-thirds of the page. Create two 0.5-pt. rules stroked with Pantone 547 to divide the page.

   - Select the Line tool. Click to start the vertical rule just below the masthead, between the third and fourth column. Holding the Shift key, drag down about 4.25 in. The rule should end just above the third guide from the bottom. Its coordinates should be set as X: 35p and Y: 2.33 in. for the top-left anchor point, and a length of 25p0.

   - Create the horizontal rule spanning all four columns, just above the third guide from the bottom. It should not touch the endpoint of the vertical rule. Position it at X: 10p, Y: 6.65 in., with a length of 33p0.

   - Select and stroke both lines with Pantone 547 and assign them 0.5-pt. weight.

2. The first story fits in the first three columns in the top section defined by the rules you just placed. Create a text frame that fits inside that section and spans from the left margin guide to the right edge of the third column. Size the frame as:

   X: 10p0     W: 24p6
   Y: 2.25 in     H: 4.2688 in

3. Chose File>Place and select **Exercise.TXT** from the **SF-Intro InDesign** folder. Click to Show Import Options and click Choose (Macintosh) or Open (Windows).

4. In the Import Options dialog box for Microsoft Word 6.0-7.0 there are several options. Defaults include Import Index Entry Fields, Import Condensed/Expanded Spacing as Kerning, and Import Tables. Since the newsletter is in columns, check the Import Page Breaks Before Paragraph option, then select As Column Break Before. Click OK.

*Hold the shift key while transforming to constrain the proportions or angle of the transformation.*

*When using the Direct Selection tool to edit endpoints of a rule, hold the Shift key to constrain the line to degree angles. Alternately, click on one of the anchor points in the Transform palette and enter precise numbers for each coordinate — the length, height, or width.*

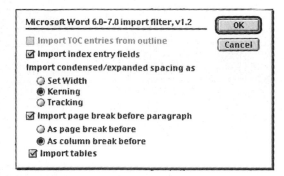

5.  Text flows across the entire text frame, so now we need to make some columns. Choose>Object>Text Frame Options. Enter "3" for the number of columns. All other variables can remain the same. Click OK.

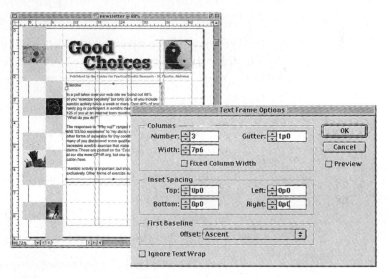

6.  Unfortunately a three-column format doesn't allow headlines to cross columns.

    • Reduce the height of the three-column frame by 0.5 in. so that it is at Y: 2.7778 in., with a height of 3.7361 in.

    • Drag a new text frame above it three-columns wide.

    • Cut the title of the article, "Exercise," and paste it into the box so that it is three-columns wide.

    • Change it to "A New Look at Exercise".

*Press the Control key (Macintosh), or right-click (Windows), while clicking in the text with the Type tool to access the Properties menu.*

7. Style the headline text as 24 pt., ATC Mai Tai Bold, flush left.

8. We need to clean up each article before it is styled by checking the spelling and replacing certain characters.

   - With the Selection tool, click on the text overflow symbol (the box with the red "X").

   - With the loaded text icon, draw a text frame on the pasteboard. The text will flow into the frame so all text in the article will be visible during cleanup.

9. We need to change every occurrence of the "%" symbol to the word "percent" with a space in front of it.

   - With the Type tool selected, place the cursor at the beginning of the article (not the headline) and choose Edit>Find/Change.

   - In the Find/Change dialog box enter "%" in the first field and "[space]percent" in the second field. Don't type the word "space", just press the Spacebar.

   - Select Document in the Search pop-up menu.

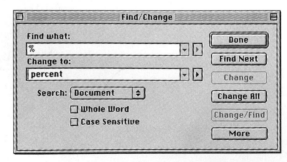

10. Click Find Next to locate the first "%". When it's highlighted, click Change, then Find Next again. At the next "%," click Change/Find — it's faster. Since there are going to be several replacements and every occurrence needs the same treatment, click Change All the third time. At the message telling how many replacements were made, click OK.

*Special characters to search for:*

*Return:* ^p
*Tab:* ^t
*En dash:* ^=
*Em dash:* ^_
*En space:* ^n
*Em space:* ^m
*Non-breaking space:* ^s
*Discretionary hyphen:* ^-
*Copy and paste from the text if you don't know or cannot remember the symbols.*

*Always place the cursor at the top of the text before starting a spell check, find, or find/change operation. Click at the top again after each, since the cursor marks where the last search ended, at the bottom of the text.*

11. This story contains two returns at the end of every paragraph. This is not typography, but Find/Change can help even with special characters that aren't ordinarily visible. The extra paragraph returns (¶) must be removed, but not every "¶" because that would run all the paragraphs together. Select Type>Show Hidden Characters, if it is not already selected, to reveal the paragraph returns.

12. With the Type tool selected and the Find/Change dialog box open, click before the first word of the first paragraph and drag up to select the "¶". Choose Edit>Cut.

    • In the Find/Change dialog box, click in the Find What field and choose Edit>Paste. The result is "^p" which will find all paragraph returns. Paste in another "^p" to find every occurrence of two ¶'s in a row.

    • In the Change field type "^p" to replace two ¶'s with one ¶.

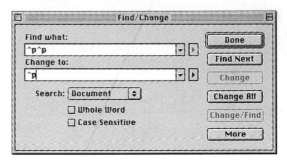

13. Click Find Next. When the cursor highlights the first pair of paragraph returns, click Change/Find. When it highlights the second pair of paragraph returns, click Change All. InDesign should return a message saying five replacements were made. Click OK. Repeat to verify that there are no more double paragraph returns.

14. We'll check the story for spelling errors. Place the cursor at the beginning of the article, choose Edit>Check Spelling and click Start.

15. Each misspelled or unlisted word will be highlighted. Here are some clues about how to handle each in this article.

| Select correct spelling | Action | Ignore |
| --- | --- | --- |
| exercize(s) — exercise(s) | *Change All* | and — *capitalization error* |
| exersize — exercise | *Change* | percent — *capitalization error* |
| guarentee — guarantee | *Change* | ranged — *capitalization error* |
| physicial — physical | *Change* | Hartlett — *proper name* |
| unstablizing — destabilizing | *Retype* | www.CHPR.org — |
| various — Various | *Change* | *could Add to Dict.* |
| | | Tai — *foreign language* |

## Establish Styles

1.  Three type-style formats for the body of this newsletter are used repeatedly. Creating three paragraph style sheets will make the newsletter more consistent and decrease the time required to lay it out.

    • From the Paragraph Styles palette Options menu, choose New Style. Name it "1 Col. Body".

    • Base the style on No paragraph style and make the Next Style Same Style.

    • Place the cursor in the Shortcut field and hold the Command/Control key while typing "1" on the numeric keypad. Click Next.

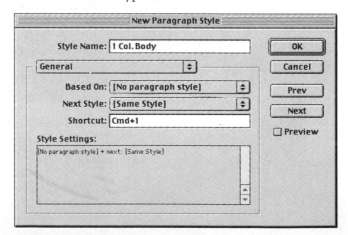

*Although we've used the Next Style feature, this function is inactive when working with imported text. It is useful only when typing text directly into the document.*

2.  In the next dialog box, Indents and Spacing, choose Left Justify (not Left) in the Alignment pop-up menu. Enter "1p" for the first line indent and click Next.

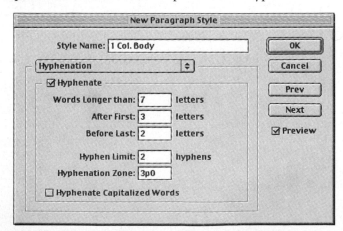

3. In the next dialog box, Drop Caps and Composer, make sure that Adobe Multi-Line Composer is selected. The next two dialog boxes, Justification and Tabs, do not need to be changed, so skip them by choosing Hyphenation in the drop-down menu under the style name.

4. The hyphenation parameters depend on the style sheet a company or publication has chosen to follow. They also depend on the layout of the publication, since narrow columns must, as a matter of practicality, hyphenate more frequently than wide columns. Check Hyphenate to allow hyphenation in this style and enter these rules for hyphenation:

   Words Longer than 7 Letters can be hyphenated.
   After First 3 Letters it's OK to hyphenate the word.
   Before Last 2 Letters it's OK to hyphenate the word.
   Hyphen Limit: 2 Hyphens in consecutive lines
   Hyphenation Zone: 3p0 from end of line. (This feature isn't applied when using Multi-line Composer.)
   Hyphenate Capitalized Words: uncheck to prevent their hyphenation.

5. Choose Keep Options from the same drop-down menu. This dialog box provides control of widow and orphan (single) lines at the beginning or end of a column or page. The first section is commonly used to keep headings and subheads with their respective paragraphs. Since this is a body-copy style, leave Keep with Next at "0" and check Keep Lines Together. Use the default of 2 Lines at the start and end of a paragraph.

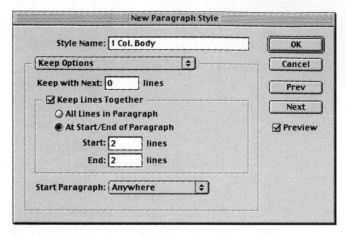

6. Choose Basic Character Formats from the same drop-down menu. Make the following selections for this style — ATC Colada, Plain (Macintosh) or Regular (Windows), 8-pt. type with 10-pt. leading. The Kerning should be set to Metrics and the Tracking set to 0. Set the Case and Position to Normal. Ligatures should remain the only choice selected in the bottom section.

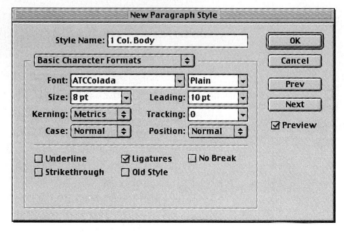

7. Select the Character Color and make certain that Black is chosen. Click Next.

8. Review all of your selections in this dialog box and click OK to save the style.

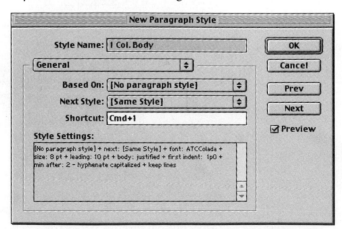

9.  This will be the main body style of the newsletter. However, two articles will be set across two columns, which requires a slightly larger type size to be read easily. We'll create another style named "2 Col. Body" based on the 1 Col. Body style.

    •  Select 1 Col. Body in the Paragraph Styles palette and click on the New button at the bottom.

    •  Double-click on the New style and name it "2 Col. Body".

    •  Designate a shortcut for it by placing the cursor in the field and holding Command/Control while typing "2" on the keypad.

    This dialog box now indicates that this style will be based on 1 Col. Body and that it will be followed by the Same Style.

10. From the drop-down menu under the style name, choose Basic Character Formats, because the size and leading are the only parameters that differ between the two styles. In the Basic Character Formats dialog box change the Size from 8 pt. to 9 pt. and the Leading from 10 pt. to 11 pt.

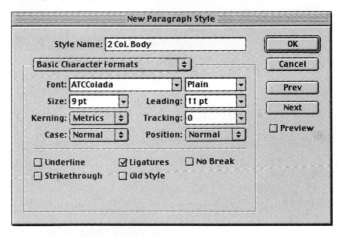

Click OK to save this style.

11. We are now ready to style the body copy of this article's text. With the Type tool, highlight the text from the first word, "In", down to "Good Choices," just before the numbered list. Click once on 1 Col. Body in the Paragraph Style palette.

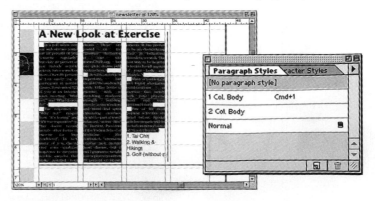

*If your keyboard does not have an "end" key, press the Down Arrow until the balance of the story is highlighted.*

12. The numbered list needs to be styled differently. Place the Type tool before "1. Tai Chi". Hold Command/Control Shift and press the End key to select the text to the end of the story. Style the type as ATC Flamingo, Regular, 8/10.

    Set the Paragraph palette to Flush Left, with a Left Indent of 0p4 and a First Line indent of 0p0. Set the Space Above to 0p0, and Uncheck Hyphenate.

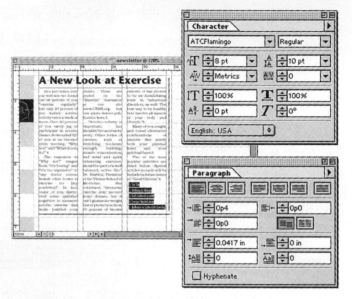

13. Save this formatting to use in the rest of the newsletter.

    • Click on any of the numbered-list items, then click on the create new style icon at the bottom of the Paragraph Styles palette to create a new style.

    • Double-click on the new style. The dialog box that appears will display all of the character and paragraph styling just completed.

    • Name this style "Tables". Click OK

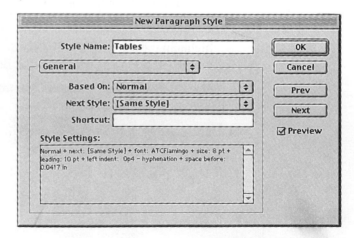

14. Highlight the headline text to capture its typographic formatting for later use.

   - Click on the create new style icon in the Character Styles palette to create a new style.

   - Double-click the New Style and name it "Mai Tai Head".

   - Assign a keyboard shortcut of your choice. Click OK.

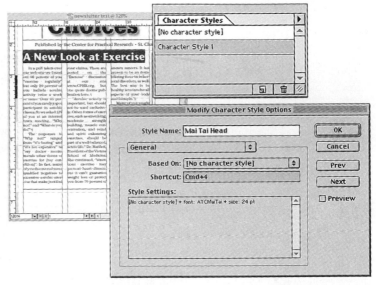

*Instead of changing the content of a frame through the Object menu, you may simply click the Type tool in the frame.*

15. If necessary, select the headline text frame and move it down, closer to the copy and away from the masthead rule. The position in the Transform menu should be set as X: 10p0, and Y: 2.3333 in.

16. This article is finished. Delete the extra frame on the pasteboard. Save the file and continue.

17. Shift your view of the page to the right column. Select the Rectangle Frame tool and create a frame in the one-column space to the right of the page. Size it as:

    X:  35p6      W:  7p6
    Y:  2.3125 in  H:  4.2601 in

18. Select the frame with the Selection tool. Check to see that it has a Stroke and Fill color of None and choose Object>Content>Text.

19. Place the text file **Multivariable.TXT** from the **SF-Intro InDesign** folder into this frame. Check Show Import Options and remember to check the option Import Page Breaks Before Paragraphs so that the text imports as a Column Break, rather than as a Page Break.

*Notice the many extraneous paragraph returns in the imported text.*

20. Stretch the right side of the frame off the page to see the overset text. For this article, four text modifications need to be made before the text is styled. Use the Find/Change feature to search for and replace the following; be certain the extent of the search is limited to Story.

| Find: | double paragraph returns | ^p^p |
| Change to: | single paragraph return | ^p |
| | | |
| Find: | double space after periods | .__ (period, space, space) |
| Change to: | single space after period | ._ (period, space) |
| | | |
| Find: | single open quote ' | ^[ |
| Change to: | double open quote " | ^{ |
| | | |
| Find: | single close quote ' | ^] |
| Change to: | double close quote " | ^} |

When finding right single quotes, don't automatically click Change All, because if you do, the program will locate and change apostrophes as well as single quotes.

*If the text styles don't match the attributes the text was just assigned, click on No Paragraph Style or No Character Style to negate the previous assignments and any local styling.*

*Notice that the extra returns and spaces have been stripped, and the quotation marks have been corrected.*

21. Run spell check on this story.

| Select correct spelling | Action | Ignore |
| --- | --- | --- |
| elluded – eluded | *Change* | Multivariable |
| | | MIT |

22. This article is ready to style. Highlight the body of the article (from "Researchers question why…" to the end) and assign it the 1 Col. Body paragraph style. Leave the text highlighted and select Align Right in the Paragraph palette. Resize the frame to fit within the column limits.

23. Highlight the headline "One just isn't Enough" and style as ATC Flamingo, Regular. Set the Size to 20 pt., with a Leading of 20 pt. Save this Character Style as "Flamingo Head".

24. From the Paragraph palette, Right Align the text with a Left Indent of 0p0, and a First Line Indent of 0p0. Set the Space Below to 0p3 and uncheck Hyphenate.

25. Flush right, two-line headlines don't work well when the top line is longer. Place a soft return (Shift-Return/Enter) after the word "just".

26. The text is overset. Apply tracking of –2 to the entire article.

Sometimes the program doesn't produce desirable hyphenation, violating grammatical rules, typographic rules, or good design. You can insert a special character — a discretionary hyphen that specifies your preference as to where to break the word or not break the word at all.

27. At the bottom of this article, "finding" is hyphenated. To prevent hyphenation, place a discretionary hyphen at the beginning of the word by holding Command/Control Shift while typing a hyphen. Unfortunately that forces the word "medical" to hyphenate to the last line, not a very appealing result. Place a discretionary hyphen before "medical" as well.

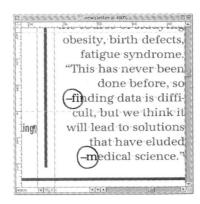

28. Delete the paragraph marker (¶) at the end of the article to remove the overset mark. This will ensure that when you give the document a final check, you won't need to wonder whether there is still text to be placed.

29. This article is complete. Save the file and continue.

*The properties menu for type — Control-click (Macintosh) or right-click (Windows) — can also be used to place a discretionary hyphen. Alternatively, press Command/Control-Shift-hyphen.*

## *Work with Threaded Text*

1. Shift your view of the page so that the four-column space remaining to fill is at the bottom of the page. Instead of four narrow columns, we will build two text frames, each two columns wide, and thread the article text through them and to the second page. Drag a text frame with the Type tool starting at the 6.75-in. guide and spanning the left two columns. It should start a little above the horizontal guide and include the first gutter (indicated by the guides) but not the second. The Transform palette should read:

   X: 10p0    W:    16p0
   Y: 6.6657 in   H:    1.9 in

2. Place the text file **Attitude check-up.TXT** from the **SF-Intro InDesign** folder. Link this text first before editing and styling it. With the Selection tool, click on the plus symbol at the right of the box. Click and drag a two-column frame to the right, using the guides to match the height of the first column.

   | | |
   |---|---|
   | Attitude check-up<br><br>   Thoughts are the blood stream of the mind. That's the claim Dr. Gunther Ancara pronounces in his thesis, "Pump Up your Mind". Dr. Ancara, Professor psycho-theism at Yucatan University, has spent 25 1/2 years studying the medical progres- | |

3. To thread the text file to the second page, click on the plus symbol in this second frame and go to page 2.

   | | |
   |---|---|
   | Attitude check-up<br><br>   Thoughts are the blood stream of the mind. That's the claim Dr. Gunther Ancara pronounces in his thesis, "Pump Up your Mind". Dr. Ancara, Professor psycho-theism at Yucatan University, has spent 25 1/2 years studying the medical progres- | sion of two tribes: one, a native culture in the mountains of Brazil, the other, a small neighborhood in Munich, Germany. In an interview about his paper, published by the American journal of Psycho-health, Dr. Ancara stated, "I set out to help others [in the peace-corp] and ended up helping myself." |

4. On page 2, locate the guide that is 6 in. down the page. Click where that guide intersects the left side of the third text column and drag a one-column frame to the bottom page margin.

5. Thread that frame to the fourth and last frame. This frame should be the same height as the last and occupy the bottom of the fourth column on page 2.

   | | | |
   |---|---|---|
   | |    Dr. Ancara became personally enthralled with the clinical study when he realized that the thread which resurfaced in his study of the two "tribes" was how | their individual and group attitudes correlated to overall health. "More than environment or physical conditions," he concluded, "healthy, happy members of each tribe practiced hope- |

6. Return to page 1 and highlight the first line "Attitude check-up". Set the text to ATC Sunset Plain (Macintosh) or Regular (Windows), 14/18. Save the Character Style as

"Sunset Head". In the Paragraph palette, designate the head to be Flush Left with a Space Below of 0p7.

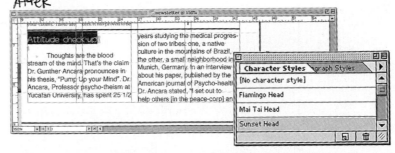

7. Now select the body text of this article. Select what is visible on page 1, then press Command/Control-Shift and press the End key to select the rest. Click on 2 Col. Body in the Paragraph Styles palette.

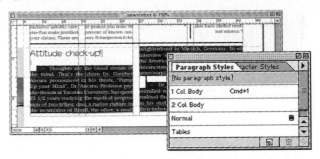

8. Place the cursor at the beginning of the text and use Find/Change to replace all double paragraph returns with single returns.

9. This article was also written with tabs at the beginning of each paragraph. Find/Change these and replace them with nothing in the Change field.

10. Notice that each time the title "Pump Up Your Mind" is mentioned in the article, "your" is lower case. Use Find/Change to correct this. Check to search for the Whole Word and to be Case Sensitive.

11. A note from the author states that "Dr. Gunther Ancara" should be "Dr. Günther Ancara". Highlight the "u" in Gunther on the second line and select Type>Replace Character. Choose ATC Colada from the pop-up menu at the bottom. Scroll through the characters until you find the lower case "u" with an umlaut "ü". Select it and click Replace, then click Done.

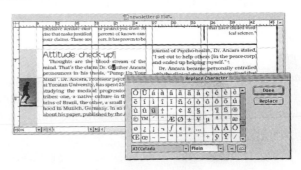

*Be certain to proof this article yourself. Toward the end is a word that the dictionary did not catch as incorrect— "tieing."*

12. Return to the layout window and find the phrase "…has spent 25 1/2 years…" in the first paragraph. Use the Type>Replace Characters command to replace 1/2 with the single character  . Delete the space between "25" and "1/2".

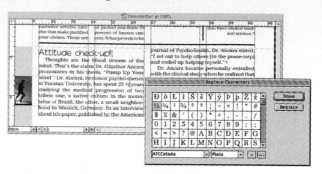

13. Check this story for spelling errors.

| Select correct spelling | Action | Ignore |
|---|---|---|
| entralled — enthralled | *Type "h"* | Günther |
| ellivates — elevates | *Change* | Ancara |
| cholesteroal — cholesterol | *Change* | LDL |
| artieries — arteries | *Change* | Ancara's |
| Dr — needs a period Dr. | *Change* | |
| peace-corp — Peace Corps | *Retype* | |

14. Type the jump line — "continued on page 2" — just after 'mature attitudes.'" at the end of the paragraph in the second column.

15. Click on Flamingo Head in the Character Style palette and create a new style, based on it by dragging Flamingo Head to the new icon in the palette. Name it "Jump Line". Change the Size to 8 pt., the Leading to 10 pt., and the Font Style to Regular Oblique. Designate the Tracking as -10. Click OK.

16. Select the text just created and assign it the Jump Line style. Press Shift-Tab immediately before the Jump Line text to align the text with the right margin.

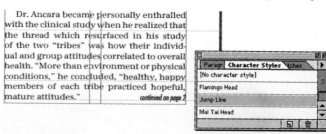

17. Go to page 2. Highlight the rest of the text in this article, and style it as 1 Col. Body. Now locate the hyphenated word at the end of the first paragraph on this page. "Carotid" is hyphenated undesirably. Place a discretionary hyphen (Command/Control-Shift) before the word to prevent it from hyphenating.

*A **jump line** tells where an article continues, or where it began.*

*Sometimes a text frame must be enlarged beyond the guides so that the last line of text can flow and sit on the guide itself.*

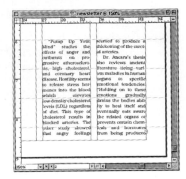

18. Save the file and continue.

## Correct Bad Justification

1. With the Selection tool, drag the first-column text frame slightly longer at the bottom, so that the last line of text displayed sits on the page margin.

2. This text contains some unsightly "rivers" as did the first article on page 1.

   • To make them more obvious, choose Edit>Preferences>Composition.

   • Click to highlight Keep Violations and H&J Violations. Click OK.

   • Look through the publication. Several lines are highlighted in light and dark yellow. For the most part, this indicates undesirable spacing. We can improve this by tightening the parameters for letter and word spacing in justified text.

3. This section of text has many lines highlighted in bold yellow, indicating a severe spacing problem.

   • Highlight the text of this article with the Type tool from the beginning of the paragraph on this page to the end of the story that is overset.

   • From the Paragraph palette Options menu, choose Justification and click Preview.

   • Enter these parameters, but do not click OK:

*Page layout programs use percentage specifications for word spacing, letter spacing, and character or glyph scaling to justify both left and right margins of a column of text. These are the specifications for paragraphs in the Justification dialog box.*

|  | Min. | Desired | Max. |
|---|---|---|---|
| Word | 80% | 90% | 110% |
| Letter | -10% | 0% | 0% |
| Glyph | 99% | 100% | 101% |

These parameters should reduce the number of strongly highlighted lines to only five and make the justified text more balanced visually within the narrow column.

   • Click Cancel.

*Adjustments to justified spacing can warp the shape of characters and quickly create illegible typography. Every font, size, and column length will react differently. Apply such adjustment consistently within a document to more evenly distribute justified type.*

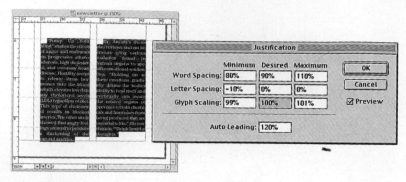

4. Return to page 1. Notice that the Exercise article also contains many lines that are highlighted in dark yellow. Highlight the text of the first article, "A New Look at Exercise" with the Type tool. Choose Justification from the Paragraph palette Options menu and enter the same parameters as above.

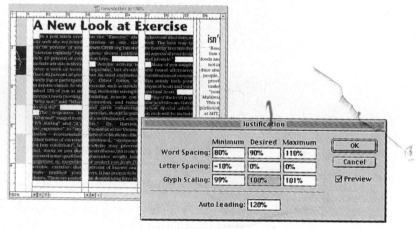

These parameters should reduce the number of strongly highlighted lines in this article substantially, making it more balanced visually. Click Cancel.

5. Now that you have evidence that these settings work, you will save them to the 1 Col. Body style. In the Paragraph Styles palette, double-click on 1 Col. Body. Choose Justification in the top pop-up menu and enter:

|        | Min. | Desired | Max. |
|--------|------|---------|------|
| Word   | 80%  | 90%     | 110% |
| Letter | -10% | 0%      | 0%   |
| Glyph  | 99%  | 100%    | 101% |

Click OK. The "Exercise" article and the second half of the "Attitude" article on page 2 will change as you previewed. The single-column article, "One just isn't Enough," will not change because its text is not justified.

6. Since the copy is set tighter, a bit of shifting is required. For the "Exercise" article on page 1, drag the top of the body text frame down the equivalent of one line of type. The coordinates of the upper-left anchor point should now be set as X: 10p0 and Y: 2.9028 in. Nudge the headline text frame down to set the coordinates at X: 10p0 and Y: 2.4826 in.

*Maintaining a consistent baseline across several columns is a subtle design attribute that improves the look and readability of a page.*

7. Go to page 2 and add a jump line at the top of the first column of the continued "Attitude" article.

- Drag a text frame across the third column on the page. Into it type "Continued from Attitude Check-up".

- Assign it the Jump Line character style and change its justification to Flush Right.

- Snug the text frame to the type and position it just above the article copy (Y: 5.8264 in.).

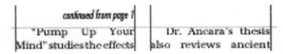

8. Shorten the text frame so all text fits within the live area. Save the file and continue.

## Add Text with Tabs

1. Shift your page view to see the top of page 2. Change the margins for page 2 only. Choose Layout>Margins and Columns and enter 2p6 (0.4167 in.) for both the Top and Bottom Margins.

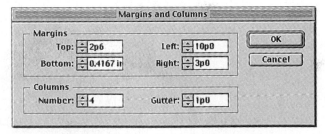

2. Select the Rectangle Frame tool and drag a frame from the top-left margin guide across all four columns to the sixth guide down from the top (4.5 in.) Make sure its Stroke and Fill are set to None.

- Click the Type tool in the frame to convert it to a text frame.

- Place the file **Eastern diet.TXT** from the **SF-Intro InDesign** folder.

3. Select all of the text in this frame and assign the 2 Col. Body paragraph style.

4. Place your cursor at the top of the text. Use Find/Change to remove the double paragraph returns, but do not remove any tabs.

5. Be sure the Text cursor is at the beginning of the article and run a spell check.

| Select correct spelling | Action | Ignore |
|---|---|---|
| neceesary — necessary | *Change* | all abbreviations |
| Spinich — Spinach | *Change* | in…to |
| Portabella — Portobello* | *Retype* | |
| mushrooms - Mushrooms | *Change* | |

- We will add "Portobello" to the dictionary. To do so, click the "Add" button. When adding it to the dictionary, also click Hyphenation. Change the hyphenation priority by deleting one of the tildes between the "r" and the "t" so that this becomes less acceptable than Porto-bello.

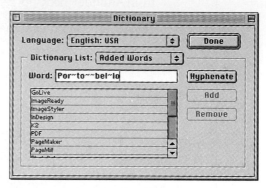

6. We'll modify this frame so the text fits more logically.

- Resize the text frame to fit in the first two columns only, and lower the top edge to the first horizontal guide.

- Create a second text frame in the other two columns, from the top guide down to the fifth guide (3.75 in.)

- Marquee both frames with the Selection tool. Click the plus symbol at the bottom of the left frame, then click in the link box at the top of the right frame to thread text to it.

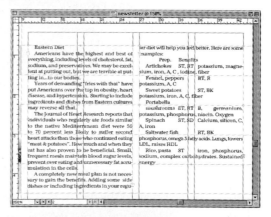

7. Now we'll create the headline for the article.

- Delete the first line of the copy, "Eastern diet".

- Drag a new text frame across all four columns between the margin guide and the top horizontal guide.

- Type: "Is an Eastern diet infusion for you?"

- Assign the Mai Tai Head character style to this headline.

- Change the local styling of this headline only to 22 pt.
- Align the headline left.

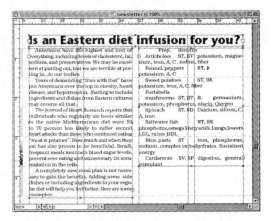

8. With the Type tool, select the copy in the right text frame to the end of the text file, and assign to it the Tables paragraph style. From the Paragraph Style palette Options menu, choose Duplicate Style and name it "Tables 2". Change the attributes for this new style. Indents and Spacing should be set with a Left Indent of 9p0, a First Line Indent of –9p0, and the Space Before set to 0p6. Create two tabs, both left justified. Set the First tab to 4p0 and the Second tab to 9p0.

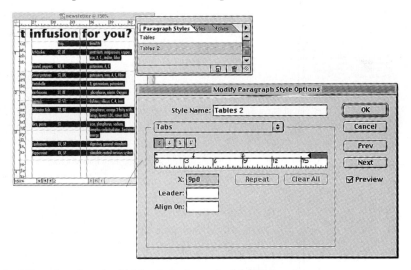

Click OK and assign the Tables 2 Style to the highlighted text.

9. Highlight the first line of this table. Drag the name Tables 2 in the Paragraph Style palette to the new icon to duplicate it. Double-click on Tables 2 Copy and rename it "Tables Head". The General settings for Next Style should be set as Tables 2. The Basic Character Formats should be set as ATC Flamingo Extra Bold, Normal at 9 pt. Move and change the left align tabs to center align them at 6p and 11p6. Assign a Space after of 0p6.

*Both character and paragraph styles show a plus sign (+) next to the style name in the palette when local styling has been applied.*

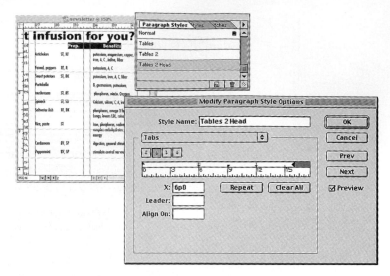

For the Paragraph Rules, click the Rule Below On with a Weight of 0.5 pt., Width set to Column, and Offset to p4. Click OK.

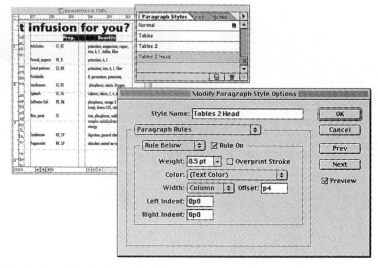

10. Highlight the last line in the table, "Peppermint…". From the Paragraph palette Options menu, choose Paragraph Rules and assign a Rule Below with the same parameters as you just created for Tables 2 Head (0.5 pt. Weight, 0p4 Offset).

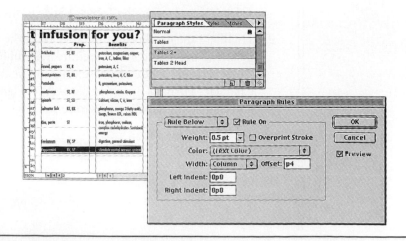

11. Certain lines require different Space Before settings to even out the vertical spacing. Place the Type tool cursor in the following lines of text and style locally:

"Sweet Potatoes…" Space Before: 1p0
"Spinach…" Space Before: 1p0
"mushrooms…" Space Before: 0p0
"Peppermint…" Space Before: 0p0

12. Highlight the text "B, germanium, potassium," in the mushrooms line. Cut this copy. Place your cursor to the left of the ¶ mark in the "Portobello" line and type one Tab. The cursor should be blinking in the third column of the table. Paste the copy here. If a return was pasted with this copy, delete it.

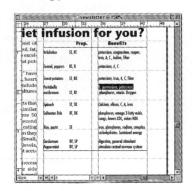

13. In the benefits listed for Rice and Pasta, you'll find the letters "NA2". For this chemical symbol, highlight the "2". In the Character palette Options menu, choose Subscript. The same specifications you entered in Preferences in step 2 will apply to all subscripts and superscripts here. Place the cursor between the "A" and the subscripted "2". In the Character palette, increase the kerning value between these two characters to 50 units.

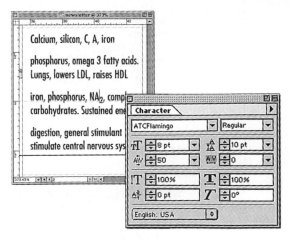

## Insert Inline Graphics

You are now ready to insert graphic symbols to replace the abbreviations that were imported with the text file.

1. With the newsletter still open, open the template document **Food Icons.INDT** from the **SF-Intro InDesign** folder in a new window. There you will find seven placed graphics and a key for identification. Configure your screen so that both the table section of the newsletter file, at about 150% magnification, and the Food Icons window are visible simultaneously. These images will replace the two-letter abbreviations in the table.

2. For the "Artichokes…" line, the abbreviations listed are "ST" and "RT". Click on the "Food Icons" window to make it active.

   • With the Selection tool, click on the placed image of a steaming pot (with the label "Steamed-ST" below it).

   • Copy the graphic to the clipboard (Command/Control-C).

   • Click on the Newsletter window, to make it active, and change to the Type tool.

   • Highlight the letters "ST" and paste (Command/Control-V) the graphic in place of the letters.

   • Continue highlighting and pasting until all the "ST" abbreviations have been replaced with the icon.

3. Return to the Food Icons file.

   • Click on the roasted chili pepper (with the label "Grilled/Roasted-RT" below it), and copy it to the clipboard.

   • Activate the Newsletter window, change to the Type tool, and replace every "RT" with the icon, deleting the comma and space following the Steamed icon.

   • Continue highlighting and pasting until all the "RT" abbreviations have been replaced with the icon.

4. Continue copying and pasting the appropriate images for each listing in the table, deleting the commas and spaces between icons. Drag only one set of images (spice and beverage) for the last entry "Cardamom & Peppermint." The table should look something like the image that follows, when all graphics have been copied into the newsletter file.

*If you accidentally delete graphics from the Food Icon file, close the file and reopen it. It is a template file, so even if you try to save over the original, the computer will not allow you to do so without your specific instructions.*

*In addition to dragging and dropping, graphics can be transferred, file to file, using Copy (Command/Control C) and Paste (Command/Control V).*

*InDesign template documents cannot be accidentally altered. On the Macintosh, they are called "Stationery Documents." We will use the generic term **template** here as a matter of clarity.*

5.  Save the file and continue.

6.  Below the table, create a legend that identifies what the icons mean. Create a text frame, in any manner you prefer. It should be sandwiched between the next two horizontal guides. Make the width of the frame across two columns, but narrower than the column guides.

    X:  27p10     W:   14p6
    Y:  3.8333 in  H:   0.4 in

    Choose Object>Text Frame Options. Make this a three-column text frame with a gutter of 0p8, and an inset of 0p0.

7.  Click in the text frame and select the Tables 2 paragraph style. Choose Type>Tabs. Change the left-aligned tab at 4p to a right-aligned tab by selecting the tab on the ruler and clicking on the right-aligned tab icon at the top. Close the palette.

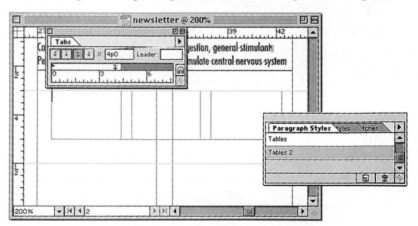

8.  Type the following text, separating the words with paragraph returns "¶". They will flow into the three columns as shown.

    steamed¶
    grilled/roasted¶
    fresh¶
    beverage¶
    baked    [tab]  spice¶
    salad

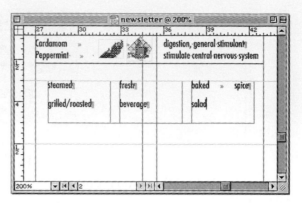

9. Switch to the Selection tool and drag another copy of each graphic into the legend next to its designation. There is no need to stay within the guides of the text frame.

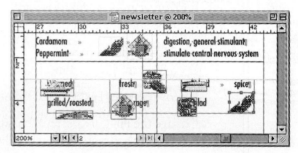

10. Choose Object>Text Wrap. With the Selection tool, click on each placed graphic and assign it a Text Wrap (second icon in the palette), with "0" Offset. If any of the text moves to a new line creating overset, move the position of that graphic away from the next line of text to prevent it from moving text inappropriately.

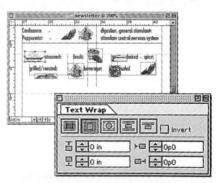

*After marqueeing an area, Shift-click on items to deselect them.*

11. Some pictures in their bounding boxes provide a tiny bit of white space that separates them from the surrounding text, some do not. If the actual image runs too close to the type with 0 offset, select the graphic and increase the offset (usually the right-side offset) to about 2 pts. Shift the pictures around, pushing the text to balance the scattered layout in the space.

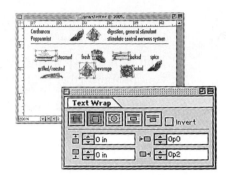

12. Save the file and continue.

## Create Borders

1. With the Rectangle tool, create a frame, using the column guides, around the text and placed graphics.

    X: 27p0     W:  16p
    Y: 3.5972 in  H:   0.7083 in

    Change the Fill to None and the Stroke to Black. Choose Object>Arrange> Send to Back.

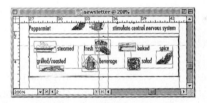

2. In the Stroke palette, assign the Weight to 1 pt., Round Cap, Miter Limit 4, Round Join, and Dash type to 0.5 pt. with a Gap of 6 pt.

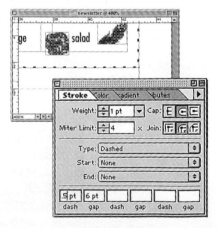

3. With the Selection tool, marquee the dotted frame around the text box and all the placed images in the legend. Be careful not to select rules, frames, or text other than those *in* the legend. Choose Object>Group. With the group selected, nudge down 2 pt. (press the Down Arrow twice).

4.  Close the Text Wrap palette. Close the Food Icons file window without saving. Save the newsletter file and continue.

5.  Shift your page view down slightly in the same column, between the legend and the continuation of the "Attitude" article.

6.  Create a rectangular frame, two columns wide, in the space left.

    X:  27p0       W:   16p0
    Y:  4.5 in     H:   1.25 in

7.  Fill the frame with Pantone 547, 10% screen from the Swatches palette. Assign a 1-pt. stoke to the frame. The stroke should be a 75% tint of Pantone 547.

    • Select Stroke in the Toolbox and click on Pantone 547 in the Swatches palette.

    • In the Color palette, drag the slider to 75% or type 75 in the percent field.

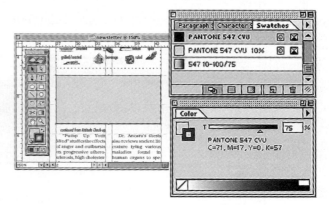

8.  Create a text frame, same size and position as the colored background frame. Click in the frame with the Type tool and place **SPCsalad.TXT** from the **SF-Intro InDesign** folder. Click in the text again and Select All (Command/Control A). From the Character palette, style the text with the Font set to ATC Flamingo, Regular, 7 pt. type with Leading of 9 pt. In the Paragraph palette, set the Justification Flush Left and all indents and paragraph spacing options to "0". Choose Type>Tabs and set a left-aligned tab at 2p0.

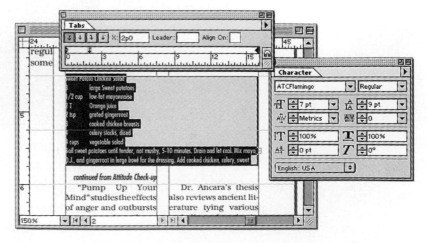

9. With the type still highlighted, select Fill in the Toolbox and choose Pantone 547 (100%) from the Swatches palette to color the text.

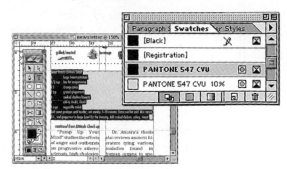

10. Highlight just the first line, "Sweet Potato Chicken Salad," and cut the text. Delete the paragraph return to move the first ingredient to the top of the frame.

11. With the Selection tool, shorten the text frame from the top to Y: 4.8 in., and H: 0.9444 in.

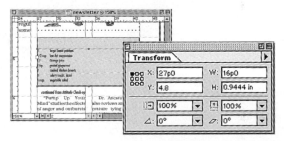

12. Choose Object>Text Frame Options and check Preview. Make this a two-column text frame with a 1p gutter with the text inset as follows:

| Top: | 0p0 | Left: | 1p0 |
|------|-----|-------|-----|
| Bottom: | 0p6 | Right: | 0p6 |

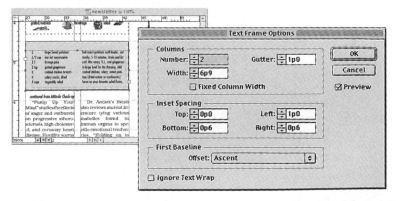

13. Create another text frame to fill the top of the colored background frame. Its bottom edge should abut the top of the recipe's text frame. Choose Edit>Paste to paste into the frame the Sweet Potato Chicken Salad text you cut from the frame in step #10.

14. Highlight the text, apply the Sunset Head from the Character Style palette, and change the Size to 10 pt.

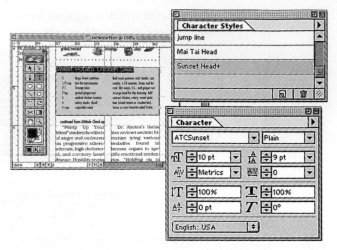

15. Select this frame with the Selection tool and choose Object>Text Frame Options. Inset the text in this frame 0p4 from the Top and 1p0 from the Left.

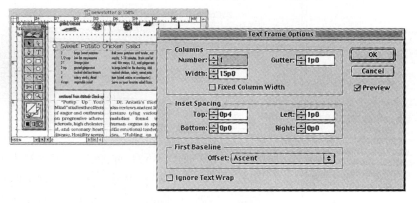

16. The recipe box is complete. Save the file and continue.

17. Shift your view of the page to the lower-left section of the page.

18. Create a text frame two columns wide from Y: 4.8704 in. to the bottom margin. Into it place the file **Eat together.TXT** from the **SF-Intro InDesign** folder. Delete the first line and the extra paragraph return. Neither Find/Change nor Check Spelling is required for this file.

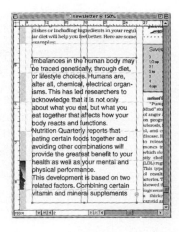

19. Select all of this text and assign the 1 Col. Body paragraph style. Change the justification for this article to Align Left.

20. In the Text Frame Options dialog box for this frame, change the specifications from 1 column to 2 columns, 1p0 gutter.

21. Above this body copy, create a text frame for the headline at Y: 4.594 in. Into it type, "What to eat together". Style this line using the Flamingo Head character style, then adjust the point size to 18 pt. Make the line flush left with "0" indents or paragraph spacing, then deselect.

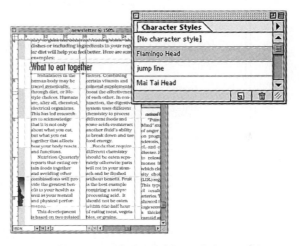

22. Select the Pen tool to add a two-sided rule around this article.

  - Click first to the right of "together" at X: 20p0 and Y: 4.7321 in.

  - Hold the Shift key for the following two clicks, to ensure that the lines created are at 90° angles. The next click with the Pen tool should be straight between the column guides of the second gutter at X: 26p5, Y: 4.7321 in.

  - The third click, still holding the Shift key, is straight down at the bottom margin guide at X: 26p5, Y: 8.5833 in.

  - With the Selection tool, select the path you just created.

23. Assign a Fill of None and a 0.5-pt. Stroke of Pantone 547 (100%) to this path.

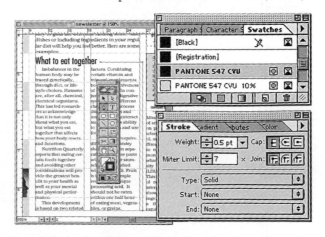

24. The two-page newsletter is now complete. Save the file and continue.

25. Review the document. Check for overset text frames, and be sure there is no text remaining to be placed.

26. Go back to page 1 and note the table text in the first article. Let's insert some space above the table. From the Paragraph palette, insert 11.5 pt. Space Above the first item (1. Tai Chi).

27. The second line of the last item should be indented to align with "Ballroom." Place the Type tool in front of "Ballroom" and press Command/Control-\, the Indent To Here command.

### *Proof the Document (Macintosh)*

1. Proof a composite of the newsletter to a color printer. (A black-and-white printer will also suffice.) First make sure that your computer is using the Adobe PS driver 8.6 or later as its default printer. You can change this in the Chooser.

2. Check the Links palette to make sure that all placed graphics are still linked.

3. Choose File>Print. From the various options in the drop-down menu under the printer name in the Print dialog box, make these changes:
   **General**
   Copies          1
   All Pages

   **Color**
   Composite
   Screening:      Default
   Accept Frequency and Angle that appears.

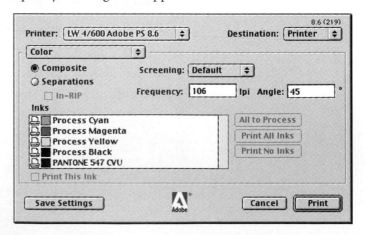

   **Page Marks**
   Check All Printer's Marks
   Uncheck Color Bars
   Bleed: 1p6

*The color printer will approximate Pantone colors using process inks. This isn't a reliable test of the color, but you can proof that the correct items will print in each spot color and that their relative tint values are accurate.*

*Note: if you first check All Printer's Marks and then uncheck Color Bars, All Printer's Marks becomes unchecked. This is an efficient way to select all but one of the printer's marks.*

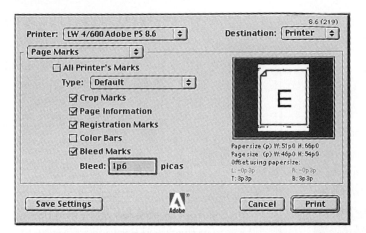

Notice that the left and right margins are now highlighted in red. If your printer does not handle paper with a wider dimension than 8.5 in., go back and turn the Printer's Marks off (you really don't need them for proofing a composite, anyway).

## PostScript Settings

Level 1, 2, 3 compatible     (Select specific PostScript level, if you know it.)
Data Format:        Binary
Font Inclusion:     All

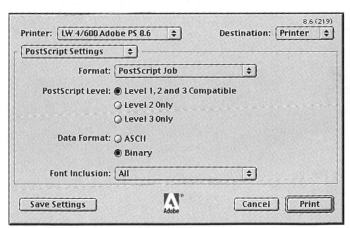

## Error Handling
Summarize on screen

## Background Printing
Background
Print Time: Normal
(Choose Foreground [No Spool File] only if you have limited hard drive space or are having difficulties printing the file.)
Click Print.

*To send separations to a black-and-white printer, choose Separations in the Color option of the Print dialog box. Select Cyan, Magenta, and Yellow in turn, and uncheck Print this Ink, so that only the Black and Pantone 547 inks will print. From the Screening pop-up menu, choose one of the combinations with a suitable resolution for your printer and an lpi ≤ 133 lpi (the maximum line screen for which the images are prepared). When each ink is selected, the Frequency field should match what is chosen in the Screening pop-up menu. The angle of Black should be 45°. For the angle of Pantone 547, check the angle of Cyan and use the same value. The angle of the spot color is critical when a grayscale and spot-color tint touch or overlap.*

4. Proof the output for position and completeness. Also check that the correct items are in Black and Pantone 547 respectively.

5. If you do not have a color printer, return to step 3, and, in the Color option of the print driver, set to print separations in addition to the composites that you just printed. You should supply both the composite and the separated proofs to your GASP.

## Proof the Document (Windows)

1. Proof a composite of the newsletter to a color printer. (A black-and-white printer will also suffice.) First make sure your computer is using the Adobe PS 4.3 driver or later as its default printer. You can change this in the Printer Setup.

2. Check the Links palette to be certain that all placed graphics are still linked.

3. In InDesign, choose File>Print. From the various tabs in the Print dialog box, make these changes:

**General**
Copies:          1

**Advanced Page Control**
All Pages

**Color**
Composite
Screening:     Default
Accept Frequency and Angle that appears.

InDesign has a built-in Preflight sequence that checks to make certain that all fonts and graphics called for in the document are online and updated. It also reports whether any color images have been left in RGB color space (not printable to an imagesetter), and which ink colors are included in the document. The Package command performs the preflight function automatically. Preflight is covered in-depth in the ATC **InDesign: Advanced Electronic Mechanicals** course book.

The color printer will approximate Pantone colors using process inks. This isn't a reliable test of the color, but you can proof that the correct items will print in each spot color and that their relative tint values are accurate.

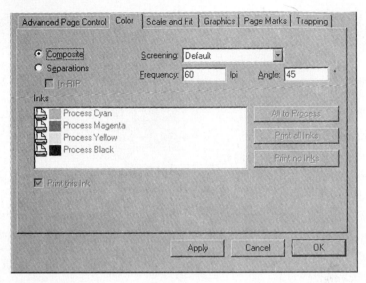

### Page Marks
Check All Printer's Marks
Uncheck Color Bars
Bleed: 1p6

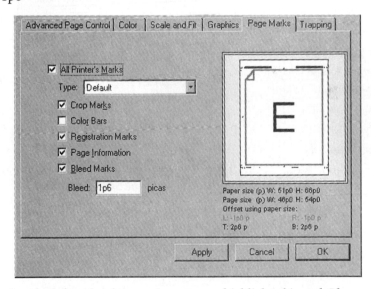

Notice that the left and right margins are now highlighted in red. If your printer does not handle paper with a wider dimension than 8.5 in., go back and turn the Printer's Marks off (you really don't need them for proofing a composite anyway).

### Graphics
Send Image Data: All
Uncheck OPI/DCS Image Replacement
Font Downloading: Complete

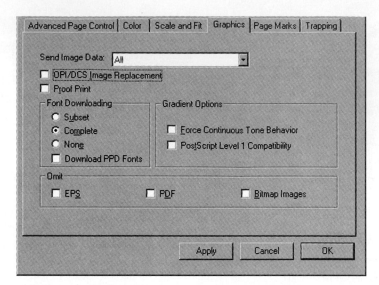

*To send separations to a black-and-white printer, choose Separations in the Color tab of the Print dialog box. Select Cyan, Magenta, and Yellow in turn, and uncheck Print this Ink, so that only the Black and Pantone 547 inks will print. From the Screening pop-up menu, choose one of the combinations with a suitable resolution for your printer and an lpi ≤ 133 lpi (the maximum line screen for which the images are prepared). When each ink is selected, the Frequency field should match what is chosen in the Screening pop-up menu. The angle of Black should be 45°. For the angle of Pantone 547, check the angle of Cyan and use the same value. The angle of the spot color is critical when a grayscale and spot-color tint touch or overlap.*

Click OK.

4. Proof the output for position and completeness. Also check that the correct items are in Black or Pantone 547 respectively.

5. If you do not have a color printer, return to step 3, and, in the Color tab of the print dialog box, set to print separations in addition to the composite you just printed. You should supply both the composite and the separated proofs to your GASP.

InDesign has a built-in preflight sequence that checks to make sure that all fonts and graphics called for in the document are online and updated. It also reports whether any color images have been left in RGB color space (not printable to an imagesetter), and which ink colors are included in the document. The Package command performs the preflight function automatically. Preflight is covered in-depth in the ATC *InDesign: Advanced Electronic Mechanicals* course book.

## *Package for the GASP*

1. Package the file to send to the Graphic Arts Service Provider for printing. Choose File>Package. First, InDesign will preflight the document, its links, and the fonts used, to be certain that all are available to package. If an alert message appears, click to View Info. If necessary, cancel the Packaging process at this time, and fix the links or fonts that it indicates are missing. When that is complete, select File>Package again.

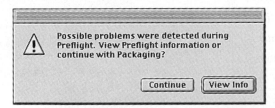

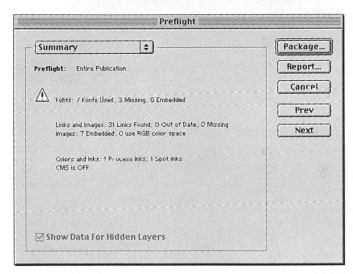

2. Once all links, fonts, and other elements have been checked, InDesign will ask to save the file. Click Save. This "save" is not yet saving the Packaged file. It is saving a final version of the document prior to packaging. This ensures that the package file has all the modifications you have made.

3. The next dialog box, Printing Instructions, provides a work order text file that will accompany the document to the Graphic Arts Service Provider. Fill in the information as shown:

   File name:   Instructions.txt        (name of info file, not the document file)
   Contact:   your name
   Company:   be creative
   Address:   your address
   Phone:   your phone number
   Email:   your e-mail address
   Instructions:   2 color newsletter, Black & Pantone 547. Front and Back, 8.5″ × 11″, 80 lb. creme, matte finish. 1/8″ Bleed.
   Trim to 7 3/4″ × 9″. Z Fold.
   Click OK.

*Deactivate or delete the ATC fonts, and eject the InDesign CD. Locate the folder you just packaged. Install or activate the fonts from this location, and open the newsletter file from this folder. You are now the Graphic Arts Service Provider. Print a composite of the document or separations to complete the process.*

4. An extended Save dialog box will appear next.

• Navigate to your **Work in Progress** folder and create a new folder called "Health Center". The document, fonts, and linked graphics will all be saved inside. (The files copied will occupy under 6 MB. If you prefer, save these files to external media.)

• At the bottom, check to Copy Fonts and Linked Graphics. Also check to Update Graphic Links in Package.

• Do not check to Include Fonts and Links from Hidden Layers.

• Check to View Report and then click Package.

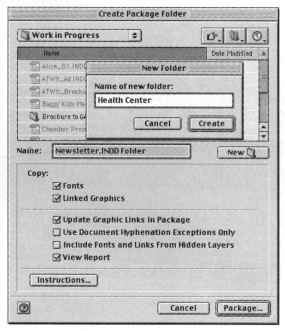

5. A Font Alert will appear, informing you to get permission to duplicate and distribute fonts. Click OK.

6. This folder can be given to the Graphic Arts Service Provider (or anyone with InDesign) and output. Close the newsletter file window.

## Notes:

## Achromatic

Having no color; therefore, completely black or white or some shade of gray.

## Acrobat

This program by Adobe Systems, Inc. allows the conversion (using Acrobat Distiller) of any document from any Macintosh or Windows application to PDF format, which retains the page layout, graphics, color, and typography of the original document. It is widely used for distributing documents online because it is independent of computer hardware. The only software needed is a copy of Acrobat Reader, which can be downloaded free.

## Adaptive Palette

A sampling of colors taken from an image, and used in a special compression process usually used to prepare images for the world wide web.

## Additive Color Process

The additive color process is the process of mixing red, green, and blue light to achieve a wide range of colors, as on a color television screen. See Subtractive Color.

## Adjacent Color

The eye will respond to a strong adjacent color in such a way as to affect the perception of the particular color in question. That is, a color having different adjacent colors may look different than it does in isolation. Also referred to as metamarism.

## Adobe Systems Incorporated

A major software developer responsible for the creation of the PostScript page description language (see PostScript), used in almost all graphic arts environments. PostScript resides in a printer or Raster Image Processor (see Raster Image Processor) and is used to convert graphics from the screen to high-resolution output. Adobe also develops the highly popular Photoshop, Illustrator, PageMaker, and Premiere graphics and video applications, in addition to a range of others.

## Adobe In-RIP Trapping

A trapping system that is active at the RIP, rather than on the desktop computer. It allows for more complex trapping than trapping routines built into Adobe programs. In-RIP trapping is a feature of the Adobe PostScript 3 page-description language.

## Adobe Multi-line Composer

Justification routine that makes hyphenation and line-ending decisions based on the parameters of a pre-efined number of lines of type.

## Adobe Single-line Composer

Justification routine that makes hyphenation and line-ending decisions based on the parameters of a single line of type.

## Algorithm

A specific sequence of mathematical steps to process data. A portion of a computer program that calculates a specific result.

## All signature folding dummy

A folding dummy in which all of the signatures that make up the job are used to determine the page arrangement for each signature. Also known as a Job Worksheet.

## ANSI

American National Standards Institute, the recognized standards-making body for the United States. ANSI code is used by some Windows computers for addressing text.

## Anti-Aliasing

A graphics software feature that eliminates or softens the jaggedness of low-resolution curved edges.

## Archival storage

The process of storing data in a totally secure and safe manner. Archiving differs from backup in that it's meant to be used to restore entire systems or networks, rather than providing quick and easy access to specific files or folders.

## Art

Illustrations and photographs in general; that is, all matter other than text that appears in a mechanical.

## Artifact

Something that is artificial, or not meant to be there. An artifact can be a blemish or dust spot on a piece of film, or unsightly pixels in a digital image.

## Ascender

Parts of a lower-case letter that exceed the height of the letter "x". The letters b, d, f, h, k, l, and t have ascenders.

## ASCII

The American Standard Code for Information Interchange, which defines each character, symbol, or special code as a number from 0 to 255 (8 bits in binary). An ASCII text file can be read by any computer, and is the basic mode of data transmission on the Internet.

## ATM (Adobe Type Manager)

A utility program which causes fonts to appear smooth on screen at any point size. It's also used to manage font libraries.

## Backing Up

The process of making copies of current work or work-in-progress as a safety measure against file corruption, drive or system failure, or accidental deletion. Backing up work-in-progress differs from creating an archive (see Archiving) for long-term storage or system restoration.

## Banding

A visible stair-stepping of shades in a gradient.

## Banner

A large headline or title extending across the full page width, or across a double-page spread.

## Baseline

The implied reference line on which the bases of capital letters sit.

## Bézier Curves

Curves that are defined mathematically (vectors), in contrast to those drawn as a collection of dots or pixels (raster). The advantage of these curves is that they can be scaled without the "jaggies" inherent in enlarging bitmapped fonts or graphics.

## Bindery marks

Marks that appear on a press sheet to indicate how the sheet should be cropped, folded, collated, or bound.

## Binding

In general, the various methods used to secure signatures or leaves in a book. Examples include saddle-stitching (the use of staples in a folded spine), and perfect-bound (multiple sets of folded pages sewn or glued into a flat spine).

## Bit (Binary Digit)

A computer's smallest unit of information. Bits can have only two values: 0 or

1. This can represent the black and white (1-bit) pixel values in a line art image. Or in combination with other bits, it can represent 16 tones or colors (4-bit), 256 tones or colors (8-bit), 16.8 million colors (24-bit), or a billion colors (30-bit). These numbers derive from counting all the possible combinations (permutations) of 0 or 1 settings of each bit: 2 x 2 x 2 = 16 colors; 2 x 2 x 2 x 2 x 2 x 2 x 2 x 2 = 256 colors; 2 x 2 x 2 x 2 x 2 x 2 x 2 x 2 x 2 x 2 x 2 x 2 x 2 x 2 x 2 x 2 x 2 x 2 x 2 x 2 x 2 x 2 x 2= 16.8 million colors.

## Bitmap image

An image constructed from individual dots or pixels set to a grid-like mosaic. Each pixel can be represented by more than one bit. A 1-bit image is black and white because each bit can have only two values (for example, 0 for white and 1 for black). For 256 colors, each pixel needs eight bits (2 8 ). A 24-bit image refers to an image with 24 bits per pixel (2 24 ), so it may contain as many as 16,777,216 colors. Because the file must contain information about the color and position of each pixel, the disk space needed for bitmap images is usually quite significant. Most digital photographs and screen captures are bitmap images.

## Bitmapped

Forming an image by a grid of pixels whose curved edges have discrete steps because of the approximation of the curve by a finite number of pixels.

## Black

The absence of color; an ink that absorbs all wavelengths of light.

## Blanket

The blanket, a fabric coated with natural or synthetic rubber wrapped around the cylinder of an offset press, transfers the inked image from the plate to the paper.

## Bleed

Page data that extends beyond the trim marks on a page. Illustrations that spread to the edge of the paper without margins are referred to as "bled off."

## Blend

See Graduated fill.

## Blind Emboss

A raised impression in paper made by a die, but without being inked. It is visible only by its relief characteristic.

## Blow up

An enlargement, usually of a graphic element such as a photograph.

## Body Copy

The text portion of the copy on a page, as distinguished from headlines.

## Border

A continuous line that extends around text; or a rectangular, oval, or irregularly-shaped visual in an ad.

## Bounding Box

The imaginary rectangle that encloses all sides of a graphic, necessary for a page layout specification.

## Brightness

1. A measure of the amount of light reflected from a surface. 2. A paper property, defined as the percentage reflection of 457-nanometer (nm) radiation. 3. The intensity of a light source. 4. The overall percentage of lightness in an image.

## Bullet

A marker preceding text, usually a solid dot, used to add emphasis; generally indicates that the text is part of a list.

## Byte

A unit of measure equal to eight bits (decimal 256) of digital information, sufficient to represent one text character. It is the standard unit measure of file size. (See also Megabyte, Kilobyte, and Gigabyte).

## Calibration

Making adjustments to a color monitor and other hardware and software to make the monitor represent as closely as possible the colors of the final printed piece.

## Calibration Bars

A strip of reference blocks of color or tonal values on film, proofs, and press sheets, used to check the accuracy of color registration, quality, density, and ink coverage during a print run.

## Callout

A descriptive label referenced to a visual element, such as several words connected to the element by an arrow.

## Camera Ready

A completely finished mechanical, ready to be photographed to produce a negative from which a printing plate will be made.

## Cap Line

The theoretical line to which the tops of capital letters are aligned.

## Caps

An abbreviation for capital letters.

## Caps and Small Caps

A style of typesetting in which capital letters are used in the normal way, while the type that would normally be in lower case has been changed to capital letters of a smaller point size. A true small-caps typeface does not contain any lower-case letters.

## Caption

The line or lines of text that identify a picture or illustration, usually placed beneath it or otherwise in close proximity.

## CCITT

International Coordinating Committee for Telephone and Telegraphy. A lossless compression method appropriate for black-and-white images.

## CD-ROM

A device used to store approximately 600MB of data. Files are permanently stored on the device and can be copied to a disk but not altered directly. ROM stands for Read-Only Memory. Equipment is now available on the consumer market for copying computer files to blank CD-ROMs.

## Center marks

Press marks that appear on the center of all sides of a press sheet to aid in positioning the print area on the paper.

## Character Count

The number of characters (letters, figures, signs or spaces) in a selected block of copy. Once used to calculate the amount of text that would fit on a given line or region when physically setting type.

## Choke

See Trapping

## Chroma

The degree of saturation of a surface color.

## Cromalin

A single-sheet color proofing system introduced by DuPont in 1971 and still quite popular in the industry. It uses a series of overlaid colorants and varnish to simulate the results of a press run.

## Chromaticity Diagram

A graphical representation of two of the three dimensions of color. Intended for plotting light sources rather than surface colors. Often called the CIE diagram.

## Cicero/Didot Point

The cicero is a unit of horizontal distance slightly larger than the pica, used widely in continental Europe. A cicero equals 0.178 inches, or 12 Didot points.

## Clipboard

The portion of computer memory that holds data that has been cut or copied. The next item cut or copied replaces the data already in the clipboard.

## Clip Gallery

A Publisher tool for previewing and inserting clip art, pictures, sounds, video clips, and animations. You can add new clips to the Gallery from other programs or from a special Microsoft site on the World Wide Web.

## Cloning

Duplication of pixels from one part of an image to another.

## CMS

See Color Management System

## CMYK

Acronym for cyan, magenta, yellow, and black, the four process color inks which, when properly overprinted, can simulate a subset of the visible spectrum. These colors form the subtractive primaries. See also color separation.

## Coated

Printing papers having a surface coating (of clay or other material) to provide a smoother, more even finish with greater opacity.

## Cold type

Type produced by photographic or digital methods, as opposed to the use of molten metal.

## Collate

To gather separate sections or leaves of a publication together in the correct order for binding.

## Collate and cut

Multiple signatures that are stacked then cut to be later placed in sequential order, drilled, and placed in three-ring binders.

## Color Balance

The combination of yellow, magenta, and cyan needed to produce a neutral gray. Determined through a gray balance analysis.

## Color Cast

The modification of a hue by the addition of a trace of another hue, such as yellowish green, pinkish blue, etc. Normally, an unwanted effect that can be corrected.

## Color Chart

A printed chart of various combinations of CMYK colors used as an aid for the selection of "legal" colors during the design phase of a project.

## Color Control Strip

A printed strip of various reference colors used to control printing quality. This strip is normally placed outside the "trim" area of a project, as a guide and visual aid for the pressman.

## Color Conversion

Changing the color "mode" of an image. Converting an image from RGB to CMYK for purposes of preparing the image for conventional printing.

## Color Correction

The process of removing casts or unwanted tints in a scanned image, in an effort to improve the appearance of the scan or to correct obvious deficiencies, such as green skies or yellowish skin tones.

## Color Gamut

The range of colors that can be formed by all possible combinations of the colorants of a given reproduction system (printing press) on a given type of paper.

## Color Key

An overlay color proof of acetate sheets, one for each of the four primary printing inks. The method was developed by 3M Corporation and remains a copyrighted term.

## Color Management System

A process or utility that attempts to manage color of input and output devices in such a way that the monitor will match the output of any CMS-managed printer.

## Color Model

A system for describing color, such as RGB, HLS, CIELAB, or CMYK.

## Color overlay

A sheet of film or paper whose text and art correspond to one spot color or process color. Each color overlay becomes the basis for a single printing plate that will apply that color to paper.

## Color Picker

A function within a graphics application that assists in selecting a color.

## Color Proof

A printed or simulated printed image of the color separations intended to produce a close representation of the final reproduction for approval and as a guide to the press operator.

## Color Scheme

A defined set of colors that is associated with a publication.

## Color Separation

The process of transforming color artwork into four components corresponding to the four process colors. If spot colors are used, additional components may be created containing only those items that will appear in the corresponding spot color layer. Each component is imaged to film or paper in preparation for making printing plates that correspond to each ink.

## Color Sequence

The color order of printing the cyan, magenta, yellow, and black inks on a printing press. Sometimes called rotation or color rotation.

## Color Space

Because a color must be represented by three basic characteristics depending on the color model, the color space is a three-dimensional coordinate system in which any color can be represented as a point.

## Color Temperature

The temperature, in degrees Kelvin, to which a blackbody would have to be heated to produce a certain color radiation. (A "blackbody" is an ideal body or surface that completely absorbs or radiates energy.) The graphic arts viewing standard is 5,000 K. The degree symbol is not used in the Kelvin scale. The higher the color temperature, the bluer the light.

## Color Transparency

A positive color photographic image on a clear film base that must be viewed by transmitted light. It is preferred for original photographic art because it has higher resolution than a color print. Transparency sizes range from 35mm color slides up to 8x10in. (203x254mm).

## Colorimeter

An optical measuring instrument designed to measure and quantify color. They are often used to match digital image values to those of cloth and other physical samples.

## Column

A vertical area for type, used to constrain line length to enhance design and readability.

## Column rule

A thin vertical rule used to separate columns of type.

## Combination signatures

Signatures of different sizes inserted at any position in a layout.

## Commercial Printing

Typically, printing on high-capacity, high-resolution presses. High-resolution commercial printing processes include offset lithography, flexography, gravure, and screen printing. Offset printing is the most widely used commercial printing process.

## Comp

Comprehensive artwork used to present the general color and layout of a page.

## Compose

To set copy into type, or lay out a page.

## Composite proof

A version of an illustration or page in which the process colors appear together to represent full color. When produced on a monochrome output device, colors are represented as shades of gray.

## Compression

A digital technique used to reduce the size of a file by analyzing occurrences of similar data. Compressed files occupy less physical space, and their use improves digital transmission speeds. Compression can sometimes result in a loss of image quality and/or resolution.

## Compression Utility

A software program that reduces a file's size for storage on a disk. If a compressed file is too large to fit onto a single disk, the compression utility compies it onto multiple disks. See Stuffit.

## Condensed Type

A typeface in which the width of the letters is narrower than that of the standard letters of the font. Condensed type can be a designed font, or the effect may be approximated by applying a percentage of normal width by a formatting command.

## Continuous Tone

An image such as an original photograph in which the subject has continuous shades of color or gray tones through the use of an emulsion process. Continuous tone images must be screened to create halftone images in order to be printed.

## Contrast

The relationship between the dark and light areas of an image.

## Copyright

Ownership of a work by the originator, such as an author, publisher, artist, or photographer. The right of copyright permits the originator of material to prevent its use without express permission or acknowledgment of the originator. Copyright may be sold, transferred, or given up contractually.

## CorelDRAW

A popular drawing program originally designed for the Windows environment, but now available also as a Macintosh program. CorelDRAW is known to create files that can cause printing and/or output problems in many prepress environments.

## Creep

The progressive extension of interior pages of the folded signature beyond the image area of the outside pages. Shingling is applied to correct for creep.

## Crop Marks

Printed short, fine lines used as guides for final trimming of the pages within a press sheet.

## Cropping

The elimination of parts of a photograph or other original that are not required to be printed.

## Crossover

An element in a book (text, line art, or other graphic)that appears on both pages of a reader spread crossing over the gutter.

## Custom printer description file

A file containing information specific to a type of output device; used in conjunction with a standard PPD file to customize the printing process.

## Data Source

A file where you store all addresses or other information for customers, friends and family, or merchants you do business with. Before you can merge a publication, you must connect your publication to a data source. See also Mail Merge.

## DCS

Acronym for Desktop Color Separation, a version of the EPS file format. DCS 1.0 files are composed of five PostScript files for each color image: cyan, magenta, yellow, and black file, plus a separate low-resolution FPO image to place in a digital file. In contrast, DCS 2.0 files have one file that stores process color and spot color information.

## Default

A specification for a mode of computer operation that operates if no other is selected. The default font size might be 12 point, or a default color for an object might be white with a black border.

## Densitometer

An electronic instrument used to measure optical density. Reflective (for paper) and transmissive (for film).

## Descender

The part of a lower-case letter that extends below the baseline (lower edge of the x-height) of the letter. The letters y, p, g, and j contain descenders.

## Desktop

1. The area on a monitor screen on which the icons appear, before an application is launched. 2. A reference to the size of computer equipment (system unit, monitor, printer) that can fit on a normal desk; thus, desktop publishing.

## Desktop Publishing (DTP)

Use of a personal computer, software applications, and a high-quality printer to produce fully composed printed documents. DTP is, in reality, an incorrect term these days. In the early days of Macintosh and PostScript technology, the term Desktop Publishing inferred that the materials produced from these systems was somehow inferior (as opposed to professional publishing). Now, the overwhelming majority of all printed materials — regardless of the quality — are produced on these systems, up to and including nationally famous magazines, catalogs, posters, and newspapers

## Dictionary

A collection of words, used by page layout programs to determine appropriate spelling and hyphenation.

## Die line

In a digital file, the outline used to mark where cutting, stamping, or embossing the finished printed piece will occur. Uses to create a particular shape, such as a rolodex card.

## Digital

The use of a series of discrete electronic pulses to represent data. In digital imaging systems, 256 steps (8 bits, or 1 byte) are normally used to characterize the gray scale or the properties of one color. For text, see ASCII.

## Digital Camera

A camera which produces images directly into an electronic file format for transfer to a computer.

## Digital Proofs

Digital proofs are representations of what a specific mechanical will look like when output and reproduced on a specific type of printing press. The difference with a digital proof is that it is created without the use of conventional film processes and output directly from computer files.

## Dingbat

A font character that displays a picture instead of a letter, number or punctuation mark. There are entire font families of pictographic dingbats; the most commonly used dingbat font is Zapf Dingbats. There are dingbats for everything from the little airplanes used to represent airports on a map, to telephones, swashes, fish, stars, balloons — just about anything. Also, a printer's typographical ornament.

## Direct-to-plate

Producing printing plates directly from computer output without going through the film process.

## Disk Operating System

Software for computer systems that supervises and controls the running of programs. The operating system is loaded into memory from disk by a small program which permanently resides in the firmware within the computer. The major operating systems in use today are Windows95/98 and WindowsNT from Microsoft, the Macintosh OS from Apple Computer, and a wide range of UNIX systems, such as those from Silicon Graphics, SUN Microsystems, and other vendors.

## Dithering

A technique used in images wherein a color is represented using dots of two different colors displayed or printed very close together. Dithering is often used to compress digital images, in special screening algorithms (see Stochastic Screening) and to produce higher quality output on low-end color printers.

## Document

The general term for a computer file containing text and/or graphics.

## Dot Gain

The growth of a halftone dot that occurs whenever ink soaks into paper. This growth can vary from being very small (on a high-speed press with fast-drying ink and very non-porous paper) to quite dramatic, as is the case in newspaper printing, where a dot can expand 30% from its size on the film to the size at which it dries. Failure to compensate for this gain in the generation of digital images can result in very poor results on press. Generally speaking, the finer the screen (and therefore, the smaller the dot) the more noticeable dot gain will be.

## Double-page Spread

A design that spans the two pages visible to the reader at any open spot in a magazine, periodical, or book.

## Downloadable Fonts

Typefaces that can be stored on disk and then downloaded to the printer when required for printing.

## DPI (Dots Per Inch)

The measurement of resolution for page printers, phototypesetting machines and graphics screens. Currently graphics screens use resolutions of 60 to 100 dpi, standard desktop laser printers work at 600 dpi, and imagesetters operate at more than 1,500 dpi.

## Drop Shadow

A duplicate of a graphic element or type placed behind and slightly offset from it, giving the effect of a shadow.

## Draw-type pictures

Object-oriented images or vector graphics) Pictures created from a series of instructions that tell the computer to draw lines, curves, rectangles, and other objects. See Bitmap Image.

## Drum Scanner

A color scanner on which the original is wrapped around a rotary scanning drum. See Scanner.

## DSC

Acronym for the Adobe Document Structure Conventions, designed to provide a standard order and format for information so applications that process PostScript, such as PressWise, can easily find information about a document's structure and imaging requirements. These conventions allow specially formatted PostScript comments to be added to the page description; applications can search for these comments, but PostScript interpreters usually ignore them. TrapWise requires that the PostScript in incoming files is formatted using conventional DSC comments, so certain functions may not work properly if the file is not DSC-conforming.

### Duotone

The separation of a black-and-white photograph into black and a second color having different tonal values and screen angles. Duotones are used to enhance photographic reproduction in two-three-or sometimes four-color work. Often the second, third, and fourth colors are not standard CMYK inks.

### Dye

A soluble coloring material, normally used as the colorant in color photographs.

### Dye Transfer

A photographic color print using special coated papers to produce a full color image. Can serve as an inexpensive proof.

### Electronic Form

An interactive form in a Web site, filled out by readers and then sent back to the owner of the Web site or stored on a Web server.

### Electrostatic

The method by which dry toner is transferred to paper in a copier or laser printer, and liquid toners are bonded to paper on some large-format color plotters.

### Element

The smallest unit of a graphic, or a component of a page layout or design. Any object, text block, or graphic might be referred to as an element of the design.

### Elliptical Dot Screen

A halftone screen having an elliptical dot structure.

### Embedding

1. Placing control codes in the body of a document. 2. Including a complete copy of a text file or image within a desktop publishing document, with or without a link (see Linking).

### Em Dash

A dash (—) that indicates the separation of elements of a sentence or clause.

### Em Space

A space that is of equal width in points to the point size. An em space in 10 point type is 10 points wide.

### En Dash

A dash (–), half the width of an em dash, that often replaces the word "to" or "through," such as 9–5 or Monday–Friday.

### Emulsion

The coating of light-sensitive material (silver halide) on a piece of film or photographic paper.

### En Dash

A dash - often used in hyphenated word pairs - that is usually half the width of an em dash.

### En Space

A space that is equal to half the width of an em space.

### EPS

Acronym for encapsulated PostScript, a single-page PostScript file that contains grayscale or color information and can be imported into many electronic layout and design applications.

### EPS (Encapsulated PostScript)

Acronym for file format used to transfer PostScript data within compatible applications. An EPS file normally contains a small preview image that displays in position within a mechanical or used by another program. EPS files can contain text, vector artwork, and images.

### Expanded Type

Also called extended. A typeface in which the width of the letters is wider than that of the standard letters of the font. Expanded type can be a designed font, or the effect may be approximated by applying a percentage of normal width by a formatting command.

### Export

To save a file generated in one application in a format that is readable in another application.

### Extension

A modular software program that extends or expands the functions of a larger program. A folder of Extensions is found in the Macintosh System Folder.

### Film

Non-paper output of an imagesetter or phototypesetter.

### Film assembly

See Stripping.

### Filter

In image editing applications, a small program that creates a special effect or performs some other function within an image.

### First signature folding dummy

A folding dummy that determines the page arrangement for a single signature layout template. This template can then be applied to a job that requires multiple signatures, and PressWise will correctly impose all the pages based on the numbering sequence and binding method specified by the first signature.

### Flat

Individual film assembled onto a carrier readied for contacting or platemaking. Referred to as a cab in gravure printing.

### Flat Color

Color that lacks contrast or tonal variation. Also, flat tint.

### Flatbed Scanner

A scanner on which the original is mounted on a flat scanning glass. See Scanner.

### Flexographic printing

A rotary letterpress process printing on a press using a rubber plate that stretches around a cylinder making it necessary to compensate by distorting the plate image. Flexography is used most often in label printing, often on metal or other non-paper material.

### Floating Accent

A separate accent mark that can be placed under or over another character. Complex accented characters such as in foreign languages are usually available in a font as a single character.

## Flop

To make a mirror image of visuals such as photographs or clip art.

## Folder

1. The digital equivalent of a paper file folder, used to organize files in the Macintosh and Windows operating systems. The icon of a folder looks like a paper file folder. Double-clicking it opens it to reveal the files stored inside. 2. A mechanical device which folds preprinted pages into various formats, such as a tri-fold brochure.

## Folding dummy

A template used for determining the page arrangement on a form to meet folding and binding requirements. See also All signature folding dummy and First signature folding dummy.

## Font

A font is the complete collection of all the characters (numbers, uppercase and lowercase letters and, in some cases, small caps and symbols) of a given typeface in a specific style; for example, Helvetica Bold.

## Font Subsetting

Embedding only part of a font. If you use only a small number of characters from a font, say for drop caps or for headlines, you can embed only the characters you used from the font. The advantage of font subsetting is that it decreases the overall size of your file. The disadvantage is that it limits the ability to makes corrections at the printing service.

## Font Substitution

A process in which your computer uses a font similar to the one you used in your publication to display or print your publication. Although the substitute font may be similar to the original font, your publication will not look exactly as you intended; line breaks, column breaks, or page breaks may fall differently, which can affect the entire look and feel of the publication.

## Force Justify

A type alignment command which causes the space between letters and words in a line of type to expand to fit

within a line. Often used in headlines, and sometimes used to force the last line of a justified paragraph, which is normally set flush left, to justify.

## Form

The front or back of a signature.

## Four-color Process

See Process Colors

## FPO

Acronym for For Position Only, a term applied to low-quality art reproductions or simple shapes used to indicate placement and scaling of an art element on mechanicals or camera-ready artwork. In digital publishing, an FPO can be low-resolution TIFF files that are later replaced with high-resolution versions. An FPO is not intended for reproduction but only as a guide and placeholder for the prepress service provider.

## Frame

In desktop publishing, (1.) an area or block into which text or graphics can be placed; (2.) a border on .

## FreeHand

A popular vector-based illustration program available from Macromedia.

## Full Measure

A line set to the entire line length.

## G (Gigabyte)

One billion (1,073,741,824) bytes (230) or 1,048,576 kilobytes.

## Galley Proof

Proofs, usually of type, taken before the type is made up into pages. Before desktop publishing, galley proofs were hand-assembled into pages.

## Gamma

A measure of the contrast, or range of tonal variation, of the midtones in a photographic image.

## Gamma Correction

1. Adjusting the contrast of the midtones in an image. 2. Calibrating a monitor so that midtones are correctly displayed on screen.

## Gamut

See Color Gamut

## GASP

Acronym for Graphic Arts Service Provider, a firm that provides a range

of services somewhere on the continuum from design to fulfillment.

## GCR

An acronym for Gray Component Replacement. A technique for adding detail by reducing the amount of cyan, magenta, and yellow in chromatic or colored areas, replacing them with black.

## GIF

An acronym for Graphics Interchange Format. A popular graphics format for online clip art and drawn graphics. Graphics in this format look good at low resolution.

## GIF, Animated

A series of GIF graphics that functions like a film loop, giving the appearance of animation. See GIF.

## Global Preferences

Preference settings which affect all newly created files within an application.

## Glyph

Any character of a font.

## Gradient fill

See Graduated fill.

## Graduated fill

An area in which two colors (or shades of gray or the same color) are blended to create a gradual change from one to the other. Graduated fills are also known as blends, gradations, gradient fills, and vignettes.

## Grain

Silver salts clumped together in differing amounts in different types of photographic emulsions. Generally speaking, faster emulsions have larger grain sizes.

## Graininess

Visual impression of the irregularly distributed silver grain clumps in a photographic image, or the ink film in a printed image.

## Gray Balance

The values for the yellow, magenta, and cyan inks that are needed to produce a neutral gray when printed at a normal density.

## Gray Component Replacement

See GCR

## Grayscale

1. An image composed in grays ranging from black to white, usually using 256 different tones of gray. 2. A tint ramp used to measure and control the accuracy of screen percentages on press. 3. An accessory used to define neutral density in a photographic image.

## Greeking

1. A software technique by which areas of gray are used to simulate lines of text below a certain point size. 2. Nonsense text use to define a layout before copy is available.

## Grid

A division of a page by horizontal and vertical guides into areas into which text or graphics may be placed accurately.

## Grind-off

The roughing up at the back (or spine) of a folded signature, or of two or more gathered signatures, in preparation for perfect binding.

## Gripper edge

The leading edge of a sheet of paper, which the grippers on the press grab to carry the paper through a press.

## Group

To collect graphic elements together so that an operation may be applied to all of them simultaneously.

## GUI

Acronym for Graphical User Interface, the basis of the Macintosh and Windows operating systems.

## Gutter

Extra space between pages in a layout. Sometimes used interchangeably with Alley to describe the space between columns on a page. Gutters can appear either between the top and bottom of two adjacent pages or between two sides of adjacent pages. Gutters are often used because of the binding or layout requirements of a job — for example, to add space at the top or bottom of each page or to allow for the grind-off taken when a book is perfect bound.

## H & J

Hyphenation and Justification. Parameters used by a page layout program to determine how a line of text should be hyphenated, or how its inter-word and inter-character space should be adjusted.

## Hairline Rule

The thinnest rule that can be printed on a given device. A hairline rule on a 1200 dpi imagesetter is 1/1200 of an inch; on a 300 dpi laser printer, the same rule would print at 1/300 of an inch.

## Halftone

An image generated for use in printing in which a range of continuous tones is simulated by an array of dots that create the illusion of continuous tone when seen at a distance.

## Halftone Tint

An area covered with a uniform halftone dot size to produce an even tone or color. Also called flat tint or screen tint.

## Hanging Punctuation

A margin alignment technique where the punctuation falls outside the margins, making the edges of the text appear more even.

## Hard Drive

A rigid disk sealed inside an airtight transport mechanism that is the basic storage mechanism in a computer. Information stored may be accessed more rapidly than on floppy disks and far greater amounts of data stored.

## High Key

A photographic or printed image in which the main interest area lies in the highlight end of the scale.

## High Resolution File

An image file that typically contains four pixels for every dot in the printed reproduction. High-resolution files are often linked to a page layout file, but not actually embedded in it, due to their large size.

## Highlights

The lightest areas in a photograph or illustration.

## Home Page

The first page readers encounter when opening a Web site.

## Hot Spot

An area on an object containing a hyperlink. An entire object can be a single hot spot, or an object can contain multiple hot spots.

## HSL

A color model that defines color based on its hue, saturation, and luminosity (value), as it is displayed on a video or computer screen.

## HSV

A color model based on three coordinates: hue, saturation and value (or luminance).

## HTML

An acronym for HyperText Markup Language. The language, written in plain (ASCII) text using simple tags, that is used to create Web pages, and which Web browsers are designed to read and display. HTML focuses more on the logical structure of a page than its appearance. HTML is used to mark, or code, the content of your design (text, graphics, sounds, and animation) so that it can be published on the Web and viewed with a browser.

## Hue

The wavelength of light of a color in its purest state (without adding white or black).

## Hyperlink

An HTML tag directs the computer to a different Anchor or URL (Uniform Resource Locator). The linked data may be on the same page, or on a computer anywhere in the world. A hyperlink can be a word, phrase, sentence, graphic, or icon. A hyperlink can also cause an action, such as opening or downloading a file.

## Hyphenation Zone

The space at the end of a line of text in which the hyphenation function will examine the word to determine whether or not it should be hyphenated and wrapped to the next line.

## ICC Profile

Using a format designed by the International Color Consortium, the profile

describes the colorspace used to create the document, based on the gamut of

the color device referenced.

## ICM

An acronym for Image Color Matching. Many, but not all, printer and monitor manufacturers use the Image Color Matching standard. ICM gives you a better idea of what the final colors in your publication will look like.

## Icon

A small graphic symbol used on the screen to indicate files or folders, activated by clicking with the mouse or pointing device.

## Illustrator

A vector editing application owned by Adobe Systems, Inc.

## Imaging

The process of producing a film or paper copy of a digital file from an output device.

## Imagesetter

A raster-based device used to output a computer page-layout file or composition at high resolution (usually 1000 - 3000 dpi) onto photographic paper or film, from which to make printing plates.

## Import

To bring a file generated within one application into another application.

## Imposition

The arrangement of pages on a printed sheet, which, when the sheet is finally printed, folded and trimmed, will place the pages in their correct order.

## Indent to Here

A special character that, when activated, causes all subsequent lines in a paragraph to indent from the left margin to that point.

## InDesign

A page layout program from Adobe Systems.

## Indexed Color Image

An image which uses a limited, predetermined number of colors; often used in Web images. See also GIF.

## Indexing

In DTP, marking certain words within a document with hidden codes so that an index may be automatically generated.

## Initial Caps

Text in which the first letter of each word (except articles, etc.) is capitalized.

## Intensity

Synonym for degree of color saturation.

## International Paper Sizes

The International Standards Organization (ISO) system of paper sizes is based on a series of three sizes A, B and C. Series A is used for general printing and stationery, Series B for posters, and Series C for envelopes. Each size has the same proportion of length to width as the others. The nearest ISO paper size to conventional 8-1/2 x 11 paper is A4.

## Internet

An international network of computer networks, which links millions of commercial, educational, governmental, and personal computers. See World Wide Web.

## Island Spread

A spread that includes more than two pages.

## ISO

The International Standards Organization.

## Internet Service Provider (ISP)

An organization that provides access to the Internet for such things as electronic mail, bulletin boards, chat rooms, or use of the World Wide Web.

## Jaggies

Visible steps in the curved edge of a graphic or text character that results from enlarging a bitmapped image.

## JPG or JPEG

An acronym for Joint Photographers Experts Group. A compression algorithm that reduces the file size of bitmapped images, named for the Joint Photographic Experts Group, an industry organization that created the standard; JPEG is a "lossy" compression method, and image quality will be reduced in direct proportion to the amount of compression. JPEG graphics produce resolution for color photographics than a GIF format. See GIF.

## Justified Alignment

Straight left and right alignment of text — not ragged. Every line of text is the same width, creating even left and right margins.

## Kelvin (K)

Unit of temperature measurement based on Celsius degrees, starting from absolute zero, which is equivalent to -273 Celsius (centigrade); used to indicate the color temperature of a light source.

## Kerning

Moving a pair of letters closer together or farther apart, to achieve a better fit or appearance.

## Key (Black Plate)

In early four-color printing, the black plate was printed first and the other three colors were aligned (or registered) to it. Thus, the black plate was the "key" to the result.

## Keyline

A thin, often black border around a picture or a box indicating where to place pictures. In digital files, the keylines are often vector objects while photographs are usually bitmap images.

## Kilobyte (K, KB)

1,024 (210) bytes, the nearest binary equivalent to decimal 1,000 bytes. Abbreviated and referred to as K.

## Knockout

A printing technique that represents overlapping objects without mixing inks. The ink for the underlying element does not print (knocks out) in the area where the objects overlap. Opposite of overprinting.

## L*a*b

The lightness, red-green attribute, and yellow-blue attribute in the CIE Color Space, a three-dimensional color mapping system.

## Landscape

Printing from the left to right across the wider side of the page. A landscape orientation treats a page as 11 inches wide and 8.5 inches long.

## Laser printer

A high quality image printing system using a laser beam to produce an image on a photosensitive drum. The image is transferred to paper by a conventional xerographic printing process. Current laser printers used for desktop publishing have a resolution of 600 dpi. Imagesetters are also laser printers, but with higher resolution and tight mechanical controls to produce final film separations for commercial printing.

## Layer

A function of graphics or page layout applications in which elements may be hidden from view, locked, reordered or otherwise manipulated as a unit, without affecting other elements on the page.

## Layout

The arrangement of text and graphics on a page, usually produced in the preliminary design stage.

## Leaders

A line of periods or other symbols connecting the end of a group of words with another element separated by some space. For example, a table of contents may consist of a series of phrases on separate lines, each associated with a page number. Promotes readability in long lists of tabular text.

## Leading ("ledding")

Space added between lines of type. Usually measured in points or fractions of points. Named after the strips of lead which used to be inserted between lines of metal type. In specifying type, lines of 12-pt. type separated by a 14-pt. space is abbreviated "12/14," or "twelve over fourteen."

## Letterspacing

The insertion or addition of white space between the letters of words.

## Library

In the computer world, a collection of files having a similar purpose or function.

## Ligature

Letters that are joined together as a single unit of type such as œ and fi.

## Lightness

The property that distinguishes white from gray or black, and light from dark color tones on a surface.

## Line Art

A drawing or piece of black and white artwork, with no screens. Line art can be represented by a graphic file having only one-bit resolution.

## Line Screen

The number of lines per inch used when converting a photograph to a halftone. Typical values range from 85 for newspaper work to 150 or higher for high-quality reproduction on smooth or coated paper.

## Linking

An association through software of a graphic or text file on disk with its location in a document. That location may be represented by a "placeholder" rectangle, or a low-resolution copy of the graphic.

## Lithography

A mechanical printing process used for centuries based on the principle of the natural aversion of water (in this case, ink) to grease. In modern offset lithography, the image on a photosensitive plate is first transferred to the blanket of a rotating drum, and then to the paper.

## Lossy

A data compression method characterized by the loss of some data.

## Loupe

A small free-standing magnifier used to see fine detail on a page.

## LPI

Lines per inch. See Line Screen.

## Luminosity

The amount of light, or brightness, in an image. Part of the HLS color model.

## LZW

The acronym for the Lempel-Ziv-Welch lossless data- and image-compression algorithm.

## M, MB (Megabyte)

One million (1,048,576) bytes (220) or 1,024 Kilobytes.

## Macro

A set of keystrokes that is saved as a named computer file. When accessed, the keystrokes will be performed. Macros are used to perform repetitive tasks.

## Mail Merge

The process of combining a data source with a publication to print a batch of individually customized publications.

## Margins

The non-printing areas of page, or the line at which text starts or stops.

## Mask

To conform the shape of a photograph or illustration to another shape such as a circle or polygon.

## Masking

A technique that blocks an area of an image from reproduction by superimposing an opaque object of any shape.

## Master

Underlying pages or spreads containing elements common to all pages to which the master is applied.

## Match Print

A color proofing system used for the final quality check.

## Mechanical

A pasted-up page of camera-ready art that is to be photographed to produce a plate for the press.

## Medium

A physical carrier of data such as a CD-ROM, video cassette, or floppy disk, or a carrier of electronic data such as fiber optic cable or electric wires.

## Megabyte (MB)

A unit of measure of stored data equaling 1,024 kilobytes, or 1,048,576 bytes (1020).

## Megahertz

An analog signal frequency of one million cycles per second, or a data rate of one million bits per second. Used in specifying computer CPU speed.

## Menu

A list of choices of functions, or of items such as fonts. In contemporary software design, there is often a fixed menu of basic functions at the top of the page that have pull-down menus associated with each of the fixed choices.

## Metafile

A class of graphics that combines the characteristics of raster and vector graphics formats; not recommended for high-quality output.

## Metallic Ink

Printing inks which produce an effect of gold, silver, bronze, or metallic colors.

## Midtones or Middletones

The tonal range between highlights and shadows.

## Misregistration

The unwanted result of incorrectly aligned process inks and spot colors on a finished printed piece. Misregistration can be caused by many factors, including paper stretch and improper plate alignment. Trapping can compensate for misregistration.

## Modem

An electronic device for converting digital data into analog audio signals and back again (MOdulator-DEModulator). Primarily used for transmitting data between computers over analog (audio frequency) telephone lines.

## Moiré

An interference pattern caused by the out-of-register overlap of two or more regular patterns such as dots or lines. In process-color printing, screen angles are selected to minimize this pattern.

## Monochrome

An image or computer monitor in which all information is represented in black and white, or with a range of grays.

## Monospace

A font in which all characters occupy the same amount of horizontal width regardless of the character. See also Proportional Spacing.

## Montage

A single image formed by assembling or compositing several images.

## Mottle

Uneven color or tone.

## Multimedia

The combination of sound, video images, and text to create a "moving" presentation.

## Nested signatures

Multiple signatures that are folded, gathered, and placed one inside another, and then saddle-stitched at the spine.

## Nesting

Placing graphic files within other graphic files. This unacceptable practice often results in errors in printing.

## Network

Two or more computers that are linked to exchange data or share resources. The Internet is a network of networks.

## Neutral

Any color that has no hue, such as white, gray, or black.

## Neutral density

A measurement of the lightness or darkness of a color. A neutral density of zero (0.00) is the lightest value possible and is equivalent to pure white; 3.294 is roughly equivalent to 100% of each of the CMYK components.

## Noise

Unwanted signals or data that may reduce the quality of the output.

## Non-breaking Space

A typographic command that connects two words with a space, but prevents the words from being broken apart if the space occurs within the hyphenation zone. See Hyphenation Zone.

## Non-reproducible Colors

Colors in an original scene or photograph that are impossible to reproduce using process inks. Also called out-of-gamut colors.

## Normal Key

A description of an image in which the main interest area is in the middle range of the tone scale or distributed throughout the entire tonal range.

## Nudge

To move a graphic or text element in small, preset increments, usually with the arrow keys.

## Object-oriented art

Vector-based artwork composed of separate elements or shapes described mathematically rather than by specifying the color and position of every point. This contrasts to bitmap images, which are composed of individual pixels.

## Oblique

A slanted character (sometimes backwards, or to the left), often used when referring to italic versions of sans-serif typefaces.

## Offset

In graphics manipulation, to move a copy or clone of an image slightly to the side and/or back; used for a drop-shadow effect.

## Offset Lithography

A printing method whereby the image is transferred from a plate onto a rubber covered cylinder from which the printing takes place (see Lithography).

## OLE

An acronym for Object Linking and Embedding. When you add an object to a publication as a linked object, you can use another program while you're in Publisher to make changes to the object. But unlike an embedded object, a linked object can be easily updated to match changes made to the original document (called the source document) in your source program. Likewise, any changes you make to the linked object in your publication will also appear in the source document (and any other documents that are linked to that object).

## Online Publishing

Preparing documents for viewing on monitors, such as through CD distribution or the Internet.

## Opacity

1. The degree to which paper will show print through it. 2. Settings in certain graphics applications that allow images or text below the object whose opacity has been adjusted, to show through.

## Opaque Inks

Inks which are not designed to interact with other inks. Their pigment is so dense that, when they overprint another color ink, there is no interaction between them.

## OPI

Acronym for Open Prepress Interface. 1. A set of PostScript language comments originally developed by Aldus Corporation for defining and specifying the placement of high-resolution images in PostScript files on an electronic page layout. 2. Incorporation of a low resolution preview image within a graphic file format (TIF, EPS, DCS) that is intended for display only. 3. Software device that is an extension to PostScript that replaces low-resolution placeholder images in a document with their high-resolution sources for printing.

## Optical Disks

Video disks that store large amounts of data used primarily for reference works such as dictionaries and encyclopedias.

## Orphan

A single or partial word, or a partial line of a paragraph appearing at the bottom of a page. See widow.

## Output device

Any hardware equipment, such as a monitor, laser printer, or imagesetter, that depicts text or graphics created on a computer.

## Overflow area

Where Publisher stores text that will not fit in a text frame or chain of connected text frames, or in a cell of a table whose size is locked. You cannot see text that's stored in the overflow area.

## Overlay

A transparent sheet used in the preparation of multicolor mechanical artwork showing the color breakdown.

## Overprint

A printing technique that lays down one ink on top of another ink. The overprinted inks can combine to make a new color. The opposite of knockout.

## Overprint Color

A color made by overprinting any two or more of the primary yellow, magenta, and cyan process colors.

## Overprinting

Allowing an element to print over the top of underlying elements, rather than knocking them out (see Knockout). Often used with black type.

## Package

Prepare a document for delivery to a service provider by putting the document file, together will all linked files in one folder. Fonts may or may not be included in the package, based on the licensing parameters.

## Page Description Language (PDL)

A special form of programming language that describes both text and graphics (object or bit-image) in mathematical form. The main benefit of a PDL is that makes the application software independent of the physical printing device. PostScript is a PDL, for example.

## Page Layout Software

Desktop publishing software such as InDesign used to combine various source documents and images into a high quality publication.

## Page Proofs

Proofs of the actual pages of a document, usually produced just before printing, for a final quality check.

## PageMaker

A popular page-layout application produced by Adobe Systems.

## Palette

1. As derived from the term in the traditional art world, a collection of selectable colors. 2. Another name for a dialog box or menu of choices.

## Panose

A typeface matching system for font substitution based on a numeric classification of fonts according to visual characteristics.

## Pantone Matching System

A system for specifying colors by number for both coated and uncoated paper; used by print services and in color desktop publishing to assure uniform color matching. One of the most widely used color-matching systems in commercial printing.

## Parallel fold

A folding method in which folds of a signature are parallel.

## Pasteboard

In a page layout program, the desktop area outside of the printing page area, on which elements can be placed for later positioning on any page.

## PCX

Bitmap image format produced by paint programs.

## PDF (Portable Document Format)

Developed by Adobe Systems, Inc. (and read by Adobe Acrobat Reader), this format has become a de facto standard for document transfer across platforms.

## Perfect Binding

A binding method in which signatures are "ground off" at the spine of the book and then bound with adhesive, so each page is glued individually to the spine.

## Perspective

The effect of distance in an image achieved by aligning the edges of elements with imaginary lines directed toward one to three "vanishing points" on the horizon.

## Photoshop

The Adobe Systems image editing program commonly used for color correction and special effects on both the Macintosh and PC platforms.

## Pi Fonts

A collection of special characters such as timetable symbols and mathematical signs. Examples are Zapf Dingbats and Symbol. See also Dingbats.

## Pica

A traditional typographic measurement of 12 points, or approximately 1/6 of an inch. Most DTP applications specify a pica as exactly 1/6 of an inch.

## PICT/PICT2

A common format for defining bitmapped images on the Macintosh. The more recent PICT2 format supports 24-bit color.

## Pixel

Abbreviation for picture element, the smallest element capable of being produced by a monitor, scanner, or other light-transmitting device. If a pixel is turned on it has color. If it is turned off it appears as a blank space. Pixels can vary in size from one monitor to another. A greater number of pixels per inch (ppi) results in a higher resolution.

## Plug-in

A program that works within a primary program to extend the features of the core program.

## PMS

See Pantone Matching System

## PMT

Photo Mechanical Transfer - positive prints of text or images used for paste-up to mechanicals.

## PNG

Portable Network Graphics format that uses adjustable, lossless compression to display 24-bit photographs or solid-color images on the Internet or other online services.

## Point

A unit of measurement used to specify type size and rule weight, equal to (approximately, in traditional typesetting) 1/72 inch. Note: Font sizes are measured completely differently from leading, even though they're both specified in points, and the only way you can verify font size on your hard copy is by measuring it against the designated sizes you'll find on an E-scale.

## Polygon

A geometric figure consisting of three or more straight lines enclosing an area. The triangle, square, rectangle, and star are all polygons.

## Portrait

Printing from left to right across the narrow side of the page. Portrait orientation on a letter-size page uses a standard 8.5-inch width and 11-inch length.

## Positive

A true photographic image of the original made on paper or film.

## Posterize, Posterization

The deliberate constraint of a gradient or image into visible steps as a special effect; or the unintentional creation of steps in an image due to a high LPI value used with a low printer DPI.

## Postprocessing Applications

Applications, such as trapping programs or imposition software, that perform their functions after the image has been printed to a file, rather than in the originating application.

## PostScript

1. A page description language developed by Adobe Systems, Inc. that describes type and/or images and their positional relationships upon the page. 2. An interpreter or RIP (see Raster Image Processor) that can process the PostScript page description into a format for laser printer or imagesetter output. 3. A computer programming language.

## PostScript Printer Description file

(PPD) Acronym for PostScript Printer Description, a file format developed by Adobe Systems, Inc., that contains device-specific information enabling software to produce the best results possible for each type of designated printer.

## PPI

Pixels per inch; used to denote the resolution of an image.

## Preferences

A set of defaults for an application program that may be modified.

## Preflight Check

The prepress process, in which the printing service verifies that fonts and linked graphics are available, traps your publication, makes color corrections or separations, and sets final printing options.

## Prepress

All work done between writing and printing, such as typesetting, scanning, layout, and imposition.

## Prepress Proof

A color proof made directly from electronic data or film images.

## Press sheet

In sheet-fed printing, the paper stock of common sizes that is used in commercial printing.

## Primary Colors

Colors that can be used to generate secondary colors. For the additive system (i.e., a computer monitor), these colors are red, green, and blue. For the subtractive system (i.e., the printing process), these colors are cyan, magenta, and yellow.

## Printer Command Language

PCL — a language, that has graphics capability, developed by Hewlett Packard for use with its own range of printers.

## Printer driver

The device that communicates between your software program and your printer.

## Printer fonts

The image outlines for type in PostScript that are sent to the printer.

## Process colors

The four transparent inks (cyan, magenta, yellow, and black) used in four-color process printing. A printing method in which a full range of colors is reproduced by combining four smitransparent inks. Process-color printing is typically used when your publication includes full-color photographs or multicolor graphics, and when you want the high resolution and quality that printing on an offset press provides. See also Color separation; CMYK.

## Profile

A file containing data representing the color reproduction characteristics of a device determined by a calibration of some sort.

## Proof

A representation of the printed job that is made from plates (press proof), film, or electronic data (prepress proofs). It is generally used for customer inspection and approval before mass production begins.

## Proportional Spacing

A method of spacing whereby each character is spaced to accommodate the varying widths of letters or figures, thus increasing readability. Books and magazines are set proportionally spaced, and most fonts in desktop publishing are proportional. With proportionally spaced fonts, each character is given a horizontal space proportional to its size. For example, a proportionally spaced "m" is wider than an "i."

## Pt.

Abbreviation for point.

## Pull quote

An excerpt from the body of a story used to emphasize an idea, draw readers' attention, or generate interest.

## QuarkXPress

A popular page-layout application.

## Queue

A set of files input to the printer, printed in the order received unless otherwise instructed.

## QuickDraw

Graphic routines in the Macintosh used for outputting text and images to printers not compatible with PostScript.

## RAM

Random Access Memory, the "working" memory of a computer that holds files in process. Files in RAM are lost when the computer is turned off, whereas files stored on the hard drive or floppy disks remain available.

## Raster

A bitmapped representation of graphic data.

## Raster Graphics

A class of graphics created and organized in a rectangular array of bitmaps. Often created by paint software, fax machines, or scanners for display and printing.

## Raster Image Processor (RIP)

That part of a PostScript printer or imagesetting device that converts the page information from the PostScript Page Description Language into the bitmap pattern that is applied to the film or paper output.

## Rasterize

The process of converting digital information into pixels at the resolution of the output device. For example, the process used by an imagesetter to translate PostScript files before they are imaged to film or paper. See also RIP.

## Reflective Art

Artwork that is opaque, as opposed to transparent, that can be scanned for input to a computer.

## Registration

Aligning plates on a multicolor printing press so that the images will superimpose properly to produce the required composite output.

## Registration Color

A default color selection that can be applied to design elements so that they will print on every separation from a PostScript printer. "Registration" is often used to print identification text that will appear outside the page area on a set of separations.

## Registration marks

Figures (often crossed lines and a circle) placed outside the trim page boundaries on all color separation overlays to provide a common element for proper alignment.

## Resample

Alter the resolution of an image. Downsampling averages the pixels in an area and replaces the entire area with the average pixel color at the specified resolution. Subsampling chooses a single pixel and replaces the entire area with that pixel at the specified resolution; it is not recommended for high-resolution printing.

## Resolution

The density of graphic information expressed in dots per inch (dpi) or pixels per inch (ppi).

## Retouching

Making selective manual or electronic corrections to images.

## Reverse Out

To reproduce an object as white, or paper, within a solid background, such as white letters in a black rectangle.

## RGB

Acronym for red, green, blue, the colors of projected light from a computer monitor that, when combined, simulate a subset of the visual spectrum. When a color image is scanned, RGB data is collected by the scanner and then converted to CMYK data at some later step in the process. Also refers to the color model of most digital artwork. See also CMYK.

## Rich Black

A process color consisting of sold black with one or more layers of cyan, magenta, or yellow.

## Right Indent Tab

An option to position the text at the right indent position following the insertion of the Right Indent Tab command.

## Right Reading

A positive or negative image that is readable from top to bottom and from left to right.

## Right Alignment

Straight right edge of text with a ragged, or uneven, left edge.

## Right-angle fold

A folding method in which any successive fold of a signature is at right angles to the previous fold.

## RIP

See Raster Image Processor

## ROM

Read Only Memory, a semiconductor chip in the computer that retains startup information for use the next time the computer is turned on.

## Rosette

The pattern created when color halftone screens are printed at traditional screen angles.

## Rotation

Turning an object at some angle to its original axis.

## RTF

Rich Text Format, a text format that retains formatting information lost in pure ASCII text.

## Rubylith

A two-layer acetate film having a red or amber emulsion on a clear base used in non-computer stripping and separation operations.

## Rules

Straight lines, often stretching horizothally across the top of a page to separate text from running heads.

## Running Head – (header)

Text at the top of the page that provides information abot the publication. Chapter names and book titles are often included in the running head.

## Saddle-stitching

A binding method in which each signature is folded and stapled at the spine.

## Sans Serif

Sans Serif fonts are fonts that do not have the tiny lines that appear at the top of and bottom of letters.

## Saturation

The intensity or purity of a particular color; a color with no saturation is gray.

## Scaling

The means within a program to reduce or enlarge the amount of space an image will occupy by multiplying the data by a scale factor. Scaling can be proportional, or in one dimension only.

## Scanner

A device that electronically digitizes images point by point through circuits that can correct color, manipulate tones, and enhance detail. Color scanners will usually produce a minimum of 24 bits for each pixel, with 8 bits each for red, green, and blue.

## Scheme color

One of the colors defined in a color scheme. If you fill an object with a scheme color, the object's color changes whenever you choose another color scheme for that publication.

## Screen

To create a halftone of a continuous tone image (See Halftone).

## Screen Angle

The angle at which the rulings of a halftone screen are set when making screened images for halftone process-color printing. The equivalent effect can be obtained electronically through selection of the desired angle from a menu.

## Screen Frequency

The number of lines per inch in a halftone screen, which may vary from 85 to 300.

## Screen Printing

A technique for printing on practically any surface using a fine mesh (originally of silk) on which the image has been placed photographically. Preparation of art for screen printing requires consideration of the resolution of the screen printing process.

## Screen Shot

A printed output or saved file that represents data from a computer monitor.

## Screen Tint

A halftone screen pattern of all the same dot size that creates an even tone at some percentage of solid color.

## Search Engine

A program that uses keywords supplied by Web users to search databases of Web sites and other resources the the World Wide Web for information on a specific topic. Search engines create indexes of Web sites, which are then searchable databases. See World Wide Web.

## Section

A range of pages having a different numbering sequence from other pages in the document. For example, the frontmatter, projects, glossary, and index all have their own numbering systems.

## Selection

The act of placing the cursor on an object and clicking the mouse button to make the object active.

## Self-Cover

A cover for a document in which the cover is of the same paper stock as the rest of the piece.

## Separation

See Color separation.

## Serif

A line or curve projecting from the end of a letterform. Typefaces designed with such projections are called serif faces.

## Service Bureau

A business that specializes in producing film for printing on a high-resolution imagesetter. An organization that provides services, such as scanning and prepress checks, that prepare your publication to be printed on a commercial printing press. Service bureaus do not, however, print your publication. To find out if you need to use a service bureau, talk to your printing professional.

## SGML

Standard Generalized Markup Language, a set of semantics and syntax that describes the structure of a document (the nature, content, or function of the data) as opposed to visual appearance. HTML is a subset of SGML (see HTML).

## Shade

A color mixed with black: a 10-percent shade is one part of the original color and nine parts black. See tint.

## Sharpness

The subjective impression of the density difference between two tones at their boundary, interpreted as fineness of detail.

## Shortcut

1. A quick method for accessing a menu item or command, usually through a series of keystrokes. 2. The icon that can be created in Windows95/98 to open an application without having to penetrate layers of various folders. The equivalent in the Macintosh is the "alias."

## Silhouette

To remove part of the background of a photograph or illustration, leaving only the desired portion.

## Skew

A transformation command that slants an object at an angle to the side from its initial fixed base.

## Small caps

A type style in which lowercase letters are replaced by uppercase letters set in a smaller point size.

## Smart Quotes

The curly quotation marks used by typographers, as opposed to the straight marks on the typewriter. Use of smart quotes is usually a setup option in a word processing program or page layout application

## Snap-to (guides or rulers)

An optional feature in page layout programs that drives objects to line up with guides or margins if they are within a pixel range that can be set. This eliminates the need for very precise, manual placement of an object with the mouse.

## Soft or Discretionary Hyphen

A hyphen coded for display and printing only when formatting of the text puts the hyphenated word at the end of a line.

## Soft Return

A return command that ends a line but does not apply a paragraph mark that would end the continuity of the style for that paragraph.

## Spectrophotometer

An instrument for measuring the relative intensity of radiation reflected or transmitted by a sample over the spectrum.

## Specular Highlight

The lightest highlight area that does not carry any detail, such as reflections from glass or polished metal. Normally, these areas are reproduced as unprinted white paper.

## Spine

The binding edge at the back of a book that contains title information and joins the front and back covers.

## Spot Color

Any pre-mixed ink that is not one of or a combination of the four process color inks, often specified by a Pantone swatch number.

## Spot-color Printing

The printing method in which one or two colors (or tints of colors) are produced using premixed inks, typically chosen from standard color-matching guides. Unlike process colors that reproduce color photographs and art, spot colors are typically used to emphasize headings, borders, and graphics, to match colors in graphics, such as logos, and to specify special inks, such as metallic or varnish.

## Spread

1. Two abutting pages. Readers Spread: the two (or more) pages a reader will view when the document is open. Printers Spread: the two pages that abut on press in a multi-page document. 2. A trapping process that makes the lighter color larger.

## Stacking Order

The order of the elements on a PostScript page, wherein the topmost item may obscure the items beneath it if they overlap.

## Standard Viewing Conditions

A prescribed set of conditions under which the viewing of originals and reproductions are to take place, defining both the geometry of the illumination and the spectral power distribution of the light source.

## Step-and-repeat

A layout in which two or more copies of the same piece are placed on a single plate. This is useful for printing several copies of a small layout, such as a business card, on a single sheet. Also called a multiple-up layout.

## Stet

Used in proof correction work to cancel a previous correction. From the Latin; "let it stand."

## Stochastic Screening

A method of creating halftones in which the size of the dots remains constant but their density is varied; also known as frequency-modulated (or FM) screening.

## Stripping

The act of manually assembling individual film negatives into flats for printing. Also referred to as film assembly.

## Stroke, Stroking

Manipulating the width or color of a line.

## Stuffit

A file compression utility.

## Style

A set of formatting instructions for font, paragraphing, tabs, and other properties of text.

## Style Sheet

A file containing all of the tags and instructions for formatting all parts of a document; style sheets create consistency between similar documents.

## Subhead

A second-level heading used to organize body text by topic.

## Subscript

Small-size characters set below the normal letters or figures, usually to convey technical information.

## Subset

When exporting documents as EPS or PDF files, the ability to include only the portion of a font that actually appears in the document. This is particularly useful when decorative drop caps are used, or when a specific symbol is used from a pi font.

## Substitution

Using an existing font to simulate one that is not available to the printer.

## Subtractive Color

Color which is observed when light strikes pigments or dyes, which absorb certain wavelengths of light; the light that is reflected back is perceived as a color. See CMYK and Process Color.

## Superscript

Small characters set above the normal letters or figures, such as numbers referring to footnotes.

## SWOP

Specifications for Web Offset Publications

## System Folder

The location of the operating system files on a Macintosh.

## Tabloid

Paper 11 inches wide x 17 inches long.

## Tagged Image File Format (TIFF)

A common format for used for scanned or computer-generated bitmapped images.

## Tags

The various formats in a style sheet that indicate paragraph settings, margins and columns, page layouts, hyphenation and justification, widow and orphan control and other parameters.

## Template

A document file containing layout and styles by which a series of documents can maintain the same look and feel. A model publication that you can use as the basis for creating a new publication. A template contains some of the basic layout and formatting, and perhaps even some text and graphics that can be re-used in future publications.

## Text

The characters and words that form the main body of a publication.

## Text Attribute

A characteristic applied directly to a letter or letters in text, such as bold, italic, or underline.

## Text Converters

Files that convert word-processing and spreadsheet documents created in other programs into files that you can import into Publisher.

## Text Wrap

See Wrap.

## Texture

1. A property of the surface of the substrate, such as the smoothness of paper. 2. Graphically, variation in

tonal values to form image detail. 3. A class of fills in a graphics application that give various appearances, such as bricks, grass, etc.

### Thin Space

A fixed space, equal to half an en space or the width of a period in most fonts.

### Thumbnails

1. The preliminary sketches of a design. 2. Small images used to indicate the content of a computer file.

### TIFF (.tif)

An acronym for Tagged Image File Format. A popular graphics format. See Tagged Image File Format.

### Tile

1. A type of repeating fill pattern. 2. Reproduce a number of pages of a document on one sheet. 3. Printing a large document overlapping on several smaller sheets of paper.

### Tint

1. A halftone area that contains dots of uniform size; that is, no modeling or texture. 2. The mixture of a color with white: a 10-percent tint is one pat of the original color and nine parts black. See shade.

### Tip In

The separate insertion of a single page into a book either during or after binding by pasting one edge.

### Toggle

A command that switches between either of two states at each application. Switching between Hide and Show is a toggle.

### Tracking

Adjusting the spacing of letters in a line of text to achieve proper justification or general appearance. You may want to squeeze letters closer together to fit into a frame, or spread them apart for a special effect.

### Transfer Curve

A curve depicting the adjustment to be made to a particular printing plate when an image is printed.

### Transform

Application of rotation, shear, scaling or other effects to an object.

### Transparency

A full color photographically produced image on transparent film.

### Transparent Ink

An ink that allows light to be transmitted through it.

### Trapping

The process of creating an overlap between abutting inks to compensate for imprecise registration in the printing process. Extending the lighter colors of one object into the darker colors of an adjoining object. This color overlaps just enough to fill areas where gaps could appear due to misregistration.

### Trim

After printing, mechanically cutting the publication to the correct final dimensions. The trim size is normally indicated by marks on the printing plate outside the page area.

### Trim page size

Area of the finished page after the job is printed, folded, bound, and cut.

### TrueType

An outline font format used in both Macintosh and Windows systems that can be used both on the screen and on a printer.

### Type 1 Fonts

PostScript fonts based on Bézier curves encrypted for compactness that are compatible with Adobe Type Manager.

### Type Family

A set of typefaces created from the same basic design but in different weights, such as bold, light, italic, book, and heavy.

### Typesetting

The arrangement of individual characters of text into words, sentences, and paragraphs.

### Typo

An abbreviation for typographical error. A keystroke error in the typeset copy.

### UCR (undercolor removal)

A technique for reducing the amount of magenta, cyan, and yellow inks in neutral or shadow areas and replacing them with black.

### Undertone

Color of ink printed in a thin film.

### Unsharp Masking

A digital technique (based on a traditional photographic technique) performed after scanning that locates the edge between sections of differing lightness and alters the values of the adjoining pixels to exaggerate the difference across the edge, thereby increasing edge contrast.

### Uppercase

The capital letters of a typeface as opposed to the lowercase, or small, letters. When type was hand composited, the capital letters resided in the upper part of the type case.

### Utility

Software that performs ancillary tasks such as counting words, defragmenting a hard drive, or restoring a deleted file.

### Varnish Plate

The plate on a printing press that applies varnish after the other colors have been applied.

### Varnishing

A finishing process whereby a transparent varnish is applied over the printed sheet to produce a glossy or protective coating, either on the entire sheet or on selected areas.

### Vector Graphics

Graphics defined using coordinate points, and mathematically drawn lines and curves, which may be freely scaled and rotated without image degradation in the final output. Fonts (such as PostScript and TrueType), and illustrations from drawing applications are common examples of vector objects. Two commonly used vector drawing programs are Illustrator and FreeHand. A class of graphics that overcomes the resolution limitation of bitmapped graphics.

### Velox

Strictly, a Kodak chloride printing paper, but used to describe a high-quality black & white print of a halftone or line drawing.

### Vertical Justification

The ability to automatically adjust the interline spacing (leading) to make columns and pages end at the same point on a page.

## Vignette

An illustration in which the background gradually fades into the paper; that is, without a definite edge or border.

## Visible Spectrum

The wavelengths of light between about 380 nm (violet) and 700 nm (red) that are visible to the human eye.

## Watermark

An impression incorporated in paper during manufacturing showing the name of the paper and/or the company logo. A "watermark" can be applied digitally to printed output as a very light screened image.

## Web Press

An offset printing press that prints from a roll of paper rather than single sheets.

## Web Site

One or a collection of Web pages stored on a computer on the World Wide Web.

## White Light

Light containing all wavelengths of the visible spectrum. Also known as 5000°k lighting.

## White Space

Areas on the page which contain no images or type. Proper use of white space is critical to a well-balanced design.

## Widow

A short line ending a paragraph, which appears at the top of the page. See orphan.

## Wizard

A utility attached to an application or operating system that aids you in setting up a piece of hardware, software, or document. A Publisher tool that helps you create a publication or change an object in a publication.

## World Wide Web

(commonly shortened to WWW, or simply Web) The popular multimedia branch of the Internet that presents not just text, but also graphics, sound, and video. On the Web, exploring (sometimes called surfing) can all be done with point-and-click simplicity, and users can easily jump from item to item, page to page, or site to site using hyperlinks. See Internet.

## WYSIWYG

An acronym for "What You See Is What You Get," (pronounced "wizzywig") meaning that what you see on your computer screen bears a strong resemblance to what the job will look like when it is printed.

## X-height

The height of the letter "x" in a given typeface, which represents the basic size of the bodies of all of the lowercase letters (excluding ascenders and descenders).

## Xerography

A photocopying/printing process in which the image is formed using the electrostatic charge principle. The toner replaces ink and can be dry or liquid. Once formed, the image is sealed by heat. Most page printers currently use this method of printing.

## Zero Point

The mathematical "origin" of the coordinates of the two-dimensional page. The zero point may be moved to any location on the page, and the ruler dimensions change accordingly.

## Zip

1. To compress a file on a Windows-based system using a popular compression utility (PKZIP). 2. A removable disk made by Iomega (a Zip disk) or the device that reads and writes such disks (a Zip drive).

## Zooming

The process of electronically enlarging or reducing an image on a monitor to facilitate detailed design or editing and navigation.

# OFFICE PROCEDURES AND TECHNOLOGY

## FOR COLLEGES

### TENTH EDITION

**PATSY J. FULTON, Ph.D., CPS**

Chancellor
Oakland Community College
Oakland County, Michigan

SOUTH-WESTERN
PUBLISHING CO.

Executive Editor: Carol Lynne Ruhl
Developmental Editor: Inell Bolls-Gaither
Developmental Editor: Penny Shank
Production Manager: Deborah M. Luebbe
Senior Production Editor: Mark R. Cheatham
Production Editor: Denise A. Wheeler
Acquisitions Editor: Randy R. Sims
Coordinating Editor: Angela C. McDonald
Marketing Manager: Colleen J. Thomas
Senior Designer: James DeSollar
Photo Researcher: Kimberly A. Larson

*Cover photo by Peter Saloutos*

Copyright © 1994

by SOUTH-WESTERN PUBLISHING CO.
Cincinnati, Ohio

2   3   4   5   6   7   H   99   98   97   96   95   94

Printed in the United States of America

Fulton, Patsy J.
    Office procedures and technology for colleges / Patsy J. Fulton.—
    10th ed.
        p.      cm.
    Rev. ed. of: General office procedures for colleges. 9th ed. 1988.
    Includes index.
    ISBN 0-538-61418-8
    1. Office practice.   2. Universities and colleges—Business management.
    I. Fulton, Patsy J. General office procedures for colleges.   II. Title.
    HF5547.5.F84   1994
    651-dc20                                                          92-36568
                                                                        CIP

# PREFACE

Career opportunities for an office assistant are numerous, and increased job opportunities are expected through the year 2005. During this period, the office will continue to be a challenging and ever-changing place to work due to new technologies and the changing roles of office assistants. The office assistant must commit to continual learning as the workplace changes. The purpose of this text-workbook is to help the office assistant develop the knowledge and skills that will be demanded on the job and to develop communication, human relations, and time and stress management skills which will assist the office assistant in a changing work environment.

*Office Procedures And Technology For Colleges* is written for college students and office professionals. The individuals who use this book will find contextual material that prepares the reader for work in the office and office applications that allow the reader to practice the skills learned in the chapter.

## TEXT-WORKBOOK ORGANIZATION

*Office Procedures And Technology For Colleges* consists of fifteen chapters organized into six parts.

Part 1, entitled Succeeding in Your Diverse Office Environment, includes two chapters: Chapter 1, The Electronic Office and Chapter 2, Effective Relationships. Chapter 1 stresses current and projected office trends and the qualities and skills needed by the office assistant. Continued professional growth is presented as essential for today and the future. Chapter 2 introduces the cultural diversity that is present in the work force today. Types of discrimination are presented along with actions that might be taken when faced with discrimination. Effective verbal and nonverbal communication techniques are discussed.

Part 2, Processing Technological Information, consists of three chapters: Chapter 3, An Overview of Word and Data Processing; Chapter 4, Software Applications; and Chapter 5, Reprographics—Copiers and Procedures. Chapter 3

presents how information is created, input electronically, and output through printers and video display monitors. In Chapter 4, software programs, functions, selection, and care of hardware and software are discussed. Chapter 5 presents various types of copiers, features, and processes. Fax machines are included as a type of copier.

Part 3, Communicating Effectively, includes three chapters: Chapter 6, Composing and Transcribing Letters; Chapter 7, Office Documents; and Chapter 8, Telephone Procedures. The office assistant composes routine letters, and Chapter 6 helps the student become proficient at writing these letters. Chapter 7 provides information and practice in preparing the various office documents that are the responsibility of an office assistant. These documents include business reports, presentations, memorandums, financial records, payroll records, and expense reports. The telephone remains an integral part of the office, and Chapter 8 stresses proper telephone techniques, along with the types of telephone equipment available.

Part 4, Managing Time and Information, consists of three chapters: Chapter 9, Time and Stress Management; Chapter 10, Office Mail; and Chapter 11, Records Management. Managing time and stress continues to be an issue in our fast-paced world. Chapter 9 presents the causes of stress and stress reducers along with numerous effective time management techniques. The way mail is received in an office today includes not only the traditional paper mail but also electronic and voice mail. Chapter 10 discusses effective procedures for handling these types of mail. In Chapter 11 the types of records management classification systems and the basic indexing rules are presented. The student is given information on the proper storage and retrieval of correspondence through paper and electronic systems.

Part 5, Planning Travel and Conferences, includes two chapters: Chapter 12, Travel Arrangements, and Chapter 13, Meeting and Conference Planning. The business executive of today travels extensively, and Chapter 12 presents the office assistant's responsibilities in planning and making trip arrangements, along with duties while the executive is away and upon his or her return. Chapter 13 prepares the office assistant for making arrangements for meetings, conferences, and conventions. Teleconferencing is also presented in this chapter.

Part 6, Beginning and Moving Ahead in Your Career, consists of two chapters: Chapter 14, Office Ethics and Environment, and Chapter 15, Career Planning. Ethical behavior is needed in all positions in the business world. Chapter 14 stresses the importance of ethical behavior along with presenting environmental factors which make the office a quality place to work. The last chapter, Chapter 15, presents strategies for finding and succeeding on the job. Detailed information is given on preparing the resume and letter of application, in addition to interviewing techniques.

## TEXT-WORKBOOK FEATURES

A profile of a successful office employee is given at the beginning of each of the six parts of this text-workbook. These successful employees allow the readers of this text-workbook to understand why they have been successful by presenting their background and the attributes that have contributed to their success. Each individual highlighted in the profile also gives some advice to the beginner in the field.

An overview introduces each chapter, with General Objectives following this overview. These objectives will help the student understand what he or she is expected to achieve. At the end of each chapter, a Chapter Summary is included as a review of the important points of the chapter. A Terminology Review follows the chapter summary. The terminology review provides a quick reference for the student in understanding the terminology presented in the chapter. Discussion Items provide eight questions or statements for the student to answer at the end of each chapter, allowing the student to achieve mastery of some of the major concepts presented in the chapter. The Case Study provides a realistic office situation. By analyzing and responding to the case the student will be able to deal with similar situations that occur on the job. As culminating activities at the end of each chapter, the Office Applications will

provide challenging activities for the student to perform. Each office application is tied directly to the general objectives that are given at the beginning of the chapter. In completing most of these office applications the student will be working for TriCounty Regional Planning Agency. The agency is introduced in Chapter 1, and an organization chart and the role of the student are presented.

A Reference Guide and Appendix are provided as the last two sections of the text-workbook. The reference guide consists of the following sections: business math, capitalization, care of diskettes, grammar, numbers, often misused words and phrases, proofreader's marks, punctuation, spelling rules, and word division. The appendix includes an explanation of the template disk and how it might be copied.

## STUDENT SUPPLEMENTARY ITEMS

Some of the Office Applications include the use of a template disk. These applications are identified by the icon shown in the margin. Template disks are free to users of the commercial word processing software listed below. (An ASCII version of the files is also on each disk to enable the instructor to use the template with other programs.)

| Software | Stock No. |
|---|---|
| *WordPerfect*®,[1] *MicroSoft Word*®,[2] IBM, 5¼" | KF40JH81G |
| *WordPerfect*®,[1] *MicroSoft Word*®,[2] IBM, 3½" | KF40JH88G |

## INSTRUCTOR SUPPLEMENTARY ITEMS

The Instructor's Manual consists of an introduction that provides information about the parts of the text-workbook along with teaching tips and reference materials.

Several transparency masters for use in each chapter are also provided in the last section of the Instructor's Manual.

Six tests (one for each part), along with a final exam, are provided free to the instructor upon request. These tests include true/false, multiple-choice, matching, and essay questions.

---

[1] *WordPerfect*® is a registered trademark of WordPerfect Corporation.
[2] *Microsoft*® is a registered trademark of Microsoft Corporation.

## MESSAGE TO THE STUDENT

As you prepare for employment in the challenging office field, it is hoped that you will seriously apply the knowledge you learned in each chapter in producing the office applications. In doing so, you will develop the skills needed in the office of today. There are numerous opportunities awaiting you if you will commit to not only applying your knowledge and skills in this course but to ongoing professional development as you are employed. Enjoy the course, and may your success be great.

## ABOUT THE AUTHOR

Patsy J. Fulton is Chancellor of Oakland Community College in Oakland County, Michigan. Her past experience in the office includes six years working as a secretary with various levels of responsibility. She also holds the CPS certification. She has taught for seven years at the community college level. Subjects she has taught include keyboarding, shorthand, office machines, office procedures, business communications, and bookkeeping. In addition to her teaching experience, she has held numerous administrative positions including Business/Social Science Division Chairperson and Vice-President of Instruction. Her position prior to accepting the position as Chancellor of Oakland Community College was as President of Brookhaven College in Dallas, Texas. Her educational credentials include a B.B.A., an M.B.Ed., and a Ph.D. Her most recent honors include Who's Who in American Education 1992-93; Outstanding Alumnus, University of North Texas; and Transformational Leader in the Community Colleges.

## CONCLUSION

Thanks to the following instructors for their helpful reviews of this text-workbook:

*Brenda A. Breton, Westbrook College, Portland, Maine*

*Donald L. Crawford, West Georgia College, Carrollton, Georgia*

*Madge Lewis Gregg, W. A. Berry High School, Birmingham, Alabama*

*Sandra B. Hemmer, Mid-Florida Technical Institute, Orlando, Florida*

*Ken F. Howey, CPS, York Technical College, Rock Hill, South Carolina*

*Joyce Lawson, ITT Technical Institute, Houston, Texas*

*Sharon Massen, University of LaVerne, Naples, Italy*

*George A. Mattsey, South Suburban College, South Holland, Illinois*

*Susan Mitchell, Detroit College of Business/Warren Campus, Warren, Michigan*

*Barbara J. Moran, Alpena Community College, Lexington, Kentucky*

*Pam Roadruck, U.S. Grant Career Center, Bethel, Ohio*

*Sue Robertson, Monroe Community College, Rochester, New York*

My thanks also to Fred Keithley, Director of Human Resources for the North Central Texas Council of Governments in Arlington, Texas for his assistance in designing TriCounty Regional Planning Agency, the fictional company used in this text-workbook.

*Patsy J. Fulton*

# CONTENTS

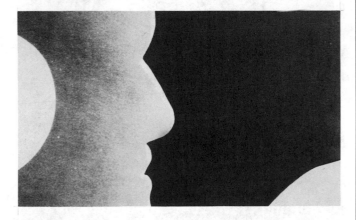

## Part 2
## Processing Technological Information

## Part 3
## Communicating Effectively

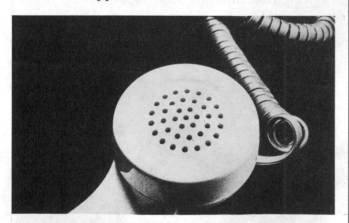

**Part 4**
**Managing Time and Information**

**Part 5**
**Planning Travel and Conferences**

### Part 6
### Beginning and Moving Ahead in Your Career

# 371

# 393

# 421
## REFERENCE GUIDE

# 435
## APPENDIX

# 437
## INDEX

# PART 1

## SUCCEEDING IN YOUR DIVERSE OFFICE ENVIRONMENT

# MICHELLE A. GOMEZ

Professional Secretary
Albert Halff Associates
Dallas, Texas

## A Success Profile

I attribute my success to a combination of the education I received at Bradford School of Business in Dallas, Texas, and the training I received through the many diverse positions I have been lucky enough to hold. In business school I majored in accounting but also received very strong secretarial training. I graduated at the top of my accounting class and was offered a job as a full-charge bookkeeper two weeks before I graduated. I accepted the position, and for the duration of that job I did not use my secretarial skills much.

My next position was in a small office where I was both the secretary and accountant for a CPA. My boss shared an office with another man and his secretary, who was the president of Big D Chapter of Professional Secretaries International (PSI). Through her I learned the difference between being "just a secretary" and being a true "professional secretary." I joined PSI shortly after that and then sat for the Certified Professional Secretary (CPS) exam. I passed my CPS exam in 1987.

Eventually I had intended to get my CPA license and leave the secretarial field. However, I found more and better opportunities in the secretarial field. It was through a contact in PSI that I found my current employer, Albert H. Halff Associates, Inc. I truly enjoy being the secretary to Raul Wong, Jr., Senior Vice President of Albert Halff Associates. No two days are ever alike and I think that is what keeps me interested. I would have to say that the variety of work and the people contact are my favorite parts of my job. I would have a hard time performing as well as I do if I were to get bored with my job. However, the constant interruptions, rushes, and snap decisions that make it so exciting can also be very stressful. A secretary has to learn to be an expert at time management and prioritizing.

I would say that the most crucial characteristics and skills that a secretary must have are the ability to manage time, versatility, the willingness and desire to learn, and a professional attitude. By maintaining a professional attitude and giving a 100 percent effort toward everything you do, you will most likely be able to learn the other required skills.

Everyone needs a release from all the stress and tension of a busy career, and my personal hobbies that help with this are drag racing and swimming. I also have a lot of interest in psychology (probably so I can deal more effectively with people). I am determined to learn how to play golf this year and tennis within the next two years.

I have been a member of PSI for six years. I cannot give PSI enough compliments. I have grown so much through this organization, both professionally and personally. I would strongly encourage every secretary to join a professional organization. You can learn much about managing and delegating through positions that you hold in professional organizations.

# 1 The Electronic Office

The office of today is an electronic office that is dominated by the computer. Desktop computers are highly visible on most office workers' desks. The typewriter, which was such a mainstay of the office a few short years ago, is rarely seen in the office today. The typewriter revolutionized the way work was processed from the time it was invented in 1874 until the introduction of the electric typewriter in 1934. However, the office of the 90s is synonymous with the processing of work with a desktop computer.

In addition to the changes in equipment in the electronic office, the role and scope of the office assistant has changed dramatically. The office assistant is considered an integral part of the office team. The office assistant now assumes not only information processing duties but also creates correspondence, solves problems, and makes decisions.

## GENERAL OBJECTIVES

*Your general objectives for this chapter are to*
1. **Develop a knowledge of the office environment of today.**
2. **Identify the role and responsibilities of the office assistant.**
3. **Cite office trends.**
4. **Identify qualities and skills necessary for the office assistant.**
5. **Identify and use effective decision-making techniques.**
6. **Develop an understanding of the importance of professional growth.**

## TECHNOLOGY IN THE OFFICE

In addition to the ever-present computer, what other technologies exist in the office today? Let's take a snapshot of the 90s office. Once a document is input on the desktop computer, a hardcopy or printout can be produced on a printer. Often the printer is a laser printer which operates very fast and produces print-like copy. The telephone that sits on the desk of the office assistant has numerous features, including the capacity for **voice mail** (messages that are sent over telephone wires to be called up at the receiver's telephone in another location). The **fax (facsimile)** machine, which is readily available to the office assistant, is another means of sending messages over telephone wires. Documents may be sent from one office to another office at a distant location in a matter of seconds through the use of the fax. The electronic calculator on the office assistant's desk is small in size but capable of complex mathematical calculations, including storage and recall of specified numbers.

Various software packages exist for performing different jobs on the computer. One software package used by the office assistant is known as **spreadsheet software.** This software provides for the automatic calculation of complex numerical data. Another software package used by the office assistant processes graphics (illustrations).

The copying machine, which is used extensively, produces copies in various sizes and collates them (arranges them in order). Collating and sizing are just two of the numerous features available on the photocopier.

Through the desktop computer the office assistant may send and receive mail electronically (called electronic mail). Through **electronic mail,** the office assistant sends messages from one computer to another computer, usually at another location within the same building.

### Information Age

Is this snapshot of the electronic office a complete one or a static one? The answer to both of these questions is a resounding no. The world we live in today is called the **information age**. This name has been adopted due to the tremendous explosion of knowledge that has occurred and the magnitude of the information that is available to us today.

The computer is an integral part of this information age; in fact, the information age was made possible due to the advent of the computer. And, new computer technological breakthroughs are occurring daily. Consider for a moment the computer of the 1940s which was large and slow, requiring three to five seconds to complete a multiplication. Now, compare that to the desktop computer of today which can store huge amounts of data on a small disk and print that data out in seconds. Due to the continued breakthroughs in computer technology, changes in office technology will continue to occur and the knowledge explosion of our information age will also continue.

**Illus. 1-1** The computer of the 1940s was large and slow, requiring three to five seconds to complete a multiplication.

*Credit: Photo courtesy of Unisys Corporation.*

### The Role of the Office Assistant

Businesses used the title of secretary in their offices for years, and that title continues to be used extensively today. However, additional titles that reflect the changing office include administrative assistant, office assistant, office manager, word processing specialist, administrative secretary, and executive secretary. To reflect the multiple duties expected in the office support role today and the changing nature of the role, the term used throughout this book is office assistant.

What are the responsibilities of the office assistant? Certainly, they are varied. Below is a list of some of the basic responsibilities:

- Keyboarding information
- Transcribing (from notes or machine)
- Preparing and processing outgoing mail
- Processing and distributing incoming mail
- Preparing financial reports
- Copying correspondence
- Ordering, storing, and inventorying office supplies
- Filing correspondence
- Telephoning
- Researching information
- Making travel reservations
- Composing routine correspondence
- Keeping the executive's calendar
- Scheduling appointments
- Performing receptionist duties—greeting and assisting callers
- Coordinating meetings
- Establishing priorities and organizing work
- Effectively communicating with individuals both within and outside the office

In addition to these responsibilities, the office assistant has to be almost a wonder worker. Ads for office assistants spell out characteristics such as someone who

1. has confidence, poise, and the ability to deal with confidential matters;

2. has excellent people, communication, organizational, and time management skills;

3. is able to perform in a fast-paced environment;

4. has a positive attitude, flexibility, detail accuracy, professional image, and phone voice;

5. has good judgment in resolving problems and handling sensitive situations.

As you can see from this list and from the job description in Figure 1-1, skills alone are not sufficient. There are numerous personal qualities and traits that are essential to the effective functioning of the office assistant.

**Figure 1-1**  Job Description of the Office Assistant

## JOB DESCRIPTION

JOB TITLE:       Office Assistant

COMPANY:       TriCounty Regional Planning Agency (TRPA)

DEPARTMENT:   Office of the Director

REPORTS TO:    George Andrews, Director

SKILLS AND TRAINING: The position of Office Assistant requires excellent organizational, oral and written communication, and human relations skills. The position requires the ability to screen and establish priorities on projects and to deal with supervisors in three counties contiguous to the district location. Exceptional courtesy and the ability to understand people are important.

Basic skills include accurate and fast keyboarding (70 wpm); computer skills with knowledge of word processing, spreadsheet, and graphics software; transcription ability; calculator and copying machine operation; and filing competence, with a general knowledge of electronic filing. Excellent grammar and composition skills are also essential since the office assistant must compose routine correspondence.

EDUCATION AND EXPERIENCE: Two years of office experience; certificate from a business school or a two-year associate degree.

DUTIES:   1. Keying letters, reports, memorandums, and other correspondence
2. Using spreadsheet and graphics software packages
3. Operating a computer
4. Checking reports on a calculator
5. Composing routine correspondence
6. Filing correspondence
7. Planning meetings and conferences
8. Making travel arrangements
9. Working with county supervisors
10. Researching information for reports

## Office Trends

In addition to technological changes, other occurrences in our society are affecting the office. Some of these events are the labor force changes, the educational level of the work force, changes in the types of businesses, and the workweek hours.

**The Labor Force**   The labor force is expected to grow through the 1990s. However, it will grow at a slower rate than in the 1980s. The civilian labor force totaled 121.7 million in 1988 and is expected to reach 141.1 million in the year 2000. This increase of 16 percent represents a slowing in both the numbers added to the labor force and the rate of labor force growth. Notice Figure 1-2 which shows a 27 percent growth in the labor force from 1976-1988 but just a projected 16 percent growth from 1988 to 2000.

In the future, the labor force will also be more diverse than it has ever been. White non-Hispanics have historically been the largest component of the labor force. However, these numbers have been dropping. By the year 2000, it is expected that white non-Hispanics will make up

**Figure 1-2** Chart of Labor Force Growth

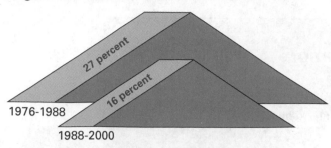

*Source: Bureau of Labor Statistics.* Occupational Outlook Handbook, *1990–91 edition, p. 8.*

74 percent of the labor force, with African Americans, Hispanics, Asians, and other ethnic groups accounting for about 26 percent of the labor force. African Americans, Hispanics, Asians, and other racial groups will account for an even greater number of those entering the labor force (33 percent). Women will continue to be a large part of the labor force. It is projected that by the year 2000 four out of five women between the ages of 25 and 54 will be in the labor force, with the labor force almost evenly divided between male and female.

Due to lower birth rates, the number of people of ages 16 to 24 in the labor force will continue to decline through the 1990s (see Figure 1-3). The picture will be different for workers in the age range of 25 to 54 years of age. These

**Figure 1-3** Age Distribution in the Labor Force, 1976–2000

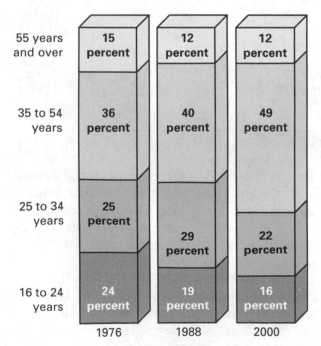

*Source: Bureau of Labor Statistics.* Occupational Outlook Handbook, *p. 9.*

workers are projected to account for 71 percent of the labor force, up from 69 percent in 1988.

**Educational Level**  The educational level of the population continues to rise. Figure 1-4 shows that between 1976 and 1988 the proportion of the labor force ages 18 to 64 with at least one year of college increased from 32 to 42 percent. The number of people with four years of college or more also increased. Of the 32 percent in 1976 who had at least one year of college, 16 percent had four years or more. By 1988, the number with four years or more of college had risen to 22 percent.

**Figure 1-4**  Educational Levels of the Labor Force, 1976–1988

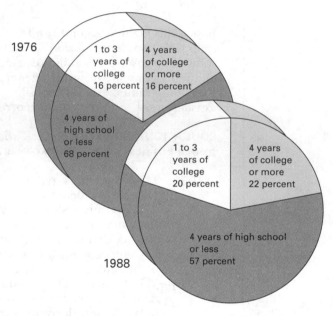

*Source: Bureau of Labor Statistics.* Occupational Outlook Handbook, *1990–91 edition, p. 9.*

Due to the complexity of the jobs of the future, the educational level of the labor force is projected to be even higher by the year 2000. The importance of education in the work force can be seen by looking at employment rates. Consistently, those individuals with one or more years of college have higher employment rates than those individuals with four years of high school or less. A college or a business school education does not guarantee success in the job market; however, it does provide a greater opportunity for success.

**Types of Businesses**  Service businesses are projected to grow more rapidly than other types of businesses between now and the year 2000.

Employment in this area is expected to rise 28 percent to 44.2 million by the year 2000 as compared to 34.5 million in 1988; the service businesses will account for one-half of all new jobs. Figure 1-5 depicts this growth.

**Figure 1-5** Percent Change in Employment, 1988–2000, by Type of Business

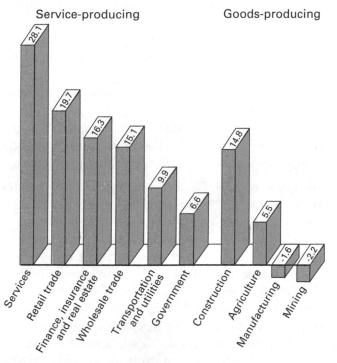

Service-producing          Goods-producing

*Source: Bureau of Labor Statistics,* Occupational Outlook Handbook, *1990–91 edition, p. 10.*

Service jobs will be found in all levels of government, banking, hospitals, data processing, and management consulting. Health care and business services will be the two largest categories of growth within the service field. New technology and a growing and aging population will increase the demand for health services; this area is projected to grow from 8.2 million in 1988 to 11.3 million in 2000. The business services field, including computer and data processing services, is expected to grow from 5.6 million in 1988 to 8.3 million in 2000.

**Office Hours**   Although many offices still adhere to the traditional office hours of from 8 a.m. to 5 p.m., the tradition is changing. The change has been brought about largely by the number of women with small children in the work force with the resultant need to establish more flexible hours. The four-day week, flextime, and job-sharing are gaining acceptance where these arrangements improve employee satisfaction and produc-

tivity. With a **four-day week**, employees work the usual number of hours (35 to 40); however, the hours are compressed into four days. For example, a 35-hour week consists of three days of nine hours each and a fourth day of eight hours.

Another departure from the eight-to-five workday is the **flextime** approach (the staggering of working hours to enable an employee to work the full quota of time but at periods most convenient for the individual). Under this plan, all employees do not report to work at the same time nor do they leave work at the same time. For example, in a 35-hour week, one employee may come to work at 7:30 a.m. and work until 3:00 p.m. (with 30 minutes for lunch). Core hours in this company (hours when everyone is in the office) might be from 9:30 a.m. until 2:30 p.m. Such a plan allows an employee to adjust his or her work hours to accommodate his or her life-style. Variations in arrival and departure times also help reduce traffic congestion at the traditional peak hours. Thus, less time may be required to commute, and the pressure and tension of meeting a fixed schedule are reduced.

Still another departure from the traditional workday is the **job-sharing** plan. Under this arrangement, two part-time employees perform a job that otherwise would be held by one full-time employee. Such a plan may be suitable for families having small children where one or both spouses want to work on a part-time basis. Job-sharing can also be suitable for workers who want to ease into retirement by reducing the length of their workday.

As more and more women with small children come into the work force, a more common employee benefit is child care for preschool children. A company may have a child care center on-site, giving the mother an opportunity to have lunch with her child or to attend to her child if an emergency arises. Or, the company may lease a facility at a location close to the company. This trend is expected to continue to grow.

With the technological advances of today, some companies allow their employees to work at home. For example, an employee might have an office set up in his or her home with a computer and any related equipment that is necessary. Correspondence that is prepared can be sent to the office by **modem** (a device that operates through telephone lines to transmit data from one computer to another). At the office, the document may then be printed out and mailed. Or the employee may print and mail the document at home.

Obviously, there are any number of ways in which the work can be coordinated between the employee at home and the employees who are working at the office site. Usually, an employee working at home will need to go into the office on occasion, perhaps one day a week or one day every other week.

Employers are also beginning to give employees special types of leave to accommodate their changing life-styles. Although maternity leave has been an accepted practice for many years, paternity leaves are now being given. In some families, the father may wish to take off from work to help care for the new baby. Companies are honoring these needs. Developmental leaves are also granted by some employers for such things as going back to school and working in another business on a loan arrangement.

**Illus. 1-2** With the technological advances today, some companies allow their employees to work at home.

## QUALITIES AND SKILLS OF THE OFFICE ASSISTANT

If the office assistant is to succeed in a world of technology and rapid change, certain qualities and skills are needed. It is important that you begin now to develop these qualities and skills.

## Change Orientation

Since change will continue to play such an important role in the office world, you must not only learn to cope with it but you must be effective in a changing environment. In order to do so, you must accept and prepare for change and be creative and flexible in dealing with it.

**Accept and Prepare for Change** Recognize that change will occur and try to predict the changes you will face. One of the things that you do know is that technological changes will continue, so be prepared to deal with technology. Take courses in school that give you the skills necessary to be comfortable and productive with computers. Continue to learn on the job. Realize that continual changes in equipment, software, and various other aspects of technology will require continued learning.

**Be Creative and Flexible** Creativity can be defined as the ability to combine existing ideas or things in new ways. When a change occurs, it is usually possible to connect that change to some already existing idea or way of doing something. For example, if your office is establishing an electronic filing system, the rules of filing that you learned in a manual system are still applicable. You will be using these rules in new ways.

Creativity demands flexibility. The flexible person is able to see that multiple options exist in most situations, and this person is free to choose from a wide variety of options. Through being creative and flexible—being willing to try new ideas and to experience new situations—you can deal with change successfully. Following are some steps that you can take to help you deal with change:

1. Understand why it is necessary to change; determine what circumstances have occurred that have necessitated change.
2. Determine what objectives will be achieved by the changes which are proposed.
3. Establish guidelines for achieving these objectives.
4. Determine the benefits or rewards that will occur as a result of the change.
5. Once the change has occurred, evaluate the effectiveness of the change and your effectiveness in working through the change.

## Dependability

Dependability means many things. It means being at work on time, being back from morning and afternoon breaks at the appropriate time, and maintaining a good attendance record (rather than calling in sick when you are not sick). It also means the willingness to stay late and finish an important assignment or come in early, if necessary, to prepare for an event. Yet another aspect of dependability is being willing to accept and complete a rush job in the time allotted without complaining about what is being asked of you. A truly dependable person can be counted on to get the job done.

## Human Relations Skills

As an office assistant you will come in contact with a number of people. Within the company you will work with co-workers, your supervisor, and executives. Contacts outside the company will include customers and other visitors to your office. All these people will be different; they will have different backgrounds and experiences. If you are to be effective, you will need to accept, understand, and work well with them. Human relations skills are like most of our other skills. We must constantly develop and improve these skills if we are to grow in our abilities.

## Confidentiality

On many occasions you will work with information that is highly confidential. Your job is to maintain confidentiality. You should never discuss confidential information that you keyboard or hear from your co-workers. You may be asked directly about a specific topic by a co-worker. Even though you consider the co-worker to be capable of keeping information confidential, you should never divulge the confidential information. Your answer if you are asked directly should be merely: "I cannot give you that information; it is confidential." You should not be apologetic about telling someone that you cannot give out information. Remember, your employer expects you to behave in an ethical manner. Being careful not to transmit confidential information is behaving ethically.

## Oral and Written Communication Skills

Office workers spend the majority of their time communicating with others. Such communication may be in the form of written letters and memorandums, telephone calls, or face-to-face conversations. Regardless of the form it takes, you must be extremely proficient in the communications area.

You must express yourself accurately and concisely in written correspondence. You must communicate your needs clearly and tactfully in verbal communications.

**Illus. 1-3** Communication may be in the form of written letters and memorandums, telephone calls, or face-to-face conversations.

## Integrity

**Integrity** is defined as the adherence to a code of behavior. In the office environment, the code of behavior means in part that you are honest. It means that you do not take equipment or supplies from the office for your personal use. It means that you spend your time on the job performing the duties of the job—not making and receiving numerous personal phone calls. It also means that you uphold high standards of ethical behavior. You do not engage in activities in which your morals or values may be questioned. You do not participate in office gossip, particularly that which can be malicious or harmful to others.

## Initiative

**Initiative** is defined as the ability to begin and to follow through on a plan or a task. In the office, initiative means the ability to take the tasks given to you and complete them in an appropriate manner. It also means having the ability to set goals for yourself once the parameters of the job or task are understood. No employer likes to have to tell the office assistant each move to make. The most highly valued office assistant has the ability to analyze a task, establish priorities, and see the work through to completion. This assistant takes the initiative to make suggestions to the employer about needed changes or revisions and is truly worth her or his weight in gold.

## Decision Making

Increased use of technology in the office requires the office assistant to make more decisions than ever before. The office assistant may make decisions about software purchasing, filing systems, appropriate media for transmission of communications, and numerous other decisions which involve the use of technology. In addition, the office assistant may be involved in handling certain types of personnel problems, composing and producing reports, and analyzing the use of office space. If the office assistant is to be successful in these endeavors, he or she must understand how to make effective decisions. Some help for understanding the various aspects of decision making and becoming an effective decision maker is given in the section in this chapter entitled "Effective Decision Making." You will want to read this section carefully.

## Technical Skills

Office assistants are expected to be knowledgeable of and skilled in the use of office equipment such as computers, photocopiers, and telecommunications equipment. Keyboarding (or typewriting as it has been commonly referred to in the past) is still the major skill required for all office positions. There is no way that an assistant can be proficient on a computer without a high level of keyboarding skill. To determine your keyboarding skill businesses usually give a five-minute straight copy test that will be scored for speed and accuracy. The majority of businesses expect a keyboarding speed of between 60 and 80 words per minute, with a high level of accuracy. Most businesses consider one error per minute to be acceptable accuracy on a five-minute test.

Obviously, the higher your keyboarding skill and the greater your accuracy, the greater the marketability of your skill. A business may want to determine your keyboarding skill prior to employment by asking you to produce documents such as letters, memorandums, and reports while timing you on the length of time it takes you to complete these documents.

## English Skills

Another skill that is absolutely essential for the office assistant is a mastery of the English language. The office assistant must know how to apply the rules of grammar, punctuation, and capitalization. It is essential that the office assistant be able to spell and proofread copy, producing a final product that is error free. Many times the employer expects the office assistant to be the English expert, relying on the assistant to correct any grammatical errors that the employer may make. In addition to having the English skills necessary to produce grammatically correct written correspondence, the office assistant must use correct grammar when speaking. On a daily basis the office assistant represents the company to the outside public via the telephone. It is most important that after a conversation with the office assistant a caller is left with a favorable impression of the company.

## Organizational Skills

Another skill that is frequently listed in job advertisements is the ability to organize work. You as an office assistant must establish priorities, determining what needs to be done first. You must organize your work space and keep items such as pens, paperclips, letterhead, and envelopes in an appropriate place so that they may be found quickly and easily when needed. You must organize the files, whether they be paper or electronic files, so that correspondence can be found quickly when needed. You must organize your time so that your work flows smoothly and tasks are finished as needed. Chapter 9 on time and stress management will help you understand more about organizing your work and time.

## EFFECTIVE DECISION MAKING

In your role as an office assistant you will make decisions daily. It is important that you make good decisions. These decisions might include deciding the type of format to use in preparing a report, deciding what to say to a difficult customer, or determining the type of filing system that should be established. As the support role increases in complexity, the office assistant is called on to not only make more decisions but also to make more difficult decisions. An understanding of the decision-making process will assist you.

A **decision** is the outcome or end product of a problem, concern, or issue that needs to be addressed and solved. The process by which a decision is reached includes five steps. You should systematically follow these steps in making a decision. The steps are depicted in the flowchart in Figure 1-6.

**Figure 1-6**   Decision-Making Steps

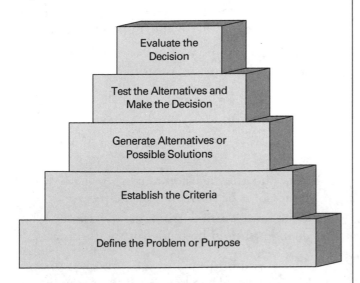

## Define the Problem or the Purpose

The first step is to define the problem or the purpose. This step may sound simple, but it is usually the most difficult of the steps. In attempting to define the purpose or problem, it is helpful to ask yourself a series of questions that may include the following:

1. What decision am I trying to make or what problem am I trying to solve?
2. Why is this decision necessary?
3. What will be the outcome of this decision?

Assume that you are completing your education and are ready to look for a position as an office assistant. Your answers to the three questions given above might be as follows:

1. I am attempting to make a decision about an appropriate career position.
2. The decision is necessary because
   a. I am finishing my education;
   b. I need money to support myself; and
   c. I want to be employed in some meaningful work.
3. The outcome of the decision will be that I will be employed in a job that supports my financial needs and provides me with work that I enjoy doing.

By asking yourself these three questions, you have helped to identify your purpose. You have discovered that you not only want to find a job, but you want to find a job that provides you with sufficient money to support yourself and one where you will be engaged in meaningful work that you enjoy. In other words, your purpose is not merely to find any job available.

When you finish answering the questions, it is a good idea to frame the problem or purpose into a statement. The statement you might frame in this situation could be

> My purpose is to find an office assistant position where I can make enough money to support myself and one that provides me with meaningful work which I can enjoy.

## Establish the Criteria

The next step in the decision-making process is to determine the criteria you need to make a sound decision. In setting your criteria, there are three questions that you may ask.

1. What do I want to achieve?
2. What do I want to preserve?
3. What do I want to avoid?

Your answers to these questions in the job situation example might be

1. I want to learn new skills and grow on the job; I want to be promoted to positions of greater responsibility and higher pay.
2. I want to use the skills that I have learned. I want to stay in the city in which I presently live.
3. I want to avoid travel time of more than 30 minutes from where I live.

By asking and answering these questions, you are able to determine several criteria that are important to you as you look for a position.

## Generate Alternatives or Possible Solutions

The next step in the decision-making process is to begin generating alternatives or possible solutions. For example, by reading the want ads in the paper, by talking with friends and acquaintances about possible positions, and by applying with job placement agencies you can begin to determine the office assistant positions available and of interest to you. Since you want to live close to home, find out what businesses are in your area. In order to project the income you need to support yourself, it is important to determine your budget. When making out a budget, be realistic about your expenditures and project your needs and not your wants. Find positions that pay accordingly. Promotion opportunities are important, so find a company that will provide a career ladder for you. Make a list of all the companies that have positions available that match your particular needs and goals.

## Test the Alternatives and Make the Decision

The effective decision maker tests each alternative using this system.

1. Eliminate ideas that are unrealistic or incompatible with your needs or the situation.
2. Give more thought to the alternatives that seem appropriate in the situation.
3. Select the alternative that appears the most realistic, creative, or appealing.

In the job situation, once you have identified several companies that match your needs and goals, set up job interviews. As you prepare for the interviews and during the interviewing process, give careful consideration to the steps presented here.

**Illus. 1-4** Promotion opportunities are important, so find a company that will provide a career ladder for you.

## Evaluate the Decision

The last step in the decision-making process is evaluating the decision. Evaluation serves two purposes:

1. Evaluation helps you decide if you have made the right decision for the immediate situation.
2. Evaluation helps you improve your decision-making skills for the future.

In evaluating your decision, here are some questions you can ask yourself:

1. What was right about this decision? What was wrong?
2. How did the decision-making process work? How can it be improved in the future?
3. What was learned from the decision? What changes should be made for the future?

Let's assume that the job you chose is not working out; you have been with the company for one year and there have been no promotional opportunities. In evaluating your initial decision, you discover that you did not look carefully at what career paths were available in the company. You made the mistake of assuming because it was a large company that opportunities would be available to you. You have learned that in the future as you look for a job you will be more careful in analyzing growth opportunities. If you know people within the company where you are applying, you will ask them about opportunities available. You will talk with the interviewer about the importance of growth opportunities for you.

## PROFESSIONAL GROWTH

You have learned in this chapter that it is essential for you to continue your professional growth if you are to be successful in the office of today and tomorrow. That professional growth can be through formal educational opportunities in a school, through seminars provided by your company or outside firms, through reading office periodicals, and through participating in professional organizations.

## Continuing Education

Most community colleges, vocational schools, and universities offer courses at night and on Saturdays.

Some even offer courses on Sunday. You may want to take additional business courses that relate to your position or enhance your promotional opportunities. For example, if you have a position where you need to supervise one or two employees, you may wish to take a course in management. If you find yourself not managing your time properly, you may want to attend a one-day seminar on time management. Such special interest seminars are frequently available through outside consultants at a nominal fee. Most businesses will grant you the time away from work to attend such seminars and will usually pay your registration fee.

## Periodicals and Newspapers

There are several periodicals available with timely articles to assist you in enhancing your knowledge and skills. Some of these are

### Office Publications

*From Nine to Five*
Dartnell Corporation
4660 Ravenswood Avenue
Chicago, IL 60640

*Modern Office Technology*
Penton/IPC, Inc.
1111 Chester Avenue
Cleveland, OH 44114

*The Office*
Office Publications, Inc.
1600 Summer Street
Stamford, CT 06904

*The Office Professional*
212 Commerce Boulevard
Round Rock, TX 78664

*The Secretary*
Professional Secretaries International
301 E. Armour Boulevard
Kansas City, MO 64111

*Today's Office*
Hearst Business Communications
645 Stewart Avenue
Garden City, NY 11530

*Words*
Association of Information Systems Professionals

104 Wilmot Road, Apt. 201
Deerfield, IL 60015

*Working Woman*
P. O. Box 10132
Des Moines, IA 50340

### Business Publications

*Administrative Management*
Automated Office, LTD
Dalton Communications
1123 Broadway
New York, NY 10010

*Business Week*
McGraw-Hill, Inc.
1221 Avenue of the Americas
New York, NY 10020

*Management World*
Administrative Management Society
1101 Fourteenth Street, NW
Suite 1100
Washington, DC 20005

*The Wall Street Journal*
Dow Jones Company, Inc.
200 Liberty Street
New York, NY 10281

## Professional Organizations

Professional Secretaries International is the largest organization of secretaries, with chapters throughout the United States, Puerto Rico, and Canada, as well as affiliate associations in 30 foreign countries. PSI publishes *The Secretary* and administers a certification program for secretaries. In order to receive the certification, you must pass a test covering the following areas:

- Behavioral science in business
- Business law
- Economics and management
- Accounting
- Office administration and communication
- Office technology

The certification entitles you to put the letters CPS (Certified Professional Secretary) after your name. These letters are highly respected in the secretarial field and indicate that you have achieved the highest professional standard.

**Illus. 1-5** PSI publishes *The Secretary* and administers a certification program for secretaries.

Other organizations which can be of help to you are

1. **Association of Records Managers and Administrators (ARMA)**
   This association sponsors the Certified Records Manager (CRM) designation.
2. **National Association of Legal Secretaries**
   This association sponsors the Professional Legal Secretary administration; it also publishes the NALS *Docket*.
3. **National Association of Educational Office Personnel**
   This association sponsors the Professional Standards Program and publishes *The National Educational Secretary, Beam,* and *Crossroads*.

**Illus. 1-6** Professional Secretary Certificate

**professional Secretaries international®**

through its department

**institute for certification**

certifies that

# George Silva

has met the requirements of and satisfactorily completed
an established program of examinations and
has been awarded the rating of

**certified professional Secretary®**

| Dean institute for certification | 19-- | International President Professional Secretaries International |

## YOUR COMPANY

Throughout this course you will be working for the TriCounty Regional Planning Agency, 3232 Six Flags Drive, Arlington, TX 76005-5888. The agency works with the counties of Collin, Hunt, and Kaufman. While Collin County reflects an urban/semi-urban character, the other two counties are predominantly rural. More than 150,000 persons live in Collin County; Hunt and Kaufman Counties each have only one-fifth as many residents.

### Role of TriCounty Regional Planning Agency

TCRPA was established by the three counties in 1975 to address common problems and needs, to develop and maintain programs and systems, and to promote the orderly development of the region. The Agency's primary programs include

1. Services to the elderly
2. Transportation planning
3. Health planning
4. Data services

## Organization and Staffing

The agency is organized around a Policy Board of eleven local elected officials who hire the Executive Director. The Executive Director hires the staff, now numbering 32. Figure 1-7 depicts the formal lines of reporting for the key staff and the agency's overall structure. Other professional and support staff are not shown.

### Your Position

You work as an office assistant, reporting to Mr. George Andrews, Executive Director. You have been employed by the agency for six months. Your duties are varied, including preparing letters, memorandums, reports, filing, answering the telephone, greeting callers, making travel arrangements, and setting up meetings. You also work with the board members, the managers within the agency, and the supervisors in the three counties. Your job demands not only that you have a high degree of skill and knowledge of the agency but that you have very effective human relations and communications skills.

**Figure 1-7** Organizational Structure, TriCounty Regional Planning Agency

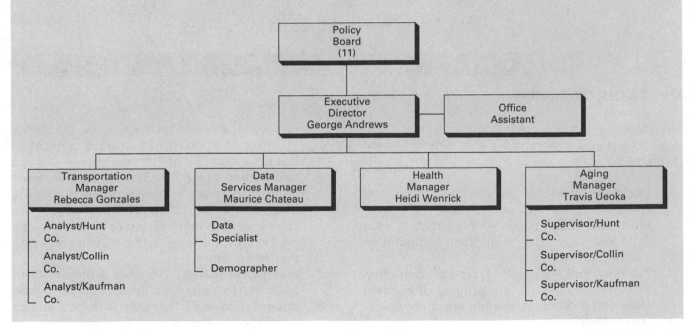

## CHAPTER SUMMARY

This summary will help you remember the important points covered in this chapter.

1. The office of today is constantly changing due to increased technology. We live in an information age which has made the growth of technology possible.
2. The office assistant position may have several titles, some of which are secretary, administrative assistant, word processing specialist, administrative secretary, executive secretary, and office assistant. The responsibilities of the office assistant are many and varied. They include keyboarding information, processing mail, preparing correspondence, ordering supplies, filing, composing, making travel arrangements, scheduling appointments, and written and oral communications.
3. The work force of the 1990s will be smaller, with the average age and the level of education increasing. Service businesses will grow more rapidly than any other type of business, with health care and business services being two of the fastest growing areas. In addition, office hours will become more flexible, with flextime, the four-day week, and job-sharing in operation in many companies.
4. Essential qualities and skills for the office assistant are handling change, dependability, effective human relations skills, excellent oral and written communication skills, integrity, initiative, decision-making skills, technical skills such as keyboarding and knowledge of computers, English skills, and organizational skills.
5. The steps of effective decision making are
   a. define the problem or the purpose;
   b. establish the criteria;
   c. generate alternatives or possible solutions;
   d. test the alternatives and make the decision; and
   e. evaluate the decision.
6. Professional growth in the form of course work at colleges or business schools, attending seminars, participating in professional organizations, and reading periodicals and newspapers is extremely important in order to keep current in the office field.

## TERMINOLOGY REVIEW

The following terms were introduced in this chapter. To help you understand them, definitions are given below.

1. **Decision** (*page 10*) A decision is the outcome or end product of an action.
2. **Electronic mail** (*page 3*) Mail that is sent from one computer to another computer at another location.
3. **Fax (facsimile)** (*page 3*) A type of copier that electronically sends an original document from one location to another via communication networks.
4. **Flextime** (*page 7*) Flextime is the staggering of working hours to enable each employee to work the full quota of time but at periods that match both employer and employee needs.
5. **Four-day week** (*page 7*) Work schedules are more flexible now than ever before; the four-day week where employees work the standard number of hours in four days rather than five is an example of this flexibility.
6. **Information age** (*page 3*) Our age has been referred to as the information age due to the tremendous explosion of knowledge. The computer is an integral part of this knowledge explosion and allows us to produce more data than ever before.
7. **Initiative** (*page 9*) Initiative is the ability to begin and to follow through on a plan or a task.
8. **Integrity** (*page 9*) Integrity is the adherence to a code of behavior.
9. **Job-sharing** (*page 7*) Under job-sharing, two part-time employees perform a job that otherwise would be held by one full-time employee.
10. **Modem** (*page 7*) A modem is an electrical device that converts computer signals into telephone signals and back again.

11. **Spreadsheet software** *(page 3)* An electronic worksheet that is divided into rows and columns and can be used to analyze and present business data.

12. **Voice mail** *(page 3)* Voice mail refers to messages which are sent over telephone wires to be called up at the receiver's telephone in another location.

## DISCUSSION ITEMS

To demonstrate your understanding of the information presented in this chapter, respond to the following items.

1. Discuss the office environment of today.
2. Enumerate the responsibilities of the office assistant.
3. Explain flextime and job-sharing.
4. What type of organizational skill does the office assistant need?
5. What do the letters CPS mean? What are the parts of the CPS exam?
6. Explain the first step in the decision-making process.
7. What role does evaluation have in decision making?
8. Why is professional growth important? Name three ways in which you might grow professionally.

## CASE STUDY

Josefina Morales, secretary to Travis Ueoka, Aging Manager, has been in the hospital for two weeks. You were asked by Mr. Andrews, Executive Director, to assume Josefina's duties during her absence. The first week you had some trouble keeping up with both jobs since your duties are heavy; however, you managed to do so by eating lunch at your desk and working thirty minutes overtime each day. This week you have not been able to get several tasks finished for Mr. Ueoka even though you have worked an hour late for each of the last three days. Mr. Ueoka was nice about the first missed deadline; however, he let you know today that it is imperative that his work be done on time.

You are tired and discouraged; you don't know how you are going to handle everything. And, to make matters even worse, Mr. Andrews told you today that Josefina will be out three more weeks.

Using the decision-making process outlined in this chapter, answer the following questions:

1. What is the problem?
2. What do you need to achieve?
3. What do you want to avoid?
4. What alternatives do you have?
5. What decision should you make?
6. How will you evaluate your decision?

## OFFICE APPLICATIONS

### Office Application 1-1 (*Objective 1*)

In this chapter you learned that the business world of today and the projected world of tomorrow are different from the business world of yesterday. Read three articles in business periodicals on the following topics:

1. Equipment used in the office today
2. Equipment trends
3. Skills required in the office today

Use recent articles (no more than six months old). Prepare a short summary of the articles using an unbound report format. For format you may wish to check a reference manual (for example, House, C.R., and K. Sigler. *Reference Manual for the Office.* Cincinnati: South-Western Publishing Co., 1989) or a keyboarding textbook. Include a list of the references you used at the end of your report.

## Office Application 1-2 (*Objectives 2, 3, 4, and 6*)

Interview two office assistants from two local businesses. Ask the individuals the questions listed below. (You might want to team with a class member on this project.)

1. What are your responsibilities? Are these responsibilities listed on a job description? (If so, ask if you might have a copy of the job description.)
2. What qualities do you consider important for the office assistant?
3. What types of equipment are being used in your office? Have you seen changes in equipment in the last year? Do you anticipate changes in the next year?
4. Is there a certain educational level required for your job?
5. How do you handle your own professional growth? What periodicals or newspapers do you read?
6. Are you a member of a professional organization? If so, what is the name of the organization?

Write a report of your findings; be prepared to give an oral report to the class.

## Office Application 1-3 (*Objective 2*)

An additional office assistant is being added to TriCounty. Mr. Andrews has rewritten the job description for this position. He has already given the first draft to you to be keyboarded. He now asks you to check over the job description that you have previously keyed to determine if there are additional skills or requirements that should be added. Using the information you learned in this chapter, make the appropriate changes.

*With a template disk:* Load the stored file OA1-3. Make any changes that are necessary. Print out one copy and turn the copy in to your instructor.

*Without a template disk:* Use the job description given on page 21 of your text. In preparing the document, allow one inch top and side margins. Triple space after the main heading. Turn in one copy to your instructor.

## Office Application 1-4 (*Objective 3*)

Teaming with two other members of your class, research the labor force demographics of your area, determining the average age of the labor force, the number of women in the labor force, and the educational level of the labor force. You may wish to check with the local Chamber of Commerce, the Bureau of Labor Statistics, or other sources which maintain area demographics. Write a short paragraph of your findings in report format, giving the sources of your information at the end of the paragraph.

### Office Application 1-5 (*Objective 4*)

Review the classified advertisements for office positions in your local newspaper. (The Sunday edition will yield the most listings.) Locate at least ten different positions. Note what skills are needed in each position, the experience required, and the salary, if given. Bring your advertisements to class. Be prepared to give an oral report on the positions listed (the titles used), the skills needed, the experience required, and the salary offered.

### Office Application 1-6 (*Objective 4*)

*With a template disk:* Load the stored file, OA1-6. Follow the directions given on the template. Save the document, proofread the copy, and print two copies. Turn in one copy to your instructor.

   *Without a template disk:* Complete the exercises on pages 23-29 of this text. Turn in the exercises to your instructor.

### Office Application 1-7 (*Objective 5*)

Assume that you have completed your office program and you are ready to apply for a position. How are you going to determine the type of position you should seek? How will you select the type of company, the location of the company, determine the job advancement opportunities, and so forth? Go through the process of making the decision, listing the steps of the process. Write up the procedure in report form, and turn in your report to your instructor.

### Office Application 1-8 (*Objective 5*)

Contact a local business executive. Ask him or her to identify an important decision that has been made in the last six months. Then, ask him or her to review how the decision was made. What steps were taken in making the decision? Ask the individual to identify how decisions are evaluated. Give an oral report to the class of your findings.

### Office Application 1-9 (*Objective 6*)

Go to your school or local library and identify the periodicals available for the office assistant. List these periodicals, giving the addresses where they may be ordered and the number of times the periodicals are published each year. Turn in your list to your instructor.

# 2 Effective Relationships

If you are to be effective in the office of today, you must have excellent human relations skills. You will spend a large portion of your time as an office assistant working with others. In fact, studies show that 90 percent of the office assistant's day involves contact with people. These people may be people within your office or people outside your office. Many times the office assistant is the company's first contact with a prospective customer. The way in which you handle that contact is extremely important. If you use good human relations skills, you give the prospective customer a good impression of the company and perhaps make him or her want to do business with your company. Conversely, if you make a bad first impression, he or she may never call on your company again. In this chapter, you will learn effective communication techniques.

## GENERAL OBJECTIVES

*Your general objectives for this chapter are to*
1. **Develop an awareness and understanding of a culturally diverse work force.**
2. **Explain the communication process.**
3. **Identify communication barriers.**
4. **Identify the types of nonverbal communication.**
5. **Use effective communication techniques.**
6. **Identify types of discrimination and steps that may be taken to counter discrimination.**

## A MULTICULTURAL LABOR FORCE

The labor force of today can be described as **culturally diverse**. You learned in Chapter 1 that the labor force will grow even more culturally diverse. By the year 2000 if you are African American, Hispanic, Asian, or among other ethnic groups, you will be 33 percent of the minority groups entering the labor force and 26 percent of the existing labor force. If you are white and non-Hispanic you will be 67 percent of the existing labor force. Such

cultural diversity demands that the office worker not only understand diversity but accept and respect it.

### Assumption of Sameness

One of the fundamental truths of human behavior is that we expect everyone else to behave just like we do. Why? It is quite natural. Think for a minute about how you learned certain behaviors. How did you learn that it was not okay to play in the street? You learned by some significant person in your life telling you that it was not okay or dangerous, and you learned by observing that others did not play in the street. We learn how to function in the world by observing, imitating, and internalizing the behavior of those around us. We have no reason for believing that other people might behave differently than ourselves. And, certainly we have no reason for believing that other cultures or ethnicities might behave in different ways if we have not been around other cultures.

Another point worthy of mention about our lack of understanding of others is that most of our conditioning operates subconsciously. We are not even aware that we have expectations about how people should behave based on how we behave. Edward T. Hall, a noted anthropologist, in his book *The Hidden Dimension* states, "Most of culture lies hidden and is outside voluntary control, making up the warp and weft of human experience. It penetrates to the roots of the nervous system and undermines how one perceives the world." Today, in our global village age, we are well aware that the world is composed of an enormous mix of people with different beliefs and different practices from our own. However, awareness through our conscious intellect is no match for what a lifetime of conditioning has taught us.

In order to break out of this conditioning, we must develop an understanding of some of the cultural differences among people in our world.

Here are a few of those differences for you to consider.

## Cultural Differences

People of different cultures often view space very differently. For example, in Mexico houses are often built behind walls, with even the front of the house hidden. In the United States, if our neighbor built a wall around her house we would probably feel shut out and wonder what indeed was happening behind the wall.

Another space difference is reflected in the distance we keep when coming in contact with people. For example, in the United States we only get very close to an individual (three to six inches) if there is an intimate relationship with the person or if we are going to whisper something of a top secret nature. We maintain a distance of from 20 to 36 inches if we are talking to an acquaintance. When we are speaking in public to a group of people, we maintain a distance of from 6 to 20 feet. In contrast, the interaction distance in Latin America is much less. In fact, people cannot talk comfortably with one another unless they are very close to the distance that suggests an intimate relationship to North Americans. The result of such space differences is that North Americans may find themselves moving away from Latin Americans when they talk. North Americans may think the Latin American is being too familiar and may feel crowded or even hostile toward the Latin American. The Latin American, on the other hand, may think that the North American is distant, cold, withdrawn, or unfriendly.

Now, consider some differences between North Americans and the Japanese. Generally

**Illus. 2-1** Today in our global village age, we are well aware that the world is composed of an enormous mix of people.

speaking, North Americans are very individualistic and entrepreneurial in many business situations. In general, North Americans are much more concerned about their own careers and their personal success than about the welfare of the organization or group. For North Americans, it is generally every person for him or herself. Generally, North Americans are not considered to be extremely loyal to a company. The Japanese, on the other hand, are extremely loyal and the team is of utmost importance. Friendship is often accorded more importance than in the United States; when a Japanese makes a friend, the friend is usually a friend for life. The Japanese take a dim view of anyone who changes the rules of the game once an agreement has been reached. The Japanese expect to make a profit when negotiating a contract; however, their considerations in computing the bottom line are much more inclusive than in the United States. In the United States, the bottom line is restricted to dollars and cents, while in Japan it includes an evaluation of possible contributions to national welfare, relationships within the company, and networks of people.

In North America or in Germany, keeping others waiting can be a deliberate put-down or a signal that the individual is very disorganized and cannot keep to a schedule. Being five minutes late calls for a brief apology; ten or fifteen minutes needs a more elaborate apology or a telephone call warning of the delay. In other cultures such as France or Mexico, time is not nearly so important. Being thirty minutes late to an appointment is perfectly acceptable, and there certainly would be no thought of an apology.

## Culturally Appropriate Expectations

Now that you understand certain cultural differences, let's take one situation and work through it using the model which is presented in Figure 2-1. The use of the steps outlined in this model will help you become aware of cultural differences and develop appropriate cultural expectations.

Assume that you have grown up in North America and your culture has taught you to keep a distance of approximately 20 inches when you are talking to an acquaintance. You have recently gone to work for an advertising company, and one of your co-workers, Carlos, is from Latin America. Each time Carlos talks with you he stands very close. You find yourself backing away from him and feeling uncomfortable. The two of you work

**Figure 2-1** Cultural Difference Model

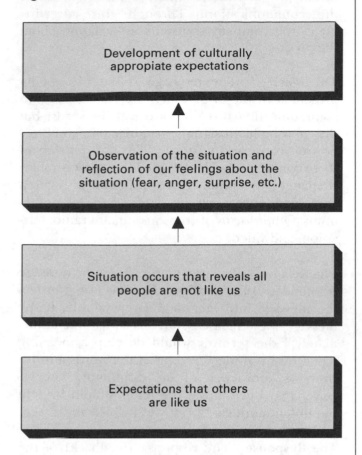

Development of culturally appropiate expectations

↑

Observation of the situation and reflection of our feelings about the situation (fear, anger, surprise, etc.)

↑

Situation occurs that reveals all people are not like us

↑

Expectations that others are like us

**Illus. 2-2**

## Pepper . . . and Salt

THE WALL STREET JOURNAL

"Mr. Gottlieb recently read one of those books on Japanese management techniques."

*Credit: From* The Wall Street Journal—*permission Cartoon Features Syndicate.*

together each month on a report. This month, as the report deadline approaches, you begin to dread having to go through this experience. You have also noticed that Carlos has been less friendly with you during the month. What is going on? Both of you are uncomfortable, but neither of you understands why. You have decided that Carlos is trying to be familiar with you; Carlos has decided that you dislike him. He sees you as distant and unfriendly. Both of you are at the first step in the model; you have expectations that all other people are like you.

Now, move to the second box in the model. When you experience some discomfort from a situation involving someone of a different culture, force yourself to think carefully about the situation. Allow yourself to realize that all other people have not had your experiences and background. Thus, they may be very different than you. They may think differently; they may act differently. Being aware of these differences is a start in understanding people of other cultures.

Once you are aware of these cultural differences, the next step is to move to the third box in the model. Practice a kind of retrospective awareness, taking time to recall the situation and exactly

what happened. Think about the feelings that you had during the experience. Did you feel anger? surprise? uncomfortableness? shock? Ask yourself why you felt that way. What in your background contributed to you feeling as you did?

Awareness of cultural differences and reflection on our feelings during an incident are not sufficient, however. We must move to the fourth and last box. We must be able to develop appropriate cultural expectations. In order to help us understand a situation, we may need to seek specific cultural knowledge by talking with the individual about his or her culture or by doing some reading. From this point, we can then develop culturally appropriate expectations. In the example given, you come to understand that Carlos is not being familiar with you; he is merely behaving appropriately according to his culture. He understands that you are not being unfriendly; you, too, are merely behaving according to your culture.

Once culturally appropriate expectations develop, you may not only find yourself understanding others' behavior but you may find yourself modifying your behavior in order to accommodate the other individual. However, this will not always be the case. In every culture there may be behaviors that are not culturally acceptable to us. And, this is as it should be. We cannot expect that we will like everything about another culture since we do not even like or approve of everything about our own culture. The goal is to be aware that people from other cultures behave differently and to understand and accept their behaviors as cultural differences—not as a negative statement about how these individuals may feel about us or the culture in which we live. Is it easy? No, it is not. As our global village becomes even smaller, all of us must constantly work to understand each other better. Is it worth it? Yes. Our world will be a better place if cultural diversity is accepted and respected.

## VERBAL AND NONVERBAL COMMUNICATION

In understanding a culturally diverse labor force, you have already learned that both verbal and nonverbal communication are important and can be the source of many misunderstandings due to people of different cultures viewing situations differently. In order to help you in communicating with people of other cultures in addition to people of your own culture, let's take a look at the process of communication and communication barriers, including nonverbal communication barriers.

### The Communication Process

The process of communication involves the exchange of ideas and feelings through the use of symbols, such as words or gestures. The elements of the communication process are the originator, the message, the receiver, and the response.

**The Originator** The **originator** is the sender of the original message. The originator transmits information, ideas, and feelings through speaking, writing, or gesturing. Although the originator is often a person, the originator may be a company, a committee, or even a nation. For example, in the advertisements you see on television about a par-

ticular product, the company is the originator of the communication. Through this advertisement, the company transmits information about the product.

**The Message** The **message** is the idea being presented by the originator. The symbols used in communicating this idea are usually words; but they may be hand signals, gestures, or a combination of words and gestures. The transmission of these symbols usually takes the form of face-to-face exchanges, telephone conversations, or written correspondence such as letters and memorandums. Other forms of transmission are radio, television, and video.

**The Receiver** The person for whom the message is intended is the **receiver.** The receiver transfers the message into meaning. For example, if the message was "Please send this letter out immediately," the receiver would develop a meaning based on his understanding of the words and his previous knowledge of the originator. The receiver may decide that the letter should be sent out in ten minutes.

**The Response** The **response** (feedback) of the receiver lets the originator know whether the communication is understood. The response may be verbal or nonverbal (such as a nod of the head, a smile, or lifting the eyebrows). If the response of the receiver indicates to the originator that the communication was misunderstood, then the originator can send the message again, perhaps in a different manner. Notice the communication model depicted in Figure 2-2.

**Figure 2-2** Communication Model

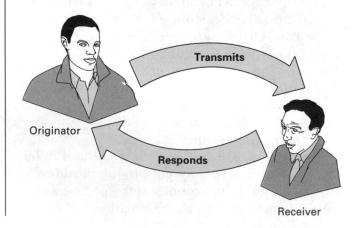

## Communication Barriers

In order for people within an organization to function productively, it is essential that there be effective communication. The information that is received among employees must be received and interpreted appropriately. However, this is not always the case. You have already learned that communication barriers can exist due to differing cultural backgrounds. Barriers can also exist due to differing educational and social backgrounds. By understanding these barriers, you can become a more effective communicator.

**Hearing the Expected**   All of us are guilty of sizing up an individual and then only hearing what we think that individual should say. Assume that you believe that all employers are hard-driving, demanding individuals. Your employer, in reality, may be a caring, thoughtful individual. Yet, when this person gives you a job to do, you immediately assume that he or she is being demanding. For example, if your employer asks you to change the text of a letter, you may decide that she is a perfectionist and will never be satisfied with your work.

**Ignoring Conflicting Information**   If you already have predetermined feelings about a subject, you tend to ignore new information on the subject. This new information may be valid, but you have made up your mind otherwise. For example, assume that you believe that Hard Rock is the only worthwhile music. You attend a music concert in which a wide range of music is presented from Hard Rock to the classics. You really enjoy listening to all of the music, but you refuse to admit it. You have already made up your mind that all music except Hard Rock is worthless. So, you refuse to accept that you truly enjoyed the other music that was presented at the concert.

**Evaluating the Source**   It is difficult for us to separate what we hear from our feelings about the person saying it. If you like the person, you tend to accept what the person says. If you dislike the person, you tend to ignore what the person is saying. Consider this statement: "The first time I met Jane Rogers I disliked her. She acted like she knew everything, and I decided she really knew nothing."

**Viewing Things Differently**   Consider the following example of two people viewing things differently. Assume that you feel that work is fun, and your friend feels that work is drudgery. Both you and your friend notice an office group in which people are laughing and enjoying life. To you, the

**Illus. 2-3**  In order for people within an organization to function productively, it is essential that there be effective communication.

laughter means that the office is a pleasant place to work. People are enjoying their work and much is being accomplished. However, your friend sees the same situation altogether differently and assumes that everyone in the office is "goofing off." No work is being accomplished. After all, how could you be laughing and getting any work done?

**Using Word Barriers**  Words mean different things to different people. Even such simple words as great, small, good, and bad are open to interpretation by the listener. In fact, communication theorists say that a word in and of itself has no meaning. A word only has the meaning given to it by the communicator. Consider the following example of miscommunication with a word. Assume that your employer tells you that your productivity must be increased. You associate the word *increased* with the word *unrealistic*. You think that you are presently producing all that you can produce, and you fear that you are in danger of losing your job. Your employer does not consider the situation in this way at all. He does expect you to increase your productivity (but only slightly). He believes you are a good employee and that you are very capable of improving your productivity with some training on the computer. You leave the conversation afraid and upset; he goes away thinking that you understand his meaning and are ready to get additional training on the computer.

Technological change has also contributed to word barriers. Today, due to our computer age, we talk about local area networks, read-only memory, modems, desktop publishing, and so forth. If you are working with a computer specialist and you have little knowledge of computers, you may have trouble listening to what he or she is saying since you are not able to interpret the meaning of the words. Terminology that is not understood by the majority of the population should be defined by the speaker.

**Noticing Differences in Position**  Breakdowns occur many times because of differences in position. For example, because of your supervisor's position, you may be hesitant to tell your supervisor that you do not understand certain instructions. You may feel that you will be considered stupid if you admit that you do not understand. But if you do not understand, how can you perform? You can save hours of wasted time by admitting that you do not understand. Certainly you want to try to understand instructions the first time someone gives them to you. You should always listen carefully to work instructions. But if you do not understand the explanation, tell your supervisor that you do not understand. Wasting your supervisor's time and your time by doing the job incorrectly causes more problems.

**Listening Ineffectively**  Studies show that the average person spends 70 percent of his or her day communicating, with 45 percent of that communication time spent listening to others. However, most authorities agree that listening is the weakest link in the communication process. You might be thinking, "Well, if I can hear it, I am listening." However, it doesn't work that way. Hearing is more than the mere perception of sound. Registering sound vibrations is hearing, while listening implies making sense out of what is heard. Research studies show that most of us listen with only 25 to 50 percent efficiency. In other words, 50 to 75 percent of what we hear is never processed.

**Listening** is the complete process by which oral language, communicated by a source, is received, recognized, attended to, comprehended, and retained. The listener attends to the oral language of the source with the intent of acquiring meaning. Thus, the main components of listening are not located in the ears, just as the main components of seeing are not located in the eyes. Our ears hear the sound vibrations to which we attend and comprehend, but our listening is based on our needs, desires, interests, previous experiences, and learning. As you can see, listening is a complex phenomenon involving the total individual. As we listen, our process of thought, which is composed of many separate and independent concepts, flows into ideas and emotions and affects what we hear.

## Barriers to Effective Listening

Do you consider yourself a good listener? Take the Listening Effectiveness Test in Figure 2-3 to determine your listening effectiveness at present. Rate yourself by checking the Always, Sometimes, or Never column. Once you have finished the test, return to this section and continue your reading.

How did you do? If you are like most of us, your score can probably be improved. Improvement comes by understanding what causes poor listening and then working on effective listening techniques. There are numerous characteristics that produce poor listening behaviors. Consider the following ineffective listeners.

**The Talker**  Unfortunately, many of us are so intent on discussing what has happened to us that we have difficulty waiting for the other person to finish talking so that we can start talking. In fact, many times the eager talker will interrupt the speaker to get his or her point across. Such individuals absorb little of what the other person says. In addition, they usually are planning their story while the other person is talking. Such behavior allows the listener to hear little other than the sound of the speaker's voice.

**The Attention Faker**  Have you ever talked to someone who made good eye contact with you while you were talking but when it came time for the person to respond you realized that she or he had not heard a word? Or, have you ever sat in a classroom and intently watched the instructor during an entire lecture but were unable to answer any questions about what was said? Most of us are good at adopting an outward posture that leads the speaker to believe we are listening when actually we are thinking of something else.

**The Easily Distracted**  Most people speak approximately 125 words a minute, yet it is believed that the brain can process information at about 500 words a minute. Listening allows plenty of time for the mind to wander. Unless the listener is committed to hearing the speaker, it is easy to become distracted. Distraction can be in the form of **external noises** or movement, either inside or outside the room. For example, when passing a classroom, have you ever watched the number of eyes that follow you down the hall?

**Figure 2-3**  Listening Effectiveness Test

---

**Listening Effectiveness Test**

1. When people talk to me, I find it difficult to keep my mind on the subject at hand.

   Always _____     Sometimes ___✓_____     Never _____

2. I listen only for facts.

   Always _____     Sometimes ___✓_____     Never _____

3. Certain words and ideas can prejudice me against a speaker to the point that I cannot listen objectively to what is being said.

   Always _____     Sometimes ___✓_____     Never _____

4. When I think a speaker has nothing worthwhile to say, I deliberately turn my thoughts to other things.

   Always _____     Sometimes ___✓_____     Never _____

5. I can tell by a person's appearance if he or she will have something worthwhile to say.

   Always _____     Sometimes ___✓_____     Never _____

6. When someone is talking to me, I try to make the person think I am paying attention even when I am not.

   Always ___✓_____     Sometimes _____     Never _____

7. I am easily distracted by outside sights and sounds.

   Always _____     Sometimes ___✓_____     Never _____

8. I interrupt the speaker to get my point across.

   Always _____     Sometimes _____     Never ___✓_____

9. When someone else is talking, I plan what I will say next.

   Always _____     Sometimes ___✓_____     Never _____

10. I frequently criticize the speaker's delivery or mannerisms.

   Always _____     Sometimes ___✓_____     Never _____

11. I use the difference between the talking time of the speaker and my own comprehension time to analyze and relate the speaker's points.

   Always _____     Sometimes ___✓_____     Never _____

12. I am aware of the nonverbal communication of others.

   Always _____     Sometimes ___✓_____     Never _____

13. I try to understand what the other person is feeling as he or she talks.

   Always _____     Sometimes ___✓_____     Never _____

14. I ask questions when I do not understand what the speaker is saying.

   Always _____     Sometimes ___✓_____     Never _____

How did you do? To be the most effective listener, you should have checked "never" on the first ten questions and "always" on the last four questions.

---

Distractions can also be in the form of **internal noise**, such as a problem that is bothering you. You may take the time in between the speaker's words to think about your problem; however, in doing so, you may tune out the speaker for several minutes. When you finally tune back in, the speaker is usually on another point and you are lost.

**The Outguesser**   Have you ever known someone who would never let you finish a sentence but always finished it for you? That person may have assumed time was being saved, but on the contrary, time was actually lost. Many times the outguesser makes an inaccurate assumption concerning your message. You, therefore, have to stop and explain to the outguesser that he or she has not made a correct assumption about what you were going to say. Such behavior causes not only a time problem, but generally an emotional problem as well. The speaker becomes upset with the listener's behavior; attempted communication often stops.

## Nonverbal Communication

Nonverbal communication can be another barrier to effective communication. Have you ever talked with someone who verbally agreed with what you said but had a frown on his face and his arms crossed? You knew that you could not trust what he was saying because his body language was telling you the opposite. Most of us come in contact with similar situations daily. What we say and what we write are important communication elements. However, what we convey nonverbally is also extremely valuable in understanding the total communication process. Let's consider four elements of nonverbal communication.

**Body Language**   Various body motions or gestures have meaning. For example, you may observe one person talking with another person. Do you think the message that is being sent is being received? Your answer is probably no. Why? Let's look at the clues that caused you to say no. One person is leaning forward in her chair, with a smile on her face, earnestly trying to get a message across to the other individual. However, the other individual has her arms crossed, is frowning, and is leaning back in her chair. All of these signs indicate that the message is not being received. Something about the message or the speaker is blocking her from truly listening to what is being said.

Although body language is extremely important, one gesture alone does not have significant meaning. In evaluating body language, consider all the gestures a person makes along with what that person says. For example, when you are communicating with someone do not make the mistake that a frown indicates that the person disagrees with what you are saying. If you are concerned about the body language, ask for an explanation. You might say something such as, "You are frowning; is there something wrong?" Such a statement gives the person with whom you are talking a chance to explain his or her behavior.

**Voice Quality**   A loud tone of voice is usually associated with anger; a soft tone of voice with calmness and poise. Two people talking softly with each other usually indicates that they are at ease. The loudness or softness of the voice and the pitch of the voice are nonverbal behaviors that reveal something about an individual. A person's voice will usually be pitched higher when he or she is tense, anxious, or nervous. Also, a person usually talks faster when angry or tense. In contrast, a low pitch and a slow pace usually indicate an intimate or relaxed tone. Other forms of nonverbal voice communication include the nervous giggle; a quivering, emotional voice; and a breaking, stressful voice.

**Time**   Another important nonverbal communicator is time. Think about the implications time has for the North American people. In a school situation, a late term paper or project usually results in a penalty for the student. In a business situation, habitually late reports may cause an employee to be fired. An applicant who is late for a job interview may forfeit the chance of getting the job. (Remember, though, that you learned in the earlier part of this chapter that all cultures do not treat time as North Americans do. For example, in Mexico being on time does not have nearly the importance that it does in North America.)

**Space**   Do you have a certain desk in a classroom that you consider yours? Do you feel pushed out of your place if someone else occupies that desk? Do you consider particular areas in your home your territory? The act of laying claim to and defending a territory is termed **territoriality. Proxemics** is the study of the personal and cultural use of space.

North Americans use space in particular ways in offices. People who have the same level or positions will generally be allocated the same amount of space. For example, the president's office will usually be larger than the vice-president's office. The desk of the president will generally be larger and more expensive than the desk of the vice-president. There may be art on the wall of the president's office but no art on the wall of the personnel manager, for example.

North Americans also use space to communicate in personal relationships. For example, has anyone ever asked you not to breathe down their neck? This common expression is used in North America to indicate that a person is getting too close in the communication process. Americans do not communicate at a close range unless there is a very close friendship or an intimate relationship involved. In contrast, as you have already learned, Latin Americans treat space in relationships very differently. Even in a casual acquaintance, the Latin American will come up close to another individual to communicate.

## EFFECTIVE COMMUNICATION TECHNIQUES

Since communication is so important in effective human relations, how may you communicate better? Here are several techniques that will help you become a more effective communicator.

1. *Use active listening.* **Active listening** implies that you are involved with the speaker. You are not merely hearing what the speaker is saying; you are truly listening to him or her.
2. *Get ready to listen.* Stop paying attention to the miscellaneous thoughts that constantly run through your mind. Direct all your attention to the speaker. Daydreaming is one of the leading causes of poor listening.

**Illus. 2-4** Active listening implies that you are involved with the speaker.

3. *Listen for facts.* Catalog the speaker's words. Use the differential time between how long it takes the speaker to say the words (an average of 125 words a minute) and how long it takes you to comprehend them (approximately 500 words a minute) in order to review the key ideas presented. Raise questions in your mind about the material. Relate what the speaker is saying with your own experience. Mentally repeat key ideas or associate key points with related ideas. Listening is not a passive activity in which you act as a sponge to soak up what is being said. Good listening is hard work, and it requires concentration and active participation on your part.
4. *Watch for nonverbal communication.* What forms of nonverbal communication is the speaker using? Observe the speaker's eyes, hands, and body movements. Do the nonverbal communications agree with what the speaker is saying?
5. *Remove distractions.* Don't doodle, tap your pencil, shuffle papers, and so forth while the speaker talks. Try to eliminate noise distractions. If a conversation is taking place in a noisy environment, move to another location. Control the physical environment as much as possible.
6. *Ask questions.* When you are not sure that you understand something that is being said, ask questions. Such questions clear up the information and show the speaker that you are interested in what is being said.
7. *Use mnemonic devices to remember key ideas.* A **mnemonic device** is a formula, word association, or rhyme used to assist the memory. For example, if a person says that her objections to a jogging program include boredom with the activity, exhaustion in the process, and the time required, you might develop the mnemonic device of BET to remember these ideas.
8. *Organize what you hear.* A listener who can identify the speaker's main points and the pattern of the speaker's remarks certainly has an advantage over the listener who simply listens to the words.
9. *Minimize your mental blocks and filters.* All of us have certain biases and prejudices. However, if we are aware of these blocks, we can control them. You may have heard people say,

"You can't talk to CPAs; they only know how to deal with figures," "Don't try to deal with a union person," or "Give me the old equipment any day." In such statements, you can hear prejudices. **Stereotyping** is taking place—an entire group of people or things is being evaluated based on one individual, one experience, or one thing. Listening behaviors are improved if you become aware of your own blocks and filters, as well as the speaker's blocks and filters.

10. *Be sensitive to the receiver's world.* Whether the communication is written or oral, you need to be aware of and sensitive to the receiver's point of view. Realize that the person receiving the information has needs and problems just as you do. This person may have had a difficult day and may have trouble understanding or accepting what you are communicating. Try to understand this person's needs.

11. *Use direct, simple language.* It is important to use direct, simple language in both written and oral communications. It is easier for us to use language when we talk than when we write. Written communication is many times sprinkled with big words and long sentences. Why? The writer is probably attempting to impress the reader with his or her vocabulary and literary genius. However, the reverse is usually true. The reader is unimpressed. So, whether the communication is written or oral, use direct, simple language.

12. *Utilize feedback.* When communicating with someone, listen totally to what that person is saying, not just to the words. Remember, there are many ways to communicate; these ways include words, gestures, facial expressions, tone of voice, time, and space. If you do not feel that you are understanding what a person is saying to you, ask for clarification. If when you are speaking you feel that the other person does not understand, try to explain your point in a different manner. Ask questions and pause at times to give the other person an opportunity to respond.

13. *Time messages carefully.* Have you ever blurted out one of your urgent problems to your supervisor just to discover that this person was so busy with his or her own problem that you were not heard? You need to be aware of what is going on in the world of the receiver.

We can cause problems for ourselves by trying to communicate with someone when that person is not ready to receive our communication. Stop, look, and observe what is going on in the world of the receiver before you attempt to communicate.

14. *Take notes.* Taking notes is sometimes beneficial. However, communication blocks can occur if note taking is not done properly. Here are some suggestions for effective note taking:

    a. Determine whether you need to take notes. Consider your goals, your concentration and retention abilities, and whether you will immediately use the information or use it at some later point.

    b. Identify the pattern of the message. Reflect that pattern in your notes.

    c. Only take down the main points of the message. Do not record every word.

    d. Keep your notes clear. Avoid doodling or making other marks on your notes which may confuse you as you reread your notes.

    e. Read over your notes immediately after the presentation. If you feel you need to expand on a point, do so at that time.

    f. Categorize and file your notes so that they are easily available when you need them.

**Illus. 2-5** Taking notes during a meeting is sometimes beneficial.

## TYPES OF DISCRIMINATION

You have learned that biases and prejudices can get in the way of communication. One prejudice that is very apparent in our world and one that needs special treatment is discrimination. **Discrimination** may occur in many forms—by race, gender, or age, or it may involve sexual harassment. In fact, discrimination has been so prevalent in our society that laws have been enacted which address the issue. Title VII of the Civil Rights Act of 1964 makes discrimination illegal if it is based on national origin, ethnic group, sex, creed, age, or race. Title VII was extended to cover federal, state, and local public employers and educational institutions through the Equal Employment Opportunity Act of 1972. This amendment to Title VII also gave the Equal Employment Opportunity Commission the authority to file suit in federal district courts against employers in the private sector on behalf of individuals whose charges were not successfully resolved. Now, let's individually consider four types of discrimination—racial, gender, age, and sexual harassment.

### Racial Discrimination

Why does racial discrimination or prejudice occur? Racial tensions have occurred in the United States from the time the first white settlers drove out the native Americans and set up a system of labor based on black slavery. **Prejudice** is based mainly on ignorance, fear, and cultural patterns. As groups of people are viewed in certain roles and with certain characteristics, those attitudes are learned and accepted by one generation and passed on to the next. Changing learned attitudes is a slow process. However, strides toward reducing racial prejudice are being made today, and it is imperative that even greater strides be made in the future.

### Gender Discrimination

As Title VII covers racial discrimination, it also covers gender discrimination. Employees may not advertise a job specifically for a male or female. A person may apply for any job, and the hiring decision must be based on whether or not the individual has the knowledge and skills needed for the job, not on whether the person is male or female. Neither can employee pay be based on whether a person is male or female. The Equal Pay Act, a 1963 amendment to the Fair Labor Standards Act, prohibits pay discrimination because of gender. Men and women performing work in the same establishment under similar conditions must receive the same pay if their jobs require equal skill, effort, and responsibility. For the most part, organizations are sensitive to this issue today and take measures to assure that gender discrimination does not occur.

However, if an individual believes he or she is being discriminated against because of gender, it is possible to take legal action against the organization or individual engaging in such discrimination.

### Age Discrimination

Title VII also covers age discrimination. No distinction can be made in age, either in the advertising or hiring process or once an employee is on the job. For example, an organization cannot advertise in the paper for a young person for a particular job nor can an organization specify a particular age for a position that is available. Individuals, regardless of age, must be treated equally in the advertising and hiring process. Discrimination because of age remains illegal once a person is on the job. In addition, a person cannot be dismissed because of his or her age. Mandatory retirement policies are illegal due to Title VII provisions. Some companies do have early retirement options in place that provide special benefits to long-time employees who choose to retire early. For example, an employee with twenty years of service to a company may retire at age 55 and receive a lump sum payment.

### Sexual Harassment

**Sexual harassment** has been defined by the Equal Employment Opportunity Commission (EEOC) as harassment arising from sexual conduct which is unwelcome by the recipient and which may be either physical or verbal in nature. Three criteria for sexual harassment are set forth.

1.  Submission to the sexual conduct is made either implicitly or explicitly as a condition of employment.
2.  Employment decisions affecting the recipient are made on the basis of the recipient's acceptance or rejection of the sexual conduct.
3.  The conduct has the intent or effect of substantially interfering with an individual's work performance or creates an intimidating, hostile, or offensive work environment.

Sexual harassment in the office can take many forms. It may be verbal in nature (such as suggestive comments and demands or sexual jokes), pressure for sexual activity, unwanted body contact, or rape.

The Civil Rights Act makes the organization responsible for preventing and eliminating sexual harassment. The organization is liable for the behavior of its employees whether or not management is aware that sexual harassment has taken place. The organization is also responsible for the actions of nonemployees on the company's premises. Because of these liabilities, many organizations have published policy statements which make it clear to all employees that sexual harassment is a violation of the law and of company policy. These policy statements generally include a clearly defined grievance procedure so that an employee has a course of action to take if sexual harassment does occur.

## ACTIONS AGAINST DISCRIMINATION

If you are the victim of racial, gender, or age discrimination or sexual harassment, you should take steps to see that such treatment does not continue. Here are some steps that you can take.

1.  Know your rights. Get current on the laws that deal with your civil rights. Know your company's policies and grievance procedures. In addition to the basic Title VII Act and the amendments of this act previously mentioned, you should be aware of the Pregnancy Discrimination Act which amended Title VII in 1978. This act makes it clear that discrimination on the basis of pregnancy, childbirth, or related medical conditions is unlawful, including refusal to hire or promote pregnant women or to offer them the same fringe benefits or insurance program.

2.  Keep a record of all discrimination infractions, noting the dates, incidents, and witnesses (if any).

3.  File a grievance with your company, if appropriate. Know your company policies and follow the procedures. If a grievance policy does not exist, file a complaint with your employer in the form of a memorandum describing the incidents. Identify the individuals involved in the discriminatory action, and request that disciplinary action be taken.

4.  If your employer is not responsive to your complaint, you may file charges of discrimination with the federal and state agencies that enforce civil rights laws. The Civil Rights Act of 1964 established the Equal Employment Opportunity Commission (EEOC) to ensure that violations of the act are exposed. The EEOC hears complaints of employees who think that they are discriminated against and sees that appropriate actions are taken. Check your local telephone directory for the address and telephone number of the EEOC office in your city. Your state may also have civil rights offices which can assist you; check your local directory for these offices.

5.  Confront the offender. Let the offender know that his or her behavior is unwanted and unacceptable. There is a chance that the offender was not aware that his or her behavior was offensive.

6.  Talk to friends, co-workers, and relatives. It is important to avoid isolation and self-blame. You are not alone; discrimination does occur in the workplace.

7.  Consult an attorney to investigate legal alternatives to discriminatory behavior.

## COMMUNICATION IMPROVEMENT—CONSTANT

If we are truly to develop effective relationships in the workplace, we must constantly work on communication in all forms. We must understand that our workplace is diverse, that different cultures exist, and that all of us view situations in different ways. We must work to overcome the numerous communication barriers that exist, including discriminatory barriers. We must recognize that constant attention and effort to improve communication are essential. Improvement in communication must be an ongoing, ever-present process. If we are diligent in our efforts, a more effective workplace will be the result.

## CHAPTER SUMMARY

This summary will help you remember the important points covered in this chapter.

1. The labor force of today is a culturally diverse one, and that diversity demands that we accept and respect cultural differences. If we are to improve in our cultural relations, we must understand that others do not necessarily behave in the same manner that we do. We must seek to understand the differences in behaviors by observing situations, reflecting on our feelings when differences occur, and then developing appropriate expectations of people of other cultures.
2. The elements of the communication process include the originator, the message, the receiver, and the response.
3. Communication barriers include:
   a. Hearing the expected
   b. Ignoring conflicting information
   c. Evaluating the source
   d. Viewing things differently
   e. Word barriers
   f. Differences in position
   g. Ineffective listening
   h. Nonverbal communication
4. Four elements of nonverbal communication are:
   a. Body language
   b. Voice quality
   c. Time
   d. Space
5. Techniques you can use for more effective communication include the following:
   a. Listen actively.
   b. Get ready to listen.
   c. Listen for facts.
   d. Watch for nonverbal communication.
   e. Remove distractions.
   f. Ask questions.
   g. Don't anticipate the speaker.
   h. Use mnemonic devices to remember key ideas.
   i. Organize what you hear.
   j. Minimize your mental blocks and filters.
   k. Be sensitive to the receiver's world.
   l. Use direct, simple language.
   m. Utilize feedback.
   n. Time messages carefully.
   o. Take notes.
6. Title VII of the Civil Rights Act of 1964 makes discrimination illegal if it is based on national origin, ethnic group, sex, creed, age, or race.
7. If you are a victim of racial, gender, or age discrimination or sexual harassment, actions you can take include:
   a. Keeping a record of infractions.
   b. Filing grievances with the company.
   c. Being knowledgeable of the laws.
   d. Filing charges with federal and state agencies.
   e. Confronting the offender.
   f. Consulting an attorney.

## TERMINOLOGY REVIEW

The following terms were introduced in this chapter. To help you understand them, definitions are given below.

1. **Active Listening** (page 39) Active listening is listening to a speaker with understanding, not merely hearing the speaker.
2. **Culturally diverse** (page 31) A labor force that is culturally diverse includes representatives of numerous cultures, including Asians, Hispanics, Blacks, native North Americans, Germans, French, and so forth.
3. **Discrimination** (page 40) An act based on bias or prejudice.
4. **External noise** (page 36) External noise refers to the physical sounds that stand in the way of communication. For example, loud music is external noise that may get in the way of your hearing.
5. **Internal Noise** (page 38) Internal noise comes from different backgrounds, experiences, and perceptions that cause a person to interpret a communication in a certain way. Internal noise is a learned response—learned

through environment, culture, and the significant people in a person's life.

6. **Listening** *(page 36)* The complete process by which oral language, communicated by a source, is received, recognized, attended to, comprehended, and retained.

7. **Message** *(page 34)* The idea being presented by the originator in the communication process.

8. **Mnemonic device** *(page 39)* A mnemonic device is a formula, word association, or rhyme used to assist the memory.

9. **Originator** *(page 34)* The sender of a message in the communication process is known as the originator.

10. **Prejudice** *(page 41)* Prejudice is defined as an adverse judgment or opinion formed beforehand or without knowledge or examination of the facts; a preconceived preference or idea; a bias.

11. **Proxemics** *(page 38)* The study of the personal and cultural use of space.

12. **Receiver** *(page 34)* The person for whom the message is intended in the communication process.

13. **Response** *(page 34)* The method by which the receiver lets the originator know whether or not the communication is understood.

14. **Sexual harassment** *(page 41)* Harassment arising from sexual conduct which is unwelcome by the recipient and which may be either physical or verbal in nature.

15. **Stereotyping** *(page 40)* Evaluating an entire group of people or things based on one individual, one experience, or one thing.

16. **Territoriality** *(page 38)* The act of laying claim to and defending a territory.

## DISCUSSION ITEMS

To demonstrate your understanding of the material presented in this chapter, respond to the following items.

1. What is meant by the "assumption of sameness"?
2. List and describe the elements of the communication process.
3. List and explain four barriers to effective communication.
4. Define listening. How does the speed with which we talk become a barrier to effective listening?
5. Describe how time can be a nonverbal communicator.
6. Define active listening. How is it used in communication?
7. What are the organization's responsibilities in sexual harassment?
8. Give five steps an employee may take when discrimination occurs.

## CASE STUDY

Maurice Chateau, Data Service Manager at Tri-County Regional Planning Agency, hired a new data specialist six months ago. The individual he hired is female. Her entry salary was $25,000. Policy provides for a performance review after an individual has been with the agency for a period of six months. The manager's review must be signed by the Executive Director, George Andrews. Mr. Chateau has given the new data specialist, Erica Forum, a below standard rating. She is upset with the rating. Following the grievance procedure of the agency, she asks for an appointment with Mr. Andrews to discuss her review. Here is her view of the situation as she reports it to Mr. Andrews.

I was employed at a salary of $25,000. I discovered after I had been on the job for a month that the other data specialist, a male, was brought in at a salary of $27,000. I know that his experience and education is not greater than mine. I talked with Mr. Chateau at that point about my salary, stating that I thought I should have received a higher salary. He told me that he would "make it up to me" during the mid-year review period. Now, not only does he not recommend a salary increase for me, but he gives me a below standard rating. Never once has he said anything about my performance being below standard before my review. In fact, he has often praised me. In fact, he has told me that I am able to produce more work than the other data specialists. I am quite upset with both my salary and my review. I don't understand why this is happening. The only thing that I can think of is that Mr. Chateau is prejudiced against women. I am ready to file a gender discrimination suit unless something is done.

Answer the following questions about the case:

1. Taking into consideration what you have learned in this chapter, what would you do if you were Mr. Andrews?
2. Do you believe Erica should file a gender discrimination suit at the present time?
3. What steps would you recommend Erica take?

## OFFICE APPLICATIONS

### Office Application 2-1 (*Objective 1*)

*With a template disk:* Load the stored file OA2-1. Follow the directions given on the template. Save the document, proofread the copy, and print two copies. Turn in one copy to your instructor.

*Without a template disk:* Complete the exercise on page 49 of this text. Turn in the exercise to your instructor.

### Office Application 2-2 (*Objective 1*)

Read at least two articles or chapters from two books on cultural diversity, and write your findings in report format. Report to your class; turn in your report to your instructor. Check your local library for recent articles and books. Here are some possibilities for you.

Dondon, John C., and Fathi S. Yousef. *An Introduction to Intercultural Communication.* New York: Macmillan Publishing Company, 1975.

Hall, Edward T. *Beyond Culture.* New York: Doubleday, 1976.

Hall, Edward T., and Mildred Reed Hall. *Understanding Cultural Differences.* Maine: Intercultural Press, Inc., 1990.

Storti, Craig. *The Art of Crossing Cultures.* Maine: Intercultural Press, Inc., 1990.

### Office Application 2-3 (*Objectives 2 and 3*)

Judith Milling is a department manager for First Word Processing. She has a problem with two employees. Here is the situation.

David Wilkerson and Fusako Goro are office assistants; both report to Judith. Fusako has been having some personal problems. She has come in late twice during the last month. Each time David has made a remark (that the entire office heard) about Fusako coming in late. Fusako did not respond to his remarks. Last week, Fusako called in sick, but that evening David saw Fusako at the grocery store. The next morning (again while the entire office listened) David said, "It's a shame you were sick yesterday; but you weren't so sick last night, were you?" Fusako informed him that it was none of his business. Today, Fusako was ten minutes late coming back from lunch. When she came in David remarked, "I wish I were the office pet." Fusako yelled, "Get off my back, will you? You aren't my boss!"

Judith thinks that Fusako will soon solve her personal problems; and since she has been a good employee, Judith thinks Fusako deserves another chance. However, Judith is very concerned about David's actions. David's work production has been good; however, Judith has never talked with him about his human relations skills. Now she is wondering if she has made a mistake since the entire office is being disrupted.

1. Who is the originator in this communication situation? Who is the receiver?
2. Explain the communication problem between Fusako and David.
3. Describe the communication problem between Judith and David.
4. Should Judith talk to David and Fusako about their behavior? If so, what should she say?

## Office Application 2-4 (*Objective 3*)

Review the communication barriers listed in this chapter. Keep a record of the barriers that you face for a period of three days. Record what was said—the barrier. Also, record what was done to eliminate the barrier or what you think should have been done to eliminate the barrier. Write your findings in report format and turn them in to your instructor.

## Office Application 2-5 (*Objective 4*)

Read two articles from recent periodicals or chapters from books on non-verbal communication. Report your findings orally to your class.

## Office Application 2-6 (*Objective 4*)

Spend two hours on one day in the school cafeteria or in another public place frequented by students. Observe the nonverbal behaviors that occur. Write a report on the types of nonverbal behaviors that you observed. If you were able to observe any communication problems that occurred because of these nonverbal behaviors, record that in your report also. Turn in your report to your instructor.

## Office Application 2-7 (*Objective 5*)

Maintain a five-day log of the time you spend speaking and listening. You won't be accurate to the minute, but make a concentrated effort to record the amount of time spent on each activity. Also record the effective and ineffective behaviors you engaged in while listening and speaking. At the end of the five-day period, analyze your log. How much time did you spend speaking? How much listening? What effective behaviors did you engage in? What ineffective behaviors occurred? Determine ways in which you can improve your communication. Write a report identifying these improved communication techniques you plan to follow. Turn in your report to your instructor.

## Office Application 2-8 (*Objective 5*)

Your instructor will read an article to you. Apply the effective communication techniques you learned in this chapter. Your instructor will ask you some questions at the conclusion of the article. Answer the questions in writing. Your instructor will then lead the class in a discussion of the correct answers to discover if any communication barriers occurred.

**Office Application 2-9 (*Objective 5*)**

*With a template disk:* Load the stored file, OA2-9. Follow the directions given on the template. Save the document; proofread the copy; print two copies. Turn in one copy to your instructor.

*Without a template disk:* Complete the exercise on pages 51-52. Turn in the exercise to your instructor.

**Office Application 2-10 (*Objective 6*)**

Choose one of the following activities:

1. Interview two office managers concerning discrimination that has occurred on the job. Report your findings orally to your class.

2. Read two recent articles on how to lessen discrimination on the job. Report your findings orally to your class.

## OFFICE APPLICATION 2-1

For this activity assume that you work for a newspaper. The following letters have been written to Dear Deborah (one of the columnists). You work for the columnist and sometimes draft replies to correspondence. When correspondence comes in you either key it into the computer or use a scanner to put it on the computer. Both of these letters were previously keyed. Now, you have been asked to draft a reply for the columnist to review.

These letters have been written by individuals who have been in the United States for less than one year. In the context of what you have learned in this chapter, what would be your response to each? Write your response to each situation below the particular situation.

*Letter 1:*

Dear Deborah:

I am Korean. I do speak English but sometimes I use the wrong word and people make fun of me. Because of this type of behavior, I have found it more comfortable to stay with my Korean friends. However, I know that my English and knowledge of American ways will not improve unless I make an effort to mix with Americans. Now I am making that effort.

My problem is that my Korean friends are beginning to reject me; they have decided that I do not care about them. When I am with them, they make remarks about my drifting away from my roots. And, sometimes my American friends laugh at me when I make a mistake in English. I do not think that they mean any harm; however, it does hurt my feelings. I feel like I am making the total effort and that they are not willing to meet me halfway. What can I do?

_____

_____

_____

_____

_____

_____

_____

_____

_____

_____

_____

_____

_____

*Letter 2:*

Dear Deborah:

I am from Mexico. There are four people in my class who are also from Mexico. When we are together, we speak only Spanish. One day in the cafeteria, a group of American students passed us and made a remark about the "dumb Latinos" who couldn't learn the English language. I immediately wondered how many of them could speak Spanish. At least my group is making an attempt to learn another language. I felt angry and confused. My whole group felt that way also. We really do like America and want to become a part of it. What advice do you have for us?

_____

_____

_____

_____

_____

_____

_____

_____

_____

_____

_____

_____

_____

Read the following case and then answer the questions given at the end.

Ruth Squires is a computer programmer at a local bank. One evening, after spending two hours working overtime on a program, Ruth decided to go to Swann's Department Store to return a blouse she had bought. The blouse did not fit properly. She had to wait approximately 15 minutes before she could get anyone to help her. When she finally did get a salesperson, here is what happened from Ruth's frame of reference.

I told the clerk I wished to return the blouse since it didn't fit. She examined the blouse. Then, in what sounded to me like a very accusing voice, she told me that I could not return the blouse because I had worn it. I told her that I hadn't worn it; I had only tried it on. At this point she practically accused me of lying and said that there was makeup on the blouse, so obviously I had worn it. By this time, other people waiting for service were listening to our conversation. I was embarrassed, but I again assured her that I had not worn the blouse. Then I examined the blouse for any makeup stains. I could find none, and I told her so. She completely lost control and said that people like me caused the department store to lose money since we were always trying to cheat. My face was red, but I tried to keep my composure. I told her I wanted to see the manager; she told me that wouldn't do any good. But I stood my ground and insisted on seeing the manager.

1.  What communication barriers did the clerk use?

    _____

    _____

    _____

    _____

    _____

    _____

2.  What communication barriers did Ruth use?

    _____

    _____

    _____

    _____

    _____

3.  How should Ruth and the salesperson have handled the situation to avoid such a confrontation?

    _____

    _____

    _____

    _____

    _____

    _____

# PART 2

## PROCESSING TECHNOLOGICAL INFORMATION

## JOSIE LUKACS, CAM

Administrative Assistant
The Sheraton Centre Hotel
Toronto, Ontario, Canada

### A Success Profile

When I completed a three year diploma in secretarial science, theoretically I was ready to take the plunge into the business world and become a good secretary. As time went by, although I was acquiring sufficient knowledge and practical experience, I felt a need to enhance my career. I was seeking a professional association where I could network with people of similar backgrounds, enhance my career growth, and assist in my personal and professional development. By joining the local chapter of Professional Secretaries International I satisfied these needs. My achievements in PSI have been numerous, some of which include the following:

- I served on the Board of Directors of the Toronto Chapter.
- I was featured on the front cover of *Canadian Secretary* magazine, October, 1990.

- I was instrumental in forming the first PSI Executive Advisory Board in Ontario.
- Through my networking in PSI, I developed an interest in the Canadian Institute of Certified Administrative Managers (CICAM), applied for the CAM designation, and was certified in March, 1988.

Once you have learned to develop professionalism in your chosen field, it can only serve to have a positive impact on your personal growth. Over the years I have developed my self-esteem and self-confidence which has led me to make dramatic changes in my personal life. I have learned to develop a positive attitude toward myself and toward life in general.

I am a native Torontonian of Northern Italian background. I graduated from Ryerson Polytechnical Institute with a secretarial science diploma. Prior to joining the Sheraton Centre Toronto, Hotel and Towers, I worked for both small and large consulting engineering firms. Presently, I am administrative assistant to David Ogilvie, Director of Marketing, and Glory Jarjoura, Director of Sales. I continually upgrade myself by enrolling in both outside courses, as well as in-house training programs.

There are many fun parts to my job; however, I feel that ongoing communication with clients is the most fun, especially when I can resolve a problem for them. Providing this type of service makes my job more interesting and helps me achieve job satisfaction.

If you are starting out in the office assistant field, here is my advice:

- Be a team player; offer assistance to colleagues; don't wait to be asked.
- Be a leader, not a follower.
- Develop good communication with fellow workers and management.
- Continue to upgrade your educational opportunities.
- Set specific goals and strive to achieve them.
- Become certified in your profession.
- Be loyal to your company as long as you work for it.

# 3 An Overview Of Word And Data Processing

Have you ever wondered how we lived in a world without computers? For most of us today, such a world is hard to imagine. Computers are an ever-present part of our daily existence. We encounter them at grocery stores, banks, department stores, schools, and churches. We have computers in our homes. Computers control systems on our cars. It is certainly no surprise that the computer and the processing of information have become synonymous in today's offices. We process words and data through the computer.

**Word processing** has typically been referred to as the organizing of words through the use of electronic equipment, particularly a computer or electronic typewriter. Thus, if a letter or memorandum is prepared on a computer, it is referred to as word processing. **Data processing** has traditionally meant the manipulation of figures through the use of a computer. For example, if your employer asks for a report giving the current population of the elderly in Collin, Hunt, and Kaufman counties along with the projected population by 2000, the manipulation of the data would be referred to as data processing. In the past, word processing and data processing functions were separate functions in the office, with the office assistant mainly responsible for the word processing function. However, with the advent of the microcomputer, the role of the office assistant has changed dramatically. More and more offices have integrated word processing and data processing systems. Software packages are available that allow the office assistant to use word processing and data processing. Your success as an office assistant is dependent upon your ability to use the computer to manipulate both words and data. This chapter will help you gain the skills and knowledge necessary for success. The focus is on the processing of information—how it is created, input, stored, and output for use.

## GENERAL OBJECTIVES

*Your general objectives for this chapter are to*
1. **Identify methods of information creation.**
2. **Define methods of inputting information.**
3. **Input information using a computer or typewriter.**
4. **Identify and use storage devices.**
5. **Output information.**
6. **Classify computer systems.**
7. **Discuss future computer directions.**

## INFORMATION CREATION

Information is created in the office today in a variety of ways. For example, your employer may create a longhand draft or a draft on the computer or typewriter. Other means of creating information include machine dictation or dictation directly to the office assistant. As an office assistant it is your responsibility to understand how to work with each of these means of creating information. You may also be in a position to help your employer understand efficient methods of creating information. The following sections of this chapter will help you to be efficient with the methods of creation and help you to analyze the most productive method to use in a particular situation.

### Draft Copy

Draft copy that the office assistant receives may be in the form of longhand drafts, printed drafts that have been keyboarded on a computer or typewriter, or drafts which have been stored on a computer diskette. (A **diskette** is a floppy magnetic storage medium for the microcomputer.) Since computer technology has become so pervasive, many originators of documents who used to handwrite or dictate to an office assistant now have computers in their offices. It is now more common for these persons to use computers to create original drafts.

**Longhand**   Some originators find it easier to handwrite documents. In certain instances longhand has its advantages. For example, if statistical tables are included, these tables may be handwritten easier than they can be set up on the computer by an originator unaccustomed to using a computer in this manner. The originator may also be at a location where he or she needs to compose a letter and does not have any other supplies except a pad and pencil. Some originators may not be entirely comfortable with a dictating unit or computer and may find that they express themselves better when they are able to see their words written down. Thus, even though computers are used extensively today, the longhand draft is still a widely used form of creating correspondence.

① Longhand has some distinct disadvantages, however. One of the main disadvantages is that longhand is slow. At top speed, an individual writes only about 40 words per minute. When composing in longhand, the rate generally drops to 10 to 15 words per minute. ② Another disadvantage of longhand is that it is not always legible to others. The office assistant may have to check numerous times with the originator, losing valuable time in the process.

**Printed Drafts**   Some originators are comfortable composing at a keyboard and will provide the office assistant with a **hard copy** (printed paper copy) of a draft. The inputting is generally done on a computer; however, it may be done on a typewriter. These drafts often contain editing marks made by the originator as he or she reads the copy. If you

are to be effective in producing the final correspondence, you must not only have good transcription techniques but you must also be aware of the meaning of various proofreader's marks. Figure 3-1 shows a memo with proofreader's marks in it. The meaning of these proofreader's marks is given in the Reference Guide on page 428.

**Disk Drafts**   More and more originators are using computers. It is also fairly common for an originator to take a small computer with him or her when traveling or to have a computer at home. Some automobiles have keyboards installed as part of their electronic equipment. With the convenience and availability of computers, the originator can keyboard information while at home or traveling, store the information on a disk, and either take the disk or mail it to the office assistant. The originator may also have a **modem** on the home computer so that information may be sent over telephone lines back to the office assistant's computer.

This method of creating correspondence is a time-saver not only for the originator but for the office assistant as well. The role of the office assistant becomes one of editing and formatting the copy in final-draft form. Much of the work of keyboarding is already done for the office assistant.

## Machine Dictation

Another method of creating information is by machine dictation. Some of the advantages of machine dictation follow.

1. Dictation equipment can be available whenever and wherever the originator wants to dictate. It can be used at home, at the office, or while the originator is traveling.
2. Machine dictation ties up only one person's time during the dictation; the office assistant does not have to take the information down as is true in alpha or symbol systems such as speedwriting or shorthand.
3. Machine dictation may be transcribed at any time.
4. Dictation equipment allows the originator to dictate, rewind and review what has been said, and make corrections. It also allows the *transcriber* (the individual producing the document) to rewind and review what has been said.

Regardless of these advantages, there are disadvantages to machine dictation. The cost of

**Figure 3-1** Memo With Proofeader's Marks

---

## FROM THE OFFICE OF THE DIRECTOR

TO:       All Staff

FROM:     George Andrews

DATE:     Current

SUBJECT:  Seminar

On Wednesday, April 15 [14], at 2 p.m. in the Conference Room, Mr. Mark Dupree will

be conducting a session on stress management. He has done extensive work in

the field; I have heard him present, and he is a very dynamic presenter. Please

make arrangements to be at this session. It will conclude by 4 p.m.

Give Janice a call at 4803 [4902] if you will not be able to attend. Otherwise, I will

see you there.

---

buying dictation machines, installing them, and training people to use them is expensive. Time and effort must be expended in determining the most effective dictation equipment for the company. Selecting the wrong equipment can result in added expense and frustration. For example, the equipment must be compatible with other equipment in the office. Also, dictation equipment must be kept in good working condition at all times.

The three basic types of dictation equipment are portable units, desktop units, and centralized systems. So that you may understand more about this equipment, these three types are explained below.

**Portable Units**   Portable units are very useful for people who travel frequently. They may be used in a car, in a hotel, in an airport, on an airplane, or in any location convenient to the originator. Portable units are battery powered and small enough to be placed in a pocket or briefcase. The media used by portables are standard cassettes, minicassettes, or microcassettes. The standard cassette

is 2½ inches by 4 inches. Minicassettes are 2 inches by 1¼ inches, while microcassettes are slightly smaller at 1¾ inches by 1¼ inches. Although the

**Illus. 3-2** Portable dictation units are very useful for people who travel frequently.

microcassette is approximately one-third the size of the standard cassette, it provides as much dictation time as the standard cassette. Microcassettes are used on lightweight hand-held units—some of these units weigh only a few ounces and fit comfortably in a pocket or purse. For compatibility, most companies will purchase portables that use the same recording media as their desktop or centralized system.

**Desktop Units** Desktop machines are just that—machines that fit on a desktop. Desktop machines are available in three configurations—a unit for dictation, a unit for transcription, or a combination unit for both dictation and transcription. The transcription unit is equipped with a headset, which is used to hear the dictation, and a foot pedal, which is used to control the starting and stopping of the tape. The foot pedal can also be used to advance or reverse the tape. In addition, the transcription unit is equipped with controls that regulate the volume, the tone, and the speed at which the tape is played.

Combination units are equipped for dictation by plugging in a microphone. Dictation is recorded on the cassette by speaking into the microphone. The same unit is then used to transcribe the dictation. The microphone is unplugged and the headset and foot pedal are attached to the unit. Desktop machines use minicassettes or standard cassettes for recording dictation.

**Illus. 3-3** Desktop dictation machines are available in three configurations—a unit for dictation, a unit for transcription, or a combination unit for both dictation and transcription.

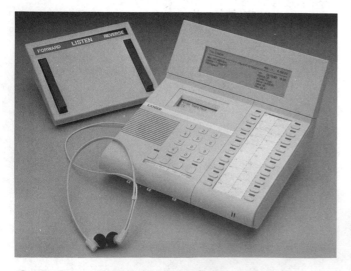

*Credit: Courtesy Lanier Voice Products.*

**Centralized Dictation Systems** With a centralized dictation system, one or several recording machines receive the dictation of a number of individuals. The machines that receive the dictation are in a centralized area; however, the originators who dictate may be located at various places throughout the building or at an off-site location. When dictating from an off-site location, the originator can do so via the telephone. The correspondence is transcribed by an office worker, who is probably at a different location than the originator, and the correspondence is returned to the originator for his or her signature. A centralized recording system is particularly useful to the originator who has only a small amount of correspondence to dictate and who does not need a full-time office assistant.

Centralized dictation systems utilize either analog or digital technology. Analog systems use cassettes or **endless loop tape**. An endless loop is a tape, joined at the ends, that is permanently housed in the tank of the recorder. When the tape is full, new dictation is added by erasing the oldest dictation on the tape. With either cassette or endless loop tape, information is recorded and reviewed in sequence. To reach a document, an operator must scan the document sequentially by the order of recording. Such scanning is known as **serial access.**

Digital systems receive dictation in analog form; then a computer switches the analog signals to digital signals that are stored on a disk. Transcription of any document can occur out of sequence since digital systems permit **random access.** For example, a document dictated on Friday at 3:00 p.m. can be retrieved and transcribed before a document dictated on Thursday at 2:00 p.m. In comparison, serial access would not allow for documents to be transcribed out of sequence. For added efficiency, information on the disk can be flagged for priority, allowing transcribers to quickly locate which section should be processed first. Digital systems can also interface with a microcomputer for recording, assigning, tracking, analyzing, and controlling dictation jobs. Although digital systems will probably not replace analog systems for some time, digital systems are considered the future technology for dictation machines.

**Machine Transcription Techniques** Regardless of the type of transcription unit you may use, your efficiency depends on the utilization of good techniques. Listed here are some techniques that will help you become more efficient.

ity printouts and is being used more and more in the office today. When using a printer, you get a hard copy (a paper copy). With the video display monitor, you get a soft copy (the information appears on the screen only).

11. Computers may be classified into three types: mainframe systems, minicomputer systems, and microcomputer systems. The computer used by the office assistant is the microcomputer, or personal computer as it is often called. In fact, in many offices today, everyone has a microcomputer on his or her desk. Laptop computers are a special type of portable microcomputer which may be used by the executive while he or she is traveling or outside the office.

12. The future directions of computers include the vanishing of distinctions between the microcomputer, the mainframe, and the minicomputer as the microcomputer becomes more and more powerful. It is also projected that the office of the future will have integrated application programs which allow linkages between the microcomputer, minicomputer, and mainframe. There will also be software applications which will allow, for example, linkages between various office functions such as telephoning, conferences, and setting up meetings.

## TERMINOLOGY REVIEW

The following terms were introduced in this chapter. To help you understand them, definitions are given below.

1. **Alphanumeric keypad** *(page 62)*  A keypad that contains a character set which includes letters, numbers, and special symbols.

2. **Auxiliary storage devices** *(page 64)*  Storage outside the computer itself; such storage is often on a floppy disk or tape.

3. **Bits** *(page 65)*  The storage of information within the computer memory is in the form of a code which utilizes a 1 or a 0. These 1s or 0s are called bits.

4. **Byte** *(page 65)*  A basic data structure used by computers, consisting of a series of bits that represents a letter, number, or symbol. A byte consists of eight bits.

5. **Central Processing Unit (CPU)** *(page 64)*  Electronic circuitry that executes stored program instructions. It consists of the control unit and the arithmetic/logic unit.

6. **Cursor control keypad** *(page 62)*  The portion of an electronic keyboard that controls the movement up, down, left, and right of the cursor on the screen.

7. **Daisy wheel printer** *(page 66)*  An impact printer with a round, flat type element.

8. **Data processing** *(page 55)*  The manipulation of alphanumeric data.

9. **Density** *(page 66)*  The amount of data stored on an external storage device such as a tape or disk.

10. **Digital scanner** *(page 63)*  A device that scans charts, maps, and other graphic documents and converts them into digital data so they can be reproduced on a video display monitor.

11. **Disk** *(page 65)*  A round, flat, double-sided sheet of pliable plastic that is magnetically treated and coated in a protective vinyl jacket. It is used as an auxiliary storage device for the computer.

12. **Diskette** *(page 55)*  A single magnetic disk on which data is recorded as magnetic spots.

13. **Dot matrix printer** *(page 66)*  An impact printer that forms characters by projecting tiny metal bristles or pins in patterns.

14. **Endless loop tape** *(page 58)*  A long piece of magnetic recording tape that stays inside the recording device and stores dictation for many documents.

15. **Facsimile machine** *(page 62)*  A machine that is capable of scanning, encoding, and reproducing information through the electronic transmission of documents over telephone lines.

16. **Function keypad** *(page 62)*  The portion of an electronic keyboard that controls specific processing functions of the computer.

17. **Graphics tablet** *(page 62)*  A tablet attached by a cable to a computer which allows you to draw or trace a picture on the surface of the tablet and displays the picture on the computer screen.

18. **Hard copy** *(page 56)*  Printed paper output.

19. **Hard disk** *(page 66)*  A high-volume storage device made of rigid plastic, aluminum, or

ceramic and magnetically treated. A hard disk is stored within the computer.

20. **Icon** *(page 68)* A system under which processing options are displayed as pictures or graphic symbols.

21. **Impact printer** *(page 66)* A printer which has a print mechanism that strikes against a ribbon that transfers an image to paper.

22. **Intelligent character recognition** (ICR) *(page 62)* A photosensitive device that reads handwritten copy, as well as printed copy, for input into a computer system.

23. **Laptop computers** *(page 64)* A special type of microcomputer which is portable enough to be taken when traveling.

24. **Laser disk** *(page 66)* A durable, nonmagnetic storage medium of great capacity which is created by laser light beams.

25. **Light pen** *(page 62)* A pen-like input device used to make entries on the face of a video display monitor. The pen is called a light pen because of its sensitivity to light on the screen.

26. **Mainframe** *(page 63)* A large computer that has access to billions of characters of data and is capable of processing data very quickly.

27. **Microcomputer** *(page 64)* The smallest of the computer systems; it is also called a personal computer and is small enough to sit on a desktop.

28. **Microprocessor** *(page 64)* A general purpose processor, containing the arithmetic, logic, and control functions on a chip. The microprocessor was developed in 1969 by an Intel Corporation design team.

29. **Minicomputer** *(page 63)* A smaller computer than the mainframe with more limited storage capacity. Generally used by smaller firms that do not have large-scale computer demands.

30. **Modem** *(page 56)* The word is taken from MOdulator-DEModulator, a device that translates digital signals into analog waves or performs analog-to-digital conversions, allowing computers to utilize telephone lines for direct communication.

31. **Mouse** *(page 62)* A small, hand-operated device that controls the cursor.

32. **Nonimpact printer** *(page 67)* A printer that causes images to be printed without actual contact between the print mechanism and the paper.

33. **Optical character reader** (OCR) *(page 62)* A photosensitive device that reads keyboarded text for input into a computer system.

34. **Program** *(page 64)* A set of instructions that enables the computer to carry out specific applications.

35. **Random access** *(page 58)* The ability to read from records without regard to the order in which they have been recorded.

36. **Serial access** *(page 58)* The ability to scan a document only in the order in which it was recorded.

37. **Soft copy** *(page 66)* Computer output displayed temporarily on a screen.

38. **Touch screen** *(page 62)* A screen with sensors that allows the user to select commands without a keyboard.

39. **Word processing** *(page 55)* The use of a computer to create, edit, revise, format, or print text.

## DISCUSSION ITEMS

To demonstrate your understanding of the information presented in this chapter, respond to the following items.

1. Identify and explain four methods of creating information.

2. List four tips which can help you in transcribing shorthand notes.

3. List and explain the advantages of machine dictation over shorthand dictation.

4. List and explain four methods of inputting information.

5. Identify the parts of the CPU.

6. List four ways in which information may be stored.

7. Explain the difference between impact and nonimpact printers.

8. List and explain three classifications of computers.

Recently, Angelica Bohlcke, the secretary to Heidi Wenrick, health manager, received an optical character reader. She didn't know how to use it and, since you have had one for six months, you offered to help her learn how. You spent an hour with her one day explaining the functions of the OCR and showing her how to use it. While you were doing so, she kept saying things such as, "I hate to learn new equipment. I really did not want to get an OCR, but Ms. Wenrick insisted. I have too much to do to be bothered with this machine." You kept assuring her that it could save her time, but she didn't seem to hear you. You have noticed on several occasions since your training session with her that she was keyboarding correspondence which she had a hard copy for. You knew it would have saved her time to use the OCR, but you didn't feel that it was your job to tell her how to do her work.

This last week your employer, Mr. Andrews, approached you, stating that Angelica is extremely busy and asking if you would help her. You said yes, but you felt extremely angry at having been asked to help someone who doesn't seem to want to help herself. After a week of assisting Angelica with her work, you really are out of patience. It seems to you that Angelica spends a tremendous amount of time on the phone on personal calls; you have also discovered that she really does not know how to use her software package. She spends much of her time looking up directions and complaining that she hates computers. She also continues to waste time by not using the OCR when it would be most beneficial.

Answer the questions below concerning the case.

1. Identify the problems in this situation. What problems does Angelica have? What are your problems?
2. What should you do about the situation? Should you talk with Angelica? with Mr. Andrews? with Ms. Wenrick? Or should you keep your mouth shut and do as much of the work as you can?

**OFFICE APPLICATIONS**

### Office Application 3-1 (*Objectives 1 and 2*)

Interview two secretaries or office assistants from businesses in your area. Ask them the following questions:

1. How is information created in your company?
2. Do you take shorthand?
3. Do you use a dictation machine?
4. Do the executives keyboard the information on a computer and give the disk to the office assistants to edit and revise?
5. How do you input information?
6. What suggestions do you have for efficiency in creating and inputting information? Are there special techniques that you use?
7. What types of computer systems are used in your company?
8. What types of software packages do you use?

Write your findings in report format. Present your findings to the class. Turn in your report to your instructor. If you have a computer available, prepare your report on a computer, labeling your disk as given in Office Application 3-2; for example, you might use RWDP2-3, which means:

> R (report)
> WDP (word and data processing)
> 2-3 (February 3)

Print out an additional copy of your report for filing. Start a folder labeled "to be filed." You will determine how to file the report in Chapter 11.

### Office Application 3-2 (*Objectives 3, 4, and 6*)

Figure 3-4 on page 74 is a letter that your employer, Mr. Andrews, has given you to produce. Mr. Andrews wrote the letter in longhand and then made some changes to it. Examine the proofreader's marks in the letter, and make the necessary changes. Refer to the proofreader's marks given in your text if you are not familiar with some of the marks. The letter is to be signed by Mr. Andrews. Make sure to use the current date.

If you have a computer available, input the letter on the computer, proofread the letter, and save it on a floppy disk. Key the date on line 14, allow one inch side margins, and double-space between paragraphs in the body of the letter. Print two copies of the letter. Save one copy and turn in the other copy to your instructor. As you proofread, do the following:

a. Call the document up on the screen.

b. Proofread first for content. You may want to put a piece of paper under each line so that your eyes will stay on the particular line.

c. Proofread all dates, names, and numbers carefully. Be certain to check for accuracy on spelling of names; check also for accuracy on dates and numbers.

d. If you have a spell checker on your software package, use it.

For this office application and others to follow, you will need to have one floppy disk if you are using a computer throughout the course. As you input a particular piece of correspondence on the disk, you must give the correspondence a file name so that you may retrieve it. This letter is to be filed with the caption "L" first which means that it is a letter, followed by the initials of the addressee, along with the month and day of the letter. The letter is to Wanda Briscoe, thus the letter will be filed on the computer as LWB, followed by the month and day you are keyboarding the letter. For example, if you are keyboarding the letter on September 28, the letter will be filed as follows:

**LWB9-28** (L stands for letter, WB stands for the initials of the addressee, 9 for September, and 28 for the day of the month)

Throughout this course, you are to label the correspondence in this manner.

### Office Application 3-3 (*Objectives 3, 4, and 6*)

Since Mr. Andrews is on his way to a meeting, he decides to quickly review the letter you produced in Office Application 3-2 and give verbal instructions to you for its revision. You review the letter with him and take notes about his concerns:

1. Mr. Andrews asks that you delete the punctuation after the salutation and complimentary close.

2. There are a few unnecessary words and phrases Mr. Andrews does not like. He dislikes the phrase "contained cities" at the end of the first sentence of the second paragraph—please delete the word "contained". Also, delete the word "Additionally" at the beginning of the second sentence of the third paragraph.

3. Rewrite the second sentence of the last paragraph to read "Call me if you have questions or if I may assist you."

Make the necessary changes, proofread the letter, save it on a floppy disk, and print two copies of the letter. Turn in one copy to your instructor. Place the second copy of your letter in your "to be filed" folder which you started in Office Application 3-2.

### Office Application 3-4 (*Objectives 3, 4, and 6*)

Mr. Andrews is revising the Policy and Procedures Manual. He gives you the information listed in Figure 3-5 on page 75 to be keyboarded.

*With a template disk:* Load the stored file, OA3-4. Paragraph 1 of the material has been keyboarded previously by you, and you merely have to make the changes to it noted in Figure 3-5. Make the necessary changes and add item number 2 from Figure 3-5. Format the document as described in the following paragraph. Save the document, proofread the copy, and print two copies. Turn in one copy to your instructor; place the second copy in your "to be filed" folder.

*Without a template disk:* Key the entire document shown in Figure 3-5 using one inch side, top, and bottom margins. Double-space the document. Allow a 2 inch top margin on the first page by placing the heading at line 12. Make one copy of the final document. Turn in one copy to your instructor; place the second copy in your "to be filed" folder.

### Office Application 3-5 (*Objectives 5 and 7*)

Go to your school or local library and research the following topics, using at least three current periodicals as references. Some periodicals that you might want to consider using include *Personal Computing* and *Modern Office Technology*.

a. Types of computer systems available with an explanation of these systems.

b. Projected future directions of the electronic office.

Prepare your findings in report format, and make or print two copies of your report. Turn in one copy to your instructor; place the second copy in your "to be filed" folder.

If you are inputting this report on a computer, the file should be labeled with R (for report), the initials of the title of the report, and the date you are keying the report.

**Figure 3-4**   Handwritten Letter for Office Application 3-2

Ms. Wanda Briscoe
Executive Administrator, Kaufman County
Kaufman County Courthouse
P.O. Box 1436
Kaufman, TX 75142

Dear Ms. Briscoe:

~~The purpose of this letter is to~~ welcome ~~you~~ to the TriCounty Regional Planning Agency region and congratulate ~~you~~ on being appointed as Kaufman County's Executive Administrator. We look forward to working with you and the County Commissioners on issues and programs of a regional nature. By the way of background, the TRPA offers planning, coordination, and technical assistance services to the three counties as well as their contained cities. The various functions in which we are involved include transportation, data services; aging services; and health planning. Each of the three counties has identified these as regional issues and, as a result, they are ones on which we focus the majority of our attention. Emerging issues which the counties are now discussing include the disposal of solid waste and the assurance of adequate water supplies. Should you wish to discuss these or other programs, I would be happy to meet at your convenience. Additionally, the key staff of each program is available to provide specific information and technical assistance. The program managers are: Rebecca Gonzales, Transportation; Maurice Chateau, Data Services; Heidi Wenrick, Health Planning; and Travis Ueoke, Aging.

I will follow this letter with a call in the hopes ~~of meeting with~~ that we can meet ~~you~~ soon. ~~Please do not hesitate to~~ call me or the managers if you have questions or if we may assist you ~~in any way.~~ ~~Again, welcome to the region;~~ My phone number is 333-4300.

Sincerely,

TRICOUNTY REGIONAL PLANNING AGENCY   *center* ]
Policies and Procedures

Chapter:   Personnel
Subject:   Drug Free Workplace

History

1.   Scope and Prohibition.  It is the policy of TriCounty to
     provide all employees with a working environment that is
     free of the problems associated with abuse of controlled
     substances.  The term controlled substances is defined as
     those drugs listed in Schedules I through IV of Section 203
     of the federal Controlled Substances Act, 21 U.S.C. 812.
     The use of non-prescription controlled substances is in-
     consistent with the behavior expected of employees and sub-
     jects TriCounty and its employees to unacceptable risks of
     workplace accidents and interferes with all employees'
     ability to perform their assigned duties in an efficient and
     effective manner.  The non-prescription use, sale, posses-
     sion, distribution, dispensation, manufacture, or transfer of
     controlled substances on TriCounty property or property
     under TriCounty control by any employee is a basis for im-
     mediate suspension without notice.

2.   Drug Free Workplace Act of 1988

     a.   The Act:  The Drug Free Workplace Act of 1988 became ef-
     fective on March 18, 1989.  The Act itself applies only to those
     employees who work directly on the subject of a grant, and
     certain others regardless of employee status; however, the Board
     has determined to extend the concept of the Act to all employ-
     ees.  Therefore, any employee who is convicted of a controlled
     substance-related violation in the workplace under state or fed-
     eral laws or who pleads guilty, or nolo contendre to such
     charges, must notify TriCounty within five days of such convic-
     tion or plea.  Failure to do so is grounds for suspension
     without notice.  Employees who are convicted or please nolo con-
     tendre to such drug related violations and who are not
     terminated must successfully complete a drug abuse assistance or
     similar program as a condition of continued employment.  If
     termination occurs, the District shall not reemploy the person
     unless he successfully completes a drug rehabilitation program.
     In addition, if a grant employee or other employee covered by
     the Act so notifies TriCounty, TriCounty must report this to the
     granter agency within teen days of the notice.  TriCounty is not
     rquired to report an employee who is not covered by the Act.
     TriCounty shall give notice to all employees concerning Board
     policy, procedure, and potential penalties thereunder.

*(handwritten margin notes: "left align with "T" in "The"", "to", "e", "e", "e", "plead", "center")*

# 4 Software Applications

Chapter 3 was an overview of word processing and data processing. In Chapter 3 you learned how information is created, how it is input to a computer, and how the information is output from the computer. You also learned about various types of computer systems and printers. You now have a basic knowledge of the process of producing documents using the computer. Your role as an office assistant does not demand that you have detailed knowledge of the interworkings of a computer. If you have problems with the functioning of a computer, computer technicians are readily available who have the expertise to repair the computer or explain what the problem is and how it can be corrected.

Your role, however, does demand that you understand software applications and have a detailed knowledge of the software package you are using. Also, many times you are expected to select or help select the appropriate software package. This chapter is not designed to give you a detailed knowledge of one software package; such knowledge and skill must come through working daily with a package. However, it is designed to help you understand several types of software programs that are on the market and some of the capabilities these programs have. This chapter is also designed to help you learn some of the basic functions that all software packages have.

## GENERAL OBJECTIVES

*Your general objectives for this chapter are to*
1. **Identify and explain various types of software programs.**
2. **Describe and use basic software functions.**
3. **Explain how to select software.**
4. **Explain how to care for computer systems and software.**

## SOFTWARE PROGRAMS

As you work with software programs on your microcomputer, you will realize there are three types of disks you will be using—DOS disks, software applications disks, and data disks. The DOS disk is used to start the computer system and to control software and files. The software applications disk is loaded into the computer after the DOS disk, and it contains special applications such as word processing. The data disk is the disk on which you record any data that you are producing. For example, if you are keyboarding a letter to be sent to a mailing list of 100 people, that letter and the mailing list would be on data disks. Now let's examine each of these types of disks.

**Illus. 4-1** The software applications disk is loaded into the computer after the DOS disk, and it contains special applications such as word processing.

### DOS Disk

**DOS** means *disk operating system.* DOS is a collection of programs that gives you control of your computer's resources. DOS controls the use of disk drives for storing and retrieving programs and data. The DOS for a microcomputer is generally on a floppy disk, and it must be loaded into a computer before any other software programs can be loaded. For example, if you are going to use a word processing package which is on a floppy disk, you must first load the disk operating system into the machine. There are several operating systems being used in offices today. One of the most frequently used operating systems is *MS-DOS*,[1] which is also called PC-DOS. Figure 4-1 shows some basic MS-DOS commands with a general description of what these commands do.

**Figure 4-1**  MS-DOS Commands

| COMMAND | USE |
| --- | --- |
| DIR | Directory—a listing of all files on the disk. |
| DEL | Delete a file. |
| DISKCOPY | Copy all files on a disk to another disk. |
| FORMAT | Prepare a disk for use. |
| RENAME | Give a file a new name. |
| TIME | Enter the current time. |
| COMP | Compare two files to see if they are identical. |

## Applications Software Disks

Applications software disks are disks containing the software program. These disks are used after the internal DOS program is loaded into memory. Sometimes internal DOS and applications software are on the same disk.

To help you understand how DOS and applications software disks function, consider this situation. Assume that you have purchased *WordPerfect*[2] software. *WordPerfect* is the applications software in this situation and it must be installed on your computer. However, before you begin installing *WordPerfect,* you must install DOS, the Disk Operating System. DOS programs are generally stored on one or more diskettes that were probably purchased with the computer. To install DOS, insert the DOS disk in the disk drive of the computer and follow a series of commands to load the program. After the DOS is loaded, remove the DOS disk from the computer and insert the *WordPerfect* disk. *WordPerfect* is installed on the computer by following a series of commands, beginning with

keying the word "install." *WordPerfect* displays a welcome screen and asks whether you want to continue with the installation. To continue with the installation you would have to respond to the prompts given on the screen.

Books containing DOS explanations and instructions are available, along with detailed instructions for installing *WordPerfect.* This short, concise explanation is given to help you understand the concept of DOS and software applications software. As an office assistant you are not expected to be an expert on either.

## Data Disks

Data disks are used concurrently with applications software disks. These disks allow you to store the files that you are creating on the computer. DOS and applications software disks contain files when they are purchased. These files allow you to give operating instructions to the computer. On the other hand, data disks contain no files when purchased. Data disks are empty disks ready to receive documents created by you once the disks have been formatted. When you **format a data disk** you actually prepare the disk for holding data files and a file directory. Instructions are available with software applications programs that give specific instructions as to how to format a data disk.

Let's address the previous situation—you have purchased *WordPerfect* applications (word processing) software. You have the DOS and *WordPerfect* applications software installed on your computer. You are now ready to produce documents. Your employer, Mr. Andrews, has given you a longhand draft of a letter to Cordelia Mendoza, a report on the demographics of the area, and a memorandum to all of the staff. You insert a formatted data disk and begin to key in the documents.

## Word Processing Applications

A wide selection of word processing packages is available. Each package has its advantages and uniqueness. Word processing packages allow the originator to create, edit, format, store, and print documents.

You learned in Chapter 3 that documents may be created by longhand, printed drafts or drafts on disks keyed by your employer, machine dictation, or shorthand dictation. The office assistant may also create routine documents. For example, if you have worked at a company for a period

---

[1] *MS-DOS* is a registered trademark of Microsoft Corporation.

[2] *WordPerfect* is a registered trademark of WordPerfect Corporation.

of time and your employer is comfortable with your composition skills, he or she may ask that you compose a letter. If so, the most productive method is to compose directly at the computer.

Once a document has been created and input into the computer through a word processing program, it can be edited, formatted, stored, and printed. You have already learned that documents can be stored on tapes and disks. The most popular method of auxiliary storage for the microcomputer is a disk. **Editing** refers to making changes in a document to correct errors or improve the content of the document. **Formatting** refers to adjusting the appearance of the document to make it look appropriate and attractive. You will learn more about editing and formatting in later sections of this chapter.

Word processing packages have helped the office assistant to increase productivity tremendously and produce a high quality product. If you have ever used a typewriter you will understand the advantages of a word processing package. Some people think of word processing as merely a glorified typewriter, and in some ways it is. However, consider some of the advantages of word processing over typewriting. The information that you input on a microcomputer is stored in the computer's memory; you can see what you keyboard on the screen before it is printed; and, you can make immediate changes easily, such as correcting errors and revising sentences. Another important feature of word processing is that it allows you, or an originator, to change a document significantly at a later date without rekeying the entire document. Word processing packages are sophisticated tools that are a part of our everyday existence in the office.

## Word Processing Helps

Some word processing packages have additional capabilities we have not yet discussed. For example, there are packages that will check your spelling, provide a list of words that you might use in the document, check your grammar and style, and print out individualized letters for mailing lists of thousands of names.

**Spell-Checker Programs** If you have misspelled words in a document, a spell-checker will find them. Once you finish a document, you activate the spell-checker. The spell-checker goes through your document and compares each word in your document with words that it has in its dictionary.

If it finds a word that has been misspelled it highlights the word and gives you the correct spelling of the word so you may then correct the spelling on the screen. Some spell-checkers will display all the words from their dictionaries that are close in spelling or in sound to the word you keyed. That is, the program tries to help you by displaying all the words that it thinks you may be trying to spell. To correct the highlighted word, follow the commands given on the spell-check program.

Spell-checker programs have thousands of words in their dictionaries, with typical directories having approximately 120,000 words. However, if the program finds a word that is not on its list, it assumes that you have misspelled or miskeyed the word, highlights it, and lets you decide whether it is misspelled or not. Spell-checkers do not recognize proper names or acronyms, so they are highlighted also to let you check if the spelling is correct. Some spell-checkers let you create your own auxiliary dictionary. For example, if you use certain acronyms or write to certain individuals, you can put these words in a dictionary.

**Thesaurus Programs** A **thesaurus** is a book of selected words that mean the same thing (synonyms) and words that have opposite meanings (antonyms). If you have ever been stuck on just the right word to use, you will understand the value of a thesaurus. A thesaurus program gives you access to a powerful vocabulary, electronically. Here is how the program works.

Assume that you have used "powerful" in your document as in the phrase "powerful vocabulary" in the preceding paragraph. However, you are not happy with that word—you would rather use another word but you are not sure what word to use. You place your cursor on "powerful" and then activate the thesaurus program by striking the appropriate keys. The program provides a list of synonyms and antonyms for "powerful." The program lists "forceful" and "strong" as synonyms for "powerful," and "weak" and "powerless" are listed as antonyms. After you activate the program and receive the list of words, select the word you wish to use. The program immediately replaces the word you used initially with the word you have selected.

**Grammar and Style Programs** No software program can make you an accomplished writer. That is something you must do through study, hard work, and practice. However, there are programs that can help you with your writing skills. A

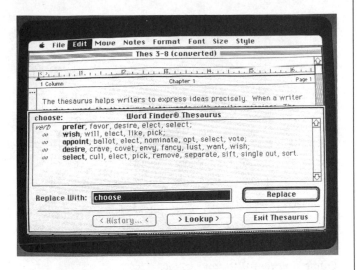

grammar or style program can identify unnecessary words, verbose phrases, and patterns that appear throughout your writing. These programs also have the capability of identifying run-on sentences and spelling errors that would not be detected by a spell-checker. For example, assume that you keyboard the following sentence:

Let me here from you immediately.

A spell-checker would not pick up the error *here* since it is correctly spelled; however, a grammar and style program would let you know that the correct word is *hear*.

**Form Letter Programs**  In the past you may have received a letter with your name keyed at the top that looked different than the print style used in the body of the letter. You knew immediately that it was a form letter, and your tendency may have been to throw it in the trash without reading it. But, with the advent of form letter programs, also known as mail-merge programs, you cannot always tell when you receive a form letter. With the use of these programs most letters look as if they had been individually keyed and addressed. Form letter programs work in the following way.

A letter is created and stored using a word processing program. However, you do not key in the individual's name and address. Rather, you key a predefined symbol in the place of the letter address and salutation. (The names and addresses of the individuals receiving the letter are stored in another location.) Then, instruct the program to print, on letterhead, a letter to each individual you have named. As the program prints a letter, it replaces the symbols with the name and address from the mailing list.

## Spreadsheet Programs

Have you ever done complex mathematical calculations manually and found yourself spending hours in the process? If so, you can appreciate the advantages of a spreadsheet program. With **spread-sheet** technology, mathematical calculations are done by the computer. See Figure 4-2 for a depiction of both a manual and computerized spreadsheet.

Basically, a spreadsheet works in this manner. You begin by entering the raw data in the spreadsheet along with formulas that indicate the types of calculations you need. For example, assume that your employer asks you to total the

**Figure 4-2**  Manual Spreadsheet and Computerized Spreadsheet

| | JAN | FEB | MAR | APR | TOTAL | MIN | MAX |
|---|---|---|---|---|---|---|---|
| SALES | 1750 | 1501 | 1519 | 1430 | 6200 | 1430 | 1750 |
| COST OF GOODS SOLD | 964 | 980 | 932 | 943 | 3819 | 932 | 980 |
| GROSS MARGIN | 786 | 521 | 587 | 487 | 2381 | 498 | 770 |
| | | | | | | | |
| NET EXPENSE | 98 | 93 | 82 | 110 | 383 | 82 | 110 |
| ADM EXPENSE | 77 | 79 | 69 | 88 | 313 | 69 | 88 |
| MISC EXPENSE | 28 | 45 | 31 | 31 | 135 | 28 | 45 |
| TOTAL EXPENSES | 203 | 217 | 182 | 229 | 831 | 179 | 243 |
| AVERAGE EXPENSE | 68 | 72 | 61 | 76 | 227 | 60 | 81 |
| | | | | | | | |
| NET BEFORE TAXES | 583 | 304 | 405 | 258 | 1550 | 258 | 583 |
| FEDERAL TAXES | 303 | 158 | 211 | 134 | 806 | 134 | 303 |
| NET AFTER TAX | 280 | 146 | 194 | 124 | 744 | 124 | 280 |

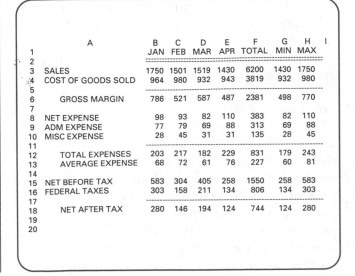

actual population figures for three counties for the last five years and project the increase for the next five years. This fairly complex problem can be done quickly by using a spreadsheet program. The spreadsheet program will compute the projections for you after you tell the program what percentage to use in the projection. Also, you can store the information on a disk. Then, if you need to make further projections, you can easily do so.

Still another advantage of the spreadsheet is that you can change a value easily and the computer will recalculate the figures. For example, assume that you first projected a five percent increase for one of the counties and a six and seven percent increase for the other two counties. Then you receive some additional information that leads you to believe that the five percent increase will go down to three percent. You can go back into the program and change the 5 to a 3; the program will automatically calculate the change and give you the new figures.

## Database Management Programs

A **database management program** is software that helps you organize data in a way that allows fast and easy access to it. The program acts as a very efficient filing system. Consider this situation. You work for an art museum. You keep computerized records of all paintings that the museum owns. Museum personnel are often interested in finding out how many paintings exist in the collection by a particular artist or how many paintings the museum owns covering a certain subject matter. Through the use of a database program you can retrieve this information quickly. If you want to know what paintings the museum owns by the artist Chagall, for example, enter the appropriate code and the list appears on the screen. If you want to know all the paintings covering the subject matter of landscape, enter the appropriate code and the list appears on the screen.

Consider another example of how database programs can be of assistance. Personnel records often include a photo database. Employers use such files for employee identification. Assume that company executives are gathered for a meeting in the boardroom. At one point, Gerald Adams is presenting data. One of the executives wants to know more about Gerald's background. After the presentation, the executive goes back to his office and keys in the appropriate database codes. In moments the face of Gerald Adams appears on

**Illus. 4-3** Personnel records often include a photo database.

*Credit: Courtesy Pictureware, Inc.*

the screen along with educational and career information.

## Graphics Programs

Graphics programs allow you to show words, numbers, and data in the form of pictures. Information can be presented in the form of a graph, pie chart, or bar chart. A considerable amount of information can be presented succinctly and meaningfully in graphic format.

There are a number of advantages to using graphics to present data. Graphics generally can hold the attention of the reader, or any audience, more than information that is presented in words and figures. Also, a graph or chart can easily show a trend that may be lost in long columns of numbers. Most businesses use graphs to help the reader or the audience see and analyze data and to make a positive impression on them. Numerous graphics programs are available.

## Desktop Publishing

In the past, if a business wanted to publish an in-house newsletter it had two choices—the traditional publishing process or word processing. Neither choice was very satisfactory. The traditional publishing process has been very costly to businesses. In fact, in many businesses, the cost of publications is second only to personnel costs. Many businesses spend hundreds of thousands of dollars annually on publishing. Publications are a major expense for other types of organizations also. Consider an educational institution.

**Illus. 4-4** Most businesses use graphs to help the reader or the audience see and analyze data and to make a positive impression on them.

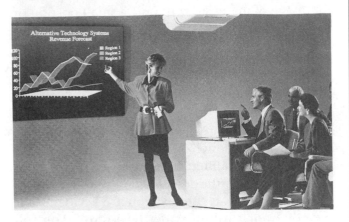

*Credit: Courtesy Electrohome Ltd.*

**Illus. 4-5** Preparing information in camera-ready format on-site can save a company a considerable amount of money in the printing process.

*Credit: Courtesy Xerox Corporation.*

Thousands of dollars are spent on schedules, catalogs, program brochures, and numerous other types of publications that are necessary so that students will have the information they need. The second choice, using word processing, did not allow the originator to use graphics and illustrations that were necessary, and thus the quality of the document suffered.

Now, with the use of **desktop publishing**, a quality in-house newsletter can be produced quickly and easily. Companies may also use desktop publishing to get documents **camera-ready** (ready to be photographed) for printing by an outside printing company. Preparing information in camera-ready format on-site can save a company a considerable amount of money in the printing process.

Now, let's consider some of the ways you, as an office assistant, may use desktop publishing. Assume that your company distributes an in-house newsletter once a month to let all employees know what is happening in the company. You may have the responsibility for keying the newsletter on a desktop publishing program. You learned in Chapter 3 that input devices include the keyboard, mouse, scanner, light pen, and so forth. The input devices used in desktop publishing are the keyboard, mouse, and scanner. Text is entered by using the keyboard. A mouse may be used to make menu selections and to move blocks of text and graphics on the screen. Already existing text and graphics can be entered into the desktop publishing system by using a scanner. Since the quality of the printer is very important in desktop publishing, most businesses will use a laser printer as the output device.

## Integrated Programs

An **integrated program** is a software program that typically includes word processing, spreadsheet, graphics, and database programs all in one. The concept is very appealing and is expected to grow in the future. Let's discuss some of the advantages of integrated programs.

An integrated program is especially useful when numbers and graphs need to be included in reports. With an integrated package, you do not need to learn a completely different program for word processing, graphics, and spreadsheets. You can move a table of spreadsheet numbers or graphs into the contextual matter quickly and easily. Without an integrated package, moving spreadsheet data and graphics into a word processing program is not simple. There is no common command structure and limited ease of transfer between programs.

Some of the disadvantages of the integrated programs are that usually the individual functions, such as word processing and graphics, are not as strong as they are in stand-alone programs. For example, if you need state-of-the-art word processing and state-of-the-art database management, you would probably be better served by buying two stand-alone programs. Integrated packages have also been rather expensive, and you have to pay for all the functions in the package when you may need to use only two or three functions. The integrated programs also require more computer memory than do stand-alone programs. There are several integrated programs on the market. These programs include *Framework IV*,[3] *Symphony*,[4] and *Microsoft Works*.[5] The choices available continue to expand as new developments occur. As the number of these programs increases, it is anticipated that the cost will decrease.

## BASIC SOFTWARE FUNCTIONS

You learned earlier that the Disk Operating System, or DOS, must be installed in the computer first. For example, let's assume that you are using a microcomputer with two disk drives. These disk drives are called drive A and drive B. The DOS disk is placed in drive A and DOS is **booted up**. This process loads DOS into the computer's memory. Then, the DOS disk is removed from drive A and the word processing program disk or other type of program is inserted in drive A. Then you must get the program started by striking the appropriate keys.

What about drive B? What goes in that drive? Remember, you learned earlier in this chapter that three types of disks are used—the DOS disks, software disks, and data disks. So far, two of these disks have been discussed—the DOS and the software disks, both which have been loaded in drive A. Now, assume that you want to store what you are going to input on an auxiliary storage device so that you may revise the information at a later time. In this case, you load your formatted data disk in drive B. (The data disk is the third type of disk mentioned earlier.) As you will recall, formatting means preparing a disk for holding data files and a file directory. As you put the document in the computer, you will temporarily use the storage that is built into the machine to save the information. However, as you already learned, all internal memory storage is limited. So, you will want to store the information on the auxiliary storage device which in this case is the formatted data disk in drive B. To do so, you merely key **B:** along with the name of the document. Now that you understand how the three disks are loaded, consider some of the other basic software functions that you will use.

[3] *Framework IV* is a registered trademark of Ashton-Tate a Borland Company.

[4] *Symphony* is a registered trademark of Lotus Development Corporation.

[5] *Microsoft Works* is a registered trademark of Microsoft Corporation.

## Scrolling

On a word processing program you may type page after page of material, with only a small portion of it showing on the screen. Most screens can display about 24 lines of text at a time. As you continue to type new lines, the earlier lines move up and off the screen into the computer's memory. If you want to see a line that has disappeared from the screen, move the cursor to the top of the screen and continue to press the up arrow on the keyboard until the copy you want appears. This process is called **scrolling.** It lets you see any part of the document on the screen whenever you desire. This function treats the text you are keying as if it were on a long roll of paper or a scroll. You roll the scroll up or down on the screen to get to the particular part of the copy that you want to display by moving the cursor. See Figure 4-3 which illustrates the scrolling process.

Now, let's take an example and see how scrolling works. Assume that you have keyed a document that contains approximately 60 lines. You are at the end of the document, and you want to proofread the entire document. What appears on the screen as you have finished the document are the last 24 lines of copy. You want to start to proofread at the beginning of the document. By using the cursor up (or up arrow) key or the PgUp key, both located on the right side of the keyboard, the first part of the document will appear on the screen. You can now proofread the first 24 lines. Use the cursor down (down arrow) key to scroll down to the remaining lines of the document.

## Editing

One of the distinct advantages of word processing is that you can make corrections and revisions easily. Assume that you have keyed a document, stored it on a data disk (the disk in the B drive in this example), and printed it out for your employer's signature. He or she decides to make several changes. Your employer makes the changes on the printed copy and hands it back to you. You then retrieve the disk on which the document was stored, load it into the computer, and call up the appropriate file. Your employer has decided to add several sentences to the letter. You move the cursor to the point where the sentences need to be added, space appropriately, and add the sentences.

Your employer has also decided to change a portion of two sentences. You need to key over

**Figure 4-3**  Scrolling

On college campuses, computers may soon be as common as pizza and dirty laundry. Many colleges, including Dartmouth, Carnegie-Mellon, Lehigh, and Drexel, require or strongly recommend that students purchase computers. Drexel, which requires each entering freshman to purchase a personal computer and software, has

thoroughly integrated computers into its curriculum.

Drexel's ambitious development of a computer-assisted curriculum has received strong student and faculty support. Faculty members developed software with the help of student and professional programmers. For instance, a chemistry professor designed software that helps students understand molecular structure by seeing the arrangements of atoms displayed on the computer screen. A program written by a mathematics professor shows students how to solve complex algebra problems. An English professor created software that helps students write more coherently.

Drexel's integration of computers into its curriculum has had a positive effect on the school's morale. A study shows that as students and faculty become more adept at using computers, they tend to feel more optimistic about the future.

the existing text. On *WordPerfect* (one type of word processing package available), you may do so by using the *Typeover* mode. You place the cursor where you want the new text to begin. Then press *Ins* to turn off *Insert* mode and turn on Typeover mode. The Typeover mode indicator appears at the lower left of the screen. You then type the new text and press Ins again to return to Insert mode. All of these changes can be made quickly and easily.

## Using Windows

Windows may also be used in the editing process. The window process gives you two or more "sheets of paper" to work with at once, if you like. For example, assume that you have two documents that have tables in them. Two columns of the tables are the same on both documents. You need

to make changes to the tables. Through the use of the window function, both tables will appear on the screen at one time. You can type in both windows and switch back and forth between them with ease. Or, assume that you need to refer to spreadsheet data as you are keying the narrative of a report. You can refer to the spreadsheet data by using a window while you are working with the narrative. Windows offer menu systems which are easy to use, the ability to transfer data among different types of files, and user-friendly prompts.

**Illus. 4-6**  Windows offer menu systems which are easy to use, the ability to transfer data among different types of files, and user-friendly prompts.

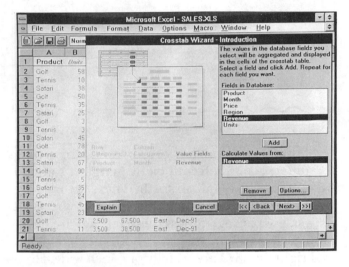

*Credit: Courtesy Microsoft Corporation.*

## Formatting

The ability to format is another advantage of a word processing program. The format of a document is the way the document appears on the page. Format refers to the size of the margins, the organization of text, the space between the lines, and other factors that affect appearance. Assume that you have prepared a report for your employer. A portion of a report is shown in Figure 4-4. Notice in the first draft of the report, the heading is not centered and the report is double-spaced. Your employer has asked that you single-space it to conserve paper, put the side headings in bold, and make the left margin 1½ inches so that the report may be bound. Through the formatting function of a word processing program you can make these changes.

To illustrate how easily it might be done, consider the change of the left margin. A word

**Figure 4-4**  Report Before and After Formatting

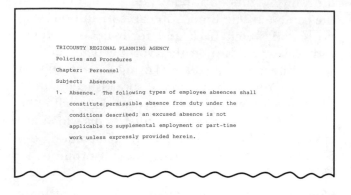

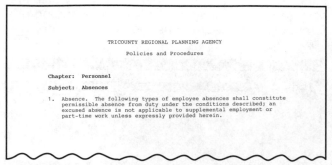

**Figure 4-5**  Line Spacing Screen

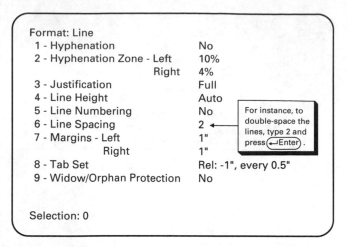

processing program has certain standard setting for line spacing, left and right margins, top and bottom margins, and so forth. These settings are called **default settings** (settings used by the word processing package unless these settings are deliberately changed by the user). Both the default left and right margins are usually one inch wide. However, you can easily change the margins by accessing the format menu and replacing the default settings for the left margin with ''1.5.'' When the margin settings are changed, most word processing software automatically adjusts the text to accommodate your new margin settings. This is called **automatic reformatting.**

## Using Menus and Prompts

A **menu** is defined as an on-screen list of command choices. Here is how you might use a menu. Assume that you want to change the line spacing from single to double. You access the Format menu by utilizing the appropriate keys; in *WordPerfect,* you use *Shift-F8.* The full-screen Format menu appears. You select *Line* by pressing 1; the next menu appears. Select line spacing by pressing 6 and then insert 2 for double-spacing. Notice Figure 4-5 which illustrates the concept. Any number of menus are available on software packages including file, edit, layout, search, tools (including spell and thesaurus), font, graphics, and help menus.

A **prompt** is a signal that the computer is waiting for data or a command from the user. Here is how a prompt works. Assume that you have keyed a document and have underscored several words in the document. As you edit the document, you decide to change one of the underscored words. A message, or prompt, will appear at the bottom of the computer screen asking if you want to delete the underscored or highlighted area. You answer the prompt by choosing *Y* for yes or *N* for no and proceed with your editing.

Consider another example of how a prompt works. You work for a police department and you receive a report that a police officer has reason to suspect that a car with a license plate beginning with AZP might be stolen. The officer is not certain of the remainder of the plate but thinks it is 646 or 648. You ask the computer to display all stolen cars in the state with licenses beginning with AZP. The computer gives you the list and prompts:

Do you wish details for a specific number from this list?

Yes (Y) or no (N)

You discover that there is a stolen car on the list with the number AZP646, so you type *Y,* and the computer provides another prompt:

Type specific license number

You do so and receive details about the make and year of the car, its owner, address, and so forth.

## Creating Macros

Tasks which are performed repeatedly can be done more quickly and efficiently by using a macro. A <u>**macro** is a series of prerecorded keystrokes assigned to a single key or key combination</u>. Macros can automate simple tasks, such as the complimentary close on a letter, or they can perform complex operations. Macros may be used in any number of situations. Let's assume that you key interoffice memorandums often. You want to use the same heading on all memorandums. Using a macro to create the memo heading allows you to press only a few characters rather than keying in all of the heading each time you prepare a memo.

Another way you might use macros is to change the default right and left margins. Assume that the default margins are each one inch. Frequently you need to change the margin to 1½ inches. Creating a macro allows you to make the margin change quickly. These illustrations are only a few of the ways that you might use macros. What you need to remember is that if you are performing repetitive tasks on a computer, a macro can help you be more efficient.

Certainly, word processing programs contain numerous other features. Only a few have been presented here so that you will have some understanding of what can be done. After using a program for a period of time, you will become very knowledgeable about its features and proficient in the use of them.

## SOFTWARE SELECTION

In addition to being knowledgeable about a particular software package and able to use that package well, you may be asked to select or have input to the selection of software which your company plans to use. Here are some questions that you should ask when selecting software.

1. Do you have the hardware requirements for the software? For example, the program may require 256K of memory and MS-DOS.

2. What software support is available? Support may be in the form of tutorials, classes by the vendor, and hotline assistance.

3. What documentation is available? The program should have an instruction manual which is well organized and easy to read. An

**Pepper . . . and Salt**

THE WALL STREET JOURNAL

*Credit: From* The Wall Street Journal—*permission Cartoon Features Syndicate.*

index, a glossary of terms, a quick reference guide, illustrations, and examples are helpful. Visual clarity is a mark of effective documentation. Sections in a manual should be separated with durable tabbed pages. There should be ample white space, pictures, and examples so that you have no trouble following the written text.

4. Is the program **user friendly**? In answering that question, here are some items that you should check.

   a. Is the menu organized well and easy to understand?
   b. Are the commands logical and easy to remember? The fewer keystrokes a command takes, the better.
   c. Does the help screen really provide the help needed? The commands for displaying the help screen should be easy to remember, and the displays themselves should be easy to read.

5. Does the program offer what you need? For example, does it offer mailmerge? automatic page numbering? bypassing of menus? a spell-checker? a thesaurus?

6. If it has a graphics package, does the graphics package require a color monitor?

7. Does the program automatically save your document to a hard disk periodically? This feature can save you considerable anguish in

case of a power failure or a careless move on your part. Some programs let you determine how often you want the computer to automatically save your material. For example, you might tell the computer to save material every 20 or 30 minutes.

8. Is the vendor known for providing good service? You certainly may have trouble with a package after purchasing it. Will the vendor assist you? Will the vendor replace the software if it doesn't work correctly?

9. What is the reputation of the software? You can check with individuals who have used the software. You can also read reviews in computer periodicals such as *InfoWorld, PC Magazine,* and *Byte.*

10. Are you going to be working with others in the office? If so, standard word processing documents will be essential. It will be necessary for you to talk with these individuals and agree on a package that will serve all of your needs.

## SOFTWARE AND COMPUTER CARE

Once you have selected and purchased your software, you must take appropriate care of it. It is also essential that your computer be appropriately maintained. Here are some suggestions for you in performing these functions.

### Software Care

When working with floppy disks, you need to store and protect them properly. Carelessness can destroy untold hours of work on a floppy disk. You should always do the following:

a. Handle a disk at the top near the label.

b. Do not remove a floppy disk from its protective cover.

c. Do not bend a floppy disk.

d. Do not write on the cover of a floppy disk. Write on an adhesive label before applying it to the disk cover. Remove old labels which may be on a disk before applying a new label.

e. Store 5¼ inch floppy disks in their paper jackets, standing on their edges in specially designed containers.

f. Magnets can erase information on floppy and hard disks, so keep them away from disks. Also keep paper clips away from disks.

g. Do not store disks close to a telephone. A ringing telephone can create a magnetic field.

h. Keep floppy disks away from water and other liquids. Dry them with a lint-free cloth if they should get wet.

i. Keep floppy disks out of direct sunlight and away from radiators and other sources of heat.

j. Apply write-protect tabs to disks containing data that should not be changed. The **write-protect notch** is an indentation on the outside edge of the floppy disk. When the notch is uncovered, you can add new data, erase data, or place data on the disk. A **write-protect tab** can be placed over the notch to prevent any changes from accidentally occurring.

**Illus. 4-8** Both 3½ and 5¼ inch disks should be stored in specially designed containers.

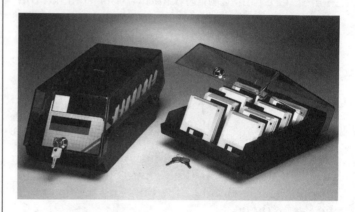

*Credit: Ring King Visibles, Inc.—a Hon Industries Company.*

### Computer Care

Here are some tips for keeping your computer in good working order.

a. Vacuum the printer periodically and wipe surface areas with a clean cloth.

b. To keep the disk-drive read/write heads clean, use an approved head-cleaning kit.

c. Keep soda, coffee, or anything crumbly away from the computer since it can ruin a keyboard.

d. Clean the surface area of the keys with a mild cleansing agent.

e. Use a can of compressed air (with a narrow nozzle) to blow out residue between and under the keys.

f. Turn off the monitor and wipe your screen clean with a mild cleanser.

g. Do not place a computer near an open window, in direct sunlight, or near a heater. Computers work best in cool temperatures, below 80 degrees Fahrenheit.

h. Do not smoke near a computer. Smoking adds tar and particle matter to the air; these particles can find their way into the computer.

i. Periodically delete files you no longer need from your hard drive. If you think you might need the files at a later time, put them on a floppy disk. When you've purged your files, take a look at your directory structure. Having hundreds of files in one directory will slow the file-search process, which impairs the overall performance of your computer. Purge your directory also.

### Security Procedures

There are several steps that can be taken to prevent theft or destruction of computer hardware or software. A few of these steps are listed here.

a. Bolt down equipment or lock computer furniture.

b. Arrange for outside computer facilities if your equipment is stolen or there is a malfunction. For example, an entity such as TriCounty Regional Planning Agency might make arrangements with another planning agency to use their computer facilities if a malfunction occurs at TriCounty.

c. **Backup** is a way of protecting data by copying it and storing it in more than one place. Backup all material that is on the hard disk with a floppy disk.

d. Use a surge protector which is a device that prevents electrical problems from affecting data files. (The computer is plugged into the surge protector and the surge protector is plugged into an outlet.)

e. Store the backup material in a separate location.

f. Frequently change the password or access code for individuals who have access to classified information.

### Computer Viruses

Computer viruses are serious maladies that can cause major computer impairment. What is a computer virus? Is it a computer with a disease? No, it is actually a computer program with unauthorized instructions. It is called a virus because it is contagious; it can pass itself on to other programs in which it comes in contact. Here is one example of how a computer can get a virus.

A computer programmer secretly inserts a few unauthorized instructions in a computer operating system program. The disk with the infected operating system is used and copied onto other files. The virus spreads to another disk, and the process is repeated. After the infected disk is copied a number of times, the virus can cause all data in the files affected to be erased.

How can viruses be prevented? Although there are programs called vaccines which can prevent viruses, protection against viruses depends more on common sense than acquiring vaccines. Viruses tend to show up on free software acquired through friends or through bulletin board systems.

**Bulletin board systems** use data communications to link personal computers in providing public-access message systems. These bulletin boards are similar to bulletin boards you see in grocery stores and student lounges. Someone leaves a message; however, the person picking up the message does not necessarily know the person who left the message. To get access to someone else's computer, all you really have to know is that computer's bulletin board phone number. Anyone who has a personal computer can set up a bulletin board. It takes a computer, a phone line, a couple of disk drives, and limited software. Tell a few people about your board, and you are in business. If you use disks received through bulletin board programs, you should put write-protection tabs on the other disks that you are using with these programs.

As you will recall from what you have learned earlier, a write-protect tab keeps new information from being saved to a disk. If an attempt is made to write on the protected disk, a warning message appears on the screen. With such a precaution, a virus that may be on the disk cannot be transferred to other disks you are working with. Figure 4-6 graphically depicts the development and transmission of a computer virus.

### SOFTWARE—A VALUABLE TOOL

You have learned in this chapter that software is a valuable tool that is used extensively by the office assistant. Software not only increases the produc-

**Figure 4-6** Infection from a Computer Virus

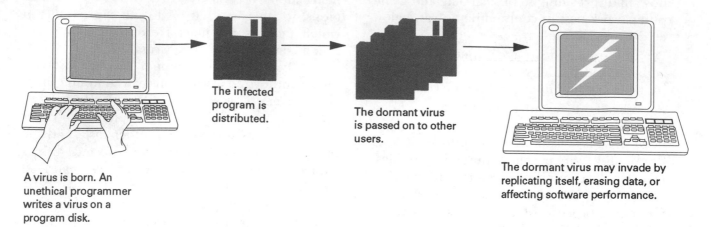

A virus is born. An unethical programmer writes a virus on a program disk.

The infected program is distributed.

The dormant virus is passed on to other users.

The dormant virus may invade by replicating itself, erasing data, or affecting software performance.

tivity of the office employee but it also improves the quality of the work. You now understand some of the major functions of software programs. By properly selecting software, using it efficiently, and taking caution with storage and security on your disks and computer, you will find your microcomputer to be an extremely efficient partner in performing your daily tasks.

## CHAPTER SUMMARY

The following summary will help you remember the important points of this chapter.

1. Word processing packages allow the originator to create, edit, format, store, and print documents. Such packages are used extensively in the office. Packages also exist that will check your spelling; provide a list of words which might be used in the document (a thesaurus package); check your grammar and style; and create form letters. Some of these packages are built into the word processing program. For example, a number of word processing programs contain spell-checkers within the program.

2. A spreadsheet program simulates an accountant's worksheet. The user of the spreadsheet keys in the raw mathematical data and the function to be performed. For example, if columns are to be added, the user keys in the appropriate instruction. The calculations are automatically made through the formulas which are built into the spreadsheet program.

3. Database programs help you organize data in a way that allows fast and easy access to it. The program acts as a very efficient filing system.

4. Graphics programs allow you to show words, numbers, and data in the form of pictures. Many of these programs have the capability of producing color graphics.

5. Desktop publishing packages allow you to produce print quality products that include graphics and the reproduction of photographs. With desktop publishing you may also prepare camera-ready copy for an outside printing company.

6. Integrated programs contain a combination of word processing, spreadsheet, graphics, and database functions. It is expected that there will be an increase in integrated programs in the future.

7. Some of the basic functions of a software package include scrolling, editing, formatting, windows, menus and prompts, and macros. With these functions you can revise material easily and change the organization of the text, the space between lines, the size of the margins, and so forth.

8. When selecting software, be certain that the hardware that you have will support the software program; that appropriate documentation is available to help you; that the services provided by the vendor are sufficient for your needs; and that the program is user-friendly.

9. Take appropriate care of your software. The floppy disk should never be taken from its pro-

tective cover; it should not be bent; it should be stored in its paper jacket, standing on its edge; and it should be kept out of direct sunlight and away from magnets.

10. You should keep your computer in good working order by vacuuming the printer periodically, cleaning the surface area of the keys with a mild cleansing agent, cleaning the screen of the monitor, keeping the computer away from direct sunlight, and not smoking next to a computer.

11. To secure your computer and software, bolt down the equipment or lock computer furniture; backup all material on the hard disk with a floppy disk; store the backup material in a separate location; and frequently change the password for individuals who have access to classified information.

## TERMINOLOGY REVIEW

The following terms were introduced in this chapter. To help you understand them, definitions are given below.

1. **Automatic reformatting** *(page 84)* In word processing, this is the automatic adjustment of text to accommodate changes to the default settings. For example, if the default setting of single-spacing is changed by the user to double-spacing, then all text is automatically changed to double-spacing.

2. **Backup** *(page 87)* Backup is a way of protecting data by copying it and storing it in more than one place.

3. **Booting** *(page 82)* Loading the operating system into memory.

4. **Bulletin board system** *(page 87)* A bulletin board system uses data communication to link personal computers in providing public-access message systems.

5. **Camera-ready** *(page 81)* Camera-ready means getting a document ready to photograph previous to printing.

6. **Database management program** *(page 79)* A database management program is software that helps you organize data in a way that allows fast and easy access to it. The program acts as a very efficient filing system.

7. **Default settings** *(page 84)* Settings automatically used by a program unless the user specifies otherwise, such as specific side, top, and bottom margins.

8. **Desktop publishing** *(page 81)* A technology that allows the generation of characters in a broad range of typefaces and allows for the production of graphics, photographs, and so forth. With desktop publishing, a high quality product can be produced within the office without the assistance of an outside typesetter.

9. **DOS** *(page 76)* DOS means *disk operating system;* it controls the use of disk drives for storing and retrieving programs and data.

10. **Editing** *(page 78)* Editing refers to making changes in a document to correct errors or improve the content of the document.

11. **Formatting** *(page 78)* Formatting refers to adjusting the appearance of a document to make it look appropriate and attractive.

12. **Formatting a data disk** *(page 77)* Preparing a disk for holding data files and a file directory.

13. **Integrated program** *(page 81)* A set of software that usually includes word processing, spreadsheet, graphics, and database programs all in one.

14. **Macro** *(page 85)* A macro is a series of prerecorded keystrokes assigned to a single key or key combination. Macros allow you to automate simple and complex repetitive tasks.

15. **Menu** *(page 84)* A menu is an on-screen list of command choices.

16. **Prompt** *(page 84)* A prompt is a signal that the computer is waiting for data or a command from the user.

17. **Scrolling** *(page 82)* A word processing feature that allows the user to move to and view any part of a document on the screen.

18. **Spreadsheet** *(page 79)* An electronic worksheet divided into rows and columns that can be used to analyze and present business data.

19. **Thesaurus** *(page 78)* A list of synonyms (words that have the same meaning) and antonyms (words that have opposite meanings).

20. **User friendly** *(page 85)* This phrase refers to software that is easy for a beginner to use.

21. **Write-protect notch** *(page 86)* The write-protect notch is an indentation on the outside edge of the floppy disk. When the notch is uncovered, you can add new data, erase data, or place data on a disk.

22. **Write-protect tab** *(page 86)* A write-protect tab can be placed over the write-protect notch to prevent any changes on the disk.

## DISCUSSION ITEMS

1. Explain the difference between an applications software disk and a data disk.
2. What is a spell-checker and how is it used?
3. What are the advantages of using a spreadsheet program?
4. What are the advantages of using a graphics program?
5. Explain some of the advantages and disadvantages of integrated programs.
6. Describe scrolling.
7. What is the difference between a menu and a prompt?
8. List eight suggestions of appropriate ways to care for floppy disks.

## CASE STUDY

The software package that you are presently using at TriCounty is not meeting your needs. It does not have a spell-checker, and you believe that one would save you a number of hours in proofreading. Also, you are frequently asked to write routine letters and memorandums for Mr. Andrews. Sometimes you need help selecting the most appropriate word. You believe that a thesaurus would help you. The documentation that you have with the present software is not well written. If you want to perform a function that you have not performed before, it takes a long time to find it in the manual and it is difficult to understand the instructions.

You have told Mr. Andrews that you are not happy with the package and believe that a more appropriate one can be found. You have not discussed it with the other office personnel; it is important that you all use the same package since many times you work on the same projects and need to share floppy disks. Mr. Andrews has told you that he will support your efforts to get another package, but he wants you to make a recommendation to him about what that package should be. Answer the questions below concerning this case.

1. What are the important considerations for you in looking at a new software package?
2. What questions should you ask of a software vendor?

## OFFICE APPLICATIONS

### Office Application 4-1 (*Objectives 1 and 3*)

Visit a software store and check out the types of software packages they have available for word processing, spreadsheet, graphics, and desktop publishing. Also check to see what integrated programs are available. Prepare a report giving your findings. Include a section in the report on "Recommendations," recommending the packages you would purchase in each area and stating your reasons for your recommendations. Review the material in your text on selecting software before you make your trip to the software store. If you are using a computer in preparing your report, store your information on your "report" disk. Label the report, "Reports SWR3-2 (software recommendations; use the date you are keyboarding the report; 3-2 is given as an example). Print out an additional copy of your report for filing and place in your folder labeled "to be filed."

### Office Application 4-2 (*Objective 2*)

Mr. Andrews gives you a portion of the Policy and Procedures Manual on absences to keyboard. You need to make the changes he noted in the copy and keyboard the remainder of the document. Allow a 2 inch top margin on the first page. Allow a 1 inch top margin on the second page. Allow 1 inch side margins and a minimum 1 inch bottom margin on all pages of your document. Single-space the document.

*With a template disk:* Load the stored file, OA4-2. Only a portion of the document is on the template. Key the remainder of the document. Correct the document as shown on pages 92-94. Proofread the document; save the copy; print two copies. Turn in one copy to your instructor. Place the second copy in your "to be filed" folder.

*Without a template disk:* Complete the entire exercise given on pages 92-94 of this text. Make two copies of the final document. Turn in one copy to your instructor; place the second copy in your "to be filed" folder.

### Office Application 4-3 (*Objective 4*)

Talk with a local vendor of computer systems; ask him or her to explain to you how to care for a microcomputer. Report your findings to the class.

### Office Application 4-4 (*Objectives 3 and 4*)

Interview an office assistant of a local business. Ask the following questions.

1.  Do you select software? If so, what criteria do you use in your selection?

2.  How do you care for your computer?

Report your findings to the class.

TRICOUNTY REGIONAL PLANNING AGENCY *center* ]

Policies and Procedures

Chapter: Personnel

Subject: Absences

------------------------------------------------------------------

1. <u>Absence</u>. The following types of employee absences shall constitute permissible absence from duty under the conditions described; an excused absence is not applicable to supplemental employment or part-time work unless expressly provided herein.

   a. <u>Sick Leave</u>

      (1) <u>Benefit Accrual</u>. Sick leave benefits shall accrue to full-time employees from the first day of employment, at a rate of one day per month of the employment year. No sick leave benefits shall accrue or be used under contracts for supplemental employment or part-time work.

      (2) <u>Maximum Accrual</u>. The maximum sick leave benefits which may accrue to eligible employees shall be ~~sixty-six~~ *fifty* (~~66~~ *50*) days. [ Sick leave shall be credited as earned, but may be approved by the Personnel Office beyond the accrued amount, provided that employees with less than six months service shall not be approved for more than six days' leave. ]

      (3) <u>Uses</u>. Sick leave may be used only

         (a) For illness of the employee;

         (b) With the prior approval of the employee's supervisor, for medical or dental emergencies or appointments, and when such

cannot be scheduled after duty hours;

(c) For maternity leave, to the extent of accrued benefits, to

be applied at the beginning of the leave period;

(d) For illness of ~~children~~ *spouses,* and other dependents living in the

household.  An employee may not use more than ten days of

sick leave per year for this purpose.

(4) <u>Benefit Adjustments</u>

    (a) <u>Job-related Injury</u>:  An employee who is absent from work due

to job-related injury shall be eligible for sick leave pay,

provided that the sick leave pay shall be reduced by an

amount equal to worker's compensation benefits paid.

    (b) <u>Disability</u>:  An employee who is absent from work due to a

disability and who is covered by optional short-term or

long-term disability plans that are offered by Tricounty,

may be eligible for disability pay under the terms and

conditions of the plan.

(5) <u>Termination of Employment</u>:  Unused accrued sick leave shall be

forfeited upon termination of employment with Tricounty. In the

event *that* an employee has received sick leave benefits in excess of

days earned to the date of termination, there shall be deducted

from such employee's final compensation check an amount equal

to such excess.

b. <u>Bereavement or Family Illness</u>:  Absence due to the death or critical

illness in the immediate family of an employee (not to exceed three

days at any one time) may be granted without loss of pay upon

approval of the employee's supervisor. "Immediate family" means

spouse, child, father, *father-in-law,* mother, *mother-in-law,* brother, sister, or grandparent of the employee or other person who occupies a position of similar

significance in the family of the employee.

c.  Birth or Adoption of a Child: Leave may be granted for a maximum of

one full day without loss of pay for an employee to be with his wife

at the birth of their child or for an employee to be at the court

proceeding for adoption of a child.

d.  Required Court Appearance: An employee will be excused with pay for

court appearance when subpoenaed as a witness.  This privilege does

not apply to court cases involving an employee's personal business.

e.  Jury Duty: An employee may be granted leave of absence without loss

of pay when called for jury duty.  If absence for jury duty would

seriously impair the operation of Tricounty, the supervisor may

request the judge to defer to a later date the employee's duty.  An

employee called for jury duty shall immediately report such notice

to his supervisor.

f.  Extenuating Circumstances: For reasons not covered by other leave,

an employee may be paid for absence not to exceed two days per

year.  Such leave may not be accumulated from one year to the

next.  Such leave is subject to approval under appropriate

procedures of Tricounty.

# 5 Reprographics—Copiers and Procedures

Have you ever tried to make a copy of a document at school or at the office and been told that the copier is not working? If so, you understand the importance of the copier in the office today. When the office copier fails, work grinds to a halt and frustration increases. Americans generate billions of images on copiers each year—studies done by copier companies have shown that the number is as high as 400 billion.

The information age has given us the capability of generating more and more data and with that capability has come the need to transmit the information to people throughout the organization. As organizations have become multinational, transmitting information does not merely mean sending it to individuals within a particular building or a even a particular state. Many times it means sending the information to a branch of the company in Europe, Asia, Africa, or South America.

As an office assistant you need to be familiar with the types of copiers available and their features. In addition to using the copier numerous times each day, you may also be involved in the decision making when your office is determining what type of copier to buy. This chapter will help you to gain the knowledge you need about copiers and procedures.

## GENERAL OBJECTIVES

*Your general objectives for this chapter are to*
1. **Become familiar with the use of centralized and decentralized copy centers.**
2. **Identify the types of copiers available.**
3. **Use copiers to reproduce documents.**
4. **Identify the features available on copiers.**
5. **Explain copier maintenance and selection procedures.**
6. **Determine when and what to copy.**

## REPROGRAPHICS DEFINED

**Reprographics** is the process of making copies of correspondence, reports, and various other documents. The process of making copies is not confined to one type of copier. Copies may be made on copy machines, on FAX machines, and through computer keyboard commands. These commands instruct a photocopier to reproduce copies of information that has been keyed.

Still other reprographic possibilities today include making copies from electronic easels. For example, an executive may produce a chart on an electronic easel while delivering a presentation. Once the executive finishes the chart he or she can make copies for everyone in the room by pushing a button on the easel. Reprographics refers to any piece of mechanical or electronic equipment that produces multiple copies of an original document.

## CENTRALIZED AND DECENTRALIZED CENTERS

If you work in a large organization, usually there will be a centralized center where copies are made in addition to decentralized centers where each worker can make his or her own copies. Centralized and decentralized centers serve different functions and exist for different reasons. If you work in a small organization you probably will have decentralized copiers. To help you learn more about the functions of both, read the following paragraphs.

### Centralized Copy Centers

**Centralized copy centers** exist to serve the large-volume copying needs of an organization. For example, if you routinely need 500 copies of reports,

**Illus. 5-1** Still other reprographic possibilities today include making copies from electronic easels.

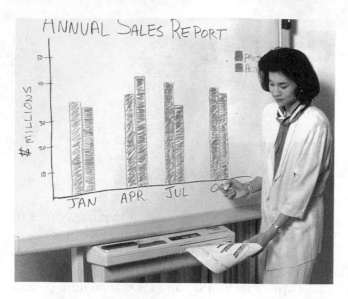

with each report ranging from 25 to 50 pages in length, it would not be cost effective or efficient to have the office assistant make the copies. Such copying projects would tie up his or her time and reduce the number of other duties that could be handled. And, if you work in a large organization where there are 200 people each day needing this volume of copy work, you can quickly understand that a centralized center would be the most efficient way to produce the work. A centralized center, then, is a center where the employees are involved in the reproduction process as a large portion of their job. However, they usually do more than just make copies—they collate, staple, bind, and so forth.

Consider the various functions that are performed in a centralized copy center. Assume that you are ready to have a report reproduced and you are going to have it done by the centralized copy center. Here are some of the questions that you will be asked:

- How many copies do you need?
- What type of paper do you need? color? weight? size?
- Do you want the report collated?
- Do you want the report copied on both sides of the paper?
- Do you want the report bound?
- Do you need the copy reduced or enlarged?

- Do you want a cover to be placed on your document?
- When do you need the copies?

The functions of a centralized center include processing all the documents that are to be produced and setting priorities in order to meet deadlines. The personnel in charge must order and keep on hand various types, sizes, and colors of paper, and must produce the copies according to instructions. In order to maintain the required inventory, copy center personnel must have knowledge of various weights, finishes, colors, and sizes of paper.

Copy center personnel must also be familiar with the types of equipment available and how it functions. Many times it is necessary to **collate** materials (assemble them in numerical or logical sequence). It may also be necessary to hole punch and/or bind materials. Large volume copy machines will collate materials. Collators are also available that operate independently of copiers. Equipment that will both punch and bind materials is available for both softcover and hardcover binding. Stapling equipment is available along with equipment that folds, inserts in envelopes, seals, and meter-stamps mail. In addition to being familiar with equipment functions, copy center personnel are also responsible for maintenance of the equipment, ensuring that it is in top working condition at all times so that breakdowns are kept to a minimum.

Some companies combine the printing function and the mail room function, thus employees need to have a knowledge of mailing equipment and procedures. Employees in a centralized center might prepare mail for distribution internally as well as externally. For example, if you want all managers within the company to get a certain report, the center would reproduce the document and send it through interoffice mail to all managers.

### Decentralized Copy Centers

Both large and small companies use **decentralized copy centers**, in which copying machines are located in proximity to the employees. For example, there may be one copying machine located in each department of the company. This gives employees immediate access to a copying machine. Small numbers of copies can be made quickly and easily. Any employee in the area can make a copy; it is not necessary to wait for someone else to do it for you.

Although the advantages of a decentralized system are numerous, and such a system is essential in the office of today, there are disadvantages. Since all employees have access to the copy machine, copying may be excessive. Also, since all employees are using the machine, costs may escalate with no information as to which department is incurring the greatest cost. Another problem with a decentralized system is that someone in the area must be responsible for the maintenance of the machine and for assisting personnel if a problem arises.

Although copiers are relatively easy to use, there are functions on most machines which require some assistance. To maintain the machine, paper must be added, toner must be put into the machine, paper must be ordered, the screen must be cleaned occasionally, and a maintenance technician must be called when a serious problem arises. Some companies solve this problem by designating a **key operator** who has the responsibility for maintaining the machine, assisting personnel, ordering paper, and so forth.

**Illus. 5-2** Both large and small companies use decentralized copy centers, in which copying machines are located in proximity to the employee.

*Credit: Courtesy Xerox Corporation.*

## COPIER CATEGORIES

There are basically four categories of copiers available—personal copiers, low-volume copiers, mid-volume copiers, and high-volume copiers. These divisions are based on the monthly copy volumes each copier can handle and the speed at which the copier operates. For example, assume a copier can produce 25 copies per minute and produces 28,000 copies per month. This machine is considered a low-volume copier.

### Personal Copiers

**Personal copiers** are used in small offices and in homes. Typically, these machines are low-cost units that turn out fewer than 500 copies per month at a speed of approximately 10 copies per minute. On most models users can copy on plain paper, on business cards, and on transparencies. Many personal copiers also include features such as enlarging, reducing, and color capability. These copiers are lightweight, portable, small, and can be placed on top of a desk. As one of the fastest growing segments in the copier market, these copiers are marketed by discount office products firms, by direct mail, through retail outlets, and through dealers.

### Low-Volume Copiers

**Low-volume copiers** are also called convenience copiers. These machines typically produce 10 to 30 copies per minute and up to 30,000 copies per month. Making up the largest portion of the copier market, they are used in small offices as the only copier and in large offices as satellite machines in decentralized centers.

### Mid-Volume Copiers

**Mid-volume copiers** generate between 30 and 70 copies per minute, producing approximately 50,000 copies per month. These machines have more features than low-volume copiers, with some of the standard features being automatic paper feed, automatic duplexing (copying on both sides of the paper), document editing, programmable memory, highlight color, reduction/enlargement, and more. Mid-volume copiers are floor-console models and are found in semi-central or satellite copying locations to serve walk-up users.

*Credit: Courtesy Xerox Corporation.*

## High-Volume Copiers

**High-volume copiers** are used in the centralized copy center. They are capable of meeting the speed, volume, and quality requirements of an entire organization. These copiers are capable of producing copies at very high speeds, in excess of 70 copies per minute (some copiers producing as much as 150 copies per minute), with monthly volumes as high as 500,000 copies. These copiers are the most expensive of the copiers, selling for $70,000 and up, as compared to a personal copier that can be purchased for approximately $1,000.

High-volume copiers may also be referred to as duplicators, which generally means that they produce the greatest number of copies per minute (90 or more copies per minute). These copiers/duplicators include a full complement of features. For example, the on-line sorter of the copier/duplicator allows copies to go directly from the machine to the sorter without operator intervention. As multiple copies of each page of a document are produced, each is automatically separated into bins. In other words, these machines perform the collating function. In addition, these machines include a finishing function. The unit receives the copies, jogs (straightens or evens the stack of copies), staples, and deposits each set in a removable tray.

**Illus. 5-4** High-volume copiers are used in the centralized copy center.

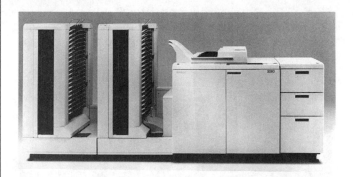

*Credit: Photo courtesy of Konica Business Machines, U.S.A., Inc.*

## OFFSET PRINTING

When it is necessary to produce large quantities of a document, offset printing is used. For example, publishers of newspapers use the offset process in printing papers. Although an office assistant does not run an offset press, it will help you to have some knowledge of the process.

Offset presses print from offset masters which may be paper or metal. The paper master (also called a mat) is prepared by keying the information on the master or drawing or writing on the master. However, in most cases a metal master is used. Offset metal masters are not directly imaged (keyed or typed on). They are produced by photographing the image of an original onto the metal plate with a special camera or using a copying machine to transfer the image from the original to the metal plate.

The principle behind offset printing is that grease and water do not mix. The master is placed on a cylinder of the offset press. The cylinder comes in contact with rollers that have ink and water on them. The ink adheres to the grease on the master, and the water prevents the ink from adhering to other parts of the master. The image is then inked on this master cylinder and transferred from the master to a blanket or intermediate cylinder. Next, the image is transferred, or offset, from the blanket cylinder to copy paper fed through the machine when an impression roller presses the copy paper against the blanket cylinder.

**Illus. 5-5**  When it is necessary to produce large quantities of a document, offset printing is used.

## TECHNOLOGICAL ADVANCES

With ongoing technological advances, changes in copiers occur frequently. More recent developments in the copier field have brought about color copying, digital copying, and intelligent copier/printers.

### Color Copying

Although color copying has been around for approximately 20 years, it has now awakened from its dormant state. User demand for full-color copies and for attention-getting communications has spurred the demand. Color imaging technology has traditionally been classified according to the method of producing the color, with some of the major methods being electrophotographic, thermal transfer, xerographic, and cycolor.

With the electrophotographic process the color image is produced with chemicals on photographic stock in the same manner as a color photograph is developed and printed. Thermal transfer machines use heat and pressure to fuse the colors on a coated ribbon to the surface of the paper. Xerographic technology is the same type of technology used in black and white copying machines. This process will be explained in more detail later. Cycolor is a recent technology which uses film coated with color-impregnated capsules. When an image is projected onto the film, different colors within the light spectrum trigger chemical reactions in the appropriate capsules. A receiver sheet is mated automatically with the film and the two pass through pressure rollers, causing the unexposed capsules to burst, blending the dyes.

### Digital Copiers

Copier users want a copier that can do more than one thing at a time; digital copiers satisfy that concern. Digital copiers can serve as a printer, make multiple copies, and electronically transmit the copies. The electronics of digital copiers give users the ability to manipulate images and create changes. Digital copiers have two main components—the scanner and the printer. Scanned images go into the computer of the copier where the image is converted into digital signals and manipulated. Then, the signal is passed to a laser or LED (light emitting diode) printer where the digital signal is converted to an image on a conductive surface which produces the copy.

One of the advantages of digital copying is that an image needs to be scanned only once, regardless of the number of copies required. Through software the image may be manipulated. When making transparencies, digital copiers can enlarge headlines and delete extraneous information to create a bold visual image. For poster-boards, where detail is needed, users may combine digital highlighting and framing techniques for quality poster displays. Digital technology can also be used with color copying and can provide clearer copies in both color and black and white than its analog counterpart.

### Intelligent Copier/Printers

An **intelligent copier/printer** can create images from hard copy or from computer instructions. These copiers are high-volume copiers that may receive input from a computer, optical character recognition unit, or prerecorded magnetic media. For example, information can be keyed into a microcomputer and sent by electronic signals to the intelligent copier where the required number of copies are printed. To be considered intelligent, a copier needs to have, at a minimum, a significant amount of memory. The intelligent copier uses microprocessor technology that allows it to accept input from one or more machines and to provide hard copy output. The capability to input electronic signals from other equipment and to format output in various layouts makes these copiers true information distributors.

In addition to the printing capabilities, the intelligent copier can operate as an electronic mail device. A letter prepared on a word processor can be stored in the copier. When delivery is de-

Illus. 5-6   An intelligent copier/printer can create images from hard copy or from computer instructions.

*Credit: Courtesy Xerox Corporation.*

sired, the letter can be sent via the phone lines to another intelligent copier. At the receiving end, the mail can be distributed on demand via a display monitor or as hard copy.

### COPIER FEATURES

In addition to making copies of correspondence, reports, and other documents, copiers are able to perform numerous other functions. There are basic features that all copiers can handle, and then there is a variety of special features available on other copiers. Both the basic features and several of the special features are presented here.

### Basic Features

Copiers usually handle the two standard sizes of paper—8½ by 11 inches and 8½ by 14 inches. The paper tray, which feeds the paper through the machine, may be adjusted for different paper sizes or there may be separate trays. If there are separate trays, one tray holds the 8½ by 11 inch paper and another tray holds the 8½ by 14 inch paper. The trays snap in and out of the copier for reloading the paper. If there is a single tray, the appropriate paper size for the task being performed must be placed in the tray. Some copiers are fitted with a roll of continuously fed paper that is cut to specific lengths as it is fed through the machine. Since roll-fed machines allow a variety of different size copies to be reproduced, they are especially suitable in applications where odd-size copies are required.

Another basic feature of copiers is the copy counter. Before starting to copy material, the counter is set for the number of copies needed. When the appropriate number of copies has been made, the copier will automatically stop. Also copiers are equipped with an exposure control which controls the lightness or darkness of the copies being produced. For example, if a copy is too light, a button may be pushed instructing the machine to make the copies darker.

Copiers are also equipped with features that indicate the cause of a machine malfunction. For example, if the paper path is jammed, the copier will indicate this problem; if the paper stock is low, the copier will indicate that paper needs to be added. When the toner in the machine needs to be replaced so that clear, dark copies can be produced, the machine will let the operator know that also.

## Special Features

Due to technological advances, many special features are available today on copiers. A number of these special features are explained here.

**Autoduplexing**  Duplexing, copying on both sides of a sheet of paper, is a special feature that is available on numerous copiers. Copies may be made on both sides of the paper by merely pushing the proper buttons; there is no need for the operator to intervene.

**Reduction and Enlargement**  Reduction and enlargement of material being copied is possible through the use of a zoom lens. Users can select from a range of reduction or enlargement modes. For example, an original might be reduced (made smaller) to 60 or 80 percent of its size. This feature is helpful when material is copied from a computer printout. Most computer paper is larger than the standard 8½ by 11 inch paper. With the reduction feature, the printout may be reduced to the standard size paper that can be placed conveniently in reports, along with other information that is being produced.

The enlargement feature on a copier allows for material to be copied larger than the original material. For example, if there are details on the original that need to be larger for ease of reading and clarity, the enlargement feature can accomplish this.

**Illus. 5-7**  Reduction and enlargement of material being copied is possible through the use of a zoom lens.

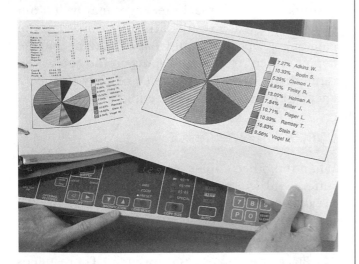

**Color Reproduction**  Some copiers offer more than one color in the machine at any given time, allowing the operator to change colors simply by pressing a button. For example, copies can be made in black, blue, green, red, or brown ink, which can match letterhead paper or be used for various other purposes. There are also copiers that allow for spot, accent, or highlight color on documents. With such a feature, the operator has the ability to add one color to a black and white copy.

**Digital Editing**  Copiers that have an editing function scan the image and convert it to digital signals. Then, using control keys or a wand, the operator can mask, move, and manipulate the copy to alter the image. For example, a paragraph in a letter may be moved to another location, a line or a word in the letter may be deleted, or a heading may be centered on the page.

**Automatic Document Feed**  This device holds a stack of originals and feeds them automatically into the copier. Such a device eliminates the need to raise the copier cover and position each original. Once the copy is made, the original feeds out into a tray of the machine.

**Diagnostics**  Some copiers are equipped with microprocessors that monitor and identify copy status and problems and display the findings on a readout panel. Some machines can automatically call a remote service center via a modem (electronic device that converts computer signals into telephone signals) and relay the problem. Also, some problems can be repaired remotely through the modem; other problems can be corrected by the service center dispatching a local serviceperson.

**Collate and Staple**  Some copiers automatically sort copies to bind, while others collate internally and produce the collated copies in staggered sets. Some copiers can also staple collated sets of material.

**Interrupt Key**  This key is a device that permits the operator to stop the copier at any point in the copying process. This key is useful in emergency situations when the operator wishes to discontinue the copy cycle.

**Repeat Key**  This key resets the number of copies after the first set has been run.

**Form Feeder**  This device automatically feeds unburst 11 by 15 inch computer forms over the platen of the copier.

**Sheet Bypass**  This device allows the operator to hand feed a single sheet of paper without using the paper tray.

**Help Button** This user-friendly feature allows the inexperienced operator to get help. The help button will flash instructions step-by-step, so that an operator can produce copies correctly.

**Transparency Reproduction** A number of copiers can produce transparencies that are used in presenting material on an overhead projector.

**Job Recovery** Sometimes it is necessary for you to interrupt the copying of a large project in order to make a few copies of another document. The job recovery mode stops the copier and remembers how many copies have been made. When you are ready to finish the project, the machine will automatically pick up where it left off and make the required number of copies.

**Automatic Folding** Some copiers will fold 11 by 17 inch copies to an 8½ by 11 inch size. With this feature, drawings and schematics can be kept in a legible size and convenient format for handling and distribution. The fold can also be offset (not folded to the edge of the paper) so that folded materials can be placed in three-ring binders.

## COPYING PROCESSES

Several processes may be used in copying materials. The main processes are given here.

### Xerography

**Xerography** was introduced in 1960 when Xerox introduced the 913 copier. This process is also called the **electrostatic process.** It is based on the principle that unlike electrical charges attract each other and like charges repel each other. It is also based on the principle that electrostatic coatings, such as selenium, have the unique property of holding an electrostatic charge in the dark and losing the charge when exposed to light, such as that reflected from the white areas of an original. This method exposes a positively charged drum or cylinder surface within the copier to light reflected through lenses and mirrors from the original document. When light from the white areas of the original strikes the drum, the positive charge disappears. A negatively charged black powder or liquid called a **toner** adheres to the portion of the drum surface still charged. A sheet of plain paper that has been given a positive electrostatic charge is passed over the drum, and a copy is produced.

### Lasography

The term **lasography** was coined to describe the role of laser technology in the copying process. Lasers are high energy, concentrated light sources that are used for scanning and recording images at high speed. Because the laser can be controlled by electronic impulses, it can be operated by digital signals from a computer, thus enabling satellite and facsimile transmission of plate images to remote printing locations.

### Fiber Optics

**Fiber optic** copiers have few moving parts and are small and lightweight. Rather than using mirrors and lenses to transfer electrical charges of an image to a drum, optic fibers transmit light from the original to the drum. Optic fibers are made up of rows of tiny glass fibers encased in a thin resin wafer. Each fiber functions as a miniature lens, focusing its tiny segment of the total image on the drum. Fiber optics has been used mainly in the low-volume copiers.

## QUALITY OF COPIES

How often have you seen a poorly copied document? Your answer is probably, "frequently." A number of errors may be made in copying. The original may not be inserted straight, resulting in copies which are not positioned well on the page. The copy may be so light that it is difficult to read, resulting from the need to put in toner or some malfunction of the machine. Pages may be left out of a document as a result of the office assistant not collating properly. Liquid paper may be on the copier screen, resulting in spots on the copies. To remind you of the importance of copy quality, a checklist for your use is presented in Figure 5-1.

## COPIER MAINTENANCE

When the office copier is inoperable, productivity suffers and frustrations increase. Many times the breakdown could have been avoided if proper maintenance had occurred. Here are some suggestions to help minimize copier breakdowns.

1.  Place the copier appropriately. There needs to be adequate space around the copier for storing supplies, toner (ink, in powder or liquid form, used to develop the image on the

**Figure 5-1**   Copier Quality Checklist

---

#### Quality Checklist

1. Keep paper clips and staples away from the copier in order to prevent any copier malfunction.

2. Check the screen to see that it is clean; be certain there is no liquid paper or other spots on the screen.

3. Know exactly how many copies you need to make.

4. Ask these questions about the copies:
   - Is the copy free of spots?
   - Is the copy easy to read? Is the ink dark and clear?
   - Is the copy straight on the page?
   - If the original was in pencil, can the copy be read?
   - If color has been used, did the color reproduce well?
   - Have all pages of the document been copied?
   - Have the pages been collated correctly?

5. Did you leave the copy room straight and orderly?

---

paper), and other essentials. Supplies should never be stacked on top of the copier; paper clips and staples falling into the machine can cause major repair bills. The copier should be in a room that has good ventilation and temperature control.

2. Read the instructions concerning the use of the copier. The vendor will have information about how the copier works and limited directions are usually printed on the machine itself. Don't a punch button if you do not understand what the button does. If you don't understand after reading the instructions, seek assistance. Many offices designate a key operator. This person is responsible for simple repairs, assisting fellow workers, ordering supplies, and calling for repair persons.

3. Be conscious of consistent problems. If one problem keeps recurring, inform the key operator, if there is one in your company. If not, call the repair person and inform him or her of the consistent problem. Such information will usually help in repairing the copier.

4. Heed the messages given by the copier. When the control panel indicates that toner should be added, do so or notify the key operator that toner is needed.

5. Use the proper paper. Do not try to force the machine to accept paper for which it was not designed. Do not attempt to run paper through the copier that has been folded or that has rough edges since paper jams may result. Before placing paper in the machine, fan the stack. The paper will feed through the copier easier if you do so.

6. Be careful. Do not attempt to make repairs or retrieve a jammed sheet unless you know the proper procedures. If you are making minor repairs, take off any dangling or large jewelry that might get caught in the machine. Also, be certain that the copier is not too hot before attempting minor repairs.

## ABUSES OF COPYING

Although for many years we have had the technology to reduce the amount of paper in the office, the reverse has been true. The amount of paper has increased, and the ease of copying material has contributed to that increase. It has been estimated, by the copier industry, that as many as 20 to 25 percent of all copies made are unnecessary. For example, an employee may make ten copies of a document when he or she knows that only eight are actually needed. The additional copies are made "just in case" they are needed, and most of the time the employee winds up throwing the extra copies away.

To help in ensuring accountability and to get the copies charged to the appropriate department, many companies use computer-driven copier control units. The first copy controller was the Keycounter introduced in 1966. Today many types of controllers are available, including keypad-entry models, credit and debit card units, and microprocessor-controlled systems that interface with computers. Controllers can count copies made, restrict access, and provide reports on copy costs. They can also identify who is making copies and calculate the cost per copy.

With copy controllers data is fed directly into a computer, accessed by using a printer, or read from the system's display. Keypad systems are the most widely used. To make a copy, the user enters an account number on a keypad and access is granted or denied. Another option is a magnetically coded card. Here is how the card might work. The office assistant may be issued the card by business office personnel. The card is good for a set number of copies, for example, 500 copies. When the card is inserted into the machine, accounts can be automatically tallied, sorted, and charged back to the appropriate division or department. A supervisor can enter the system and examine and delete accounts as needed. When the 500 copies have been run, the office assistant is issued another card. Some companies allow employees to buy cards and use the copier for personal copying of a limited nature.

Each employee in a company should be extremely ethical in the use of the copying machine. Being ethical in such a situation means that you should not copy documents for your own personal use, you should be consistently prudent in making the appropriate number of copies, and you do not copy restricted materials, such as copyrighted materials or materials that you are prohibited from copying due to certain rules.

## THE COPYRIGHT LAW

The modern concept of copyright had its statutory beginnings in the British copyright law of 1710, known as the Statute of Anne, which for the first time recognized the author's right of protection. In the United States the first federal copyright act, which covered books, maps, and charts, was passed in 1790. Throughout the nineteenth century, U.S. copyright law was expanded to protect prints, music, photographs, paintings, and drawings. Because of the heavy use of copying machines, the notice of *fair use* was incorporated into law in the 1970s. The fair use clause allows material to be copied where the intended use is private, educational, or journalistic, and where the amount to be copied is limited. Libraries have been given certain larger copying rights, although these are also carefully spelled out. An excerpt from the law on fair use is given in Figure 5-2.

Some additional highlights of the law which you need to be familiar with include:

1. Securities of the United States (money, postage stamps, bonds) may not be reproduced.
2. Birth certificates, passports, draft cards, naturalization and immigration papers may not be reproduced.

**Figure 5-2** Excerpt from Law on Fair Use

### The Federal Copyright Law
### P.L. 94-553

106. The fair use of a copyrighted work including such use by reproduction in copies of phone records or by any other means specified by that section, for purposes such as criticism, comment, news reporting, teaching (including multiple copies for classroom use), scholarship, or research is not an infringement of copyright. In determining whether the use made of a work in any particular case is a fair use, the factors to be considered shall include:

(1) The purpose and character of the use, including whether such use is of a commercial nature or is for nonprofit educational purposes;

(2) The nature of the copyrighted work,

(3) The amount and substantiality of the portion used in relation to the copyrighted work as a whole, and

(4) The effect of the use upon the potential market for or value of the copyrighted work.

3. Driver's licenses, automobile registrations, and certificates of title may not be reproduced.
4. Documents that contain the personal information of an individual are protected by the Right of Privacy Act. They may not be reproduced without the individual's permission.
5. Material that retains a copyright cannot be reproduced without the owner's permission, although the fair use provision of the law cited earlier allows some exception to this provision.

Further technological advances have impacted the copyright process even more. For example, software packages present a problem concerning copying. Almost all software is copyrighted and contains statements to the effect that under the copyright laws neither the documentation nor the software may be copied, photocopied, reproduced, translated, or reduced to any electronic medium or machine-readable form without prior written consent from the company.

As you use copying machines in the office, you need to be aware of the copyright law. Many companies have legal counsel who may advise you if you have questions concerning the legality of making copies.

## COPIER SELECTION

Since a copier is used so extensively, it is important that consideration be given to the type of copier that will best serve the needs of the business. Here are some questions to ask before selecting a copier.

1. How many copies will be made per month on the machine?
2. What features do you need in a copier? Is reduction and enlargement essential? editing? duplexing? collating?
3. Will color copying be needed? If so, you need to ask these additional questions:
   a. Can color be reproduced with a high degree of accuracy?
   b. What is the cost per copy? Since color copiers are more expensive than black and white copiers, you need to be certain that the expense can be justified.
   c. Is the service good?
4. Ask for a demonstration of the copier. Ask these questions of yourself or the vendor as the machine is being demonstrated:
   a. Are the copies clean and crisp?
   b. Is there a clear definition between black and white areas?
   c. Are the grays in photos clear?
   d. Is the machine easy to operate?
   e. Is the interior easily accessible for removing jammed paper and replacing toner?
5. Ask these questions about the vendor:
   a. Is the vendor an authorized representative for the brand?
   b. Does the vendor have an established reputation?
   c. Does the vendor carry parts for the brand?
   d. Does the vendor provide quick, reliable service?
   e. What is the cost of service? Is a service contract available? If so, how much does it cost?
6. What is the purchase price of the machine?
7. What is the cost per copy?
8. What is the cost of supplies, especially toner?

## FACSIMILE MACHINES

A **facsimile** machine (fax) is a type of copier that electronically sends an original document from one location to another via communication networks. With a fax you may communicate with other persons within the same building, in the same city, across the nation, or across the world. The fax has become a standard piece of office equipment, and sales of these machines have been increasing each year. The fax process combines copying technology and telephone or satellite communications. There are two basic steps in the fax transmission:

1. The original document is placed on a facsimile machine. Then, the document is converted into electronic signals that are transmitted over communication networks to a receiving fax machine.
2. The receiving unit converts the electronic message to its original form and prints a copy of the received document.

There are two types of fax machines—analog and digital. The oldest type is the analog machine. This type is also the slowest, with a typical low-speed machine taking approximately two minutes to transmit each page. Digital machines are much faster, taking an average of 20 seconds to transmit

**Illus. 5-8** A facsimile machine is a type of copier that electronically sends an original document from one location to another via communication networks.

*Credit: Courtesy Xerox Corporation.*

a page. With a digital system messages are converted into binary electronic signals as in computers. These systems use special communication networks rather than the ordinary telephone lines that are used in analog systems. There are any number of features available on a fax; the following are several of these features.

## Fax Features

There are a number of special features that are available on fax machines. Several of these features, along with a short explanation of each feature, are presented here.

**Faxboards** Fax functions can be added to microcomputers, minicomputers, or mainframes through the use of computer boards or boxes. These units do not need a dedicated telephone line (a line devoted to the fax machine alone) and are compatible with most message switching systems. They allow an office with a computer to communicate directly with a facsimile machine and vice versa. A graphic showing how a system might work for the mini/mainframe computer and the microcomputer is shown in Figure 5-3.

Faxboard benefits include enhanced time and money savings over regular facsimile machines since information is communicated directly from the computer. Another benefit is increased broadcasting capabilities since users have access to computer memory, which allows more information to be stored and transmitted.

**Integration of Computer Printer and Fax Machine** Through special devices that connect to your printer, plain-paper faxes can be received directly on the laser printer. A delay feature on the device lets you specify the time of transmission.

**Autodialers** Special equipment (called autodialers) will automatically redial a busy number after a minute or two and store from 20 to 100 numbers into memory for one-button code dialing. Some devices can dial preset numbers when line charges are the lowest, so you can transmit information at the cheapest rate. This feature is called "delayed send" and is available on the more expensive fax models.

**Color Fax** Color fax makes it possible to scan any high resolution color image and transmit it anywhere in the world in a few minutes via standard telephone lines. Images can be edited and output to a full-color printer, color display monitor, or other output device. A color system will

**Figure 5-3** Fax from Minicomputer/Mainframe or Microcomputer

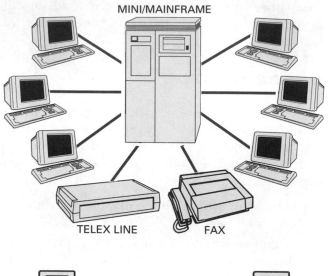

MINI/MAINFRAME

TELEX LINE    FAX

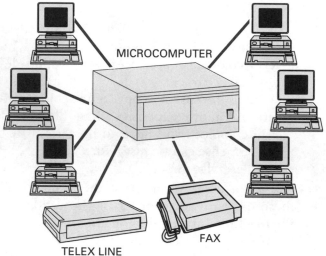

MICROCOMPUTER

TELEX LINE    FAX

transmit and receive color photographs, color slides, video images, color documents, and transparencies.

The printing system on a color fax performs much like a laser printer in that it loads the entire page into memory before printing. A color fax system can also be used as a color copier, as a color scanner, and as a color printer peripheral for a computer. Notice Figure 5-4 which illustrates the components of a color fax.

**Identifiers** Most fax machines will transmit an identifying header with each page showing the date and time of transmittal. Figure 5-5 on page 108 shows a fax transmittal with an identifying header. If the fax has a journal feature, it is possible to print out periodic or on-demand logs of the date, time, total number of pages, and source or destination for all documents handled.

**Figure 5-4** Fax Can Produce Color

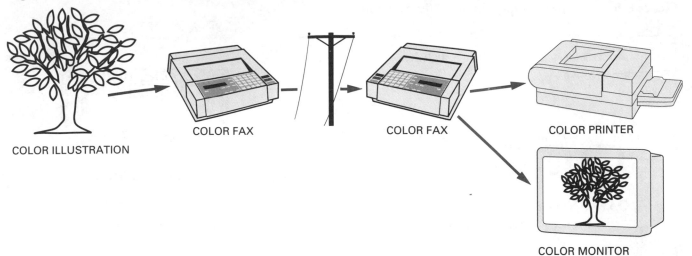

COLOR ILLUSTRATION     COLOR FAX     COLOR FAX     COLOR PRINTER

COLOR MONITOR

**Printing Process** The standard fax printer uses a *thermal* (heat) process, which is silent and inexpensive, yielding a soft-look image which can smear and fade with age. The paper is waxy and hard to write on. However, many machines now print on plain paper (as copiers do) in a thermal-transfer process.

**Portable Fax** A portable fax (a telephone handset and a small fax machine) will fit in a briefcase. These machines are available for slightly over $1,000; most come with autodialers and thermal-transfer printers.

If the executive is traveling and does not have a portable fax machine, the U.S. Postal Service is now putting fax machines in post office lobbies across the country. Some hotels have credit-card-operated fax machines in their lobbies, and many office supply stores offer sending and receiving fax services.

**Confidential Fax** Devices are available that will electronically store incoming faxes until addressees want to retrieve them. These devices come with confidential mailboxes and memory that will allow several pages of storage. Some vendors offer fax mailboxes which allow you to forward the contents from the vendor fax mailbox into your own fax machine at your office or home.

**Elimination of Junk Fax** Businesses have had problems with junk mail clogging up the fax machines. In fact, some states have passed laws that restrict the flow of unsolicited information over telephone lines. With a special device attached to your fax you can eliminate the receipt of junk faxes. The device requires that the sender know your security code as well as your fax number. If the sender does not know the security code, the machine blocks the message. Another way of controlling junk fax is to purchase a fax machine that only allows communication with user-selected numbers stored in the machine's memory.

**Publications by Fax** Some newspapers, magazines, and newsletters are now offering fax editions to subscribers. Such services allow you to receive the information immediately; U.S. mail service delivery or carrier delivery of newspapers is no longer necessary.

### Fax Networks

If a business is using multiple machines, a fax network can be created. However, an efficient network requires an understanding of the applications. A company needs to understand how the fax machines are going to be used and how much they will be used. With this understanding there are benefits to be gained by moving the information as quickly as possible.

By using a hub machine for relay broadcasting and reception from remote machines, businesses can achieve significant savings. For example, a company headquartered in Texas with a number of offices in California can transmit a document to a hub machine in Arizona where it can be relayed to the California offices, thus saving long-distance charges. Networks can also exist within the confines of one location of an organization. For example, a hospital may move information from the laboratories to the physicians and to various other individuals within the hospital who will use the information. They would have fax machines rather than communicating via telephone

## LETTER PLAN

Now that you understand effective letter writing principles, consider the planning of a letter. In anything you set out to do, it is a good idea to have a plan in mind. This advice certainly holds true when writing a business letter. You save yourself and the reader a considerable amount of time and effort by carefully planning what you want to say.

### Consider Your Audience

Who will receive your letter? How much does the person receiving your letter know about the subject? Is the reader familiar with technical jargon that might be used? What is the educational level of the reader? All of these questions are important ones to ask yourself as you begin to compose a letter.

Assume that you work in the computer department in your company and you are writing a letter to a vendor requesting information about computer software. Since you are writing a vendor, you can assume that the individual knows much about the subject. Be specific about the information you are requesting. Ask the technical questions that need to be asked. In such a situation it would be appropriate to use computer jargon. For example, you might ask the vendor for the latest in *dBase*[1] software. Now, assume that you are working with someone in your organization who is not in the computer department and who has little knowledge of software. You would not use *dBase* to describe a software package; you would talk in terms of what the software package is capable of doing, explaining any technical terms that you might use.

### Gather Your Facts

Before you begin to write a letter, gather all the necessary facts. Ask yourself the "W" questions: what? why? when? where? and who? Once you have answered these questions, you will have the information needed to accomplish your letter writing purpose. Consider another situation described below.

The office workers at TriCounty Regional Planning Agency need help in writing effective letters. Your employer, George Andrews, asks you to find a good film on the subject and to order it for

---

[1] *dBase* is a registered trademark of Ashton-Tate.

viewing by the office staff. What do you need to know before you can accomplish your purpose?

1. What is the purpose of the film?
2. Who should see the film?
3. When should the film be shown?
4. What is Mr. Andrews willing to pay for rental of the film?
5. From what companies can letter writing films be obtained?

### Determine What You Want to Say

Once you have gathered your facts, determine what you want to say. At this point do not be concerned with how you are going to say it or the order in which you will say it. Merely jot down the points that you want to make.

For example, here are some questions you may want to ask when ordering the film:

1. Is the film available for rental?
2. What is the rental price?
3. When is the film available?
4. Are other films available on the subject?

### Decide on the Order of Presentation

The third step in writing a letter is to determine the order of the presentation. There are two basic approaches in developing a letter—the deductive approach and the inductive approach. The **deductive approach** goes from the general to the specific. For example, if you use the deductive approach in writing the letter about the film, you let the reader know that you are interested in all the films available on business letter writing. Thus, you ask for a listing of all the films that are available. You then identify your particular interest in a film and give the specific information for ordering this film. Conversely, the **inductive approach** goes from the specific to the general. In using this approach you give specific information on the film at the beginning of the letter and then ask for general information on all films.

The situation usually dictates whether the inductive or deductive approach is best. In a sales letter, for example, it is usually best to use the deductive approach. Your goal is to get the reader in a favorable frame of mind before trying to sell a specific product. You, therefore, begin with general statements that attempt to stimulate interest. Furthermore, letters in which the main message is bad news should usually be written deductively.

Negative messages are received better when an explanation precedes them. Thus, you begin the letter with a general explanation of why something is not possible and go on to the specifics of the situation.

Figure 6-1 is an example of the deductive approach when the answer is no. When the message is a positive one the inductive approach is usually used. You begin with the specific—stating the positive. You may then go to the general at the end of the letter. Figure 6-2 is an example of the inductive approach.

## Make an Outline

You may be asking yourself, "Why should I prepare an outline? If I have all the facts, if I know what I want to say, and if I know the order in which I want to say it, then why can't I just say it?" After writing several letters you will be able to skip the outline stage. However, for the beginning writer it is a good idea to put your thoughts in outline form. It may seem time-consuming, but it actually saves time and money. Making an outline forces you to get your thoughts on paper; and, in the process, you may discover that you do not have all the facts you need. An outline also helps you to see the relationship between topics and to determine whether your letter is in logical order. It is much easier to change an outline than it is to change a finished product.

## Develop an Effective Beginning

Now that you have completed the preceding steps you are ready to write the letter. The first paragraph is the most important paragraph of any letter. It should get the reader's attention and prepare the reader for what follows. This paragraph sets the tone for the entire letter. The effective opening emphasizes the reader's interest; it

**Figure 6-1** Using the Deductive Approach When Saying "no"

TriCounty Regional
Planning Agency

3232 Six Flags Drive
Arlington, TX 76025-5888
(817) 245-6800

September 20, 19--

Mr. Robert J. Mercer
Concerned Citizens Association
973 Market Avenue
Duncanville, TX 75116-1846

Dear Mr. Mercer

Your suggestion to build a fund for the purchase of a new fire truck for Duncanville's fire station is commendable. I hope you are able to meet your goal.

Every year TriCounty contributes several thousand dollars to worthy causes. Your proposal is certainly worthwhile; however, we have already expended this year's budget on such causes. If you are still in need of our help next year, let us know. We will be happy to consider your project.

Good luck in your efforts. Our town needs more civic-minded groups such as yours.

Sincerely

George Andrews

George Andrews
Executive Director

aa

uses the "you" approach. Here is a good example of how you might start the letter to order the film:

> Is your film "Writing Effective Business Letters" available on a rental basis? Our office workers need some help in letter writing, and your film sounds as if it would be a good aid for us.

Can you see the difference in the above beginning paragraph and the following one?

> I saw your film "Writing Effective Business Letters" advertised in a company brochure. If it is available, my company would like to rent this film to show to our office workers.

**Figure 6-2** The Inductive Approach for a Positive Message

**TriCounty Regional Planning Agency**

3232 Six Flags Drive
Arlington, TX 76025-5888
(817) 245-6800

August 15, 19--

Mr. Harold Edwards
Mercer National Bank
301 Main Street
Dallas, TX 75202

Dear Mr. Edwards:

Yes, I will be delighted to speak to your office assistants on February 21 at 10 a.m. concerning "Listening--How Do We Do It More Effectively?" I am pleased that you thought of me, and I am looking forward to the session.

There are some things I need to know about the audience. First, how may people do you expect to be in attendance? What is the background of these people? Have you had any sessions on listening in the past? If so, what has been the topic of these sessions and how were they received by the audience?

Please let me hear from you within a week so that I may begin preparing my remarks.

Sincerely,

*Patricia Martin*

Patricia Martin
Office Assistant

*Inappropriate Ending:* I regret that we cannot comply.
*Appropriate Ending:* May we serve you in another way?

*Inappropriate Ending:* I trust you will give this matter your attention.
*Appropriate Ending:* Please act soon on this matter.

*Inappropriate Ending:* I hope you will mail your order today.
*Appropriate Ending:* Mail your order today to get a quick response.

*Inappropriate Ending:* Thank you in advance for responding to this request.
*Appropriate Ending:* Your immediate response will insure that the order reaches you within a week.

Here is an appropriate ending to the letter requesting information about film rental:

Since we are eager to help our employees write more effective letters, could you let us know immediately if this film is available?

The first example sets the tone from the reader's point of view; the second example addresses only the writer's needs.

## Develop an Effective Ending

The closing of the letter is also important because it sets the tone for action. It should reinforce goodwill and inspire the reader to do what you are requesting. Never end a letter by expressing doubt, demanding compliance with your request, or thanking the reader in advance. Thanking the reader in advance is trite and implies that you are sure the reader will do what you ask. Note the differences between the following types of endings.

## TYPES OF LETTERS WRITTEN BY AN OFFICE ASSISTANT

As an office worker, you will most likely write letters to request information, order materials, respond to requests for information and materials, and communicate goodwill. If you compose these letters effectively you will be an asset to your company.

## Composing Routine Letters

Use the same approach in writing routine letters that you would use in any letter; that is, gather your facts, determine what you need to say, decide on the order of presentation, and develop an effective beginning and ending. Also keep in mind the characteristics of a good letter—completeness, conciseness, courteousness, accuracy, positivism, and the "you" approach.

**Writing Order Letters**   A routine letter that you may frequently write is the order letter. Order letters are generally written when printed purchase orders are unavailable. The order letter is a direct letter and, as such, should state clearly, concisely, and accurately what materials or products are being ordered. Before you attempt to write this letter, know exactly what materials you want, what quantity you want, and the necessary specifications. If you fail to give accurate specifications you may receive materials which you had no intention of ordering. Following is a checklist of information that should be included in the order letter:

1. *Quantity.* Give the number of units, pounds, yards, reams, and so forth.
2. *Description of materials.* Give the catalog number (if available), size, color, material, weight, finish, quality, and style.
3. *Price.* List the price per unit and the total price for the items.
4. *Method of payment.* Charge to an established account or include a check.
5. *Shipment.* If you have a preference as to how the items should be shipped, state that preference.

The order of your letter presentation should be as follows:

1. Direct statement of need
2. Tabulation of items
3. Shipping and payment methods
4. Date materials are requested

Figure 6-3 presents a sample order letter.

**Writing Inquiry Letters**   Another routine letter that you may write frequently is the letter of inquiry. Such letters ask for information about prices, products, services, and people.

When writing inquiry letters, you should include the following:

1. Begin with your objective. The direct approach is convenient for the reader because it lets the reader know immediately what your concerns are and it saves misunderstandings. You may wish to begin this letter with a question. Such an approach can be advantageous, since questions stand out and immediately call attention to your purpose.

2. Give all the necessary facts concerning your inquiry. If you do not explain in enough detail, or if you assume the reader has some knowledge that he or she does not actually have, you make it difficult for the reader to respond to your inquiry.
3. End with goodwill. Just as you would end a face-to-face inquiry with an expression of goodwill, so should you end a letter. Use specific words selected for the situation rather than a general statement of goodwill. For example, "If you can get the conference information to me by Friday, I shall be delighted" is much better than "Thank you for your prompt attention to this matter."

Figure 6-4 is an example of a letter of inquiry.

## Answering Routine Letters

Not only will you write order letters and inquiry letters, but you will also answer these letters. If your answer is positive, use the direct approach. Such an approach gives the reader what he or she wants at the beginning of the letter. However, if your answer is negative, use an indirect approach. Bad news is better received if an explanation precedes it. The indirect approach, therefore, allows you to give the information first, and it cushions the disappointment for the reader.

**Saying "Yes"**   To write a routine letter when the answer is positive, follow these steps:

1. Respond to the request.
2. Explain any necessary details.
3. End with a statement of goodwill.

Since yes is an extremely positive word, you may wish to start with it. For example, you might say:

```
Yes, the management conference sounds
like a challenging one.  I will be happy
to speak on the topic of "Listening."
```

In the next paragraph of a routine letter of response you should give any additional information needed. Here is an example:

```
My flight is American Airlines 345, ar-
riving at 2 p.m. Thursday, October 22, at
JFK.  Will someone meet me at the airport?
Also, do you want me to make my own res-
ervation at the hotel or will you make it
for me?  My flight back to Dallas leaves
at 6 p.m. on Friday, October 13. Therefore,
I will need to be at the airport by 5 p.m.
```

**Figure 6-4** Letter of Inquiry

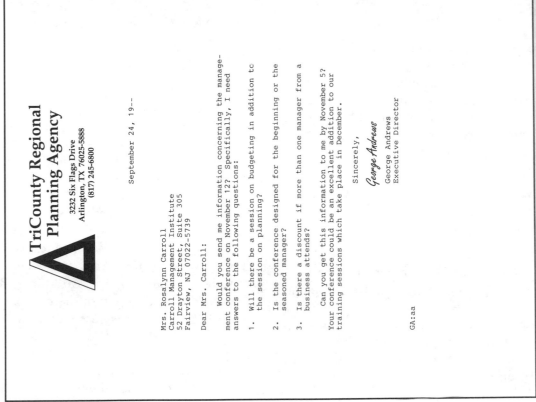

**TriCounty Regional Planning Agency**

3232 Six Flags Drive
Arlington, TX 76025-5888
(817) 245-6800

September 24, 19--

Mrs. Rosalynn Carroll
Carroll Management Institute
52 Drayton Street, Suite 305
Fairview, NJ 07022-5739

Dear Mrs. Carroll:

Would you send me information concerning the management conference on November 12? Specifically, I need
answers to the following questions:

1. Will there be a session on budgeting in addition to
the session on planning?

2. Is the conference designed for the beginning or the
seasoned manager?

3. Is there a discount if more than one manager from a
business attends?

Can you get this information to me by November 5?
Your conference could be an excellent addition to our
training sessions which take place in December.

Sincerely,

*George Andrews*

George Andrews
Executive Director

GA:aa

**Figure 6-3** Order Letter

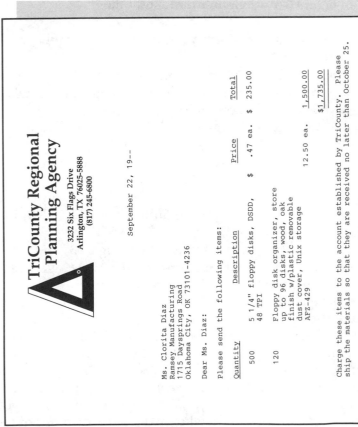

**TriCounty Regional Planning Agency**

3232 Six Flags Drive
Arlington, TX 76025-5888
(817) 245-6800

September 22, 19--

Ms. Clorita Diaz
Ramsey Manufacturing
1715 Daysprings Road
Oklahoma City, OK 73101-4236

Dear Ms. Diaz:

Please send the following items:

| Quantity | Description | Price | Total |
|---|---|---|---|
| 500 | 5 1/4" floppy disks, DSDD, 48 TPI | $ .47 ea. | $ 235.00 |
| 120 | Floppy disk organizer, store up to 96 disks, wood, oak finish w/plastic removable dust cover, Unix storage AFZ-429 | 12.50 ea. | 1,500.00 |
|  |  |  | $1,735.00 |

Charge these items to the account established by TriCounty. Please
ship the materials so that they are received no later than October 25.

Sincerely,

*George Andrews*

George Andrews
Executive Director

rl

Close your letter with a statement of goodwill.

```
Thank you for asking me to speak. I am
looking forward to a chance to talk over
old times with you.
```

**Saying "No"**   In almost every situation in which a negative answer must be given, there is a reason. That reason should be explained before you say no. If the reason is stated sincerely and courteously, most readers will understand. They may not be happy, but they will be able to accept and appreciate your refusal. Here is a good plan to follow in writing a refusal:

1. Begin with a statement that acknowledges the request.
2. Explain why you must refuse.
3. Refuse.
4. Propose an alternative if one is possible.
5. End with a courteous and friendly statement.

In a previous example (Figure 6-2 on page 125), a yes answer was given to a speaking engagement. Now consider the rejection of a similar invitation as presented in Figure 6-5.

### Composing Goodwill Letters

Consider the examples of goodwill letters of appreciation and congratulations presented in Figure 6-6 on the following page and in Figure 6-7 on page 130.

Goodwill letters give a chance to express sincerity and ingenuity. For example, Figure 6-8 on page 130 is certainly not the usual letter written to customers. However, the goodwill letter gives you a chance to be creatively different. As you write goodwill letters let your creativity show, convey a positive viewpoint, and call attention to the reader by using the "you" approach.

### BUSINESS LETTER TRANSCRIPTION

In addition to a letter being well written, it is also important that the letter be arranged attractively on quality stationery. When you open a letter the first impression that you receive is based on the way the letter is placed on the page and the quality of the stationery. Since first impressions often are lasting ones, you must know how to place a letter on the page and how to select the right type of paper. In addition, as an office-support employee, it is your responsibility to address the envelope correctly and properly fold and insert the letter for mailing.

### Selecting the Proper Stationery

The standard size of stationery used for business letters is 8½ inches by 11 inches, and the standard weight of paper is 20- to 24-pound paper. The weight of the paper is determined by the weight of a ream of paper. A ream of paper consists of 500 sheets that are 17 by 22 inches. Two thousand sheets of 8½ by 11 inch paper are cut from one ream. The weight of the paper is printed on the box or package. For example, if the label on the end of the ream reads "Sub 20," that particular ream is 20-pound paper. Other sizes of paper that may be used for business letters are 8½ by 5½ inches, which is referred to as baronial, and executive-size stationery, which is 7¼ by 10½ inches.

The letterhead on business stationery customarily shows the name, address, and telephone number of the company. Additional features may be the logo and slogan of the company. The term letterhead is used because this information is usually placed at the top of the page. However, the information is sometimes placed at the side or even at the bottom of the stationery. Figure 6-9 on page 131 shows several types of letterheads. White is the traditional color of stationery; however, off-white and ivory colors are used frequently. Some companies even select colors such as yellow, light brown, and blue.

### Placing Letters Appropriately

A letter should be well balanced on a page. In order to achieve the appropriate balance, the top, bottom, right, and left margins should resemble a frame around a picture. The right margin should be as even as possible, and all margins should appear to be an equal distance from the edge of the page. There should be as few word divisions at the ends of lines as possible, and there should never be more than two end-of-line word divisions in a row.

Table 6-2 on page 131 indicates the proper side margins for short, average, and long letters, as well as letters that use a standard line length. Your first step is to recognize the length of the letter. You will need some practice in making these estimates from longhand materials, shorthand notes, or from a dictating machine. You are not expected to count each word in a letter. Letter placement should become an intuitive process. However, when you first begin keying letters you will probably need to make a rough count of the words.

**Figure 6-6** Letter of Appreciation

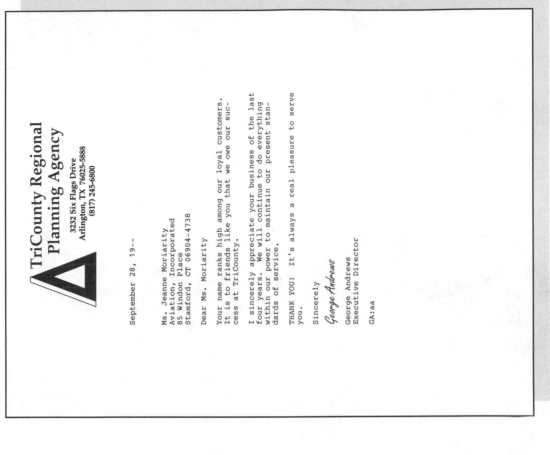

**TriCounty Regional Planning Agency**

3232 Six Flags Drive
Arlington, TX 76025-5888
(817) 245-6800

September 28, 19--

Ms. Jeanne Moriarity
Aviation, Incorporated
85 Windon Place
Stamford, CT 06904-4738

Dear Ms. Moriarity

Your name ranks high among our loyal customers.
It is to friends like you that we owe our success at TriCounty.

I sincerely appreciate your business of the last
four years. We will continue to do everything
within our power to maintain our present standards of service.

THANK YOU! It's always a real pleasure to serve
you.

Sincerely

*George Andrews*

George Andrews
Executive Director

GA:aa

---

**Figure 6-5** Letter of Refusal

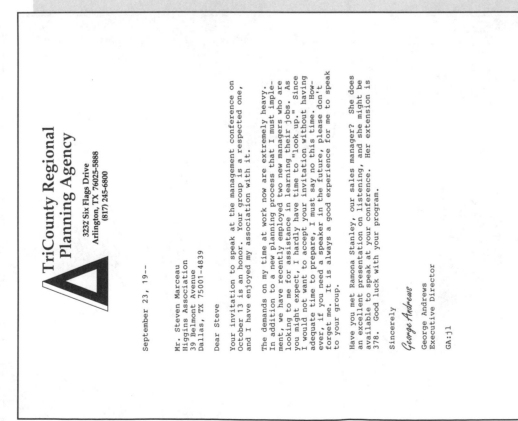

**TriCounty Regional Planning Agency**

3232 Six Flags Drive
Arlington, TX 76025-5888
(817) 245-6800

September 23, 19--

Mr. Steven Marceau
Higgins Association
39 Belmont Avenue
Dallas, TX 75001-4839

Dear Steve

Your invitation to speak at the management conference on
October 13 is an honor. Your group is a respected one,
and I have enjoyed my association with it.

The demands on my time at work now are extremely heavy.
In addition to a new planning process that I must imple-
ment, we have recently employed two new managers who are
looking to me for assistance in learning their jobs. As
you might expect, I hardly have time to "look up." Since
I would not want to accept your invitation without having
adequate time to prepare, I must say no this time. However, if you need a speaker in the future, please don't
forget me. It is always a good experience for me to speak
to your group.

Have you met Ramona Stanley, our sales manager? She does
an excellent presentation on listening, and she might be
available to speak at your conference. Her extension is
378. Good luck with your program.

Sincerely

*George Andrews*

George Andrews
Executive Director

GA:jl

**Figure 6-8** Letter of Goodwill

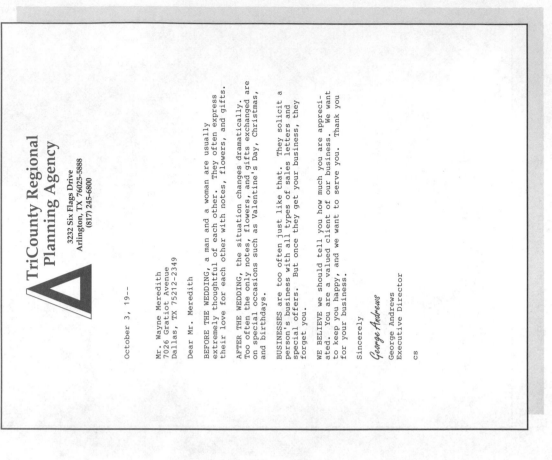

October 3, 19--

Mr. Wayne Meredith
7026 Gratiot Avenue
Dallas, TX 75212-2349

Dear Mr. Meredith

BEFORE THE WEDDING, a man and a woman are usually extremely thoughtful of each other. They often express their love for each other with notes, flowers, and gifts.

AFTER THE WEDDING, the situation changes dramatically. Too often the only notes, flowers, and gifts exchanged are on special occasions such as Valentine's Day, Christmas, and birthdays.

BUSINESSES are too often just like that. They solicit a person's business with all types of sales letters and special offers. But once they get your business, they forget you.

WE BELIEVE we should tell you how much you are appreci- ated. You are a valued client of our business. We want to keep you happy, and we want to serve you. Thank you for your business.

Sincerely

*George Andrews*

George Andrews
Executive Director

cs

---

**Figure 6-7** Letter of Congratulations

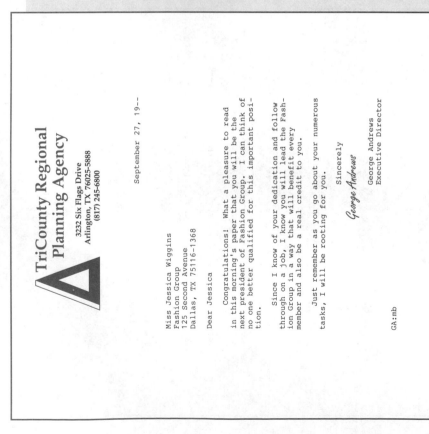

September 27, 19--

Miss Jessica Wiggins
Fashion Group
125 Second Avenue
Dallas, TX 75116-1368

Dear Jessica

Congratulations! What a pleasure to read in this morning's paper that you will be the next president of Fashion Group. I can think of no one better qualified for this important posi- tion.

Since I know of your dedication and follow through on a job, I know you will lead the Fash- ion Group in a way that will benefit every member and also be a real credit to you.

Just remember as you go about your numerous tasks, I will be rooting for you.

Sincerely

*George Andrews*

George Andrews
Executive Director

GA:mb

**Figure 6-9** Types of Letterheads

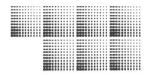

Women in Business
7885 SOUTH MARIPOSA AVENUE
LOS ANGELES, CA 90005 4800

TC Twin Cities Industries, Inc.
525 Marquette Avenue
Minneapolis, Minnesota 55402-1234

AMICOLA beverage, inc.
*For a World of Refreshment*
Wachovia Bank Tower
129 West Trade Street
Charlotte, NC 28202-6311

SALT LAKE
SUPPLY COMPANY
54 West South Temple
Salt Lake City, UT 84101-6531

**Table 6-2** Letter Placement

| LETTER CLASSIFICATION | WORDS IN BODY OF LETTER | SIDE MARGINS |
|---|---|---|
| Short | Up to 100 words | 2" |
| Average | 101-200 words | 1½" |
| Long | 201-300 words | 1" |
| Standard 6½" line* | Varies | 1" |

*In many offices, the same line length is used for all letters regardless of classification.

You learned in Chapter 4 that software packages come with default settings—settings that are built into the program and are automatically used unless the originator specifies other settings. Default margin settings are generally one inch for each side. In Table 6-2, notice that a standard 6½ line letter uses 1-inch left and right margins. Many offices adopt the default settings as the standard margins to be used on all letters; therefore, there is no need to change the default settings. If you need to change the default settings for a very short letter, you may do so by calling up the appropriate menu (for example, the Setup menu) and inserting a 2-inch or even a 1½-inch margin in place of the 1-inch margin.

### Basic Parts of a Letter

Most business letters contain a number of parts. It is important to know what these parts are and to know the correct format for them.

**Dateline** The dateline varies in vertical placement according to the letter length. For example, in a short letter the dateline is placed on line 18 from the top edge of the paper; in an average letter the dateline is placed on line 16; and in a long letter the dateline is placed on line 14. When a window envelope is used, the dateline is placed on line 12. If a standard 6½ inch line is used, the dateline is placed on line 16. (Note that when a deep letterhead prevents use of these dateline positions, the date should be placed a double space below the last line of the letterhead.) The first line of the letter address is placed on the fourth line below the date.

**Letter Address** The letter address provides all the necessary information for mailing the letter. This information includes the recipient's name, title, company name, street number and name, city, two-letter state abbreviation, and ZIP Code. As discussed above, three blank lines are left between the date and the first line of the letter address. The keyboard operator must use judgment in placing the letter on the page so that it appears properly balanced.

**Salutation**   The salutation in a letter serves the same purpose as a greeting. The salutation is typed one double-space below the letter address. It must agree in number with the letter address. Notice in this example that the letter is addressed to an entire company and the salutation is plural in number.

```
Jong Equipment Corporation
134 Magnolia Avenue
Woodland, CA 91364-6784
```

```
Ladies and Gentlemen
```

If you are writing a letter to an individual, the most appropriate salutation to use is the individual's name. For example, if the letter is addressed to Mr. Arnold Borchgrave, the salutation should be:

```
Dear Mr. Borchgrave
```

Other appropriate salutations are as follows.

One person, sex unknown:
```
Dear A. L. Schuster
```

One person, name unknown, title known:
```
Dear Personnel Manager
Dear Purchasing Agent
```

One woman, title preference unknown:
```
Dear Ms. Sabin
```

Two or more women, titles known:
```
Dear Ms. Perez, Mrs. Li, and Miss Stein
```

If all women are married:
```
Dear Mrs. Perez, Mrs. Li, and Mrs. Stein
```
*or*
```
Dear Mesdames Perez, Li, and Stein
```

If all women are unmarried:
```
Dear Miss Perez, Miss Li, and Miss Stein
```
*or*
```
Dear Misses Perez, Li, and Stein
```

If all women use Ms.:
```
Dear Ms. Perez, Li, and Stein
```
*or*
```
Dear Mses. (or Mss.) Perez, Li, and
Stein
```

A woman and a man:
```
Dear Ms. Perez and Mr. Wallace
```

An organization composed entirely of women:
```
Ladies
```
*or*
```
Mesdames
```

An organization composed entirely of men:
```
Gentlemen
```

An organization composed of women and men:
```
Ladies and Gentlemen
```

The person dictating a business letter may specify the salutation to be used, but in many offices a standard salutation is used for all routine letters. However, sometimes you will not be told to use a special salutation when one should be used. It will be expected that you will use the salutation that best reflects the relationship between the parties.

For example, Mr. Eric Strickland may be answering a letter from Mr. Joseph D. Hall. Mr. Hall used the salutation "Dear Eric" in writing to Mr. Strickland and signed his letter "Joe." Even though the standard instructions are to use a salutation such as "Dear Mr. Hall" unless other instructions are given, you should assume that a more personal salutation such as "Dear Joe" should be used in this letter. If Mr. Hall knows Mr. Strickland well enough to address him as "Dear Eric" and to sign his letter "Joe," he certainly would not expect a reply to carry the salutation "Dear Mr. Hall."

**Illus. 6-3**   Use the salutation that best reflects the relationship between the parties.

**Body**   The body of a letter contains the message. It begins a double-space below the salutation or a double-space below the subject line (if the letter contains a subject line). The body is single-spaced, but double-spaced between paragraphs. A very short letter can be double-spaced to create a page that looks balanced. Paragraphs begin block style at the left margin, except in the modified block letter with indented paragraphs (see Figure 6-12 on page 136). In this letter style paragraphs are indented five spaces. In general, an effort should be made to have at least two paragraphs in a letter without the paragraphs being extremely long or short.

**Complimentary Close**   The purpose of the complimentary close is to provide a courteous ending. The most commonly used complimentary closes are "Very truly yours" and "Sincerely." Two others that are frequently used are "Yours very truly" and "Sincerely yours." The complimentary close is keyed at the left margin in the block letter or at the center of the page in the modified block letter. It is placed a double-space below the end of the body with only the first letter of the first word capitalized.

**Signature**   The name and title of the individual writing the letter are keyed four line spaces below the complimentary close. If the name and title are short, they may be placed on the same line and separated by a comma. But if the name and title are relatively long, the name is keyed on the first line (a comma is not used after the name) and the title is placed on the second line. The general rule is to make the lines as even as possible.

**Reference Initials**   Reference initials are placed even with the left margin and a double-space below the title of the writer. The recent trend is to key only the keyboard operator's initials in lowercase letters. However, it is also acceptable to use the originator's initials in all capitals, followed by a colon or a slash, and then followed by the keyboard operator's initials. Notice the examples presented in Figures 6-10 and 6-11.

### Special Parts of a Letter

The parts of a letter discussed in the preceding paragraphs are found in virtually all business letters; however, certain letters have other parts. These special parts of a letter are discussed below.

**Attention Line**   If a letter is addressed to an organization, an attention line may be used to direct the letter to the proper person or department within the organization. The attention line is placed on the second line of the letter address and even with the left margin. The placement of the attention line in the block letter style is shown in Figure 6-10.

The use of an attention line does not change the salutation. For example, if a letter is addressed to a company with an attention line of "Attention Mrs. Chen," the salutation is still "Ladies and Gentlemen," not "Dear Mrs. Chen."

**Subject Line**   The writer of a letter may feel that the letter will be clearer if the subject to be discussed is indicated at the beginning of the letter. In that case, a subject line is used. The subject line is placed a double-space below the salutation. After the subject line there is a double-space before the body of the letter. The subject line is keyed even with the left margin if the block letter style is used. If the modified block letter style is used, the subject line may be centered, may begin at the left margin, or may be indented five spaces (if the paragraphs are indented). The word SUBJECT or abbreviation RE may precede the subject line, but it is not essential to use these words. The subject line can be shown in capitals, in capitals and lowercase, or in capitals and lowercase and underlined. Here are several examples of how the subject line may be keyed:

```
Dear Dr. Kallaus

AMERICAN MEDICAL ASSOCIATION


Dear Dr. Kallaus

SUBJECT:  American Medical Associ-
ation


Dear Dr. Kallaus

RE:  American Medical
     Association
```

**File Number**   In some businesses a file or reference number is inserted at the beginning of a letter to facilitate the filing of correspondence. When such a number is used, it may be inserted a double-space below the date or placed opposite the dateline, ending at the right margin. A file reference number is used in Figure 6-10.

A company using a file reference number in a letter expects the one answering the letter to refer to the file number. This reference can be made in the following ways: A reference to the file number may be made in the first paragraph of the letter, or the file number may be treated as a subject and typed in the usual subject line position.

**Figure 6-11** Modified Block Letter Style, Blocked Paragraphs, Mixed Punctuation

## DRISCOLL & SMITH, Inc. fine furniture
Louisville, KY 40219-8866

September 17, 19--

Mr. George Andrews
TriCounty Regional Planning Agency
3232 Six Flags Drive
Arlington, TX 76005-5888

Dear Mr. Andrews:

Several weeks ago you placed an order with us for five desks to be manufactured according to your specifications. You approved the plan we submitted and asked us to let you know when the desks would be ready for finishing.

The desks are ready for finishing. We were very fortunate in finding some unusual wood that we believe will match very closely the other furniture in your office. It was necessary for us to make some slight changes in the hardware because it was impossible to obtain exactly what you had in mind.

Will you come in within the next week so we can decide on the proper finish for the desks? We can also decide at that time whether you want any special drawer pulls. If you can telephone us and let us know what day you will come, we can be sure that our furniture expert is here at that time.

It is certainly a pleasure to work with you on this order, and we believe you will be satisfied with the finished product.

Sincerely yours,

*A. H. Rice*

A. H. Rice
Sales Manager

AHR:bh

If we do not hear from you soon, we will assume you are no longer interested.

---

**Figure 6-10** Block Letter Style, Open Punctuation

## ATLANTIC PAPER CO.
3500 Appalachian Avenue    Atlanta, GA 30325-3427

October 17, 19--

In reply, refer to
File No. 637-1

TriCounty Regional Planning Agency
Attention Mrs. A. Chen
3232 Six Flags Drive
Arlington, TX 76005-5888

Ladies and Gentlemen

Thank you very much for your recent fine order for corrugated boxes and wrapping paper. The shipment of the corrugated boxes will be sent within ten days.

Usually we are able to make immediate shipment on wrapping paper, but a shortage of certain types of paper pulp has resulted in manufacturing delays. We are quite sure, however, your wrapping paper can be sent within the next month.

If you are in immediate need of wrapping paper, may we suggest that you let us send a limited supply of a lighter grade? We have quite a stock of this paper on hand. If we do not hear from you, however, we shall assume that it will be satisfactory to go ahead with your order for wrapping paper and ship it next month.

Very truly yours

*E. James Pullman*

E. James Pullman
Manager

kr

pc Jane Kelly

**Enclosure Notation** When reference to an enclosure is made in the body of the letter, a notation of the enclosure should be made by keying "Enclosure" or "Enc." a double-space below the reference initials. For example:

```
pjf

Enclosures 2
```

**Copy Notation** When additional copies are made for distribution to various persons, reference to each recipient is commonly made in the copy notation so that the addressee knows to whom copies were sent. The copy notation is keyed a double-space below the enclosure, if used, or below the reference initials if there is no enclosure. When more than one person is to receive a copy, list each person on a succeeding line, indented three spaces from the left margin. The notation may be keyed as follows:

```
pc William C. Mack (pc means photocopy)
```

*or*

```
Copy to William C. Mack
```

**Blind Copy Notation** If the person who receives the original letter does not need to know that a copy is being sent to a particular person, a blind copy notation is used. To make the notation, the original letter is removed from the machine and the notation is keyed on the carbon copy or on the photocopy one inch from the top of the paper at the left margin. An example is shown here:

```
bc Linda K. Turner
```

**Mailing Notation** When mailing notations such as SPECIAL DELIVERY and REGISTERED MAIL are keyed on the letter, they are shown even with the left margin, a double-space below the date, and in all capitals. These notations may be keyed on the original and the file copy or keyed only on the file copy. Other special notations such as CONFIDENTIAL or PERSONAL are also keyed in the same location.

**Postscript** A postscript is used to add a personal note to a letter or to emphasize a point the writer is making. A postscript should not be used for something that is forgotten in the letter. Place a postscript either a double-space below the reference initials or the enclosure notation, whichever is the last line. The initials "P.S." or the word "postscript" need not be used. Notice the example presented in Figure 6-11.

**Second-Page Headings** When keying the second page of a letter, use plain bond paper. Letterhead paper is to be used for the first page only. A heading consisting of the name of the addressee, the page number, and the date is to be single-spaced, an inch (on line 6) from the top of the sheet, and in one of the following forms.

Block form (used when the letter is in block style):

```
Ms. Ellen Sumter
Page 2
September 12, 19--
```

Horizontal form (Used when the letter is in modified block style):

```
Ms. Ellen Sumter    2    September 12, 19--
```

Double-space between the heading and the first line of the body of the letter.

The last paragraph of the letter's preceding page should contain at least two lines, and the first paragraph of the letter's second page should contain at least two lines. A word should not be divided at the end of the first page of the letter.

**Punctuation** The two most common types of punctuation used in business letters are discussed below.

1. *Open punctuation.* No punctuation follows the salutation or the complimentary close.

2. *Mixed punctuation.* A colon is used after the salutation and a comma is used after the complimentary close.

## Use an Acceptable Letter Style

There are four basic letter styles—**block style**, **modified block style** with either blocked paragraphs or indented paragraphs, and the **AMS simplified style**. These styles are presented in Figures 6-10, 6-11, 6-12, and 6-13. In each style notice where the date, letter address, salutation, and closing lines begin.

The block and modified block styles are used more frequently than the AMS simplified style; however, this style is extremely efficient. It was adopted by the Administrative Management Society because of its timesaving features. Notice in Figure 6-13 that the letter has no salutation or complimentary close. Notice also that a subject line is used. This subject line, keyed in all capitals, is three line spaces below the letter address. The body begins three lines spaces below the subject line. The writer's name and title are positioned at least four line spaces below the body and in all capitals. The name and title are keyed on the same line.

**Figure 6-12** Modified Block Letter Style, Indented Paragraphs, Open Punctuation

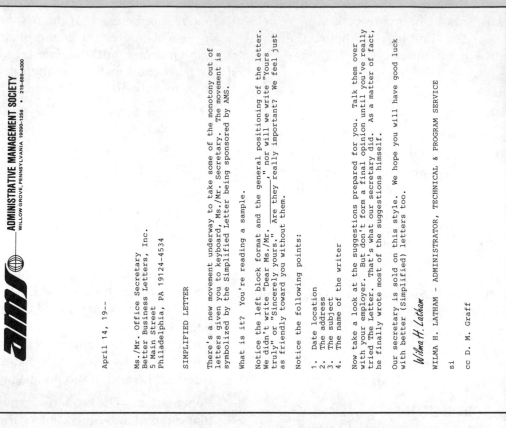

**Figure 6-13** AMS Simplified Letter Style

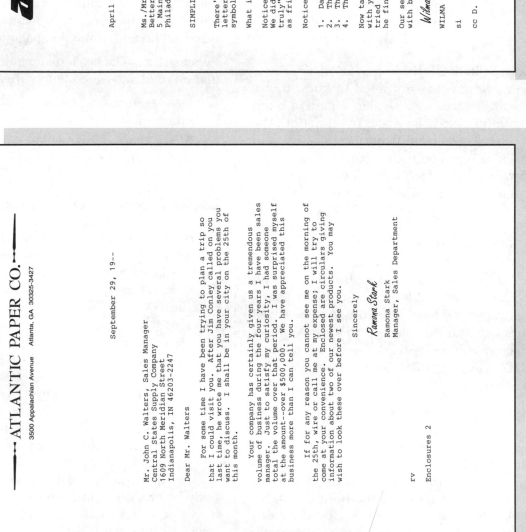

## Preparing Envelopes Correctly

Envelopes match the letterhead stationery in quality, design, and color. The address on the envelope must be correct, legible, and placed in the appropriate location. To speed the delivery of mail, the United States Postal Service has installed Optical Character Recognition (OCR) equipment in many post offices. This scanner electronically reads and sorts envelopes. Certain changes in the addressing of an envelope have occurred as a result of the OCR.

The OCR scanner starts reading from the bottom line and is programmed to read the city, state, and ZIP Code first. Therefore, any extra lines that fall below the last line of the address prevent the OCR from locating the address. Such notations as the attention line, please forward line, and a confidential notation cannot be placed in the lower left corner of the envelope. The attention line should be keyed as the second line of the letter address. The please forward and confidential notations should be typed three line spaces below the return address and even with that address. Notice the examples presented in Figure 6-14.

**Figure 6-14**

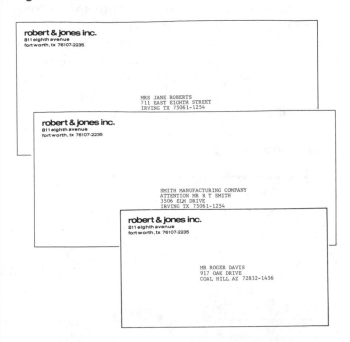

**Abbreviations**   Two-letter state abbreviations are recommended by the United States Post Office. These recommended abbreviations are presented in Table 6-3.

**Table 6-3**   Recommended Postal Abbreviations

| NAME | STANDARD ABBREVIATION | TWO-LETTER ABBREVIATION | NAME | STANDARD ABBREVIATION | TWO-LETTER ABBREVIATION |
|------|------------------------|--------------------------|------|------------------------|--------------------------|
| Alabama | Ala. | AL | Montana | Mont. | MT |
| Alaska | Alaska | AK | Nebraska | Nebr. | NE |
| Arizona | Ariz. | AZ | Nevada | Nev. | NV |
| Arkansas | Ark. | AR | New Hampshire | N.H. | NH |
| California | Calif. | CA | New Jersey | N.J. | NJ |
| Colorado | Colo. | CO | New Mexico | N. Mex. | NM |
| Connecticut | Conn. | CT | New York | N.Y. | NY |
| Delaware | Del. | DE | North Carolina | N.C. | NC |
| Dist. of Columbia | D.C. | DC | North Dakota | N. Dak. | ND |
| Florida | Fla. | FL | Ohio | Ohio | OH |
| Georgia | Ga. | GA | Oklahoma | Okla. | OK |
| Hawaii | Hawaii | HI | Oregon | Oreg. | OR |
| Idaho | Idaho | ID | Pennsylvania | Pa. | PA |
| Illinois | Ill. | IL | Rhode Island | R.I. | RI |
| Indiana | Ind. | IN | South Carolina | S.C. | SC |
| Iowa | Iowa | IA | South Dakota | S. Dak. | SD |
| Kansas | Kans. | KS | Tennessee | Tenn. | TN |
| Kentucky | Ky. | KY | Texas | Tex. | TX |
| Louisiana | La. | LA | Utah | Utah | UT |
| Maine | Maine | ME | Vermont | Vt. | VT |
| Maryland | Md. | MD | Virginia | Va. | VA |
| Massachusetts | Mass. | MA | Washington | Wash. | WA |
| Michigan | Mich. | MI | West Virginia | W. Va. | WV |
| Minnesota | Minn. | MN | Wisconsin | Wis. | WI |
| Mississippi | Miss. | MS | Wyoming | Wyo. | WY |
| Missouri | Mo. | MO | | | |

**Envelope Address** On No. 10 envelopes (9½" by 4⅛") the address begins approximately 14 lines from the top and approximately five spaces from left of center. The address is keyed in block style and is single-spaced. The No. 10 envelope is the size most commonly used in business offices. On small envelopes ( 6½" by 3⅝"), the address begins approximately 12 lines from the top and ten spaces left of the center.

**Mailing Preparation** To fold a letter for a No. 10 envelope, fold slightly less than one third of the letter up toward the top. With the edges even at the sides, crease the fold. Fold down the top of the sheet to within one-half inch of the bottom fold. With the edges even at the sides, crease the fold. Insert the letter into the envelope with the last crease toward the bottom of the envelope. Frame A in Figure 6-15 shows this process.

**Figure 6-15**

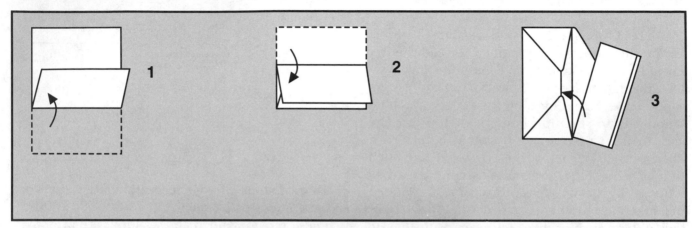

**Frame A** Folding a Letter for a No. 10 Envelope

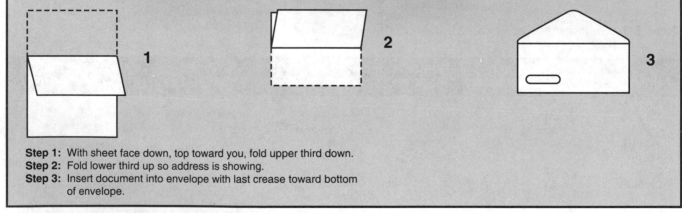

**Step 1:** With sheet face down, top toward you, fold upper third down.
**Step 2:** Fold lower third up so address is showing.
**Step 3:** Insert document into envelope with last crease toward bottom of envelope.

**Frame B** Folding a Letter for Window Envelope (Full sheet)

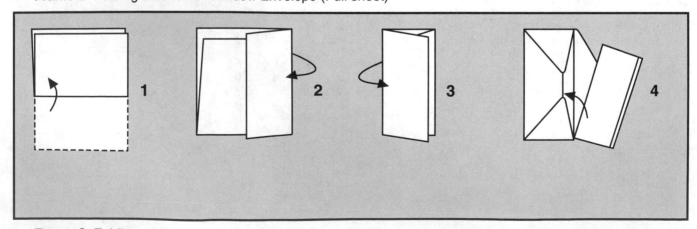

**Frame C** Folding a Letter for a Small Envelope

To fold a letter for a window envelope, with the sheet face down, top toward you, fold the upper third down. Then, fold the lower third up so the address is showing. Insert the letter into the envelope with the last crease at the bottom. Frame B in Figure 6-15 shows this process.

Even though a small envelope is infrequently used in a business office, you need to know how to fold and insert a letter into such an envelope. Fold the letter from the bottom to within one-half inch of the top. With the edges even at the sides, crease the fold. Then, fold from right to left a third of the sheet's width. Next fold another third of the sheet's width from left to right to within one-half inch of the last crease. Insert the letter into the envelope with the last creased edge inserted first, as shown in Frame C in Figure 6-15.

## MAILABILITY

From what you have learned in this chapter, you should now understand the importance of effective business letter writing. You should also know how to compose routine letters and transcribe letters properly. Producing a mailable letter requires that the techniques and steps presented in this chapter be followed. Failing to follow these techniques and steps may produce a letter that is not considered mailable. For example, as you compose and prepare the letters assigned to you in this chapter and turn them in to your instructor, you may get a letter back from your instructor with the notation that it is "not mailable." This means you have not fulfilled some of the requirements of an acceptable business letter. In the office, as you apply the techniques learned in this chapter, your employer may, on occasion, give you back a piece of correspondence, telling you that it cannot be mailed due to errors in the copy. A mailability checklist is given in Figure 6-16. This checklist can be valuable to you as you compose the letters in this unit. This list can also be valuable to you on the job. After you finish a piece of correspondence, it is an excellent idea to review it using such a checklist.

**Figure 6-16** Mailability Checklist

1. Does the letter satisfy these requirements?
   a. Is it complete?
   b. Is it concise?
   c. Is it courteous?
   d. Is it accurate?
   e. Is it positive?
   f. Does it use the "you" approach?
2. Is it placed appropriately on the page? Are the top, bottom, and side margins correct? (Do the margins resemble a frame around a picture?)
3. Is the dateline appropriately placed? Is the date correct? (Have you used the current date?)
4. Is the letter address correct? Is it appropriately placed?
5. Is the salutation correct? Is it appropriately placed?
6. Are the complimentary close and signature lines correct and appropriately placed?
7. Are the reference initials in the appropriate place?
8. If there are enclosures, has such been noted on the letter?
9. If there are special letter parts such as attention lines and subject lines, are they correct and appropriately placed?
10. If a copy is to be sent to another individual, is it noted on the letter in the appropriate place?
11. Are correct letter and punctuation styles used?
12. Does the envelope address match the letter address?
13. Is the appropriate envelope format used?
14. Is the letter free of grammatical and punctuation errors?
15. Is the letter free of any misspelled words? (Have you used a spell-checker if one is available to you?)
16. Is the letter folded and inserted correctly in the envelope?

## CHAPTER SUMMARY

The following summary will help you remember the important points of this chapter.

1. The effective business letter is complete, concise, courteous, accurate, positive, and uses the "you" approach.

2. Before writing a business letter a planning process should take place. The process includes considering your audience, gathering the facts, determining what to say, deciding on the order of presentation, outlining, and developing an effective beginning and ending.

3. When answering a letter positively, use the inductive approach; respond to the request, explain any necessary details, and end with a statement of goodwill.

4. In answering a letter negatively, use the deductive approach; begin with a statement that acknowledges the request, explain why you must refuse, refuse, propose an alternative if one is possible, and end with a courteous and friendly statement.

5. The basic parts of a business letter are

   a. Dateline

   b. Letter address

   c. Salutation

   d. Body

   e. Complimentary close

   f. Signature

   g. Reference initials

6. Some of the special parts of a business letter include the following:

   a. Attention line

   b. Subject line

   c. File number

   d. Enclosure notation

   e. Copy notation

7. The most common forms of punctuation are open punctuation and mixed punctuation. In open punctuation there is no punctuation after the salutation and complimentary close. In mixed punctuation there is a colon after the salutation and a comma after the complimentary close.

8. Letter styles include the following:

   a. Block letter style: Everything is keyed flush with the left margin.

   b. Modified block letter style with blocked paragraphs: Date and closing are centered; paragraphs are blocked.

   c. Modified block letter style with indented paragraphs: Date and closing are centered; paragraphs are indented.

   d. AMS simplified letter style: Salutation and complimentary close are eliminated, and everything is positioned flush with the left margin. The subject line is shown in all capital letters, and the writer's name and title are keyed in all capital letters.

9. The United States Post Office now uses OCR scanners to speed the processing of mail by rapid reading and sorting of envelopes.

10. Envelopes are prepared in the following manner:

    a. All lines are single-spaced.

    b. The name and address are keyed in all capital letters with no marks of punctuation.

    c. For a No. 10 envelope, the address is keyed 14 lines down and five spaces to the left of the center.

    d. For a small envelope, the address is keyed 12 lines down and ten spaces to the left of the center.

## TERMINOLOGY REVIEW

The following terms were introduced in this chapter. To help you understand them, definitions are given below.

1. **Accurate** *(page 122)* When writing a letter, get the facts before you start to write the letter. Check all information carefully.
2. **AMS simplified style** *(page 135)* All lines begin flush with the left margin, there is no salutation or complimentary close, and a subject line is used.
3. **Block style** *(page 135)* All lines of a letter are flush with the left margin.
4. **Complete** *(page 119)* A letter is complete if it gives the reader all the information needed so that the writer achieves the results intended.
5. **Conciseness** *(page 120)* Conciseness in letter writing means expressing the necessary information in as few words as possible.
6. **Courteousness** *(page 121)* Courteousness in letter writing means using good human relations skills.
7. **Deductive approach** *(page 123)* The deductive approach in letter writing means going from the general to the specific.
8. **Inductive approach** *(page 123)* The inductive approach in letter writing goes from the specific to the general.
9. **Mnemonic device** *(page 120)* A device such as a formula or rhyme used to assist the memory.
10. **Modified block style** *(page 135)* The dateline and complimentary close begin at center in the modified block letter style. The paragraphs may be indented or blocked.
11. **Positivism** *(page 122)* Positivism gives the reader a favorable association with a person, a service, or a product. A positive tone is set by the words chosen and by the way they are used.
12. **"You" approach** *(page 122)* The "you" approach means placing the reader at the center of the message.

## DISCUSSION ITEMS

To demonstrate your understanding of the information in this chapter, respond to the following items.

1. Discuss four ways of keeping business letters concise.
2. Explain how you can achieve good human relations in writing letters.
3. What does positivism mean in letter writing?
4. Illustrate the difference between the "you" approach and the "we" approach.
5. Differentiate between an inductive and a deductive approach to letter writing.
6. If you were responding negatively to a request, would you handle it differently than a positive response? If so, how?
7. What is meant by cliched words and phrases?
8. What influence has the OCR had on addressing envelopes?

## CASE STUDY

Maurice Chateau, data services manager, asked his secretary to write a letter to Ruth Hart congratulating her on becoming city manager of Carrollton. Ruth worked for Mr. Chateau at TriCounty five years ago. Here is the draft of the letter that his secretary wrote:

Dear Ms. Hart:

I want to congratulate you on becoming City

Manager of Carrollton. I recognized your talent during the years that you worked for me. I know that you will do an excellent job for Carrollton.

Again, my congratulations on your success.

The secretary is not happy with the letter, and she asks that you critique it. What suggestions would you make to her?

## OFFICE APPLICATIONS

### Office Application 6-1 (*Objective 1*)

Collect five business letters that you receive through the mail. Any type of business letter will be acceptable—for example, a sales letter or inquiry letter. Using the effective letter characteristics given in this text, critique the letters. Pick one letter to rewrite. Present the critique orally to your class along with the rewritten letter.

### Office Application 6-2 (*Objective 1*)

Rewrite the following sentences and apply the effective letter-writing techniques that you learned in this chapter.

1.  Your kind letter of October 8 was received today.
2.  I wish to thank you for your recent order.
3.  As per my letter of November 5, the typewriter is unsatisfactory.
4.  Please send us the information at your earliest convenience.
5.  The repair costs on the photocopier were less than usual.
6.  Thank you in advance for responding to my request.
7.  A preponderance of businesspersons was consulted on this esoteric matter.
8.  People's propensity to consume goods is insatiable.
9.  You will receive the merchandise without any more delay.
10. You will not be sorry if you buy one of our new seat belts.

### Office Application 6-3 (*Objective 1*)

Each of the sentences below is intended to be the beginning sentence of a letter. Rewrite these sentences so they will be effective.

1.  I received your order today and wanted to thank you for it.
2.  Enclosed please find my check in the amount of $510.36 in payment for your Order 34560.
3.  I regret to inform you that the seat belts you ordered are no longer being manufactured.
4.  This check affirms my intent to subscribe to your weekly investment publication, *Financial News*.
5.  I hope you will send us your subscription renewal today.

### Office Application 6-4 (*Objectives 2 and 4*)

Write a letter for each of the following situations. If you are using a microcomputer, store your letters on your data disk, giving them an appropriate file name (use the initials of the addressee, along with the month and day of the letter).

1.  You have been asked to order the following office supplies from Douglas Office Supply, 7891 Loop 12, Arlington, TX 76025-5622.

a. 10 printer ribbons
b. 5 boxes of computer paper
c. 10 packages of diskette labels
d. 10 boxes of floppy disks

Visit a computer supply store to get the specifications needed for ordering these supplies. Then, compose and transcribe the letter using the AMS simplified letter style. Print the letter on the letterhead given at the end of this chapter then print out an additional copy on plain paper for a file copy and put it in your folder labeled "to be filed." Address the preprinted TriCounty envelope also provided at the end of this chapter. Fold the letter for mailing, and attach the envelope with a paper clip.

2. You are interested in ordering *The Office Professional* for the office support personnel at TriCounty. You will need 10 copies. This publication is printed once each month, with the yearly subscription price being $20. The address of *The Office Professional* is 210 Commerce Boulevard, Round Rock, TX 78664-2189. Compose and transcribe the letter using an appropriate letter style. Print the letter on the letterhead provided at the end of this chapter. Print an additional copy on plain paper for a file copy, and put it in your folder labeled "to be filed." Address the preprinted TriCounty envelope also provided at the end of this chapter. Fold the letter for mailing and attach the envelope with a paper clip.

3. You have been asked by Mr. Mike Rowse, Temporary Office Workers, 3986 East Commerce, Dallas, TX 75001-4839, to participate in a panel discussion on the topic of office communication. You would like to do so, but your current work load is extremely heavy and Mr. Andrews feels he needs you on the job. Write a letter to Mr. Rowse saying no to his request. Use an appropriate letter style. Print the letter on the TriCounty letterhead provided at the end of this chapter. Print an additional copy on plain paper for a file copy, and put it in your folder labeled "to be filed." Address the TriCounty envelope also provided at the end of this chapter, fold the letter for mailing, and attach the envelope with a paper clip.

4. One of your friends, Monica Sanchez, has just received a promotion to office manager for Roger Steel, 309 Mockingbird Avenue, Arlington, TX 76010-2674. Write a letter of congratulations to her, using an appropriate letter style. Print the letter on the letterhead provided at the end of this chapter, and print an additional copy on plain paper for a file copy. Put this file copy in your folder labeled "to be filed." Address the TriCounty envelope also provided at the end of this chapter, fold the letter for mailing, and attach the envelope with a paper clip.

### Office Application 6-5 (*Objective 3*)

Identify the numbered parts of the business letter on page 145.

### Office Application 6-6 (*Objectives 2 and 4*)

You have keyed two letters for Mr. Andrews. He has made some changes in the letters and now he asks that you correct them. As you are correcting the letters, you notice that you have inadvertently used incorrect letter styles.

# △ TriCounty Regional Planning Agency

**3232 Six Flags Drive**
**Arlington, TX 76025-5888**
**(817) 245-6800**

TriCounty Regional
Planning Agency

3232 Six Flags Drive
Arlington, TX 76025-5888
(817) 245-6800

# TriCounty Regional Planning Agency

3232 Six Flags Drive
Arlington, TX  76025-5888
(817) 245-6800

TriCounty Regional
Planning Agency
3222 Six Flags Drive
Arlington, TX 76025-5888
(817) 245-6800

# TriCounty Regional Planning Agency

3232 Six Flags Drive
Arlington, TX  76025-5888
(817) 245-6800

**TriCounty Regional**
**Planning Agency**

3232 Six Flags Drive
Arlington, TX 76025-5888
(817) 245-6800

# 7 Office Documents

As you learned in Chapter 6, there are numerous letters written every day in most offices. In addition to letters, there are a number of other documents prepared on a daily basis. Most interoffice correspondence takes place in the form of interoffice memorandums. A variety of reports are written detailing special projects of the company or reflecting new directions of the company. These reports often include statistical material, charts, and graphs.

Financial records make up a large portion of the correspondence in the office. Take a moment to consider a few of the essential financial records that a company must maintain. You, as an employee, are concerned with getting a paycheck each week, semimonthly, or every month. To insure that you are paid the proper amount, your company must keep detailed records of your earnings, the amount of social security tax withheld, the amount of income tax withheld, and any other deductions for such items as group insurance and retirement plans. Your company must correctly prepare your payroll check, issue numerous other checks, and make bank deposits. The financial picture of the company must be reported to the board of directors and to the owners of the company.

As an office assistant you will probably be heavily involved with producing interoffice memorandums and reports. You must be able to present the information given to you in a format that is consistent with the requirements of the business. You must also be able to produce mailable copy free of errors. You may not be directly involved in handling the financial transactions of a business, since usually departments such as payroll, purchasing, the controller's office, and so forth handle the financial transactions. However, a knowledge of some of these transactions will help you to understand the total operations of the business. This chapter will help you develop the necessary skills and knowledge in the areas mentioned.

**Illus. 7-1** A variety of reports are written in the business office detailing special projects or reflecting new directions of the company.

## GENERAL OBJECTIVES

*Your general objectives for this chapter are to*
1. **Prepare business reports and presentation drafts.**
2. **Use reference sources.**
3. **Prepare interoffice memorandums.**
4. **Write checks.**
5. **Use appropriate types of endorsements.**
6. **Complete deposit slips.**
7. **Reconcile a bank statement.**
8. **Prepare an expense report.**
9. **Prepare financial records.**
10. **Perform mathematical computations with a calculator.**

## BUSINESS REPORTS

Numerous reports are prepared in a typical office. These reports may be informal reports consisting of two or three pages, or they may be formal reports containing a table of contents, the body of the report (with footnotes), appendices, and a bibliography. They may be either single-spaced or double-spaced. Single-spacing reduces the amount of paper needed; for this reason, many business reports are single-spaced. However, if the report is long, it is easier to read if it is double-spaced.

Your role in preparing these reports may involve doing a limited amount of research for your employer, and certainly your role will include keying the report, producing the final copies, and distributing them to the appropriate individuals.

## Steps in Preparing a Report

A number of steps are usually followed in the preparation of a report. In preparing the report, the writer usually

1. Prepares a summary of what should be included in the report.
2. Gathers the information for the report (if research is necessary, it is done at this point).
3. Prepares an outline of the report. (This outline may or may not be a detailed outline.)
4. Writes the report and gives it to the office assistant for keyboarding.
5. Reads, edits, and returns the report to the assistant for rekeying.
6. Reads the report again, after appropriate changes are made and after copies are printed and distributed.

## Reference Sources

If you are called upon to research information for your employer, you need to be familiar with the major sources of information. Several of these sources are given here.

**Almanacs and Yearbooks** Almanacs and yearbooks provide a record of notable events and statistical information, such as population and production figures. *Information Please Almanac* and the *World Almanac and Book of Facts* are two such publications.

**Government Publications** Numerous informational and statistical publications are available from the United States government. The *Monthly Catalog of United States Government Publications* provides a comprehensive listing of all publications issued by the various governmental departments and agencies.

Following are some of the government publications available and a brief synopsis of what is contained in each:

- *The Statistical Abstract of the United States* gives statistics concerning population, climate, employment, military affairs, social security, banking, transportation, agriculture, and related fields.
- *The Survey of Current Business* reports on the industrial and business activities of the United States.
- *The Monthly Labor Review* publishes labor statistics, standards, and employment trends.
- *International Financial Statistics Yearbook* traces financial statistics for more than 125 countries. It covers income to central governments, grants, aid, and such financial obligations as debt repayments and other financing.

**Illus. 7-2** If you are called upon to research information for your employer, you need to be familiar with the major sources of information.

**Reference Guides** One of the most frequently used reference guides is the *Reader's Guide to Periodical Literature*. A selected list of magazines is indexed in each issue. It is easy to use. Articles may be looked up in subject and author indexes and there is extensive cross-referencing. Another reference guide that you may find helpful is the *Business Periodicals Index*. It contains a list of articles published in selected business magazines. These listings are cataloged alphabetically by the subject of the article and by the author. *Books in Print* contains listings of books published since 1900. This index lists each book by author, by title, and by one or more subjects. There are also special guides for reference readings, two of which are the *Medical and Health Care Books and Serials in Print* and *Scientific and Technical Books and Serials in Print.*

**Computer Reference Sources**   Several computer networks exist that allow you to do research through a microcomputer. A communications network allows the microcomputer or terminal user to access other computers in order to obtain information. If you don't live near a network number you can connect to the network through long-distance telephone service. From these networks, information services such as Predicasts, Dun's Marketing Services, Dialog, and UMI/Data Courier can be reached. Substantial amounts of information are available from these sources. Some of the topics that can be accessed over these networks include information on international business; demographic, economic, and financial statistics; industry trends and developments; corporate planning; management techniques; and mergers and acquisitions. Once you decide what references you wish to review you can receive an abstract or summary of the reference through your terminal and print the abstract on your printer.

Airline and travel information is also available on the computer. Travel routes and schedules may be keyboarded into the computer and several possible flights are given from which to choose. The *Official Airline Guide,* which lists arrivals and departures for all airlines around the world, is another source available, along with the *Mobil Travel Guide to Hotels, Motels, and Inns,* and a hotel reservation service.

The *Dow Jones* service can give you current quotes of stocks traded on the New York, American, Midwest, and Pacific stock exchanges as well as quotes from the national over-the-counter market. This service also lets you search for stories of interest that have appeared in *The Wall Street Journal, Barron's,* and the *Dow Jones News Service.* Numerous other databases are available, a few of which are *Books in Print* and *Reader's Guide to Periodical Literature.*

## Report Format

There are a number of software packages available that can assist you as you prepare reports. You have already been introduced to some of these software packages in previous chapters (for example, spell checkers, thesaurus, punctuation, and grammar checkers). You have also learned that integrated software programs provide word processing, spreadsheet, and graphics in one program. These integrated programs can be used quite successfully in preparing a report. Desktop publishing is also helpful in that it allows you to use graphics, pictures, different types and sizes of fonts, and other features that can enhance the appearance of the report. Many word processing packages contain footnote and endnote commands that make it relatively easy to insert footnotes in the report. There are also commands that help you create a table of contents, an index, and a list of bibliographic references.

**Margins**   With the exception of the first page, if a report is to be unbound, margins should be one inch on both sides and at the top and bottom. (For a one inch top margin, the first line should be line 7.) The heading for the first page should begin 2 inches from the top (at line 13). If the report is to be topbound, an additional two lines are added for the binding. If the report is to be leftbound, one-half inch is added to the left margin to provide for the binding. Thus, the left margin of a leftbound report may be 1½ inches.

Software packages have *default* margins (settings that are in effect each time you start the program). The default margins for most word processors is usually one inch on all sides. Many offices now use the default one inch margin even in leftbound reports, since it does not require that margins be changed and many binding methods do not require a full half inch. However, if necessary, the default margins can be easily changed by using a screen such as the Document Initial Codes screen and inserting the appropriate margins. Notice Figure 7-1 which illustrates the default margins that are on a word processing software package.

**Headings**   The main heading is prepared in all capitals and centered. It is followed by a double-space if a secondary heading is used or by a quadruple space if no secondary heading is used. Side headings are placed at the left margin and are underscored with the first letter of major words capitalized. Double-space before and after a side heading. Paragraph headings are underscored and indented, with only the first word capitalized and with a period at the end of the heading. Double-space before a paragraph heading. Figure 7-2 shows the position of the title and various types of headings on an unbound report.

**Figure 7-1** Default Margin Settings

```
Format:  Line

1 - Hyphenation              No

2 - Hyphenation Zone - Left  10%
                    Right    4%

3 - Justification            Full

4 - Line Height              Auto

5 - Line Numbering           No

6 - Line Spacing             1

7 - Margins - Left           1"
            Right            1"

8 - Tab Set                  Rel: -1", every 0.5"

9 - Widow/Orphan Protection  No

Selection:  0
```

**Figure 7-2** Proper Business Report Format (Unbound Report)

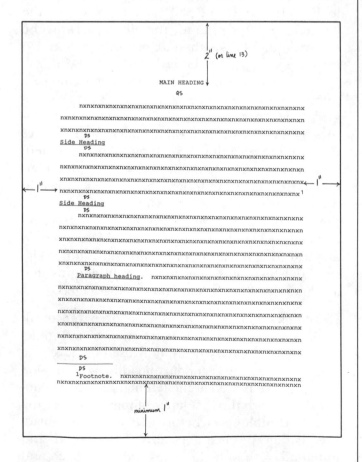

**Page Numbers** The first page of a report is unnumbered. On leftbound and topbound reports, the second and subsequent pages are numbered on line 6 (one inch from the top) at the right mar-

gin. The body of the report begins a double-space below the page number. On topbound reports, all page numbers are centered at the bottom of the page on line 62. The word "page" should not be keyed; only the number itself should appear. Most software packages have an automatic pagination feature which allows you to place the page number at the top or bottom of the page and at the left, right, or center. Or, you can have the page number appear at alternating positions—the left side of even pages and the right side of odd pages, if you are duplexing a report.

**Footnotes and Endnotes** Footnotes and endnotes are references used to cite the source of any quoted or paraphrased material. When notes are placed on the same page as the quoted or paraphrased material they are called footnotes. When they are placed at the end of a manuscript they are called endnotes. Figure 7-3 shows a partial page of endnotes. Notice that this page (Figure 7-3) is headed "endnotes."

Footnotes are often separated from the text by a 1½ inch dividing line that is preceded by a double-space and followed by a double-space. The footnotes themselves are single-spaced with a double-space between the footnotes. They are numbered consecutively throughout the text of the document with superscripted or superior (raised) figures. Figure 7-4 illustrates a footnote. Software packages now make it relatively easy to include footnotes in a manuscript.

**Figure 7-3** Partial Page of Endnotes

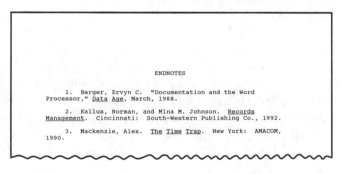

**Figure 7-4** A Footnote

**Textual Citations** Another method of documentation is the textual citation method. Both the footnote and endnote methods require the use of superscript figures in the text, and footnotes require that the information be put at the bottom of the page. Textual citation references require neither. With the textual citation method, the surname of the author, the publication date, and the page number is given in the text. These text citations are keyed to a list of works cited, arranged in alphabetical order by author name, placed at the end of the document. An example of the textual citation method is given in Figure 7-5. When using footnotes, a bibliography is prepared at the end of the report which lists all references cited in alphabetical order. The heading REFERENCES or BIBLIOGRAPHY may be used above textual citations.

**Figure 7-5** The Textual Citation Method

```
One of the more difficult aspects of speech
preparation is going from ideas on paper to
sharing ideas aloud with an audience.  Throughout
the process of sifting through information and
organizing thoughts, it is important to consider
your impact upon the audience (Flacks, Rasberry,
1982, 120).
```

**Bibliography or References** The bibliography, or reference page, identifies all sources used within the report. When preparing a separate bibliography or reference page, use the same margins as for the first page of the report. The heading BIBLIOGRAPHY is generally used and is placed 1½ inches (line 10) from the top. Figure 7-6 illustrates a bibliography. A quadruple space follows the title. When endnotes or textual citations are used, the heading ENDNOTES or REFERENCES (either one is acceptable) is keyed 1½ inches from the top. Each entry in a bibliography is arranged alphabetically by author name. Individual items are single-spaced with a double-space between items. The first line of each item starts at the left margin; additional lines are indented five spaces.

**Table of Contents** A table of contents, often simply titled CONTENTS, lists each major division in the report and the number of the first page of each division. When preparing the table of contents, use the same margins that are used for the first page of the report. If the report is unbound, the heading CONTENTS is placed 1½ inches (line 10) from the top. The title is centered and is in all

**Figure 7-6** Bibliography Format

```
                          BIBLIOGRAPHY

Bennis, Warren.  Why Leaders Can't Lead.  San Francisco:
    Jossey-Bass Publishers, 1990.

Bly, Robert.  Iron John.  New York:  Addison-Wesley Publishing
    Company, Inc., 1990.

Fulton, Patsy J.  Office Procedures and Technology for Colleges.
    Cincinnati:  South-Western Publishing Co., 1994.
```

capital letters. A quadruple space is left between the title and the table itself.

**Title Page** Although a title page is not essential and is not used on all reports, the appearance of a report of more than five or ten pages can be enhanced with a title page. The title page contains the essential facts that identify the report. The information on a title page generally includes the title of the report, the person or group for whom the report was prepared, the person or group who submitted the report, and the date of the report. The title of the report is centered approximately 2½ inches from the top of the page, with the other information centered in the middle third and lower third of the sheet. Figure 7-7 shows a title page. With graphics packages that are now available, attractive borders can be easily created for the title page.

## PRESENTATIONS

Executives often give presentations within the company or outside the company for professional or civic groups. Your responsibility may include doing research for a presentation. When doing research for a presentation, you may prepare an abstract of a particular article for the executive's review. *Abstracting* is the process of taking the most important ideas in an article or book and recording them in your own words. When preparing abstracts it is essential that you develop the ability to pick out the important points and express them in summary form. Such abstracts can save the executive a great deal of reading time. Abstracts are generally prepared on note cards.

Another task that you might have in assisting the executive with a presentation is preparing his or her notes. Before beginning such a task, be certain that you understand how the executive wants the notes prepared. Some individuals work best

**Figure 7-7** Title Page of a Report

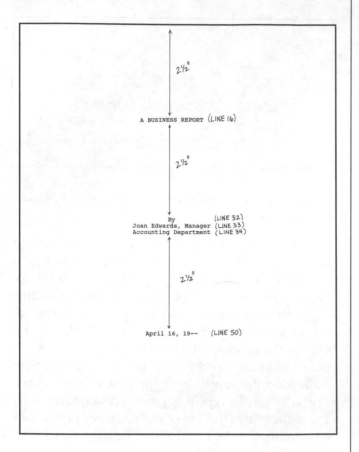

6. If the executive is using handouts it is a good idea to color-code or number the handouts so that the executive may refer to the coding as he calls the audience's attention to the handout. Always place the handouts (with the appropriate number) in order so that the executive does not have to sort them while delivering the presentation. Highlight the text of the speech to call attention to when the handouts are to be presented.

7. If transparencies are used, number these also in the order in which they will be presented. Highlight the text of the speech with a colored marker to call attention to when the transparency is to be presented. Transparencies can be made easily on a copier. Merely substitute the transparency film for the paper in the copier's paper tray, place your original on the platen of the copier, and press the print button. Transparencies may also be made in color. There are many films on the market capable of producing color transparencies on clear film in purple, red, blue, or green. Be certain to make transparencies in print large enough to be read from any point in the room. You should always check out the transparencies in the room where the presentation is to be made (if possible) to be certain that they can be read from the back of the room.

**Illus. 7-3** Some individuals work best from note cards when giving presentations.

from note cards. If that is the case, you may prepare an outline on 5 inch by 3 inch or 4 inch by 6 inch cards. Generally individuals like to have a considerable amount of space between points; thus, it is a good idea to use quadruple spacing. Also, many times it is important that the letters be as large as possible for ease in reading; you might want to prepare it in all caps. Put a number on each card so there will be no confusion as to the order.

Some executives prefer to present from a word-for-word format; therefore, they want the entire text keyed. Again, it is important that the presentation be easy to read with adequate space between the lines. Following are some suggestions for keying the presentation:

1. Use quadruple spacing.
2. Use a large print style; key in all caps.
3. Use a short writing line so that the eye does not have to travel across the entire page; a 4 inch or 5 inch line is suggested.
4. Number the pages.
5. Place the completed copy in a presentation folder; a dark color (black, navy, or brown) is usually best.

## MEMORANDUMS

Frequently, written information is sent to other individuals within the office. This correspondence is written as an interoffice memorandum. Some companies may use special interoffice memorandum forms with the guide words (*To, From, Date, and Subject*) preprinted on the form. However, with the use of software packages, it is simpler to place the appropriate heading on a plain sheet of paper rather than to be concerned about placement on a form. Figure 7-8 depicts an interoffice memorandum.

Memorandums are usually prepared in block style. Double-space between the guide words and the message and single-space the paragraphs, unless it is an extremely short memorandum. Often interoffice memorandums are addressed to several people. The general practice is to alphabetize the names or list them according to position. Titles such as Mr., Miss, Mrs., Ms., and the like, should not be used. Specially designed envelopes are used by most businesses to transmit interoffice memorandums. These envelopes are reusable and are large enough to accommodate an 8½ inch by 11 inch sheet of paper without having to fold it.

**Figure 7-8** Interoffice Memorandum

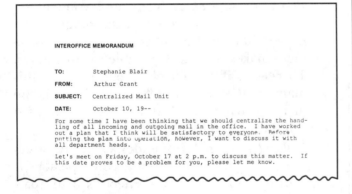

## FINANCIAL RECORDS

Today offices handle most of their financial records via the computer. Your involvement with these records may be very minimal, unless you are employed in one of the financial departments of your firm; for example, the accounting department, payroll department, purchasing department, and so forth. If the company is a large one, a mainframe computer is probably used to prepare payroll (with income tax, social security, and other deductions figured automatically) and to generate numerous other financial records. Many companies generate purchases through the computer. If your company is a small one, the microcomputer may be used to generate financial records.

There are a number of financial software programs available. One of the ways in which you as an office assistant might be involved with financial records includes the purchasing of office supplies. For example, if your company is a relatively large one, purchase requisitions may be generated via the computer. If you wish to order ten reams of letterhead, you would generate your order by calling up the appropriate screen on your computer and keying the order information. This input would then be sent to the purchasing department where various orders for paper would be batched to insure efficiencies in purchasing, and then the order would be developed. Your involvement with the budgeting may involve keying in budget figures once a year for the annual budget and keying in budget adjustments when necessary. Your involvement in payroll may merely involve preparing the appropriate forms to record your vacation or sick leave. Regardless of your involvement with financial records, a knowledge of these transactions will help you to understand more about the operations of the business.

### Banking

In most companies banking records are computer-generated and maintained. In fact, personnel checks are often deposited by **direct deposit** which means that a check is never written. Funds are transferred automatically from the company's account to the employee's bank. In a small company checks may still be written by hand. However, if you do not write checks in your office, you certainly will be writing them in your personal life. The information presented here will be helpful to you both professionally and personally.

**Checks Defined**   A **check** is an order in writing directing the bank to pay cash from the **drawer's** account to the **payee**. Most financial obligations of businesses, as well as of individuals, are paid for by check. Checks provide an easy way to transfer money, and canceled checks serve as receipts. Most businesses use a special type of check called a **voucher check**. This check has a detachable portion (a voucher) on which is written the check's purpose. The voucher is sent to the payee with the check; it is not detached from the check by the office assistant. In contrast, a check stub is detached from the check and remains in the checkbook of the company issuing the check. The purpose of the purchase is noted on the stub. A voucher check is shown in Figure 7-9.

**Figure 7-9** Voucher Check with Detachable Stub

## Check Writing

If you are preparing a check manually, the correct procedures should be followed. Here are the steps:

1. The check voucher, stub, or register should be filled out first with the date, amount, and purpose of the check. As has been explained, the voucher is used by most businesses. The stub or register is used more for personal or personal/business transactions. A **stub** is a short leaf of paper attached to the spine of the checkbook. A **check register** is a separate form for recording the checks that have been written. Check registers are provided by banks for personal accounts. Personal checks are less cumbersome to carry with you. Checks with check stubs attached are generally used for individuals who have small businesses that they operate from their home. The check stub allows for the recording of more detailed information.

2. The date should be entered in the space provided on the check.

3. The name of the payee should be written in full and as far as possible to the left in the space provided.

4. The amount of the check must be written twice. It is first written in figures after the dollar sign. The figures should be placed as close as possible to the printed dollar sign so that no additional figures can be inserted. The amount of the check is then written on the following line with words for the dollar amount and figures for the cents. Express cents in fractions of 100. The words should begin as far as possible to the left. If the written amount does not fill the entire space, draw a line through the excess space.

5. Erasures or changes should be avoided in writing checks. If a mistake is made, write *void* across the face of the check and the check voucher, stub, or register.

6. In the lower left-hand corner of many checks, there is a section with the word "memo." This space is used to put account numbers of the bills you are paying or the purpose of the check.

## Check Depositing

In addition to writing checks, you may be required to make deposits to your company's account. Here is some information you should know in order to make the deposit correctly.

*Endorsements*  Before a check can be deposited, it must be endorsed. An **endorsement** is a written signature by the holder of the check for the purpose of transferring ownership. The endorsement is written on the back of the check. A rubber stamp may be used instead of a signature if the check is to be deposited only. The following types of endorsements are used.

1. *Blank endorsement.* A **blank endorsement** requires only the signature of the payee or the present holder of the check. A blank endorsement makes the check payable to any holder. Therefore, if the check is endorsed in this manner, it should not be sent through the mail because if it is lost, anyone who finds it can turn it into cash.

2. *Full endorsement.* A **full endorsement** transfers ownership of a check to a definite person or firm to whose order the check is made payable. The name of the person to whom the check is payable is written above the signature of the holder.

3. *Restrictive endorsement.* A **restrictive endorsement** transfers the ownership of a check for a specific purpose. For example, if a person has several checks to deposit at a time when it is not convenient to go to a bank, the checks can be endorsed with a restrictive endorsement so that they are not cashed for any other reason. Figure 7-10 shows all the types of endorsements.

*The Deposit Slip*  Banks supply special blank forms known as **deposit slips** on which the following information is to be recorded:

1. The account number and the name of the individual or the business to whose account the

**Figure 7-10** Types of Check Endorsements

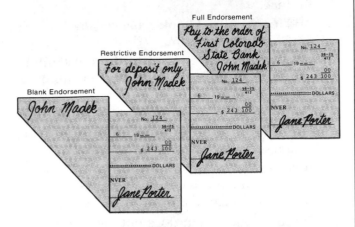

4. A list of the checks or other items to be deposited, with listing by ABA (American Bankers Association) transit number.

5. The total of the deposit.

The ABA number is printed in the upper right portion of the check. Notice in Figure 7-11 the numbers 32-56 that indicate the ABA transit number that has been assigned to the bank. The number 3110, appearing below the line, is a Federal Reserve number that is used by banks in sorting checks. This Federal Reserve number is not used in listing the checks. The transit number and the Federal Reserve number may also appear on the check with a slash mark between them instead of on two separate lines. In addition to listing the check by the ABA number, checks may also be listed according to the name of the bank or the city in which the bank is located.

deposit is to be credited. (If this information is not preprinted, you must record it.)

2. The date on which the deposit is made.

3. A list of the currency and coins to be deposited.

**Figure 7-11** Deposit Slips

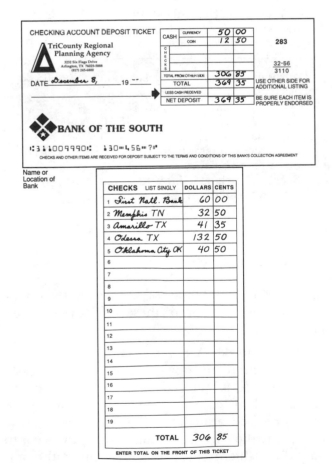

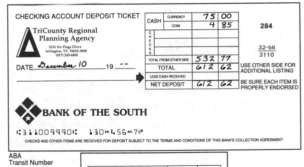

Checks and deposit slips are processed electronically. In order to aid in this processing the depositor's account number is preprinted in magnetic ink characters in a uniform position at the bottom left of the check (see Figure 7-11).

**Bank Statement Reconciliation**   Periodically (usually on a monthly basis) the bank prepares a bank statement for each depositor. The statement shows the amounts deposited and withdrawn, bank service charges, interest, and the account's balance for the month. The depositor should verify the statement balance by checking it against the balance shown on either the last check stub or on other accounting records. Proving the accuracy of the bank statement and the check register is called **reconciling the bank statement**.

Reconciling the bank statement involves closely comparing the bank statement with the company records of deposits and withdrawals. In addition, bank service charges and any other special fees must be taken into consideration, although these charges usually are not known until the bank statement is received. Below are procedures for reconciling a bank statement. (Most bank statements include a form to be completed that gives the steps to follow in reconciling the statement.)

1. Look at the check register to see that all check amounts have been deducted from the preceding balances and that all deposit amounts have been entered and added to the balance.

2. Sort, in numerical order, the canceled checks that have been returned by the bank. Usually a statement is accompanied by the checks that have been paid by the bank. Some banks use **check truncation.** With this process, the bank keeps the checks rather than returning them to the drawer. A monthly statement is issued listing the number and amount of each check that has been cashed. If a check is needed for some reason, the drawer may request it.

3. If checks are returned by the bank, verify each check with the corresponding check register. Place a check mark on the register.

4. On a separate sheet of paper, list the numbers and the amounts of the checks that are outstanding. An **outstanding check** is an issued check that has not yet been cashed by the bank nor deducted from the depositor's account. Total the outstanding checks.

5. Add the total unlisted deposits to the bank balance.

6. Add to the checkbook balance any interest earned on the checking account.

7. Deduct the total amount of the outstanding checks from the balance shown on the bank statement.

8. Deduct from the checkbook balance any service charges or special fees. If there are any charges, they will be shown as separate deductions on the bank statement. The checkbook balance and the balance on the bank statement should agree after these steps.

9. If the reconciliation does not balance after a careful verification, the discrepancy should be brought to the attention of the bank. However, errors are seldom traced to faulty bookkeeping by the bank.

The computation in Table 7-1 shows how the balance on the bank statement in Figure 7-12 is reconciled with the company's checkbook balance of $9,418.25.

**Table 7-1**   Bank Statement Reconciliation (see Figure 7-12)

| | |
|---|---|
| Bank balance, June 1 ............................ | $9,563.83 |
| Less checks outstanding: | |
| No. 790 .............................. $62.50 | |
| No. 792 ................................ 19.10 | |
| No. 808 ................................ 24.60 | |
| Total checks outstanding ......................... | $106.20 |
| Correct bank balance .............................. | 9,457.63 |
| Checkbook balance, June 1 ..................... | 9,418.25 |
| Add: Interest earned ...................................... | 39.38 |
| Correct checkbook balance .................. | $9,457.63 |

## Special Bank Services

Banks offer special types of services that you may find beneficial. Some of these services are given here.

**Cashier's Check**   A check issued by a bank and drawn on the bank's own funds is called a **cashier's check**. A cashier's check can be purchased by giving the bank cash or a check for the amount of money desired; a small fee is required by the bank for writing the check. Recommended practice is to have the cashier's check made payable to the purchaser of the check; the purchaser then endorses

**Figure 7-12** Bank Statement

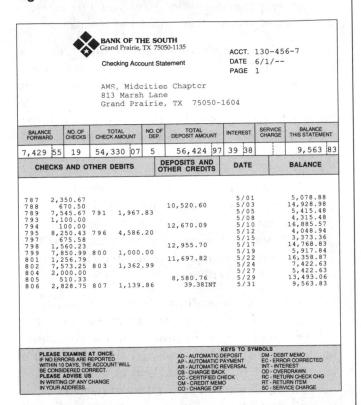

it to the person to whom payment is to be made. The canceled check becomes proof of payment. A cashier's check is shown in Figure 7-13.

**Certified Check** A **certified check** is a check that is guaranteed by the bank on which it is drawn. In order to certify a check, a bank official investigates the drawer's account to see if there are sufficient funds to cover the check. If there are, the word *certified* is stamped on the face of the check and an official signature is added. The drawer's account is immediately charged for the amount of the check. A small fee is usually charged to certify a check.

**Bank Money Order** A **bank money order** is sold by the bank and states that a certain amount of money is to be paid to the person named on the money order. Normally cashable at any bank in the United States or abroad, the money order is negotiable and can be transferred by endorsement. The maximum amount for which a money order can be made varies depending on the bank where you purchase the money order. If you want to send an amount larger than the maximum, any number of money orders may be purchased and issued to the same payee.

**Traveler's Checks** The American Express Company and most banks and travel agencies issue a special type of check called a **traveler's check** which facilitates paying for expenses when traveling. Traveler's checks are sold in various denominations. A small fee may be charged, depending on the amount purchased. When traveler's checks are purchased, each check must be signed by the purchaser. When cashed, each traveler's check must be countersigned by the purchaser in the presence of the person who cashes the check.

**Safe-Deposit Box** Most banks have large vaults that contain small boxes known as **safe-deposit boxes**. These boxes are available for the convenience of individuals and businesses wishing to store articles of value or important papers for safekeeping. There is a rental charge for the use of these boxes.

**Figure 7-13** Cashier's Check

The bank has strict rules about access to safe-deposit boxes. At the time a safe-deposit box is rented, the renter must register his or her signature. The renter is then given a key. Two keys are required to open a safe-deposit—box—the renter's and a duplicate key kept by the bank. If more than one person is authorized to have access to the box, each must register his or her signature. Each time the box is used, the person's name must be registered and the time in and the time out is recorded.

**Illus. 7-4** Safe-deposit boxes are available in banks for the storage of valuable articles or important papers.

*Credit: Courtesy Diebold, Inc.*

## Electronic Banking

Electronics has revolutionized the banking industry. **Electronic fund transfers** (EFTs) allow customers to obtain money, to transfer funds from one account to another, to deposit money, and to pay bills without the use of checks or the services of a bank teller. Simply stated, EFTs use computer and electronic technology as a substitute for checks and other paper forms of banking. The services listed below utilize electronic fund transfers.

**Automated Teller Machine**  Automated teller machines (ATMs) allow customers to obtain cash, to deposit cash or checks, to transfer money from a checking account to a savings account, and to borrow money without writing a check or going to a bank. You will see ATMs in supermarkets, shopping malls, airports, and other highly frequented locations.

To use an ATM, you insert a magnetically encoded plastic card (similar to a credit card) into an electronic terminal and enter your own confidential personal identification number (PIN). The amount of money you requested is then delivered from the machine.

**Direct Payroll Depositing**  Some companies directly deposit an employee's wages. The employee's net pay is withdrawn from the company's bank account and is deposited directly into the employee's bank account. Use of direct payroll depositing eliminates the writing of paychecks, relieves the employee of the inconvenience of going to the bank, and decreases the possible loss or theft of paychecks. In some areas of the country, the federal government deposits social security payments directly into the recipients' bank accounts rather than issuing social security checks.

**Automatic Bill Payment**  It is also possible to automatically pay some bills such as utility bills, mortgage payments, and insurance premiums. For example, the bank deducts the amount of the bill from the customer's account and adds the same amount to the account of the utility company. The customer receives a copy of the paid utility bill for his or her records.

**Point-of-Sale Transfer**  Point-of-sale (POS) systems allow the electronic transfer of money from a purchaser's bank account to a store's bank account. For example, a cashier or salesperson can pass a customer's bank-issued card through a reader attached to a POS terminal that functions as a cash register. The amount of the purchase is deducted from the customer's checking account and added to the store's account. Transferring funds at the moment of purchase is a compelling reason for merchants to install point-of-sale systems. Funds available to a merchant at the moment of purchase accelerate the merchant's cash flow and reduce the number of bad checks and fraudulent credit card charges, both of which are costly to banks and merchants.

## Payroll Records

An understanding of the payroll records and reports that are required by law is essential, not only for the person who works in the payroll department but also for every individual who receives a paycheck. If you work in the payroll department, you must be familiar with these records and reports in order to perform your job. If you receive a paycheck, you need to be familiar with the payroll laws in order to understand the deductions that will be taken from your gross earnings each pay period. The laws and acts that relate to payroll are the Federal Insurance Contribution Act (social security), the Fair Labor Standards Act, income tax laws, and federal and state unemployment compensation acts.

**Federal Income Tax** Employers are required to withhold, for federal income tax purposes, amounts that are determined by a formula or tax table. Amounts vary depending on the salary and the number of tax exemptions claimed by the employee. Each employee must fill out a copy of Form W-4 that shows the number of exemptions. Notice the W-4 Form in Figure 7-14. The amount of income taxes withheld by employers is paid quarterly or monthly by the business to the Internal Revenue Service.

**Federal Insurance Contribution Act (Social Security)** Social security provides income upon retirement, benefits for survivors in the event of the employee's death, and hospital and medical insurance (Medicare) for persons 65 years of age or older. In order to pay for the benefits that you collect upon retirement, both you and your employer contribute an equal amount of money each pay period to the federal government. The amount of that contribution and the base on which it is paid changes frequently. The base means the total amount of your salary that is used in figuring the FICA tax. To determine the percentage and the base at the present time, you can check with your local social security office. The government accumulates the money in an account and pays you the benefits when you retire or pays benefits to your survivors in the event of your death.

Each employer and employee must have a social security number. Under the provisions of the Tax Reform Act of 1986, everyone age two or older must have a social security number. To obtain a number you must file an application with the so-

**Figure 7-14** W-4 Form

Form **W-4** Department of the Treasury Internal Revenue Service

**Employee's Withholding Allowance Certificate**

▶ **For Privacy Act and Paperwork Reduction Act Notice, see reverse.**

OMB No 545-0010

19--

1 Type or print your first name and middle initial — Last name: Robert H. Gausnell

2 Your social security number: 310-48-8293

Home address (number and street or rural route): 7448 Chesterfield Avenue

3 ☐ Single ☐ Married ☒ Married, but withhold at higher Single rate.
**Note:** *If married, but legally separated, or spouse is a nonresident alien, check the Single box.*

City or town, state, and ZIP code: Boise Idaho 83709-8282

4 If your last name differs from that on your social security card, check here and call 1-800-772-1213 for more information . ▶ ☐

5 Total number of allowances you are claiming (from line G above or from the Worksheets on back if they apply) — 5: 2

6 Additional amount, if any, you want deducted from each paycheck . . . . . . . . . . . . . . . — 6: $

7 I claim exemption from withholding and I certify that I meet **ALL** of the following conditions for exemption:

- Last year I had a right to a refund of **ALL** Federal income tax withheld because I had **NO** tax liability; **AND**
- This year I expect a refund of **ALL** Federal income tax withheld because I expect to have **NO** tax liability; **AND**
- This year if my income exceeds $600 and includes nonwage income, another person cannot claim me as a dependent.

If you meet all of the above conditions, enter the year effective and "EXEMPT" here . . . ▶ 7 19

8 Are you a full-time student? (**Note:** *Full-time students are not automatically exempt.*) . . . . . . . . . 8 ☐ Yes ☒ No

Under penalties of perjury, I certify that I am entitled to the number of withholding allowances claimed on this certificate or entitled to claim exempt status.

Employee's signature ▶ Robert H. Gausnell    Date ▶ March 9 , 19--

9 Employer's name and address (Employer: Complete 9 and 11 only if sending to the IRS) | 10 Office code (optional) | 11 Employer identification number

cial security office or post office near you. You will receive a card with your number on it. The Social Security Administration recommends that every three years you request a statement of your earnings to make sure that they have been reported properly. In order to get this statement, send a letter requesting the information, along with your date of birth and social security number, or send Form SSA-7004-PC to the Social Security Administration, P.O. Box 57, Baltimore, MD 20203.

**Unemployment Compensation Tax** This tax provides some relief to those who become unemployed as a result of economic forces outside their control. To finance the program, all employers covered by the law are subject to federal and state taxes. The state employment rate and the wage base subject to the tax vary from state to state. The federal portion of the tax is calculated at 6.02 percent on a wage base (which varies) paid to each employee per year.

**Fair Labor Standards Act** The Fair Labor Standards Act requires that businesses engaged in interstate commerce keep a record of hours worked and pay a minimum hourly wage. In addition, the law requires that certain employees be paid at a rate of at least 50 percent greater than the regular hourly rate for all time worked in excess of 40 hours during a workweek. All persons are not covered by this law. Businesses basically have two ways of paying employees—through salaries (at a monthly or weekly rate) or through wages at a rate per hour. Most hourly employees are covered by this law. Most administrative or executive positions are paid through a monthly salary; these individuals are not covered by this law.

**Other Deductions** There are many other deductions that may be made from wages. Common examples are local or state income taxes, union dues, group insurance, and hospitalization insurance. An example of a payroll check with a list of deductions is shown in Figure 7-15.

## Expense Reports

With the amount of travel that most executives do today, the office assistant frequently needs to prepare expense reports. Generally, before the executive travels there must be some type of leave request filled out that includes the time of travel and the projected cost of the travel. Many companies have accounts with airlines; therefore, once flight arrangements are made, the company is billed directly for the flight expense. When the executive

**Figure 7-15** Payroll Check

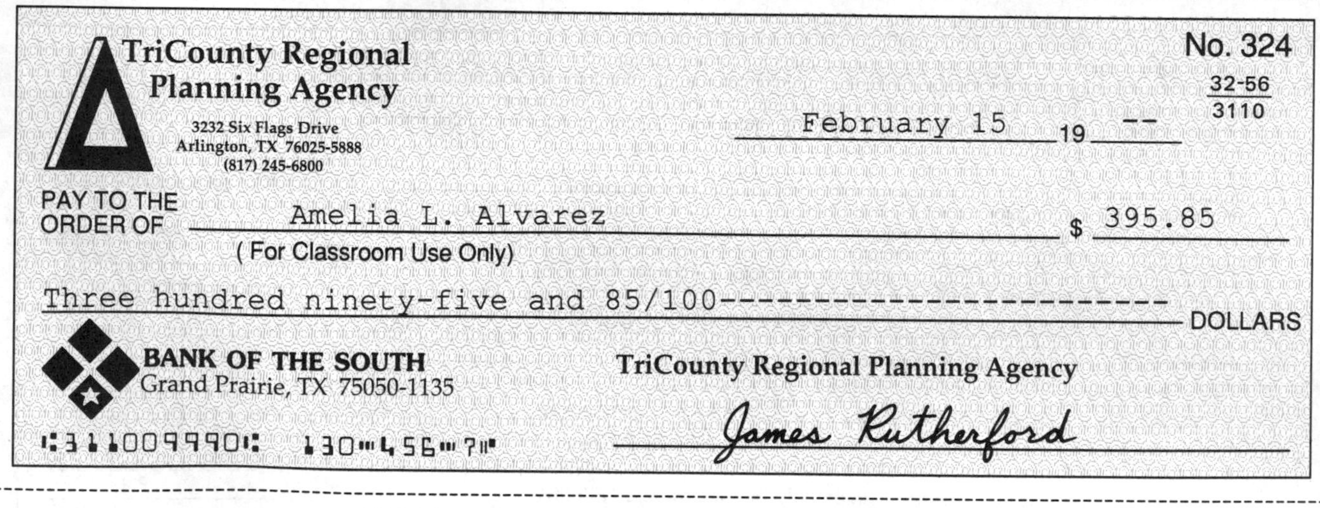

TriCounty Regional Planning Agency
3232 Six Flags Drive
Arlington, TX 76025-5888
(817) 245-6800

No. 324
32-56
3110

February 15 19 --

PAY TO THE ORDER OF Amelia L. Alvarez $ 395.85
(For Classroom Use Only)

Three hundred ninety-five and 85/100---------------------- DOLLARS

BANK OF THE SOUTH
Grand Prairie, TX 75050-1135

TriCounty Regional Planning Agency
James Rutherford

⑆311009990⑆ 130⑈456⑈7⑈

STATEMENT OF EMPLOYEE EARNINGS AND PAYROLL DEDUCTIONS

TriCounty Regional Planning Agency

| PERIOD ENDING | HOURS | EARNINGS | | TOTAL EARNINGS | FEDERAL INCOME TAX | FICA TAX | HOSP. INS | OTHER | TOTAL DEDUCTIONS | NET PAY |
|---|---|---|---|---|---|---|---|---|---|---|
| | | REGULAR | OVERTIME | | | | | | | |
| 2/15/-- | 90 1/2 | 484.00 | 20.63 | 504.63 | 61.50 | 30.28 | 12.00 | 5.00 | 108.78 | 395.85 |
| YEAR-TO-DATE TOTALS | | 1408.00 | 20.63 | 1428.63 | 169.30 | 85.72 | 36.00 | 15.00 | 306.02 | 1122.61 |

returns, an expense report needs to be prepared in order to document the travel and to provide for reimbursement for the expenses of the executive. Figure 7-16 shows an expense report.

As an office assistant your responsibility is to prepare the expense report. Most companies require that receipts be submitted for such items as airfare (even though the company is billed directly for the flight costs), hotel bills, registrations, and car rentals. Receipts may not be required for meals, taxi fares, and similar expenses; however, some companies limit the amount of money that can be charged for meals. Mileage for use of a personal automobile is usually reimbursed at a rate established by the Internal Revenue Service. When you prepare the expense report, you should check to see that all necessary receipts are attached, that the correct amounts are given on the expense report, that the form is filled out properly, and that the total amounts are computed correctly.

**Illus. 7-5** With the amount of travel that most executives do today, the office assistant frequently needs to prepare expense reports.

**Figure 7-16** Expense Report

## ▲TriCounty Regional Planning Agency — WEEKLY EXPENSE REPORT

| | | SUNDAY | MONDAY | TUESDAY | WEDNESDAY | THURSDAY | FRIDAY | SATURDAY | TOTALS |
|---|---|---|---|---|---|---|---|---|---|
| NAME George Andrews | SAVE NO / ENDING SPEEDOMETER | | | | CHANGED DRIVER'S LISCENSE NO | | | | TR NO S |
| WEEK ENDING | SATURDAY November 19 | SUNDAY | MONDAY | TUESDAY | WEDNESDAY | THURSDAY | FRIDAY | SATURDAY | TOTALS |
| PERSONAL MOTEL OR HOTEL Bent Tree Inn | | | | | | | | | |
| CITY Chicago | | | | | | | | | |
| STATE Illinois | | | | | | | | | |
| ROOM CHARGE (ATTACH RECEIPT) | 11 | 90 00 | 90 00 | | | | | | 180 00 |
| BREAKFAST | | 5 00 | 4 00 | 5 25 | | | | | |
| LUNCH | | 8 25 | 8 50 | 8 75 | | | | | |
| DINNER | | 12 00 | 15 00 | 13 00 | | | | | 79 75 |
| TOTAL MEALS → | 12 | 25 25 | 27 50 | 27 00 | | | | | |
| OTHER PERSONAL | 13 | | | | | | | | |
| COMPANY OWNED AUTOMOBILE GAS-OIL | 14 | | | | | | | | |
| OTHER OPERATING (INCLUDE PARKING TOLLS, TAXES, AND FEES) | 15 | 8 00 | 6 00 | | | | | | 14 00 |
| PARTS AND REPAIRS | 16 | | | | | | | | |
| MISCELLANEOUS (EXPLAIN - ATTACH RECEIPT IF OVER $25.00) ENTERTAINMENT | 17 | | | | | | | | |
| OTHER TRANSPORTATION (AIR FARE CAR RENTAL) | 18 | 362 71 | | | | | | | 362 71 |
| MISC. OTHER (EXPLAIN - ATTACH RECEIPT IF OVER $25.00) | 19 | | | | | | | | |
| TOTAL FOR DAY | | 485 96 | 123 50 | 27 00 | | | | | WEEK'S EXPENSES 636 46 |

EXPLANATION OF ENTERTAINMENT AND MISCELLANEOUS

| | | |
|---|---|---|
| | INCREASE MY ADVANCE | 21 |
| | DECREASE MY ADVANCE | 22 |
| | ISSUE CHECK | 23 636 46 |

PLEASE SIGN *George Andrews*

## Statements of Financial Condition

There are two basic statements depicting the financial condition of a business; these statements are the **balance sheet** and the **income statement**. Your company may title them differently and there may be supplementary statements, but the basic concept will be the same. A company needs to know what its assets and liabilities are and whether it is making a profit. Or, if it is a nonprofit organization, such as TriCounty Regional Planning Agency, the organization must know if funds are being expended appropriately and if the organization is living within its budget.

**Balance Sheet**   The balance sheet shows the condition of the business on a certain date—how much it owns and how much it owes. In order to interpret a balance sheet you must have an understanding of the major sections of it. Notice the balance sheet that is shown in Figure 7-17. It contains three main sections—assets, liabilities, and owner's equity.

The assets of a business are the properties or economic resources owned by the business. There are two major classifications of assets—current assets and plant and equipment. Current assets consist of cash and assets that are reasonably expected to be turned into cash or be sold or consumed within a short period, usually one year. Notice in Figure 7-17 that merchandise inventory is listed under current assets. This inventory will be sold during the course of the business operations. Plant and equipment assets are relatively long-lived assets that are held for use in the production or sale of other assets or services. Notice in Figure 7-17 that land and buildings are listed under plant and equipment.

Another asset category that may be included on the balance sheet is long-term investments. Stocks, bonds, and promissory notes that will be held for more than one year appear under this classification.

Liabilities are the debts of the business. Current liabilities are debts that must be paid within a year. Long-term liabilities are debts that are not due and payable for a comparatively long period, usually more than one year. Common long-term liability items are mortgages payable, bonds payable, and notes payable.

The owner's equity, or capital, section of the balance sheet shows the interest of the owner or owners of a business in its assets. From this section you can tell if the business is owned by one person, a partnership, or a corporation. Notice in the illustration that common stock and retained earnings are listed under the owner's equity section. This business is a corporation. The investment of the stockholders (owner's equity) is shown in the common stock. The amount of past earnings that have not been distributed to the owners is shown in the retained earnings.

**Income Statement**   Another financial statement that reflects the financial picture of a business is an **income statement**. The income statement covers the activities of a business for a certain period of time. It shows the total amount of money earned and the total amount of expenses involved in earning the money. Figure 7-18 shows a typical income statement. This income statement covers a one year period. (Notice that the heading indicates the period of time covered by the statement.)

The first section of the income statement is the income section. This section shows the total amount of sales the company has made and the cost of the merchandise that was sold. The difference between these two items is the gross profit on sales. If there were no other expenses in connection with the sales, the gross profit would be the amount of net income earned by the business. However, additional expenses are incurred in the operation of a business. For example, the employees must be paid and insurance and utilities must be paid. Notice under Operating Expenses that these costs are itemized. The total amount of operating expenses is deducted from the gross profit on sales to arrive at the net income from operations. Any other income or expense is computed and the net income is obtained.

**Personal Assets, Liabilities, and Income**   Just as a business or organization must know what it has, what it owes, and how much its income is, so must an individual. Before you enrolled in school you had to know if you were going to be able to pay your tuition, buy your books, and pay your living expenses. In the process of determining what you would need and the amount of money you had to finance your needs, you may have discovered that you could not finance your education on your own. Thus, you may have applied for and received a student loan. Many students do so, and it is a good way to receive a postsecondary education if you do not have the money available from other sources. However, when you apply for and receive a loan, you accept certain responsibilities. Just as a

**Figure 7-18**  Income Statement

**GRIFFITH CORPORATION**
**Income Statement**
**For Year Ended December 31, 19--**

| | | | |
|---|---|---:|---:|
| **Sales** | | | $415,100 |
| **Cost of Goods Sold** | | | |
| Merchandise Inventory, January 1 | | $38,500 | |
| Purchases | | 294,675 | |
| Merchandise Available for Sale | | $333,175 | |
| Less Inventory, December 31 | | 51,000 | |
| Cost of Goods Sold | | | 282,175 |
| Gross Profit on Sales | | | $132,925 |
| **Operating Expenses** | | | |
| Selling Expenses | | | |
| Sales Salaries and Commissions | $28,575 | | |
| Advertising Expense | 19,300 | | |
| Miscellaneous Selling Expense | 2,500 | | |
| Total Selling Expenses | | $50,375 | |
| General Expenses | | | |
| Officers' Salaries | $23,060 | | |
| Office Salaries | 8,300 | | |
| Depreciation, Office Equipment | 1,800 | | |
| Insurance | 2,050 | | |
| Utilities | 2,790 | | |
| Total General Expenses | | 38,000 | |
| Total Operating Expenses | | | 88,375 |
| **Net Income from Operations** | | | $ 44,550 |
| **Other Expenses** | | | |
| Interest Expense | | | 5,000 |
| Net Income before Estimated Income Tax | | | $ 39,550 |
| Estimated Income Tax | | | 15,100 |
| Net Income after Income Tax | | | $ 24,450 |

---

**Figure 7-17**  Balance Sheet

**GRIFFITH CORPORATION**
**Balance Sheet**
**December 31, 19--**

**Assets**

| | | | |
|---|---:|---:|---:|
| **Current Assets** | | | |
| Cash | | $22,240 | |
| Accounts Receivable | $41,500 | | |
| Less Allowance for Bad Debts | 2,500 | 39,000 | |
| Merchandise Inventory | | 105,725 | |
| Supplies | | 4,000 | |
| Prepaid Insurance | | 2,900 | |
| Total Current Assets | | | $173,865 |
| **Plant and Equipment** | | | |
| Office Equipment | $18,000 | | |
| Less Accumulated Depreciation | 8,100 | $9,900 | |
| Factory Equipment | $276,000 | | |
| Less Accumulated Depreciation | 163,500 | 112,500 | |
| Buildings | $125,000 | | |
| Less Accumulated Depreciation | 20,000 | 105,000 | |
| Land | | 35,000 | |
| Total Plant and Equipment | | | $252,400 |
| **Total Assets** | | | $456,265 |

**Liabilities**

| | | | |
|---|---:|---:|---:|
| **Current Liabilities** | | | |
| Accounts Payable | $38,600 | | |
| Estimated Income Tax Payable | 15,100 | | |
| Salaries and Wages Payable | 1,965 | | |
| Interest Payable | 1,250 | | |
| Total Current Liabilities | | $56,915 | |
| **Long-Term Liabilities** | | | |
| Mortgage Payable | $50,000 | | |
| Notes Payable, Due December 31, 2000 | 22,500 | | |
| Total Long-Term Liabilities | | 72,500 | |
| Total Liabilities | | | $159,415 |

**Owner's Equity**

| | | | |
|---|---:|---:|---:|
| Common Stock | | $150,000 | |
| Retained Earnings | | 156,850 | |
| Total Owner's Equity | | | 306,850 |
| Total Liabilities and Owner's Equity | | | $435,265 |

business must pay back any money that it has borrowed, so must you. Before you obtain your loan you will need to consult the financial aid office of your school. This office will be able to provide you with a considerable amount of information as to what types of loans are available, what the payback interest will be, when you will need to start paying back your loan, and other necessary information about loans.

A number of students in our society are failing to pay back their loans in a timely manner. This failure has caused our federal government to set up more stringent guidelines for schools as they administer loans. A defaulted loan also has several long-term penalties for you. Here are some of them:

- Loss of future student loans and other federal and state assistance
- Negative comments to national credit bureaus that can hurt your credit rating
- Initiation of court action
- Assignment to collection agencies
- Withholding of federal tax refunds
- Loss of deferment and monthly payment options

When you accept a loan you accept certain responsibilities. Some of these responsibilities are listed below.

- Use the loan for educational purposes.
- Provide proper documentation to the lender when requesting a deferment.
- Contact your lender upon graduation or within 90 days of the end of your grace period to obtain a repayment schedule.
- Repay your loan according to the repayment schedule.
- Notify your lender promptly and in writing if you do not enroll in school during the period for which your loan was intended. Notify your lender if you withdraw from school or attend classes on less than a half-time basis, transfer to another school, or if you change your name, address, or phone number.

## MANUSCRIPT AND STATISTICAL COPY PROOFREADING

It is always important that you proofread well. However, when you are working with both the written word and numerical copy it is doubly important that you proofread well. As you have learned, you can use a spell-checker on manuscript copy. However, you cannot use a spell-checker on statistical copy, since the computer does not know if you have put in the correct figures. In Chapter 3 you were given some proofreading tips for manuscript copy and you also learned the commonly used proofreader's marks. You may need to review those tips. To help you in proofreading statistical copy, study and practice the techniques given here.

- Proofread with another person. Have the person read the numbers from the source document while you check the computer screen or the printed copy.
- For numbers in a column, read down the column rather than across the page. If the table includes totals, the amounts in each column should be added and the totals verified. If you are using spreadsheet software, this step is not necessary since the computer will add the totals automatically. Your task with spreadsheet software is to be certain that you have entered the correct figures for calculation.
- Once the document has been finished, file the draft document along with the final document so that any questions can be answered as to what the original figures were.
- If you are not using spreadsheet software and there are computations in the copy, use a calculator to check the numbers. Run a tape of the numerical data. For example, if you are going to be adding several columns, run a tape of the addition. When you finish the tape, check the tape against the numbers on the original copy.
- In checking a tape, place the tape as close to the copy as possible. Check the figure on the original copy and then check the figure on the tape to see that it corresponds. Place a check mark by each number on the tape when its accuracy has been verified. Another method is to ask another person to read you the figures from the tape as you check the original document.
- If you have extremely large figures it is a good idea to read them in groups. For example, if the figure is 14,530,203, read 14  530  203.

## OFFICE DOCUMENT DIVERSITY

As you have discovered from the variety of office documents presented in this chapter, the office assistant is involved in handling many different types of documents. The complexity of these documents varies greatly. Some documents are relatively easy to prepare; others are quite involved and complex. The knowledge and skills that you have acquired in this chapter will help you to handle the various documents that you are given effectively and with speed and accuracy.

## CHAPTER SUMMARY

The following review will help you remember the important points of this chapter.

1. Numerous business reports are prepared in offices. These reports may be informal, containing two or three pages; or they may be formal, containing a table of contents, the body (footnotes or endnotes), appendices, and a bibliography.

2. The office assistant may be called upon to do research and should be familiar with the basic reference sources, some of which are almanacs and yearbooks, government publications, and reference guides. Computer networks are also available that allow you to do research through a microcomputer. Information such as stock quotes, periodical indexes, and reference works containing specialized scientific, legal, and economic information is available.

3. An unbound business report is prepared with top, side, and bottom margins of one inch except for the first page which begins two inches from the top. If the report is leftbound, an additional one half inch is required for the binding.

4. Interoffice memorandums are prepared frequently by the office assistant and are used to send written information to other departments within the same company.

5. A check is an order in writing that directs the bank to pay cash from the depositor's account. When writing a check, the check stub should be filled out first. The amount should be written twice on the check. The figures should be placed as close as possible to the printed dollar sign so that no additional figures can be inserted. When writing the amount of the check in words, the words should begin as far to the left as possible in the space provided. No erasures or changes should be made on the check.

6. There are three types of endorsements—a blank endorsement, a full endorsement, and a restrictive endorsement. A blank endorsement requires only the signature of the payee. A full endorsement transfers ownership to a definite person or firm to whose order the instrument is made payable. A restrictive endorsement transfers the ownership for a specific purpose.

7. Balancing a bank statement with a checkbook balance is called reconciling the bank statement. Reconciliation should occur after the bank statement is received, usually monthly.

8. Some of the special services offered by a bank include cashier's check, certified checks, bank money orders, traveler's checks, and safe-deposit boxes.

9. Electronic technology has revolutionized the banking industry, making possible the automatic transfer of funds without the use of checks or other paper documents traditionally needed to complete a financial transaction. Some of the types of electronic fund transfers include automatic bill payment, point-of-sale transfer, automated teller machines, and direct payroll depositing.

10. All businesses keep payroll records. These records involve federal income tax deductions, social security, unemployment compensation tax, and requirements due to the Fair Labor Standards Act. The Fair Labor Standards Act requires that businesses engaged in interstate commerce keep a record of hours worked for all hourly employees and pay a minimum hourly wage plus time-and-a-half for overtime work.

11. The office assistant is responsible for preparing an expense report when an executive returns from a trip. Receipts must be obtained and the total amount of money spent on the trip must be recorded.

12. There are two basic statements that depict the financial condition of a business. These statements are the balance sheet and income statement. The balance sheet shows how much a business owns and how much it owes. An income statement gives the net income of a company for a particular period of time.

13. Just as it is important that a business knows what it has and what it owes, it is also important for an individual to know this information. As a student, you may have borrowed

money through some type of loan program to pay your tuition and other school expenses. Your responsibility here is to know when you will be expected to pay back the loan and make your loan payments in a timely manner. A defaulted loan can have several long-term disadvantages for you, including a negative credit rating and initiation of court action against you.

14. As you prepare manuscript and statistical copy, it is important that you proofread well. When proofreading statistical copy, it is a good idea to proofread with someone else. Another suggestion is to run calculator tapes on columns of addition, subtraction, and so forth and to proofread long numbers in groups.

## TERMINOLOGY REVIEW

The following terms were introduced in this chapter. To help you understand them, definitions are given below.

1. **Balance sheet** *(page 186)* The balance sheet is a financial statement of a business or individual, showing the condition of the business or individual on a certain date—how much is owned and how much is owed.

2. **Bank money order** *(page 181)* A bank money order is sold by the bank and states that a certain amount of money is to be paid to the person named in the money order. A bank money order is normally cashable at any bank in the United States or abroad, is negotiable, and can be transferred by endorsement.

3. **Blank endorsement** *(page 178)* This endorsement requires only the signature of the payee or the holder of the check.

4. **Cashier's check** *(page 180)* A check issued by a bank and drawn on the bank's own funds is called a cashier's check.

5. **Certified check** *(page 181)* A check that is guaranteed by the bank on which it is drawn is called a certified check.

6. **Check** *(page 177)* A check is an order in writing directing the bank to pay cash from the drawer's account to the payee.

7. **Check register** *(page 178)* A check register is a separate form for recording the checks that have been written.

8. **Check truncation** *(page 180)* Check truncation is a process whereby the bank keeps the check rather than returning it to the drawer at the end of the month. The monthly statement lists the number of the check and the amount of the check but no check is sent back to the drawer.

9. **Deposit slip** *(page 178)* A deposit slip is a special form used by the bank to record a deposit of money to an account.

10. **Direct deposit** *(page 177)* A company may deposit money directly into the bank account of the employee from the company's bank account for payroll purposes; in such a case, a check is never written.

11. **Drawer** *(page 177)* The individual or company who orders the bank to pay cash is the drawer.

12. **Electronic fund transfer** *(page 182)* The transfer of money from one account to another without the use of checks or the services of a bank teller is referred to as electronic fund transfer.

13. **Endorsement** *(page 178)* A written signature by the holder of the check for the purpose of transferring ownership is known as an endorsement.

14. **Full endorsement** *(page 178)* A full endorsement transfers ownership of the check to a definite person or firm to whose order the check is made payable.

15. **Income statement** *(page 186)* The income statement is a financial statement that reflects the financial picture of a business for a certain period of time. It shows the total amount of money earned and the total amount of the expenses involved in earning the money.

16. **Outstanding check** *(page 180)* A check that has been issued but neither cashed by the bank nor deducted from the depositor's account is known as an outstanding check.

17. **Payee** *(page 177)* The individual or company to whom a check is made payable is the payee.

18. **Reconciling the bank statement** *(page 180)* Proving the accuracy of the bank statement and the check register is called reconciling the bank statement.

19. **Restrictive endorsement** *(page 178)* A restrictive endorsement transfers the ownership of a check for a specific purpose.

20. **Safe-deposit box** *(page 181)* Safe-deposit boxes are available at banks for the convenience of individuals and businesses wishing to store articles of value or important papers for safekeeping.

21. **Stub** *(page 178)* A stub is a short leaf of paper attached to the spine of the checkbook.
22. **Traveler's check** *(page 181)* Traveler's checks are checks sold in various denominations, purchased from banks or other agencies, and used by travelers as a safer method of paying for purchases than bills or coins. Identification is required when cashing a traveler's check.
23. **Voucher check** *(page 177)* A voucher check is a special type of check with a detachable portion on which is written the check's purpose.

## DISCUSSION ITEMS

To demonstrate your understanding of the information in this chapter, respond to the following items.

1. List and explain four reference sources.
2. Explain the differences between a footnote, an endnote, and a textual citation.
3. Explain the procedures for reconciling a bank statement.
4. List and explain three types of special services that a bank offers.
5. Define EFT and explain how it is used.
6. Explain the advantages of a restrictive endorsement.
7. What is the Fair Labor Standards Act and how does it affect business?
8. Explain the differences between a balance sheet and an income statement.

## CASE STUDY

Martin Klug, an employee in the payroll department, has been ill for a week. You have been asked to help with the work of that department during his absence. During this time you have seen the payroll records for several of the executives who work for TriCounty.

On your coffee break, one of your best friends, Monica Helms, asks you if you have discovered what any of the executives make. You tell her that you have. She then asks you to tell her what one of the top executives makes. You have been a friend of Monica's for a long time, and you trust her. You definitely feel that if you give Monica the information she will not repeat it to anyone else in the firm. What should you do?

## OFFICE APPLICATIONS

### Office Application 7-1 (*Objectives 1 and 2*)

Research the latest developments in electronic banking (for example, electronic fund transfers). Review at least two current sources (within the last year). Write your findings in report format, listing your reference sources. Entitle the report "Electronic Banking." Use the appropriate side headings. Your report should be approximately three typewritten pages. Print two copies of your report. Turn one copy in to your instructor and place the other copy in your "to be filed" folder.

### Office Application 7-2 (*Objectives 1 and 2*)

Mr. Andrews has been asked to do a presentation at the next AMS (Administrative Management Society) meeting on effective leadership characteristics. He asks that you do some research on the topic. In doing the research, use at least three sources. Prepare a draft of your findings for his review, listing your reference sources. Use quadruple spacing in keying the draft so that he will have ample space to write any comments.

### Office Application 7-3 (*Objective 2*)

Using reference sources from the library, look up the following information. Record your answers, giving the reference sources you used.

1. Who were the U.S. senators from your state in 1991?
2. What was the population of New York state in 1992?
3. What is the average education of individuals in the U.S. today?
4. List two jobs where the employment possibilities for the next five years are expected to increase.
5. Find two articles dealing with business ethics, and prepare an abstract of these two articles.

### Office Application 7-4 (*Objective 3*)

Mr. Andrews gave you three interoffice memorandums to key yesterday. You did so, and today he gave them back to you with changes to be made.

*With a template disk:* The three interoffice memorandums are stored on template OA7-4. Retrieve the documents and make the necessary changes which are shown on pages 195-196 of your text.

*Without a template disk:* Key the three interoffice memorandums given on pages 195-196 of your text; make all the necessary corrections.

### Office Application 7-5 (*Objective 3*)

Mr. Andrews asks that you compose an interoffice memorandum to the four managers informing them of a meeting to be held on November 12 at 2:00 p.m. in Conference Room C. The meeting will last approximately two hours; the topic will be strategic directions for the next five years. Compose and prepare the memorandum, making the appropriate number of copies.

### Office Application 7-6 (*Objective 4*)

Mr. Andrews is the treasurer of the local AMS chapter. He asks that you prepare voucher checks, using the information given below and the checks provided on pages 197-198. Begin numbering the voucher checks with 100 under the Voucher No. heading.

| | |
|---|---|
| December 2 | Pay Maynard Office Company, 3781 Beech Street, Arlington, TX 76008, for office supplies, Invoice 34890 for $159.34. |
| December 4 | Pay John T. Snyder & Sons, 1872 Harrison Road, Arlington, TX 76006, for computer supplies, Invoice 7891 for $58.95. |
| December 5 | Pay Marriott Corporation, 345 Valley View Avenue, Arlington, TX 76006, for banquet charges, Invoice 7720 for $345.75. |

**Office Application 7-7 (*Objective 5*)**

On a separate sheet of paper, identify the types of endorsements shown on page 199. Explain what type of endorsement you would use in each of the following situations:

1. TriCounty received a check from J. T. McElroy Corporation for transportation consulting. You plan to send the check to the bank through the mail. What type of endorsement should you use?

2. You are depositing your payroll check. You are at the bank and are personally handing the check to the bank teller. What type of endorsement should you use?

**Office Application 7-8 (*Objective 6*)**

Using the forms on pages 201-202, prepare a deposit slip for the following deposits for AMS, Midcities Chapter. Page 201 shows the front of the deposit slip and page 202 shows the back.

1. The following deposit is made on December 4.

    | | |
    |---|---|
    | Currency | $150.00 |
    | Coin | 15.75 |
    | Checks: | |
    | John McIlvain, 21-52 | $125.00 |
    | Judy Terry, 84-118 | 125.00 |
    | Roger Meyer, 19-130 | 125.00 |
    | Billy Smith, 18-451 | 100.00 |

    (The number after the name is the ABA transit number)

2. The following deposit is made on December 8.

    | | |
    |---|---|
    | Currency | $225.00 |
    | Coin | 10.25 |
    | Checks: | |
    | LaVerne MacTavish, 32-103 | 125.00 |
    | Carl Thomas, 73-633 | 125.00 |

**Office Application 7-9 (*Objective 7*)**

On page 203 is a statement from the bank for the checking account of the Midcities Chapter of AMS for the month of December. After verifying the canceled checks with your check stubs, you find that checks 48 ($15) and 49 ($18.75) are outstanding. In the space below the bank statement, reconcile the bank balance with the check stub balance of $891.78. Take into account the service charge and interest on the statement.

**Office Application 7-10 (*Objective 8*)**

After a business trip, Mr. Andrews gave you his receipts for the week ending Saturday December 13 (see page 205). In addition to these receipts, Mr. Andrews spent the following amounts. Prepare an expense report using the form on page 206.

| | |
|---|---|
| Dinner, December 7 | $15.50 |
| Breakfast, December 8 | 8.50 |

Lunch, December 8 .........................................7.75
Dinner, December 8 ......................................21.50
Breakfast, December 9 ..................................5.25
Lunch, December 9 .........................................8.50
Dinner, December 9 ......................................14.50
Breakfast, December 10 ................................5.75
Lunch, December 10 .......................................9.50
Dinner, December 10 ....................................18.75
Breakfast, December 11 ................................5.25
Lunch, December 11 .....................................10.50
Dinner, December 11 ....................................12.75
Breakfast, December 12 ................................5.25
Lunch, December 12 .......................................8.75
Air Fare .....................................................550.75
Taxi Service, December 7 ............................12.00
Taxi Service, December 12 ...........................14.00

## Office Application 7-11 (*Objectives 9 and 10*)

Mr. Andrews gives you the Departmental Expenditures for Fiscal Years 1991-1992 and 1992-93 (see page 207) and asks that you project the expenditures for each department for the next two years using an 8 percent increase for Transportation and Health, a 6 percent increase for Aging, and a 4 percent increase for Data Services for each year. Use a calculator in doing the math; attach your tape to the document. The heading for the document will be as follows:

TRICOUNTY REGIONAL PLANNING AGENCY
DEPARTMENTAL EXPENDITURES AND PROJECTED EXPENDITURES

The column heading for the projected expenditures will be:

Projected Expenditures
(years of projections)

Key the report and print two copies; hand in one to your instructor and place the second copy in your "to be filed" folder.

INTEROFFICE MEMORANDUM

TO:        Rebecca Gonzales

FROM:      George Andrews

SUBJECT:   Transportation Study

DATE:      Current date

Last week I discussed with you the need to do a transportation
study in Hunt County.

Please let me know *by next Wednesday (put in mo. & date)* ~~immediately~~ if you have made contact with the
appropriate individuals and when the projected beginning and
completion date of the study will be.

*Thanks for your help here.*

---

INTEROFFICE MEMORANDUM

TO:        Heidi Wenrick

FROM:      George Andrews

SUBJECT:   Smoking Cessation Sessions

DATE:      Current date

Since we have implemented a no-smoking policy throughout the
organization, it is important that we begin smoking cessation
sessions for our employees.

Please have a plan to me by next Monday that includes the number
and type of sessions which will be conducted. *The plan should
include the projected budget for the sessions. Also, add this activity to your*
Thanks for your attention to this important matter. *work plan for
the year.*

INTEROFFICE MEMORANDUM

TO:        Travis Ueoka

FROM:      ~~Patsy Fulton~~ *George Andrews*

SUBJECT:   Aging Activities

DATE:      Current date

I recently read an article about the importance of exercise for senior citizens.  Are we providing some type of exercise activities in Hunt, Collin, and Kaufman counties?  If so, what type of activities are we providing?  ~~If not, let's talk~~

Please give my office a call *on Monday* to set up a time so that we might discuss what is happening in this area. *Donna can check my calendar and give you a date. Plan to spend approximately an hour with me.*

**No. 110**

AMS, Midcities Chapter
813 Marsh Lane
Grand Prairie, TX 75050-1604

32-56
3110

_____ 19 _____

PAY TO THE
ORDER OF _____ $ _____
(For Classroom Use Only)

_____ DOLLARS

**BANK OF THE SOUTH**
Grand Prairie, TX 75050-1135

AMS, Midcities Chapter

⑆3110099901⑆ 130⑆456⑆7⑈

_____

| INVOICE NUMBER | NET AMOUNT | DESCRIPTION |
|---|---|---|
| | | |
| | | |

| DATE | VOUCHER NO. | CHECK NUMBER | AMS , Midcities Chapter<br>Grand Prairie, TX |
|---|---|---|---|
| | | | |

DETACH AND RETAIN THIS STATEMENT - IF NOT CORRECT, PLEASE NOTIFY US PROMPTLY.

---

**No. 111**

AMS, Midcities Chapter
813 Marsh Lane
Grand Prairie, TX 75050-1604

32-56
3110

_____ 19 _____

PAY TO THE
ORDER OF _____ $ _____
(For Classroom Use Only)

_____ DOLLARS

**BANK OF THE SOUTH**
Grand Prairie, TX 75050-1135

AMS, Midcities Chapter

⑆3110099901⑆ 130⑆456⑆7⑈

_____

| INVOICE NUMBER | NET AMOUNT | DESCRIPTION |
|---|---|---|
| | | |
| | | |

| DATE | VOUCHER NO. | CHECK NUMBER | AMS , Midcities Chapter<br>Grand Prairie, TX |
|---|---|---|---|
| | | | |

DETACH AND RETAIN THIS STATEMENT - IF NOT CORRECT, PLEASE NOTIFY US PROMPTLY.

No. 112

32-56
3110

**AMS, Midcities Chapter**
**813 Marsh Lane**
**Grand Prairie, TX  75050-1604**

_____ 19 _____

PAY TO THE
ORDER OF _____ $ _____
(For Classroom Use Only)

_____ DOLLARS

**BANK OF THE SOUTH**
Grand Prairie, TX  75050-1135

**AMS, Midcities Chapter**

⑈311009990⑈   130⑈456⑈7⑈

_____

| INVOICE NUMBER | NET AMOUNT | DESCRIPTION |
|---|---|---|
|  |  |  |
| DATE | VOUCHER NO. | CHECK NUMBER | AMS , Midcities Chapter<br>Grand Prairie, TX |

DETACH AND RETAIN THIS STATEMENT - IF NOT CORRECT, PLEASE NOTIFY US PROMPTLY.

No. 113

32-56
3110

**AMS, Midcities Chapter**
**813 Marsh Lane**
**Grand Prairie, TX  75050-1604**

_____ 19 _____

PAY TO THE
ORDER OF _____ $ _____
(For Classroom Use Only)

_____ DOLLARS

**BANK OF THE SOUTH**
Grand Prairie, TX  75050-1135

**AMS, Midcities Chapter**

⑈311009990⑈   130⑈456⑈7⑈

_____

| INVOICE NUMBER | NET AMOUNT | DESCRIPTION |
|---|---|---|
|  |  |  |
| DATE | VOUCHER NO. | CHECK NUMBER | AMS , Midcities Chapter<br>Grand Prairie, TX |

DETACH AND RETAIN THIS STATEMENT - IF NOT CORRECT, PLEASE NOTIFY US PROMPTLY.

Voucher Checks For Use in Office Application 7-6

① Bonita Melrose

Pay to the order of
② Jack Yesco
Bonita Melrose

For deposit only
③ Bonita Melrose

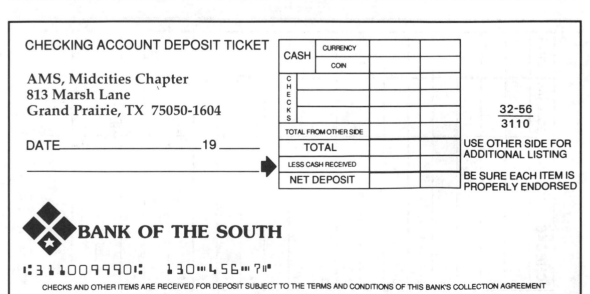

CHECKING ACCOUNT DEPOSIT TICKET

AMS, Midcities Chapter
813 Marsh Lane
Grand Prairie, TX 75050-1604

DATE_____19_____

| CASH | CURRENCY | | |
| | COIN | | |
| C H E C K S | | | |
| | | | |
| | | | |
| TOTAL FROM OTHER SIDE | | |
| TOTAL | | |
| LESS CASH RECEIVED | | |
| NET DEPOSIT | | |

32-56
3110

USE OTHER SIDE FOR
ADDITIONAL LISTING

BE SURE EACH ITEM IS
PROPERLY ENDORSED

◆ BANK OF THE SOUTH

⑆3110099⑉0⑆ 130⑈456⑈7⑆

CHECKS AND OTHER ITEMS ARE RECEIVED FOR DEPOSIT SUBJECT TO THE TERMS AND CONDITIONS OF THIS BANK'S COLLECTION AGREEMENT

---

CHECKING ACCOUNT DEPOSIT TICKET

AMS, Midcities Chapter
813 Marsh Lane
Grand Prairie, TX 75050-1604

DATE_____19_____

| CASH | CURRENCY | | |
| | COIN | | |
| C H E C K S | | | |
| | | | |
| | | | |
| TOTAL FROM OTHER SIDE | | |
| TOTAL | | |
| LESS CASH RECEIVED | | |
| NET DEPOSIT | | |

32-56
3110

USE OTHER SIDE FOR
ADDITIONAL LISTING

BE SURE EACH ITEM IS
PROPERLY ENDORSED

◆ BANK OF THE SOUTH

⑆3110099⑉0⑆ 130⑈456⑈7⑆

CHECKS AND OTHER ITEMS ARE RECEIVED FOR DEPOSIT SUBJECT TO THE TERMS AND CONDITIONS OF THIS BANK'S COLLECTION AGREEMENT

---

CHECKING ACCOUNT DEPOSIT TICKET

AMS, Midcities Chapter
813 Marsh Lane
Grand Prairie, TX 75050-1604

DATE_____19_____

| CASH | CURRENCY | | |
| | COIN | | |
| C H E C K S | | | |
| | | | |
| | | | |
| TOTAL FROM OTHER SIDE | | |
| TOTAL | | |
| LESS CASH RECEIVED | | |
| NET DEPOSIT | | |

32-56
3110

USE OTHER SIDE FOR
ADDITIONAL LISTING

BE SURE EACH ITEM IS
PROPERLY ENDORSED

◆ BANK OF THE SOUTH

⑆3110099⑉0⑆ 130⑈456⑈7⑆

CHECKS AND OTHER ITEMS ARE RECEIVED FOR DEPOSIT SUBJECT TO THE TERMS AND CONDITIONS OF THIS BANK'S COLLECTION AGREEMENT

Deposit Slip For Use in Office Application 7-8

## Slip 1

| CHECKS LIST SINGLY | DOLLARS | CENTS |
|---|---|---|
| 1 | | |
| 2 | | |
| 3 | | |
| 4 | | |
| 5 | | |
| 6 | | |
| 7 | | |
| 8 | | |
| 9 | | |
| 10 | | |
| 11 | | |
| 12 | | |
| 13 | | |
| 14 | | |
| 15 | | |
| 16 | | |
| 17 | | |
| 18 | | |
| 19 | | |
| TOTAL | | |

ENTER TOTAL ON THE FRONT OF THIS TICKET

## Slip 2

| CHECKS LIST SINGLY | DOLLARS | CENTS |
|---|---|---|
| 1 | | |
| 2 | | |
| 3 | | |
| 4 | | |
| 5 | | |
| 6 | | |
| 7 | | |
| 8 | | |
| 9 | | |
| 10 | | |
| 11 | | |
| 12 | | |
| 13 | | |
| 14 | | |
| 15 | | |
| 16 | | |
| 17 | | |
| 18 | | |
| 19 | | |
| TOTAL | | |

ENTER TOTAL ON THE FRONT OF THIS TICKET

## Slip 3

| CHECKS LIST SINGLY | DOLLARS | CENTS |
|---|---|---|
| 1 | | |
| 2 | | |
| 3 | | |
| 4 | | |
| 5 | | |
| 6 | | |
| 7 | | |
| 8 | | |
| 9 | | |
| 10 | | |
| 11 | | |
| 12 | | |
| 13 | | |
| 14 | | |
| 15 | | |
| 16 | | |
| 17 | | |
| 18 | | |
| 19 | | |
| TOTAL | | |

ENTER TOTAL ON THE FRONT OF THIS TICKET

**BANK OF THE SOUTH**
Grand Prairie, TX 75050-1135

Checking Account Statement

ACCT. 203-924-4
DATE 12/1/--
PAGE 1

AMS, Midcities Chapter
813 Marsh Lane
Grand Prairie, TX 75050-1604

| BALANCE FORWARD | NO. OF CHECKS | TOTAL CHECK AMOUNT | NO. OF DEP. | TOTAL DEPOSIT AMOUNT | INTEREST | SERVICE CHARGE | BALANCE THIS STATEMENT |
|---|---|---|---|---|---|---|---|
| 750 53 | 8 | 292 00 | 1 | 467 00 | 5 25 | 4 20 | 926 58 |

| CHECKS AND OTHER DEBITS | | DEPOSITS AND OTHER CREDITS | DATE | BALANCE |
|---|---|---|---|---|
| 4 2 | 25.00 | 467.00 | 11/05 | 1,192.53 |
| 4 3 | 50.00 | | 11/07 | 1,142.53 |
| 4 4 | 75.00 | | 11/15 | 1,067.53 |
| 4 5 | 100.00 | | 11/16 | 967.53 |
| 4 6 | 12.00 | | 11/18 | 955.53 |
| 4 7 | 5.00 | | 11/22 | 950.53 |
| 5 0 | 10.00 | | 11/25 | 940.53 |
| 5 1 | 15.00   4.20SC | 5.25INT | 11/31 | 926.58 |

**PLEASE EXAMINE AT ONCE.**
IF NO ERRORS ARE REPORTED
WITHIN 10 DAYS, THE ACCOUNT WILL
BE CONSIDERED CORRECT.
**PLEASE ADVISE US**
IN WRITING OF ANY CHANGE
IN YOUR ADDRESS.

**KEYS TO SYMBOLS**

AD - AUTOMATIC DEPOSIT
AP - AUTOMATIC PAYMENT
AR - AUTOMATIC REVERSAL
CB - CHARGE BACK
CC - CERTIFIED CHECK
CM - CREDIT MEMO
CO - CHARGE OFF

DM - DEBIT MEMO
EC - ERROR CORRECTED
INT - INTEREST
OD - OVERDRAWN
RC - RETURN CHECK CHG
RT - RETURN ITEM
SC - SERVICE CHARGE

Room No. _210_

Customer _George Andrews_

| Date | Charges |
|------|---------|
| 12/10 | $90.00 |
| 12/11 | $90.00 |
| TOTAL | $180.00 |

Paid _One hundred eighty 00/100_ _____ Dollars

Cash ☒  Check ☐  Credit card ☐  Other ☐

**MAXWELL HOTEL**
**555-8900**
**18245**

_Jessica Capps_
Clerk

---

Room _311_

**Manhattan Manor**
**New York • 555-6200**

Customer _George Andrews_

| Date | Charges | Balance |
|------|---------|---------|
| 12-7 | $105.00 | |
| 12-8 | $105.00 | |
| 12-9 | $105.00 | $315 |

_R. H. Goldford_
**Signed**

---

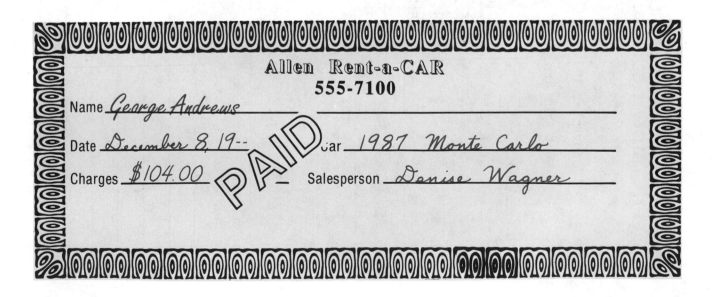

**Allen Rent-a-CAR**
**555-7100**

Name _George Andrews_

Date _December 8, 19--_  Car _1987 Monte Carlo_

Charges _$104.00_  Salesperson _Denise Wagner_

PAID

# ▲ TriCounty Regional Planning Agency

**NAME** George Andrews

**WEEK ENDING** SATURDAY November 19

**PERSONAL**
**MOTEL OR HOTEL** Bent Tree Inn
**CITY** Chicago
**STATE** Illinois

SAVE NO. ENDING SPEEDOMETER — CHANGED DRIVER'S LISCENSE NO — TR NO. S

| | | SUNDAY | MONDAY | TUESDAY | WEDNESDAY | THURSDAY | FRIDAY | SATURDAY | TOTALS |
|---|---|---|---|---|---|---|---|---|---|
| 11 | ROOM CHARGE (ATTACH RECEIPT) | 90 00 | 90 00 | | | | | | 180 00 |
| | BREAKFAST | 5 00 | 4 00 | 5 25 | | | | | |
| | LUNCH | 8 25 | 8 50 | 8 75 | | | | | |
| | DINNER | 12 00 | 15 00 | 13 00 | | | | | |
| 12 | TOTAL MEALS | 25 25 | 27 50 | 27 00 | | | | | 79 75 |
| 13 | OTHER PERSONAL | | | | | | | | |
| 14 | COMPANY OWNED AUTOMOBILE — GAS-OIL | | | | | | | | |
| 15 | OTHER OPERATING (INCLUDE PARKING, TOLLS, TAXES, AND FEES) | 8 00 | 6 00 | | | | | | 14 00 |
| 16 | PARTS AND REPAIRS | | | | | | | | |
| 17 | MISCELLANEOUS ENTERTAINMENT (EXPLAIN - ATTACH RECEIPT IF OVER $25.00) | | | | | | | | |
| 18 | OTHER TRANSPORTATION (AIR FARE, CAR RENTAL) | 362 71 | | | | | | | 362 71 |
| 19 | MISC. OTHER (EXPLAIN - ATTACH RECEIPT IF OVER $25.00) | | | | | | | | |
| | **TOTAL FOR DAY** | 485 96 | 123 50 | 27 00 | | | | | 636 46 |

EXPLANATION OF ENTERTAINMENT AND MISCELLANEOUS

WEEK'S EXPENSES 636 46

| | | |
|---|---|---|
| 21 | INCREASE MY ADVANCE | |
| 22 | DECREASE MY ADVANCE | |
| 23 | ISSUE CHECK | 636 46 |

PLEASE SIGN *George Andrews*

TRI-COUNTY REGIONAL PLANNING AGENCY
DEPARTMENTAL EXPENDITURES
FISCAL YEARS 1991-92 AND 1992-93
(Presented in 000's)

| Department | Fiscal Year 1991-92 Expenditures | Fiscal Year 1992-93 Expenditures |
|---|---|---|
| Transportation | $8,700 | $9,500 |
| Data Services | 796 | 876 |
| Health | 1,936 | 2,229 |
| Aging | 2,500 | 3,780 |
| Total Expenditures | $13,932 | $16,385 |

# 8 Telephone Procedures

Ever since Alexander Graham Bell made his first telephone call to Thomas Watson in 1876 the telephone has grown to be one of our most important means of communication. Studies have shown that communicating with others is necessary in 90 percent of all office jobs; and, much of that communication takes place over the telephone. Verbal contact within the office and with business customers is so important that the executive often has a telephone in his or her car and utilizes the telephones now available on planes. It is easy to understand why the telephone plays such an important role; it is a fast, easy way to transmit information over long or short distances. And, although we have many other methods of communication that are fast and easy (such as the facsimile machine that you learned about in Chapter 5), the telephone will remain an important communication element. Why? In addition to being fast and easy, the telephone adds a personal touch. Since you are able to hear the other person's voice you can detect sincerity, happiness, and even anger through the tone of voice used. In a world in which high technology is used extensively, the telephone allows for an added dimension of humanness to communication.

In this chapter you will learn how to use the telephone effectively. You will also learn about various types of telephone systems and special types of telephone equipment and features.

## GENERAL OBJECTIVES

*Your general objectives for this chapter are to*
1. **Develop and use proper telephone techniques.**
2. **Use a telephone directory correctly.**
3. **Develop an understanding of the types of telephone systems, equipment, and features available.**

## TELEPHONE TECHNIQUES

Since the telephone is an essential part of our day-to-day existence, there is no doubt you have used the telephone since you were very young. You may be thinking, "Why should I study effective telephone techniques; I already know how to use the telephone?" But, chances are you do make errors when using the telephone. And, you probably have been treated rudely or unprofessionally over the telephone a number of times. The mistakes people make over the telephone are numerous. What are they? Here are some examples.

People sometimes forget, when they are using the telephone, that the person on the other end of the line is a human being. Somehow it is easier to be rude when you cannot see the person. Our tone of voice over the telephone often depicts anger, irritation, or frustration. We sometimes ignore the telephone. Have you ever called an office and had the telephone ring approximately ten times before someone answered it? We sometimes put people on "hold" and leave them there for an inordinately long period of time without even asking if they wish to be placed on hold. We sometimes answer the phone while eating and the person on the other end of the line gets a garbled and sometimes unintelligible response. These are merely a few of the mistakes we make; you can no doubt add to this list of unpleasant telephone experiences.

As an office assistant it is essential that you represent your company well over the telephone. A client or customer may be gained or lost by the manner in which you represent your company when you answer the telephone. Follow the suggestions given in the following sections for being more effective over the telephone.

## Keep a Smile in Your Voice

When you have customers or visitors in your office, a cheerful smile, a cup of coffee, and a magazine will keep the in-person callers happy, even when you have to keep them waiting. However, these services cannot be provided over the telephone. Thus, you must rely on your voice and your manner to make the voice-to-voice contact as pleasant as the face-to-face contact.

A voice that makes the caller feel as if a smile is coming through the receiver is a winning one. But how do you develop such a smile in your voice? One way is to smile as you pick up the telephone receiver. If you are smiling, it is much easier to project a smile in your voice. Treat the voice on the other end of the line as you would treat a person who is standing in front of you. Let the individual know that you are concerned. Maintain a caring attitude. Never answer the phone in a voice that is curt or rude. Do not speak in a monotone. Be expressive, much as you would when talking with someone face-to-face.

**Illus. 8-1**  A voice that makes the caller feel as if a smile is coming through the receiver is a winning one.

## Be Natural and Considerate

Be yourself. Don't adopt an affected tone of voice over the telephone. The person who tries to impress usually appears insincere. Use a vocabulary and a tone of voice that expresses your best natural self.

Let the caller know that you want to help. When it is necessary to leave the phone to get information ask, "Will you please wait, or may I call you back?" If the caller decides to wait, then thank the caller for waiting upon returning to the telephone.

People always appreciate courtesy. Use the words *thank you* and *you're welcome* often. Such amenities let the caller know that you care.

When the telephone rings, answer it promptly—on the first or second ring if possible. If you wait too long to answer the call you may lose a valuable caller.

## Be Attentive and Discreet; Avoid Slang

Listen politely to what the other person says. Don't interrupt. If the caller is unhappy about some situation, allow the caller to explain why. Most of a person's anger can be vented in telling the story. Therefore, it becomes easier to handle an unhappy person after you have listened to his or her problem. Use good listening skills. Listen for facts and for feelings. Be patient. Don't evaluate. Try to understand the words that the speaker uses, and act on what the speaker says.

Be discreet if your employer is unavailable. Carefully explain why your employer cannot answer the telephone. You may say, "Mr. Andrews is away from his office now; I expect him back in approximately an hour. May I have him call you when he returns?" Never say, "He's not in yet" (at 10:00 a.m.); "He's gone for the day" (at 3:00 p.m.); or "He's playing golf" (at any time during the day). A good rule to remember is: *Be helpful, but not specific.*

It is neither businesslike nor in good taste to use slang.

| Avoid | Say |
|---|---|
| Yeah | Certainly or yes |
| Uh-huh | Of course |
| Bye-bye | Goodbye |
| Huh? | I did not understand *or* would you please repeat that? |
| OK | Yes |

## Identify Yourself

If you work in a large company, chances are that the first person to answer the telephone will be a receptionist. He or she will probably identify the company. The caller will then ask for a specific person or department. As an office assistant in Mr. Andrews' office, you might answer, "Mr. Andrews' office, Rebecca Martinez." Other possible ways to answer the phone are with the company name or with the company name and your name.

## Take Messages Courteously

If you are answering the telephone for someone who is out of the office or for someone who cannot answer at the time, offer your assistance. Say, "Mr. Andrews is out of the office. May I take a message or have him call you when he returns?" Then, make a note of the message for Mr. Andrews. Be certain that you get the information correct. Repeat the information to the caller (such as the phone number, name, and date or time) to be sure that you have accurately received the message.

Mark all appropriate boxes on the telephone message pad. For example, if the caller requests that your employer return the call, the "please call" box should be checked. If the message is urgent, the "urgent" box should be checked. A telephone message form is shown in Figure 8-1.

**Figure 8-1** Telephone Message Form

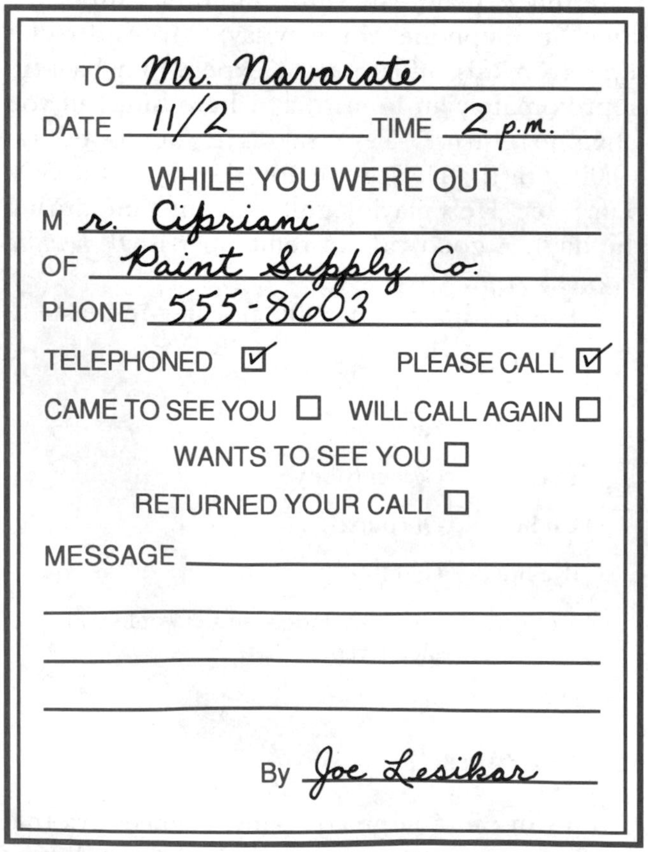

TO _Mr. Navarate_
DATE _11/2_ TIME _2 p.m._
**WHILE YOU WERE OUT**
M _r. Cipriani_
OF _Paint Supply Co._
PHONE _555-8603_
TELEPHONED ☑     PLEASE CALL ☑
CAME TO SEE YOU ☐   WILL CALL AGAIN ☐
WANTS TO SEE YOU ☐
RETURNED YOUR CALL ☐
MESSAGE _____
_____
_____
_____
By _Joe Lesikar_

## Transfer Calls Carefully

It is frequently necessary to transfer a call to another extension. Before you transfer a call, explain to the caller why you must transfer the call.

Make sure the caller is willing to be transferred. For example, you may say, "Mr. Andrews is out, but Jane Rowe can give you the information. May I transfer you to her?" You may also want to give the caller the extension number of the person to whom the caller is being transferred in case there is an equipment malfunction and the transfer does not go through. The caller can then call that number without having to call you again.

Be certain that you know how to transfer a call on your telephone. Nothing is more aggravating to a caller than to be told that he or she is going to be transferred and then the caller is lost due to incorrect transferring procedures.

## Ask Questions Tactfully

Care should be used in asking questions, especially when answering telephone calls for others. Ask only necessary questions such as "May I tell Mr. Andrews who is calling?" or "When Mr. Andrews returns, may I tell him who called?" Never ask, "Who's calling?" Many people are offended by such a blunt question; it may imply that your boss is not available to the caller. If your boss is not in or cannot take the call for some reason, ask about the nature of the call so that it can be referred to someone else. For example, you may say, "If you can tell me the nature of your call, perhaps I can help you or refer you to someone else."

## Leave Word When You Are Away From Your Telephone

Leave word with the person who answers your telephone while you are away. Information about where you are going and when you expect to return is a courtesy. Give the person who answers your phone enough information so an uninformed response such as "I don't know" will not be necessary.

## Speak Distinctly

Make sure the caller can understand what you say. You can't speak distinctly with gum, candy, or a pencil in your mouth, nor should you shout. A loud voice sounds gruff and unpleasant over the telephone. It is equally unpleasant to listen to someone who whispers. When you talk over the telephone, you should do the following:

1. Place the receiver firmly against your ear so that a good seal is obtained.

2. Place the center of the mouthpiece about

three fourths of an inch from the center of your lips.

3. Speak in a pleasant, normal voice. Watch the speed of your voice; do not talk too fast or too slow. Speak at a moderate rate. A pleasant voice is friendly, cordial, cheerful, interested, and helpful.

**Illus. 8-2** A loud voice sounds gruff and unpleasant over the telephone.

## Use Words to Identify Letters; Enunciate Numerals

Use words to identify letters in the spelling of names and places when necessary. Some words, letters, and numbers are difficult to understand over the telephone. Table 8-1 is a list of words commonly used to designate letters of the alphabet. Table 8-2 shows recommended methods of pronunciation for numerals.

## Avoid Sexism

Although this is changing, some people still assume that all secretaries are females and all execu-

**Table 8-1**   Using Words to Identify Letters

| | |
|---|---|
| **A** as in **Alice** | **F** as in **Frank** |
| **B** as in **Bertha** | **G** as in **George** |
| **C** as in **Charles** | **H** as in **Henry** |
| **D** as in **David** | **I** as in **Ida** |
| **E** as in **Edward** | **J** as in **John** |

**Table 8-1**   *(continued)*

| | |
|---|---|
| **K** as in **King** | **S** as in **Sugar** |
| **L** as in **Lincoln** | **T** as in **Thomas** |
| **M** as in **Mary** | **U** as in **Union** |
| **N** as in **Nellie** | **V** as in **Victory** |
| **O** as in **Ocean** | **W** as in **William** |
| **P** as in **Peter** | **X** as in **X-ray** |
| **Q** as in **Queen** | **Y** as in **Young** |
| **R** as in **Robert** | **Z** as in **Zero** |

**Table 8-2**   Pronunciation of Numerals

| NUMERAL | SOUNDED AS | FORMATION OF SOUNDS |
|---|---|---|
| 0 | oh | Long *O* |
| 1 | wun | Strong *W* and *N* |
| 2 | too | Strong *T* and *OO* |
| 3 | th-r-ee | A single roll of the *R* and lone *EE* |
| 4 | fo-er | Long *O* and strong *R* |
| 5 | fi-iv | *I* changing from long to short, and strong *V* |
| 6 | siks | Strong *S* and *KS* |
| 7 | sev-en | Strong *S* and *V* and well-sounded *EN* |
| 8 | ate | Long *A* and strong *T* |
| 9 | ni-en | Strong *N*, long *I*, and well-sounded *EN* |

tives are males. If you answer the telephone and the voice on the other end is female, do not assume that she is a secretary and ask to speak to her employer. When addressing anyone use terms that connote respect. Do not refer to a woman as a girl, a young lady, a beautiful young thing, or any other term that can be construed as sexist in nature. Also, do not refer to a man as a boy.

## Place Calls Properly for Your Supervisor

Supervisors usually place their own calls to save time and to create favorable impressions. However, you may work for someone who does not wish to place calls. If so, identify your supervisor's name before you transfer the call. For example, you may say, "Mr. Andrews of TriCounty Regional Planning Agency is calling," and then transfer the call to Mr. Andrews.

If your supervisor is not available or makes another call after you place one for him or her, provide some subtle training for your supervisor. For example, before you place the call you might say, "Mr. Andrews, I am going to place the call that you requested to Mr. Hill. Are you going to be in for a few minutes?" It may be that he or she is unaware that such habits are discourteous and irritating to the person being called, implying that the other person's time is not valuable.

### Plan Your Call

If you are not certain of the telephone number, refer to the telephone directory. If the number is not in the directory, check with directory assistance. After checking with directory assistance, make a note of the number for future calls. There are a number of different types of telephone files that may be purchased, such as wheel files or card files. Keeping a list of frequently called numbers in such a file will save you much time.

Take a few moments to plan your call before you make it. Know the purpose of your call and know what you intend to say. Once you get the person on the telephone, state your purpose clearly and concisely. For example, you might say, "This is John Chin of TriCounty Regional Planning Agency. I'm calling to verify your attendance at the Board of Directors meeting tomorrow at 3:00 p.m. in Conference Room A." Certainly, you may exchange some pleasantries with the individual you are calling. The main idea, though, is to get your message across without wasting the time of the individual you are calling.

### TELEPHONE DIRECTORIES

It is important that you are familiar with the type of information that is in a telephone directory and that you use the directory as efficiently as possible. Telephone directories in large cities have two separate directories—the yellow pages and the white pages. Some large cities have a third directory, with the white business pages being a separate directory.

### White Pages

The white pages of a directory generally contain three parts. One section is an alphabetic listing of the names, addresses, and telephone numbers of individuals. This directory is called the residence white pages. The additional sections are an alphabetical listing of the names, addresses, and telephone numbers of businesses, referred to as the business white pages, and the blue pages, which are an easy reference for locating telephone numbers of local, state, and federal government offices. Federal government numbers are listed under the U.S. Government by the various departments, bureaus, and agencies of the federal government. State agencies are listed under the name of the state and then under the name of the particular department, bureau, or agency. County and city government numbers are listed by the name of the county or city and by the department, bureau, or agency.

### Yellow Pages

The yellow pages list the names of particular businesses according to the service the business provides. For example, assume that you are interested in purchasing a computer but you are not aware of any companies in your area that sell computers. You would logically look under computers in the yellow pages. The category may be broken down as follows:

Computers and Computer Equipment—Dealers—New

Computers and Computer Equipment—Dealers—Used

Computers and Computer Equipment—Renting and Leasing

Computers and Computer Equipment—Service and Repair

The companies specializing in each area are listed alphabetically. Since the yellow pages are used as a sales mechanism for businesses, many businesses choose to also print a large advertisement in the yellow pages giving more information about their company.

### Front Pages of the Directory

Both the white pages and the yellow pages of telephone directories have important information. If you are to use the telephone book as effectively as possible, you need to be knowledgeable about the information that is contained in the front. The front of the white pages contains emergency phone numbers, police, fire, and ambulance, along with other emergency numbers such as suicide prevention and poison center numbers. This information is usually given on the inside front cover. Page one of the front pages includes a table of contents for the remainder of the front pages. Some of the information provided includes telephone repair numbers; information on making collect, person-to-person, and calling-card calls; directory assistance information; area codes and foreign country and city codes; a time and area code map; calling services; and services for the disabled. Products and services for the disabled include products and services for the hearing impaired such as light flashers, volume control receivers, and tone ringers; and products for the speech and vision impaired such as voice synthesizers, artificial larynxes, and large button telephones.

The front cover of the yellow pages also contains information on emergency numbers. In addition, the front pages also contain information such as numbers to call to get weather forecasts, national and international news, business news, stock market updates, maps of the area, educational opportunities, and transit systems in the area.

**Illus. 8-3** One of the products for the vision impaired is the Card-Dialer.

*Credit: Courtesy of AT&T archives.*

## TELEPHONE SYSTEMS

The many changes in technology, along with the 1984 court order that forced AT&T (American Telephone and Telegraph) to give up its monopoly of the industry and to divest itself of its local companies, have brought about new equipment and services provided by several companies. Before 1984, all equipment was rented from AT&T and all services were provided by AT&T. Now, companies may buy or rent their equipment from several different companies. Long-distance service may also be purchased from several companies.

In the past, telephone systems have been **analog systems**. Analog systems transmit data in continuous, smooth sound waves. **Digital systems**, in contrast, transmit data in the form of digital signals—discrete on/off signals. The telephone network is shifting to an all-digital network because of the advantages offered by digital technology. These advances include greater reliability, lower maintenance, and the ability to mix media over a single line. For example, voice, video, and data may be sent over the same telephone line. Digital networks allow for the transmission of facsimile, which you learned about in Chapter 5, and E-mail (electronic mail), which you will learn about in Chapter 10.

The new technology has also brought the **Integrated service digital network (ISDN)** that allows a telephone system to be connected to a computer system for retrieval of information. It is projected that ISDN will be the driving force for telephone system technology through the first half of the 1990s. ISDN is intended to provide a set of standards around which all equipment manufacturers can build their products. Thus, a telephone system designed by one manufacturer can make use of applications designed by another manufacturer.

There are basically three types of telephone systems available. These systems include single-line systems, key systems, and PBX (private branch exchange) systems. The following paragraphs will help you understand more about these systems.

### Single-Line Systems

Single-line telephone systems are used in homes and in small offices. As the name implies, these telephones have only a single line available. These telephones are operated by push buttons or rotary dials. However, today you rarely see a rotary dial telephone. Single-line telephones come in table models, wall models, or models with the push button in the handset.

## Key Telephone Systems

A key system includes a group of push-button desk telephones interconnected to allow a group of people to share several outside lines plus make intercom calls to each other. Key systems function with a **key service unit (KSU)** which operates a maximum number of phones and lines, depending on system size. For example, a key system may handle 32 phone lines and 72 phones. A key system permits the user to select an outside or an internal line. Internal lines are used for conversations within the company and for paging purposes.

Key systems may have a variety of features. For example, the system may have an electronic memory that allows for the storage of frequently called numbers. When you use a number frequently, you may give that number a one-digit code; and thus you only have to press one button when calling the number. Key systems have switching devices that automatically switch calls to another line if one line is busy. Another feature will automatically dial a busy number for you and alert you as soon as the call goes through; you do not have to spend your time redialing a number.

## PBX Systems

If the company is a large one, a PBX system may be needed. **PBX (Private Branch Exchange)** is the general name used for the office switchboard and the descendants of the PBX, one of which is the PABX (Private Automatic Branch Exchange). On a manual PBX system, an operator answers the call and forwards it to the individual requested. On a PABX system, a computer controls the system. A PABX system may be an analog system or a digital system. A digital PABX can link computers and other electronic equipment into a network in addition to directing telephone calls. The term PBX is used generically to mean any type of PBX, both manual and automatic. Although a few manually operated PBXs remain in use today, most are completely automatic; no operator is needed to operate the system.

A PBX system is more complex than a key system, but it is also more flexible, it can accommodate more phones, and it is more expensive. A PBX system can accommodate 10,000 or more telephones. The cost of a PBX system depends on its size, how many lines are needed, projected expansion, and the number of features wanted. However, it generally costs from two to three times what a key system costs. For example, a key system

**Illus. 8-4** If the company is large, a Private Branch Exchange (PBX) system may be needed.

Credit: Courtesy of AT&T archives.

might cost $200 per phone, while a PBX system might cost $600 per phone.

As with all technologies, key systems and PBXs have improved and will continue to do so. With the change from electromechanical equipment to electronic equipment, systems can now keep reports on calls made, how long the call lasted, where it went, which employee made the call, and how much it cost. PBX systems are also available that allow the company to add users without throwing away the old equipment. For example, you can buy a PBX which accommodates about 150 users and build up the PBX to the point that it can service 30,000 users.

## SELECTION OF A TELEPHONE SYSTEM

Since a telephone system is so important and the number of options available today are so extensive, many companies employ an experienced telecommunications professional or consultant for advice on equipment purchases and implementation. Here are some of the considerations when purchasing a system.

Cost is a primary factor. Although the telecommunications market is very cost competitive, there are wide fluctuations in cost. It is wise to examine the specifications carefully in order to determine the cost of the standard features and the cost of the optional features. In addition, the cost of running and maintaining the system should be considered. A reliable system will save money in ongoing maintenance. Some suppliers will offer maintenance contracts, which are generally flat fees as insurance for multiple service calls.

Another factor to consider is system flexibility. A telephone system should be easy to expand. For example, a software-driven system is more flexible because product enhancements may be implemented more easily and cost-effectively by loading new software than by installing new or additional hardware. The ability to move telephones between systems and facilities is also important. This ability is known as **migration**. For example, a large company that has locations throughout the nation and frequently adds and moves locations can standardize equipment that can migrate from one location to another. In addition, if an office needs to expand its system from a key system to a PBX, the telephones may be retained, thus protecting a capital investment.

Voice and data switching capability is also an important consideration. A company needs to be sure that a telephone system has the capability to meet both existing and future needs. A PBX system equipped with data handling capabilities allows data transmission and reception between users and equipment, such as computers, that are linked to the system.

## SPECIAL TYPES OF EQUIPMENT

In addition to regular telephone equipment there are several types of special telephone equipment available. This equipment can assist the employee in being more productive and in providing for unique needs.

### Cellular Telephones

Individuals often need to maintain contact with a central location while moving between different locations. **Cellular technology** makes it possible to have a fully functional telephone in the car, the briefcase, or even a coat pocket. Cellular technology breaks a large service area down into smaller areas called cells. Each cell is served by a low-powered receiver-transmitter.

As the mobile caller moves from one cell to another cell, a mobile telephone switching office automatically moves the call from one cell to another cell. The mobile telephone switching office interfaces with a land-based subscriber to complete the mobile calls to fixed locations serviced by telephone lines.

### Portable Pagers, Cordless Telephones, and Speakerphones

Portable pagers are signaling devices that alert the holder to contact a phone number for a message. Two-way conversations are not possible as they are with a cellular telephone. Pagers are usually clipped to your pocket or belt; and when someone in the office wants to speak to you, the pager emits a sound. You then call the office from the nearest telephone.

The cordless telephone was introduced in the early 1980s. These telephones allow a person to communicate a short distance from the base station without interconnecting wires. Cordless telephones have a base station and a handset. The base station is a unit with electronic circuits that communicates with the handset. The base station plugs into both the telephone jack and an electrical outlet. The handset functions as a portable telephone with a receiver and a transmitter; rechargeable batteries provide power for the handset.

**Illus. 8-5**

**Illus. 8-6** Cellular technology makes it possible to have a fully functional telephone in the car, the briefcase, or even a coat pocket.

The handset may be carried to distances of approximately 900 feet and used as a telephone.

Sometimes there is a need for several people in one office to talk with one or more people at another location. Speakerphones are available for such occasions. A speakerphone has a built-in transmitter and volume control that permits both sides of a telephone conversation to be amplified. A speakerphone makes it possible to consult files, take notes, or walk around the room while on the phone.

## TELEPHONE FEATURES

Numerous special features are available to telephone users. Following is a description of some of the features you may encounter.

1. **Call restriction** allows the organization to eliminate unauthorized telephone calls. Here is how it works. If an individual is authorized to make long-distance calls, he or she is given an authorization code. This code must be keyed into the telephone before the long-distance call will be processed. Call restriction also enables the company to keep track of the calls people make and discourages individuals from making personal long-distance calls. A computer printout can be provided to the supervisor each month with a listing of the calls made by telephone number. Call restriction is often used in high traffic areas of an organization such as the lobby, mail room, and employee breakroom in order to discourage unauthorized use of the telephone.

2. **Station messages detail recording (SMDR)** allows businesses to produce detailed traffic reports by logging each incoming and outgoing call. These reports allow managers to analyze traffic patterns, to determine telephone requirements, and to evaluate employee workload.

3. **Least-cost routing** automatically connects a given call to the lowest cost long-distance provider. You learned earlier that with the breakup of the AT&T monopoly in 1984, other companies are now in the telephone market. Long-distance services are available from numerous companies, a few of which are AT&T, MCI, and US Sprint. Since most companies make numerous long-distance calls daily, this least-cost routing option can save considerable dollars for an individual company.

4. The **liquid crystal display (LCD)** feature allows the user to see the number dialed, prompts the user with instructions, and displays the number of minutes the individual remains on the telephone. For incoming calls, an LCD also displays the number of the incoming caller.

**Illus. 8-7** The liquid crystal display feature allows the user to see the number dialed, prompts the user with instructions, and displays the number of minutes the individual remains on the telephone.

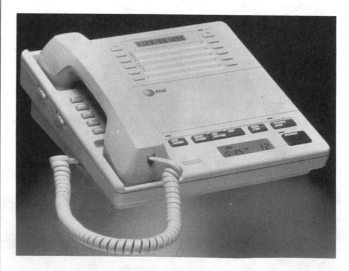

*Credit: Courtesy of AT&T archives.*

5. **Speed dialing** allows the user to store the telephone numbers that are used most often. Once the numbers have been stored in the memory of the telephone, they may be retrieved by keying in a one- or two-digit code rather than the entire number.

6. **Call timing** is a feature that is beneficial to firms, such as accounting and law firms, who bill clients for the time spent handling their business. The system tracks the call by client, with some systems having the capability to record the total time spent for an individual client during a determined period of time.

7. **Call forwarding** permits a telephone call to be automatically forwarded to another telephone number.

8. **Call waiting** allows a call to a busy telephone to be held while a beeping tone notifies the called party that a call is waiting. He or she can then answer the second call while the first caller "holds" on the line.

9. **Automatic call back** permits a caller to give instructions to a busy station to call back as soon as the busy station is free.

10. **Identified ringing** provides distinctive ringing tones for different categories of calls. For example, internal calls may ring one long ring while outside calls may ring two short rings close together.

11. **Call holding** allows a user to place a caller on hold while dialing or talking to another person and then return to the caller on hold.

12. **Automatic call stacking** allows calls to arrive at a busy station and be automatically answered by a recorded wait message.

13. **Conference calling** allows the caller to talk with several people in different places at the same time. If your telephone has a conference call feature, you may set up the conference call in a few moments by using this feature. For example, assume your company is in Ohio. You want to talk with an individual on the third floor of your building (while you are on the first floor); with an individual in one of your offices in California; and with another individual in one of your offices in New York. With the conference call feature on all of your telephones, you may have the call underway in a short period of time. If you do not have a conference call feature on your telephone, you may set up a conference call by calling a conference call operator and giving the individual the various numbers you wish to call and the time you want your call to go through. If you are using a conference operator, you should plan to call the operator several minutes before you expect to talk with the individuals. In this instance, it usually is not possible to make the conference call immediately.

**Illus. 8-8** Conference calling allows the caller to talk with several people in different places at the same time.

## LONG-DISTANCE SERVICES

Due to our nation becoming more global, with businesses having locations not only in the United States but abroad, long-distance calls are made more frequently. There are various types of services available for long-distance calling; several of these are explained here.

### Direct Distance Dialing (DDD)

Direct distance dialing is an arrangement whereby it is possible to dial long-distance numbers in other parts of the United States and in other countries on a station-to-station basis. In order to use DDD, it is necessary to dial a "1" plus the area code when you are charging the call to the number from which you are calling and when you are willing to talk with anyone who answers. Procedures for making a long-distance call when you are charging the call to another number or when you wish to talk with a particular individual are given later on in this section. Area codes are listed at the front of the telephone book alphabetically by state (within the United States) and for selected foreign countries and cities.

Assume that you want to call Allentown, Pennsylvania from Michigan. Through checking the front pages of the telephone book, you will discover that the area code for Allentown is 215. You then key "1" plus "215" plus the number of the business you wish to call. If you wish to call a number in a foreign country, you would key the international access code, which is available from your long-distance company, plus the country code, city code, and the local number of the company or person. For example, if you were calling Melbourne, Australia, you would do the following:

**Key:**

| 011 | + | 61 | + | 3 | + | local number |
|-----|---|-----|---|---|---|-------|
| (International Access Code) | | (Country Code) | | (City Code) | | |

### Person-to-Person and Collect Calls

Person-to-person calls are more expensive than direct number calls; however, it is sometimes essential to make such a call. The procedure for making person-to-person calls varies according to the area of the country. You need to consult your local directory for the procedure in your area. However, in most areas, the call may be made by keying "0" plus the area code and the telephone number. When you have completed keying, the operator will come on the line and ask for calling information. You then give the operator the name of the person you are calling.

A call to a distant point may be made collect, sometimes referred to as reversing the charges. When placing such a call, consult your local directory for the procedure. Usually the procedure is the same as placing a person-to-person call. Key "0" plus the area code and the telephone number. The operator then asks for calling information. You give your name and state that the call is being made collect. The person answering the call has to accept the charges before conversation can begin.

### Calling Card Calls

Many businesses now provide their executives with calling cards that allow the executive to make calls while traveling and charge the call to the company. Also, an individual has the option of receiving a calling card for personal telephone calls that allows the call to be charged to a home telephone.

The procedure for using a calling card is usually the same as a person-to-person or collect call.

You key "0" plus the area code and the number. The operator will come on the line and ask for your calling card number or you will hear a recording asking that you key in your calling card number.

**Illus. 8-9** Many businesses now provide their executives with calling cards that allow the executive to make calls while traveling and charge the call to the company.

*Credit: Courtesy of AT&T archives.*

### Wide Area Telecommunications Service (WATS)

**WATS** is a cost-effective way to make outgoing long-distance calls if a large quantity of long-distance calls are made regularly. The fee per call is reduced as more long-distance calls are made. Assuming that a large number of long-distance calls are made, the fee per call is less than the regular long-distance rate. There are two types of WATS services available—intrastate and interstate. Intrastate WATS permits calling within a state. Interstate WATS permits calling within a specified band or bands extending outward from the originating state. Bands are the number of divisions or service areas into which the United States is divided.

### 800 and Foreign Exchange Service

The 800 service permits an individual to call a business toll free. Companies that use this service are listed in the telephone directory with an 800 number. Then the customer making the call is not charged a long-distance fee for the call. Charges to the company with the 800 listing are based upon the number of subscribed service bands, the amount of usage, and the time at which the usage occurs. For measuring usage charges, the hours of the day and days of the week are divided into rate periods. Lower rates are in effect for the evenings and weekends.

With the **foreign exchange service (FX)**, a company can obtain a local number for a plant or subsidiary of the business in a city that is remote from a company's main office and arrange for all calls to that number to be filled as local calls. For example, a company with headquarters in Michigan and a branch office in Dallas could use FX to have the Michigan number listed in the Dallas directory; calls from Dallas to Michigan or from Michigan to Dallas would be treated as local calls. A leased line (one that the business leases from the telephone company) connects the subscriber's telephone to a central office in the foreign exchange area. Since it is a two-way service, FX per-

mits the business subscriber to call any number in the foreign exchange area and permits people from the foreign exchange area to call the business without a long-distance number. FX does not refer to international calls.

## Time Zones

When you are placing long-distance calls to points within the United States or abroad, time zones and time differences are extremely important. For example, if you are in San Antonio, Texas (which is on Central Standard Time), you would not want to call Los Angeles, California (which is on Pacific Standard Time) at 8:00 a.m. It would only be 6:00 a.m. in California, and the office would not be open. Before you make any long-distance calls, be certain that you consider the possible time differences. If you are not sure of the time differences, check a time zone map. There will be one in the front pages of your telephone directory. Notice Figure 8-2 which indicates the time zones and the area codes for the United States.

**Figure 8-2**  Area Code and Time Zone Map

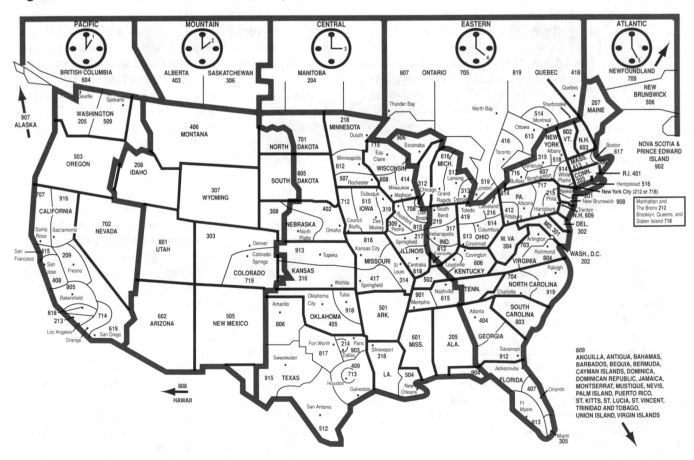

## TELEPHONE COSTS

Businesses spend a considerable amount of money each year on telephone services. You have already learned some ways that new technological advances help to control costs by displaying the time an individual is on the phone via the LCD, restricting access to long-distance usage, and providing computer printouts for supervisors to know how many calls were made and by whom. As an office assistant, there are certain other steps you can take to reduce telephone costs. Some of these follow:

1. Make operator-assisted calls only when necessary.

2. Do not make personal calls on company time unless absolutely necessary. If you must make personal calls during the workday, make them during your breaks or at your lunch hour.

3. Always take messages accurately so your employer does not waste time calling an incorrect number.

4. Keep a directory of frequently used numbers so that you do not have to waste time looking up telephone numbers.

5. Always check time zones so that you will not call another part of the country at a time when the business is not open.

## CHAPTER SUMMARY

The following review will help you remember the important points of this chapter.

1. Working with the telephone is an extremely important part of the office assistant's job duties, and calls must be received and placed effectively. There are numerous telephone techniques that can help you to be more effective. Some of these are to keep a smile in your voice and be natural, considerate, attentive, and discreet. The office assistant should answer calls promptly, transfer calls carefully, ask questions tactfully, speak distinctly, enunciate clearly, avoid sexism, and plan calls carefully.

2. Understanding how and when to use the telephone directory is important. The white pages of the telephone directory generally include the residents' telephone numbers and addresses. A separate section called the business white pages contains telephone numbers and addresses of businesses by alphabetical listing. Also, a part of the white pages are the blue pages, which are an easy reference for locating telephone numbers of local, state, and federal government offices.

3. Helpful information listed in the front of the white pages includes emergency phone numbers (police, fire, and ambulance), along with other emergency numbers such as suicide prevention and poison center numbers. Also included in the front pages is information on making collect, person-to-person, and calling card calls, along with area codes and foreign country and city codes.

4. Telephone systems are shifting to using digital technology rather than analog technology due to the advantages of digital technology. These advantages include greater reliability, lower maintenance, and the ability to mix media over a single line. Voice, video, and data may be sent over the same telephone line. Another result of digital technology is the Integrated Service Digital Network (ISDN) that allows a telephone system to be connected to a computer system for retrieval of information.

5. There are three basic types of telephone systems available—single-line systems, key systems, and PBX (private branch exchange) systems. A single-line system, as its name implies, has only a single line available. A key system is a push-button system that is capable of handling approximately 32 phone lines and 72 phones. A PBX system is more complex, more flexible, can accommodate more phones, and is more expensive than a key system. It can accommodate 10,000 or more phones.

6. When purchasing a telephone system, cost, flexibility, and voice and data switching capability are important considerations.

7. Special types of telephone equipment include cellular telephones, portable pagers, cordless telephones, and speakerphones. Cellular technology makes it possible to have a fully functional telephone in a car, a briefcase, or even a coat pocket.

8. There are numerous special features available on a telephone. Some of these features are call restriction, SMDR (station messages detail recording), least-cost routing, liquid crystal display (LCD), speed dialing, call timing, call forwarding, call waiting, automatic call stacking, and conference calling.

9. Long-distance services available include direct distance dialing (DDD), person-to-person calls, collect calls, calling card calls, WATS (Wide Area Telecommunications Service), 800 service, and FX (Foreign Exchange Service).
10. Telephone costs may be saved by making operator-assisted calls only when absolutely necessary; by not making personal calls on company time; by taking messages accurately; by keeping a directory of frequently used numbers; and by always checking time zones before placing a call.

## TERMINOLOGY REVIEW

The following terms were introduced in this chapter. To help you understand them, definitions are given below.

1. **Analog systems** *(page 213)* Analog systems transmit data in continuous, smooth sound waves. This type of system has been used in the past exclusively in telephone systems.
2. **Automatic call back** *(page 217)* This feature permits a caller to give instructions to a busy station to call back as soon as the busy station is free.
3. **Automatic call stacking** *(page 217)* Through automatic call stacking, calls arrive at a busy station and are automatically answered by a recorded wait message.
4. **Call forwarding** *(page 217)* Telephone calls may be automatically forwarded to another telephone number using the call forwarding feature.
5. **Call holding** *(page 217)* With call holding, a user can place a caller on hold while dialing or talking to another person and then return to the caller on hold.
6. **Call restriction** *(page 216)* This feature allows an organization to eliminate unauthorized telephone calls; an individual must have an authorization code to place a long-distance call.
7. **Call timing** *(page 217)* This feature allows for the tracking of calls by client and is useful in organizations such as accounting and law firms when clients are billed for the time spent in handling their business.
8. **Call waiting** *(page 217)* With call waiting, a call to a busy telephone is held while a beeping tone notifies the called party there is a call. He or she can then answer the second call while the first caller "holds" on the line.
9. **Cellular technology** *(page 215)* Cellular technology is the technology that makes it possible to have a fully functional telephone in a car, a briefcase, or even a coat pocket. Cellular technology moves a mobile call from one cell to another through a mobile telephone switching office and interfaces with a land-based subscriber to complete the mobile calls to fixed locations serviced by telephone lines.
10. **Conference calling** *(page 217)* This feature allows the caller to talk with several people in different places at the same time.
11. **Digital systems** *(page 213)* Digital systems transmit data in discrete on/off signals. Telephone systems are switching to digital systems.
12. **Foreign exchange service (FX)** *(page 219)* This service allows a company to obtain a local number for a plant or subsidiary of the business in a distant city and arrange for all calls to that number to be filled as local calls.
13. **Identified ringing** *(page 217)* This feature provides distinctive ringing tones for different categories of calls.
14. **Integrated service digital network (ISDN)** *(page 213)* ISDN is a system that allows a telephone to be connected to a computer system for retrieval of information.
15. **Key service unit (KSU)** *(page 214)* KSU is a type of key telephone system which operates a maximum number of telephones and lines with interconnected push-button desk telephones. This service allows a group of people to share several outside lines plus make intercom calls to each other.
16. **Least-cost routing** *(page 216)* Least-cost routing is a feature that automatically connects a call to the lowest cost long-distance carrier.
17. **Liquid crystal display (LCD)** *(page 216)* This feature on a telephone allows the individual to see the number keyed, prompts the user with instructions, and displays the number of minutes the individual remains on the telephone.
18. **Migration** *(page 215)* Migration is the ability to move telephones between systems and facilities.
19. **Private branch exchange (PBX)** *(page 214)* PBX is the general name for the office switchboard and its descendants. Automatic PBXs are known as PABXs (private automatic branch exchanges); however, the term PBX is used to mean any type of PBX (both manual and automatic).

We actually can gain new energy by taking time to play. Maslow, a noted psychologist, talks about letting the child in us live. Too often as adults we have forgotten how to relax and, with complete abandon, enjoy the world around us. Some individuals writing in the field of creative energy urge us to take "joy breaks"—to actually have toys at our desk and to stop for two to five minutes to play when we feel overtired or nonproductive. Such play allows us to release built-up tensions, to open blocked thinking, and to trigger creative ideas. Take a few moments now and write down several things that are fun for you that you can do in a two-to-five minute break from your job.

**Know the Difference Between Achievement and Perfection** Perfectionism can be defined as a

**Illus. 9-2** Learn to take breaks and relax in order to avoid negative stress.

**Figure 9-1** Perfectionist Test

propensity for setting extremely high standards and being displeased with anything else. Although many of us are taught that it is important to do everything perfectly, this is not possible. Are you a perfectionist? Do you believe that everything you do must be done extremely well? Read the statements in Figure 9-1, and check those which apply to you. If you respond positively to all of the statements, you have probably bought into a negative, perfectionist pattern of behavior. Begin now to rethink how you view your work.

Certainly, it is important to achieve and to do things well; however, no human being can be perfect. And to blame oneself continually for not doing everything extremely well is to tie yourself up in energy-draining behaviors. Thomas Edison was asked one time how he came to hold so many patents. He answered that he dared to make more mistakes than ten other people put together and had learned from each of them. Edison knew that the creative process involves trial and error—failure and success.

Unless we are willing to risk failure, we will never grow and learn. Think for a moment about the last time that you did something that you considered perfect. What did you learn? Your answer probably was that you did not learn anything. We do not learn and grow from doing something extremely well. In order to learn and grow, we have to risk trying something new. For example, let's assume that you are asked to make a presentation at one of your professional meetings. You have

1. If I don't do something well, I feel like I am a failure. _____

2. When I make a mistake, I spend many hours rethinking how I might have done it better. _____

3. I have a reputation of being someone who is hard to please. _____

4. When I am playing a sport (tennis, golf, basketball), I get angry with myself if I do not play my best game. _____

5. I will not start a project unless I know everything there is to know about what I am to do. _____

6. I don't like to try new things. _____

7. I lose patience with others when they don't do things well. _____

8. I expect every piece of work I produce to be perfect. _____

never made a presentation to the group before, and the idea scares you. However, you decide to accept the challenge and you make the presentation. Did you do it perfectly? No, but you learned in the process, and your next presentation will be better because you made the first one. When we do something the first time or even the second or third time, it is healthy to evaluate how it went. You can ask yourself these questions:

1. Where did I make mistakes?
2. What can I learn from my mistakes?
3. If I had it to do over, what would I do differently?

Once you have asked and answered these questions, let it go. You have risked and grown; you will be a more complete person because of it.

**Recognize Your Limits**   It is most important that you recognize when you are working too hard. We have different energy levels; you may be able to work ten hours a day quite successfully. Your friend may be able to work only eight hours a day. How do you know when you are working too hard? People react in different ways to stress, but here are some symptoms of stress:

| | |
|---|---|
| Anxiety | Panic attacks |
| Headaches | Muscular neck pain |
| High blood pressure | Muscular chest pain |
| Phobias | Insomnia |
| Gastrointestinal problems | Jaw pain |

If you identify these symptoms, where can you go for help? Most insurance programs provide for counseling services through psychologists or psychiatrists. These trained individuals can help you discover the causes of your stress and how to alleviate it. Some hospitals provide stress reduction clinics and individual psychotherapy. Another source is to check with your family physician; he or she can provide sources of assistance.

There must be other things in your life besides work or you will quickly become nonproductive. You have already learned that you must take time to play. It is also important that you take time out in other ways. All of us need some time alone. People who are highly creative and people who are extremely productive seem to require significant time alone with their own thoughts. Time alone for you may mean that you get up early in the morning before your family and spend time admiring the beauty of the day. It may mean that you spend 30 minutes when you come home in the evening listening to music.

It is also important to spend quality time with your family and friends. So much of our energy is given to our work that many times we arrive home exhausted and merely want to flop on the couch. But, relationships with family and friends are essential to being a fully functioning individual. Through caring and nurturing relationships we refuel our tank and help others refuel their tanks.

We also need to take time off from the job. How many people do you know that seem to pride themselves on the fact that they haven't taken all of their vacation days in years? They seem to feel that if they aren't on the job, the company will fold. Of course, quite the contrary is true. All of us need to take extended time away from the job. Sometimes it is important to go to a different part of the country. Leaving the location of our day-to-day life can help us relax and let the issues or concerns of our daily existence go.

**Exercise**   Cardiovascular specialists have found that regular exercise can lower blood pressure, decrease fats in the blood, reduce joint stiffness, control appetite, and decrease fatigue. Exercise changes the chemistry in the body, getting rid of toxins and producing endorphins and other hormones which increase creativity and silence negative self-talk. You will be more patient, calmer, more receptive to others, and a better listener after twenty to thirty minutes of aerobic exercise.

What type of exercise should you do? There are many exercises that are good for your body— swimming, walking, and bicycling, to name a few. Participate in an exercise that you enjoy. What time of day should you exercise? It depends on you. You may find it better to exercise in the morning. Contrary to what you may think, there are many exercise opportunities at this time of day. Several television channels offer instructor-led aerobic exercise programs. Fitness centers and the YMCA and YWCA open as early as 5:30 a.m. to accommodate people exercising before work. Determine a regular time of the day that you will exercise and then do it. When you begin exercising, go slowly. Train your body; don't strain it. If you have any medical problems, be sure to consult your doctor about the type of exercise that is best for you.

**Illus. 9-3** It is important to spend quality time with your family and friends.

**Eat Right** What you eat or do not eat affects your overall health. Excessive intake of fat, sugar, salt, and caffeine contributes to poor health and to certain diseases such as hypertension and heart disease. Six ounces of coffee contain 180 milligrams of caffeine; six ounces of tea contain 70 milligrams; and twelve ounces of cola contain 45 milligrams. Nervousness, insomnia, headaches, and sweaty palms have been related to 250 milligrams of caffeine. Excessive amounts of caffeine can cause an individual to exhibit the same clinical symptoms as an individual suffering from anxiety.

The average American consumes more than 126 pounds of sugar a year. Excessive sugar consumption can lead to an increase in triglyceride levels in the blood which can cause cardiovascular disease. Too much salt can lead to an increase in blood pressure and to the development of hypertension. The wisest course of action for an individual is to lower the intake of fat, sugar, salt, and caffeine in the diet.

Your diet should include plenty of fresh fruits and vegetables. Drinking six to eight glasses of water a day is also very healthy. Whole grain breads with high fiber are good for your body. Maintaining a balanced, healthy diet will help keep your energy level high and your stress level low.

## TIME MANAGEMENT

In the previous sections you learned that negative stress can reduce productivity, cause health problems, and even lower self-esteem. You also learned that we live in an information age in which changes in technology are impacting our jobs and even our careers. We are expected to be continual learners in order to keep up with the demands of our jobs. In addition, divorces continue at a high rate and more and more people are single parents, demanding added time and responsibilities in caring for children. All of these demands place constraints on our time.

For many of us, the vicious cycle begins when we feel we have too much to do in too little time. Decisions are made in haste and actions are taken under pressure. Planning is abandoned. Our effectiveness is diminished; deadlines are missed; productivity is reduced. Tempers build, and we become irritable with individuals on the job and our families at home.

You can see that there is a very close connection between time and stress. If we do not manage ourselves well in relation to the time we have, we become stressed. This stress in turn affects the way we do our job and the way we relate to people in our personal life. The vicious cycle continues, and individuals that are caught in it sometimes feel that they can do nothing to correct the situation. They feel out of control. But you can be in control of your time; and you must be in control if you are to be a productive employee at work and a caring, nurturing individual in your relationships at home. **Time management** is the way we manage ourselves in relation to time. We cannot actually manage time since time is finite. There is only so much time in a day; we cannot control how much time we have. However, we can control how we choose to use the time that we have. This section is about ways in which you can control yourself in relation to time and thus control your stress.

### Time Defined

**Time** is a resource, but it is a unique resource. It cannot be bought, sold, borrowed, rented, saved, or manufactured. It can be spent, and it is the only resource that must be spent the minute it is received. Every one of us receives the same amount of time to spend each day; we all have 24 hours each day to manage in relation to our professional and personal goals. We cannot speed up the clock or slow it down. Much is written in the literature about managing time; however, it really is not possible to manage time. Time passes at the same rate each minute, hour, and day. What is possible is to manage ourselves in relation to the time available. And, that is where the difficulty occurs. Many of us do not even understand how we are spending our time; we do not understand our time wasters; and we certainly are not taking steps to manage ourselves more effectively in relation to our time. Many of us haven't realized that once we have wasted time, it's gone; and it cannot be replaced.

## Time Wasters

Before we begin to analyze how you might do a more effective job in managing yourself in relation to your time, let's look at some of the common time wasters. You will probably find that you have been guilty of most of these behaviors.

**Poor Telephone Usage**   The telephone can be a time saver, but it becomes a time waster when you do not use it properly. Let's discuss some of the errors we make in using the telephone. We are often afraid of offending people, so we let them take more of our time on the telephone than is necessary. Certainly, it is important to exchange certain amenities; for example, saying good morning or good afternoon and doing so in a pleasant voice. But, we often allow ourselves to be caught up in hearing about the individual's latest vacation or how the family is doing. In other words, we sometimes allow our calls to be turned into a social occasion rather than a business occasion. Another way the phone can be a time waster is tied up with our need to know. All of us need to know enough about a situation to get our job done effectively, but we don't need to hear all of the details of a project. Still another way that the phone can be a time waster is when you fail to give and get the proper information. For example, you may fail to ask the caller what he or she wants to discuss with your employer. Or, you may fail to write the correct telephone number on the message pad. Taking personal calls on the job also becomes a time waster for many individuals. Certainly, there are times when there are emergency situations at home that necessitate a call. But, spending thirty minutes on a personal call several times each day becomes an unacceptable time waster.

**Inadequate Planning**   Many individuals never plan what needs to be done on a particular day. Consider this situation. Assume that your employer has told you on a Friday afternoon that you must get out a report by Monday afternoon; you understand that it is a high priority job. However, you do not plan how long it will take you to do the job, nor do you block any time on your calendar for the production of the job. On Monday morning you have numerous interruptions including telephone calls, visitors, and one crisis after another. You do not begin the report until Monday afternoon at 4:00 p.m. As you get into the report, you see that it is very involved; there is no way that you will be able to finish your work by 5:00 p.m. At 5:00 p.m. your employer asks for the report. You are unable to produce it since you have not planned well.

**Improper Handling of Visitors**   As an office assistant, your responsibility is to make visitors feel comfortable and welcome. However, that does not mean that you must entertain the visitors while they are waiting to see your employer. Sometimes that is the mistake that office assistants make. They spend too much time in conversation with office callers. Another mistake that occurs all too frequently in the office has to do with visiting with other office employees. Consider this situation. Robin, a good friend of yours, usually drops by about 8:30 a.m. to talk. You always enjoy seeing her, and you never intend to visit for long. However, your visits rarely take less than 15 minutes, and sometimes you spend as much as 30 minutes talking with her. You have used 15 to 30 valuable minutes on a social call and have thus been unproductive in your work.

**Disorganization**   Does your desk have a mountain of file folders, with their contents spilling out onto your desk? Perhaps it also has a desk calendar open to last Wednesday and an old coffee cup with some coffee remaining in it from yesterday. Half-finished projects; half-finished memorandums; a stack of filing that is three weeks old. Disorganized individuals are a serious liability to their organization. They cannot be depended upon to provide information in a timely manner to others. They forget where the information is; they never meet deadlines because they have not written them down. They waste an enormous amount of their own time and other people's time in searching for files, phone numbers, reports, and so on.

**Illus. 9-4** Disorganized individuals are a serious liability to their organization.

**Procrastination** Procrastination is defined as postponing or needlessly delaying a project or something that has to be done. Many of us are guilty of procrastination. We postpone a project because we are afraid that we will fail at it, because we aren't interested in the work, and even because we are angry with the person who delegated it to us. Of course, we don't want to admit any of these real reasons, so we make excuses. We say, "I have too many other projects; I can't add this one to the list right now. I don't have what I need to do the job. Before I can get started, I need to consult with Mr. Weinberger. There really is no rush to begin; it's not due for three weeks." Procrastinators are late for meetings, put off handling projects, and don't return telephone calls. Procrastinators may be such relaxed, easy-going people that the procrastination does not bother them as much as others. But, they can create stress for themselves with their last-minute efforts, and the stress they put on other members of their work group is significant.

**Ineffective Communication** Communication is a critical skill that is too often not well understood. We often take it for granted. We assume that if we know how to talk we can communicate. Such is not the case. **Ineffective communication** occurs frequently. This is communication in which the message intended by the originator is not understood by the receiver. If communication is to be effective, a number of factors must be in place. Everyone involved in the communication process must understand how words are being used. The communicator must choose the best channel to get the message across. For example, the communicator must determine whether the best channel is a letter, a telephone conversation, or a face-to-face meeting. The communicator must give enough information so that the recipient understands but not so much that the recipient tunes out. The communicator must understand what is happening in the world of the recipient at the time of the communication. For example, the communicator must ask whether the recipient is too busy to really hear the message or whether the recipient may be distracted by loud noises in the environment. Or perhaps the recipient is concerned about a project that is not going well and is thus unable to hear the message.

## Time Management Techniques

You have considered the importance of time management and you understand that time is a resource that must be used well. You have looked at some of the time wasters that we all face. Now it is time to understand how you might do a better job of managing yourself in relation to time. This area is one that all of us must work on constantly. We never will become such effective time managers that we can forget about the constraints of time. However, if we pay attention to effective management techniques, we will find that not only do we seem to have more time to get our tasks done but that we have reduced the stress in our lives considerably.

**Set Goals** A **goal** is an objective, a purpose, or an end that is to be achieved. The idea of establishing goals makes many people feel uncomfortable. It has something to do with writing the goal down and then being expected to do it. It's like setting New Year's resolutions. How many of us set New Year's resolutions in good faith and then fail to reach any of them? If we even allow ourselves to think of these resolutions at a later date, we feel a vague sense of guilt about not having accomplished what we set out to do. Goal setting can produce this same type of hesitancy and guilt. But, if we are to accomplish anything on our job and in our personal lives, setting goals is essential. There is an old Chinese proverb that states if you don't know where you are going, any road will take you there. And, so it is. If we don't establish our goals, we become very undirected and may wind up someplace we didn't intend to go.

**Organizational Goals** Most all organizations are involved in strategic and organizational planning. When these plans are written, there are very definite goals to be accomplished and deadlines established in meeting these goals. Employees are usually brought into the planning process at some point. In fact, in many companies employees are asked to write action plans that reflect what they will be accomplishing to meet the goals of the organization. Then, during evaluation time, the employees are evaluated on how well they have met these goals.

If you are a part of your company's planning process, you will have a chance to understand where the company is headed. The company may ask you to write your own goals to show what you will accomplish in helping the company meet its goals. If you are not part of this formal process, it is still important that you set professional goals for yourself. In the day-to-day operations of the business, these goals may take the form of a monthly, weekly, and daily planning guide as to what you need to produce. In your long-range career planning, setting goals may take the form of identifying where you want to be in the company in five years, determining the education that you want to achieve, or establishing goals that mean a job or career change for you.

**Personal Goals** Personal goal setting is also important. This goal setting can take the form of deciding how much quality time you need to spend with your family and setting that time aside. It can also take the form of deciding when you want to purchase a house or a car and establishing goals so that you will have the resources to do this when the designated time arrives. It can take the form of planning in such personal areas as marriage and childbearing.

**Goal Attributes** There are certain attributes that effective goals must have. A goal must be achievable. A goal should stretch you so that you will have the opportunity for growth. A goal must be specific and measurable, with a deadline attached. A goal should be written down. A goal must be flexible. See the detailed explanation below.

1. *A goal should stretch you.* A goal should motivate you to do more than you have been doing; it should motivate you to reach a higher level of accomplishment. For example, assume that on your job you have several reports to prepare each month. The use of a spreadsheet software package would help you to prepare the reports more efficiently. You set your goal to learn a spreadsheet package; such a goal stretches you to use your intellect in learning a new process.

2. *A goal must be attainable.* Just as your goals should stretch you, they also should not be unrealistically high. You will only frustrate yourself with an unrealistically high goal, and you may also destroy your motivation to continue to set goals.

3. *A goal must be specific and measurable.* If your goal is vague and unspecific, you will not know when you have achieved it. For example, "to become a more effective communicator" is a goal that is too vague. How can you become a more effective communicator? You should determine behaviors in which you are going to be engaged in accomplishing your goal. You might say that you are going to listen 75 percent of the time to others; that you are going to use paraphrasing (repeating what you have said in different words) to help others to understand your communication; or that you are going to use direct and simple language when you are communicating. Then, establish methods for measuring the accomplishment of your goals. In the communication situation, you might determine that you are going to ask three people within the company with whom you have had communication problems if your communication is more effective.

4. *A goal must have a deadline.* Deadlines perform an extremely important function in goal setting. They allow us to track to see if the goal has been accomplished. A goal without a deadline is a dream. In the communication example given above, you might set yourself a deadline of three months to improve your communication. At the end of that three month period you should check to see if your communication has improved.

5. *A goal should be written down.* If a goal is not written down, it is easy to forget the goal or to change your mind about it. Serious goal setters write down their goals and check periodically to see where they are in the accomplishment of their goals.

6. *A goal should be flexible.* Sometimes conditions external to you impact your goals to the point that you cannot accomplish them. When this happens, don't cling stubbornly to something that is no longer possible. But, don't be too

quick to mark off your goal. It may be that by working smarter you can offset the external factors or you may be able to revise your goal or establish a different time frame for completion.

**Analyze Your Time**  Although you might feel that you know exactly how you spend your time, most of us in reality do not. It is a good idea to check periodically how you are spending your time. You might be surprised at what is taking your time, and you might also discover some time wasters as you analyze your time.

*Log Your Time*  One way to determine how you spend your time is to chart on a time log the amount of time you spend in various daily activities. Certainly, you should not become a slave to the log. It is not important that you be accurate to the second or minute. However, it is important that you are faithful to the process for a period of time so you might have a realistic picture of how you are spending your time. How long should you use the log? Usually, a week will be adequate to get a good picture of time usage. However, if a number of unusual things happen during the week, you might want to record your time for another week. Figure 9.2 shows one illustration of a time log.

**Figure 9-2**  Time Log

| | DAILY TIME LOG | | |
|---|---|---|---|
| Name *Alexander Proos* | Day *Monday* | Date *11-16* | |
| **Time** | **Activity** | **Priority*** | **Interruptions (nature of)** |
| 8:30 | Keyboard report | 1 2 3 | |
| 9:30 | Set up meeting | 1 2 3 | |
| 10:00 | Write memos | 1 2 3 | |
| 11:30 | Return calls | 1 2 3 | |
| 12:00 | Lunch | 1 2 3 | |
| 1:00 | Keyboard letters | 1 2 3 | |
| 2:30 | Filing | 1 2 3 | |
| | | 1 2 3 | |
| | | 1 2 3 | |
| | | 1 2 3 | |
| | | 1 2 3 | |
| | | 1 2 3 | |

*Circle the number which indicates the importance of the activitiy. Priority code:
1 — Urgent, 2 — Do today, and 3 — Do when convenient

*Analyze the Log*  Your next step is to analyze your time log in an attempt to discover ways in which you can improve the management of your time. Ask yourself these questions:

1. What was the most productive period of the day? Why?
2. What was the least productive period of the day? Why?
3. Who or what accounted for the interruptions?
4. Can the interruptions be minimized or eliminated?
5. What activities needed more time?
6. On what activities could I spend less time and still get the desired results?
7. Do I have all my supplies and materials ready before beginning an activity?

*Prepare an Action Plan*  After you analyze your log, you must do something about how you spend your time. Make an action plan for yourself. Determine the positive steps you will take to increase your time management efficiency.

**Use Good Techniques**  In deciding how you will manage yourself in relation to your time, you will want to use some of the techniques given here. Obviously, there are a number of techniques that you may use; a sampling is presented here.

*Set Priorities*  Many times it will be impossible for you to do everything that you are asked to do in one day. Thus, you must be able to set priorities—to distinguish between the most important and least important jobs and determine the order in which they should be completed. If you are new to a job, you probably will have to have some help from your employer to determine what tasks are the most important. But once you learn more about your position and your employer, you should be able to establish priorities on your own.

*Plan Your Activities*  A big help in planning is to establish a "to do" list. Put all of your tasks, activities, and projects on this list. Number each item. Include everything on your desk, in work piles, phone messages, reading, and so forth. Review your list. Mark the most important items A; less important items B; and those remaining C, or cross them off if they are not worth your time. Use your numbered list, with priorities in place, to

1. Stack papers in priority order; the A's in one pile, the B's in another pile, and the C's in a third pile. You will probably want to put the C's in a drawer so that your attention will be freed for the A's and B's.
2. Mark telephone message slips A, B, or C.

Set up a list of projects that need to be done during the month. Plan the next day in late afternoon or evening when today is fresh on your mind. Put down on your "to do" list what must be done the next day, again establishing priorities.

Estimate time needed for activities and tasks to make scheduling more realistic. This type of planning will take time initially, but when you become adept at planning it will take less time. However, the time spent in planning saves you time overall. Figure 9-3 illustrates a "To Do" list.

***Conquer Procrastination*** Pick one area where procrastination plagues you and conquer it. As-

**Figure 9-3** To Do List

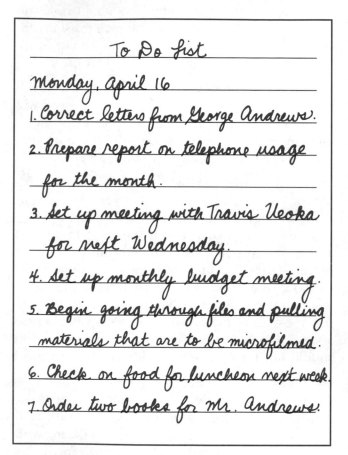

To Do List

Monday, April 16

1. Correct letters from George Andrews.

2. Prepare report on telephone usage for the month.

3. Set up meeting with Travis Ueoka for next Wednesday.

4. Set up monthly budget meeting.

5. Begin going through files and pulling materials that are to be microfilmed.

6. Check on food for luncheon next week.

7. Order two books for Mr. Andrews.

sume that you always put off filing. You find yourself having two and three weeks of filing stacked on your desk, and you are constantly having to rummage through the papers for something your employer needs. In your priorities, set aside 20 or 30 minutes each day (or whatever time you need) to do the filing; put it on your "to do" list. Check it off when you have accomplished it. Other ways in which you might conquer procrastination include the following:

1. Focus on one problem at a time.
2. Give yourself deadlines and meet them.
3. Tackle the most difficult problems first.
4. Don't let perfectionism paralyze you; don't be afraid to make mistakes.
5. Recognize that you have developed the habit of putting things off, and take steps to correct the habit. For example, set up a new routine that contrasts with your old one. Create whatever visual reminders you need; you may make a sign for your desk reminding you not to procrastinate. Don't let yourself make exceptions by saying, "It's okay to procrastinate on this job." A lapse is like a skid in a car; it takes much more effort to recover than to maintain control from the outset.

***Handle Paper Once*** Do you ever find yourself rereading a piece of paper or shuffling it from the top of the stack to the bottom of the stack several times? Most of us do. In fact, most time management experts claim that handling paper over and over is the biggest paperwork time waster. The basic rule is to handle paper once. Read it, route it, file it, or answer it. Get it off your desk as quickly as possible.

**Illus. 9-5**

*Credit: Reprinted by permission: Tribune Media Services.*

*Organize Your Work Area* When you are working on a project, clear your desk of materials that relate to other projects. Put these materials in a file folder, label the folder with the name of the project, and place the folder in your drawer. Keep the items on your desk to a minimum so that you have the space to work.

Keep in and out trays on your desk, and label the trays so that it is clear which is for incoming material and which is for outgoing material. If space permits, you may wish to have a tray for material to be filed on your desk. An alphabetic file sorter will help you put materials to be filed in alphabetical order quickly. Keep frequently used supplies such as pencils, pens, and paper clips in the center drawer of your desk. Paper will generally go in the side drawer of your desk. Divide your paper into letterhead, plain bond, memorandum pads, and other types of paper that you use.

*Reduce Interruptions* As an office assistant, part of your responsibility is to screen calls for your employer. A skilled assistant can get the information needed without offending the caller. A polite, businesslike approach is essential. For example, you may say to the telephone caller, "I'm sorry; she's not available at the moment. May she return your call when she is free?" Then, it is your responsibility to take down the name, phone number, company affiliation of the caller, and purpose of the call. If the caller does not volunteer this information, you might say, "May I add a brief note as to what this call is about so she can be prepared when she returns your call?" Repeat the name, number, and message to the caller to confirm your understanding of it.

When you are placing calls, group them if possible. For example, if you have six calls to make, you may save time by making all the calls at once. Know the time of day when you can most likely reach people to save the likelihood of playing "telephone tag" with the individual. It is generally easier to get people during the early morning hours before they get tied up in meetings and in making outside calls. Set a time limit for your calls. A three-minute egg timer may look strange on your desk, but it can serve the purpose nicely. Don't let yourself get drawn into social chitchat. If you find yourself being drawn in, you can use statements such as this to extricate yourself: "Pete, I have a minor emergency here to handle so I must hang up. It was good talking with you." Limit your personal calls to emergency situations, and ask that your friends not call you at work.

*Set Up Appointments For Visitors* Discourage people from dropping by unexpectedly to see you or your employer. If a visitor drops by to see your employer and he or she is busy, ask, "May I help you?" or "May someone else help you?" If no one else can help, ask, "May I set up an appointment for you?" Make visitors to your office welcome, but do not feel that you must make small talk with them. Provide them with reading materials and continue with your duties. Discourage your co-workers from dropping by to socialize with you. Breaks are usually provided in the morning and in the afternoon. If you want to socialize, meet your co-workers for a break or for lunch. Make it clear that during working hours it is your responsibility to work.

**Take Advantage of Time Management Systems** There are any number of systems that will allow you to utilize your time well. The system may be a manual one or an electronic one.

*Manual Systems* One type of manual system is a calendar that allows you to record all appointments for the day, week, month, and year. Planning systems are also available; they include calendars but are much more than a calendar. For example, the system may include a calendar with two pages for each day. On one page, there are places to record your prioritized daily tasks and your appointments. On the other page you may record events of the day. Also included are monthly planning calendars for future years, pages to record values and goals, telephone/address directories, and delegation sheets.

Another type of manual system is a **tickler file**. This file is a chronological record of items to be completed. The system may be one that you design yourself or one that you purchase. If you are setting up the system, a guide for the current month is placed in the front of the file followed by a separate guide for each day of the month. At the back of the file are guides for each month of the year. To use this file, you write notes on index cards and file them behind the appropriate dates. Purchased systems are available which adhere to the same type of format using a folder system.

*Electronic Systems* An **electronic calendar system** allows you to electronically record calendar events, reserve office resources, and update

**Illus. 9-6** Manual planning systems include calendars, pages to record values and goals, telephone/address directories, and delegation sheets.

**Illus. 9-7** An electronic calendar system allows you to electronically record calendar events, reserve office resources, and update and modify lists quickly.

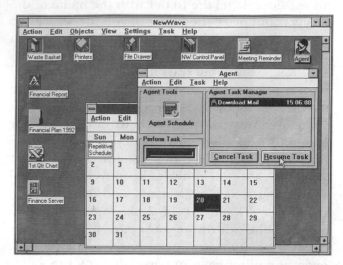

*Credit: Photo courtesy of Hewlett-Packard Company.*

not lost in getting busy signals or in being told that the individual is not available.

## YOUR POWER AND POTENTIAL

Tom Peters, in his book *Thriving on Chaos*, states that "To succeed in a competitive global business

**Illus. 9-8** If you are to thrive in the business world of today, you must be able to realize your full power and potential.

and modify lists quickly. For example, assume that you wish to schedule a meeting with several executives in your company. Each executive's calendar is maintained on a personal computer. To schedule the meeting, call up the calendars of the executives and determine a free date and time for all parties. Then schedule the meeting on the electronic calendar of each executive. With such a system you are freed from the task of making numerous telephone calls to determine when the executives might be free for a meeting.

Another timesaving electronic system is the **voice mail system**. The office professional must make numerous telephone calls in the course of accomplishing routine tasks. Many times the office professional plays telephone tag with other office employees. With voice mail, a message can be left for the individual. The receiving party dials the message center to retrieve the messages. Time is environment we must learn not only to survive in this chaos of rapid change, but thrive on chaos." If you are to thrive in the business world of today, to master the multitude of changes that will be coming your way in the form of technology, and to be productive and happy in your work, you must be able to realize your full power and potential.

When you are negatively stressed to the point of burnout on your job and when you are con-stantly fighting too few hours in the day to ac-complish what you must accomplish, you are not able to realize your full power and potential. By putting to use the techniques presented in this chapter you will have the chance not only to succeed in your job but to thrive in a world in which rapid change will continue for years to come.

## CHAPTER SUMMARY

The following review will help you remember the important points of this chapter.

1. Stress can be caused by a number of factors, some of which are overwork, personal prob-lems, and distressing work conditions. Contin-ual exposure to these factors over a period of time can cause negative stress which is harm-ful to an individual's health. Some of the symp-toms of stress are anxiety, headaches, high blood pressure, jaw pain, gastrointestinal prob-lems, muscular neck pain, and insomnia.
2. Stress reducers include
   a. Balancing work and play
   b. Knowing the difference between achieve-ment and perfection
   c. Recognizing your limits
   d. Exercising
   e. Eating right
3. Time is a unique resource. It cannot be bought, sold, borrowed, rented, saved, or manufac-tured. It can be spent, and it is spent by each of us every day. It is not possible to manage time. What is possible is to manage ourselves in rela-tion to the time available.
4. Time wasters can include
   a. The telephone
   b. Inadequate planning
   c. Visitors
   d. Disorganization
   e. Procrastination
   f. Ineffective communication
5. You can manage yourself in relation to time by setting both organizational and personal goals.
6. A goal must have certain attributes:
   a. A goal should stretch you.

b. A goal must be attainable.
   c. A goal must be specific and measurable.
   d. A goal must have a deadline.
   e. A goal should be written down.
   f. A goal should be flexible.
7. If you are to effectively manage yourself in rela-tion to your time, you must know how you spend your time. One way to do so is to log the time you spend on various activities for a pe-riod of time. Then, analyze how you are spend-ing your time. Ask yourself if there are certain activities that you could spend less time on and whether some of your interruptions can be minimized or eliminated. Prepare an action plan listing how you intend to improve the way you manage yourself in relation to time.
8. Good time techniques include
   a. Setting priorities.
   b. Planning your activities.
   c. Conquering procrastination.
   d. Handling paper only once.
   e. Organizing your work area.
   f. Reducing interruptions.
   g. Setting up appointments for visitors.
9. Take advantage of time management systems. Time management systems include planners which incorporate calendars, pages to record values and goals, telephone directories, and delegation sheets. Electronic calendar systems allow you to electronically record calendar events, reserve office resources, and update and modify lists quickly. Voice mail systems al-low you to leave messages for individuals with-out having to redial if the line is busy or no one answers.

## TERMINOLOGY REVIEW

The following terms were introduced in this chapter. To help you understand them, definitions are given below.

1. **Burnout** *(page 236)*  When an employee consistently has low productivity and low motivation and has a general attitude of disinterest in the job, it is referred to as burnout.

2. **Chronic stress** *(page 236)*  Chronic stress is the experience of negative stress (stress that is harmful to our body and mind) for an extended period of time.

3. **Distress** *(page 236)*  Negative stress or stress that is harmful to our body is referred to as distress.

4. **Electronic calendar system** *(page 245)*  An electronic calendar system is a system in which the daily calendar of an individual is input and maintained on a microcomputer.

5. **Ergonomics** *(page 236)*  Ergonomics is the study of the effects of the work environment on the health and well-being of employees.

6. **Goal** *(page 241)*  An end objective or the purpose toward which an endeavor is directed is called a goal.

7. **Ineffective communication** *(page 241)*  Communication in which the receiver does not understand what has been said or is unclear about the message being sent by the originator is referred to as ineffective communication.

8. **Perfectionism** *(page 237)*  A propensity for setting extremely high standards and being displeased with anything else is called perfectionism.

9. **Procrastination** *(page 241)*  Needlessly postponing or delaying a project or something that has to be done is called procrastination.

10. **Productivity** *(page 236)*  Productivity refers to the amount of work produced on the job. That work may be in goods or services. If the productivity is not at an acceptable level, it is referred to as low productivity.

11. **Stress** *(page 236)*  Stress is the body's response to a demand placed upon it.

12. **Tickler file** *(page 245)*  A chronological record of items to be completed is called a tickler file.

13. **Time** *(page 239)*  Time is a unique resource which cannot be bought, sold, borrowed, rented, saved, or manufactured. It can be spent, and it is spent by each of us every day.

14. **Time management** *(page 239)*  The effective management of ourselves in relation to the time that is available is known as time management.

15. **Voice mail system** *(page 246)*  A voice mail system operates via the telephone and allows voice messages to accumulate in a mailbox for later retrieval by the recipient.

## DISCUSSION ITEMS

To demonstrate your understanding of the information in this chapter, respond to the following items.

1. List and explain three causes of stress.

2. Explain how perfectionism can be related to stress.

3. Identify and explain four time wasters.

4. What is meant by the statement, "Time management is a misnomer"?

5. What are the attributes that an effective goal must have?

6. Explain how a time log can be beneficial in managing yourself in relation to time.

7. List three ways in which you might conquer procrastination.

8. Explain how time management systems can help you utilize time effectively.

## CASE STUDY

Antonio Previno, a new employee of TriCounty Regional Planning Agency, has become a problem employee for you. You have been asked by your employer to help him with the job, and you are trying. Although you have given him extensive instructions on handling the telephone, he still does not handle it properly. From the beginning of his employment he has asked you questions about each job that he does. Now that he has been here six weeks you think he should be able to work on his own. However, each day he comes to you at least six or seven times with questions about his work.

The amount of time that you spend with Antonio is impacting your own work. Last week you were late with a report for Mr. Andrews, and you felt extremely guilty for being late. Your relationship with Mr. Andrews has always been good, and he has been complimentary of your work. However, you could tell that he was not pleased with your lateness even though he didn't say anything.

Recently you have been having some problems at home. Although you do not live at home (you have your own apartment), you attempt to help your mother when she needs you. She has had pneumonia and has been in the hospital for two weeks. You go by each morning before work and each evening after work, and you have been taking her gowns home with you to launder.

The last few weeks have been tough. You have always liked your work, but you are beginning to feel that you really need a vacation. In fact, you have thought of looking for another job. Antonio is really getting on your nerves.

Respond to these questions about the case:

1. What is the problem?
2. What can be done about the problem?
3. Are there stress or time techniques which might be successfully employed?

## OFFICE APPLICATIONS

### Office Application 9-1 (*Objectives 1, 2, and 3*)

Analyze the two cases presented here, then respond to the items following the cases.

Two of your friends (Georgia and Harold) who work in offices in your building are having problems; they have both told you their situations which are given here.

*Georgia's Situation:*

Georgia has worked for a company for three years. Recently, she was promoted to administrative assistant for the president of the company. The job is a demanding one. Her responsibilities include setting up meetings, making travel arrangements for the president and the Board of Trustees, arranging meals before the monthly Board meetings, and responding to calls from the Board of Trustees about various items. In addition, she supervises two office assistants and takes minutes at the board meetings and the biweekly staff meetings called by the president, along with numerous other projects.

Georgia is attempting to employ a new office assistant, since one assistant has recently left for another position. This task is taking a long time. She is using a temporary employee until she can employ someone full time.

Georgia has two children, and she and her husband are in the process of getting a divorce. Her husband has fought her throughout the process. The situation at home has been difficult.

## ACTION PLAN

In order to make more effective use of my time, I will engage in the following activities for a period of three days:

| Activity | Date |
|---|---|
|  |  |
|  |  |
|  |  |
|  |  |
|  |  |
|  |  |
|  |  |
|  |  |
|  |  |
|  |  |

# 10 Office Mail

The electronic age that we live in is generating more mail than ever before. National trends have shown as much as a 35 percent increase in mail over a two-year period. These trends are expected to increase in the future. This increase in mail includes not only first-class mail, but second- and third-class mail also. The cost of handling both incoming and outgoing mail is a significant expense to businesses of all sizes. If mail is not handled as expeditiously as possible, thousands of dollars can be lost by the company. For example, assume that you allow an order letter to remain on your desk for several days. The customer ordering the materials may become upset due to your lack of response and cancel the order. Such action, or lack of action on your part, may result in the loss of a customer for your company, which in turn can mean the loss of immediate and prospective sales. Inefficiency in handling outgoing mail can also cost your company thousands of dollars. The failure to address mail properly, to use the proper postage, and to use the ZIP + 4 code can result in both increased postal costs and increased delivery time.

As an office assistant, your mail duties usually include preparing the incoming mail for your employer to review and preparing the outgoing correspondence to be mailed. In addition to the traditional paper mail that you process, you will also be involved in processing electronic messages. For example, most offices send and receive large volumes of mail within the company via the computer. As an office assistant you will have the responsibility of sending and receiving this mail.

## GENERAL OBJECTIVES

*Your general objectives for this chapter are to*
1. **Efficiently handle incoming and outgoing mail.**
2. **Identify classes of mail and determine which class should be used when preparing outgoing mail.**
3. **Identify special mail services.**
4. **Develop an understanding of electronic message systems and use selected systems.**
5. **Recognize the importance of recycling paper.**

## INCOMING MAIL

In a large office the mail probably comes into a central mail room where it is sorted according to the company's departments. There are a number of ways that the mail may be distributed. A mail room employee may deliver the mail to individual offices; the mail may be picked up by the office assistant at the mail room; or the mail may be delivered by electronic means.

A traditional mail cart used in delivering mail has larger rear wire wheels to enable it to roll easier on and off elevators and thresholds. The cart will accommodate both letter and legal size folders. An electronic cart uses a photoelectric guidance system to follow invisible chemical paths painted on carpeting, floor tile, or other surfaces. Mail is placed in selected trays for pickup by the person to whom it is addressed.

In small offices, the post office may deliver mail directly to the office or a mailbox may be maintained at the post office. In such an office, you may have the responsibility of taking packages to the post office for processing, purchasing stamps, and preparing all outgoing mail.

### Sorting Mail

Once you receive the mail in your office or department, you must do a preliminary mail sort. If there are several individuals within the department, sort the mail according to the person addressed. An alphabetical sorter is handy if you are sorting mail for a number of individuals. Once the mail is sorted, place the mail for each individual into separate stacks. When this preliminary sort is

**Illus. 10-1** An electronic mail cart uses a photo-electric guidance system to follow invisible chemical paths painted on carpeting, floor tile, or other surfaces.

*Credit: Courtesy of Bell & Howell Company.*

completed, sort each person's mail in the following order:

1.  *Personal and confidential mail.* Mail that is marked personal or confidential on the outside of the envelope should not be opened by the office employee. Place this mail to one side so that you do not inadvertently open it.

2.  *Mailgrams, special delivery, and registered, or certified mail.* This mail is important and should be placed so that the individual to whom it is addressed will see it first.

3.  *Regular business mail.* Mail from customers, clients, and suppliers is also considered important and should be handled promptly.

4.  *Interoffice communications.* This mail is generally received in an interoffice envelope that is distinctive in its design and color.

5.  *Advertisements and circulars.* This mail is relatively unimportant and can be handled after the other correspondence is answered.

6.  *Magazines and catalogs.* These materials should be placed at the bottom of the correspondence stack since they may be read at the executive's convenience.

## Opening Mail

Mail may be opened in the mail room or it may be opened in the individual's office. If the mail is opened in the mail room, an automatic mail opener is usually used. Mail opening systems today are extremely efficient, with some systems having the capability of opening as many as 30,000 envelopes an hour. Mail opened in an individual's office is usually opened by hand, using an envelope opener. When opening mail, follow these procedures:

1.  Have the supplies that you need readily available. These supplies include an envelope opener, a date and time stamp, routing and action slips, a stapler, paper clips, and a pen or pencil.

2.  Before opening an envelope, tap the lower edge of the envelope on the desk so that the contents will fall to the bottom and will not be cut when the envelope is opened.

3.  Place the envelopes face down with all flaps in the same direction.

4.  Open the letters by running them through a mail-opening machine or by using a hand envelope opener.

5.  Empty each envelope. Carefully check to see that everything has been removed.

6.  Fasten any enclosures to the letter. Attach any small enclosures to the front of the letter. Enclosures larger than the letter should be attached to the back.

7.  Mend any torn paper with tape.

8.  If a personal or confidential letter is opened by mistake, do not remove it from the envelope. Write "Opened by Mistake" on the front of the envelope, add your initials, and reseal the envelope with tape.

9.  Stack the envelopes on the desk in the same order as the opened mail in case it is necessary to refer to the envelopes. It is a good practice to save all envelopes for at least one day in case they should be needed for reference; then the envelopes may be thrown away.

## Keeping Selected Envelopes

Certain envelopes should always be retained. Keep the envelope when one or more of the following situations exist:

1.  *An incorrectly addressed envelope.* Your supervisor may want to call attention to this fact when answering the correspondence.

2. *A letter with no return address.* The envelope will usually have the return address.

3. *A letter written on letterhead with a different return address than that written on the envelope.* For example, a person may write a letter on a hotel's letterhead and write the business address on the envelope.

4. *A letter without a signature.* The envelope may contain the writer's name.

5. *An envelope that has a postmark that differs significantly from the date on the letter.* The letter date may be compared with the postmark date to determine the delay in receiving the letter.

6. *A letter specifying an enclosure that is not enclosed.* Write "No Enclosure" on the letter and attach the envelope.

7. *A letter containing a bid, an offer, or an acceptance of a contract.* The postmark date may be needed as legal evidence.

### Date and Time Stamping, Reading, Underlining, and Annotating

All correspondence should be date and time stamped. Most companies provide you with some type of date and time stamp. This may be a manual stamp on which you change the date each morning and rotate the clock face to the appropriate time. Or it may be an automatic date and time stamper.

There are several reasons why it is important to date and time stamp mail. The main reason is that it furnishes a record of when the correspondence was received. For example, a letter may arrive too late to handle the matter mentioned in the letter. Therefore, the stamped date of receipt is a recorded confirmation of the day the letter was received and of the resultant inability to take care of the matter. Or the correspondence may not be dated. The date stamped on the letter, therefore, shows approximately when the correspondence was written.

After you date and time stamp the correspondence, you should read each piece of material to note the important information. Then reread the correspondence and underline the important words and phrases with a colored pen or pencil. This process enables executives to scan letters for important facts and thus saves them time. However, you must be thrifty in underlining. Underlining too much of the correspondence defeats its purpose—which is to save the executive time in the reading process.

Annotations, or explanatory notes, assist the executive in answering correspondence. For example, if a check should have been enclosed with a letter and was not, the words "Check Missing" should be annotated in the letter margin. If a bill is received, check the computations; if the computations are wrong, note that on the bill. If a check is enclosed with a letter, examine the check to see that it is made out for the right amount. Annotate any deviations. The purpose of annotating is the same as underlining—it is meant to save the executive time. Whatever you as an office worker can do to assist in this important task will be appreciated.

**Illus. 10-2** All correspondence should be date and time stamped with an apparatus such as this electronic stamper.

### Preparing Mail for the Executive

Many times a piece of correspondence cannot be answered without referring to previous material. As you read the correspondence, note whether additional materials are needed. If so, pull that information from the file and attach it to the correspondence. On the front of the correspondence, annotate, "See attached letter dated July 18." Again, such a procedure saves time for the executive, and it is much better to get this information before you are asked to get it. This approach will enhance your efficiency in the eyes of the executive.

After you have completed the preliminary mail sort and have opened, date and time stamped, underlined, and annotated, you are ready to do a final sort and to place the mail on the executive's desk. It is a good practice to place the mail in various folders. Such a practice preserves confidentiality. Furthermore, placing the mail in various folders helps the executive see, at a glance, what mail needs to be handled first. Folders are available from office supply stores that have preprinted labels on them; for example, "urgent," "respond," "miscellaneous," and "signature." You might wish to purchase these folders. Or, you might wish to make your own labels, using colored folders or manila folders. Colored folders add some efficiency in that the executive knows at a glance (without reading the label) what mail is most urgent. For example, you might use red for the urgent mail; this folder should always be placed on the top of the stack. Although a signature folder is not needed for incoming mail, it is important to have one for outgoing mail. Again, with such a folder, the executive is able to quickly find and handle the correspondence that needs to be signed.

The final sort is one that you will probably want to work out with your employer to be sure that his or her needs are met. However, here is one suggestion for final sorting. Separate the mail into the following three groups:

1. *Urgent mail.* This folder includes unopened, confidential letters; mailgrams, special delivery, registered, or certified mail; and top priority first-class mail.
2. *Regular mail.* This folder includes routine correspondence and interoffice correspondence.
3. *Miscellaneous.* This folder includes advertisements, circulars, magazines, and catalogs. It is the lowest priority of mail and can be read at the executive's convenience.

### Routing Mail

For mail or other materials that should be referred to other departments or to specific individuals, a referral slip or a routing slip as shown in Figure 10-1 should be used.

Usually the person who refers or routes materials signs only his or her initials on the routing slip. The blank on the first line of the routing slip may be filled in with the word "letter," "article," "report," and so forth. If a copying machine is available, copies of letters, memorandums, and similar materials may be made. Each person concerned would then be sent a copy rather than circulating the original. Such an approach obviously uses more paper, but it saves time. When you are making a decision as to how to route, you need to consider how quickly the information needs to reach the individuals.

**Figure 10-1** Referral and Routing Slips

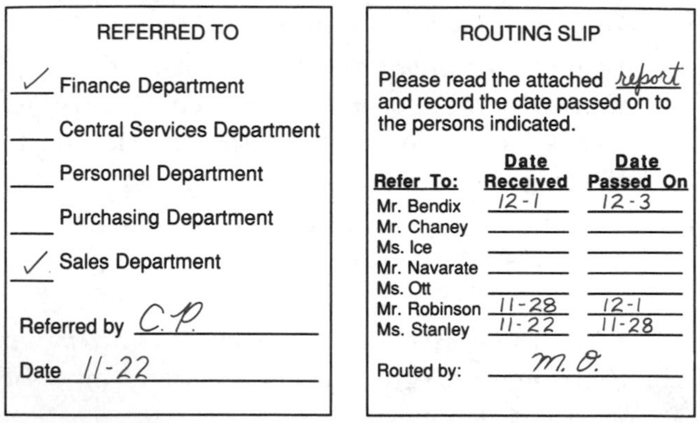
REFERRED TO

✓ Finance Department
___ Central Services Department
___ Personnel Department
___ Purchasing Department
✓ Sales Department

Referred by C.P.

Date 11-22

ROUTING SLIP

Please read the attached report and record the date passed on to the persons indicated.

| Refer To: | Date Received | Date Passed On |
|---|---|---|
| Mr. Bendix | 12-1 | 12-3 |
| Mr. Chaney | | |
| Ms. Ice | | |
| Mr. Navarate | | |
| Ms. Ott | | |
| Mr. Robinson | 11-28 | 12-1 |
| Ms. Stanley | 11-22 | 11-28 |

Routed by: M.O.

## OUTGOING MAIL

Procedures for handling outgoing mail vary depending upon the size of the business. In large companies, personnel in the mail department handle most of the work of sending out the mail. However, in a small company, the individual may be totally responsible for getting correspondence ready for mailing.

### Preparing Correspondence for Mailing

Whether you are working in a large or small company, you should follow these procedures before mailing correspondence.

1. Address the envelopes carefully. Check to see that the envelope address and the letter address are identical.
2. Check each letter or memorandum to see that it is signed.
3. See that any special mailing notations are keyed both on the letter and on the envelope.
4. Make sure that all enclosures are included. When an enclosure is smaller than the letter, staple it to the upper left corner of the letter.
5. If enclosures that are too large to be sent with the letter are sent in a separate large envelope, be sure that the address on the large envelope is correct also. Mark the large envelope with the appropriate class of mail. For example, if the enclosures are to go first class, indicate that on the envelope.

6. Place all interoffice correspondence in appropriate envelopes with the name and department of the addressee listed on the envelope.

If a mail room employee applies postage and seals your mail, neatly stack your correspondence for the employee who picks it up.

**Processing Mail**  Most large companies have postage meters for processing outgoing mail. Postage meters are electronic, high-volume mailing machines that are capable of processing thousands of envelopes an hour. The envelopes are fed into the machine and are stacked, sealed, meter-stamped, and counted in one continuous operation. Electronic postage meters also have the capacity to handle special rates, such as registered, certified, return receipt requested, special delivery, and international mail.

Mailing systems are also available that are comprehensive computerized systems that manage each step of the mail process. These systems will **bar code**, which is the process of printing the

ZIP code on the lower right portion of the envelope in bar code format. Such systems will also print postage, produce management information reports, and produce funds management reports. A bar code is shown in Figure 10-2.

**Figure 10-2**  Envelope With Bar Code

PEARONE INC
PO BOX 8932
CLEVELAND OHIO 44101-4950

PLACE STAMP
HERE
THE POST OFFICE
WILL NOT DELIVER
MAIL WITHOUT
PROPER POSTAGE

**PEARONE INC**
PO BOX 8932
CLEVELAND OH 44101-4950

**Sealing and Stamping**  In a small office you may be responsible for sealing and stamping your own mail. To seal a number of envelopes quickly, place them in a row on the desk with the flaps facing up. Run a moist sponge across the flaps and press down the flap for each envelope. You can also save time by purchasing stamps in rolls. Place the envelopes to be stamped face up on the desk. Before detaching the stamp from the roll, pass the stamp over a moist sponge, place it on an envelope, and then detach the stamp from the roll.

## Using Postal Publications

The *Postal Bulletin* has complete and official postal information. Current information is published weekly in supplement form. Other publications that may assist you with the mailing process are the *Domestic Mail Manual*, the *International Mail Manual*, and the *National ZIP Code and Post Office Directory*. These publications are available for a fee from the Superintendent of Documents, U.S. Government Printing Office, Washington, D.C. 20402-9371.

Your local post office has brochures on such topics as wrapping parcels for mailing, addressing mail, abbreviations for use with the ZIP Code, and your local ZIP Code directory. If you need help in a specific area of mailing procedures, you should call the customer service number listed under United States Government, U.S. Postal Service, in your telephone directory.

**Illus. 10-3**  Most large companies have electronic postage meters for processing outgoing mail.

*Credit: Pitney Bowes, Inc.*

# DOMESTIC MAIL CLASSIFICATIONS

Domestic mail includes the following:

1. Matter deposited in the mail for local delivery.
2. Matter transmitted from one place to another within the United States.
3. Matter transmitted to, from, or between the possessions of the United States.

Domestic mail is divided into four classes:

1. First-class mail
2. Second-class mail
3. Third-class mail
4. Fourth-class mail or parcel post

## First- and Second-Class Mail

First-class mail consists of letters, post cards, greeting cards, personal notes, checks, and money orders. First-class letters may not be opened for postal inspection. All first-class mail is given the fastest transportation service available. If first-class mail is not letter size, it should be marked "First Class." First-class mail over 12 ounces is called Priority Mail. More details on Priority Mail will be presented under the section on special classes of mail.

Second-class mail is generally used by newspapers and other periodical publishers who meet certain postal requirements. However, the general public can use second-class mail for sending newspapers, magazines, and other periodicals. No handwritten messages can be sent by second-class mail. There is no weight limit for this class of mail. Second-class mail should not be sealed and should be marked "Second-Class."

## Third-Class Mail

Third-class mail, sometimes called advertising mail, may be used by anyone, but is used most often by large mailers. Third-class mail includes printed materials and merchandise parcels that weigh less than 16 ounces. Two rate structures are available for this class—a single-piece rate and a bulk rate.

You may have occasion to send printed matter, booklets, and other material by third-class mail with an accompanying letter. This material can sometimes be placed in a large envelope with the letter attached to the outside. The large envelope requires postage at the third-class rate (maximum weight up to, but not including, 16 ounces),

and the smaller envelope containing the letter requires postage at the first-class rate. The entire package, however, is treated as third-class mail by the post office. If material sent in an attached envelope weighs 16 ounces or more, the fourth-class rate is used.

If third-class mail consists of merchandise or books, a letter may be enclosed with postage added to the package. There should be an endorsement "Letter Enclosed," below the postage.

## Fourth-Class (Parcel Post) Mail

Fourth-class (parcel post) mail is used for packages that weigh 16 ounces or more. Packages mailed between larger post offices in the continental United States are limited to 40 pounds and 84 inches in length and girth combined. (Parcels weighing up to 70 pounds and 100 inches in length and girth combined should be sent by priority mail.) Parcels up to 70 pounds and 100 inches in length and girth combined can be mailed to and from smaller post offices and from any post office in Hawaii and Alaska. Your local post office has information to assist you on the sizes and weights that can be mailed to particular locations.

A package should not usually contain a communication other than one that identifies the contents, such as a sales slip or an invoice. However, first-class mail may be sent with a parcel-post package in one of the following ways:

1. Enclosed in the package with the package marked "First-Class Mail Enclosed" below the postage.
2. Enclosed in an envelope and attached to the outside of the package. The address should be on both the parcel and the envelope. The entire package travels as fourth-class mail.

Previously, if a piece of first-class material was attached to a second- or fourth-class mailing, the postal service required postage for both pieces. As a result of a recent ruling, a piece of first-class mail that is incidental (related) to the matter mailed via another class, except nonmerchandise third-class mail, does not require the separate, additional postage.

## SPECIAL MAIL SERVICES

In addition to knowing the different classifications of mail, you should be familiar with special postal services as well. Such services, when used appropriately, can enable you to be more efficient in processing outgoing mail.

### Priority and Express Mail

First-class mail that weighs more than 12 ounces must be sent as priority mail. **Priority mail** cannot exceed 70 pounds in weight, and the maximum size for any item is 108 inches in combined length and **girth** (measurement around the thickest part). A higher postal rate is charged for priority mail; therefore, use it only when necessary.

Through **Express Mail Next Day Service** you can mail letters or packages at a designated express mail post office by 5:00 p.m. on any business day and be assured of delivery to the required destination by 3:00 p.m. of the next day. Express mail has a considerably higher postage rate than first-class mail; therefore, you should use it only for mail that must be delivered overnight. Letters and parcels sent by express mail are insured against loss or damage at no additional cost.

**Illus. 10-4** Special postal and delivery services can enable you to be more efficient in processing outgoing mail.

### Registered Mail

Registered mail provides protection and evidence of receipt for first-class and priority mail. When this service is used, the post office guarantees delivery and, if the mail is lost, becomes responsible to the sender for the declared value of the mail up to $25,000. Registered mail must be sealed. It is most frequently used in sending money and valuable papers such as stocks, bonds, contracts, and bids.

A receipt is always issued to the sender of a registered letter. For a small, additional fee, a return receipt showing the signature of the recipient and the date received will be furnished to the sender. For an additional fee, the address where delivered will be shown. The sender may also, upon payment of an additional fee, restrict the delivery of registered mail to the addressee only or to someone named by the sender in writing. Registered mail service, with return receipt requested or demanded, is sometimes used in writing credit letters and other letters when the writer wants to verify that the addressee received the letter.

Whenever letters or packages are sent by registered mail, a record should be kept showing the name and address of the addressee, the contents of the package, its value, and the postage paid. The receipt issued by the post office for each registered piece should be kept with the record. The registry fee is governed by the value of the contents.

### Insured Mail

Only third- and fourth-class mail are insurable. The maximum liability of the post office is $500. When a package is insured, a receipt is issued by the post office and the package is stamped "Insured." This receipt should be kept by the sender as it will be needed if a claim for loss or damage is made. If a package is lost or damaged in the mail, a claim for the amount of the loss may be made at the post office where the package was mailed or received. Simply present the insured mailing receipt and invoice on the damaged parcel or the damaged article itself along with the container or wrapper showing evidence of insurance, postage, and address of sender. If an article valued at more than $500 is to be sent by mail, it can be sent by registered mail and be covered for loss. A return receipt is available on parcels insured for $25 or more for an additional fee.

### C.O.D. Service and Special Delivery

An article that has not been paid for may be sent by mail and the price and the cost of the postage may be collected from the addressee. This is called **C.O.D.**, collect-on-delivery, or cash-on-delivery service. C.O.D. service may be used for merchandise sent by parcel post, first-class, or third-class. However, the merchandise must have been ordered by the addressee. Fees charged for this service include insurance protection against loss or damage. C.O.D. service is not available to foreign countries.

Special delivery service is available for all classes of mail. It provides delivery during prescribed hours that extend beyond the regular hours of ordinary mail delivery. Special delivery mail is also delivered on Sundays and holidays. This service is available to all customers served by city carriers and to other customers within a one-mile radius of the delivery post office.

The purchase of special delivery does not always mean the article will be delivered by special messenger; special delivery may be delivered by a regular mail carrier. All mail sent by special delivery should be marked prominently with the words "Special Delivery."

### Special Handling and Certified Mail

Special handling service is available for third- and fourth-class mail only, including insured and C.O.D. mail. It provides for preferential handling in dispatch and transport, but it does not provide for special delivery. A special handling fee must be paid on parcels that require special care. Special handling does not mean special care of fragile items. Anything breakable should be packed with adequate cushioning and marked "Fragile."

Certified mail provides the sender with a mailing receipt. A record of delivery is maintained at the addressee's post office. It is used for items with little intrinsic value that are sent and handled as ordinary mail. A return receipt, which provides the sender proof of delivery, may be obtained for an additional fee.

### Return Receipts/Postal Money Orders

The return receipt gives the sender proof of delivery. It is available on mail that is insured for more than $25 and on certified, registered, and C.O.D. mail. The return receipt identifies who signed for the item and the date it was delivered. For an additional fee, you can get a receipt showing the exact address of delivery.

Money orders are available at all post offices in amounts up to $500. If a money order is lost or stolen, the customer receipt may be presented to the post office, and the money order will be replaced. Copies of paid money orders are available for two years after the date they are paid.

### MAILING COSTS

Mailing costs are continuing to escalate. Some large companies in the United States report mailing costs for postage, equipment, and salaries at several million dollars per year. In one year the average cost of mailing a first-class letter increased 19 percent. How are companies coping with the ever-increasing costs of mailing? The answer for many companies is use of technology and efficient methods of handling mail. Cost containment methods include ZIP + 4 bar coding, in-house presorting, lightweight mailing envelopes, and up-to-date mailing lists. Presorting and bar coding are only done with relatively large volume mailing (500 or more pieces of mail), and these functions would generally be performed in the mail room of the company.

In presort mailing, the mail is organized into five-digit, three-digit, and residual categories. In barcode sorting, a bar code (similar to bar codes used on grocery products) is printed on the lower right portion of envelope. This bar code allows the postal service to sort the mail more quickly and efficiently.

The office assistant is not usually involved in performing this presorting and bar coding. However, the office assistant would be involved in the other cost containment items mentioned here and should have knowledge of presorting and bar coding in order to be able to suggest less costly methods of mailing.

### The ZIP Code

In devising the five-digit code, the United States and its possessions were divided into ten geographic areas. Each area consists of three or more states or possessions and each has been assigned a number between 0 and 9. This number is the first digit of any ZIP code. Notice Figure 10-3. Together, the first three digits of any ZIP code number stand for a particular sectional center or a metropolitan city. The last two digits of a sectional center ZIP code number stand for one of the associated post offices served by the sectional center or one of the delivery areas served by the city post office.

For example, in the ZIP code number 45237, the 4 designates the national area. The 5 designates a subdivision within the region. The 2 designates a section center, and the 37 designates a specific post office or delivery area within a multi-ZIP coded city. The ZIP 45237 designates a delivery area in Cincinnati, Ohio. The ZIP + 4 code is an expanded ZIP code designed to improve service. National implementation of ZIP + 4 occurred in October, 1983. This nine-digit ZIP further identi-

**Figure 10-3** ZIP Code Explanation

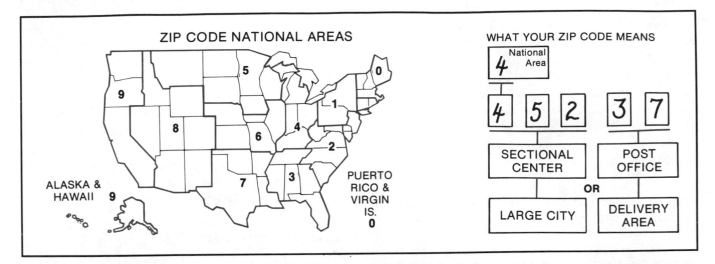

fies the destination of correspondence and permits even greater mailing productivity.

By using the ZIP + 4 code, in addition to presort and bar codes, first-class mail can qualify for discounts from the United States Postal Service. When addressing the envelopes or packages using the ZIP + 4 code, the following guidelines should be used:

- The address should be machine-printed or typewritten.
- Only capital letters should be used.
- Each line of the address should be flush with the left margin.

- No punctuation should be used except the hyphen in the ZIP code.
- For best results, the address should be printed in black, preferably on white paper.
- Lines of print should be parallel to the bottom edge of the envelope.

Figure 10-4 illustrates the proper use of the ZIP + 4 code.

Using these guidelines helps increase the accuracy and speed of the sorting process. In Chapter 3 you learned that an OCR (optical character reader) scans keyboarded characters that are then

**Figure 10-4** Envelope With ZIP + 4 Code

TriCounty Regional
Planning Agency

3232 Six Flags Drive
Arlington, TX 76025-5888
(817) 245-6800

GRATIOT PRINTING CORPORATION
3450 BIG BEAVER ROAD
TROY MI 48304-3491

encoded into electronic signals and read by a computer. OCRs are used by the United States Postal Service in reading and sorting mail. The OCR reads each character separately and does not register differences in size. In many type styles, a comma could be read as a nine or a period as a 0, thus producing errors. If all capital letters are keyboarded, the beam on the OCR can scan all the way across the line in one continuous motion. If the letters are capital and lowercase, the beam has to go up and down, thus increasing the time of the sorting process.

**Illus. 10-5** Optical character readers are used by the United States Postal Service in reading and sorting mail.

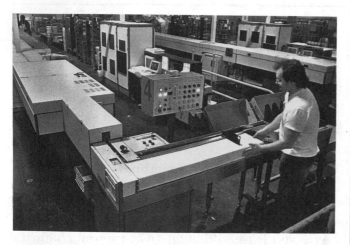

*Credit: U.S. Postal Service.*

## Mailing Lists

Keeping an up-to-date mailing list eliminates the loss that is caused by sending out incorrectly addressed mail. To keep the list up-to-date, notice must be taken of returned mail, change of address, and change of name. The mailing list should be kept on a computer file, and changes in names or addresses can be inserted easily. Also, with the mail merge function on many software packages, mailing lists can be alphabetized quickly and easily.

## Proper Postage and Mail Service

Be certain that you are applying the correct postage. Do not try to guess the weight of packages or large envelopes. Mail rooms have equipment that will apply the correct postage. If your company does not have a mail room, you should have scales for weighing the mail or take it to the post office for mailing.

Place all mail for one individual or for one branch office in the same envelope. If more than one letter is written to an individual in one day, you can save the company money by placing these letters in the same envelope. If mail is sent daily to branch offices, you should hold all the mail for the branches until the end of the day; then, place the mail in one envelope.

Use the correct type of mail service. For example, if mail that can be sent third-class is sent first-class, the company will pay more postage than is necessary. If you are not sure what type of mail service should be used, check with the mail room or the postal service.

## SPECIAL PROBLEMS

There are some special problems in sending mail that you, as an office employee, may encounter. Some of these special problems are covered here.

### Currency/Mail Retrieval

Currency should generally not be sent through the mail. However, sometimes you may find it necessary to mail small amounts of money. If you are mailing coins, you should tape the coins to a small card and insert the card with the letter, or place the card inside a folded plain sheet of paper. Bills should be folded inside the letter. If bills are being sent without a letter, they should be folded inside a plain sheet of paper.

Certainly you should be extremely careful to have all information correct before you mail a piece of correspondence. However, if you discover that you have sent an important piece of mail incorrectly, you may call the post office and ask that the correspondence be held. Then you must go to the post office and fill out the necessary form to retrieve the mail. For identification purposes, you must present an envelope addressed the same as the incorrectly mailed item. If the correspondence has left the post office, it can still be stopped at the destination post office by calling or telegraphing the post office. You must pay for the telephone call or the telegram.

### Incorrectly Addressed Mail

If you receive mail for someone who is unknown at the company where you work, you should mark the mail "Not Known at This Address" and put it in the outgoing mail. If you receive mail for someone who is no longer with the company but you know the person's new address, merely cross out the old address and write the new address in ink. If you open mail that does not belong to your company, you should write "Opened by Mistake" on the envelope, reseal the envelope with tape, and place it in the outgoing mail.

### Change of Address and Forwarding

If the company you work for changes its address, you should notify the local post office of the change. The post office will ask that you fill out a change-of-address card. Mail will then be forwarded to the new address for one year.

First-class mail can be forwarded without charge. For second-, third-, and fourth-class mail, the addressee must pay the postage for having the item forwarded.

If a piece of correspondence fails to arrive at its destination in a reasonable length of time, you can ask the post office to trace the item. You should report to the post office how the item was mailed—first class, registered, insured, and so forth. If the lost mail was insured or registered, you may file a claim for reimbursement.

## ELECTRONIC MESSAGES

An **electronic message** is the noninteractive communication of text, data, images, or voice messages between a sender and a recipient by utilizing telecommunication links. Five types of electronic messages include computer-based message systems (CBMS), voice mail, telegrams, mailgrams, and Telex.

### Computer-Based Message Systems

**Computer-based message systems**, often called E-mail (electronic mail), allow individuals who are connected to the system to communicate quickly and efficiently via a computer. Computer-based message systems can handle long or short documents for almost instantaneous review by the receivers. The computer-based message system, or E-mail, has become a commonly used method of sending information to individuals within a company. Any number of options are available to you with E-mail software. Notice the options given in Figure 10-5. You may send a message, view a message, process calendars, and so forth.

**Figure 10-5** Electronic Mail Options

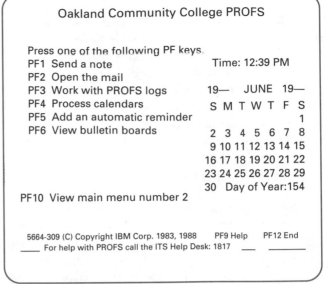

**Sending the Message** Your job as an office assistant may include sending E-mail messages for your employer. In order to send a message, you must have the access code or password of the individual for whom you are sending the message. Using the procedures designed by the software package that you are using, log onto the E-mail system. Then, from the main menu of the package, select "send a note" or a similar option that allows you to send a message (notice that Figure 10-5 has this "send a note" option). From that point, the message is keyed just as you would key any message on a computer (Figure 10-6 shows the message display screen). You also have the ability to designate

**Figure 10-6** Electronic Mail Message Display Screen

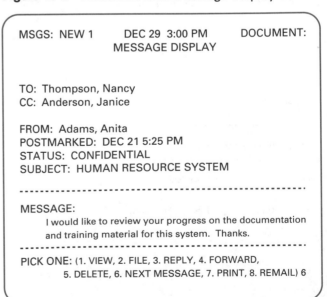

whether the mail being sent is urgent or confidential. The display screen in Figure 10-6 shows the confidential status of the mail being sent.

**Receiving a Message**   Your employer may choose to access his or her own E-mail or have you access the E-mail and print out a copy. However, most office assistants will be receiving and sending E-mail on their own as part of their daily responsibilities. You should check your E-mail on a periodic basis, possibly two or three times a day, depending on the volume that you receive. If you receive the E-mail for your employer, check his or her mail two or three times a day.

**Viewing the Mail**   To view the mail, key in either your access code or your employer's access code. After accessing the E-mail system, the "in-box" appears. Figure 10-7 depicts an in-box. Once the in-box appears, select the items that you want to view. For example, in Figure 10-7, assume you want to view the first item. You would key in "PF1" and the first item would appear on the screen as in Figure 10-8. Once the correspondence in the in-box has been viewed, you need to act on the message. Notice in Figure 10-8 that these options appear at the bottom of the in-box. You can forward the message, erase the message, reply to the message, and so forth.

**Replying to the Mail**   With E-mail, you can respond immediately to the mail received. Within minutes or seconds after you receive the correspondence, the sender may have a reply. The message is keyed on the computer, the appropriate

**Figure 10-7**   Electronic Mail In-Box

```
┌──────────────────────────────────────────────┐
│              OPEN THE MAIL                     │
│                                                │
│  Press the PF key for the document you want.   │
│  Or, if you want to view all of these          │
│  documents, type ALL here and press ENTER ──►  │
│                                                │
│  ----- FROM -----  ---TO---  TYPE  DUE         │
│                                    DATE  DOCUMENT NO. │
│  PF1 MCCOMDEN--OCC  Patsy Fulton  Note         │
│      Subject: HOLIDAY DATES        06/03/— 11:29 │
│                                                │
│  PF2 RTSAUNDE--OCC  Patsy Fulton  Forward      │
│      Subject: corrected encumbrances  06/03/— 10:25 │
│                                                │
│  PF3 JSSLOAN--OCC   Patsy Fulton  Forward      │
│      Subject: finaid               06/02/— 21:27 │
│                                                │
│                                  Screen 1 of 1 │
│  PF9 Help  PF10 Next Screen  PF11 Previous Screen  PF12 Return │
└──────────────────────────────────────────────┘
```

**Figure 10-8**   Electronic Mail Note Screen

```
┌──────────────────────────────────────────────┐
│              VIEW THE NOTE              E01     │
│  From: MCCOMDEN--OCC       Date and time  06/03/— 11:29:31 │
│  To: PJFULTON--OCC    Patsy Fulton             │
│                                                │
│  Subject: HOLIDAY DATES                        │
│                                                │
│  TONY JARSON'S ANNUAL C.O. PARTY IS SCHEDULED FOR FRIDAY, │
│  DECEMBER 20. IT IS USUALLY IN THE LATE AFTERNOON AT FOX AND │
│  HOUNDS IN BLOOMFIELD HILLS.                   │
│                                                │
│  THE OCC COLLEGE GALA IS SCHEDULED FOR DECEMBER 8. WE HAVE │
│  PAID THE 300.00 DEPOSIT TO RESERVE LOVETT HALL AT GREENFIELD │
│  VILLAGE, DEARBORN.                            │
│                                                │
│  SHIRTS AND TOWELS ARE TO BE PICKED UP WEDNESDAY. GREEN WITH │
│  WHITE IMPRINT. I WILL HAVE THE FLOWERS DELIVERED TO C.O. FRIDAY │
│  SO WE WILL TAKE THEM WITH US.                 │
│                                                │
│  WORKING ON PICNIC DETAILS NOW. WILL ADVISE LATER IN THE DAY │
│  REGARDING OPTIONAL DATES FOR YOUR CALENDAR DECISIONS. │
│                                                │
│  cc: PHJEFFRE--OCC    Patricia Jeffrey         │
│  PF1 Alternate PFs  PF2 File NOTE  PF3 Keep  PF4 Erase  PF5 Forward Note │
│  PF6 Reply  PF7 Resend  PF8 Print  PF9 Help  PF10 Next  PF11 Previous │
│  PF12 Return                                   │
└──────────────────────────────────────────────┘
```

software procedures are followed, and the message is transmitted to the in-box of the receiver.

**Forwarding the Mail**   In a regular mail system, forwarding can take a day or two to accomplish. With E-mail, forwarding to another individual takes place in a matter of seconds. You merely key in the appropriate number on your computer, and the mail is forwarded to the mailbox of the receiver. (Notice again in Figure 10-8 the "forward note" notation.)

**Filing the Mail**   If you receive information on your computer in-box that you need to refer to again, it should be filed. Filing can take place by printing out a copy of the correspondence and filing it in a standard file drawer, or it can take place electronically by filing it on the computer. Notice in Figure 10-9 the message is filed by selecting the appropriate response at the bottom of the screen.

## Voice Mail

A **voice mail** system operates like a mailbox for voice messages via the telephone. When you reach an unattended phone that is connected to a voice message system, you hear a message. This message may tell you how to reach another extension number or leave a message. If you leave a message, it is stored in the receiver's mailbox. By keying an access code, the receiver can pick up his or her messages from the voice mailbox. Following is a list of some of the advantages of voice mail.

1.   Voice mail can speed communications by getting messages through, even when there are

**Figure 10-9** Electronic Mail Reply to Message Screen

```
MSGS:  NEW 0         DEC 29, —  3:00 P.M.        DOCUMENT:
                       REPLY TO A MESSAGE


TO: Adams, Anita
BC: (YOURSELF)


SUBJECT: Human Resource System
ORIGINAL MESSAGE TEXT:
     I would like to review your progress on the documentation
     and training material for this system. Thanks.


REPLY TEXT:
     I will have the material you requested on Monday, Jan 5, 1990.
     Are you free that day?


CERTIFIED? (Y/N)  N
FILE THIS REPLY? (Y/N)  N


CONFIDENTIAL? (Y/N)  N   ACTING FOR:
URGENT? (Y/N)  N   EXECUTE? (Y/N)  Y
```

time zone differences. For example, if a user wants to send a message from California to New York at 4:00 p.m., the New York office will probably be closed since it is 7:00 p.m. in New York. However, with voice mail, the message can be sent right away, and the receiver can have it when he or she arrives at work the following morning.

2. Voice mail can make office workers more productive by eliminating repeated telephone calls when the individual called is not available.

3. Voice mail can cut down on extraneous conversation. (For example, a normal phone conversation lasts four or five minutes while a voice message averages 30 seconds to a minute.)

4. Voice mail can provide the frequent traveler with the ability to communicate with the office at any time.

5. Voice mail can cut down on internal memorandums.

### Telegrams and Mailgrams

There are two classes of Western Union telegrams—the regular telegram and the overnight telegram. The regular telegram can be sent any time of the day or night. Western Union guarantees delivery of telegrams to major U.S. cities within five hours by messenger or 2½ hours by telephone. The minimum charge is based on 15 words, excluding the address and signature; an additional charge is made for each additional word.

An overnight telegram can be sent at any time up to midnight for delivery the next morn-

ing. The overnight telegram is less expensive than the regular telegram. The minimum charge is based on a 100-word message; an additional charge is made for each word over 100.

The **mailgram** combines Western Union and post office services. Mailgrams are sent over Western Union communication networks to the post office near the addressee. After the Mailgram is routed through Western Union to the post office, the message is printed out on high-speed equipment. Then, it is inserted into an envelope for delivery the next business day by regular postal carriers.

### Telex and TWX

Telex was introduced in 1958 by Western Union. TWX was first introduced by the Bell System and later purchased by Western Union. Both systems transmit information from one location to another through teletypewriters. These machines comprise a two-way communication network capable of sending and receiving messages around the world in a fast, economical manner. Teletypewriters can accept messages even when unattended. They turn on automatically when called and answer back automatically.

### INTERNATIONAL MAIL

International mail service is divided into two general categories: postal union mail and parcel post. Postal union mail is further classified as LC Mail and AO Mail.

**Illus. 10-6** Telex machines comprise a two-way communication network capable of sending and receiving messages around the world.

Credit: Western Union.

## Postal Union Mail

The two categories of postal union mail are **LC mail** (letters and cards) and **AO mail** (other articles, such as printed matter, small packets, and the like). The postage for letters and cards mailed to Canada and Mexico is the same as for the United States. To other countries the rates are higher. Rates on letters to countries other than Canada and Mexico are charged at a fixed rate for a half ounce.

## Parcel Post

The postal service ships packages to countries by two different methods: air parcel post and surface parcel post. Air parcel post ensures delivery in 10 days or less. Surface parcel post items are sent by boat and may take up to two months for delivery. Packages to be sent overseas by parcel post should be packed carefully and must be accompanied by a customs declaration document that describes the package's contents. Since rates, weight limitations, and other regulations vary from country to country, the office assistant should obtain information from the post office about requirements for a particular mailing.

## RECYCLING

You have learned in this chapter that there is a significant increase in the amount of mail generated yearly. This increase in mail means that more and more paper products are being used, and thus more and more trees are being cut down to produce the paper. Nearly 76 percent of the municipal waste generated in the United States today is buried in landfills. But the landfills are closing at the rate of one per day, and there is a shortage of available land to establish more landfills. Paper and paper products constitute over 35 percent of solid waste in landfills. According to American Paper Institute statistics, the average office worker discards 2.5 pounds of paper each week or 80 percent of an office's waste.

The realization that our nation is losing its forests, that we are running out of landfill space, and the concern about the high cost of trash removal have caused many companies to take action. Recycling bins in which paper is sorted by various types (for example, white bond paper and computer paper) are common in offices. This paper is then bought by businesses engaged in recycling. Once the paper is recycled, it is again available for purchase in various weights, finishes, and colors.

Current recycling efforts save more than 200 million trees a year. Recycled paper uses 64 percent less energy and 58 percent less water in production, compared to virgin papers. In addition, manufacturing recycled paper produces 74 percent less air pollution and 35 percent less water pollution than virgin paper production processes.

Businesses are also finding creative applications for shredders in the recycling of paper. Shipping departments of typical companies can spend several hundred dollars per week on plastic pellets for packaging. These pellets are not biodegradable, and many states have banned their use in packaging. By shredding used paper and using it for packaging, a company can not only address environmental concerns but can also save money.

**Illus. 10-7** Current recycling efforts, such as this paper shredding operation, save more than 200 million trees a year.

*Credit: Allegheny Paper Shredders Corporation.*

## CHAPTER SUMMARY

The following review will help you remember the important points of this chapter.

1. Incoming mail is sorted, opened (with the exception of confidential mail), and date and time stamped by the office assistant.
2. Outgoing mail should be carefully prepared by (a) checking the envelope address against the letter address; (b) checking to see that all correspondence has been signed; (c) checking to see that special mailing notations are keyed on the letter and envelope; (d) determining that any enclosures are included; and (e) properly addressing envelopes for material that must be sent in a separate envelope.
3. Domestic mail includes first-, second-, third-, and fourth-class mail. First-class mail consists of letters, post cards, and similar types of mail. Second-class mail consists of newspapers and periodicals. Third-class mail includes mail that cannot be classed as second-class and weighs up to 16 ounces. Fourth-class mail includes mail weighing 16 ounces or more.
4. Special mail services include priority mail, Express Mail, registered mail, insured mail, C.O.D. service, special delivery, special handling, certified mail, return receipts, and money orders. Through Express Mail Next Day Ser-

vice, letters and packages are delivered to the required destination in one day.
5. Mailing costs may be decreased by using the ZIP + four code, ZIP + 4 bar coding, in-house presorting, up-to-date mailing lists, and by selecting the proper postage and mail service.
6. Electronic message systems involve the noninteractive communication of text, data, images, or voice messages between a sender and a recipient by utilizing telecommunication links. They include computer-based message systems (E-mail), voice mail, telegrams, mailgrams, Telex, and TWX.
7. International mail is divided into postal union mail and parcel post mail. Postal union mail consists of letters, cards, small packets, and the like. Parcel post mail consists of packages.
8. The increase in the amount of paper used in offices today has brought a corresponding need to reduce the amount of waste from discarded paper. Nearly 76 percent of the municipal waste generated in the United States today is buried in landfills. Landfills are closing at the rate of one per day, and there is a shortage of available land to establish more landfills. Efforts are being made to recycle the used paper in offices. Current efforts save more than 200 million trees a year. It is anticipated that recycling efforts will continue to increase.

## TERMINOLOGY REVIEW

The following terms were introduced in this chapter. To help you understand them, definitions are given below.

1. **Bar code** *(page 269)* A bar code in relation to mail refers to the ZIP code that is printed in bar code format on the lower right portion of an envelope. Bar coding increases the efficiency of the sorting process and thus speeds up mail delivery.
2. **C.O.D.** *(page 271)* An article that has not been paid for may be sent by mail and the price and the cost of the postage may be collected from the addressee. This service is called collect-on-delivery or cash-on-delivery service.

3. **Computer-based message systems** *(page 275)* Computer-based message systems (also called E-mail) allow the delivery of electronic messages via a computer.
4. **Electronic message** *(page 275)* An electronic message is defined as the noninteractive communication of text, data, images, or voice messages between a sender and a recipient by utilizing telecommunication links.
5. **Express Mail Next Day Service** *(page 271)* Letters or packages that need to be delivered in one day may be sent via Express Mail Next Day Service offered by the United States Postal Service.
6. **Girth** *(page 271)* Distance around the thickest part of an object; in this chapter girth

refers to determining the size of a package for mailing.

7. **LC mail and AO mail** *(page 278)* International postal union mail is divided into two categories—LC mail and AO mail. LC mail consists of letters and cards, and AO mail consists of all other articles.

8. **Mailgram** *(page 277)* A mailgram combines Western Union and post office services to deliver messages in one day by regular postal carriers.

9. **Priority mail** *(page 271)* First-class mail that weighs more than 12 ounces is sent by priority mail.

10. **Voice mail** *(page 276)* Voice mail operates essentially as a mailbox for voice messages via the telephone.

## DISCUSSION ITEMS

To demonstrate your understanding of the information in this chapter, respond to the following items.

1. Identify five situations in which incoming mail envelopes must be retained.

2. Explain how underlining and annotating assist the executive.

3. Discuss three types of special mail services available.

4. List three procedures that can help reduce mailing costs.

5. Assume that you need to retrieve a piece of mail that has been incorrectly mailed. How do you go about doing it?

6. What are the advantages of certified mail and insured mail?

7. Name and describe four types of electronic messages.

8. Why has recycling become so important today?

## CASE STUDY

Roger Martin is a clerk in the central mail room. He has been with the company for six months. Roger seems like a nice young man who is eager to succeed on his job, but he has made several mistakes. These mistakes were as follows:

1. You had a very important item to mail, and you requested that it be insured for $250. Roger failed to have the package insured.

2. Roger picks up mail from you in the morning and in the afternoon. On several occasions, he has inadvertently left your outgoing mail at other desks in the building. The employees at these desks have returned the mail to you.

3. On three mornings this week (and on several previous occasions), Roger has missed you on his mail run—he has neither picked up your outgoing mail nor brought you the incoming mail.

Each time Roger has made a mistake, you have talked with him about the error. He has been extremely apologetic and has made the excuse that he still has a lot to learn. However, the last time you called a mistake to his attention, he seemed to be quite defensive about the mistake. What should you do now?

## OFFICE APPLICATIONS

### Office Application 10-1 (*Objective 1*)

You receive the incoming mail listed below for Mr. Andrews, Ms. Gonzales, and Mr. Ueoka. Identify the general and special handling procedures to follow in opening the mail. Separate each individual's mail for individual folders with labels of "urgent," "regular mail," and "read." Prepare a report to be submitted to your instructor. The headings of your report should be as follows:

I.   Opening the Mail

    A.   General Procedures
    B.   Special Handling Procedures

II.  Arrangement of Mail in Individual Folders

    A.   Mr. Andrews' Folder
       (List of items in folder)
    B.   Ms. Gonzales's Folder
       (List of items in folder)
    C.   Mr. Ueoka's Folder
       (List of items in folder)

Here is the list of incoming mail you are to handle:

1.   Confidential letter addressed to Ms. Gonzales
2.   *The Wall Street Journal* addressed to Mr. Andrews
3.   A new product advertisement addressed to the director of TriCounty
4.   A letter addressed to Regina Kinseth who is no longer with TriCounty
5.   A letter addressed to Mr. Ueoka, with enclosures
6.   A certified letter addressed to Mr. Andrews
7.   An insured letter addressed to Mr. Ueoka
8.   An interoffice memorandum addressed to Mr. Andrews
9.   A catalog of computer supplies addressed to Mr. Andrews
10.  A letter with no letterhead address sent to Mr. Andrews
11.  An interoffice memorandum addressed to Ms. Gonzales
12.  A letter addressed to Ms. Gonzales. The envelope has an incorrect address for TriCounty.
13.  A letter addressed to Mr. Andrews which states that a check is enclosed. No check is enclosed.
14.  A letter to Mr. Ueoka. The letter is dated two weeks ago; however, the postmark date is only two days ago.
15.  A letter to Mr. Andrews that refers to a letter written two weeks ago by Mr. Andrews
16.  A bill addressed to Mr. Andrews from Carvell Manufacturing
17.  A special delivery letter to Mr. Andrews

18. *U.S. News & World Report* addressed to Ms. Gonzales
19. A memorandum from Jo Fowler addressed to Mr. Andrews
20. A memorandum from Alan Raye to Mr. Andrews

### Office Application 10-2 (*Objectives 1 and 2*)

Mr. Andrews asks you to mail the correspondence listed below. How will you prepare each item for the outgoing mail? Prepare a report of your response, with the title of the report "Preparing Items for Mailing."

1. A letter with enclosures that must be sent in a separate envelope
2. Five memorandums to be sent to Greco Company
3. A letter that is to be sent SPECIAL DELIVERY
4. A memorandum to be sent to the health manager
5. A first-class letter that is to be sent with a package that weighs more than 16 ounces
6. A memorandum to be sent to the transportation manager
7. A letter that has two enclosures
8. A letter that is confidential
9. A first-class letter to be sent with third-class material
10. An outgoing letter that has Mr. Andrews' name and title on it, but no signatures

### Office Application 10-3 (*Objective 3*)

Indicate the class of mail or special service that should be used in sending the items listed below. Set up a two-column table with the special headings "Correspondence" and "Mail Classifications."

1. A newspaper
2. A periodical
3. A photocopy of a letter
4. A booklet that weighs 15 ounces
5. A catalog that weighs 24 ounces
6. An important letter that weighs 14 ounces
7. A $75 check
8. An important package that has a value of $5,000
9. Two books with a value of $25
10. A letter for which Mr. Andrews wants proof that it has reached its destination
11. A package that weighs 10 pounds and is valued at $150. The receiver is to pay for the goods upon receipt.

### Office Application 10-4 (*Objectives 1, 2, and 5*)

Visit the mail room of your school or a local business. Ask the following questions.

1. What procedures do you use in handling incoming mail?
2. What procedures do you use in handling outgoing mail?

3. What types of equipment do you use?

4. Do you do any presorting or bar coding?

5. Is paper recycled in your business? If so, what advantages do you experience from this recycling?

Prepare the answers to the questions in report format, identifying the people you interviewed and the company affiliation. Turn in your report to your instructor.

### Office Application 10-5 (*Objective 4*)

You are asked by your employer, Mr. Andrews, to set up a meeting with all the managers (Maurice Chateau, Rebecca Gonzales, Travis Ueoka, and Heidi Wenrick). The meeting is to be scheduled for February 10 from 9:00 a.m. until 11:00 a.m. in conference room A. The subject of the meeting is strategic planning. Using a computer, write the memorandum to set up the meeting. By rereading the information in your text on electronic message systems, explain how this message would be transmitted through an E-mail system. Turn in your memorandum, along with your explanation of how it would be sent, to your instructor.

### Office Application 10-6 (*Objective 4*)

Visit an office employee who uses E-mail on the job. Ask him or her to explain how E-mail is used in the office. Report your findings in an oral report to the class.

### Office Application 10-7 (*Objective 5*)

Read two recent articles on recycling. Prepare a report, identifying your reference sources. Turn in your report to your instructor.

# 11 Records Management

Today's office generates vast amounts of information. In fact, a national management consulting firm estimates that paper records are growing at the rate of 8 percent annually, creating hundreds of billions of documents each year. And, although 95 percent of all records are still maintained in paper form, microfilm, microfiche, and computer storage are also used extensively.

One of the biggest complaints of executives is that it is often difficult and sometimes impossible to find essential information when it is needed. This inability to find a document quickly is not only a frustrating process but a costly one as well. Studies have shown that the cost of finding one piece of information that has been misplaced can exceed $100. On the other side of this equation is the office assistant who consistently sees a mountain of paper records that seems to grow each day. Many times there is very little help for the office assistant in understanding the process of records management, including records retention and storage. Office assistants often complain about having to maintain materials; it is a process enjoyed by few. Too often it is a task that is put off until everything else is done; and since everything else never seems to get done, the materials that need to be stored accumulate.

This chapter is designed to help you understand the importance of storing records correctly and to teach you procedures and processes designed to handle the task with efficiency. As an office assistant you will not be able escape the process. If you understand how to do it well, you can learn to take pride in files that are in order and documents that are arranged and found quickly and easily. In this chapter you will learn the alphabetic indexing rules, classification systems, and the basic storage procedures. You will also become familiar with basic storage supplies and the use of micrographics and computerized storage systems.

## GENERAL OBJECTIVES

*Your general objectives for this chapter are to*
1. **Identify and use the basic classification systems.**
2. **Follow proper storage procedures.**

**Illus. 11-1**

## WIZARD OF ID
## BY BRANT PARKER & JOHNNY HART

*Credit: By permission of Johnny Hart and Creators Syndicate, Inc.*

3. **Learn and apply the basic alphabetic indexing rules.**
4. **Become familiar with supplies and equipment used in records management.**
5. **Discuss records transfer and retention.**
6. **Use basic micrographics storage systems.**
7. **Explain computerized storage systems.**

## RECORDS MANAGEMENT TODAY

A **record** is any type of recorded information, whether that information has been recorded in letter form, report form, as a blueprint, as a map, or in some other form. Records contain information about an organization—its functions, policies, procedures, decisions, and operations. The record that we traditionally expect in the office is in paper form. And, although for a number of years the concept of the paperless office has been possible from a technical standpoint, you have just learned that paper continues to be the major form for accumulating information. Paper does have its advantages. Some of these advantages are

1. It's affordable in offices large and small.
2. It is not vulnerable to power surges and accidental keystrokes that can destroy computerized information.
3. Most people are comfortable in working with paper documents, finding a certain reassurance in actually holding the information in hard copy form.

So, it is anticipated that paper documents will not be replaced. However, as technology continues to grow, it is also anticipated that other forms of records—microfilm, microfiche, hard disks, floppy disks, and optical disks—will continue to grow and the percentage of records held in these various forms will increase.

**Records management** is the systematic control of records from the creation of the record to its final disposition. In order for a records system to function there must be information, equipment, and people. Information is generated by many sources and may appear, as mentioned, on a piece of paper or in a magnetic form. Equipment in a records system includes all of the hardware used in processing the records. People include the necessary personnel to get the right record to the right person at the lowest cost.

If you work in a small office you may have the total responsibility for preparing the correspondence and carrying it through the records manage-

ment cycle from distribution to storage, retrieval, and final disposition. If you work in a large office there may be a centralized records management department that stores records, determines retention schedules, makes decisions on equipment, and disposes of records. Your responsibilities for records management in such a company will probably be limited to your immediate office needs—creating, storing, and retrieving information.

## COMPUTER RECORDS

Even though paper records still exist, office assistants are responsible for maintaining records on the computer. How? One of the main computer records that is your responsibility is the maintenance of outgoing or internal correspondence on your microcomputer. As you have learned in earlier chapters, the microcomputer is standard equipment for the office assistant. You will prepare numerous pieces of correspondence on this microcomputer daily. You must be able to store the correspondence so that you can instantly retrieve it for editing or review purposes by you or your employer.

**Illus. 11-2** On a daily basis, the office assistant prepares numerous pieces of correspondence on a microcomputer.

As an example, assume that you have prepared a letter for your employer's signature. You print out a copy for your employer; he or she makes changes in the copy and returns it to you for editing. You must retrieve the letter from computer storage and perform the editing function. Remember, you learned in Chapter 3 that you may store information on the computer internally (for example, the hard drive) or externally (a floppy disk). Now, assume that the letter is mailed. You have decided that you will not store a paper copy of any outgoing correspondence but will maintain it in computer storage. Two weeks later your employer asks you for a copy of the letter. You are able to return to your computer storage, retrieve the letter, and print out a copy for your employer—all within a few minutes. Notice the illustration of this process shown in Figure 11-1. Such retrieval demands that you understand the basic rules of storing records. In the following sections of this chapter, you will develop the skills that will allow you to retrieve correspondence quickly from computer or manual storage.

## CLASSIFICATION SYSTEMS

Although records may be classified in various ways, there are several basic classification systems. Five classifications are presented here.

1. Alphabetic storage
2. Subject storage
3. Geographic storage
4. Numeric storage
5. Chronological storage

These classification systems may be used in computer or paper systems. As you are learning the classification systems, it is easier to apply the concepts to a paper system. Thus, the material presented here refers to paper systems. Once you have the knowledge, it may be transferred to computer systems.

### Alphabetic Storage

**Alphabetic storage** is a system of storage in which records are stored by the names of people, organizations, agencies, and businesses. This classification is one of the most commonly used and is found in one form or another in almost every office. With alphabetic storage, the name of the company, the person, or the organization addressed determines the filing order of outgoing correspondence. The name of the company, the individual, or the organization writing the letter determines the filing order of incoming correspondence. A manual alphabetic storage arrangement is shown in Figure 11-2.

**Figure 11-1**  Process of Computer Storage of Records

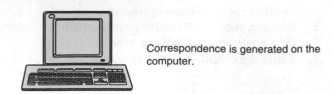
Correspondence is generated on the computer.

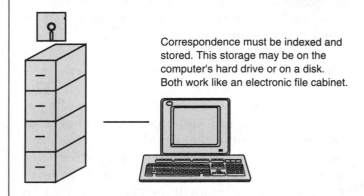
Correspondence must be indexed and stored. This storage may be on the computer's hard drive or on a disk. Both work like an electronic file cabinet.

The correspondence is printed out.

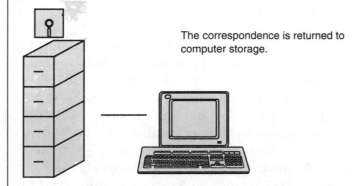
The correspondence is returned to computer storage.

Alphabetic storage has the following advantages:

1. It is a direct system. There is no need to refer to anything except the file itself to find the name.
2. The dictionary order of arrangement is simple to understand.
3. Misfiling is easily checked by alphabetic sequence.
4. It is less costly to operate than other storage methods.

**Figure 11-2** Manual Alphabetic Storage

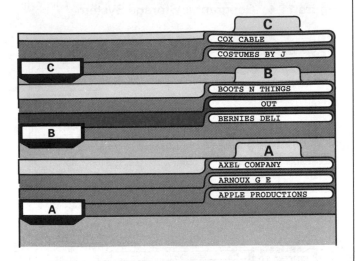

5. Only one sorting is required.
6. Papers relating to one correspondent are stored in the same location.

Some disadvantages of alphabetic storage are as follows:

1. Misfiling may result when rules are not followed.
2. Similarly spelled names may cause confusion when stored under the alphabetic method.
3. Related records may be stored in more than one place.
4. Expansion may create problems, especially if the expansion takes place in one section of the file where there is no room remaining in that particular section for the insertion of more guides and folders.
5. Excessive cross-referencing can congest the files.
6. Confidentiality of the files cannot be maintained since the file folders bearing names are instantly seen by anyone who happens to glance at a folder.

## Subject Storage

With subject storage, correspondence is filed according to the subject of the material. Although subject order is useful and necessary in certain situations, it is the most difficult and most costly method of classification to maintain. Each piece of correspondence must be read completely to determine the subject. And, it is a difficult method to control since one person may read a piece of correspondence and determine that the subject is one thing, and another person may read it and decide that the subject is something entirely different. For example, one person classifying records concerning personnel grievances may determine that the subject is "grievances" while another person may determine that the subject is "personnel—grievances."

A necessary part of subject storage is an index. An index is a list of all subjects under which a piece of correspondence may be stored. Without an index it is almost impossible for the subject storage method to function satisfactorily. The list should be kept up-to-date as new subjects are added and old ones eliminated. When new subjects are added, the index provides guidance to avoid the duplication of subjects. The index may be kept on standard sheets of paper and stored in a notebook or on index cards and stored in a card file box. A subject list kept on sheets of paper provides an easier way to see at a glance which subjects exist in the file than does a card index. When subjects are added to the list, however, the sheets must be reworked and updated. With a card index, a card indicating the new subject is simply inserted in the index. A subject index is shown in Figure 11-3.

**Figure 11-3** Subject Index

```
            SUBJECT INDEX

    ACCOUNTING
        BUDGET
        FINANCIAL STATEMENTS
        INVOICES

    ADVERTISING
        AGENCIES
        NEWSPAPER
        RADIO
        TELEVISION

    COMMITTEES
        STAFF DEVELOPMENT
        UNITED WAY

    PERSONNEL
        DEVELOPMENTAL LEAVE
        GRIEVANCES
        SALARIES
        VACATIONS
```

Subject storage has the following advantages:

1. Correspondence about one subject is grouped together.
2. The system can be expanded easily by adding subdivisions.

Some disadvantages of the subject storage are as follows:

1. It is difficult to classify records by subject.
2. Liberal cross-referencing is necessary since one piece of correspondence may contain several subjects.
3. The system does not satisfactorily provide for miscellaneous records.
4. It is necessary to keep an index of subject headings contained in the subject storage.
5. Preparation of materials for subject storage takes longer than any of the other methods, since each piece of correspondence must be thoroughly and carefully read.

## Geographic Storage

**Geographic storage** is an arrangement in which related records are grouped by place or location. For example, the main divisions may be states, counties, cities, and sales territories. The breakdown into geographic divisions and subdivisions must, of course, fit the type of business, its organization, and its need for specific kinds of information. Geographic records are particularly appropriate for sales records stored by location. For example, the guides used may indicate the state of the sales. The folders may then be arranged by the city or town within the state and, finally, alphabetically by individuals or companies within the city. If there are several folders for one particular city, special guides may be inserted to show an alphabetic breakdown within the city. A geographic arrangement is shown in Figure 11-4.

The advantages of geographic storage are as follows:

1. It provides for grouping of records by location.
2. The volume of correspondence within any given geographic area can be seen by glancing at the records.
3. It allows for direct storage if the location is known.

**Figure 11-4**  Geographic Storage System

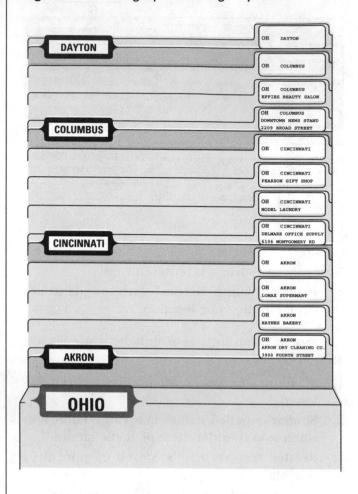

The disadvantages of geographic storage are as follows:

1. Multiple sorting increases the possibility of error and is time-consuming.
2. The complex arrangement of guides and folders makes storage more difficult.
3. Reference to the card file is necessary if the location is not known.
4. It takes longer to set up than does the alphabetic storage method.

## Numeric Storage

With **numeric storage**, guides and folders are assigned numbers and are arranged in numeric sequence. A numeric system has four parts:

1. An accession log
2. An alphabetic card index
3. The main numeric file
4. A miscellaneous alphabetic file.

**Illus. 11-3** Alphabetic storage is a system in which records are stored by the names of people, organizations, agencies, and businesses.

*Credit: © Charles Harbutt, Magnum Photos, Inc.*

The alphabetic card index file is first consulted to determine the number assigned to the client or company. If it is a new client or company (one with which the office has not previously done business), the accession log must be consulted for the next available number. A page from an accession log is shown in Figure 11-5. Once the number has been determined or assigned, the correspondence is placed in the appropriate number file. If there is little correspondence with a particular client or company, it may not be necessary to set up a separate file. In such a case, the correspondence is placed in the miscellaneous alphabetic file. A numeric classification is shown in Figure 11-6.

The numeric storage system has the following advantages:

1. Expansion is unlimited.

**Figure 11-5** Accession Log

| | | Page 105 |
|---|---|---|
| Number | Name | Date |
| 504 | Travel World | 3/16/-- |
| 505 | M E Baker | 3/16/-- |
| 506 | Browning Supply Co | 3/17/-- |
| 507 | Jan Chinook | 3/17/-- |
| 508 | | |

2. It is confidential; a card file must be consulted before records or important papers can be located.

3. Once an index card is prepared and a number is assigned to a piece of correspondence, arranging by number is quicker than arranging alphabetically.

4. Misfiled folders are easily located because numbers out of place are easier to locate than misfiled alphabetic records.

5. All cross-references appear in the card file and do not congest the file folders or drawers.

6. A complete list of the names and addresses of correspondence is instantly available from the alphabetic card file.

7. In an office using the numeric classification system, orders, invoices, ledger accounts, and correspondence of one customer all bear the same number, making reference to them easy.

**Figure 11-6** Numeric Storage System

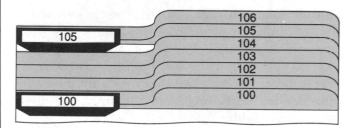

Some disadvantages of the numeric storage system include the following:

1. It is an indirect method. The card file must be consulted before a paper can be filed.

2. More equipment is necessary; therefore, the cost is higher.

3. Numbers may be transposed without being detected.

4. Since two classifications of storage are involved—alphabetic arrangement and numeric arrangement—the disadvantages of the name ordering classification are also disadvantages of the numeric arrangement.

5. If the card file and the accession book are not kept carefully, one correspondent's papers might be assigned several numbers and filed in several folders.

6. As the numbers used become larger, it is harder to remember them and misfiling can easily result.

## Numeric Storage Variations

**Terminal Digit Storage**   Terminal digit storage is one variation of straight numeric storage. In a straight numeric arrangement, as the files increase, the numbers assigned become higher. However, when the numbers are several digits long, it becomes difficult to store papers. Terminal digit storage, which is designed to solve this problem, is done by final digits. For example, assume you have a legal file for Case 389023. The last, or terminal, digits, 23, would identify the drawer number. The second pair of digits, 90, would indicate the number of the file guide, and the first two digits, often called tertiary digits, 38, would be the number of the file folder in the drawer.

In a large organization where numeric storage is used extensively, research shows that terminal digit storage saves up to 40 percent of the filing costs by assuring a uniform work load among office workers, better employee relations, fewer misfiled papers, and unlimited expansion. A terminal digit arrangement is shown in Figure 11-7.

**Middle Digit Storage**   Another variation of the straight numeric classification is middle digit storage, which is similar to terminal digit storage with the exception that the two middle digits identify the drawer. The first two digits identify the guide number in the drawer, and the final two digits identify the folder.

**Block Numeric Storage**   A third variation of the straight numeric classification is block numeric storage. Round numbers (100, 200, 300, and so forth) are assigned to main subjects or groups. For example, the accounting department may be assigned 100, the human resources department 200, payroll 300. Individual folders within the accounting area would be assigned numbers such as 101, 102, and so forth. The advantages of block numeric storage include close groupings of related files and unlimited expansion. Disadvantages, as with other variations of numeric storage, are that personnel must be trained to use the system and creating and starting the system is time-consuming.

### Chronologic Storage

A **chronologic storage** system is an arrangement in which records are stored in date order. Chronologic arrangements have basic applications

1.   As tickler files
2.   As transaction files

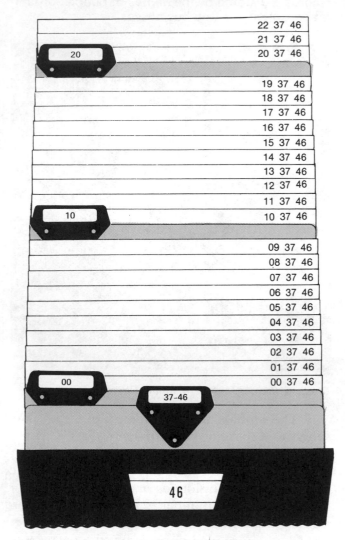

**Figure 11-7**   Terminal Digit Storage

3.   As a supplement to another classification system
4.   Within individual files.

The term *tickler file* comes from the fact that the file is used to tickle your memory and remind you to take certain actions. For example, when something must be taken care of on a certain date, a card is prepared with the necessary information and placed in date or chronologic order. The file is checked each morning to see what must be done that day. The basic arrangement of a tickler file consists of a series of 12 guides with the names of the months printed on the tabs and 31 guides with the number 1 through 31 representing each day of the month printed on the tabs. The tickler file is generally kept on the office worker's desk. A tickler file is shown in Figure 11-8.

Chronologic storage may also be used as a supplement to an alphabetic system. For example, you may keep a chronologic index with a subject ordering system. The index would contain the

**Figure 11-8** Tickler File

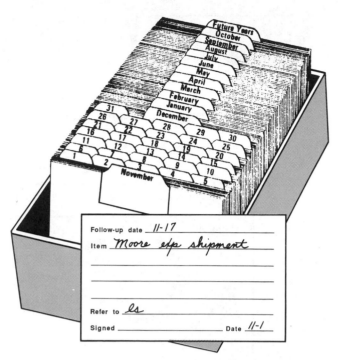

dates of the correspondence along with the name of the individual or company and the subject under which the correspondence is filed. Such a system allows you to find correspondence addressed to Leroy Hampton dated January 11. With a subject ordering system, it would be difficult to locate the correspondence given this information. By maintaining a chronologic index, you can quickly find the correspondence requested. A chronologic index is shown in Figure 11-9.

The chronologic principle is followed with all storage classifications as papers are placed within folders. The top of each paper is at the left of the folder, and the paper with the most recent date is on top so that anyone who opens a folder can see immediately the latest piece of correspondence.

## STORAGE PROCEDURES

Before material can be filed, the proper storage classification must be selected and then the proper steps followed. These steps include determining when a piece of correspondence is ready to be stored, determining whether cross-referencing is necessary, and actually storing the material in the file.

### Select the Correct Classification

You have learned the basic classifications of storing correspondence and the advantages and disadvantages of each classification. If you are setting up a new storage system in an office, you should be familiar with these methods and be able to recommend the system most appropriate for the needs of the company. If you are working with already established systems, you may be able to recommend more efficient classifications based on your knowledge.

### Follow the Proper Filing Steps

Before records can be stored in a folder they must be prepared for storing. Records must be inspected, indexed, coded, cross-referenced if necessary, and sorted before they can be filed. These steps are explained here.

**Inspect**  Incoming correspondence must never be stored until it has been read by your employer. Therefore, before sorting any incoming correspondence, be certain to **inspect** the correspondence for a release mark. This mark may be the executive's initials, a file stamp and the office worker's initials, a code or check mark, or some other agreed upon designation. Outgoing correspondence does not need a release mark since the original copy has been written by your employer or you. However, do not store the copy until the original has been signed, since changes may need to be made.

**Indexing**  The process of determining where a piece of correspondence is to be stored is called **indexing**. In alphabetic storage, indexing means determining the name that is to be used. On incoming

**Figure 11-9**  Chronologic Index

| Date | Name of Company or Individual | Subject Filed Under |
|------|-------------------------------|---------------------|
| 1-11-94 | Leroy Hampton | Advertising--Radio |
| 2-10-94 | Jonathan R Clark | Accounting--Budget |
| 3-20-94 | Patricia Irwin | Personnel--Grievance |

correspondence, the most likely name to use is in the letterhead. On outgoing correspondence, the most likely name to use is in the address.

In an alphabetic subject arrangement, indexing means determining the most important subject discussed in the correspondence. If there are two subjects, the correspondence should be stored under one subject and cross-referenced under the other. In an alphabetic geographic arrangement, the location to be used must be determined. When using the numeric classification, the name and number to be used must be determined.

**Code**   **Coding** is the marking of the correspondence by the name, subject, location, or number that was determined in the process of indexing. The correspondence may be marked by underlining, circling, or checking. Coding is important since it saves time in the refiling process. When a paper has been removed from the files and must be refiled, the office workers do not have to re-read the correspondence.

**Cross-Reference**   For correspondence that can be filed under more than one name, a cross-reference should be prepared. A **cross-reference** is an aid used to find a record stored by a name, subject, or geographic location other than the one selected for storage of the piece of correspondence. For example, if a company that you have been doing business with changes its name from *Heun and Miller Corporation* to *Carvell, Heun, and Miller Corporation,* you will want to cross-reference the correspondence under *Heun and Miller Corporation,* at least until everyone in the office is aware that the name has changed. Without cross-referencing, material from this company could be misplaced.

One method of cross-referencing is to prepare a cross-reference card or cross-reference sheet as shown in Figure 11-10. Both of these documents can be purchased at office supply stores. Another method of cross-referencing is to code the name the material is to be stored under and how it is to be cross-referenced in the upper right-hand corner of the correspondence. Then, make a copy of the document. The original correspondence is stored in the regular folder and the copy is stored in the cross-referenced file. An advantage of using the photocopying method is that if the item is looked for by the cross-referenced name first, it is not necessary to go from the cross-reference file to the regular file to obtain the correspondence. A copy of the correspondence appears in the cross-reference file.

**Figure 11-10**   Cross-Reference

```
ALLEN JAMES MR
SEE JAMES ALLEN MR
```

**CROSS-REFERENCE SHEET**

Name or Subject   *Wade John L.*

Date of item   *April 14, 19--*

Regarding   *Installation of hydraulic presses*

**SEE**

Name or Subject   *H. S. Syner Co.*

Authorized by   *J. McCathy*   Date   *4/17/--*

**Sort**   **Sorting** is the arrangement of materials in the order in which they are to be filed. Sorting should be done daily or twice per day if the filing load is heavy. When sorting materials, a sorter can be used to quickly and efficiently handle the task. The letters of the alphabet appear on the sections of the sorter. Papers can be filed in each section. And, if papers are needed before they are actually stored

**Illus. 11-4**   When sorting materials, a sorter can be used to quickly and efficiently handle the task.

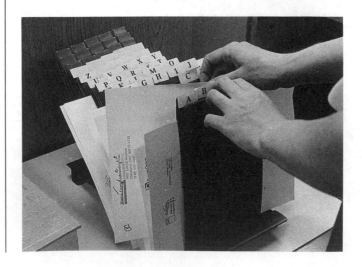

in a file cabinet, they may be quickly retrieved, since they have been placed in alphabetical order.

**Storing** **Storing** is the actual placement of materials into a folder. When storing materials, place the top of the document face forward at the left edge of the file folder. If you have more than one paper for a folder, the most recent date is placed on top. In other words, the papers are filed chronologically within the folder. Small items should be taped to a regular size sheet of paper or filed side by side so the folder will not bulge at one end. Large items should be neatly folded. Material to be filed should always be placed behind the guides. When papers need to be fastened together, a stapler may be used. No more than 50 sheets should be placed in a single folder.

## INDEXING RULES

In order to store and retrieve records effectively, a set of rules must be followed. No one, universal set of rules for alphabetic filing is followed by every business. The key is to adopt a set of rules and apply them consistently. The Association of Records Managers and Administrators, Inc. (ARMA) has published *Alphabetic Filing Rules,* containing standard rules for filing records. The rules in this chapter are written to agree with the ARMA Simplified Filing Standard Rules and Specific Filing Guidelines. The rules, along with examples of each rule in indexing order, are given here. **Indexing order** refers to the order in which units of a filing segment are considered when a record is stored.

### Rule 1: Indexing Order of Units

**A. Personal Names** A personal name is indexed in this manner:

1. The surname (last name) is the key unit.
2. The given name (first name) or initial is the second unit.
3. The middle name or initial is the third unit.

If determining the surname is difficult, consider the last name as the surname. A unit consisting of just an initial precedes a unit that consists of a complete name beginning with the same letter— *nothing comes before something.* Punctuation is omitted. See Table 11-1 (Rule 1A) for examples of indexing personal names.

**Table 11-1** Examples of Indexing Rules 1-7

*Examples of Rule 1A:*

**Index Order of Units in Personal Names**

| Name | Key Unit | Unit 2 | Unit 3 |
|---|---|---|---|
| Walter Kingscott | KINGSCOTT | WALTER | |
| Walter A. Kingscott | KINGSCOTT | WALTER | A |
| Walter Andrew Kingscott | KINGSCOTT | WALTER | ANDREW |

*Examples of Rule 1B:*

**Index Order of Units in Business Names**

| Name | Key Unit | Unit 2 | Unit 3 | Unit 4 |
|---|---|---|---|---|
| Beaumont Health Center | BEAUMONT | HEALTH | CENTER | |
| Beaver Creek Golf Club | BEAVER | CREEK | GOLF | CLUB |
| Chuck Beaver Pharmacy | CHUCK | BEAVER | PHARMACY | |

*Examples of Rule 2:*

**Index Order of Units in Minor Words and Symbols in Business Names**

| Name | Key Unit | Unit 2 | Unit 3 | Unit 4 | Unit 5 |
|---|---|---|---|---|---|
| A Bit of Honey | A | BIT | OF | HONEY | |
| At Home Laundry | AT | HOME | LAUNDRY | | |
| The $ and Shop | DOLLARS | AND | CENTS | SHOP | THE |

**Table 11-1** *(continued)*

**Examples of Rule 3:**

### Index Order of Units with Punctuation and Possessives in Personal or Business Names

| Name | Key Unit | Unit 2 | Unit 3 | Unit 4 |
|------|----------|--------|--------|--------|
| A-Z Video Company | A | Z | VIDEO | COMPANY |
| Abbey's Grooming | ABBEYS | GROOMING | | |
| North/South Printing | NORTHSOUTH | PRINTING | | |

**Examples of Rule 4:**

### Index Order of Units for Single Letters and Abbreviations in Business and Personal Names

| Name | Key Unit | Unit 2 | Unit 3 | Unit 4 |
|------|----------|--------|--------|--------|
| J. V. Hildebrand | HILDEBRAND | J | V | |
| Jas. W. Hildebrand | HILDEBRAND | JAS | W | |
| Wm. R. Hildebrand | HILDEBRAND | WM | R | |
| J K of Texas | J | K | OF | TEXAS |
| KRLD Television | KRLD | TELEVISION | | |
| U.S.A. Motors | USA | MOTORS | | |

**Examples of Rule 5A:**

### Index Order of Units for Titles and Suffixes in Personal Names

| Name | Key Unit | Unit 2 | Unit 3 | Unit 4 |
|------|----------|--------|--------|--------|
| Father James | FATHER | JAMES | | |
| S. R. Harrold II | HARROLD | S | R | II |
| S. R. Harrold III | HARROLD | S | R | III |
| S. R. Harrold, Jr. | HARROLD | S | R | JR |
| S. R. Harrold, Sr. | HARROLD | S | R | SR |
| Frederick Johns, MD | JOHNS | FREDERICK | MD | |
| Ms. Helen Johns | JOHNS | HELEN | MS | |

**Examples of Rule 5B:**

### Index Order of Units for Titles and Suffixes in Business Names

| Name | Key Unit | Unit 2 | Unit 3 |
|------|----------|--------|--------|
| Doctors' Hospital | DOCTORS | HOSPITAL | |
| Dr. Pepper Bottling | DR | PEPPER | BOTTLING |

**Examples of Rule 6:**

### Index Order of Units for Prefixes in Personal and Business Names

| Name | Key Unit | Unit 2 | Unit 3 | Unit 4 |
|------|----------|--------|--------|--------|
| Paul Alan LaFaver | LAFAVER | PAUL | ALAN | |
| MacDugal's Meat Market | MACDUGALS | MEAT | MARKET | |
| McDouglas & Edwards | MCDOUGLAS | AND | EDWARDS | |
| Mary Lou St. Marie | STMARIE | MARY | LOU | |

**Examples of Rule 7:**

### Index Order of Units for Numbers in Business Names

| Name | Key Unit | Unit 2 | Unit 3 | Unit 4 |
|------|----------|--------|--------|--------|
| 4-Cent Copy Center | 4 | CENT | COPY | CENTER |
| 4th Street Garage | 4 | STREET | GARAGE | |
| 400-410 Daniels Court | 400 | DANIELS | COURT | |
| Four Seasons Health Spa | FOUR | SEASONS | HEALTH | SPA |
| Highway 30 Cafe | HIGHWAY | 30 | CAFE | |
| Highway Service Station | HIGHWAY | SERVICE | STATION | |

**Figure 11-16** Electronic Delivery of Micrographic Images

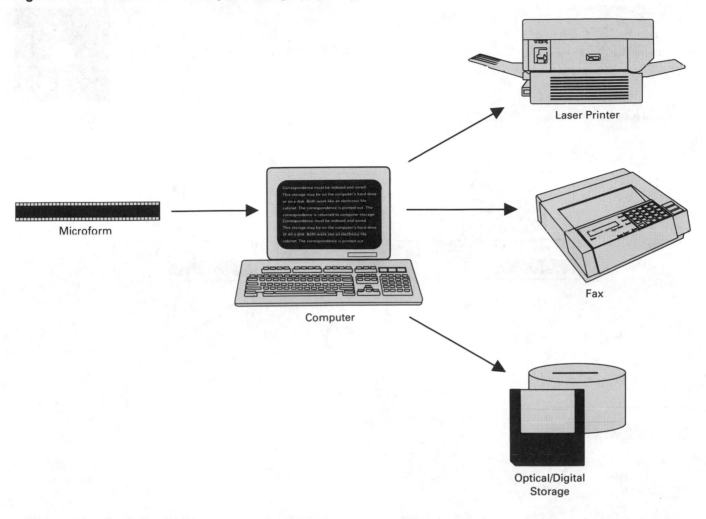

Microform

Computer

Laser Printer

Fax

Optical/Digital Storage

## ARMA

You learned earlier in this chapter that ARMA (The Association of Records Managers and Administrators, Inc.) is responsible for the filing rules that are presented in this chapter. This organization also provides conferences and seminars designed to help people increase their expertise in records management. There are more than 130 ARMA chapters in the U.S., Canada, and 20 other countries, with over 10,000 individual members. ARMA also produces publications that can assist individuals in understanding more about records management. For more information about membership, programs, and other activities, you may contact ARMA at the following address:

ARMA International
4200 Somerset Drive
Suite 215
Prairie Village, KS 66208
Phone: 913-341-3808

## RECORDS MANAGEMENT—ESSENTIAL FOR A QUALITY ENVIRONMENT

You have learned the basics of records management in this chapter. If you are to be successful as an office assistant, you must put the knowledge and skills that you have gained in this chapter to use on the job. As the amount of information produced continues to grow and technology continues to expand, the ability to manage records (file, find, store, and destroy) in a cost-effective and efficient manner is crucial. Such effectiveness can increase productivity, reduce employee and management frustration, and provide for a quality environment in which to work.

**Figure 11-17** Software Retrieval System

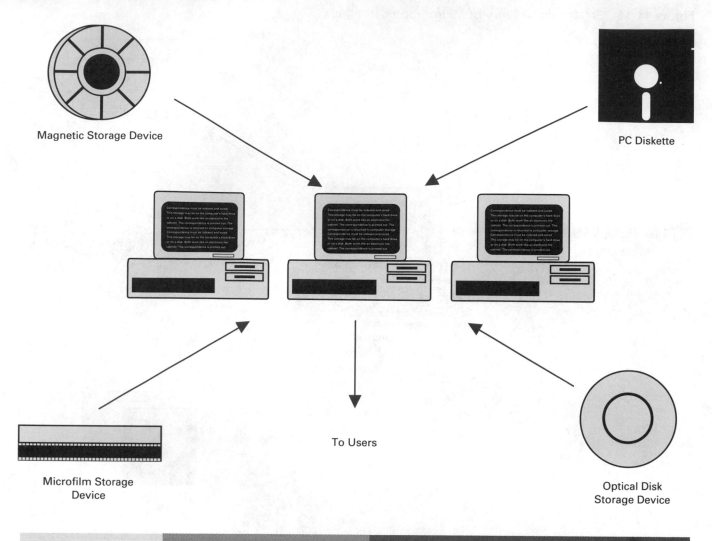

Magnetic Storage Device

PC Diskette

To Users

Microfilm Storage Device

Optical Disk Storage Device

## CHAPTER SUMMARY

The following summary will help you remember the important points of this chapter.

1.  Records management is the systematic control of records from the creation of the record to its final disposition.
2.  The main classification systems are alphabetic, subject, geographic, numeric, and chronologic. Terminal digit, middle digit, and block numeric are all variations of numeric storage.
3.  When storing information, the following steps should be taken: a) Inspect, b) Index, c) Code, d) Cross reference, e) Sort, f) Store.
4.  Efficient storage is based upon an understanding of the indexing rules. The ARMA rules are presented in this chapter.
5.  The office assistant has the responsibility of storing and retrieving documents keyed into

the microcomputer. A system must be developed that allows for the immediate location and retrieval of these items.

6.  The basic filing supplies for paper systems include file folders, file guides, file labels, and metal tabs.
7.  Basic filing equipment for manual systems includes vertical files, lateral files, open-shelf files, visible-card files, horizontal files, and mobile filing systems.
8.  When removing materials from the file, an out guide, out folder, or out card should be placed in the file from which the material is taken. Follow-up records, in the form of a card placed in a tickler file, must be maintained in case materials are not returned at the appropriate time.
9.  When papers are misplaced, several steps should be followed when looking for them, for example, look in the folder immediately in

front of and immediately behind the correct folder; look between folders; check to see if the paper has slipped to the bottom of the file drawer; and look on your employer's desk.

10. Managing records includes determining how long to keep the records as well as storing, transferring, and destroying records. Records can be divided into four categories for retention purposes—vital records, important records, useful records, and nonessential records. Retention schedules that indicate how long particular records are to be kept should be established by a business. Records may be transferred through two basic methods—the perpetual transfer method or the periodic transfer method. With the perpetual transfer method, materials are continuously transferred from active to inactive files. With the periodic transfer method, records may be transferred on a one-period, two-period, or maximum-minimum basis.

11. Software packages are available that provide help in records management. These packages allow for checking records in and out of files, following up on overdue files, maintaining a complete inventory of records, and providing data on the activity of records by user and department.

12. Micrographics refers to the technology by which information can be reduced to a microform, stored conveniently, and then easily retrieved for reference or use. Microforms are available in several different formats, with the most common formats being microfilm and microfiche. Microfilm is a roll containing a series of frames or images much like a movie film. Microfiche is a sheet of film containing a series of images arranged in rows and columns on a card.

13. The combination of micrographics and the computer has made the storage and retrieval of microforms a speedy, inexpensive, and efficient process. Computer output microfilm, computer input microfilm, and computer aided retrieval are all types of integration of micrographics and the computer. Computer output microfilm uses the computer to aid in producing and reading microfilm. With computer input microfilm, information is read from microfilm into the computer, manipulated by the computer in some way if needed, and printed or converted back to microfilm. With computer aided retrieval (CAR), the computer is used to quickly retrieve documents filed on microfilm.

## TERMINOLOGY REVIEW

The following terms were introduced in this chapter. To help you understand them, definitions are given below.

1. **Alphabetic storage** (page 286) Alphabetic storage is a system of storage in which records are stored by the names of people, organizations, agencies, and businesses.

2. **Bar coding** (page 308) Bar coding consists of placing an identifying unit on a document in bar code format, which reduces an alphabetical identifier to a series of bars. This process allows for quick retrieval of a document and is now being used in conjunction with CAR.

3. **Chronologic storage** (page 290) A chronologic storage system is one in which records are arranged in date order.

4. **Coding** (page 291) Coding is the marking of the correspondence by the name, subject, location, or number that was determined in the process of indexing.

5. **Computer aided retrieval (CAR)** (page 307) CAR is the use of micrographics and computer technology to locate and retrieve documents filed on microforms.

6. **Computer input microfilm (CIM)** (page 307) CIM is the process of transferring data from a microform to the computer.

7. **Computer output microfilm (COM)** (page 307) COM is the process of transferring data from the computer to a microform.

8. **Computer record** (page 304) A computer record is the total collection of fields of information about one item.

9. **Cross-reference** (page 292) Cross-referencing is the process of placing the original document in one location in the file and a reference sheet or card in another location in the file. This process is used when a document may be looked for under more than one name.

10. **Database** (page 304) A database is a collection of information organized for rapid search and retrieval.

11. **Field** (page 304) Is a combination of characters to form words, numbers, or a meaningful code.

12. **File management database** *(page 304)* A file management database is used to keep track of one or two relevant facts, such as names in a computer mailing list.

13. **Geographic storage** *(page 288)* Geographic storage is a file arrangement in which related records are grouped by place or location.

14. **Hanging folders** *(page 300)* Folders which hang on metal rods that are attached to the sides of a file cabinet are called hanging folders.

15. **Important records** *(page 306)* Important records are records that are necessary to the continuation of the business and are replaceable only with a considerable expenditure of time and money.

16. **Indexing** *(page 291)* The process of determining where a piece of correspondence is to be stored is called indexing.

17. **Indexing order** *(page 293)* Refers to the order in which units of a filing segment are considered when a record is stored.

18. **Inspect** *(page 291)* Inspect means to ascertain that the correspondence is ready for storing.

19. **Microfiche** *(page 307)* Microfiche is a sheet of film containing a series of images arranged in rows and columns.

20. **Microfilm** *(page 307)* Microfilm is a roll of film containing a series of images in greatly reduced size.

21. **Micrographics** *(page 307)* Micrographics refers to the technology by which information can be reduced to a microform, stored conveniently, and then easily retrieved for reference and use.

22. **Numeric storage** *(page 288)* Numeric storage is a system in which materials are assigned numbers and are arranged in numeric sequence.

23. **Nonessential records** *(page 306)* Nonessential records are those records which may be destroyed after their purpose has been fulfilled.

24. **Periodic transfer** *(page 306)* Periodic transfer is a method of transferring documents from active files to inactive files on a one-period, two-period, or maximum-minimum basis.

25. **Perpetual transfer** *(page 306)* Perpetual transfer is a method of transferring documents from active files to inactive files on a continuing basis.

26. **Record** *(page 285)* A record is any type of recorded information, whether that information be recorded in letter form, report form, blueprint form, or in some other form.

27. **Records management** *(page 285)* The systematic control of records from the creation of the record to its final disposition is called records management.

28. **Records management database** *(page 304)* A records management database is an index of stored records.

29. **Sorting** *(page 292)* Sorting is the arrangement of materials in the order in which they are to be filed.

30. **Storing** *(page 293)* The actual process of placing the document in the file folder is called storing.

31. **Useful records** *(page 306)* Records that when lost may involve delay or inconvenience to the firm.

32. **Vital records** *(page 306)* Records wich cannot be replaced and should never be destroyed.

---

## DISCUSSION ITEMS

To demonstrate your understanding of the information in this chapter, respond to the following items.

1. List and describe three storage classification systems.
2. Explain how government names are filed.
3. If you are dealing with identical names in a filing system, how should the names be filed?
4. What does "code" mean in relation to storage?
5. Define and explain the perpetual transfer method.
6. Define micrographics and explain how it is used.
7. Define CAR and explain how it is used.
8. Explain how software packages might be used in records management.

Part 4 Managing Time and Information

## CASE STUDY

Your job includes preparing reports and records management. You consistently get out the reports on time and keep the files up-to-date and well maintained. You have never had any trouble finding documents quickly. In fact, Mr. Andrews has often praised your ability. He has told you that you have "an amazing ability to find anything in a moment's notice." You are proud of your skills, enjoy working for Mr. Andrews, and are always eager to learn new and more efficient records management techniques.

One of your co-workers, Lisa, never gets her filing done. She constantly complains about how much she has to do and has asked you on several occasions to help her. You don't mind helping out, but believe she wastes her time. You feel she is an ineffective employee. However, a few weeks ago, you did help her with her filing. You worked with her for almost three days and helped her get her files up-to-date. Now, she is behind again and wants your help again. You don't believe you should be doing your job and her job too. The tension is building between the two of you. You don't want to cause any problems within the office. How should you handle the situation?

## OFFICE APPLICATIONS

### Office Application 11-1 (*Objectives 1-7*)

Interview one office worker regarding records management functions used in his or her office. Ask the questions listed below. Write your findings in a short report.

1. What storage classification is used?
2. What type of equipment is used? Are computerized systems used? If so, what are they?
3. Is a records-retention schedule available?
4. How are materials transferred and stored?
5. Does the company have full-time positions in records management? If so, what are they and what are the job duties? Obtain a copy of the position descriptions, if possible.

### Office Application 11-2 (*Objective 1*)

Indicate the subject you would use in storing the following correspondence. Place your answers on a separate sheet of paper.

1. A reminder notice for the next weekly meeting of the Administrative Management Society
2. A notice of a seminar on leadership
3. A job application from Martin Irwin
4. A copy of Mr. Andrews' expense account
5. A blueprint of a new building
6. A TV script on transportation methods of the future
7. A copy of TriCounty's financial report
8. A copy of Mr. Andrews' sick leave form

9.   A report on past due accounts

10.  A research project on a new piece of equipment

## Office Application 11-3 (*Objective 1*)

Assume that you are setting up numeric storage. Assign numbers for the following correspondence; begin your numbers with 100. Then prepare 5 inch by 3 inch cards for the alphabetic card file and alphabetize the cards. Study the indexing rules given in the chapter. Prepare a list showing how the numbers would be placed in a numeric system. Turn in your list of numbers and your 5 inch by 3 inch cards to your instructor.

- Dave Marley Ford, Incorporated
- McCoy-Hoving and Associates
- Maritime Telecommunications Corporation
- Marek Auto Service
- Paul Marco and Associates
- George W. McCormick Insurance Agency
- Mark IV Systems
- Margo's Coiffures
- Marlin-Rockwell Division
- J.A. McBride, Inc.
- Margie's Florist & Gift Shop
- Marsalis Avenue Garage
- Maresa's
- Marquee East Apartments
- McCrackin Carpet Service

## Office Application 11-4 (*Objective 3*)

On pages 317-318 are 21 groups of names. In the space provided at the right of each group, show how the names would be indexed by units and alphabetized within each group. The first group is given as an example.

## Office Application 11-5 (*Objectives 1, 2, and 3*)

Before you begin this job, you may wish to study the indexing rules given in this chapter.

*With a template disk:* Load the stored file, OA11-5. Code the names of the individual or business firm in proper order by rekeying the name in the space directly above the name as it is printed. If you have access to a sort program, arrange the names in proper alphabetic sequence. Print out and hand in a copy of your work to your instructor.

If you do not have access to a sort program, print out a copy of your work. Arrange the names in alphabetic order. Rekey the names in the proper order, and put the number of the item in parentheses at the end of the name. Print out and hand in a copy of your work to your instructor.

*Without a template disk:* Write or key, in proper indexing form on 5 inch by 3 inch cards, the names and addresses of the individuals or business firms. Place the number given by the name in the upper right-hand corner of the card. Then, alphabetize the cards. Once you have finished the alphabetizing, take a sheet of paper and list in proper order the card numbers that would be filed under each letter of the alphabet, along with the indexing order of the name. Place the number of the item in parentheses at the end of the name. Turn in this sheet to your instructor.

(1) Donald L. Sells, Jr.
4329 Mountain Drive
Juneau, AK 99801-2573

(2) San Diego Supply Co.
1181 Jefferson Road
San Diego, CA 92110-9837

(3) Russell J. Sells
600 South 29th
Arlington, VA 22202-3422

(4) Vinson Supply Company
3804 Wood Street
Hastings, NE 68901-4789

(5) Mrs. James D'Ilvetta
1405 Knoxville Avenue South
Tulsa, OK 74112-7835

(6) MacAbbott Corporation
412 Broadway
Montclair, NJ 07043-2384

(7) Capt. John Frase
427 Grand Avenue
Princeton, WV 24720-3839

(8) M. M. Stans & Co.
4500 Fifth Avenue
Pittsburgh, PA 15213-7865

(9) Ima L. McCormick
719 Superior Avenue
Cleveland, OH 44116-5684

(10) Tolbert Aircraft Shop
1800 Tremont Shop
Kansas City, KS 66103-4755

(11) John Lipinski & Sons
83 Main Street
Peoria, IL 61611-3892

(12) The L & S Lane Company
875 Willow Road NW
Albuquerque, NM 87107-8932

(13) Jones & Hardin Mfrs.
208 Holona Place
Honolulu, HI 96817-2428

(14) Universal Company
81 Branch Avenue
Portales, NM 88130-5679

(15) 7th Street Supply Company
Fall River, WI 43932-8273

(16) Capital Services
Insurance Building
Houston, TX 77012-3492

## Office Application 11-6 (*Objectives 1, 2, and 3*)

See pages 319-320 of this text for a list of addresses to use for this application. Write or key the name and address of each individual or business firm in proper indexing form on a 5 inch by 3 inch card. Place the number given by the name in the upper right-hand corner of the card. Then, alphabetize all cards. Once you have finished the alphabetizing, take a sheet of paper and list in proper order the individual or business name that would be filed under each letter of the alphabet. Turn in this sheet to your instructor. Retain your cards for Office Application 11-7.

## Office Application 11-7 (*Objectives 1, 2, and 3*)

You will use the same cards in this job as were used in Office Application 11-6. Follow these instructions for completing this job.

1. Arrange the 50 cards in alphabetical order by state. Then arrange them in alphabetical order by cities within each state. Finally, arrange the cards in alphabetical order by names of individuals or businesses within each city.

2. After arranging the cards properly, take a blank sheet of paper to prepare your solutions. On the left side, list the names of the states. After each state, list in indexing order the names of cities within each state. After each city, list the names of the businesses or individuals within that city.

3. Hand in your sheet to your instructor.

### Office Application 11-8 (*Objective 2*)

Sometimes correspondence may be called for under more than one name. When there is such a possibility, a cross-reference should be made. On page 321 you will find four cross-reference sheets. Using the following information, fill out the sheets with a pen or pencil. Use the current date.

1. A letter from Vinson Supply Company, Hastings, NE 68901-4789, asking for demographic information. Letter signed by Anne L. Frazier.

2. A letter from Ronald L. Selzer, National Airport Services Co., Washington, DC 20013-3942, asking for a transportation survey.

3. A telegram from P. R. Eads, Stillwater Products Company, Stillwater, OK 74074-8526, asking for population trends.

4. A letter from Torres and Mills, Minneapolis, MN 55660-2839, signed by Benjamin Torres, asking for advice on aging issues.

### Office Application 11-9 (*Objectives 1, 2, and 3*)

Throughout the course you have been maintaining a "to be filed" folder. Assume that you are using a subject system. Using the correspondence in the "to be filed" folder, determine how each piece of correspondence will be filed. Write that notation on the correspondence. Arrange your papers in alphabetic order and list the order on a cover sheet. Turn in your list and your correspondence to your instructor.

### Office Application 11-10 (*Objectives 4 and 5*)

Read and summarize two articles—one on supplies and equipment used in records management and one on the transfer and retention of records. Summarize the articles in report format, listing your sources. Turn in your report to your instructor.

### Office Application 11-11 (*Objective 6*)

Visit your college or public library. Locate two items that are stored on microfilm or on microfiche. Use the microfilm reader and make a hard copy of both items. Hand in your copies to your instructor.

### Office Application 11-12 (*Objective 7*)

Read and summarize two articles in current periodicals on computerized filing systems. Prepare your summaries in report format, listing your sources. Turn in your report to your instructor.

Indexing Units

| Names | | 1 | 2 | 3 | 4 |
|---|---|---|---|---|---|
| 1. John T. Baur | 1. | Bauer | Mary | Ellen | |
| Henry Elison Bowers, Jr. | 2. | Baur | John | T | |
| Mary Ellen Bauer | 3. | Bower | C | L | |
| C.L. Bower | 4. | Bowers | Henry | Elison | Jr |
| 2. Z.T. Glasier, II | 5. | | | | |
| Z. T. Glasier, Jr. | 6. | | | | |
| Alice Glazier | 7. | | | | |
| Gleason Company | 8. | | | | |
| 3. Helen Clara McBeth | 9. | | | | |
| David F. MacCormack | 10. | | | | |
| Mildred MacBeth | 11. | | | | |
| L.B. Maple | 12. | | | | |
| 4. D.A. Schwartz | 13. | | | | |
| M. Robert Swartz | 14. | | | | |
| Katherine Schwarz | 15. | | | | |
| Ethel M. Schwarzkoff | 16. | | | | |
| 5. Edward C. Albert | 17. | | | | |
| Albert's Ice Cream Shoppe | 18. | | | | |
| Alberts' Grocery Store | 19. | | | | |
| E. Charles Albert | 20. | | | | |
| 6. John T. Schklar, Jr. | 21. | | | | |
| John L. Schlanger, Sr. | 22. | | | | |
| Judge Julia Schleicher | 23. | | | | |
| Mary B. Schlick | 24. | | | | |
| 7. Five Hundred Ervay Bldg. | 25. | | | | |
| 500 Cafeteria | 26. | | | | |
| 5 Dollar Diner | 27. | | | | |
| The 500, Inc. | 28. | | | | |
| 8. Francis Q. Bourque | 29. | | | | |
| Patricia Boark | 30. | | | | |
| Patrick O'Reilly Burke | 31. | | | | |
| Iris Burk | 32. | | | | |
| 9. Moore Supplies & Equipment | 33. | | | | |
| Moore-Town Boat Repair | 34. | | | | |
| Frank H. Mohr | 35. | | | | |
| Betty Geneva Mohr | 36. | | | | |
| 10. George M. Lloyd | 37. | | | | |
| Amelia E. Lollar | 38. | | | | |
| Eugene Bahr Loyd | 39. | | | | |
| Mrs. Carmen C. Lopez | 40. | | | | |

Names for Use in Office Application 11-4

| Names | | 1 | 2 | 3 | 4 |
|---|---|---|---|---|---|
| 11. O. Edwards Shop | 41. | | | | |
| Mrs. Mary McClellan O'Connor | 42. | | | | |
| Jacqueline O. Odum | 43. | | | | |
| George Felix Oden | 44. | | | | |
| 12. Jos. A. O'Neill | 45. | | | | |
| J. George O'Neal | 46. | | | | |
| Harriet R. O'Neill | 47. | | | | |
| J. Gerald O'Neal | 48. | | | | |
| 13. The SP Printing Company | 49. | | | | |
| The Standard Oil Company | 50. | | | | |
| Standard Clothing Company | 51. | | | | |
| SFAX Television Station | 52. | | | | |
| 14. Joseph Parker | 53. | | | | |
| Allen Parks & Sons | 54. | | | | |
| Inman D. Parker, Attorney | 55. | | | | |
| O.A. Park | 56. | | | | |
| 15. Sister M. Bernadine | 57. | | | | |
| St. Louis City Library | 58. | | | | |
| San Francisco State Univ. | 59. | | | | |
| St. John's School | 60. | | | | |
| 16. M.L. DeBrum | 61. | | | | |
| Mrs. Robert G. De Spain | 62. | | | | |
| Mayor Ronald W. DeBerry | 63. | | | | |
| Carolyn De Baca, M.D. | 64. | | | | |
| 17. The V & V Deli | 65. | | | | |
| Prof. H.S. Vallery | 66. | | | | |
| Thal's & Thal's, Inc. | 67. | | | | |
| Thomasen Brothers | 68. | | | | |
| 18. Thomas Hardy Syrgley | 69. | | | | |
| Syndicated Newspaper Corp. | 70. | | | | |
| Sylvan Park Service Station | 71. | | | | |
| Jeannette K. Sylvia | 72. | | | | |
| 19. U.S. Department of Agriculture | 73. | | | | |
| U.S. Playing Card Company | 74. | | | | |
| United Dairy Farmers | 75. | | | | |
| Union Bank & Trust | 76. | | | | |
| 20. Herbert N. Jahncke | 77. | | | | |
| E.H. Jakes | 78. | | | | |
| Helen O'Toole Jackson | 79. | | | | |
| Jack & Jill's Shop | 80. | | | | |
| 21. T.W. O'Poole | 81. | | | | |
| Martin Y. Pryszanski | 82. | | | | |
| Belva D. Pyrtle | 83. | | | | |
| O.R. Poole, Sr. | 84. | | | | |

(1) Glenn Overman Company
3020 23rd Street NW
Tucson, AZ 85703-5868

(2) Mays & Suter
351 Ludlow Street
Chicago, IL 60612-3472

(3) A. L. George, Jr.
3842 Texas Avenue
Baton Rouge, LA 70805-9747

(4) D. George MacBeth
1142 Market Street
Charlotte, NC 28202-7985

(5) L. T. Stinson
2960 Flagler Street
Tampa, FL 33607-2385

(6) A. L. George, Sr.
3842 Texas Avenue
Baton Rouge, LA 70805-9747

(7) O'Neal Office Services
1710 Hampton Avenue
Columbia, SC 29204-9542

(8) Ammond Supply Co.
Decatur, GA 30016-4379

(9) Northwest Suppliers
911 Flowers Avenue
Helena, MT 59602-6589

(10) Nevada Products Company
6182 Main Street
Carson City, NV 89701-2548

(11) O'Keefe Rubber Company
1674 Chestnut Street
Decatur, AL 35601-2376

(12) Wm. A. Prangle
1800 Brooks Drive
Miami, FL 33112-2892

(13) R & W Raymond
1016 Riverside Avenue
Concord, NH 03301-9483

(14) L. M. Doutt
106 Granite Avenue
Montpelier, VT 05601-4855

(15) Western Export Corp.
Golden Gate Drive
San Francisco, CA 94107-6765

(16) Dr. Georgia Ammon
210 Doctor's Building
Hartford, CT 06107-1538

(17) Canton-Cantor
1419 South Street
Cheyenne, WY 82001-2388

(18) J. T. Crow
1231 Sixteenth Street
Seattle, WA 98106-3651

(19) J. T. Crow
1400 Sixteenth Street
Seattle, WA 98106-3652

(20) Department of Health
State of Kentucky
Frankfort, KY 40601-5752

(21) Department of Parks
State of Idaho
Pocatello, ID 83202-3899

(22) Graham Department Store
412 East Street
Madison, WI 43704-7814

(23) Olivia S. Young
21 Ocean City Drive
Atlantic City, NJ 08401-9532

(24) Barnes and Batts
4726 Wilmore Street
Decatur, GA 30012-4415

(25) San Rafael, Inc.
1708 Tremont Street
Springfield, MA 01105-8962

(26) Bertke and Young,
Attorneys
Norton, KS 67654-2435

(27) Jane's Bootery
Meadville, PA 16335-3984

(28) The Oriental Company
12 Michigan Boulevard
Chicago, IL 60611-4725

(29) Bartons' Importers
Hanover and Spring Streets
Binghamton, NY 13902-6581

(30) Leppert and Carter
Company
Carlon and Lacey Streets
St. Paul, MN 55101-7785

(31) Wilson Electric Company
Redfield, SD 57469-8992

(32) McFeatter Box Company
200 East Sixth Street
Little Rock, AR 72203-5483

(33) KRLD Television Station
1990 Stuart Avenue
Des Moines, IA 50301-9235

(34) James and Company
Fifth and Main Streets
White Plains, NY 10604-8765

(35) Bowers Show Store
119 Limestone Street
Lexington, KY 40503-7443

(36) Twelve Plus One Apartments
123 Erie Avenue
Cincinnati, OH 45205-2316

(37) 12 Step AA Club
Front Street
Columbus, OH 43210-3467

(38) 12 Hills Apartments
444 Foster Street
Boston, MA 02110-4812

(39) At Home Grocery
666 North Avenue
Kalamazoo, MI 49002-3954

(40) Deland Cigar Company
Ida Avenue and Smith Road
Dallas, TX 75203-2310

(41) Knoxville Supply Co.
100 University Street
Knoxville, TN 37906-5506

(42) Hammond Inn
Hammond, LA 70402-6812

(43) Dr. Harold Owens
504 Medical Arts Building
Johnstown, PA 15902-3495

(44) Daniel's Supply Store
1400 Cleveland Place
Denver, CO 80202-8294

(45) H.E.V. Thomasen
890 Hill Road
Rapid City, SD 57702-6275

(46) Randall Book Store
3413 Linwood Street
Davenport, IA 52802-8254

(47) Harold C. Duffy
Bristol, GA 31518-8534

(48) Helen LaMarr
3 Bond Place
Bismarck, ND 58502-4892

(49) Northwest Suppliers
300 First Street
Helena, MT 59602-6589

(50) Internal Revenue Service
Dallas, TX 75202

Data for Office Application 11-6

| CROSS-REFERENCE SHEET | CROSS-REFERENCE SHEET |
|---|---|
| Name ——————— Date ——— <br> Subject ——————— | Name ——————— Date ——— <br> Subject ——————— |
| Regarding | Regarding |
| SEE <br><br> Name ——————— Date ——— <br> Subject ——————— | SEE <br><br> Name ——————— Date ——— <br> Subject ——————— |
| | |
| CROSS-REFERENCE SHEET | CROSS-REFERENCE SHEET |
| Name ——————— Date ——— <br> Subject ——————— | Name ——————— Date ——— <br> Subject ——————— |
| Regarding | Regarding |
| SEE <br><br> Name ——————— Date ——— <br> Subject ——————— | SEE <br><br> Name ——————— Date ——— <br> Subject ——————— |
| | |

# PART 5

## PLANNING TRAVEL AND CONFERENCES

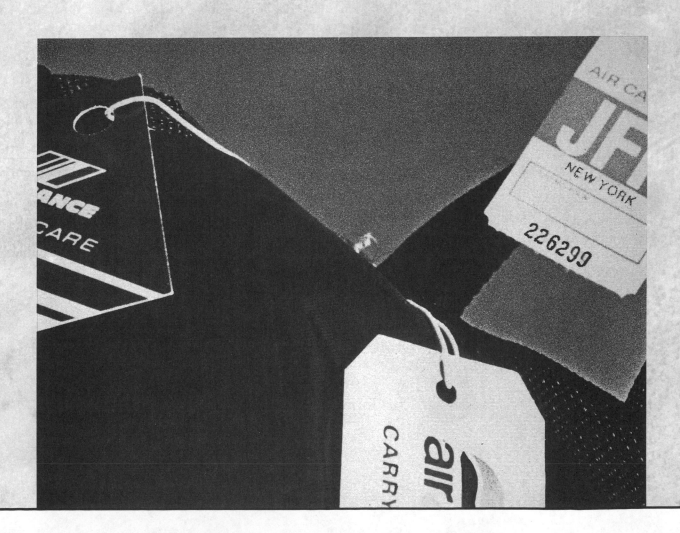

# JENNY BALDWIN

Executive Secretary
Coast of South Africa Breweries Group
South Africa

## A Success Profile

Success is rather a large word that means different things to different people. To me success means the achievement of another step—tackling a job and learning on the way how to get it done. Success is being part of a team and helping everyone on that team to work well together. Mastering a new computer package and printing off that first letter—what a feeling of success that gives you. Success means working for a fine company and having a good relationship with your employer.

I was born and educated in England and emigrated to South Africa in 1969. South Africa became my home the minute I stepped ashore. It is the most wonderful country and a fine place to develop and grow, no matter what your skills are.

Upon my arrival in Cape Town I joined the British Consulate as the telex operator and worked my way up from there. In 1985 I was approached by the regional director of the Coast of South Africa Breweries to join him as his personal assistant. It was a massive step. He is a man who thinks and moves quickly; high standards are important to him.

At the time I joined Coast of South Africa Breweries I also became a member of The Executive Secretaries Club of South Africa. We have a large membership in the Cape, and the regular monthly meetings have proven invaluable. The networking and general exposure to training courses have formed a great part of my development. The monthly lectures relate to many facets of the secretarial profession. Belonging to the club gives me a feeling of pride in my profession. I have held many leadership positions since I have been in the club, and in 1991 was honored to become the national president. The club has helped me to be more confident and to take on bigger challenges.

My advice to any secretary is to always add some laughter to the day. There is no task that cannot be made easier or more fun. My position has involved traveling throughout South Africa, and it has been tremendous fun chatting to people on planes and in airports. The world is full of interesting people, all with their own life experiences.

My advice to secretaries entering the field is to

- Learn the basic skills and learn them well; never stop learning.

- Join a professional club in your area.

- Network with secretaries in similar companies.

- Be an ambassador for your company at all times.

- Develop a dress sense for the office.

- Always look as though you are having lunch with the president; that way someday you will.

# 12 Travel Arrangements

The phrase *global economy* is often used today. What does it mean? What are its implications? It means, in part, that we now live in a world in which our economic well-being is not based on the goods and services we produce and sell in the United States alone. It is also based on the amount of business we do in Europe, in the Middle East, in the Far East, in South America, and in other countries. The converse is also true. The global economy is also based on how much business Europe, the Middle East, the Far East, South America, and other countries do with us. Its implications are many. For example, many United States owned businesses now have subsidiaries abroad; many Japanese owned businesses now have subsidiaries in the United States. Both our country and other countries take advantage of land, labor, and technical expertise available in other parts of the world in making decisions as to where a product is produced. For example, the availability of a relatively inexpensive labor force in Korea may mean that a United States clothing manufacturer will have a plant in Korea.

Thus, in addition to domestic travel to conferences, seminars, and to branches or subsidiaries located within the United States, it is not unusual today for the executive to make trips abroad for business purposes. As an office assistant you will be involved in making travel arrangements for your employer. Also, as an office assistant you may be asked to attend an occasional conference which is designed to assist you in performing your job better. In order to handle travel arrangements effectively, you must become familiar with the types of services available. This chapter will help you understand the options available to you when making the necessary travel arrangements and will show you how to handle the numerous other responsibilities associated with a trip.

## GENERAL OBJECTIVES

*Your general objectives for this chapter are to*
1. **Become knowledgeable about travel options.**
2. **Prepare itineraries.**
3. **Know what duties should be performed while the executive is traveling and when the executive returns.**
4. **Prepare expense reports.**

## METHODS OF TRAVEL

Almost all travel that the executive does will be by air. Time is an extremely important commodity to the busy executive, and he or she does not usually have the additional time that is required to go by car or by rail. If your employer is planning a trip by car or by rail, information is available from the American Automobile Association (AAA) and from the *Official Railway Guide,* published by the National Railway Publication Company, 424 West 33rd Street, New York, NY 10001. AAA can help in car trip planning by providing maps that show recommended routes and locations of restaurants and motels. The *Official Railway Guide* includes the schedules of all railroads in the United States. Information on rail travel may also be obtained by calling Amtrak or looking under the heading Railroads in your local Yellow Pages.

Since air travel is the most common method of traveling for the executive, this chapter is devoted almost exclusively to air travel arrangements. Ground transportation at the destination is presented and train travel in relation to international travel is briefly considered.

## TRAVEL ARRANGEMENTS

How travel arrangements are made depends on the company where you work. Many companies

Credit: Miami International Airport.

deal with travel agencies, and companies will often select a particular travel agency to work with the company on a regular basis. This agency then becomes knowledgeable about the particular needs of the company and the particular needs of executives within the company. Thus, efficiencies of time and fiscal resources are gained. Some large companies will have their own travel department. This department will make all travel arrangements for executives within the company. In a small office, the office assistant may deal directly with the airlines.

## Travel Agencies

Travel agencies will make all travel arrangements. They will schedule the flight, obtain tickets, make hotel reservations, and arrange car rental. The agency will also see that airline tickets are delivered to your business. Part of their service includes providing a complete itinerary which gives flight numbers, arrival and departure times of flights, hotel reservations, car rental, and any other arrangements that were requested. The company can make arrangements with the agency to bill directly to the firm or the travel agency will accept major credit cards.

Before calling a travel agency to make the arrangements, you must be ready to provide the details about when your employer wishes to travel (the dates and time of day) and your employer's preference as to a direct flight or willingness to change planes (less expensive flights are sometimes available if the individual is willing to change planes). You will have to know his or her hotel and car rental preference. Ask the travel agency to check with several airlines to determine the least expensive flight available. Airlines are extremely competitive today, and many times reduced prices are available. Companies are very aware of cost factors; and regardless of the level of the executive's position, he or she is usually interested in the lowest price available. It is a good idea as you begin to plan a trip to set up a folder with the location and date of the trip on the label. Then, as you make the arrangements, you can record all information and place it in the folder. Be prepared to give the travel agency the following types of information:

1. Employer's name and company name
2. Employer's credit card number or account number of the company
3. Preferred airlines (if he or she has a preference) along with frequent flyer number. (A frequent flyer program is an incentive program offered by most airlines that provides a variety of awards. Awards may include upgrading from coach to first class and free airline tickets after the accumulation of mileage points.)
4. Cities to be visited; dates and times of travel
5. Class of flight—first class, business class, or coach
6. Preference as to aisle or window seat; smoking or nonsmoking section
7. Food preferences—low calorie meal, low cholesterol meal, salt-free meal, and any other special needs
8. Hotel preferences—single or double room, size of bed (king or queen), number of nights, price range
9. Car rental—type of car, size, make, model; number of days of usage

Since travel agencies receive commissions from airlines, hotels, and other service industries which they use, there is generally no fee charged to the business. If you ever have the task of helping to select a travel agency for your company, determine which agencies specialize in business travel and get references from other businesses using travel agencies. You might wish to look for a travel agency that belongs to ASTA (American Society of Travel Agents) or ARTS (Association of Retail Travel Agents).

## Corporate Travel Departments

Since companies in the United States spend billions of dollars each year on travel, it may be more efficient for large companies to have their own travel department rather than having individual offices working with travel agencies. If you work for a company that has a travel department, your task is to get the information necessary about the trip and give the information to the travel department. You will need to give the department information as to the cities to be visited and the dates and times of arrivals and departures. It may be necessary to give information on hotels, flight preferences and classifications, and so forth. However, the department may keep a file on executives within the company in which flight preferences (such as aisle or window seat and food preferences), hotel preferences, and other pertinent information are maintained. Also, many companies have policies regarding flight classifications. For example, the president and vice-presidents of the company may be allowed to fly first class. All other executives may fly business class or coach. It is also the responsibility of the travel department to determine the most economical flights available; they are responsible for checking with several airlines or asking the travel agency to get the best prices. The travel department will ordinarily take care of getting any cash advances necessary for the executive and forward all tickets, itinerary, and cash advances to you.

Travel departments generally use travel agencies in booking the arrangements for executives. However, some companies subscribe to the *Official Airline Guide* published by Official Airline Guides, Inc., 2000 Clearwater Drive, Oak Brook, IL 60521. Information on fares, schedules, aircraft, and other services is provided in the guide. Also available is an electronic edition of the guide which may be used on your computer.

See Figure 12-1 which shows three screens from the electronic edition of the *Official Airline Guide.* Notice on screen no. 1 there is a list of commands for viewing schedule displays, fares displays, and hotel/motel displays. Notice on screen no. 2 there is a flight from Los Angeles to Washington leaving at 7:10 a.m. from LAX (Los Angeles International Airport) and arriving at DCA (Washington National Airport) at 4:45 p.m. The flight is NW 330, breakfast is served; there is one stop; and the travel time is 6 hours and 35 minutes. Now notice screen no. 3 (Figure 12-1) which

**Figure 12-1** Screens from Electronic Edition of *Official Airline Guide*

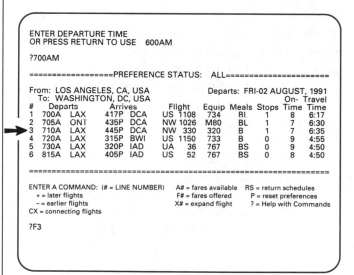

Screen No. 1

Screen No. 2

Screen No. 3

shows fares on Northwest Airlines from Los Angeles to Washington National. Line no. 3 shows a $488 round-trip fare on coach (indicated by "Q") with a required overnight stay on Saturday.

### Office Assistant Arrangements

If you work in a small company, you will probably have the responsibility of calling the airlines, hotels, and car rental agencies. It is a good idea to use comparison shopping when making these arrangements; you will want to call several companies to get the best quotes on prices and routes. Your company and your supervisor will be interested in using travel funds wisely.

Your employer may have a preferred airline, hotel, or car rental agency. Be certain that you ask before beginning to make the reservations. If he or she is attending a conference, there are probably certain hotels which have been designated by the conference planners as preferred hotels. These hotels usually have agreed to give a discount rate for people attending the conference. Again, you will want to check this information with your employer before making the arrangements.

## DOMESTIC TRAVEL

As you have already learned, executives travel most frequently by air. This section will concentrate on making air travel arrangements. In addition, there is a section on making hotel reservations and a brief section on car travel.

### Air Travel

This section will help you understand the various services that are available when traveling by air. Regardless of whether you are dealing with a travel agency, a company travel department, or are making the arrangements directly with the airlines, you need to understand what types of services are available.

**Flight Classifications**  Airlines provide two basic classes of flight—first-class and coach. Some airlines offer a third class of service which is business class.

**First-class accommodations** are more luxurious than coach. The seats are wider and farther apart, and services are extended. For example, greater quantity and quality of food is offered, and more attention is paid to presentation of the food. Cloth napkins, tablecloths, silverware, and china

dinnerware are used in first-class. Alcoholic beverages are offered without additional cost. There are more flight attendants per customer than in coach-class, which allows for greater attention to be given to the individual flyer. First-class customers are allowed to board first and to exit first. Attendants take coats and hang them up for the customer and store parcels in overhead bins. In other words, the customer is given attentive service.

**Illus. 12-2**  First-class accommodations are more luxurious than coach.

Credit: United Airlines.

**Coach-class accommodations** provide snacks, soft drinks, tea or coffee, and meals free of charge. However, seats are closer together and fewer flight attendants are available to serve the needs of the customers. Food is served with plastic plates and dinnerware and paper napkins. Since there are fewer flight attendants, meals and other services are slower in delivery than in first-class.

Some airlines offer **business class accomodations**. This class is not provided on all planes or on all routes. It is usually provided only on wide-bodied jets such as 747s or 767s and on long-distance routes. Business-class is slightly more expensive than coach. The business-class section is located directly behind first-class and in front of coach. Accommodations include more spacious seating than coach and complimentary alcoholic beverages.

**Reservations**  If you are responsible for making flight reservations, you must give the travel agent the necessary information as to destination, date and approximate time of departure, date and approximate time of return, and class of service de-

It is a dinner meeting. They will be having dinner in the Seville Room at the Four Seasons. Make the change in time on the itinerary and call the Four Seasons to make a dinner reservation for two at 7:00 p.m. If you are using a template disk, make the appropriate changes by inserting the place for the dinner reservation. If you are using the form on page 343, prepare a revised itinerary for the New York trip reflecting the changes in the appointment with Mr. Chow. Turn in your revised itinerary to your instructor.

### Office Application 12-4 (*Objectives 2 and 4*)

Mr. Andrews is taking a trip to Washington, D.C. from Monday, December 5 through Thursday December 8. He wants to leave after 11:00 a.m. on December 5 and return after 5:00 p.m. on December 8. He wants a hotel near Washington National Airport for the nights of December 5 through December 7. He will not need a car; his meetings will be at the hotel. He wants an aisle seat and low-cal meals; he will be flying coach. He prefers a queen-size bed on a no-smoking floor. Go to your school or local library and check the *Official Airline Guide* and *The Hotel and Motel Redbook* for flight and hotel information. Prepare an itinerary for Mr. Andrews, using template file OA12-4 or the form on page 345.

When Mr. Andrews returns, he gives you the following expenses (he did not get a cash advance).

- Hotel for 3 nights—$495 ($165 per night)
- Meals:
  December 5, dinner—$25
  December 6, breakfast—$8; lunch—$15; dinner—$75 (he took out a client)
  December 7, breakfast—$6; lunch—$12; dinner—$150 (for Mr. Andrews and two clients)
  December 8, breakfast—$7, lunch—$10

Prepare an expense report, using the form given on page 347.

TRAVEL ITINERARY

For:

Frequent Flyer No.

Destination:

Departure:

Flight:

Meals:

Seating:

Arrival:

Car Rental:

Hotel:

Appointments:


Destination:

Departure:

Flight

Arrival:

Hotel:

Appointments:

Destination:

Departure:

Flight:

Meals:

Seating:

Arrival:

TRAVEL ITINERARY

For:

Frequent Flyer No.

Destination:

Departure:

Flight:

Meals:

Seating:

Arrival:

Car Rental:

Hotel:

Appointments:

Destination:

Departure:

Flight

Arrival:

ENTER ONLY ONE AMOUNT PER LINE, PER DAY

ENTER ONLY ONE AMOUNT PER LINE, PER DAY

# △ TriCounty Regional Planning Agency — WEEKLY EXPENSE REPORT

| NAME | SAVE NO | ENDING SPEEDOMETER | CHANGED DRIVER'S LICENSE NO | TR NO | $ |
|---|---|---|---|---|---|

| WEEK ENDING | SUNDAY | MONDAY | TUESDAY | WEDNESDAY | THURSDAY | FRIDAY | SATURDAY | TOTALS |
|---|---|---|---|---|---|---|---|---|
| **PERSONAL** | | | | | | | | |
| MOTEL OR HOTEL | | | | | | | | |
| CITY | | | | | | | | |
| STATE | | | | | | | | |
| ROOM CHARGE (ATTACH RECEIPT) 11 | | | | | | | | |
| BREAKFAST | | | | | | | | |
| LUNCH | | | | | | | | |
| DINNER | | | | | | | | |
| TOTAL MEALS → 12 | | | | | | | | |
| OTHER PERSONAL 13 | | | | | | | | |
| **COMPANY OWNED AUTOMOBILE** | | | | | | | | |
| GAS-OIL 14 | | | | | | | | |
| OTHER OPERATING (INCLUDE PARKING, TOLLS, TAXES, AND FEES) 15 | | | | | | | | |
| PARTS AND REPAIRS 16 | | | | | | | | |
| **MISCELLANEOUS** | | | | | | | | |
| ENTERTAINMENT (EXPLAIN - ATTACH RECEIPT IF OVER $25.00) 17 | | | | | | | | |
| OTHER TRANSPORTATION (AIR FARE, CAR RENTAL) 18 | | | | | | | | |
| MISC. OTHER (EXPLAIN - ATTACH RECEIPT IF OVER $25.00) 19 | | | | | | | | |
| **TOTAL FOR DAY** | | | | | | | | |

EXPLANATION OF ENTERTAINMENT AND MISCELLANEOUS

WEEK'S EXPENSES

INCREASE MY ADVANCE 21

DECREASE MY ADVANCE 22

ISSUE CHECK 23

PLEASE SIGN _____

# 13 Meeting and Conference Planning

Meetings are a way of life in the office of today. In fact, taking a conservative estimate of time spent in meetings, office employees average four hours of meetings a week. This average increases the higher your position in the organization. It has been estimated that middle management spends approximately 35 percent of each week in meetings. Top management spends more than 50 percent of each week in meetings. And, what do these meetings cost business? Certainly the figures vary from organization to organization, but most organizations spend between 7 and 15 percent of their personnel budgets directly on meetings. For example, if you work for an organization that has a $10 million personnel budget, $700,000 to $1.5 million could be spent on meetings.

Why is it necessary to have meetings? Problems and issues within an organization often need the collective wisdom of several people to come up with the best solutions. Sitting down face to face with members of the organization in a meeting format is often the quickest and most effective means of solving these issues and problems.

As an office assistant, you will have a myriad of responsibilities when meetings are called. These responsibilities include sending out the meeting notices, preparing the agenda, arranging for the meeting room, and taking and transcribing minutes. You may need to order food and beverages, arrange for equipment, and occasionally make presentations. This chapter will help you not only understand your various duties but become more proficient in performing them.

## GENERAL OBJECTIVES

*Your general objectives for this chapter are to*
1. **Identify the responsibilities of an office assistant when meetings and conferences are held.**
2. **Prepare notices for meetings.**
3. **Prepare agendas and minutes.**
4. **Identify alternatives to meetings and conferences.**

**Illus. 13-1** Sitting down face to face with members of the organization in a meeting format is often the quickest and most efficient means of solving issues and problems.

## NECESSARY MEETINGS

Meetings are a good means of generating ideas, sharing information, and making decisions. Calling a meeting can be appropriate when

1. Advice is needed from a group of people.
2. A group needs to be involved in solving a problem or making a decision.
3. There is an issue that needs clarification.
4. Information needs to be given to a group.
5. There is a problem, but it is not clear what it is or who is responsible for dealing with it.
6. It is necessary to communicate quickly with a large number of people.

## UNNECESSARY MEETINGS

There are many meetings held each day in businesses across the United States. Not all of these meetings are productive, and not all of these meetings should be held. Meetings are not generally productive when detailed analysis and research has yet to take place, when reports must be written, and when materials must be organized as part of the preparation for the discussion. A meeting is generally not a good idea when

1. Confidential or sensitive personnel matters must be addressed.
2. There is inadequate data.
3. There is insufficient time to prepare for the meeting.
4. The information could be communicated by memo, fax, electronic mail, or telephone.
5. There is a considerable amount of anger and hostility in the group, and people need time to calm down before working together.

## ORGANIZATIONAL MEETINGS

There are several types of meetings that are held within an organization. Executives usually meet often with the people who report directly to them. These meetings are generally referred to as staff meetings. Meetings are often held with customers and clients of the business. These meetings will generally consist of only two or three people. The office assistant may have few responsibilities for these types of meetings since notices may not even be necessary.

In the case of staff meetings, often the staff is informed that they will meet every Tuesday at 9:00 a.m. They mark their calendars for that day each week, so there is no need to send out a notice. In customer or client meetings, the office assistant may have the responsibility of calling or writing the individuals involved to establish the meeting time. Other responsibilities at these meetings may include offering the individuals beverages or food and preparing materials for the executive for the meeting. Minutes are rarely taken at these meetings.

Other types of meetings within a company are more formal in nature and require the office assistant to be heavily involved in setting up the meeting, taking notes during the meeting, and engaging in follow-up activities after the meeting. These meetings include committee meetings and meetings of special task forces or project teams to accomplish a specific task.

## Determining Who Should Attend

If it is a problem-solving meeting, individuals who have knowledge of the problem and who will be involved in the implementation of it should be at the meeting. These individuals may be a fairly standard group. For example, if the issue is to establish a strategic plan for the business, the top-level executives of the business should be involved—the president, vice-presidents, and possibly the board of trustees.

One way to think about who should be at the meeting is to consider who is most affected by the problem and who can contribute to the solution. Occasionally, if the meeting group is fairly standard, it is a good idea to bring in new people such as an expert from outside the company or people from other work groups. New people can inject new life into groups, bring in fresh ideas, and help break down communication barriers that may have occurred in the group. A heterogeneous group (a group having dissimilar backgrounds and experiences) can often solve problems more satisfactorily than a homogeneous group (a group with similar backgrounds and experiences). A heterogeneous group of people brings varying views to the problem and can encourage creative thinking through the diversity that is present. However, an extremely heterogeneous group demands a skilled facilitator in order to make the meeting productive.

Although the decision as to who will be at the meetings is not the perogative of the office assistant in most cases, you may have some input into the decision if you have worked in the company for a long period of time. Also, you may occasionally call a meeting to address a specific issue among your peers. You can use the ideas presented here when these opportunities occur.

## Determining the Number of Attendees

The general rule is that no more than 15 participants should be involved in a meeting. Obviously, the number depends on the purpose of the meeting and the number of people who can best achieve the purpose. There are some advantages to having no more than seven participants in a meeting. Some of these advantages are that

1. The participants may be assembled quickly.
2. The meeting can be informal.

3. Detailed problems can be dealt with.

4. Group dynamics are easy to manage.

However, there are some disadvantages of a small group, too. Some of these disadvantages are that

1. The points of view presented are limited.

2. There may not be enough ideas to create the best solution to the problem.

3. The participants may not be willing to challenge each other's point of view due to the closeness of the group.

It is generally considered that the ideal size for problem-solving and decision-making is 7 to 15 people. This size group allows for creative *synergy* (the ideas and products of a group of people of which each is individually incapable of solving the problem). There are enough people to generate divergent points of view and to challenge each other's thinking. The basic disadvantage to this size group is that the meetings can become complex if they are not clearly structured. A facilitator and a recorder are needed to move the meeting and capture the ideas.

Certainly, there are larger meetings necessary at times. However, these meetings take on more of the characteristics of conferences where one or two people present an idea and there is little interaction with the audience.

## Selecting and Arranging the Room

The room and room arrangement impact what happens at the meeting. You probably have attended meetings where the room was too large or

**Illus. 13-2** In a large meeting, a facilitator and a recorder are needed to move the meeting and capture ideas.

Credit: R. R. Donnelley & Sons Company.

too small for the group, the participants could not be heard, the room was too cold or too hot, and the lighting in the room was not adequate or the ventilation was poor. Room inadequacies can start the meeting off in a negative manner. As you have learned already, meetings are expensive, so when a meeting is called the arrangements should allow for maximum effectiveness from the participants. If you carefully plan the room arrangements, you can help the meeting begin in a positive way.

When you know how many people are going to attend the meeting, look for a room that is the proper size to accommodate the group. Most businesses will have several conference rooms of varying sizes available. There is usually someone that schedules the conference rooms, so you may need to contact this individual to reserve the room. If you have to choose between reserving a room that is too large or one that is too small, it is generally a good idea to choose the smaller room. For example, 20 people in a room that accommodates 80 people can make the group feel intimidated by the empty space. The participants may feel like they are giving a party and no one came. Whereas, selecting a room that accommodates 20 people for a meeting of 25 people can create a feeling of community. However, if you must take a room that is too large for the participants, there are ways to make the room appear smaller. For example, you might set up chairs or tables in one corner of the room. If there are movable partitions, the partitions can be arranged around the space selected.

The arrangement of the room depends on what the objectives of the meeting are. For example, if the group is going to be reviewing materials and making notes, tables need to be set up for writing space. If a table is not available that will accommodate the number of people, you may wish to have several smaller tables grouped together. These tables may be grouped in a rectangular manner, an inverted U, or in other configurations. You also may have people arranged at a circular or oval table. Circular, oval, or rectangular arrangements work best when the purpose of the meeting is to generate ideas and discussion. These forms encourage a sense of warmth and togetherness. It is easy to make direct eye contact with everyone else in the group. If the purpose of the meeting is to solve problems, you may want to set up a semicircle arrangement or an inverted U. With this arrangement, you can have flip charts or overhead projectors at the front of the configuration. The group's attention will be focused on solutions to the problems being presented.

Check the temperature controls before the meeting. Remember that bodies give off heat, so the room will be warmer with people in it. A standard rule is to aim for about 68 degrees. Be certain that you know whom to call if the temperature gets too hot or too cold during the meeting. Nothing can be worse than a hot, stuffy room or a room that is icy cold when you are trying to make important decisions. Check the ventilation—is the air flow adequate? Is the lighting bright enough? If visuals are going to be used, can they be seen? If you have any questions about the temperature, ventilation, or lighting, you should check with building maintenance personnel well before the meeting begins. Give them a chance to correct the problem. It is a bad idea to call at the last minute about one of these areas merely because you didn't plan properly.

Before meetings consideration should be given to the smoking policy. Many companies now have smoking policies that allow smoking only in restricted areas of the building. Some organizations ban smoking completely. If your organization does not have a smoking policy, the executive in charge of the meeting may want to make the smoking rules clear at the beginning of the meeting.

### Sending Meeting Notices

If the meeting is a small, informal one, you may choose to telephone the participants. Many businesses now use electronic calendars to help with the scheduling of meetings. For example, if your supervisor asks that you set up a meeting with five people, you can check the electronic calendars of these five people to determine when a common date is available on all calendars. Such a system can save numerous calls between office assistants in establishing meeting dates.

The most common form of notification for in-house meetings is an interoffice memorandum (see Figure 13-1). This

memorandum is short and concise, stating the following:

- Date
- Starting and ending times
- Location
- Person calling the meeting
- Desired outcomes
- Materials to bring

If it is a formal meeting, such as a company board of trustees meeting, there are rules that govern the meeting notice. For example, it may be required that the meeting notice be sent to all individuals at least 24 hours before the meeting. In the case of public entities such as colleges, the notice of a board of trustees meeting usually has to be made available to the public. It may be advertised in the newspapers.

Meetings can drag on endlessly if they are not planned. Give people a starting and ending time. Begin and end the meeting on time. Generally meetings should be from one hour to no longer than 2½ hours. If people have to sit for longer than 2½ hours, they usually get restless and lose interest in the topic. If specific outcomes are expected of the group, these specific outcomes should be stated. For example, if the group is expected to develop a budget, the meeting notice should state that a budget will be developed. If individuals are expected to bring materials, let

**Figure 13-1** Interoffice Memorandum for a Meeting

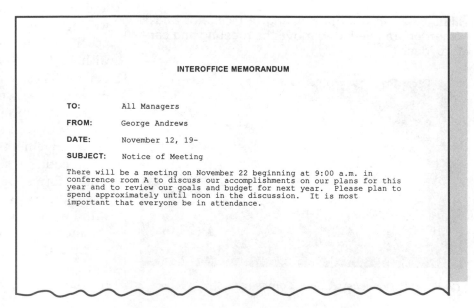

INTEROFFICE MEMORANDUM

TO:        All Managers

FROM:      George Andrews

DATE:      November 12, 19–

SUBJECT:   Notice of Meeting

There will be a meeting on November 22 beginning at 9:00 a.m. in conference room A to discuss our accomplishments on our plans for this year and to review our goals and budget for next year.  Please plan to spend approximately until noon in the discussion.  It is most important that everyone be in attendance.

them know that also. For example, if a budget is being developed, the meeting participants might be requested to bring last year's budget with them. In the case of a club meeting or similar professional meeting involving people outside the company, a letter announcing the meeting is sent out. There may be a return card with the letter so that individuals may respond as to whether or not they plan to attend.

As an office assistant, you may also have the responsibility of following up to determine if people are going to attend the meeting. Although you may ask people to let you know, there are usually some people who do not respond. The usual method of follow-up is to call the people or send them an electronic reminder. You also need to keep track of who will be at the meeting for your employer. If someone is going to be late, that needs to be noted too. You may write this information directly on a copy of the memo that went out announcing the meeting and give this to your employer. Another alternative is to prepare a special form for noting attendees.

## Preparing the Agenda

Everyone should know what to expect before coming to a meeting, and an **agenda** provides for this. An agenda is an outline of procedures or the order of business to be followed during a meeting. Participants should receive a detailed agenda at least a day, and preferably a week, before the meeting. The agenda should include the following:

- The name of the group
- The date of the meeting
- The starting and ending time
- The location
- The order of agenda items
- Action expected on agenda items
- Background materials (if appropriate)

The person responsible for presenting each agenda item should be listed. You might also wish to allocate a particular time period for the presentation of the agenda. Although this process

is not absolutely essential, it usually does remind people of the importance of time and adhering to a schedule. If time frames are not listed, the facilitator of the meeting may need to move the meeting along. The order of the agenda items can vary. Some people feel that the most difficult items should be presented first so that participants can deal with them while they are fresh. Other people feel that the difficult items should be presented last. You should check with your supervisor to determine the order that he or she prefers.

If it is a formal meeting, you may need to adhere to Robert's Rules of Order in determining the agenda order. For example, old business should come before new business on the agenda.

The action that is expected on the agenda item should be noted. You will notice in Figure 13-2 that the word *ACTION* is listed after specific agenda items. This word denotes that a decision is expected to be made on this agenda item. This approach helps participants know what is expected. If they are to make a decision, they can come prepared to do so. If a decision is not going to be made on an item, the individual in charge of the meeting needs to let the group know what will happen to the item being discussed. Is it going to be discussed at a later date? Is it going to be referred to another group for a decision? If participants understand what is expected of them, they can be better contributors.

Sometimes participants need to read or review materials before coming to the meeting. These materials can be sent out with the agenda

**Figure 13-2** Meeting Agenda

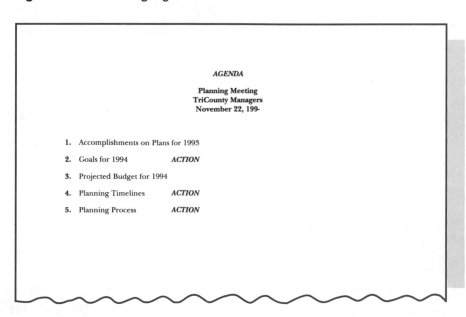

*AGENDA*

**Planning Meeting
TriCounty Managers
November 22, 199-**

1. Accomplishments on Plans for 1993
2. Goals for 1994      *ACTION*
3. Projected Budget for 1994
4. Planning Timelines      *ACTION*
5. Planning Process      *ACTION*

so that the participants can come prepared. If materials are sent out, try to keep them as concise as possible. Most people will not read long handouts.

## Preparing Materials and Equipment

Determine what materials and equipment are needed and then follow through to see that it is available at the meeting. It is a good idea to make a list of the equipment that is needed and note on the list what arrangements have been made. List who is furnishing each item; if it is your responsibility to get it, note that. Then, before the meeting begins, take your list to the room and check it against the equipment.

If the meeting is in a hotel, there is usually a special department to handle equipment needs. You will need to inform the hotel of the equipment needed, and the hotel will handle the details; however, there is generally an additional cost for this service. If the meeting is in a company conference room, you will probably be responsible for getting the appropriate materials and equipment. Here are some items that you may need:

- Notepaper, pencils, pens, and markers
- Flip charts, easels, overhead projectors, transparencies
- Tape recorders
- Telephone in the room
- Glasses, water
- Name tags (if people do not know each other)

Be certain to check out all equipment before the meeting. Remember, if anything can go wrong it usually will. Check to see that the tape recorder works; record a few words and play it back to see how well the voices are being picked up. Put one of the transparencies on the overhead projector, position it for good readability and focus the projector. There is nothing worse in a meeting than finding that the overhead projector is not working when you have numerous transparencies to present.

## Ordering Food and Beverages

If it is a morning meeting, coffee or juice can be provided for the participants; water should also be available. For an afternoon meeting, you may want to provide coffee and soft drinks. If the budget permits, you may also want to provide some type of food such as fruit, Danish, or cookies. For a luncheon meeting, you will probably have the responsibility of selecting the menu, calling the caterer, and arranging for the meal to be served. It is usually a good idea not to have a heavy lunch if you are expecting people to work after lunch. A salad or a light entree is more appropriate for a working lunch.

If it is a meeting at the office with dinner served, you may be responsible for working with an outside caterer. Due to health concerns many people do not eat red meat or eat it only sparingly. If you know the attendees, you should consider their needs and likes. If you don't know the attendees, ask the caterer to recommend several meals to you, and select from one of those meals. Be sure to ask your employer what the budget allocation is for the meal. For evening, wine may also be served (be certain to check with your employer on this possibility). You will also need to select the room carefully, being certain that it is large enough to accommodate the number of people. You will need to determine if the meal is served buffet style or banquet style.

If the dinner is at a hotel, you can usually expect a great deal of assistance from the hotel staff. They are generally very knowledgeable about making the appropriate arrangements. You will usually be responsible for selecting the menu and making arrangements for the appropriate equipment. If it is very formal, you might also wish to have table decorations and place cards. It is wise to know the group when selecting the seating arrangement; you may want to get your employer's help here. It is never good to have two people seated next to each other who do not get along well. Also, you may want to have some type of dinner music or entertainment. The hotel will generally work with you on such arrangements.

## Making A Presentation

Although the office assistant does not usually make presentations at a meeting, sometimes it is necessary to do a short presentation about the logistics of the meeting or some similar presentation. You may also have the opportunity to make presentations at a professional meeting that you attend. Here are some questions you should ask yourself if you are presenting:

- Who is my audience?
- What am I trying to get across?

- How much do they already know about the subject?
- What terms and jargon do they understand?
- What level of detail do they need?

Studies have shown that people retain about 10 percent of what they hear in a presentation and 20 percent of what they see, but about 50 percent of what they both see and hear. You might wish to consider using some type of visual to help retention. Some possibilities include transparencies, slides, and even flip charts (if the audience is small). If you use visuals, here are some tips for presenting your visuals.

- Everyone should be able to see and read the visual. Check out your visual in the room before presenting. Get at the back of the room to determine if the visual can be seen from that position.
- Don't display too much information at once. Keep three or four main ideas on each visual.
- Vary the size and color of the visuals so that everything does not look the same. Make sure you have some way of pointing to what is being talked about on the visual.

Before you go into the room to begin your presentation, it is a good idea to do some type of relaxation exercise. Deep breathing is one technique that will help to relax you. As you proceed to the front of the room to begin, pause slightly

**Illus. 13-3** Visual presentations help retention during meetings.

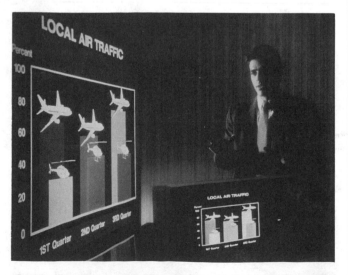

before starting your presentation. Look at your audience; then begin your presentation. Be certain to make frequent eye contact with your audience. Most people need to use some type of notes—either note cards or an outline that they use in speaking. However, you should never read your presentation and lose eye contact with the audience. Certainly, it is okay to glance at your notes occasionally but *occasionally* is the key phrase. Beginning presenters need to practice extensively before the presentation and even seasoned presenters need to practice some. If you have to present often and you are not pleased with your skills, get help. One organization that can help you is Toastmasters. You can get their number in most cities by looking under "Toastmasters" in the telephone book. After giving a presentation, go over what went right and what went wrong. Critique yourself; learn from your mistakes; try never to make the same mistake twice. But, don't dwell on the negative. Remember, most people are never happy with their public presentations. And, if you dwell on it, you will probably be more apprehensive during the next presentation.

## During the Meeting

The office assistant's responsibilities during the meeting are varied. You may be expected to greet the guests and offer them any type of refreshments that are available. You may also be expected to introduce individuals to each other. Remember, you represent the company at the meeting. Your courteousness, warmth, and friendliness can go a long way toward making people feel comfortable and getting the meeting off to a good start.

To refresh your memory as to the purpose of the meeting, review the agenda before the meeting. Your main responsibility during the meeting will probably be to take the **minutes** (a record of what happens at the meeting). Sit near the presiding officer so that you will be able to hear easily. You may want to use a tape recorder in taking notes or a laptop computer. If you are using a tape recorder, be certain that you have a sufficient supply of tapes. When using the recorder, it is a good idea to manually record the names of speakers and individuals making the motions so that you may identify them when transcribing the minutes. A laptop computer can save you time, since you can record the minutes on a disk as the meeting is occurring. After the meeting is over, you can go over the disk and edit wherever needed.

Minutes should contain a record of all important matters that are presented in the meeting. You do not need to record the minutes verbatim; you do need to record all pertinent information. Items which should be included in the minutes are

1. The date, time, and place of the meeting
2. The members present and absent
3. Approval or correction of the minutes from the previous meeting
4. Reports of committees, officers, or individuals
5. Motions made
6. Items on which action needs to be taken and the person responsible for taking the action
7. Adjournment of the meeting

## Following Up After the Meeting

Your duties after the meeting include seeing that the meeting room is left in good order, preparing the minutes, and numerous other details that need to be handled.

**Handling Routine Tasks**   Here is a list of some of the routine tasks that need to be handled after a meeting.

- Return all equipment. See that any additional tables and chairs are removed from the room. Clean up any food or beverage leftovers or notify the cleaning staff if the room needs a general cleanup.
- Prepare the minutes promptly—it is a good idea to get minutes out within 24 to 48 hours after the meeting.
- Write items on your calendar that may require future attention by you or your employer.
- Send out any follow up letters that may be necessary.
- If the meeting room is at a hotel or place where you are being charged for the room, sign for the bill.
- Evaluate the meeting. Review what happened; consider how you might improve the arrangements for the next meeting. Make notes for your files so that you may review these notes before the next meeting. If you have used a hotel or caterer, make notes about their effec-

tiveness—the quality of the food, the adequateness of the facilities, the helpfulness of the staff. Would you suggest using them again? If so, put that in your notes. If not, record that also. Keep files for all meetings for a period of time so that you may refer to them before the next meeting. It is also a good idea to keep names and telephone numbers of contact people in the files.

**Preparing the Minutes**   Although minutes are not kept for very informal meetings, they are usually kept for most meetings. Figure 13-3 illustrates minutes of a meeting. Although there is no set form for writing minutes, here are some general rules.

1. Minutes may be double- or single-spaced. Margins should be at least 1 inch. If the minutes are to be placed in a bound book, the left margin should be 1½ inches.
2. Capitalize and center the heading that designates the official title of the group.
3. Use subject captions for ease in locating various sections of the minutes.
4. Minutes may or may not be signed. Minutes of board meetings are signed, and generally minutes of professional clubs are signed. If minutes are to be signed, a signature line should be provided.
5. In composing the minutes, give the following information:
   a. Include the day, date, hour, and place of the meeting.
   b. Indicate who was present and who was absent.
   c. Record the actions taken at the meeting.
   d. Give a succinct summary of the important points of each discussion.

## CONFERENCES AND CONVENTIONS

A conference or convention is much larger in scope and number of participants than a meeting. Many executives belong to professional organizations such as the American Management Association or Administrative Management Society. These organizations generally hold at least one convention a year. Most companies encourage their executives to participate in some conferences and conventions as a means of broadening their knowledge in various fields and learning

# Figure 13-3 Minutes of a Meeting

## MINUTES—BOARD OF DIRECTORS MEETING
## ADMINISTRATIVE MANAGEMENT SOCIETY

San Francisco Chapter
September 8, 19--

**TIME AND PLACE OF MEETING**

The regular monthly meeting of the AMS San Francisco Chapter Board of Directors was held on Tuesday, September 8, in the main parlor of the Regent Hotel at 6:00 p.m. The meeting was called to order by the President, Ronald Anderson. All fifteen members were present.

**READING OF THE MINUTES**

The minutes of the July meeting were approved without reading since each member had received a copy prior to this meeting. (There was no August meeting.)

**TREASURER'S REPORT**

The treasurer's report (copy attached), showing a balance of $1,623 as of September 1, was read, received, and filed.

**UNFINISHED BUSINESS**

Ronald Anderson reported that he has received acceptance from H. R. Princeton to speak at the October meeting and that all pictures and publicity items had been turned over to the Publicity Committee.

**NEW BUSINESS**

*Application of T. A. Alexander.* The application of T. A. Alexander, substituting for Harold Georgia, Jr., of the Ramsey Business Equipment Company, was unanimously approved.

*Chapter Merit Award Qualifications.* It was suggested that the merit award qualifications be included in the Chapter bulletin for the first week of October.

*Education Teachers' Information Booklet.* Copies of the education teachers' booklet, prepared by Cindy Taylor, were distributed to the Board of Directors. Many favorable comments were made about the contents of the booklet and appreciation was expressed to Cindy and to the Brown Life Insurance Company for printing the booklet.

---

Board of Directors Meeting     2     September 8, 19--

*Speakers Bureau.* Silas Stehr, chairperson of the Speakers Bureau, said that he and the Bureau are planning to increase the number of speakers at the winter seminar so that the programs can be expanded without placing too heavy a burden on those who are willing to accept speaking assignments.

*Information Service Committee.* Mildred Gary, chairperson of the Information Service Committee, said that she has written to the national office about the Chapter's willingness to participate in any survey proposed by the national office; so far no request has been received.

*Picnic Committee.* The Picnic Committee reported that 94 adults and 40 children attended the fall picnic. The cost to the Chapter was $173.85. Several suggestions for next year's outing were included in the report. The Committee will do research on these suggestions.

*Publicity Committee.* Percy Atwater reported that approval on the solicitation of ads for the roster and the bulletin was received. He explained that the format of the bulletin would have to be changed to accommodate the inclusion of the ads. The Board of Directors approved this action.

In Percy's complete report, which is attached to these minutes, he outlined plans to establish a business education week in November to coincide with our regular education night meeting. Also, it was suggested that a committee be appointed to take care of seminars, special study groups, etc.

**ADJOURNMENT**

As there was no further business, the meeting was adjourned.

*Arthur M. Grant*

Arthur M. Grant, Secretary-Treasurer

from colleagues in other companies. As an office assistant you may be a member of Professional Secretaries International and get involved in attending or helping to plan some of their conferences.

## Before the Conference

Preparing for a regional or national conference takes months of work. Good planning will ensure a smooth, successful conference, whereas poor planning will result in a disorganized, ineffective conference. One of the major responsibilities in planning a conference is to determine the location and meeting facilities for the conference. Contact the Chamber of Commerce in the city being considered; ask for information about the city and appropriate conference and convention facilities. Request conference planning guides from the hotels and convention centers that give floor plans

of the facilities, dining and catering services, price lists of rooms, meeting rooms, and meals. Notice Figure 13-4 which shows a portion of a hotel floor plan. Once the city and hotel have been selected, detailed arrangements need to be made for meeting rooms, guest rooms, meal arrangements, and so forth.

Presenters must be contacted and travel and lodging arrangements must be made before the conference. If you are responsible for making the arrangements for a presenter, you should determine the type of accommodations required—room (single or double, queen- or king-size bed), flight preferences, arrival and departure times, rental car needs, and so forth.

There is usually some type of preregistration before the conference and registration during the conference. You may be responsible for mailing out and receiving the preregistration forms. You

**Figure 13-4** Floor Plan Showing Meeting Rooms and Facilities

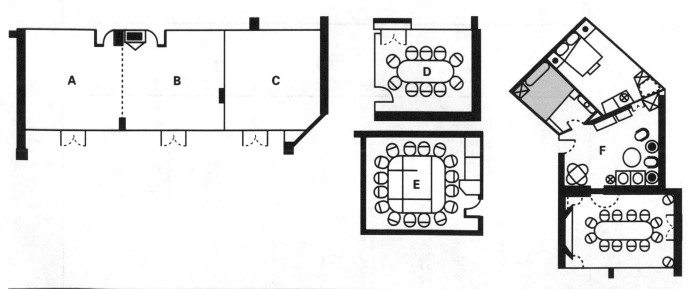

| | | **MEETING ROOM SPECIFICATIONS** | | | | **STATISTICS** | |
|---|---|---|---|---|---|---|---|
| | | Theatre | Classroom | Banquet | Reception | Dimensions | Area (Sq. Ft.) |
| A | Bobbie Layne | 45 | 35 | 46 | 60 | 24' x 24' | 576 |
| B | Billy Sims | 50 | 35 | 48 | 60 | 24' x 24' | 576 |
| A & B | Combined | 95 | 70 | 94 | 120 | 24' x 48' | 1152 |
| C | Joe Schmidt | 45 | 32 | 40 | 50 | 23' x 24' | 552 |
| D | Pistons Executive Boardroom | Conference Seating for 14 | | | | 20'3" x 17'6" | 360 |
| E | Lions Executive Boardroom | Conference Seating for 16 | | | | 20' x 22' 9" | 430 |
| F | Featherstone Conference Suite | Conference Seating for 14 | | | | | |

G. Opdyke Conference Suite also available. (Not shown)

also may be responsible for assisting with registration at the conference. If the conference is a large one, several people will be needed to staff the registration tables.

## During the Conference

Your responsibilities during the conference may include running errands, assisting in getting messages to participants, and being on hand to help solve any problems that may occur. Other responsibilities may include checking room arrangements, equipment needs, checking with the hotel on meal arrangements, and so forth. At a conference you are a representative of the company for which you work; thus, you should present an outstanding public relations image at all times. Keep a smile on your face and handle even the most difficult situations with poise and confidence.

## After Conference Details

After the conference your basic duties involve clean up and follow-up. These responsibilities may include seeing that all equipment is returned, presenters are assisted with transportation to the airport, letters of appreciation are sent to presenters, expense reports are filled out, and bills are paid. You may also be responsible for seeing that the proceedings of the conference are published and mailed to the participants. You will generally not be responsible for the writing of this report, but you may be responsible for working with the conference reporters in assembling and mailing out the report. At some conferences, tapes are made of sessions and these tapes are available for attendees. There is usually a charge for the tapes.

If others have worked with you on the conference, call a meeting to evaluate the conference. Ask these questions:

- What went right?
- What went wrong?
- Was the facility adequate?
- Were the meals good and served on time?

Keep a record of your evaluation so that you may refer to it before the next conference. Also, keep all of your files containing information about conference preparation. These files can be valuable in planning future conferences.

## TELECONFERENCING

Conferences are extremely expensive; however, technological advances have provided an alternative in the form of teleconferencing. **Teleconferencing** is a general term applied to a variety of technology-assisted, two-way (interactive) communications via telephone lines or microwaves. Two types of teleconferencing are discussed here—videoconferencing and computer conferencing.

### Videoconferencing

**Videoconferencing** is a system of transmitting audio and video between individuals at distant locations thereby eliminating the need for travel. Videoconferencing may occur with minimal equipment (a screen and a camera at each location) or with numerous pieces of equipment. For example, there might be color television cameras to transmit pictures of people and graphics, monitors to pick up people images and graphic images, microphones and speakers for audio interaction, and facsimile units for hard copy transmission of documents.

**Illus. 13-4** Videoconferencing is a system of transmitting audio and video between individuals at distant locations thereby eliminating the need for travel.

Credit: NEC Corporation.

### Computer Conferencing

Another alternative to face-to-face meetings and conferences is **computer conferencing.** Computer conferencing requires that each participant have a communicating computer. With these communicating computers, computer-to-computer conversation can take place. Individuals can stay in their offices where they have access to the necessary data and can communicate with other individuals on a common issue or concern. Information can be transmitted back and forth between a number of individuals in a very short period of time.

## ORGANIZATION, THE KEY TO EFFECTIVE MEETINGS AND CONFERENCES

You have learned in this chapter that you will have several responsibilities in setting up meetings and conferences. If you are to carry out these responsibilities well, you must stay organized. As you plan for these events, make a checklist of all the tasks that need to be accomplished before, during, and after the meeting or conference. As you plan, ask yourself these questions:

- What should I do first in getting organized?
- What should be completed before the meeting?
- When should each task be completed?
- Who is responsible for each activity?
- What should I be doing during the conference?
- What should I be doing after the conference is over?

## CHAPTER SUMMARY

The following review will help you remember the important points of this chapter.

1. Meetings are a good means of generating ideas, sharing information, and making decisions. However, there are times when a meeting should not be called. These times include when a confidential or sensitive personnel matter needs to be addressed; when there is inadequate data; when there is inadequate time to prepare for the meeting; when information could be communicated better by telephone, fax, or other means; and when there is considerable anger or hostility in a group.

2. Individuals who have knowledge of the problem and who will be involved in the solution need to be in attendance at problem-solving meetings. Before a meeting is held, one of the questions that should be given careful consideration is who should attend the meeting.

3. The general rule is that no more than fifteen participants should be involved in a meeting. The number depends on the purpose of the meeting and the number of people who can best achieve the purpose.

4. Some of the responsibilities of the office assistant in planning a meeting are (1) selecting and arranging the room; (2) sending meeting notices; (3) preparing the agenda; (4) preparing materials and equipment; (5) ordering food and beverages.

5. During the meeting the office assistant may be expected to greet guests, offer them refreshments, introduce individuals, and take minutes.

6. After the meeting, the office assistant's duties include seeing that the meeting room is left in good order, preparing the minutes, returning equipment, and handling any follow-up details that were generated as a result of the meeting.

7. The office assistant will probably not be involved in many conferences or conventions. However, if he or she is involved, the duties may include selecting the facility, working with the hotel or convention center on room arrangements and food, contacting presenters, assisting with preregistration and registration, and handling the clean up and follow-up details after the conference.

8. An alternative to having meetings and conferences is teleconferencing. Two types of teleconferences are videoconferencing and computer conferencing.

## TERMINOLOGY REVIEW

The following terms were introduced in this chapter. To help you understand them, definitions are given below.

1. **Agenda** *(page 353)* An agenda is an outline of procedures or the order of business to be followed during a meeting.
2. **Computer Conferencing** *(page 359)* Computer conferencing is a conference conducted with the use of communicating computers; it allows individuals to communicate with each other from their individual offices.
3. **Minutes** *(page 355)* Minutes of a meeting are a record of what happened at the meeting. Action taken, motions passed, and old and new business discussed all appear in the minutes. Minutes are kept for a period of time (and indefinitely in some cases) as a record of the history of the proceedings of an organization.
4. **Teleconferencing** *(page 359)* Teleconferencing is a general term applied to a variety of technology-assisted, two-way (interactive) communications via telephone lines or microwaves.
5. **Videoconferencing** *(page 359)* Videoconferencing is a system of transmitting audio and video between individuals at distant locations thereby eliminating the need for travel.

## DISCUSSION ITEMS

To demonstrate your understanding of the information in this chapter, respond to the following items.

1. Explain when meetings are necessary and when they are not necessary.
2. List and explain five responsibilities of the office assistant before a meeting.
3. Why are visuals helpful in making presentations?
4. What are the responsibilities of the office assistant during the meeting?
5. What are the responsibilities of the office assistant after the meeting?
6. What should an agenda include?
7. How should minutes be formatted?
8. List and explain two alternatives to meetings and conferences.

## CASE STUDY

TriCounty Regional Planning Agency is planning a conference for all of the planning agencies in the state. There are ten planning agencies. It is expected that 300 people will attend the conference. Mr. Andrews has asked you to take a lead role in planning the conference. He asks that you work with the other agencies in identifying speakers and presenting the list to him for final approval. You are also to work with the other agencies in selecting a facility. You are to be responsible for preregistration and registration. The conference is scheduled for May of next year (ten months away).

Planning has been going on for two months. During this time, you have held three meetings with the appropriate individuals from the other agencies. There has been a good discussion each time, but nothing has been resolved. No facility has been selected; no presenters have been identified. You are becoming anxious about the conference. You know that if you do not get a facility on contract soon there may be no place available. You also know that if you don't identify and contact presenters soon you will not be able to get anyone. You hate to go to Mr. Andrews, but you are concerned. Explain how you should handle the situation.

## OFFICE APPLICATIONS

### Office Application 13-1 (*Objective 1*)

Mr. Andrews gives you the following meetings to set up:

1. A meeting in two days with Rebecca Gonzales and Maurice Chateau to discuss their presentations at the next Board meeting.

2. A meeting with Travis Ueoka and the aging supervisors of Hunt, Collin, and Kaufman County to discuss plans for the next six months. This meeting will be held in one week.

3. A seminar on transportation issues for the late 90s to be held in three months. All managers are to be invited, along with the analysts from Hunt, Collin, and Kaufman County.

Make a list of your responsibilities for all three meetings and hand in this list to your instructor.

### Office Application 13-2 (*Objectives 2 and 3*)

Prepare a meeting notice for the meeting in situation 2 of Office Application 13-1 using a date of one week from today. Mr. Andrews gives you the following items for the agenda: (1) grant from the Kellogg Foundation; (2) facilities needs for the next year; (3) update on Project Health; (4) Federal regulations. Prepare an agenda for the meeting.

### Office Application 13-3 (*Objective 3*)

Mr. Andrews asks your help in preparing some statistical data for the seminar in situation 3 of Office Application 13-1.

*With a template disk:*

1. Load the stored file, OA13-3. Notice that the population figures for Collin, Hunt, and Kaufman counties (as of the 1990 census) appear on the disk. Mr. Andrews asks that you project the figures for 1998, using a projected increase in Collin County of 8 percent, 4 percent for Hunt County, and 6 percent for Kaufman County. Label the column "Projected Population, 1998." Prepare an appropriate heading for the table. Print out one copy for your instructor.

2. Prepare three sheets of the population figures prepared in item 1 above which will be made into overheads for use by Mr. Andrews during the seminar. Place the population figures for each county (both 1990 and projected 1998) on a separate sheet of paper. Hand in your sheets to your instructor.

3. Prepare an agenda for Mr. Andrews to use at the seminar. This agenda will be printed later as a program, with slight modifications. Your task

is to prepare the agenda only. Here are the items Mr. Andrews gives you:

| | |
|---|---|
| Welcome | George Andrews |
| Introduction of Dr. Harold Hodgkinson | Travis Ueoka |
| Demographic Presentation | Dr. Harold Hodgkinson |
| Population Figures for Collin, Hunt, and Kaufman Counties | George Andrews |

*Without a template disk:* Use the information provided on page 365 of your text. Notice that the population figures for Collin, Hunt, and Kaufman counties (as of the 1990 census) appear on this page. Mr. Andrews asks that you project the figures for 1998, using a projected increase in Collin County of 8 percent, 4 percent for Hunt County, and 6 percent for Kaufman County. Label the column "Projected Population, 1998." Prepare an appropriate heading for the table. Turn in your completed copy to your instructor.

Complete the additional two activities as given in items 2 and 3 above.

### Office Application 13-4 (*Objective 3*)

Your notes from the TriCounty board meeting appear on pages 367-368 of this text. Keyboard the minutes, and format your document similarly to the example shown in Figure 13-4 in this chapter. Turn in one copy of the minutes to your instructor.

### Office Application 13-5 (*Objective 3*)

Attend a meeting of a professional organization—either a club that you are a member of at school or some other organization. Take notes at the meeting and keyboard your notes in the form of minutes. Turn in the minutes to your instructor.

### Office Application 13-6 (*Objective 4*)

Read two recent articles on teleconferencing. Prepare a report of your findings, giving your reference sources. Turn in your report to your instructor.

|                | Population, 1990 |
| -------------- | ---------------- |
| Collin County  | 261,600          |
| Hunt County    | 41,400           |
| Kaufman County | 49,350           |

petite of our nation for mind-altering chemicals entails other costs that rival the sums that dealers squeeze out of drug users and addicts. The most obvious is crime. Research by the board of Pardons and Paroles shows that two of every three prisoners have used drugs, and the board suggests that substance abuse may be the most important reason parolees land back in prison.

## The Impact

The problem is great. It impacts our families, our cities, our states and nation, and our workplace. Daily the newspapers in almost every city in the United States report a substance abuse related accident, death, or crime. People are dying daily in car accidents caused by drunk drivers. Drug-related thefts, robberies, and killings also occur daily.

The immediate result of substance abuse in the office is higher absenteeism and illness. Drug- and alcohol-affected employees are absent an average of two to three times more than the normal employee. Staff turnover is greater. Chemically dependent people lead disorganized lives and often quit rather than face detection. Studies have shown that drug- and alcohol-affected employees perform at about two-thirds of their actual work potential, thus productivity is lowered. Shoddy work and material wastage is evident with individuals who abuse substances. Mental and physical agility and concentration deteriorate with substance abuse. Chronic drug abuse creates wide mood swings, anxiety, depression, and anger. Employees who abuse drugs are more likely to steal equipment and materials in order to get money for their substance habit. Substance abusers are also over three times more likely to cause accidents. Even small quantities of drugs in the system can cause deterioration of alertness, clear mindedness, and reaction speed.

## The Laws

In 1988, the federal government imposed sweeping new anti-drug rules on private employers in an effort to curb employee substance abuse. The Drug-Free Workplace Act of 1988 requires most federal government contractors, as well as recipients of federal grants, to take steps to ensure a drug-free workplace. Employers, under the act, are required to prepare and distribute anti-drug policy statements prohibiting any drug-related activity in the workplace. Since schools and colleges are the recipients of federal grants, they also fall under this act.

Employers that seek or enter into contracts with the Department of Defense must agree to a contract clause certifying their intention to maintain a drug-free workplace. Employers must include drug testing of employees in sensitive positions, as well as provisions for anti-drug education and training and supervisory training to detect possible drug use in the workplace.

Under the Department of Transportation rules issued in November of 1988, employees of transportation industry firms whose jobs include safety- or security-related functions must be tested for illegal drug use. These rules apply to industries regulated by the Federal Highway Administration, Federal Aviation Administration, Federal Railroad Administration, Urban Mass Transportation Administration, Research and Special Programs Administration, and the U.S. Coast Guard.

## Employer Responsibilities

Under the Drug-Free Workplace Act employers are responsible for

- Publishing a policy prohibiting the unlawful manufacture, distribution, dispensing, possession, or use of controlled substances in the workplace. The statement must specify actions that will be taken against employees who violate the policy's provisions.

- Establishing a drug-free awareness program that informs employees about the dangers of workplace drug abuse; the employer's intent to maintain a drug-free workplace; the availability of drug counseling, rehabilitation, and employee assistance programs; and the penalties that may be imposed upon employees who abuse drugs.

- Informing employees that they are required, as a condition of employment, to abide by their employer's policy and to report any criminal convictions for drug-related activity in the workplace.

- Taking appropriate personnel action against any employee convicted of a criminal drug offense.

## Company Policy

Here is a sample policy statement that a business might issue. This sample policy was excerpted from information distributed by The Bureau of National Affairs, Inc.

### Policy on Drug-Free Workplace

Employees are expected and required to report to work on time and in appropriate mental and physical condition for work. It is the intent and obligation of the company to provide a drug-free, healthful, safe, and secure work environment.

The unlawful manufacture, distribution, possession, or use of a controlled substance on company premises is absolutely prohibited. Violations of this policy will result in disciplinary action, up to and including termination, and may have legal consequences.

Employees needing help in dealing with substance abuse problems are encouraged to use our employee assistance program and health insurance plans, as appropriate.

## Outside Sources of Help

In addition to taking advantage of company programs for substance abuse help, there are numerous other options for help. Alcoholics Anonymous is an organization that has been in existence for years and provides service to anyone free of charge. The number of the local chapter may be obtained through the telephone directory. The names of other organizations may be obtained by looking in the yellow pages of the directory under "Drug Abuse and Addiction Information and Treatment" or under "Alcoholism Information and Treatment Centers." Also, in the front pages of the yellow pages there is generally a section on health that lists numbers that may be called for information and help on alcohol and drugs.

## AN ETHICAL, SAFE, AND HEALTHY WORK ENVIRONMENT

Throughout this chapter you have learned the importance of working in an ethical, safe, and

**Illus. 14-9** Many companies are committed to providing a drug-free work environment.

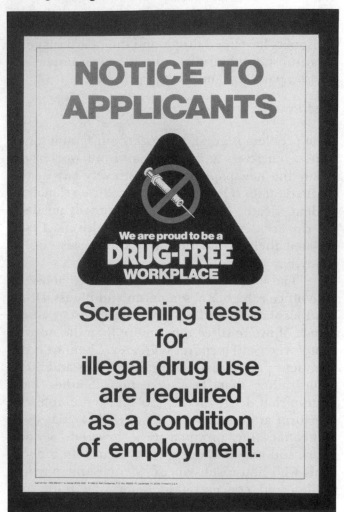

healthy work environment. The problems of our nation and world spill over into the work environment, and we are faced daily with ethical and environmental issues on the job. The business for which you work has a social responsibility to help improve the conditions not only in our workplace but in our world. You, as an office employee, also have a responsibility to help make the office and your environment a more responsible and safe place to work and live.

## CHAPTER SUMMARY

The following review will help you remember the important points of this chapter.

1. The importance of ethical behavior by businesses today is recognized by business leaders. Some of the characteristics of ethical business leaders include being socially and environmentally responsible, internationally aware, honest, and committed to employment practices that recognize diversity. The ethical leader is committed to community volunteerism, a visionary, consistent, a good listener, open, and an effective communicator. In recognizing the importance of ethical behaviors, businesses have written vision statements that outline some of the ways the business intends to behave ethically.

2. As an office assistant you are responsible for behaving in ethical ways toward your supervisor, your peers, and the clients and customers of the business. Some of the ethical behaviors you should be committed to include respecting the privacy of others, not accepting expensive gifts from clients, observing office hours, accepting responsibility, and displaying flexibility.

3. The physical environment of the office can and does affect the productivity of workers. In order to make the workplace as safe, pleasant, and healthy as possible, attention should be paid to color, lighting, acoustics, heating and air conditioning, space planning, and furniture and equipment. OSHA regulations in regard to safety should be adhered to, and precautions should be taken to ensure the personal safety and security of employees, as well as the security of information.

4. Substance abuse is a major problem in our nation and world today. This problem finds its way into our offices and causes the loss of productivity, absenteeism, numerous health problems for workers, and theft of equipment and materials.

## TERMINOLOGY REVIEW

The following terms were introduced in this chapter. To help you understand them, definitions are given below.

1. **Acoustics** *(page 379)* Acoustics is the sense of hearing or the science of sound.

2. **Bilateralness** *(page 374)* Bilateralness is defined as an initiative that affects or is undertaken by two sides equally. Bilateralness in the context of this chapter means that leaders are sometimes followers and followers are sometimes leaders.

3. **Empathy** *(page 377)* Empathy is defined as an intimate understanding of the feelings, thoughts, and motives of another. When one is empathic, he or she is demonstrating the ability to understand the feelings, thoughts, and motives of another.

4. **Ergonomics** *(page 378)* Ergonomics comes from the Greek words *ergos* and *nomos* and means the bringing together of the physiological factors that make an effective work environment and the psychological factors that explain how workers react to their environment.

5. **Ethics** *(page 371)* Ethics is defined as a systematic study of moral conduct, duty, and judgment.

6. **Flexibility** *(page 378)* Flexibility is defined as capability of being bent or being pliable.

7. **Hierarchy** *(page 375)* Hierarchy is the chain of command of the organizational structure of the company; for example, the research analyst reports to the vice-president of resource and development, and the vice-president of resource and development reports to the president.

8. **Modular furniture** *(page 379)* Walls and workstations that may be easily moved are referred to as modular furniture. The walls do not go to the ceiling and the panels generally contain electrical wiring, outlets, and lighting.

9. **Open space concept** *(page 379)* An approach to space planning that involves modular partitions and movable walls is called the open space concept.

10. **Password** *(page 382)* A password or access code is used to limit access to computer information. An individual without the appropriate

password cannot gain access to computer data.

11. **Peer** *(page 376)* A peer is someone who has equal standing or rank or someone in the organization with job responsibilities at the same level.

12. **Physical environment** *(page 378)* In this chapter, physical environment refers to the complex conditions affecting the work surroundings of the office community such as lighting, space, furniture, health, safety, and security issues.

13. **Space planning** *(page 379)* Space planning involves designing the office layout to enable efficient work patterns.

14. **Substance abuse** *(page 382)* The abuse of alcohol and drugs is referred to as substance abuse.

15. **Surge suppressors** *(page 382)* Surge suppressors are electronic devices which remove random fluctuations from the power source. They are used to eliminate the loss of computer data through power fluctuations.

16. **Uninterruptible power supply** *(page 382)* An uninterruptible power supply is a battery powered backup used in case of total power failure.

17. **Video Display Terminal (VDT)** *(page 379)* The term video display terminal refers to the computer screen. The placement of the VDT in the office workstation is a critical ergonomic concern.

18. **Visionary** *(page 373)* Someone capable of unusual perception and intelligent foresight concerning matters of the future is referred to as a visionary.

## DISCUSSION ITEMS

To demonstrate your understanding of the information presented in this chapter, respond to the following items.

1. Explain why ethics are important to business.
2. What role do leaders play in ethical behavior within the business?
3. What might a vision statement include?
4. List and describe five physiological factors that are important in an effective work environment.
5. Define ergonomics.
6. How can security controls be provided for information in the office?
7. How does substance abuse affect the work of the office?
8. List and explain the laws that apply to substance abuse.

## CASE STUDY

Mr. Ueoka gives his expense report to you each month to fill out. His expenses usually exceed $800 per month. You have noticed on several occasions that he has reported dinner with clients when you know the dinners didn't occur. He has reported these dinners at times when he has been on vacation or even on holidays. When he goes to a conference or seminar, he turns in receipts from hotels and restaurants that have movies, massages, and alcohol on them. Company policy specifically states that the employee will not be reimbursed for alcohol. Mr. Andrews signs his expense reports; however, you do not believe that Mr. Andrews checks to see what expenses have been incurred. It has been going on now for at least six months. You have not said anything, but you are beginning to believe that you are engaging in unethical behavior by not calling it to Mr. Andrews' attention. What should you do? Should you say something to Mr. Andrews or should you let it go?

Part 6   Beginning and Moving Ahead in Your Career

## OFFICE APPLICATIONS

### Office Application 14-1 (*Objective 1*)

Choose one of the following activities:

1.  Interview two executives concerning the importance of ethical behavior. Write your findings in report format, including the names of the individuals and their company affiliation.

2.  Read two recent articles on business ethics. Write your findings in report format, identifying your sources. Turn in your report to your instructor.

### Office Application 14-2 (*Objectives 2, 3, and 4*)

Visit an office in a local business or an administrative office at your school. Notice what colors, lighting, equipment, and so forth are in the office. Talk with the office assistant about what attention is paid to ergonomics. Ask what safety precautions are taken within the office and if there is a substance abuse policy. If there is, ask if you might have a copy of the policy. Using what you have learned in this chapter and what you observed at the company, prepare a report that includes the following:

a.  A layout of an office assistant's workstation, explaining what type of lighting, equipment, and furniture should be used.

b.  Safety factors that should be considered by the office assistant.

c.  A summary of what you discovered in the office you visited, including a copy of the drug abuse policy if available.

Submit your report to your instructor. Make an oral report to the class of your findings.

### Office Application 14-3 (*Objective 4*)

TriCounty has a substance abuse policy. You have recently keyed part of the policy. Mr. Andrews gives you the remaining part of the policy to keyboard.

*With a template disk:* Load the stored file, OA14-3. At the end of this file, key the handwritten information given on pages 390-392 of your text (beginning with the heading "Overview of Procedures for Action"). Save the document, proofread the copy, and print one copy and turn it in to your instructor.

*Without a template disk:* Key all the material given on pages 389-392 of your text. Make one copy, and turn it in to your instructor.

TRICOUNTY REGIONAL PLANNING AGENCY

DRUG-FREE WORKPLACE POLICY

(Insert current date)

This policy by TriCounty Regional Planning Agency sets forth policies and procedures to foster a drug- and alcohol-free workplace.

It is the intent of TriCounty:

to create and maintain a workforce and work environment that is free of alcohol and drugs, and

to comply with the requirements of the Drug-Free Workplace Act of 1988

POLICY OVERVIEW

As a responsible employer and a member of the Central Texas regional community, TriCounty is committed to the safety and well-being of its employees and its constituents.

Substance abuse by TriCounty employees detrimentally affects work performance and the safety of employees as well as eroding public confidence in TriCounty as an organization. TriCounty also recognizes that its efficient functioning is directly related to the individual performance of each employee. When the effects of substance abuse interfere with employee performance, TriCounty must consider the welfare of the organization as well as the welfare of the employee.

ACTIONS PROHIBITED

The following actions are prohibited in the workplace:

The unlawful manufacture, sale, distribution, dispensation, possession, or use of a controlled substance or the use of alcohol on agency premises is prohibited. Violations of this policy will result in disciplinary action, up to and including termination.

DRUG-FREE WORKPLACE ACT OF 1988

Employee Notification of the Law. The following will be distributed to all employees as required by the Drug-Free Workplace Act of 1988. Each employee will be required to sign a form acknowledging receipt of this notification.

Employees are required, as a condition of employment, to report any criminal convictions for drug-related activity in the workplace. (This means that any current TriCounty employee must report any such conviction within the time period specified if the employee does not want to jeopardize continued employment with the agency.) Employees must notify the Executive Director, or his designee, no later than five (5) days after a conviction.

TriCounty is required to notify the federal contracting or granting agency of any criminal convictions of employees for illegal drug activity in the work-place. This notice must be provided within ten (10) days of learning about a conviction.

An employee convicted of a workplace violation for the use of drugs or alcohol will be subject to sanctions, which may range from a requirement of satisfactory participation in a drug and/or alcohol assistance treatment program to termination from the agency. Such sanctions must be imposed within thirty (30) days of the date that TriCounty learns of a conviction.

## OVERVIEW OF PROCEDURES FOR ACTION

A supervisor who has reason to believe that an employee has ingested, inhaled, or injected a drug or has ingested an alcoholic beverage when reporting for or while on duty or who has reason to believe that an employee's performance on the job may be impaired by substance abuse must:

a) Notify Program Director.

b) Prohibit the employee from beginning work or continuing to work.

c) Counsel with the employee to determine if there may be an alcohol and/or drug abuse problem which could be affecting job performance and to discuss appropriate courses of action available to the employee.

d) Make arrangements for the employee to take a drug screening and confirmation test or alcohol test if such testing is considered necessary.

e) Prepare appropriate documentation supporting the supervisor's findings for use in any disciplinary action.

# DEFINITIONS

**Alcohol:** Alcohol or any beverage containing more than one-half of one percent of alcohol by volume which is capable of use for beverage purposes, either when alone or when diluted.

**Drug:** A controlled substance as defined by Section 1.02 of the Texas Controlled Substance Act and/or Section 202, Schedules I through V of the Federal Controlled Substance Act, including but not limited to marijuana, hashish, cocaine, heroin, morphine, codeine, opiates, amphetamines, barbiturates and hallucinogens.

**Reasonable Suspicion:** A conclusion based on personal observation of specific objective instances of employee conduct, subject to corroboration and documented in writing, that an employee is unable to satisfactorily perform his job duties due to use of drugs or alcohol. Such inability to perform may include, but is not limited to, a drop in the employee's performance level or by impaired judgment, reasoning, level of inattention or behavioral change or decreased ability of the senses.

Physical characteristics indicating reasonable suspicion may be a pattern of abnormal or erratic behavior, physical symptoms (i.e., glassy or bloodshot eyes, slurred speech, unsteady gait, poor coordination or reflexes or direct observation of drug or alcohol use). Information provided by a reliable and credible source or possession of drugs or alcohol will constitute a basis for reasonable suspicion.

The reliability of the sources of information, the reliability of the facts or information, the degree of corroboration, results of Department inquiry, personal observation and/or other factors shall be weighed in determining the presence or absence of reasonable suspicion.

Drug
Testing:      Collection of a urine specimen by medical personnel and a laboratory analysis of that specimen by Enzyme Immunoassay (EMIT) screening and, if appropriate, confirmatory testing using the Gas Chromatography/Mass Spectrometry (GC/MS) methods and procedures, or the most current and appropriate technology.

Alcohol
Testing:      Testing for blood alcohol content by a breathalyzer instrument device or drawing or collecting a blood or serum sample and laboratory analysis thereon.

Workplace:   (Also includes any reference to agency premises.) The buildings which house the offices of the NCTCOG and Regional Training Center, as well as the parking lots, driveways and grounds adjacent to those buildings.

# 15 Career Planning

*How do I go about finding the job I want?* If this question is not an important one to you at present, it will become increasingly important as you finish your schooling and look for a job. The steps that you take in applying for a job, the job interview, and the follow-up of that interview are all areas in which you must plan carefully.

The job interview is a time when you must sell the interviewer on your abilities. What skills do you have that will be beneficial for the business? What personal traits do you have that will help the business? Remember, there are probably a number of other people applying for the same job. You may have excellent skills and work well with people; but unless you can convince the interviewer that your skills are good and that you are the right person for the job, you will not be hired. This chapter, then, is important to you in that it will help you to develop skills needed to apply for a job.

## GENERAL OBJECTIVES

*Your general objectives for this chapter are to*
1. Develop strategies for success in the job search process.
2. Learn where to get information concerning job opportunities.
3. Write a letter of application.
4. Prepare a resume.
5. Learn how to conduct yourself during a job interview.
6. Fill out an application form.
7. Write a follow-up letter.
8. Determine some characteristics that will help you continue to be successful on the job.
9. Learn how to successfully leave a position.

## DEVELOPING STRATEGIES FOR SUCCESS

One of the first steps that you need to take before beginning the job search process is to understand what strategies contribute to success in finding a job and commit to developing these strategies. Throughout this course you have been developing the skills that will help you be successful on the job. Now you need to develop the strategies that will help you get the job. In this chapter we will discuss some strategies that will not only help you get the job but will help you enjoy the process of the job search.

Commit to working hard in the job search process. Finding the right job is not easy. It will take time and effort on your part. You must be willing to commit numerous hours to the process. You can expect to spend an average of three months of hard work before finding a job which is a match for you.

### Set Goals

It is extremely important that you have a clear idea of the type of job you want and the skills that you possess. You need to know the type of company which will best match your goals. Would you like to work for a service industry, a health related industry, a government agency, or a banking institution? What are your career goals? Do you plan to work for one year, five years, or twenty years? Would you like to move up in the company? Within five years, would you like to be a supervisor? All these questions are important considerations for you. Clear goals will help direct your job search into productive channels and make you work hard in getting what you want.

### Evaluate Your Communication Skills

You have learned in this course that oral, written, and nonverbal communication skills are extremely important. You have also worked on increasing your communication skills. Now is the time to use those communication skills. Most every aspect of the job search will involve communicating with others. You will need to communicate

with receptionists, office assistants, placement officers, and executives. And don't forget the importance of listening as a communication skill. Being a good listener is often more important than being a good questioner or good verbal communicator. Concentrate on using the good listening behaviors that you have learned in this course. Remember and use the information gained from others; make others feel they enjoyed talking with you and listen to what they say.

### Be Professional and Have a Positive Attitude

Remember that you are being observed. Be courteous and polite to everyone. Watch what you say and how you say it. Speak with confidence and authority. Do not be too aggressive or assertive.

Be energetic and enthusiastic. Employers are attracted to positive people. No one likes to work with a person who is negative and constantly finding fault with everyone and everything. Check out your telephone voice also. Be certain that you sound enthusiastic and upbeat over the telephone.

Demonstrate your intelligence and competence. Present yourself to the interviewer as someone who achieves results. In preparing for the job search, think through what you have done in the past. Be prepared to talk about what you have accomplished whether it be on a past job, in a leadership position in school, or in a voluntary activity in the community.

### Do Not Overdo Your Job Search or Get Discouraged

Looking for a job is hard work and is also stressful. You must be presenting your best self on each interview. It is important that you maintain your positive outlook during the process. You may need to take some time off in the job search process to rejuvenate yourself. For example, you may decide to schedule interviews for three days in succession and then take one day or two days off.

Know that you probably are not going to be offered the first job that you seek. In fact you may get many *nos* before getting a *yes*. Expect disappointments and handle them well.

### Evaluate Your Progress

Each week during the job search process evaluate your progress. What are you accomplishing? What has gone right? What has not gone so well? Are there questions that you feel you have not answered well? Work on your answers; you may get the same question again, and you want to be prepared to answer it well the second time. Look back over your goals. Are they realistic? If not, spend time in reevaluating them. Reorganize your activities and priorities if necessary. Notice Figure 15-1 which depicts the success strategies in graphic form.

**Figure 15-1** Job Search Success Strategies

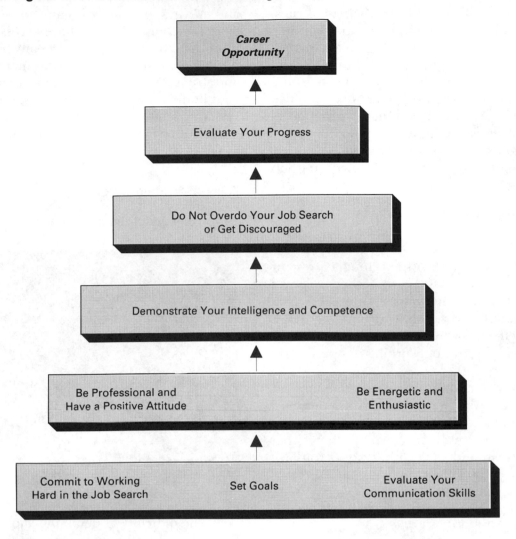

## SEARCHING FOR JOB INFORMATION

One of the first things to do is to get all the information you can about job opportunities in your community or wherever you would like to work. These suggestions are helpful in getting the needed information:

1. Register and cooperate with your college placement department.

2. Establish and use a network.

3. Make personal visits to companies where you would like to work.

4. Read the want ads in newspapers.

5. Visit state employment agencies.

6. Contact private employment agencies.

7. Watch for civil service announcements.

## Go to Your Placement Office

Many colleges maintain placement departments for the purpose of placing their graduates in positions. Your school may not have enough employment calls from employers to provide positions for all students, but on the whole you will find that the officials of your school are well informed about employment opportunities in the community and are glad to help you obtain a position. They know the employers who need entry-level workers, and they can match a job to your qualifications and abilities.

You will undoubtedly have an opportunity to discuss the matter of employment with the placement director of your school some weeks before you graduate. You should seek his or her advice and help. The placement director will try to place you in a position where you will have the best opportunity for success.

Most schools take pride in their graduates, for a school is often judged by them and their success. Your school has spent much time and money maintaining contacts with business firms in the surrounding territory, showing them that the school is in a position to furnish competent office employees, both with and without job experience. However, the school is not responsible for getting you a job. You should be exploring all the other available sources of information concerning job opportunities.

### Establish and Use a Network

**Networking** is defined in a work context as the process of identifying and establishing a group of acquaintances, friends, and even perhaps relatives who can assist you in the job search process. Network is a word that is used extensively today, but it is often not effectively implemented. As you begin the job search process, networking is a perfect vehicle to assist you.

When you are about ready to graduate and go to work, talk with acquaintances, friends, and relatives. Find people who have recently gone through the job search process. Ask them what worked for them and what didn't work. You may also learn of employment opportunities through your network. You may have some executives in your network; ask them if there are openings in their companies or if they know of any openings in other companies. Ask your family and friends if they know of any openings. Remember, though, that some firms will not employ relatives of employees. It is good advice for you to inquire whether such a policy might keep you from obtaining employment in an organization where you would like to work.

### Visit Companies

If you are particularly interested in obtaining a position with a certain company or in a particular type of business, the **direct canvass** (sometimes called cold canvass) is often the most successful procedure. This type of approach is particularly true if you have a great deal of ability, abundance of enthusiasm, and a gift for selling yourself. However, before you engage in the direct canvass approach it is a good idea to find out as much as you can about the company. There are several ways to do so. You may contact friends or relatives if they

work for the company. You may visit the library, checking publications such as *Standard and Poor's* and *Moody's*. You may obtain an annual report from the company if you have access to one. The more you know about the company before visiting it, the better able you will be to match your goals and strengths with those of the company. If you do your homework well before attempting a cold canvass, the employer may be so impressed with your qualifications and skills that you will be offered a job.

**Illus. 15-2** Before you engage in the direct canvass approach it is a good idea to find out as much as you can about the company.

The difficulty of obtaining a job in this way is that you may find it impossible to obtain an interview with the person who is actually in charge of employment. Office assistants or receptionists are often directed to say no to anyone who calls in this manner. If possible, find out who is in charge of employment before you go to the firm so that you can ask for that person specifically. You can usually find out by telephone by asking who is in charge of personnel.

Another way of canvassing a number of firms is to send out letters of application. A large number of companies can be contacted in this way, but your letter must be superior. If you receive no answer to your letter, you might call the company to ask if there are openings.

### Read the Want Ads in Newspapers

Employers typically use advertisements in local newspapers to attract applicants. Some representative ads are shown in Figure 15-2.

**Figure 15-2**  Representative Job Ads

```
GENERAL OFFICE
Stock brokerage firm needs responsible individual
who is detail oriented and has a strong math
aptitude. General office experience preferred. Key-
boarding skills of 50 to 60 wpm needed. If inter-
ested, call Ms. Burtness for an appointment at 555-
9350.
```

```
RECEPTIONIST
Downtown law firm seeks receptionist. Duties in-
clude phone, payroll, and insurance. Good bene-
fits. Call 555-3861.
```

```
SECRETARY
The Dallas News is seeking a skilled secretary to
become part of our exciting business. Interested
candidates should have knowledge of computer
systems and computer word processing software.
Keyboarding skills must be a minimum of 70 wpm.
Excellent oral and written communications skills
required. If qualified, apply in person at The Dallas
News, Houston and Main, Personnel Office, First
Floor.
```

Employment agencies also use want ads to advertise the positions they are trying to fill. These ads give an excellent review of the types of positions that are open at any time and usually provide information about the salaries offered and the qualifications required.

## Visit State and Private Employment Agencies

Most states operate employment agencies in connection with state unemployment compensation laws. An unemployed person who has previously worked can register with these offices and be referred to available jobs. If no jobs are available that match the person's qualifications, the person is eligible for unemployment compensation. A person who has never worked before can also register and be referred to jobs that are available. When registering with one of these agencies, ask to talk to the employment interviewer who is assigned to handle the kinds of jobs for which you are qualified.

There are many excellent private employment agencies that can help you get a position. Your college placement director or your business friends can name some of the reputable agencies in your community. You may also find them listed in the Yellow Pages of the local telephone directory. If you are seeking the services of private employment agencies, you should be interested mainly in those agencies that specialize in filling office vacancies.

These agencies charge a fee for finding a position. In many of the agencies, the fee is paid by the employer. However, in some of the agencies the employee must pay the fee. This fee is usually based on a certain percentage of the employee's salary for a given period of time.

## Check for Civil Service Openings

Many people are employed by the city, state, and federal governments. Many of these jobs come under civil service and are secured on the basis of competitive examinations. Information about city and state civil service jobs may be obtained from state employment agencies and by calling the Office of Personnel Management, United States Government. Also, post offices often post civil service jobs available.

## WRITING A LETTER OF APPLICATION

The **letter of application** is often the key to securing an interesting and challenging position that will give you economic security. As such, this letter may be one of the most important letters you will write. It is basically a sales letter because it tries to sell your services, skills, knowledge, and abilities. Prepare your letter thoughtfully, and rehearse what you plan to say as though you were making a sales presentation. The appearance, format, arrangement, and content of the letter are extremely important in making a good impression and in ultimately obtaining your objective—an interview.

### Goals of A Letter of Application

The three basic goals of a letter of application are to arouse interest, describe your abilities, and request an interview. These goals, with an explanation of each, are listed here.

**Arouse Interest**  You want to gain the interest of the potential employer without being cute or dull. Consider the following examples of poor beginnings.

```
I can do it! I can have those letters
flying from the computer; I can make
your company more productive.
```

```
This letter is in reply to your ad which
appeared in the News. I am interested
in the job you have to offer.
```

The first example is too cute, and the writer overused the word *I*. The second example is overused and dull. Instead, provide the employer with a brief statement of your qualifications. Let the reader know you are interested in the company and what you can do for the company, but don't oversell. Consider the following examples:

> The position you have advertised sounds both challenging and interesting. After finishing an Associate of Arts Degree in Business Information Systems and working part time as an office assistant while going to school, I believe I have the skills necessary to fill the job.

> Your employment announcement calls for an office assistant who is interested in learning and has good office skills. My training at Royal Oak College for the last two years has provided me with these skills.

In both cases you let the prospective employer know that you are interested in performing for the company. You also let the person know briefly what skills you have.

**Describe Your Abilities**   The next paragraph of the letter should describe in more detail the abilities you have and should call attention to your enclosed **resume** (also called a data sheet or vita).

> In May of this year, I will graduate from Royal Oak College. During my two years of school, I have taken courses in word processing, keyboarding, accounting, management, and office procedures. My keyboarding skill is 80 words a minute. My resume, which is enclosed, gives more details concerning my education and experience.

**Request an Interview**   Remember, the purpose of the letter is to get an interview. Therefore, you should ask directly for the interview. Here is an example.

> Please give me an opportunity to discuss my qualifications with you. My telephone number is 555-2041.

### Letter-Writing Techniques

Here are some additional techniques that will assist you as you write your letter of application:

1. The letter should look impressive. It must be neat. Prepare your letter on a good grade of

8½ inch by 11 inch bond paper. Read the letter carefully for any spelling, grammatical, or keyboarding errors. It is a good idea to run the letter through a spell checker, if possible. The letter must be free from smudges, wrinkles, or tears.

2. Keep the letter short. Put the details in the resume. Remember, the letter should attract the reader's eye and call attention to the resume.

3. Address the letter to a specific person. Never address an application letter "To Whom It May Concern." If you do not have a name, take the time to find out. Call the company and ask. Or ask the school placement office, your friend, or whomever told you about the job.

4. Use an acceptable letter style. Stay with a traditional letter style such as a block or modified block style. This is not the time to try one of the lesser used styles such as the simplified one. Some people are not familiar with this style and may assume it is incorrect.

5. Use the "you" approach. The **"you" approach** means that the writing is done from the reader's point of view. You want to discuss what you can do for the company, but from the perspective of what the company needs. Let the reader know that you understand the requirements of the position and that you have the qualifications and initiative necessary to do a good job for the company.

6. Be honest. Tell the reader what you can do, but do not exaggerate. After all, if you get the job, you will be expected to do what you said you could do. The letter of application is no time to be boastful.

A sample letter of application is shown in Figure 15-3 on page 400.

## PREPARING A RESUME

The resume is intended to relieve the application letter of many details regarding your qualifications. It provides a summary of your education and experience. Just as the letter of application is a sales letter, so the resume is a piece of sales literature. It represents a very important product—you.

To a certain degree, a resume reflects what is important in the changing business world. Thus, what is included in a resume changes from time to time. Prior to the anti-discrimination legislation of the 1960s and 1970s, almost all resumes had a section labeled "Personal Data." This section included such information as age, marital status, number of children, height, weight, and hobbies. Our laws now state that it is illegal to discriminate on the basis of age, race, gender, and so forth. Therefore, most authorities recommend that personal items be left off the resume. What the prospective employer needs to know is whether you have the qualifications for the job. However, although employers are limited by law on what they can ask you to provide, you can submit any data you wish on a resume. If you feel that some of your personal characteristics will assist you in getting the job, list them. You should analyze the job situation carefully and determine what is best for you in a given situation. A sample resume showing one acceptable format is presented in Figure 15-4.

**Illus. 15-3**

"First of all, you spelled 'résumé' wrong."

*Credit: © 1992; Reprinted courtesy of Bunny Hoest and Parade Magazine.*

## The Sections of a Resume

As you have just learned, sections of a resume may vary. There is no perfect model. Each individual needs to develop his or her own resume. However, there are certain parts that are common to most resumes. These parts are presented here.

**Career Objective** This section lets the reader know what your present and long-range career goals are. For example:

> **Career Objective:** To achieve a position as an office assistant in a law firm, with a long-range goal of being a law office manager.

**Education** In this section you should begin with your most recent education—list the school you attended last and the degree obtained (if applicable). Then list your other education in reverse chronological order. If you graduated many years ago, it is usually not necessary to list your high school. However, if you are a recent high school graduate, you should list it. It is wise to list the courses or programs that you have taken that would be helpful to you in getting the position.

**Work Experience** Just as you list your most recent education first, you should also list your most recent work experience first and then work backwards. List the company where you worked, the dates of employment, and your duties. You may want to reverse the order of education and experience on your resume. For example, if you have had excellent experience that directly relates to the job for which you are applying, you probably would want to list that first. Remember, the resume is a sales piece. You want to call attention to your best selling features first.

**Extracurricular Activities, Memberships, and Honors** If you have participated in special activities, maintained memberships in professional organizations, or achieved honors, you may wish to list these. Such activities illustrate that you have many interests and leadership qualities. Employers are usually impressed with such characteristics, which may provide you with an added advantage as you are compared to other people who also are applying.

**References** Listing references is vital since the prospective employer must verify your qualifications. Three references are considered a minimum number; five references are considered a maximum number. The most effective references are previous employers, followed by references from your instructors. Personal references are considered to be less acceptable. However, if you have limited work experience and a weak educational background, you may list one personal reference.

It is important that you choose your references carefully. Attempt to select those individuals who know your qualifications well and will take the time and trouble to respond to a reference request. Before you list a person as a reference, it is essential that you obtain permission from that person.

**Figure 15-4  Resume**

AMELIA ALVAREZ
1311 Conflans Avenue
Dallas, TX 75211-1135
555-2041

CAREER OBJECTIVE

To achieve a position as an office assistant with the long-range goal of being an office manager.

EDUCATION

Royal Oak College, Dallas, Texas, September 1991 to May 1993, Associate of Arts Degree in Office Occupations. Courses Studied: word processing, keyboarding, office machines, business math, accounting, business communications, and management.

Oakpark High School, Dallas, Texas, September 1986 to May 1990. Courses Studied: bookkeeping, office practice, and keyboarding.

WORK EXPERIENCE

Student assistant in the Business Division of Royal Oak College, September 1991 to May 1993. Responsibilities included producing tests, duplicating materials, and filing.

Receptionist, Memorial Medical Center, 110 Grace Street, Dallas, TX, June 1990 to August 1991. Responsibilities included preparing correspondence, filing, bookkeeping, and answering the phone.

EXTRACURRICULAR ACTIVITIES, MEMBERSHIPS, AND HONORS

Vice-President of Phi Kappa Theta
Dean's List
President of Phi Beta Lambda

REFERENCES

Ms. Mary Lee Patterson, Royal Oak College, 4789 Keist, Dallas, TX 75202-1133.

Dr. Morris Adams, Royal Oak College, 4789 Keist, Dallas, TX 75202-1133.

Dr. J. L. Phillips, Memorial Medical Center, 110 Grace, Dallas, TX 75211-1135.

---

**Figure 15-3  Letter of Application**

1311 Conflans Avenue
Dallas, TX 75211-1135
May 10, 19--

Ms. Marjorie Ott
Tricounty Regional Planning Agency
3232 Six Flags Drive
Arlington, TX 76005-5888

Dear Ms. Ott

Your employment announcement for an office assistant specifies an individual with good keyboarding and English skills and one who is willing to learn. My two years training in office occupations at Royal Oak College plus my one year of work experience have provided me with good skills and experiences. I am eager to get started in such a position and am willing to work hard.

During the last two years, I have completed an Associate of Arts Degree in Office Occupations from Royal Oak College. I studied word processing, keyboarding, office practices, accounting, and management. I can keyboard at 80 words a minute and am skilled at operating a computer. Prior to beginning college, I worked for one year in the office of Memorial Medical Center. While there, I acted as a receptionist and did some keyboarding and filing. The enclosed resume gives further details concerning my qualifications and experience.

May I have the opportunity to discuss my qualifications with you? You can reach me by telephoning 555-2041 between 9:00 a.m. and 4:00 p.m.

Sincerely

*Amelia Alvarez*

Amelia Alvarez

Enclosure

## Resume Format

There is no set format to be used. Use a format that is clear, concise, and fits your needs. Just as the application letter must be free from spelling and grammatical errors, so must the resume. It should be prepared on a good grade of 8½ inch by 11 inch bond paper with no keyboarding errors or smudges. For a student, a one-page resume is usually adequate. However, if you have extensive work experience, your resume may need to be two or even three pages long. Remember, the rule is to present the necessary information as concisely as possible. No prospective employer wants to read through five or six pages of material presented in a wordy manner.

## PREPARING FOR THE INTERVIEW

The interview will not be an ordeal if you adequately prepare for it. Knowledge of what to do and what to say will help eliminate a great deal of nervousness. If you use some of the techniques described in this chapter, your poise and assurance will greatly improve. Remember that you are striving to sell certain skills and knowledge that is needed in an office.

After reading your letter of application and studying your resume, the employer usually sets up an interview. In an interview, an employer will judge your appearance, personality, temperament, physical characteristics, manners, and other traits—things that cannot be put on an application. He or she wants to find out firsthand if you are friendly, cheerful, and sincere. The interview is a "sizing-up" process—an opportunity to get acquainted, both on the prospective employer's part and on yours. So, although it may be a new experience for you, approach it with confidence.

### Learn All You Can About the Company

Before you go for an interview, it is important that you learn what you can about the company. Know what size the company is, what services or product it provides, what its growth over the last few years has been, who the president of the company is, and other similar information. You may learn about the company by checking with acquaintances who work there, by going to the library and checking in publications such as *Standard and Poor's* and *Moody's,* or by checking with the local chamber of commerce.

## Check Your Personal Appearance

First impressions are important. Many people feel that appearance counts for 75 to 90 percent in an interview. You may know all the answers and be able to do the work accurately and efficiently, but you must also win the approval of your interviewer.

Dress in a businesslike manner. Wear a color and style that looks good on you. A suit is usually the most appropriate attire, with blue being an acceptable color. It is not usually a good idea to wear something brand new. You are usually more self-conscious in a new garment, and the interview is no time to add to your level of self-consciousness. Avoid extremes in clothing, makeup, and hairstyles. In other words, don't overdress or underdress.

## Think About the Questions That You May Be Asked

It is a good idea to give some thought to questions that the interviewer may ask and possible re-

**Illus. 15-4** A suit is usually the most appropriate attire for a job interview.

### Office Application 15-5 (*Objective 5*)

In order to assist you in the interviewing process, do some library research on interviewing. Check for recent books or periodicals on the interviewing process. Write a review of one article on 5 inch by 3 inch cards. Your review should include the following:

1. The source of the article
2. A summary of important points of the article
3. A short paragraph of what you learned from the article

### Office Application 15-6 (*Objective 6*)

Fill out the application form on pages 419-420 for TriCounty Regional Planning Agency. Turn in the completed form to your instructor.

### Office Application 15-7 (*Objective 8*)

Interview two office assistants who have been in the position at least three years. Ask them what personal characteristics or skills are most responsible for their success. Write your findings in report format, giving the names of the individuals interviewed. Turn in your report to your instructor.

### Office Application 15-8 (*Objective 9*)

Read two articles in books or periodicals on leaving a job. Abstract your articles, giving the reference sources. Turn in your abstracts to your instructor.

(Current date)


Mrs. Regina Meisel
Personnel Manager
Republic National Bank
One Main Place
Dallas, TX  75201

Dear Mrs. Meisel:

My friend, Georgia Cartsonis, told me that there is an opening in
your bank.  I graduated this month from Brookhaven College with an
associate degree.  My course of study was office occupations.  My
skills are good, and I am very interested in working for your
organization.

You may reach me at 620-4607.  I am willing to come in anytime for
an interview.  I look forward to hearing from you.

Sincerely,


(your name)

# △ TriCounty Regional Planning Agency

3232 Six Flags Drive
Arlington, TX 76025-5888
(817) 245-6800

Name _____ Social Security Number _____

        LAST            FIRST            MIDDLE

Present Address _____ Tel. No. _____

        NO.         STREET         CITY       STATE    ZIP

U.S. Citizen? _____

Have you ever been convicted of a crime? _____ If yes, describe in full: _____

Have you ever been employed by TriCounty? _____ When? _____

Have you ever had or do you now have a worker's compensation claim pending for an injury while working for any employer? _____

If yes, give date and nature of accident _____

List relatives working for TriCounty Regional Planning Agency

_____

        NAME                    RELATIONSHIP

List acquaintances now employed by TriCounty Regional Planning Agency

_____

_____

---

Person to be notified in case of emergency: _____

                                    NAME

Home Address _____ Tel. No. _____

Business Address _____ Tel. No. _____

---

| SCHOOL | NAME & ADDRESS OF SCHOOL | COURSE OF STUDY | DATES ATTENDED | CIRCLE LAST YEAR COMPLETED | DID YOU GRADUATE? | DIPLOMA, DEGREE, OR CERTIFICATE |
|---|---|---|---|---|---|---|
| High | | | | 1  2  3  4 | ☐ Yes<br>☐ No | |
| College | | | | 1  2  3  4 | ☐ Yes<br>☐ No | |
| Other (Specify) | | | | 1  2  3  4 | ☐ Yes<br>☐ No | |

# EMPLOYMENT RECORD

Present or Last Employment:

| Name of Firm | | Type of Business | Your Dept. Manager | | Your Job Title | Salary |
|---|---|---|---|---|---|---|
| Address | Phone | Date Started | Date Left | Reason for Leaving | | |

Previous Employment:

| Name of Firm | | Type of Business | Your Dept. Manager | | Your Job Title | Salary |
|---|---|---|---|---|---|---|
| Address | Phone | Date Started | Date Left | Reason for Leaving | | |

Previous Employment:

| Name of Firm | | Type of Business | Your Dept. Manager | | Your Job Title | Salary |
|---|---|---|---|---|---|---|
| Address | Phone | Date Started | Date Left | Reason for Leaving | | |

List Other Employers:

_____

_____

U.S. Military Experience: Branch of Service _____ Date Entered _____

Do you have a valid Drivers License? _____ Type _____ Was it ever suspended? _____

Have you ever been bonded? _____

## REFERENCES (not former employers or relatives)

| NAME AND OCCUPATION | ADDRESS | PHONE NUMBER |
|---|---|---|
| | | |
| | | |
| | | |

I hereby authorize any former employer or any other person given as reference to answer any and all questions that may be asked concerning me. The facts set forth in my application for employment are true and correct. I understand that any false statements on this application shall be considered sufficient cause for dismissal. TriCounty Regional Planning Agency is an equal opportunity employer.

Applicant's Signature _____

Applicant Leave This Area Blank

INTERVIEW EVALUATION

Application Form for Use in Office Application 15-6

# REFERENCE GUIDE

This guide provides an easy-to-use reference to English rules and basic math that you use daily in written and oral communication. To help you review the basics, it is a good idea to read through the guide at the beginning of the course and to also review it as questions arise when you are preparing materials for this course. The parts of the guide are

- Business Math
- Capitalization
- Care of Diskettes
- Grammar
- Numbers
- Often Misused Words and Phrases
- Proofreader's Marks
- Punctuation
- Spelling Rules
- Word Division

## Business Math

This section presents a review of fractions, decimals, and percentages.

**FRACTIONS** $\dfrac{2 \text{ Numerator}}{3 \text{ Denominator}}$

1. To add or subtract two or more fractions
   a. Find the lowest common denominator.
   b. Express each fraction as an equivalent fraction, having the lowest common denominator as the denominator for each fraction.
   c. Add or subtract the resulting fractions.
   d. Reduce to lowest terms if necessary.

Example:

$$\frac{1}{2} + \frac{2}{16} + \frac{5}{12}$$

The lowest common denominator of 2, 16, and 12 is 48.

$$\frac{1}{2} = \frac{24}{48}$$

$$\frac{2}{16} = \frac{6}{48}$$

$$\frac{5}{12} = \frac{20}{48}$$

$$\frac{24}{48} + \frac{6}{48} + \frac{20}{48} = \frac{50}{48} = 1\frac{1}{24}$$

2. To multiply fractions
   a. Multiply the numerators.
   b. Multiply the denominators.
   c. Reduce to lowest terms if necessary.

$$\frac{2}{15} \times \frac{3}{7} = \frac{6}{105} = \frac{2}{35}$$

3. To divide fractions
   a. Invert the second fraction.
   b. Multiply (according to the multiplication rule).

$$\frac{2}{3} \div \frac{3}{4} = \frac{2}{3} \times \frac{4}{3} = \frac{8}{9}$$

### DECIMALS

1. To convert a fraction to a decimal, divide the numerator by the denominator.

$$\frac{2}{5} = .4 \text{ because:} \quad 5\overline{)2.0}^{\;.4}$$

$$\frac{13}{20} = 20\overline{)13.00}^{\;.65}$$
$$\frac{12.0}{100}$$
$$\frac{100}{0}$$

Note: Add to the dividend as many zeros as necessary to complete the division process.

2. To convert a decimal to a fraction
   a. Delete the decimal point and use the resulting number as the numerator.
   b. Count the number of places the decimal point would have to be moved in the given decimal to get it just to the right of the units digit in the numerator. (For example, in 21.410 it will be 3 places.)

c. The denominator will be a 1 followed by as many zeros as places counted in Step 2b.

For example, to convert .414 to a fraction, use 414 as the numerator.
The decimal point has to be moved three places to the right. The denominator will be 1 followed by three zeros.

$$.414 = \frac{414}{1000}$$

3. To add and subtract decimals
   a. Place the decimal points of the numbers to be added or subtracted in a vertical column before performing the addition or subtraction.

   For example, to add 0.5, 2.30, 30.495 and 0.05, first write the numbers in a column; then add.

   | 0.5 | | 0.500 |
   |---|---|---|
   | 2.30 | | 2.300 |
   | 30.495 | | 30.495 |
   | 0.05 | or as | 0.050 |
   | 33.345 | | 33.345 |

   b. Follow the same procedure in subtraction. Place the decimal points of the numbers to be subtracted in a vertical column. Each amount must have the same number of decimal places, so it may be necessary to add zeros before performing the subtraction.

   For example, to subtract 1.9 from 2.871, add two zeros at the end of the 1.9 as follows:

   ```
   2.871
   1.900
    .971
   ```

4. To multiply decimals
   a. Multiply in the same manner as for whole numbers except the decimal point must be placed correctly in the answer.
   b. Count the number of digits to the right of the decimal point in the multiplicand and in the multiplier; then count the same number of places from right to left in the product and insert the decimal point.

   Example:
   ```
   $5.20      2 decimal places
   ×  .35     2 decimal places
   2600
   1560
   $1.8200    2 + 2 = 4 decimal places
   ```

   c. In some cases it is necessary to add zeros in the product to obtain the required number of decimal places.

   Example:   .00031 × 3.21

   ```
       3.21    2 decimal places
   × .00031    5 decimal places
        321
        963
   .0009951    5 + 2 = 7 decimal places
   ```

5. To divide decimals
   a. Change the divisor to a whole number by moving the decimal point in the divisor to the right until the divisor becomes a whole number.
   b. Move the decimal point in the dividend the same number of places.
   c. Place the decimal point in the quotient directly above the new decimal point in the dividend.

   Example: Divide 23.56 by 1.5

   ```
            1 5.706
   1.5) 23.5 600
        15
        85
        75
       106
       105
         10
          0
        100
         90
         10
   ```

## PERCENT

1. To change a percent to a fraction, drop the percent sign, place the number over 100, and reduce the fraction to lowest terms. If the numerator results in a decimal, multiply numerator and denominator by an appropriate power of 10 to clear the decimal.

   $$4\% = \frac{4}{100} = \frac{1}{25}$$

   $$5.5\% = \frac{5.5}{100} = \frac{55}{1000} = \frac{11}{200}$$

2. To change a percent to a decimal, move the decimal point two places to the left and drop the percent sign.

   $$12\% = .12$$
   $$3\% = .03$$

3. To find a certain percent of a number, convert the percent to a decimal and multiple by the number.

   Example: 34% of 500

   ```
       500
   ×   .34
      2000
      1500
   170.00 = 170
   ```

4. To calculate the percent of increase or decrease

a. Determine the amount of increase or the amount of decrease.

b. Divide the amount of increase or the amount of decrease by the reference amount.

c. Then multiply the result by 100 percent.

$$\text{Percent of increase} = \frac{\text{Amount of increase}}{\text{Reference amount}} \times 100\%$$

$$\text{Percent of decrease} = \frac{\text{Amount of decrease}}{\text{Reference amount}} \times 100\%$$

Example: Joan typed 30 letters on Wednesday and 40 letters on Thursday. Calculate the percent of increase in her letter production on Thursday as compared to Wednesday.

$$40 - 30 = 10 \text{ (Amount of increase)}$$

$$\frac{10}{30} \times 100\% = .333 \times 100\% = 33.3\%$$

5. To calculate reference values or amounts

a. Compute the percent of original value or amount by adding 100 percent plus the percent of increase.

b. Convert the percent of original value or amount to a decimal by dividing the result from the above by 100 percent.

c. Divide the original value or amount by the result from (b).

Example: Joan keyed 40 letters on Thursday. This was a 33.3 percent increase over her Wednesday letter production. Calculate the number of letters Joan prepared on Wednesday.

$$100\% + 33.3\% = 133.3\%$$

$$\frac{133.3\%}{100\%} = 1.333$$

$$\frac{40}{1.333} = 30$$

# Capitalization

In this section are summarized the rules for capitalization that will be convenient for reference purposes.

## COMMON USAGE

The following are examples of the most common usage of capitalization:

1. The first word of every sentence should be capitalized.

2. The first word of a complete direct quotation should be capitalized.

3. The first word of a salutation and all nouns used in the salutation should be capitalized.

4. The first word in a complimentary close should be capitalized.

## OUTLINE FORM

Capitalize the first word in each section of an outline form.

## FIRST WORD AFTER A COLON

Capitalize the first word after a colon only when the colon introduces a complete passage or sentence having independent meaning.

In conclusion I wish to say: "The survey shows that. . . ."

If the material following a colon is dependent on the preceding clause, the first word after the colon is not capitalized.

I present the following three reasons for changing: the volume of business does not justify the expense; we are short of people; the product is decreasing in popularity.

## NAMES

1. Capitalize the names of associations, buildings, churches, hotels, streets, organizations, and clubs.

The Business Club, Merchandise Mart, Central Christian Church, Peabody Hotel, Seventh Avenue, Administrative Management Society, Chicago Chamber of Commerce

2. All proper names should be capitalized.

Great Britain, John G. Hammitt, Mexico

3. Capitalize names that are derived from proper names.

American, Chinese

Do not, however, capitalize words that are derived from proper nouns and that have developed a special meaning.

pasteurized milk, china dishes, morocco leather

4. Capitalize special names for regions and localities.

North Central States, the Far East, the East Side, the Hoosier State

Do not, however, capitalize adjectives derived from such names or localities that are used as directional parts of states and countries.

far eastern lands, the southern United States, southern Illinois

5. Capitalize names of government boards, agencies, bureaus, departments, and commissions.

   Civil Service Commission, Social Security Board, Bureau of Navigation

6. Capitalize names of the deity, the Bible, holy days, and religious denominations.

   God, Easter, Yom Kippur, Genesis, Church of Christ

7. Capitalize the names of holidays.

   Memorial Day, Labor Day

8. Capitalize words used before numbers and numerals, with the exception of the common word, such as page, line, and verse.

   The reservation is Lower 6, Car 27.
   He found the material in Part 3 of Chapter X.

## TITLES USED IN BUSINESS AND PROFESSIONS

The following are rules for capitalizing titles in business and professions.

1. Any title that signifies rank, honor, and respect, and that immediately precedes an individual's name should be capitalized.

   She asked President Harry G. Sanders to preside.
   He was attended by Dr. Howard Richards.

2. Academic degrees should be capitalized when they precede or follow an individual name.

   Mrs. Constance R. Collins, Ph.D., was invited to direct the program.
   Fred R. Bowling, Master of Arts

3. Capitalize titles of high-ranking government officers when the title is used in place of the proper name in referring to a specific person.

   Our Senator invited us to visit him in Washington.
   The President will return to Washington soon.

4. Capitalize military and naval titles signifying rank.

   Captain Meyers, Lieutenant White, Lieutenant Commander Murphy

# Care of Diskettes

In order to prevent damage and loss of data on diskettes there are certain procedures that should be followed. Adverse forces to diskettes include dust, magnetic fields, liquids, vapors, and temperature extremes. Use the suggestions here to assure the proper handling of diskettes, prevention of data loss, and appropriate storage of diskettes.

1. Keep diskettes out of direct sunlight and away from radiators, lamps, and other sources of heat.

2. Do not leave a diskette in the trunk of a car on a hot day or leave it on the dashboard in the sunlight.

3. Avoid smoking cigarettes around a computer. Particles deposited on the diskette will cause the disk drive head to scratch the diskette surface.

4. Do not use magnets or magnetized objects near the diskette. Data can be lost from a diskette exposed to a magnetic field.

5. Do not use alcohol or thinners to clean diskettes.

6. Do not touch the diskette surface; touch only the jacket of the diskette.

7. Do not use erasers on a diskette.

8. Do not use rubber bands or paper clips on a diskette.

9. Do not place heavy objects on a diskette.

10. Keep a diskette in its protective envelope when not in use.

11. Do not leave diskettes near telephones or set a telephone on top of a disk drive since a ringing telephone can create a magnetic field.

12. Keep diskettes away from water and other liquids. Do not put your coffee or soft drink cup close to a diskette. If the diskette gets wet, dry it with a lint-free cloth.

13. Do not bend or fold a diskette.

14. If you do not want to change data on the diskette, cover the write-protect notch with a write-protect sticker before you use the diskette or make a copy of it. Stickers usually come with the box of diskettes.

15. It is a good idea to write the indexing information on an adhesive-backed label before applying it to the diskette cover. Remove any old labels; do not add new labels on top of old ones.

16. If you do write on a label after it is attached to a diskette cover, use only a felt-tip pen, not a pencil or ballpoint pen.

17. Apply the index label to the right of the man-ufacturer's label.

18. Insert the diskette carefully into the disk drive. Grasp it at the upper edge and place it in the disk drive.

19. Store diskettes in their protective envelopes; stand them on their edges. Do not store in stacks. Specially designed containers are available for proper diskette storage.

# Grammar

## SUBJECT AND VERB AGREEMENT

This section presents a review of some of the basic rules concerning subject-verb agreement.

1. When the subject consists of two singular nouns and/or pronouns connected by *or, either . . . or, neither . . . nor,* or *not only . . . but also,* a singular verb is required.

   *Jane* or *Bob has* the letter.
   Either *Ruth* or *Marge plans* to attend.
   Not only a *book* but also *paper is* needed.

2. When the subject consists of two plural nouns and/or pronouns connected by *or, either . . . or, neither . . . nor,* or *not only . . . but also,* a plural verb is required.

   Neither the *secretaries* nor the *typists have* access to that information.

3. When the subject is made up of both singular and plural nouns and/or pronouns connected by *or, either . . . or, neither . . . nor,* or *not only . . . but also,* the verb agrees with the last noun or pronoun mentioned before the verb.

   Either *Ms. Rogers* or the *assistants have* access to that information.
   Neither the *men* nor *Jo is* working.

4. Disregard intervening phrases and clauses when establishing agreement between sub-ject and verb.

   *One* of the men *wants* to go to the convention.

5. The words *each, every, either, neither, one,* and *another* are singular. When they are used as subjects or as adjectives modifying subjects, a singular verb is required.

   *Each* person *is* deserving of the award.
   *Neither* boy *rides* the bicycle well.

6. The following pronouns are always singular and require a singular verb:

   | | | | |
   |---|---|---|---|
   | anybody | everybody | nobody | somebody |
   | anyone | everyone | nothing | something |
   | anything | everything | no one | someone |

   *Everyone plans* to attend the meeting.
   *Anyone is* welcome at the concert.

7. *Both, few, many, others,* and *several* are always plural. When they are used as subjects or as ad-jectives modifying subjects, a plural verb is required.

   *Several* members *were* asked to make presenta-tions.
   *Both* women *are* going to apply.

8. *All, none, any, some, more,* and *most* may be sin-gular or plural, depending on the noun to which they refer.

   *Some* of the supplies *are* missing.
   *Some* of that paper *is* needed.

9. A collective noun is a word that is singular in form but represents a group of persons or things. For example, the following words are collective nouns: committee, company, de-partment, public, class, board. These rules determine the form of the verb to be used with a collective noun.

   a. When the members of a group are thought of as one unit, the verb should be singular.

      The *committee has* voted unanimously to begin the study.

   b. When members of the group are thought of as separate units, the verb should be plural.

      The *board are* not in agreement on the decision that should be made.

10. *The number* has a singular meaning and re-quires a singular verb; *a number* has a plural meaning and requires a plural verb.

    *A number* of people *are* planning to attend.
    *The number* of requests *is* surprising.

## PRONOUNS

Common rules concerning pronoun usage are presented in this section.

1. A pronoun agrees with its antecedent (the word for which the pronoun stands) in num-ber, gender, and person.

   *Roger* wants to know if *his* book is at your house.

2. A plural pronoun is used when the antecedent consists of two nouns joined by *and*.

   *Mary* and *Tomie* are bringing *their* stereo.

3. A singular pronoun is used when the antecedent consists of two singular nouns joined by *or* or *nor*.

   A plural pronoun is used when the antecedent consists of two plural nouns joined by *or* or *nor*.

   Neither *Elizabeth* nor *Johann* wants to do *her* part.
   Either the *men* or the *women* will do *their* share.

4. Do not confuse certain possessive pronouns with contractions that sound alike.

   | | |
   |---|---|
   | its (possessive) | it's (it is) |
   | their (possessive) | they're (they are) |
   | theirs (possessive) | there's (there is) |
   | your (possessive) | you're (you are) |
   | whose (possessive) | who's (who is) |

   As a test for the use of a possessive pronoun or a contraction, try to substitute *it is, they are, it has, there has, there is,* or *you are.* Use the corresponding possessive form if the substitution does not make sense.

   *Your* wording is correct.
   *You're* wording that sentence incorrectly.
   *Whose* book is it?
   *Who's* the owner of this typewriter?

5. Use *who* and *that* when referring to persons.

   He is the *boy who* does well in keyboarding.
   She is the type of *person that* we like to employ.

6. Use which and that when referring to places, objects, and animals.

   The card *that I* sent you was mailed last week.
   The fox, *which* is very sly, caught the skunk.

# Numbers

1. Spell out numbers 1 through 10; use figures for numbers above 10.

   We ordered *ten* coats and *four* dresses.
   About *60* letters were keyed.

2. If there are numbers above and below ten in correspondence, be consistent—either spell out all numbers or place all numbers in figures. If most of the numbers are below 10, put them in words. If most are above 10, express them all in figures.

   Please order *12* memo pads, *2* reams of paper, and *11* boxes of envelopes.

3. Numbers in the millions or higher may be expressed in the following manner in order to aid comprehension.

   *3 billion* (rather than, 3,000,000,000)

4. Always spell out a number that begins a sentence.

   *Five hundred* books were ordered.

5. If the numbers are large, rearrange the wording of the sentence so that the number is not the first word of the sentence.

   We had a good year in 1976.
   *Not:* Nineteen hundred and seventy-six was a good year.

6. Spell out indefinite numbers and amounts.

   A *few hundred* voters

7. Spell out all ordinals (first, second, third, etc.) that can be expressed in words.

   The store's *twenty-fifth* anniversary was held this week.

8. When adjacent numbers are written in words or written in figures, use a comma to separate them.

   On Car 33, 450 cartons are being shipped.

9. House or building numbers are written in figures. However, when the number one appears by itself, it is spelled out. Numbers one through ten in street names are spelled out; numbers above ten are written in figures. When figures are used for both the house number and the street name, use a hyphen that is preceded and followed by a space.

   | | |
   |---|---|
   | 101 Building | 2301 Fifth Avenue |
   | One Main Place | 122-33d Street |

10. Ages are usually spelled out except when the age is stated exactly in years, months, and days. When ages are presented in tabular form, they are written in figures.

    She is eighteen years old.
    He is 2 years, 10 months, and 18 days old.

    | *Name* | *Age* |
    |---|---|
    | Jones, Edward | 19 |
    | King, Ruth | 21 |

11. Use figures to express dates written in normal month-day-year order. Do not use "th," "nd," or "rd" following the date.

    May 8, 1987
    *Not:* May 8th, 1987

12. Fractions should be spelled out unless they are part of mixed numbers. Use a hyphen to

separate the numerator and denominator of fractions written in words when the fraction is used as an adjective.

three-fourths inch
5 5/6

13. In legal documents, numbers may be written in both words and figures.

One Hundred Thirty-Four and 30/100 Dollars ($134.30)

14. Amounts of money are usually expressed in figures. Indefinite money amounts are written in words.

$100
$3.27
several hundred dollars

15. Express percentages in figures; spell out the word percent.

10 percent

16. To form the plural of figures, add s.

Technological advances will increase in the 1980s.

17. In times of day, use figures with a.m. and p.m.; spell out numbers with the word o'clock. In formal usage, all times are spelled out.

9 a.m.
10 p.m.
eight o'clock in the evening

# Often Misused Words and Phrases

1. **A or an before the letter h**
   A is used before all consonant sounds, including *h* when sounded.
   An is used before all vowel sounds, except long *u*.

   **a** historic event, **an** honor, **a** hotel

2. **A while, awhile**
   A while is a noun meaning a short time.

   We plan to go home in **a while**.

   Awhile is an adverb meaning a short time.

   She wrote the poem **awhile** ago.

3. **About, at**
   Use either about or at—not both.

   He will leave **about** noon.
   He will leave **at** noon.

4. **Accept, except**
   Accept means to receive; it is always a verb.

   I **accept** the gift.

Except as a preposition means with the exception of.

Everyone left **except** him.

Except as a verb means to exclude.

When the sentence was **excepted**, the committee approved the report.

5. **Addition, edition**
   Addition is the process of adding.

   They plan to add an **addition** to the building.

   Edition is a particular version of printed material.

   This is the fourth **edition** of the book.

6. **Advice, advise**
   Advice is a noun meaning a recommendation.

   She did not follow my **advice**.

   Advise is a verb meaning to counsel.

   The counselor will **advise** you.

7. **All, all of**
   Use all; of is redundant. If a pronoun follows all, reword the sentence.

   Check **all** the items.
   They are **all** going.

8. **All right, alright**
   All right is the only correct usage. Alright is incorrect.

9. **Among, between**
   Among is used when referring to three or more persons or things.

   The inheritance was divided **among** the four relatives.

   Between is used when referring to two persons or things.

   The choice is **between** you and me.

10. **Appraise, apprise**
    Appraise means to set a value on; apprise means to inform.

    The house was **appraised** at $200,000.
    I was **apprised** of the situation by Jack.

11. **Bad, badly**
    Bad is an adjective and should be used after verbs of sense; badly is an adverb.

    He feels **bad** about losing. She looks **bad**.
    The football team played **badly** tonight.

12. **Biannual, biennial**
    Biannual means occurring twice a year.

    The **biannual** meeting will be held next month.

    Biennial means occurring once every two years.

    The **biennial** evaluation will be done in May.

13. **Bimonthly, semimonthly**
**Bimonthly** means every two months; **semimonthly** means twice a month.

The report will be run on a **bimonthly** basis.
I receive my paycheck **semimonthly**.

14. **Can, may**
**Can** means to be able to; **may** means to have permission.

The diskette **can** be copied.
He **may** leave when the report is finished.

15. **Capital, capitol**
**Capital** is used unless you are referring to the building that houses a government.

Austin is the **capital** of Texas.
We toured the United States **Capitol** in Washington.

16. **Cite, sight, site**
**Cite** means to quote; **sight** means vision; **site** means location.

She **cited** the correct reference.
That is a pleasant **sight**.
They **sighted** a whale.
The **site** for the new building will be determined soon.

17. **Complement, compliment**
**Complement** means to complete, fill, or make perfect; **compliment** means to praise.

His thorough report **complemented** the presentation.
I **complimented** Jane on her new dress.

18. **Council, counsel**
**Council** is a noun meaning a governing body.

The **council** meets today.

**Counsel** as a noun means advice; it also means a lawyer.
**Counsel** as a verb means to advise.

Dr. Baker's **counsel** helped Chris overcome her fears.
**Counsel** was consulted on the case.
He is there to **counsel** you.

19. **Desert, desert, dessert**
**Desert** may mean a barren or arid region with low rainfall.

We traveled through the **desert** of Arizona.

**Desert** may mean to abandon.

He **deserted** his family.

**Dessert** is a sweet usually served at the end of a meal.

We had ice cream for **dessert**.

20. **Farther, further**
**Farther** refers to distance; **further** refers to a greater degree or extent.

The store is a mile **farther** down the road.
We will discuss the matter **further** on Saturday.

21. **Good, well**
Both **good** and **well** are adjectives. **Well** is used to mean in fine health; **good** is used to mean pleasant or attractive.

I feel **well**.
She feels **good** about her job.

22. **Got, gotten**
**Got** is preferred to **gotten** as the past participle of get. It is colloquial when used for must or ought.

I've **got** to get up at 6:00 a.m.
*Improved:* I must get up at 6:00 a.m.

23. **In, into**
**Into** is a preposition suggesting motion. **In** is a preposition implying place in which.

She went **into** the room (she was on her way and not yet in the room).
She is sitting **in** the room (she is already in the room).

24. **Its, it's**
**Its** is the possessive form of it.

The family had **its** reunion yesterday.

**It's** is the contraction of it is.

**It's** probably going to rain.

25. **Percent, per cent, percentage**
**Percent** is the correct usage; not **per cent**. **Percentage** is also one word and should not be used with numbers.

26. **Principal, principle**
**Principal** as an adjective means main; as a noun it means the main person or a capital sum.

The **principal** actor was outstanding.
The **principals** in the case are present.

**Principle** is a noun meaning a rule, guide, truth; it never refers directly to a person.

She held steadfast to her **principles**.

27. **Respectfully, respectively**
**Respectfully** means in a courteous manner; **respectively** refers to being considered singly in a particular order.

She **respectfully** asked for her grade report.
The first, second, and third awards will go to Richard, Sarah, and Christine, **respectively**.

28. **Stationary, stationery**
**Stationary** means stable or fixed; **stationery** is writing paper.

The ladder seems **stationary**.
Order three boxes of **stationery**.

## 29. That, which, who

**Who** is used to refer to persons; **which** refers to animals and inanimate objects; **that** is used to refer to animals, inanimate objects, or a classification of persons.

Patricia is a woman **who** understands what she is doing.
**Which** books do you mean?
The animal **that** I saw yesterday belonged to Harold.

## 30. Who, whom

**Who** is used as the subject of a verb; **whom** is used as an object of a verb or preposition.

Send it to the people **who** asked for it.
**Whom** shall I ask first?
It does not matter **who** did what to **whom**.

# Punctuation

## PUNCTUATION

Correct punctuation is based on certain accepted rules and principles rather than on the whims of the writer. Punctuation is also important if the reader is to correctly interpret the writer's thoughts. The summary of rules given in this reference guide will be helpful in using correct punctuation.

## THE PERIOD

The period indicates a full stop and is used

1. At the end of a complete declarative or imperative sentence.
2. After abbreviations and after a single or double initial that represents a word.

| acct. | etc. | Ph.D. |
|-------|------|-------|
| U.S.  | viz. | p.m.  |
| N.E.  | i.e. | pp.   |

However, some abbreviations that are made up of several initial letters do not require periods.

FDIC (Federal Deposit Insurance Corporation)
FEPC (Fair Employment Practices Committee)
AAA (American Automobile Association)
YWCA (Young Women's Christian Association)

3. Between dollars and cents. A period and cipher are not required when an amount in even dollars is expressed in figures.

$42.65     $1.47     $25

4. To indicate a decimal.

3.5 bushels     12.65 percent     6.25 feet

## THE COMMA

The comma indicates a partial stop and is used

1. To separate coordinate clauses that are connected by conjunctions, such as *and, but, or, for, neither, nor,* unless the clauses are short and closely connected.

We have a supply on hand, but I think we should order an additional quantity.
She had to work late, for the auditors were examining the books.

2. To set off a subordinate clause that precedes the main clause.

Assuming that there will be no changes, I suggest that you proceed with your instructions.

3. After an introductory phrase containing a verb form.

To finish his work, he remained at the office after hours.
After planning the program, she proceeded to put it into effect.

If an introductory phrase does not contain a verb, it usually is not followed by a comma.

After much deliberation the plan was revoked.
Because of the vacation period we have been extremely busy.

4. To set off a nonrestrictive clause.

Our group, which had never lost a debate, won the grand prize.

5. To set off a nonrestrictive phrase.

The beacon, rising proudly toward the sky, guided the pilots safely home.

6. To separate from the rest of the sentence a word or a group of words that breaks the continuity of a sentence.

The secretary, even though his work was completed, was always willing to help others.

7. To separate parenthetical expressions from the rest of the sentence.

We have, as you know, two persons who can handle the reorganization.

8. To set off names used in direct address or to set off explanatory phrases or clauses.

I think you, Mr. Bennett, will agree with the statement.
Ms. Linda Tom, our vice-president, will be in your city soon.

9. To separate from the rest of the sentence expressions that, without punctuation, might be interpreted incorrectly.

*Misleading:* Ever since we have filed our reports monthly.

# PROOFREADER'S MARKS

| Symbol | Meaning | Marked Copy | Corrected Copy |
|---|---|---|---|
| Cap or ≡ | Capitalize | dallas, texas | Dallas, Texas |
| ∧ | Insert | two ∧ people *or three* | two or three people |
| ℓ | Delete | the man and woman ℓ | the man |
| ⊏ | Move to left | ⊏ human relations | human relations |
| # | Add space | follow # these | follow these |
| / lc | Lowercase letter | in the Fall of 1983 *lc* | in the fall of 1983 |
| ◡ | Close up space | sum mer | summer |
| tr or ∼ | Transpose | When is it | When it is |
| ⊐ | Move to right | skills for living ⊐ | skills for living |
| ∨ | Insert apostrophe | Macs book | Mac's book |
| ∨∨ | Insert quotation marks | She said, No. | She said, "No." |
| ⊔ | Move down | falle n ⊔ | fallen |
| ⊓ | Move up | straigh ⊓ t | straight |
| ¶ | Paragraph | ¶ The first and third page | The first and third page |
| No new ¶ | No new paragraph | No new ¶ The first and third page | The first and third page |
| sp | Spell out | Dr. | Doctor |
| Stet or ....... | Let it stand; ignore correction | most efficient worker | most efficient worker |
| ——— | Underline or italics | Business World | Business World |
| ⊙ | Insert period | the last word ⊙ | the last word. |

*Better:* Ever since, we have filed our reports monthly.

10. To separate words or groups of words when they are used in a series of three or more.

    Most executives agree that dependability, trustworthiness, ambition, and judgment are required of their office workers.

    Again I emphasize that factory organization, correlation of sales and production, and a good office organization are all necessary for maximum results.

11. To set off short quotations from the rest of the sentence.

    He said, "I shall be there."
    "The committees have agreed," he said, "to work together on the project."

12. To separate the name of a city from the name of a state.

    Our southern branch is located in Atlanta, Georgia.

13. To separate abbreviations of titles from the name.

    William R. Warner, Jr.      Ramona Sanchez, Ph.D.

## THE SEMICOLON

The semicolon should be used in the following instances:

1. Between independent groups of clauses that are long or that contain parts that are separated by commas.

    He was outstanding in his knowledge of typing, shorthand, spelling, and related subjects; but he was lacking in many desirable personal qualities.

2. Between the members of a compound sentence when the conjunction is omitted.

    Many executives would rather dictate to a machine than to a secretary; the machine won't talk back.

3. To precede expressions such as *namely* or *viz.*, *for example* or *e.g.*, *that is* or *i.e.*, when used to introduce a clause.

    We selected the machine for two reasons; namely, because it is as reasonable in price as any other and because it does better work than others.
    There are several reasons for changing the routine of handling mail; i.e., to reduce postage, to conserve time, and to place responsibility.

4. In a series of well-defined units when special emphasis is desired.

    *Emphatic:* The prudent secretary considers the future; he or she makes sure that all the requirements are obtained, and he or she uses his or her talents to successfully attain the desired goal.

*Less emphatic:* The prudent secretary considers the future, makes sure that all the requirements are obtained, and uses his or her talents to successfully attain the desired goal.

## THE COLON

The colon is recommended in the following instances:

1. After the salutation in a business letter except when open punctuation is used.

    Ladies and Gentlemen:      Dear Ms. Carroll:

2. Following introductory expressions, such as *the following, thus, as follows,* and other expressions that precede enumerations.

    Please send the following by parcel post:
    Officers were elected as follows: president, _____;
    vice-president, _____; secretary-treasurer, _____.

3. To separate hours and minutes when indicating time.

    2:10 p.m.      4:45 p.m.      12:15 a.m.

4. To introduce a long quotation.

    The agreement read: "We the undersigned hereby agree. . . ."

5. To separate two independent groups having no connecting words between them and in which the second group explains or expands the statement in the first group.

    We selected the machine for one reason: in competitive tests it surpassed all other machines.

## THE QUESTION MARK (INTERROGATION POINT)

The question mark should be used in the following instances:

1. After each direct question.

    When do you expect to arrive in Philadelphia?

    An exception to the foregoing rule is a sentence that is phrased in the form of a question, merely as a matter of courtesy, when it is actually a request.

    Will you please send us an up-to-date statement of our account.

2. After each question in a series of questions within one sentence.

    What is your opinion of the IBM word processor? the Xerox? the CPT?

## EXCLAMATION POINT

The exclamation point is ordinarily used after words or groups of words that express command, strong feeling, emotion, or an exclamation.

> Don't waste office supplies!
> It can't be done!
> Stop!

## THE DASH

The dash is used in the following instances:

1. To indicate an omission of letters or figures.

> Dear Mr.—
> Date the letter July 16, 19—.

2. Sometimes in letters, especially sales letters, to cause a definite stop in reading the letter. Usually the dash is used in such cases for increased emphasis. One must be careful, however, not to overdo the use of the dash.

> This book is not a revision of an old book—it is a brand new book.

3. To separate parenthetical expressions when unusual emphasis is desired on the parenthetical expression.

> These sales arguments—and every one of them is important—should result in getting the order.

## THE APOSTROPHE

The apostrophe should be used

1. To indicate possession.

> The boy's coat; the ladies' dresses; the girl's book.

   a. To form the possessive singular, add 's to the noun.

> man's work     bird's wing     hostess's plans

   An exception to this rule is made when the word following the possessive begins with an s sound.

> for goodness' sake     for conscience' sakes

   b. To form the possessive of a plural noun ending in a s or z sound, add only the apostrophe (') to the plural noun.

> workers' rights     hostesses' duties

   c. If the plural noun does not end in s or z sounds, add 's to the plural noun.

> women's clothes     alumni's donations

   d. Proper names that end in an s sound form the possessive singular by adding 's.

> Williams's house     Fox's automobile

   e. Proper names ending in s form the possessive plural by adding the apostrophe (') only.

> The Walters' property faces the Jones' swimming pool.

2. To indicate the omission of a letter or letters in a contraction.

> it's (it is), you're (you are), we'll (we shall)

3. To indicate the plurals of letters, figures, words, and abbreviations.

> Don't forget to dot your i's and cross your t's.
> I can add easily by 2's and 4's, but I have difficulty with 6's and 8's.
> More direct letters can be written by using shorter sentences and by omitting and's and but's.
> Two of the speakers were Ph.D.'s.

## QUOTATION MARKS

Certain basic rules should be followed in using quotation marks. These rules are as follows:

1. When a quotation mark is used with a comma or a period, the comma or period should be placed inside the quotation mark.

> She said, "I plan to complete my program in college before seeking a position."

2. When a quotation mark is used with a semicolon or a colon, the semicolon or colon should be placed outside the quotation mark.

> The treasurer said, "I plan to go by train"; others in the group stated that they would go by plane.

3. When more than one paragraph of quoted material is used, quotation marks should appear at the beginning of each paragraph and at the end of the last paragraph.

> "_____
> _____
> _____
> "_____
> _____
> _____" 

4. Quotation marks are used in the following instances:

   a. Before and after direct quotations.

> The author states, "Too frequent use of certain words weakens the appeal."

   b. To indicate a quotation within a quotation, use single quotation marks.

> The author states, "Too frequent use of 'very' and 'most' weakens the appeal."

c. To indicate the title of a published article.

Have you read the article, "Automation in the Office"?

He asked, "Have you read 'Automation in the Office'?"

## OMISSION MARKS OR ELLIPSES

Ellipses marks (. . . or ***) are frequently used to denote the omission of letters or words in quoted material. If the material omitted ends in a period, four omission marks are used (. . . .). If the material omitted is elsewhere in the quoted material, three omission marks are used (. . .).

He quoted the proverb, "A soft answer turneth away wrath: but. . . ."

She quoted Plato, "Nothing is more unworthy of a wise man . . . than to have allowed more time for trifling and useless things than they deserved."

## PARENTHESES

Although parentheses are frequently used as a catch-all in writing, they are correctly used in the following instances:

1. When amounts expressed in words arc followed by figures.

   He agreed to pay twenty-five dollars ($25) as soon as possible.

2. Around words that are used as parenthetical expressions.

   Our letter costs (excluding paper and postage) are much too high for this type of business.

3. To indicate technical references.

   Sodium chloride (NaCl) is the chemical name for common table salt.

4. When enumerations are included in narrative form.

   The reasons for his resignation were three: (1) advanced age, (2) failing health, (3) a desire to travel.

# Spelling Rules

1. Put *i* before *e* except after *c* or when sounded like *a* as in neighbor or weigh.

   Exceptions: either, neither, seize, weird, leisure, financier, conscience.

2. When a one-syllable word ends in a single consonant and when that final consonant is preceded by a single vowel, double the final consonant before a suffix that begins with a vowel or the suffix *y*.

   | | | | |
   |---|---|---|---|
   | run | running | drop | dropped |
   | bag | baggage | skin | skinny |

3. When a word of more than one syllable ends in a single consonant, when that final consonant is preceded by a single vowel, and when the word is accented on the last syllable, double the final consonant before a suffix that begins with a vowel.

   | | | |
   |---|---|---|
   | begin | beginning | concur | concurrent |

   When the accent does not fall on the last syllable, do not double the final consonant before a suffix that begins with a vowel.

   | | | |
   |---|---|---|
   | travel | traveler | differ | differing |

4. When the final consonant in a word of one or more syllables is preceded by another consonant or by two vowels, do not double the final consonant before any suffix.

   | | | | |
   |---|---|---|---|
   | look | looked | deceit | deceitful |
   | act | acting | warm | warmly |

5. Words ending in a silent *e* generally drop the *e* before a suffix that begins with a vowel.

   | | | |
   |---|---|---|
   | guide | guidance | use | usable |

6. Words ending in a silent *e* generally retain the *e* before a suffix that begins with a consonant unless another vowel precedes the final *e*.

   | | | | |
   |---|---|---|---|
   | hate | hateful | due | duly |
   | excite | excitement | argue | argument |

7. Words ending in *ie* drop the *e* and change the *i* to *y* before adding *ing*.

   | | | |
   |---|---|---|
   | lie | lying | die | dying |

8. Words ending *ce* or *ge* generally retain the final *e* before the suffixes *able* and *ous* but drop the final *e* before the suffixes *ible* and *ing*.

   | | | |
   |---|---|---|
   | manage | manageable | force | forcible |

9. When a word ends in *c*, insert a *k* before adding a suffix beginning with *e*, *i*, or *y*.

   | | |
   |---|---|
   | picnic | picnicking |

10. Words ending in *y* preceded by a consonant generally change the *y* to *i* before any suffix except one beginning with *i*.

    | | | | |
    |---|---|---|---|
    | modify | modifying | modifier | lonely | lonelier |

11. Words ending in *o* preceded by a vowel form the plural by adding *s*. Words ending in *o* preceded by a consonant generally form the plural by adding *es*.

    | | | |
    |---|---|---|
    | folio | folios | potato | potatoes |

12. Words ending in *y* preceded by a vowel form the plural by adding *s*; words ending in *y* preceded by a consonant change the *y* to *i* and add *es* to form the plural.

attorney    attorneys        lady    ladies

# Word Division

1. Divide words between syllables.

    moun-tain

2. Do not divide words of five or fewer letters (preferably six or fewer).

    apple    among    finger

3. Do not divide one-syllable words.

    helped    eighth

4. If a one-letter syllable falls within a word, divide the word after the one-letter syllable.

    regu-late    sepa-rate

5. If 2 one-letter syllables occur together within a word, divide between the one-letter syllables.

    continu-ation    radi-ator

6. Divide between double consonants that appear within a word. Also, when the final consonant of a base word is doubled to add a suffix, divide between the double consonants.

    neces-sary    commit-ted

7. When a base word ends in a double consonant, divide between the base word and the suffix.

    tell-ing    careless-ness

8. Divide hyphenated compound words at existing hyphens only.

    two-thirds    self-control

9. Avoid dividing a date, personal name, or address. If it is absolutely necessary, maximize readability by doing the following:
    a. Divide a date between the day and the year.
    b. Divide a personal name between the first name and surname.
    c. Divide an address between the city and state.

10. Avoid dividing figures, abbreviations, and symbols.

    $20,000    YMCA    #109

11. Do not divide contractions.

    he'll    wouldn't

12. Divide no more than three or four words on a typewritten page.

13. Avoid dividing words at the end of the first and last lines of a paragraph.

14. Do not divide the last word on a page.

15. The first part of a divided word must contain at least two letters; the latter part must contain at least three.

    around (not a-round)
    lately (not late-ly)

# APPENDIX

## Template Disk

A template disk is available for your use in this text-workbook. This template disk is to be used with specific office applications that appear at the end of each chapter. To let you know when an application is available on the template disk, the following icon is given in the margin of the office application.

This appendix will provide you with information about a template disk.

### WHAT IS A TEMPLATE DISK?

A template disk is a computer disk on which information about a particular office application is stored. When using the template disk, refer to the instructions given in the particular office application. The information given there will tell you what you are expected to do with the template disk for that application.

### HOW DO YOU COPY A TEMPLATE DISK?

Since your instructor will not have enough template disks for the entire class, you will need to copy the disk before beginning your project. You will then have one disk for your use with the office applications.

Copying instructions for a disk will vary depending upon the type of system you are using. The following information is given for copying on WordPerfect 5.1. If you are using some other word processing package, you will need to refer to the copying instructions given in the manual.

On a floppy disk system, follow these steps to make backup copies of your original disk:

1. Place a DOS disk in drive A.
2. Turn on the computer.
3. If prompted, type the current date and press Enter; then type the current time and press Enter.

4. At the **A>** prompt, type **diskcopy a: b:** and press Enter. Remove the DOS disk from drive A. Place the template disk in drive A and your blank disk in drive B. Then press Enter.
5. After you have copied the disk, press **N** at the **Copy another diskette (Y/N)? prompt**.

If your computer has one floppy disk drive and a hard disk, follow these steps to make backup copies of your disk:

1. Turn on the computer.
2. If prompted, type the current date and press Enter; type the current time and press Enter.
3. At the **C>** prompt, type **diskcopy a: a:** and press Enter.
4. When DOS prompts you to, insert the original disk and press Enter.
5. When DOS prompts you to insert a target disk, insert your blank disk and press Enter.
6. When DOS displays the prompt **Copy another diskette (Y/N)?**, press **N**.

### WHAT TYPES OF EXERCISES ARE ON THE TEMPLATE?

Examples of the types of exercises on the template include revision of a policy and procedures manual (with information already keyed on the template), sorting names in proper alphabetic sequence for a records management office application, and preparing itineraries.

### WHAT ARE THE ADVANTAGES OF USING A TEMPLATE?

Using a template disk allows you to engage in extremely realistic office situations. Almost all work done in an office today involves using a microcomputer and storing the information keyed onto a disk. Many times that information will need to be edited in some way. With the template disk, you are working with information that has been previously put on the disk and changing or adding to that information.

# INDEX

Cash-on-delivery service (C.O.D.), 271–272
CD-ROM, 66
Cellular telephones and technology, 215
Centralized dictation systems, 58
Central processing unit (CPU), 64–65
Certified check, 181
Certified mail, 272
Certified Professional Secretary (CPS), 13–14
Change, 8
Change of address, 275
Change orientation, as a quality of office assistants, 8
Check register, 178
Checks, 177
  cashier's, 180–181
  certified, 181
  depositing, 179
  outstanding, 180
  payroll, 184
  traveler's, 181
  writing, 178
Check truncation, 180
Chronic stress, 236
Chronologic storage, 290–291
Civil service employment, 397
Clichés, 121
Coding correspondence, 292–293
C.O.D. service, 271–272
Collating, 96, 101
Collect-on-delivery service (C.O.D.), 271–272
Colon, 431
Color copiers, 99
Comma, 429, 431
Communication. *See also* Communication skills
  barriers to, 35–36
  effective, 117–231, 374
  improving, 42
  ineffective, 241
  model of, 34
  nonverbal, 34–39
  process of, 34
  techniques, 39–40
  verbal, 34–39
Communication skills, 9
  evaluating, 393–394
Company policy, and substance abuse, 383–384
Completeness, as a quality of effective letters, 119–120
Complimentary close, 133

Computer-aided retrieval (CAR), 307–308
Computer conferencing, 359–360
Computer devices, 64–66
Computer input microfilm (CIM), 307
Computerized references, 173
Computer output microfilm (COM), 307
Computer records, 297, 300
  management of, 285–286
  retrieving, 304–305
Computers
  caring for, 86–87
  classifications of, 63–64
  laptop, 64
  and security, 87
  and viruses, 87–88
Conciseness, as a quality of effective letters, 120–121
Conference calling, 217
Conferences, planning, 356, 358–359. *See also* Teleconferencing; Videoconferencing
Confidentiality, as a quality of office assistants, 9
Consistency, as a leadership characteristic, 374
Continuing education, 12–13
Control unit, 65
Conventions, planning, 356, 358–359
Copier/printers, 100
Copiers
  categories of, 97–98
  color, 99
  and copying abuses, 103–104
  and copying demands, 109
  and copying processes, 102
  and copy quality, 102–103
  digital, 99
  features of, 100–102
  intelligent, 100
  maintenance of, 102–103
  selecting, 105
  technological advances in, 99–100
Copies, quality of, 102–103
Copy centers, 95–97
Copying abuses, 103–104
Copying demands, 109
Copying processes, 102
Copy notation, 135
Copyright law, 104–105
Corporate culture, 374–375

Correspondence
  annotating, 267
  coding, 292–293
  indexing, 291–292
  inspecting, 291
  reading, 267
  sorting, 292–293
  underlining, 267
Courteousness, as a quality of effective letters, 121–122
Criticism, accepting, 376
Cross-referencing, 292, 296–297
Cultural differences. *See* Cultural diversity
Cultural diversity
  and business ethics, 373
  defined, 31
  and expectations, 32–34
Culture, corporate, 374–375
Currency, as a special mail problem, 274
Cursor control keypad, 62

## D

Daisy wheel printers, 66
Dash, 432
Database, 79–80, 304
Data disks, 77
Data processing
  defined, 55
  overview of, 55–75
Dateline, 131
Date stamping, 267
Decimals, 421–422
Decision, defined, 10
Decision making, 10–12
Deductions, payroll, 184
Deductive approach, 123–124
Defining problems, as a step in the decision-making process, 11
Density, 66
Dependability, as a quality of office assistants, 8–9
Deposit slips, 178–180
Desktop publishing programs, 80–81
Dictation
  alpha, 59–61
  machine, 56–59
  symbol, 59–61
  systems, 58
  tips, 59
Dictation units, 57–58
Digital copiers, 99

Digital scanner, 63
Digital telephone systems, 213
Direct canvassing, 396
Direct deposit, 177
Direct distance dialing (DDD), 217–218
Direct payroll depositing, 182
Discrimination, 40–42
Diskettes, 55, 424–425
Disk operating system (DOS), 76–77
Disks, 65–66
applications software, 77
data, 77
density of, 66
hard, 66
laser, 66
optical, 66, 308
template, 435
Disorganization, 240
DOS, 76–77
Dot matrix printers, 66
Draft copy, 55–56
Drawer, 177

### E

Eating right, 238
Editing, 78, 82–83
Education, continuing, 12–13
Electronic banking, 182–183
Electronic calendar system, 245–246
Electronic mail, 3, 275–276
Electronic messages, 275–277
Electronic office, 3–29
Electronic typewriters, 61–62
Ellipses, 433
Emergencies, in the office, 382
Employment, changes in, by type of business, 7
Employment agencies, 397
Enclosure notation, 135
Endless loop tape, 58
Endnotes, for reports, 174
Endorsements, 178–179
English skills, 10
Envelopes
keeping selected, 266–267
preparing, 137–139
Equipment
filing, 302
for storing records, 306–307
Ergonomics, 236, 378

Establishing the criteria, as a step in the decision-making process, 11
Ethics. *See* Business ethics
Evaluating the decision, as a step in the decision-making process, 12
Exclamation point, 432
Exercise, 238
Exit interview, 410–411
Expectations, culturally appropriate, 32–34
Expense reports, 184–185, 336–337
Express mail, 271
Express Mail Next Day Service, 271
Eyestrain, 380

### F

Facsimile, 3, 62, 105–109, 308
Facts, gathering, 123
Fair Labor Standards Act, 184
Fatigue, 380
Fax. *See* Facsimile
Fax transmittal, illustration of, 108
Federal Insurance Contribution Act, 183–184
Fiber optics, 102
File management database, 304
File number, 133
Files, types of, 302
Filing, 291–293, 300–302
Financial condition, statement of, 186–188
Financial records, 177–188
First–class mail, 270
Flexibility, displaying, 378
Flextime, 7
Floor plan, illustration of conference room, 358
Footnotes, for reports, 174
Foreign exchange service (FX), 218–219
Formatting, 78, 83–84
Form letter programs, 79
Four-day week, 7
Fourth-class (parcel post) mail, 270
Fractions, 421
Full endorsement, 178
Function keypad, 62
FX. *See* Foreign exchange service

### G

Generating alternatives, as a step in the decision-making process, 11–12
Geographic storage, 288
Girth, 271
Goals
attributes of, 242–243
defined, 241
organizational, 242
personal, 242
setting, 241
Goodwill letters, composing, 128
Government names, indexing, 296
Government publications, 172
Grammar, 425–426
Grammar programs, 78–79
Graphics programs, 80
Graphics tablets, 62

### H

Hard copy, 56
Hard disks, 66
Headings, for reports, 173
Health issues, 379–380
Hierarchy, respecting the, 375–376
High-volume copiers, 97
Hotel reservations, 330–331
Human relations skills, 9

### I

Identical names, indexing, 296
Identified ringing, 217
Impact printers, 66–67
Income, personal, 186, 188
Income statement, 186, 187
Index, subject, 287
Indexing
correspondence, 291–292
examples of, 293–294, 298–299
government names, 296
initials, 295
institutional names, 296
numbers, 295
organizational names, 296
particles, 295
personal names, 293
possessives, 295

prefixes, 295
records, 291–292, 293–296
rules for, 293–296
suffixes, 295
titles, 295
Inductive approach, 124–125
Information
creating, 55–61
inputting, 61–63
managing, 233–231
outputting, 6–7
Information age, 3–4
Initials, indexing, 295
Initiative, 9
Ink-jet printers, 67
Inquiry letters, writing, 126
Inspecting correspondence,
291
Institutional names, indexing,
296
Insured mail, 271
Integrated programs, 81–82
Integrated service digital network
(ISDN), 213
Integrity, 9
Intelligent character recognition
(ICR), 62
Intelligent copiers, 100
Internal noise, 38
International mail, 277–278
Interruptions, reducing, 245
Interviews
ending, 403–404
following up, 406–407
preparing for, 401–402
starting, 402–403
and what not to do, 404
Itinerary, preparing a, 334